Policy Externalities and International Trade Agreements

World Scientific Studies in International Economics

(ISSN: 1793-3641)

World Scientific Studies in International Economics includes works dealing with the theory, empirical analysis, and evaluation of international economic policies and institutions, with topics covering international macroeconomics and finance, international trade theory and policy, as well as international legal and political economy. Monographs and edited volumes will comprise the core of the publications.

Vol. 70 *Policy Externalities and International Trade Agreements*
by Nuno Limão (University of Maryland, USA)

Vol. 69 *Economic Analysis of the Rules and Regulations of the World Trade Organization*
edited by Kamal Saggi (Vanderbilt University, USA)

Vol. 68 *International Trade, Capital Flows and Economic Development*
edited by Francisco L. Rivera-Batiz (Columbia University, USA) &
Luis A. Rivera-Batiz (University of Puerto Rico, USA)

Vol. 67 *Megaregionalism 2.0: Trade and Innovation within Global Networks*
edited by Dieter Ernst (East-West Center, USA &
The Centre for International Governance Innovation/CIGI, Canada) &
Michael G. Plummer (The Johns Hopkins University, SAIS, Italy)

Vol. 66 *International and Interregional Migration: Theory and Evidence*
edited by Francisco L. Rivera-Batiz (Columbia University, USA)

Vol. 65 *International Trade Theory and Competitive Models: Features, Values, and Criticisms*
by Ronald W. Jones (University of Rochester, USA)

Vol. 64 *Information Spillovers and Market Integration in International Finance: Empirical Analyses*
by Suk-Joong Kim (University of Sydney, Australia)

Vol. 63 *Dimensions of Trade Policy*
by Martin Richardson (Australian National University, Australia)

Vol. 62 *International Trade and Labor Markets: Welfare, Inequality and Unemployment*
by Udo Kreickemeier (TU Dresden, Germany)

The complete list of the published volumes in the series can be found at
https://www.worldscientific.com/series/wssie

70 World Scientific Studies in International Economics

Policy Externalities and International Trade Agreements

Nuno Limão
University of Maryland, USA

World Scientific

NEW JERSEY • LONDON • SINGAPORE • BEIJING • SHANGHAI • HONG KONG • TAIPEI • CHENNAI • TOKYO

Published by

World Scientific Publishing Co. Pte. Ltd.

5 Toh Tuck Link, Singapore 596224

USA office: 27 Warren Street, Suite 401-402, Hackensack, NJ 07601

UK office: 57 Shelton Street, Covent Garden, London WC2H 9HE

Library of Congress Cataloging-in-Publication Data
Names: Limão, Nuno, author.
Title: Policy externalities and international trade agreements /
Nuno Limão, University of Maryland, USA.
Description: New Jersey : World Scientific, [2018] | Series: World scientific studies in international economics ; 70 | Includes bibliographical references.
Identifiers: LCCN 2018022531 | ISBN 9789813147973 (hc : alk. paper)
Subjects: LCSH: Commercial policy. | Externalities (Economics) | International trade. | Commercial treaties.
Classification: LCC HF1411 .L53565 2018 | DDC 382/.3--dc23
LC record available at https://lccn.loc.gov/2018022531

British Library Cataloguing-in-Publication Data
A catalogue record for this book is available from the British Library.

For any available supplementary material, please visit
https://www.worldscientific.com/worldscibooks/10.1142/10234#t=suppl

Desk Editors: Sankar/Karimah Samsudin

Typeset by Stallion Press
Email: enquiries@stallionpress.com

Printed in Singapore

I dedicate this collection to my mentors and mentees — from whom I learned tremendously — and to my family — for their enduring support.

About the Author

Nuno Limão's research focuses on international trade, trade policy, and political economy. His research integrates theoretical and empirical work to examine a variety of issues, such as how governments choose among redistribution policies, the determinants of trade policy and trade agreements, and the effects of trade costs and geographic location.

Professor Limão's current research examines how firms and consumers are affected by policy uncertainty and the role of international institutions in managing such uncertainty. Professor Limão is a research associate of the National Bureau of Economic Research and the Kiel Institute for the World Economy and an Associate Editor of the *Journal of International Economics.* He received his BSc in economics from the London School of Economics in 1996 and his PhD from Columbia University in 2001.

Acknowledgements

Part of this work benefited from the financial assistance of the University of Maryland BSOS and the NSF grant SES-1360780.

I would like to thank the following publishers and journals for granting their permission to reproduce the articles in this book.

Publishers

American Economic Association
Elsevier Science
John Wiley & Sons
Oxford University Press
The World Bank Group

Journals

American Economic Journal: Economic Policy
American Economic Journal: Microeconomics
American Economic Review
European Economic Review
International Economic Review
Journal of International Economics
Review of Economic Studies
The World Bank Economic Review

Contents

Chapter 1

Introduction

The research in this volume aims to understand the impacts of international trade on policies and economic outcomes of highly interdependent countries and the role of institutions in shaping them. It comes at a critical time: the unprecedented wave of international economic integration since the 1990s was abruptly interrupted by a collapse in commerce and fears of a trade war in 2008–2009.[1] Moreover, the recent backlash against trade agreements by two of its traditional supporters threatens a wave of disintegration. The United Kingdom (U.K.) has voted to exit the European Union, and the United States (U.S.) is renegotiating and possibly abandoning some of its trade commitments.[2]

There is a myriad of interconnected facets to this latest wave of globalization with at least one unifying feature: policies have international and domestic externalities that can be addressed via agreements. I use this feature to organize the research into four parts.

Part I: International Externalities and the Role of International Trade Agreements

Part I examines how a country's trade barriers impose an externality on foreign exporters and provides an essential role for trade

[1] Carballo, Jeronimo, Kyle Handley and Nuno Limão. 2018. *"Economic and Policy Uncertainty: Export Dynamics and the Value of Agreements." NBER working paper.*

[2] Handley, Kyle and Nuno Limão. 2017. "Trade under T.R.U.M.P. policies," *Economics and Policy in the Age of Trump*, CEPR, ed. Chad Bown,141–152.

agreements. Mill (1884) argued that a country can improve its welfare by unilaterally using a small tariff.[3] This requires the country to have import market power, so its demand reduction improves its terms-of-trade. However, this is an international zero-sum game — the importers' improvement comes at the expense of the exporter, who is likely to retaliate, thus leaving both worse off. This simple insight underlies leading modern theories of reciprocal trade agreements, which have assumed that (i) countries have market power and (ii) they exert it in the absence of such agreements.[4] Both of these assumptions have been strongly questioned by many economists who more readily attribute protection to political economy incentives. But there was little econometric evidence either way until I conducted the research with Christian Broda and David Weinstein, which is presented in Chapter 2.

An importers' market power is determined by the responsiveness of its terms-of-trade to changes in its import demand, which is determined by the elasticity of foreign export supply. So, the first contribution in Chapter 2 are those elasticities for more than 800 goods in each of the 15 countries. We find that even small countries have market power, mostly in differentiated products rather than commodities. To determine if countries exploit this market power, we then analyze their tariff rates prior to entry in the World Trade Organization (WTO) and find that they are higher in products where a country has more market power. The effect is economically large and at least as important as a variable that can capture the influence of domestic special interests on trade protection.

The canonical trade models have not focused on the uncertainty motive for agreements, despite the importance that international institutions attribute to this role. The predecessor of the

---

[3]Mill, J.S. 1844. *Essays on some Unsettled Questions of Political Economy.* London: Parker.

[4]See Bagwell, K. and R.W. Staiger, 1999, "An Economic Theory of GATT," *American Economic Review,* 89, 215–248; and Grossman, G. and E. Helpman, 1995, "Trade Wars and Trade talks," *Journal of Political Economy,* 103, 675–708.

WTO was created in response to the 1930s trade war to help prevent a re-occurrence, and many regional agreements claim as a central objective to "ensure a predictable environment for business planning and investment". In Chapter 3, Giovanni Maggi and I show that international agreements that focus on reducing policy uncertainty are more likely to generate welfare gains for economies that are more specialized and less responsive to price changes. We also develop a "sufficient statistic" to quantify the gains from these agreements and show that they are relatively higher when trade costs are low and economies become very open. This provides one explanation for the recent proliferation in regional agreements — as trade costs unrelated to policy fell, countries became more open and vulnerable to foreign policy uncertainty, and thus sought agreements to reduce it.

The idea that aggregate economic uncertainty can have powerful impacts on economic activity was already noted by Keynes, and recent evidence indicates that aggregate uncertainty shocks can have negative effects on aggregate activity via firm-level investments. Until recently, research in this area has focused on uncertainty from purely economic shocks. However, policy uncertainty (about future taxes, regulatory reforms, etc.) is thought to be just as important, and, until recently, there was scarce evidence about how to measure it and identify its causal impacts. The research in Chapters 4 and 5 analyze these issues in the context of trade policy uncertainty (TPU). The trade setting is interesting both in its own right and because it provides a rich source of data and quasi-experiments. First, we can observe the "sales" taxes (tariffs) that firms face in different export markets as well as the counterfactual worst-case tariffs, which allow us to measure TPU. Second, we can also observe some investment outcomes by product and destination, which provide a rich source of variation that helps address identification issues. Third, there have been a substantial number of trade reforms, which provide a variety of settings in which to explore whether and how governments affect TPU.

In Chapter 4, Kyle Handley and I incorporate TPU in a trade model where firms decide whether to make irreversible investments to enter new markets. We show that investment and entry into export markets are reduced by TPU and that credible international agreements can reduce this uncertainty. We derive a theory-based measure of TPU and apply it to examine the entry of a developing country, Portugal, to the European Community in 1986. Employing newly available firm-level data on market entry and sales we find that (i) the accession removed Portuguese exporters' uncertainty about future European Community trade policies, and (ii) this accounted for a substantial fraction of the subsequent export growth. These results have broader implications for other agreements and, in particular, for the current debate on Brexit, since one of the possible scenarios is that the U.K. retains some preferential access to the European Union, but the uncertainty of eventual withdrawal or prospect of barriers if a trade war breaks out may considerably dampen trade between them.

In Chapter 5, we address the role of the WTO in reducing TPU. We examine the role of WTO accession in reducing TPU faced by China and how it has impacted its global integration. The WTO accession coincided with a Chinese export boom, which was particularly large towards the U.S., even though only a few of the U.S.-applied trade policies changed at that time. Our hypothesis is that this boom was fueled by a reduction in TPU. Specifically, China's WTO accession led the U.S. to end its annual threat to impose prohibitively high tariffs on Chinese imports. We estimate that the removal of this source of TPU increased Chinese exports to the U.S. by about 22%. The resulting price effects imply a considerable real income gain for U.S. consumers. This is a benefit that is frequently overlooked in the China syndrome debate that has fueled the recent backlash against trade agreements.

Part II: Domestic Externalities and the Role of International Trade Agreements

Trade policy is frequently used for redistribution within countries, either towards particular industries or factory owners that lobby the government. Certain political economy determinants of trade policy may motivate countries to commit to policy restrictions via trade agreements. This commitment motive for agreements is present if *ex ante* restrictions can improve *ex post* outcomes. For example, the current government may have different preferences from a future one, or commitment to a policy today may affect the allocation of factors and help a government address a time consistency problem.[5] Redistributive policies impose obvious domestic externalities since some groups will bear a cost. The questions then become what is the more efficient redistribution policy and whether trade agreements play any role in the choice of that policy and its magnitude.

The leading political economy models explain trade policy in a small economy as a way to redistribute income across agents, but they fail to explain why governments would ever *choose* to use certain trade policy instruments when other policies could achieve the same at lower cost. This policy choice question in the presence of political pressures also arises in other fields of economics and is an important puzzle in political economy. In Chapter 7, with Allan Drazen, I address this issue in the context of bargaining between a politician who seeks "payments" from domestic special interest groups in exchange for a redistribution policy, e.g., a production subsidy. We show that, in an initial stage, the politician has an incentive to restrict the use of efficient redistribution policies in order to subsequently extract higher payments from the special interest group.

One important policy commitment mechanism that is often used is trade agreements, which restrict tariffs, but not necessarily other trade instruments that are relatively costlier to use for redistribution. Thus in Chapter 6, with Patricia Tovar, we extend the model in Chapter 7 to address the choice between different trade

[5]See, for example, Staiger, Robert and Guido Tabellini. 1987. "Discretionary trade policy and excessive protection," *American Economic Review*, 77(5), 823–837; and Maggi, Giovanni and Andres Rodriguez-Clare. 1998. "The value of trade agreements in the presence of political pressures," *Journal of Political Economy*, 106(3), 574–601.

policies. We show that governments are more likely to constrain tariffs via international agreements in industries that have more bargaining power, even when they know that lobbies in that industry will be able to pursue and obtain redistribution via less efficient non-tariff barriers. We find empirical support for this model, and thus for the commitment motive for trade agreements.

Trade policy can and is used not only to redistribute towards special interest groups but also to ameliorate income inequality. In Chapter 8, Arvind Panagaryia and I argue that a government's concern for inequality is an important determinant of trade policy in many economies. Although trade policy is not the first-best instrument to reduce inequality, it is often supported for that purpose in opinion polls. Moreover, import protection is often higher in sectors with a large share of low-skill, low-wage workers, which strongly suggests that many governments take inequality into account when setting trade policy. We then show that this motive generates a systematic anti-trade bias, i.e., it generates trade protection rather than liberalization. Therefore, in the ongoing debates of the impact of trade liberalization on income inequality, more attention needs to be devoted to address reverse causality.

Part III: Externalities and Linkage of Cooperation Across Policies

To understand the impact of agreements, we must understand not only their motives but also their policy scope, membership, and how their rules are enforced. The appropriate scope and enforcement tools in the WTO have been under scrutiny since its inception in 1995, and more recently by countries such as the U.S. The WTO contains a dispute settlement system but has no power to enforce any of its rulings. Therefore, commitments in the WTO are only credible if its individual members have the incentive and ability to enforce them. Prior to the WTO, this enforcement relied mainly on the threat of a few large countries to raise tariffs on goods of a violating country. Two important expansions in this period led me to examine whether alternative agreement designs could enforce more cooperation.

The first change was the expansion of the policy scope in trade agreements. In the context of multilateral agreements, this expansion has occurred since the creation of the GATT. However, the largest expansion in scope was the inclusion of intellectual property rights protection in the WTO. The so-called TRIPS agreement may have increased the incentives for firms to expand trade and foreign direct investment (FDI) with developing countries. However, the threat of the U.S. using tariffs to enforce royalty payments by Indian firms was extremely controversial; as were subsequent attempts to enforce cooperation in environmental and labor issues in the WTO.

Many economists opposed this scope expansion in the WTO, arguing that linking cooperation across issues would reduce cooperation in trade policy, which is also not the first-best policy to target non-trade issues. However, there was little understanding of the impact of issue linkage on enforcement. I address this issue in Chapter 9, where I model the WTO as a self-enforcing agreement in the presence of cross-border externalities in two issues. I show under what conditions linking cooperation in the policies can increase cooperation in both (e.g., stronger environmental standards and lower tariffs) or in one at the expense of the other.

This expansion in policy scope is even more widespread in preferential trade agreements.[6] We require a framework to understand this, given the tremendous proliferation of these agreements, which have been the primary source of trade policy liberalization in the last 25 years. In Chapter 8, I provide a framework to analyze the effects of such agreements, where large countries provide market access to small ones in return for cooperation on various policies with international externalities, including intellectual property, environmental, labor, and security policies.

[6]Limão, Nuno. 2016. "Preferential Trade Agreements", *Handbook of Commercial Policy*, eds. Kyle Bagwell and Robert Staiger, Elsevier.

A second important change in the world trading system since the early 1990s has been the expansion and change in the composition of WTO membership. Specifically, the increased importance of developing countries in world trade and in the WTO, where they now account for more than two-thirds of the membership. This shift reflects the growth of these economies and their unilateral liberalizations. However, several of these countries are still individually small and thus have a limited ability to bilaterally extract and enforce trade concessions from larger developed economies — even though they would be able to do so as a group. Some developing countries have thus proposed to extend the agreement to allow for financial compensation mechanisms. In Chapter 11, Kamal Saggi and I argue that the canonical two-country model of trade agreements must be augmented to capture this new, more fragmented, trade order. We show that redesigning the WTO to include certain financial enforcement instruments is preferable to the current arrangement from both an efficiency and equity perspective. In Chapter 12, we show that such arrangements are much less valuable in a setting where countries are similar, which may help us understand why they were not adopted by the initial set of more homogeneous members.

Part IV: Policy Externalities Across Agreements: Multilateral vs. Preferential Liberalization

Countries choose both the scope of agreements and also whether to pursue them multilaterally through the WTO or only with a preferential subset of countries. Since the creation of the WTO, there has been no successful major multilateral trade negotiation; the Doha Round was launched in 2001 and is yet to be concluded. However, countries have continued to liberalize through preferential trade agreements (PTAs), as is evident from the large increase in their numbers and bilateral trade. The fraction of country pairs in the WTO that also belong to PTAs increased by a factor of 10 in that period, and in 2010 they accounted for over 50% of trade between WTO members (Limão, 2016). This raises the question of how preferential and multilateral agreements and policies interact.

A similar question about the externalities across agreements arose in the early 1990s when PTAs started to propagate at the same time that there was a stalling of the Uruguay Round, which lead to the WTO only years later. While, on average, PTAs have increased trade between members, there is a concern that they harm non-members and hinder liberalization via the WTO. The latter systematic risk was modeled by several leading theorists in the field who sought to determine whether regional agreements affect the incentive for aggregate multilateral liberalization, i.e., the likelihood for a WTO trade round. Unfortunately, we cannot test such theories econometrically as there have been very few multilateral trade rounds.

The framework I developed in Chapter 8 suggested a new approach to test the externalities across agreements. It predicts that PTAs affect multilateral incentives differentially across goods. In Chapter 13, I test for these differential incentives using detailed multilateral tariff data for the U.S. I find that the U.S. kept multilateral tariffs higher on goods it imported under PTAs. In Chapter 14, with Baybars Karacavaoli, we find similar evidence for goods that the European Union imports duty free from other PTAs.

In Chapter 15, with Marcelo Olarreaga, we quantify one of the externalities that PTAs impose on multilateral liberalization for non-members. We combine the estimates from Chapter 13 with data for up to 5,000 goods in each of the 170 countries and provide the first estimates of the welfare effects of PTAs due to lost multilateral liberalization. We also evaluate a rule designed to avoid the negative effects of PTAs on future multilateral liberalization, and find it would increase the welfare gains from a future WTO round by 10%.

I hope this collection informs and inspires others to continue to improve our knowledge of these vital economic issues.

Part I
International Externalities and the Role of International Trade Agreements

Chapter 2

Optimal Tariffs and Market Power: The Evidence

By CHRISTIAN BRODA, NUNO LIMÃO, AND DAVID E. WEINSTEIN*

We find that prior to World Trade Organization membership, countries set import tariffs 9 percentage points higher on inelastically supplied imports relative to those supplied elastically. The magnitude of this effect is similar to the size of average tariffs in these countries, and market power explains more of the tariff variation than a commonly used political economy variable. Moreover, US trade restrictions not covered by the WTO are significantly higher on goods where the United States has more market power. We find strong evidence that these importers have market power and use it in setting noncooperative trade policy. (*JEL* F12, F13)

The idea that countries set tariffs in response to their market power in international markets is a controversial result in international economics. For example, Kyle Bagwell and Robert W. Staiger (1999) argue that it provides the underlying motive for the world trading system, while Paul R. Krugman and Maurice Obstfeld (1997, 226) argue that "the terms-of-trade argument is of little practical importance." Given that the theoretical debate over optimal tariffs goes back over a century, one might ask, "What evidence is there in favor or against the notion that tariffs vary inversely with foreign export supply elasticities?" The answer is none.[1]

The theory that a country with market power in trade might gain from protection has a long history but its main insight can be summarized as follows.[2] A tariff creates consumption and production distortions, but it also creates a terms-of-trade gain if the foreign supply is inelastic, i.e., if the importer has market power. Thus, in the absence of constraints such as trade agreements,

* Broda: Graduate School of Business, University of Chicago, 5807 S. Woodlawn Avenue, Chicago, IL 60637 (e-mail: cbroda@chicagogsb.edu); Limão: Department of Economics, University of Maryland, 3105 Tydings Hall, College Park, MD 20742 (e-mail: limao@econ.umd.edu); Weinstein: Economics Department, Columbia University, 420 West 118th St., MC 3308, New York, NY 10027 (e-mail: dew35@columbia.edu). Broda and Weinstein would like to thank the National Science Foundation for generous funding under grant 0214378. Limão gratefully acknowledges the excellent research assistance of Piyush Chandra and the financial support of the International Monetary Fund research department where he was a resident scholar during part of this research. Weinstein would like to thank the Center for Japanese Economy and Business for research support. We thank Stephanie Aaronson, Fernando Alvarez, Kyle Bagwell, Alan Deardorff, Peter Debaere, Bill Ethier, John Romalis, Robert Staiger, two anonymous referees, and the editor for extremely useful and detailed comments. We also thank seminar participants at various institutions for numerous comments and suggestions (CEPR trade meeting Summer 2006, Chicago Federal Reserve, Empirical Investigations in Trade 2006, Dartmouth College, Harvard University, IMF, Midwest International Economics Spring 2006, NBER ITI meeting Winter 2006, Princeton University, Johns Hopkins University, Syracuse University, University of Chicago, University of Virginia, and University of Wisconsin). The views expressed in this paper are those of the authors.

[1] There is some evidence that changes in trade policy affect the prices of the goods that countries import (c.f. Mordechai E. Kreinin 1961; Won Chang and Alan L. Winters 2002; Robert C. Feenstra 1989). This evidence generally attributes the effect to imperfect competition in specific industries. More importantly, these studies do not argue or estimate whether countries changed their trade policies to affect their terms-of-trade, much less if they did so taking the export supply elasticity into account. Since our initial working paper, however, independent research by Bagwell and Staiger (2006) provides evidence for their theory by showing that WTO accession leads to greater tariff reductions in products with higher initial import volumes.

[2] Seminal contributions on this issue extend back to Robert Torrens (1833) and include John S. Mill (1844), Francis Y. Edgeworth (1894), Tibor Scitovsky (1942), and Harry G. Johnson (1954). Douglas A. Irwin (1996) carefully discusses the history of thought on optimal tariffs.

Originally Published in *American Economic Review* 98(5), pp. 2032–2065.

the theory predicts a positive relationship between a country's tariffs and its market power. The original derivation of such a relationship by Charles F. Bickerdike (1907) focused on the "optimal tariff" set by a welfare maximizing government. But the positive relationship between tariffs and market power also arises in more general settings that do not require welfare maximization, as we discuss in the theory section.

Our objective in this paper is to quantify the importance of the market power (or terms-of-trade) motive in trade policy. In doing so, we make three contributions. First, we estimate elasticities of export supply faced by 15 importer countries at a highly disaggregated level. Second, we use these elasticities to provide evidence that prior to constraints imposed by the World Trade Organization (WTO), these countries systematically set higher import tariffs on goods in which they have market power. Finally, we estimate similar elasticities for the United States and find that its trade restrictions that are not constrained by the WTO are significantly higher in goods where the United States has more market power. The results are robust to the inclusion of political economy variables and a variety of model specifications. The effect is statistically and economically significant relative to both other explanations and to the average tariff in the typical country. In short, we find strong evidence that countries have market power in imports and exploit it in setting their trade policy.

We rely on the methodology of Feenstra (1994) and Broda and Weinstein (2006) to estimate the export supply elasticities at the four-digit Harmonized System (HS) level over the period 1994–2003. Our sample consists of the 15 countries for which we could obtain tariff data for a large fraction of products prior to constraints imposed by WTO membership. We find that the inverse export supply elasticity faced by an importer is between one and three for the typical four-digit HS good. We also test several conjectures about these elasticities and find support for them in our estimates. For example, larger countries face less elastic export supply curves, which indicate that, on average, they have more market power than small countries. Moreover, these elasticities are positively correlated across importing countries for any given good. This is likely to be the case if importers systematically have more market power for some types of goods. We confirm this conjecture by finding that importers face much flatter export supply curves for commodities, where the inverse elasticity is 0.5, than for differentiated products, where it is 2.4.

Using these elasticities, we then estimate that, prior to WTO constraints, these countries set higher tariffs on products where they have more market power. This effect is present both when we compare median tariff rates across countries and when we compare actual tariff rates across HS four-digit goods within countries and industries. The impact of market power on tariffs is robust to many different specifications. The effect is present using continuous and discontinuous versions of the export supply elasticity measure and controlling for unobserved industry heterogeneity in *each* country. The estimate is positive and significant in the pooled sample and also positive in all countries and significant in 13 of the 15 countries studied. Moreover, we address the possibility of omitted variable bias and measurement error via an instrumental variables approach.

The result is also robust to the inclusion of variables that capture two prominent motives for protection: revenue and lobbying. As is common in recent tests of political economy models (e.g., Pinelopi K. Goldberg and Giovanni Maggi 1999), we find that the lobbying effect is strong. Nonetheless, the market power effect on tariffs remains positive and significant. It is at least as important as the lobbying motive, both in terms of the magnitude and the fraction of tariff variation explained.

The estimated effect is also economically important. In particular, we find that the countries in our sample set tariffs about 9 percentage points higher in goods with medium or high market power relative to those with low market power; in China it is 35 percentage points. This is roughly the same magnitude of China's average tariff over all goods and the same relationship between the effect and the average tariff holds for the typical country. We estimate that removing this motive for tariff setting would lead to significant increases in the prices received by foreign exporters, particularly those selling in the larger countries in our sample: China, Russia, and Taiwan.

In order to follow the theory closely, we focus on countries' tariffs prior to their WTO membership so they are set in a unilateral, noncooperative way. However, we also analyze the role of market power in shaping a subset of trade policies that are determined noncooperatively by the United States, a large member of the WTO. The United States sets nontariff barriers and statutory tariffs (i.e., rates it applies to some non-WTO members) with few or no restrictions from the WTO. We find that market power is also an important determinant of these trade policies that the United States sets unilaterally. Interestingly, we find no such effect on those US tariffs set according to WTO rules. This finding is broadly consistent with Bagwell and Staiger's theory of the WTO, and it suggests that market power would play an important role for *all* US trade policies if they were set noncooperatively, e.g., in the absence of the WTO. More generally, the results for the United States show that the importance of the terms-of-trade motive extends to WTO members, and so understanding its impact on trade policy is essential.

The paper is organized as follows. We first present the basic theory that we test. In Section II we describe the estimation methodology for the elasticities. In Section III, we describe the data and assess the validity of the elasticity estimates. We present the estimation results of the impact of market power on trade policy in Sections IV and V, and conclude in Section VI.

I. Theory

The basic theory underlying the optimal tariff argument is well established. Therefore, in this section, we provide the basic intuition for the result and show how it is robust to the inclusion of political economy considerations. We are interested in how a country sets policy in the absence of agreements. So we focus on a country that takes as given the policies of the remaining $n \geq 1$ countries.

A. *Optimal Tariffs: The Benchmark Case*

Suppose each individual has a utility defined over a numeraire good, c_0, and a vector of non-numeraire goods $u(\mathbf{c})$. Here we consider the simpler case where $u(\mathbf{c})$ is separable. Omitting the country subscript, we write this individual's utility as

$$U = c_0^h + \sum_g u_g(c_g^h). \tag{1}$$

Each individual h with income I^h chooses expenditure on each good c_g to maximize (1), subject to $c_0^h + \sum_g p_g c_g^h \leq I^h$, where p_g is the domestic price for c_g. Given this utility, the demand for each good g is simply a function of its own price, i.e., $c_g = c_g(p_g)$. Social welfare is then the sum of the individual indirect utilities, which includes income and consumer surplus:[3]

$$W = \sum_h [I^h + \sum_g \psi_g(p_g)]. \tag{2}$$

To determine income, we employ the standard assumptions in the leading endogenous trade policy models, e.g., Gene Grossman and Elhanan Helpman (1994, 1995). First, the numeraire is

[3] More specifically, $\sum_g \psi_g(p_g) \equiv \sum_g [u_g(c_g(p_g)) - p_g c_g(p_g)]$.

freely traded and produced using only labor according to a constant returns production. So, the equilibrium wage is determined by the marginal product in this sector, which we normalize to one. Second, the nonnumeraire goods are produced under constant returns to scale using labor and one factor specific to the good. This means that each specific factor earns a quasi-rent that is increasing in the good's price, $\pi_g(p_g)$. Finally, tariff revenues for each good, $r_g(p_g)$, are redistributed uniformly to all individuals. All individuals own a unit of labor and a fraction of them also own up to one unit of specific capital. If we normalize the population to be one and recall the wage is also unity, we can rewrite social welfare as

$$W = 1 + \sum_g [\pi_g(p_g) + r_g(p_g) + \psi_g(p_g)]. \tag{3}$$

The world price for each traded good $g \in G_m$ is determined by the market clearing conditions

$$m_g((1 + \tau_g)p_g^*) = m_g^*(p_g^*) \quad \forall g \in G_m, \tag{4}$$

where m_g represents home's import demand written as a function of the domestic price, $p_g = (1 + \tau_g)p_g^*$, and m_g^* is the rest of the world's export supply. From this we obtain prices as functions of the trade policy, i.e., $p_g(\tau_g)$, $p_g^*(\tau_g)$.[4]

A government choosing the tariff to maximize (3) will set it according to the following first-order condition:[5]

$$\tau_g p_g^* \frac{dm_g}{d\tau_g} - m_g \frac{dp_g^*}{d\tau_g} = 0 \quad \forall g \in G_m. \tag{5}$$

The first term represents the domestic distortion caused by the negative impact of tariffs on import levels. The second term represents the terms-of-trade effect. If the country has no market power in trade, i.e., if the export supply elasticity is infinite, then $dp_g^* / d\tau_g = 0$, and the optimal tariff is zero. Otherwise, the optimal tariff is positive and can be shown to equal the inverse export supply elasticity,[6]

$$\tau_g^{opt} = \omega_g \equiv [(dm_g^* / dp_g^*)(p_g^* / m_g^*)]^{-1}. \tag{6}$$

B. *Optimal Tariffs: Extensions*

The positive relationship between protection and the inverse elasticity, ω_g, extends to more general settings. Here we highlight a few points. The separability assumption in our model implies that the tariffs in (6) do not reflect any monopoly power in the export sector. The bottom line from studies that consider market power in the export sector is that market power may create an additional motive for the use of import tariffs (c.f. Jan de V. Graf 1949–1950 and Fernando E. Alvarez and Robert E. Lucas 2007; Daniel Gros (1987), shows this is the case even for "small" countries when products are differentiated), but this additional motive does not

[4] In a setting with many importers, the equilibrium prices also depend on other importers' tariffs. This does not affect the results here because the optimal tariff prediction takes the other countries' policies as given *and* we will focus on the case where there is a constant foreign export supply elasticity that is independent of prices.

[5] Taking $dW/d\tau_g = 0$, and using the envelope theorem, $d\psi_g(p_g)/d\tau_g = -c_g[dp_g/d\tau_g]$ and $dp_g/d\tau_g = (1 + \tau_g)(dp_g^*/d\tau_g) + p_g^*$, we obtain (5).

[6] By applying the implicit function theorem to (4), we obtain an expression for $dp_g^*/d\tau_g$, which can be used in (5) to obtain the expression in (6) after some algebraic manipulation.

eliminate the first-order incentive to impose higher tariffs in sectors in which imports are supplied less elastically.

The positive relationship between tariffs and inverse elasticities also holds *even if* the government's objective is not social welfare maximization. For example, Grossman and Helpman (1995) extend their political contributions trade model to the large country case. The noncooperative tariff that the government chooses in that model maximizes a weighted sum of social welfare and contributions, C_g, from the L organized lobbies representing specific factor owners, i.e., $aW + \sum_{g \in L} C_g$. In this case, the tariff is

$$\tau_g^{GH} = \omega_g + \frac{I_g - \alpha}{a + \alpha} \frac{z_g}{\sigma_g}, \tag{7}$$

where the last term reflects the lobbying motive for tariffs. If a is infinite, then we obtain the welfare maximizing optimal tariff. More importantly, the partial positive relationship between the tariff and ω_g holds even when the government places *no* weight on social welfare, which we can immediately see by setting a equal to zero and noting that the second term in (7) remains finite. In sum, even though the terms-of-trade motive for tariffs is often associated with a welfare-maximizing government, such a relationship can also arise even if governments care *only* about lobbies' contributions.[7]

In equation (7) the tariff for an organized group is increasing in z_g, the inverse import penetration ratio, because a given tariff generates larger benefits for a factor owner if it applies to more units sold.[8] The tariff depends negatively on the import demand elasticity, σ_g, reflecting the basic Ramsey taxation intuition that, once the terms-of-trade effect is accounted for, the tariff's distortion is increasing in this elasticity. As Helpman (1997) shows, the size and elasticity effect captured by z_g/σ_g also arises in other political economy models and so we will use this variable as one of the controls in the estimation.

The key obstacle in estimating the impact of market power on tariffs is obtaining elasticity estimates for a broad set of countries and goods. In order to achieve this, we must impose some structure on the data. We now briefly describe how the standard approach above can be extended in a way that is both compatible with our estimation of the elasticities *and* delivers the positive effect of market power on tariffs.

In the next section, we describe the system of import demand and export supply equations that we use to estimate the elasticities. This system can be derived in a setting where any foreign variety (i.e., a good imported from a particular exporter) is valued according to a CES utility function, and supply is perfectly competitive. In the appendix of our working paper (available on request), we show that the optimal tariff in a model with CES utility over foreign varieties of a given good is identical to equation (6), i.e., the inverse export elasticity. This happens when utility is separable across goods (but not varieties). The tariffs do not affect the relative demand of varieties within any given good, and hence the only distortion that is addressed by the tariff is the terms-of-trade externality.[9]

[7] In this setting, this occurs because lobbies' contributions account for all the costs and benefits of the tariffs they bid on, including the terms-of-trade gain the lobbies reap via the redistributed tariff revenue.

[8] The variable z_g is defined as the ratio of domestic production value to import value, where the latter excludes tariffs.

[9] As we prove in that appendix, there are three assumptions that imply the tariff in a good does not affect the relative demand of varieties within it; these assumptions are mainly driven by the constraints imposed by the data, sample, and estimation. First, consumption and foreign export supply elasticities within any given good are constant. Second, they are identical across varieties, i.e., exporters of that good. Third, tariffs of a given country in any given year are equal across exporters of the same good.

II. Estimating Foreign Export Supply and Import Demand Elasticities

A key reason why the impact of market power on tariffs has not been examined before is the difficulty of obtaining reliable measures of the elasticity of foreign export supply. In fact, most estimates of trade elasticities simply assume that countries face an infinitely elastic supply of exports and therefore estimate only import demand elasticities. In this section, we explain how to obtain the elasticities of foreign export supply and import demand for each good in each importing country. We do so using a methodology derived by Feenstra (1994) and extended by Broda and Weinstein (2006).[10]

We estimate the import demand and *inverse* export supply elasticities (σ_{ig} and ω_{ig}, respectively), using the following system of import and export equations:

$$\Delta^{k_{ig}} \ln s_{igvt} = -(\sigma_{ig} - 1)\,\Delta^{k_{ig}} \ln p_{igvt} + \varepsilon^{k_{ig}}_{igvt}; \tag{8}$$

$$\Delta^{k_{ig}} \ln p_{igvt} = \frac{\omega_{ig}}{1+\omega_{ig}}\,\Delta^{k_{ig}} \ln s_{igvt} + \delta^{k_{ig}}_{igvt}. \tag{9}$$

Equation (8) represents the optimal demand of country i for a given variety v of a good g—derived from a CES utility function—and (9) represents the residual export supply country i faces in that variety. Both are expressed in terms of shares, where s_{igvt} is the share of variety v of good g in country i. The equation for each variety imported by country i is differenced with respect to time t *and* a benchmark variety of the same good g imported by i, denoted k_{ig}. Thus, the difference operator we use for the shares and domestic prices is defined as $\Delta^{k_{ig}} x_{igvt} = \Delta x_{igvt} - \Delta x_{igk_{ig}t}$, where Δ stands for a simple time difference. The last parameter in (8), $\varepsilon^{k_{ig}}_{igvt} = \varepsilon_{igvt} - \varepsilon_{igk_{ig}t}$, represents demand shocks that differ across varieties, for example, ε_{igvt} includes *changes* in taste or quality for a variety v over time. Similarly, $\delta^{k_{ig}}_{igvt} = \delta_{igvt} - \delta_{igk_{ig}t}$, where δ_{igvt} includes shocks to the residual export supply when expressed as a function of importer prices. One important shock to supply is bilateral exchange rate *changes* between countries i and v. We can see how exchange rates would enter into δ_{igvt} by rewriting the domestic price as

$$p_{igvt} = (1 + \tau_{igvt})\, e_{ivt}\, p^{*}_{igvt},$$

where τ_{igvt} is some ad valorem trading cost (e.g., tariffs), and e_{ivt} is the bilateral exchange rate between i and v. In this case, k-differencing would produce

$$\Delta^{k_{ig}} \ln p_{igvt} = \Delta^{k_{ig}} \ln(1 + \tau_{igvt}) + \Delta^{k_{ig}} \ln e_{ivt} + \Delta^{k_{ig}} \ln p^{*}_{igvt},$$

so the export supply error, $\delta^{k_{ig}}_{igvt}$, contains the bilateral exchange rate shock. Since these are frequent and large, they are likely to be a more important source of variation than shocks to relative trade costs—a point that we discuss further below.

There are two important conditions needed to identify the elasticities. First, ω_{ig} and σ_{ig} are constant over varieties and this time period (but they can vary over importers and goods). Second, demand and supply shocks *relative* to the benchmark variety are assumed to be uncorrelated, i.e.,

[10] Broda and Weinstein (2006) estimate import demand elasticities for a range of imports but do not report the export supply elasticities. Feenstra (1994) reports both elasticities for eight specific products. Both studies focus only on the United States. Irwin (1988) and John Romalis (2007) report both elasticities. However, because they are estimated at the aggregate level and for only two countries (the United Kingdom and United States, respectively), they cannot be used to estimate the impact of market power on tariffs.

$E_t\,(\varepsilon^{k_{ig}}_{igvt}\,\delta^{k_{ig}}_{igvt}) = 0$. To take advantage of the latter condition, we solve (8) and (9) in terms of the errors and multiply them together to obtain:

$$(\Delta^{k_{ig}} \ln p_{igvt})^2 = \theta_{i1}\,(\Delta^{k_{ig}} \ln s_{igvt})^2 + \theta_{i2}\,(\Delta^{k_{ig}} \ln p_{igvt}\,\Delta^{k_{ig}} \ln s_{igvt}) + u_{igvt}, \tag{10}$$

$$\text{where } \theta_{ig1} = \frac{\omega_{ig}}{(1+\omega_{ig})(\sigma_{ig}-1)},\ \theta_{ig2} = \frac{\omega_{ig}(\sigma_{ig}-2)-1}{(1+\omega_{ig})(\sigma_{ig}-1)},\ \text{and } u_{igvt} = \frac{\varepsilon^{k_{ig}}_{igvt}\,\delta^{k_{ig}}_{igvt}}{\sigma_{ig}-1}.$$

Note that the new error term, u_{igvt}, is correlated with the "independent" variables in equation (10) that depend on prices and expenditure shares. However, Feenstra (1994) shows that a consistent estimator of $\boldsymbol{\theta}_{\mathbf{ig}} = (\theta_{ig1}, \theta_{ig2})$ can be obtained by averaging (10) over time. To see this we can write the "between" version of (10) as:

$$\overline{Y}_{igv} = \theta_{ig1}\,\overline{X}_{1,igv} + \theta_{ig2}\,\overline{X}_{2,igv} + \overline{u}_{igv}, \tag{11}$$

where $Y_{igvt} = (\Delta^{k_{ig}} \ln p_{igvt})^2$, $X_{1,igvt} = (\Delta^{k_{ig}} \ln s_{igvt})^2$, $X_{2,igvt} = (\Delta^{k_{ig}} \ln p_{igvt}\,\Delta^{k_{ig}} \ln s_{igvt})$, and the bars on top of these variables denote their time averages (the t subscript is dropped). The independence of errors assumption implies that $E_v\,(\overline{u}_{igv}) = 0$. Intuitively, the time-series identification problem of a single importer-good pair is solved by using the information available in all the varieties imported of that good. While data on prices and shares of a single variety can pin down a relationship between σ_{ig} and ω_{ig}, they are insufficient to determine the exact value of these elasticities. Additional varieties of the same importer-good pair provide information about how these elasticities are related, and given that the true σ_{ig} and ω_{ig} are assumed constant across varieties of the same good, this information helps estimate the elasticities.

Feenstra (1994) also notes that provided there are three varieties of the same importer-good pair that are sufficiently different in their second moments, the true underlying elasticities are exactly identified. We will slightly modify this criterion and follow the procedure in Broda and Weinstein (2006). They show that in the presence of measurement error in the prices used to compute unit values for each variety, an additional term needs to be added to (10) and a different weighting scheme should be used to estimate (11). In particular, unit values are generally better measured when based on large volumes. Therefore, the weights and the additional term are inversely related to the quantity imported of the variety and the number of periods the variety had positive imports. This implies that at least four varieties per good are needed to obtain identification.

Using this weighting scheme, we first estimate (11) to obtain $\hat{\boldsymbol{\theta}}_{\mathbf{ig}}$ and check that it implies elasticities in the set of economically feasible estimates, i.e., $\sigma_{ig} > 1$ and $\omega_{ig} > 0$ for all i and g. If this fails, we perform a grid search over the feasible values of $\boldsymbol{\theta}_{\mathbf{ig}}$. We evaluate the sum of squared errors of (11) at values of $\sigma_{ig} > 1$ and $\omega_{ig} > 0$ at intervals that are approximately 5 percent apart.[11]

The precision for the typical elasticity is obtained by bootstrapping. We resampled the data for each importer-good pair 250 times and computed estimates of the importer-good elasticity each time. The procedure used to compute these bootstrapped elasticities is similar to the one used in the estimation of the actual elasticities.

Several features of this estimation strategy help us to avoid concerns that usually make it difficult to obtain consistent estimates. First, one might be worried that if countries impose tariffs in response to demand shocks, this might cause a correlation between demand and supply shocks.

[11] We present additional details about the specific computational procedure in our working paper.

However, if these tariff changes are implemented identically across exporters of any given good g (as they often are), then that effect is purged from the export supply error in our estimation since $\Delta^{k_{ig}} \ln(1 + \tau_{igvt}) = \Delta \ln(1 + \tau_{igvt}) - \Delta \ln(1 + \tau_{igk_{ig}t}) = 0$. As a result, such tariff changes will not affect the estimates. This also implies that the *level* of tariffs on varieties or goods will not affect our estimated elasticities, which reduces the possibility of reverse causality when we estimate their effect on tariffs.[12]

Note that the double differencing is also useful in controlling for other factors that could otherwise induce a correlation of the error terms. For example, if some countries produce higher quality goods at higher cost, the time-differencing of the data will eliminate any correlation in the levels. Similarly, if the quality and cost of a good are rising, the time and k-differencing will eliminate any correlation between demand and supply as long as the trend in quality is common across exporters.

In the robustness section, we analyze if our results are sensitive to some of the identifying assumptions; for now we simply note why they may be plausible. The elasticity of substitution over varieties of a good, σ_{ig}, is a preference parameter and thus not likely to vary across the short time period we examine or across varieties for a finely defined good. The residual export supply elasticity, ω_{ig}, depends, among other things, on production elasticities and on the rest of the world's import demand elasticities, $\sigma_{j \neq ig}$. The latter should not change much over the time span of our data, six to nine years, for the reason noted above. However, we will test whether allowing for different elasticities across exporters of a given good changes the results. Finally, the assumption of independence of relative errors is likely to be reasonable because the large shocks on a yearly frequency are often due to bilateral exchange rate changes. These are captured as supply shocks in (9) and, at this frequency, they are unlikely to be correlated with demand shocks such as relative taste or quality. Ultimately, this is an empirical question, and in the appendix of our working paper, we test and find evidence that supports this assumption.

III. Data, Descriptive Statistics, and Assessment of Elasticity Estimates

A. *Data*

In order to estimate the impact of market power, we need data on tariffs, domestic production, and elasticities. In deciding what set of countries to include, we face both theoretical and empirical constraints. The theory applies to countries setting their trade policy unilaterally in a noncooperative way. Since a major function of the General Agreement on Tariffs and Trade (GATT)/WTO is to allow countries to reciprocally lower their tariffs, possibly in order to internalize the terms-of-trade effects, we focus the test on policies that countries set prior to the constraints of GATT/WTO membership. In Section V, we provide additional evidence for a set of policies set noncooperatively by a WTO member.

[12] In an extreme version of the optimal tariff argument, we may expect countries to discriminate across all different exporters of the same good. This would entail very high administrative costs and thus is not the norm. The closest countries come to such discrimination is through preferential agreements. These agreements are not important for most countries in our sample. Some of them did, however, implement such agreements during the period for which we estimate elasticities. Those differential tariff changes are reflected only on the export supply error, $\delta_{igvt}^{k_{ig}}$, since the demand equation controls for the domestic price. Thus, such shocks do not invalidate our elasticity identification assumption unless there is some other simultaneous shock to relative demand. We address the possibility that such preferential tariff changes affect both the elasticity estimate *and* the nonpreferential tariffs by using instrumental variables in the tariff estimation section.

Table 1—Data Sources and Years

	GATT/WTO	Production data		Tariff data[a]	Trade data[b]
	Accession date	Source	Years		
Algeria				93	93–03
Belarus				97	98–03
Bolivia[c]	8-Sep-1990	UNIDO	93	93	93–03
China	11-Dec-2001	UNIDO	93	93	93–03
Czech[d]	15-Apr-1993			92	93–03
Ecuador	21-Jan-1996	UNIDO	93	93	94–03
Latvia	10-Feb-1999	UNIDO	96	97	94–03
Lebanon				00	97–02
Lithuania	31-May-2001	UNIDO	97	97	94–03
Oman	9-Nov-2000			92	94–03
Paraguay	6-Jan-1994			91	94–03
Russia				94	96–03
Saudi Arabia	11-Dec-2005			91	93–03
Taiwan	1-Jan-2002	UNIDO	96	96	92–96
Ukraine		UNIDO	97	97	96–02

[a] All tariff data are from TRAINS. Countries are included if we have tariff data for at least one year before accession (GATT/WTO).

[b] Except for Taiwan, all trade data are from COMTRADE. For Taiwan, data are from TRAINS.

[c] The date of the tariffs for Bolivia is post-GATT accession but those tariffs were set before GATT accession and unchanged between 1990–1993.

[d] The Czech Republic entered the GATT as a sovereign country in 1993. Its tariffs in 1992 were common to Slovakia with which it had a federation, which was a GATT member. So it is possible that the tariffs for this country do not reflect a terms-of-trade motive. Our results by country in Table 9 support this. Moreover, as we note in Section IVC, the pooled tariff results are robust to dropping the Czech Republic.

Our tariff data come from the TRAINS database, which provides data at the six-digit HS level. We focus on the 15 countries that report tariffs in at least one-third of all six-digit goods.[13] The set of countries and the years we use are reported in Table 1. Our sample includes a nonnegligible part of the world economy and is representative of the world as a whole in some dimensions. It includes countries from most continents. The average per capita GDP in the sample is $9,000, which is similar to the 1995 world average of $8,900. The 15 countries comprise 25 percent of the world's population and close to 20 percent of its GDP (in PPP terms). This is due to the fact that it includes two of the world's ten largest economies, China and Russia, as well as several smaller but nonnegligible countries such as Taiwan, Ukraine, Algeria, and Saudi Arabia.

The trade data are obtained from the United Nations Commodity Trade Statistics Database (COMTRADE). This database provides quantity and value data at six-digit 1992 HS classification for bilateral flows between all countries in the world. As we can see from Table 1, the import data for most countries in our sample cover the period 1994–2003. For Taiwan we use the United Nations Conference on Trade and Development (UNCTAD) TRAINS database since COMTRADE does not report data for this country.

B. *Descriptive Statistics*

The choice of what constitutes a good is dictated by data availability. The more disaggregated the choice of good, the fewer varieties per good we have, and thus at some point, the elasticity estimates

[13] Unfortunately, some non-WTO countries report this tariff data for only a small share of goods, making it impossible to make meaningful comparisons across goods. Our criteria were binding only for the Bahamas, Brunei, Seychelles, and Sudan.

TABLE 2—TRADE AND TARIFF DATA SUMMARY STATISTICS

	Trade data			Tariff data				
				Rate per four-digit HS				Fraction of HS6 variation between HS4
	Number of varieties[a]	Number of HS4 goods	Median # of var. per HS4	Observations[b]	Mean	Standard Deviation	Median	
Algeria	26,466	1,100	13	739	23.8	17.4	15.6	0.95
Belarus	24,440	1,172	12	703	12.4	7.8	10.0	0.94
Bolivia	18,592	1,064	9	647	9.8	0.8	10.0	0.63
China	63,764	1,217	33	1,125	37.9	26.0	30.3	0.93
Czech Republic	61,781	1,219	30	1,075	9.5	17.6	5.1	0.87
Ecuador	22,979	1,101	11	753	9.8	5.5	10.6	0.91
Latvia	33,790	1,128	17	872	7.3	10.5	1.0	0.90
Lebanon	34,187	1,109	15	782	17.1	14.8	15.0	0.87
Lithuania	34,825	1,159	17	811	3.6	7.4	0.0	0.90
Oman	20,482	1,107	10	629	5.7	8.7	5.0	0.76
Paraguay	15,430	1,049	7	511	16.1	11.3	14.0	0.91
Russian	66,731	1,187	34	1,029	10.7	11.0	5.7	0.95
Saudi Arabia	62,525	1,202	32	1,036	12.1	2.6	12.0	0.93
Taiwan	38,397	1,215	19	891	9.7	8.5	7.5	0.90
Ukraine	37,693	1,128	18	730	7.4	7.6	5.0	0.95
Median	34,187	1,128	17	782	9.8	8.7	10.0	0.91

[a] Varieties are defined as six-digit HS, exporting country pairs.
[b] Number of observations for which elasticities and tariffs are available.

become imprecise. Therefore, in estimating (8) and (9) we define a good, g, as a four-digit HS category and a variety, v, as a six-digit good from a particular exporter. Table 2 shows that the typical country has 1,100 four-digit categories with positive imports between 1994 and 2003. The typical good in the sample contains 17 HS6-country pairs. There are between 15,000 and 66,000 varieties being imported per year by each of these countries. For instance, there were 40 different varieties of live fish (four-digit HS 0301) imported by China in 2001, among them were "trout" (HS 030191) from Australia and "eels" (HS 030192) from Thailand. The high degree of specialization of exports suggests that one should be cautious about assuming that the share of a country in world GDP is a sufficient proxy for the ability of a country to gain from a tariff. If China places a tariff on live fish, it is not clear that Thailand can easily export its eels elsewhere and receive the same price.

Table 2 also shows statistics describing the tariff data at the HS4 level. There are several important features to note. First, variation across countries accounts for one-third of the total variation. The mean across countries ranges from 4 to 38 percent, with 10 being the typical value; the range and typical values for medians are similar to the mean. Second, there is also considerable variation within countries: the standard deviation ranges from 1 to 26 percent and 9 is the typical tariff value. Finally, since we estimate the elasticities at the HS4 level we aggregate the tariff data up to that level by taking simple averages. As we can see from the last column, the precise aggregation method and focus on HS4 variation has little impact since over 90 percent of the variation in tariffs for the typical country occurs across HS4 rather than within it.

If one were to take size, as measured by GDP, as a good proxy for market power, then the data on tariff levels suggest that the skepticism regarding the optimal tariff argument is not entirely unwarranted. First, as we can see in Table 2, although China is both the largest country in our sample and has the highest tariff, Taiwan, the third largest country, has a below average tariff. The correlation between median tariff and the log of GDP is 0.48 and that between average tariffs and GDP is 0.53 If we drop China, however, those correlations fall to 0.05 and 0.10, respectively.

Data on the within-country variation also suggests that the tariff setting policies are likely to be more complex than a simple application of the optimal tariff calculus. Figure 1 portrays the

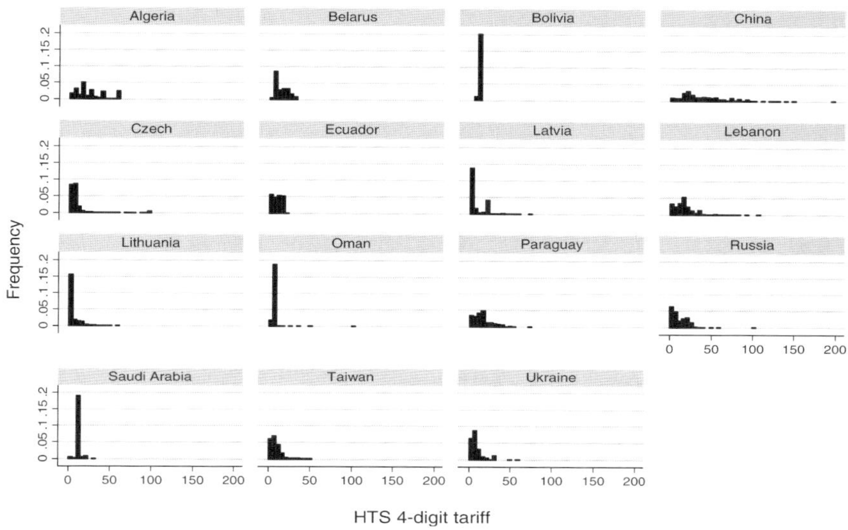

FIGURE 1. TARIFF DISTRIBUTION BY COUNTRY

within-country frequency distribution of tariffs at the four-digit level. Although most countries have large dispersion across goods, there are three with either little dispersion, such as Bolivia, or some dispersion but with most tariffs grouped into certain value bins, such as Oman and Saudi Arabia. Moreover, we observe truncation and some bunching at the lower end of distribution, where about 9 percent of all tariffs are zero.

There are a couple of important implications of the stylized facts mentioned above. First, although considering cross-country results may yield interesting insights, it may be more reasonable to focus on the effect of market power in determining tariffs across goods within countries. Second, in some countries the data seem to militate against a simple relationship in which policymakers equate the tariff level with a continuous variable such as export elasticities or degrees of political power. One can imagine many reasons for this. Perhaps policymakers are uncertain of elasticities or political connectedness and therefore divide their tariff schedule in various categories rather continuous levels; maybe policymakers employ other means of protection at their disposal when they want to achieve high levels of protection; maybe countries are averse to setting tariffs too high out of fear of retaliation; or maybe as tariffs approach prohibitive levels, there is no reason to raise them further.

All of these complications suggest that the effect of market power on tariffs may not follow the exact functional forms postulated by simple and stylized models. Thus, our focus will not be to test if the data confirm or reject the optimal tariff theory expressed in a particular functional form, but rather to estimate the impact of market power on tariffs.

C. *Elasticity Estimates*

Since we conduct the analysis at the four-digit level for each country, we estimate over 12,000 foreign export supply elasticities—far too many to present individually. Therefore, in Table 3A

TABLE 3A—INVERSE EXPORT SUPPLY ELASTICITY STATISTICS

Statistic	Observations[a]	Median[b]			Mean		Standard deviation	
Sample	All	Low	Medium	High	All	W/out top decile	All	W/out top decile
Algeria	739	0.4	2.8	91	118	23	333	47
Belarus	703	0.3	1.5	61	85	15	257	36
Bolivia	647	0.3	2.0	91	102	23	283	49
China	1,125	0.4	2.1	80	92	17	267	35
Czech Republic	1,075	0.3	1.4	26	63	7	233	18
Ecuador	753	0.3	1.5	56	76	13	243	30
Latvia	872	0.2	1.1	9	52	3	239	8
Lebanon	782	0.1	0.9	31	56	7	215	18
Lithuania	811	0.3	1.2	24	65	6	235	16
Oman	629	0.3	1.2	25	209	7	3,536	21
Paraguay	511	0.4	3.0	153	132	67	315	169
Russia	1,029	0.5	1.8	33	48	8	198	18
Saudi Arabia	1,036	0.4	1.7	50	71	11	232	25
Taiwan	891	0.1	1.4	131	90	20	241	43
Ukraine	730	0.4	2.1	78	86	16	254	34
Median	782	0.3	1.6	54	85	13	243	30

[a] Number of observations for which elasticities and tariffs are available. The tariff availability did not bind except for Ukraine, where it was not available for about 130 HS4 goods for which elasticities were computed.

[b] The median over the "low" sample corresponds to the median over the bottom tercile of inverse elasticities. Medium and high correspond to the second and third terciles.

we report their summary statistics. In theory, the inverse foreign export elasticity, ω_{ig}, can be anywhere between zero and infinity. So the median provides a useful way to characterize the estimates, as it is less sensitive to extreme values. The median inverse elasticity across all goods in any given country ranges from 0.9 to 3. It is 1.6 in the full sample, implying a median elasticity of supply of 0.6, i.e., a 1 percent increase in prices elicits a 0.6 percent increase in the volume of exports for the typical good.

As will become clear, it is also useful to consider how different the typical estimates are across terciles. The table shows that the typical estimate for low market power goods (i.e., those with inverse elasticities in the bottom thirty-third percentile of a given country) is 0,3, about five times smaller relative to medium market power goods (1.6) and 180 times smaller than high market power goods (54).

Obviously, some of the 12,000 elasticities are imprecisely estimated. The problem of outliers can be seen from the fact that when we trim the top decile of the sample in Table 3A, the means fall by almost an order of magnitude, down to 13. The same is true for the standard deviation. Since the standard errors are nonspherical, we assess the precision of the estimates via bootstrapping. In Table 3B, we report results from resampling the data and computing new estimates for each of the elasticities 250 times.[14] Table 3B indicates that the imprecision of the estimates appears to be most severe for the largest estimates, as indicated by how much higher the mean is relative to the median and by the wider bootstrap confidence intervals for elasticities in the top decile. Since there is no simple way to describe the dispersion of all estimates, we focus on the key question for our purpose, namely, whether the estimates are precise enough to distinguish between categories of goods in which a country has low versus medium or high market power.

[14] This implies calculating more than 3 million bootstrapped parameters. The results were similar when we moved from 50 to 250 bootstraps, which indicates that further increases in the number of repetitions should not change the results.

TABLE 3B— BOOTSTRAPPED STATISTICS FOR INVERSE EXPORT SUPPLY ELASTICITIES

Statistic	Low		Medium or high	
Sample	Median	Confidence interval[a]	Median	Confidence interval[a]
Algeria	0.5	[0.10 , 0.8]	5.0	[2.0 , 81]
Belarus	0.3	[0.03 , 0.5]	3.0	[0.9 , 58]
Bolivia	0.4	[0.02 , 0.6]	4.2	[1.1 , 87]
China	0.6	[0.15 , 0.8]	5.0	[1.5 , 59]
Czech Republic	0.3	[0.06 , 0.5]	3.0	[0.9 , 30]
Ecuador	0.4	[0.02 , 0.6]	3.3	[0.9 , 63]
Latvia	0.3	[0.02 , 0.4]	2.3	[0.7 , 60]
Lebanon	0.2	[0.01 , 0.3]	2.1	[0.6 , 29]
Lithuania	0.3	[0.03 , 0.5]	2.3	[0.7 , 28]
Oman	0.4	[0.04 , 0.6]	2.2	[0.6 , 35]
Paraguay	0.5	[0.03 , 0.8]	6.7	[1.9 , 98]
Russia	0.6	[0.12 , 0.7]	3.8	[1.3 , 42]
Saudi Arabia	0.5	[0.10 , 0.7]	4.1	[1.4 , 44]
Taiwan	0.3	[0.01 , 0.3]	3.0	[0.8 , 98]
Ukraine	0.6	[0.08 , 0.9]	4.5	[1.4 , 59]
Median	0.4	[0.04 , 0.6]	3.4	[1.1 , 49]

Notes: "Median" indicates the median of the 250 bootstrapped estimates for each inverse elasticity, ω_{ig}. The "low" column reports the median of that value in the bottom tercile of the sample for ω_{ig} in a country. The value in the medium or high column corresponds to the median in the rest of the sample.

[a] The lower bound of the confidence interval reported is the median lower bound over all those estimated in the relevant part of the sample; similarly for the upper bound. The individual estimates for the $1 - 2\alpha$ confidence interval are obtained via the bias-corrected percentile method (Bradley Efron 1981) using $\alpha = 0.1$.

If the answer to this question is positive, then we can address measurement error by using this categorical variable as either our market power measure or as an instrument for the continuous variable.

Before describing the results for the full sample, we consider the following specific case for Russia, where we divide goods into a low, medium, or high market power category defined by the terciles of the inverse elasticity in each country. If we rank goods by market power, we find that the median estimate for a low market power good in Russia is 0.5 with an associated confidence interval of $[0.2, 0.7]$. The corresponding values are 1.8 $[0.8, 3]$ for the median medium market power good and 33 $[3, 53]$ for the median high market power good. Thus, our estimates are sufficiently precise to statistically distinguish the median good in the low, medium, and high market power groups.

Obviously, the confidence intervals for a particular good may not be representative of those for all goods in a category. Therefore, in Table 3B we report the typical confidence interval, lower bound, and upper bound in each category to describe the range of bootstrap estimates.[15] We will be conservative and try to distinguish only between low versus medium or high market power goods. The data clearly allow us to distinguish between these goods. For example, China's typical *upper* bound for low market power goods is 0.8, whereas its typical *lower* bound for medium or high market power goods is 1.5. This lack of overlap is typical for the sample as a whole where the corresponding values are 0.6 and 1.1. Thus, as we move toward our econometric analysis of tariffs and inverse elasticities, we will be able to use a categorical classification of goods, into low versus medium or high market power, as an instrument to address measurement error explicitly.

[15] More specifically, the lower bound of the confidence interval reported is the median lower bound over all the individual confidence intervals estimated in the relevant part of the sample; similarly for the upper bound.

D. *Assessment of Elasticity Estimates*

We now turn to the question of whether our estimates themselves are plausible. In our estimation framework, we rely only on the relative levels of market power across goods, so the focus of our tests will be on the relative magnitudes, although we will discuss the levels at the end of this section. We explore the "reasonableness" of the variation in elasticities in three ways. First, we check whether the elasticities for the same good estimated using data from different countries are correlated. Second, we investigate a particular type of product characteristic, its differentiation, to assess whether the estimates fit our priors. Third, we ask whether countries have more market power when they are larger, as is often stressed by the trade literature, or if they are in more remote regions.[16]

The motivation for the tests is clearer if we note that the residual supply of exports faced by importer i, m^*_{igv}, is the difference between the production of good g in country v and any consumption in countries $j \neq i$. The export supply elasticity faced by importer i, $1/\omega_{igv}$, should be an increasing function of both the exporter's supply elasticity, denoted by λ^*_{gv}, a weighted average of other countries' demand elasticities, $\tilde{\sigma}^*_{j \neq igv}$, and a decreasing function of i's import share, m^*_{igv}/m^*_{gv}. We discuss the tests in terms of the inverse elasticity, ω_{igv}, so we summarize the relationships above as

$$\omega_{igv} = \omega(\underset{-}{\lambda^*_{gv}}, \underset{-}{\tilde{\sigma}^*_{j \neq igv}}, \underset{+}{m^*_{igv}/m^*_{gv}}). \tag{12}$$

We first examine whether we obtain similar export elasticities for a given good with different datasets. While it is clear from equation (12) that these elasticities can vary across importers, it is also clear that some goods may be more elastically supplied than others for all importers. The reason is simple: the export supply curve faced by any two importers of a given variety, i.e., from a given exporter, shares at least one common term, the value of the exporter's production. Thus, ω_{igv} and ω_{jgv} both reflect the same production elasticity, λ^*_{gv}. Moreover, ω_{igv} and ω_{jgv} should be similar because countries other than i and j also consume the good and these demand elasticities will enter identically in the export supply equation. If our estimates are reasonable, then this relationship should also be reflected in the "average" elasticities over exporters of a given good, ω_{ig} and ω_{jg}. Thus, for each country i we regress $\ln(\omega_{ig})$ for all goods against the mean of $\ln(\omega_{j \neq ig})$ computed using the data of the remaining 14 countries. We report these results in Table 4. The point estimates are all positive and significant, which indicates a very strong positive statistical relationship. Since the datasets are completely different and each elasticity was estimated independently, these results show that our measure of market power contains information about systematic variation across goods.[17]

We now ask what product characteristics drive the result above and whether they fit our priors. Our second test addresses this question by focusing on product differentiation. As we note in equation (12), we expect countries to have lower market power in goods with higher elasticity of substitution in consumption, e.g., commodities. The reason is simple: if China decreases its demand for a commodity, e.g., US soybeans, and as a consequence the price falls, then other countries will substitute toward that good and away from other sources of supply (e.g., demand less of other countries' soybeans), so the equilibrium price decline will be minimal. Such substitution

[16] In the working paper, we also show that the elasticities are consistent with the implied pass-through coefficients in other studies. These results are available upon request.

[17] We use a log specification to minimize the influence of the outliers and because the estimation procedure for the elasticities cannot yield nonpositive estimates.

TABLE 4—CORRELATION OF INVERSE EXPORT SUPPLY ELASTICITIES ACROSS COUNTRIES

	Log inverse export supply			
Dependent variable: Statistic	Beta	Standard error	R^2	Number of observations
Algeria	0.80	(0.07)	0.13	739
Belarus	0.80	(0.07)	0.14	703
Bolivia	0.82	(0.09)	0.13	647
China	0.54	(0.06)	0.11	1,125
Czech Republic	0.61	(0.05)	0.12	1,075
Ecuador	0.73	(0.08)	0.12	753
Latvia	0.57	(0.07)	0.09	872
Lebanon	0.71	(0.08)	0.11	782
Lithuania	0.70	(0.07)	0.13	811
Oman	0.39	(0.08)	0.04	629
Paraguay	0.94	(0.11)	0.14	511
Russia	0.53	(0.05)	0.11	1,029
Saudi Arabia	0.48	(0.06)	0.08	1,036
Taiwan	0.31	(0.08)	0.02	891
Ukraine	0.83	(0.07)	0.17	730
Median	0.70	(0.07)	0.12	782

Note: Univariate regression of log inverse export supply elasticities in each country on the average of the log inverse elasticities in that good for the remaining 14 countries.

TABLE 5—INVERSE ELASTICITIES BY PRODUCT TYPE

	Differentiated	Reference priced	Commodity
Median inv elasticity	2.38	0.70	0.45
Standard errors	(0.04)	(0.06)	(0.14)
p-value: Differentiated vs. refer. or commod.		0.00	0.00
Mean inv. elasticity	17.5	9.3	8.3
Standard errors	(0.71)	(0.70)	(1.23)
p-value: Differentiated vs. refer. or commod.		0.00	0.00

Notes: The number of observations for the median regression is 8,734, less than the full sample since not all HS4 can be uniquely matched to Rauch's classification. The number for the mean regression is 7,927 because we trim the top decile. The pattern of results with the top decile is similar but with higher values.

is much less likely for specialized or differentiated goods such as locomotives, aircraft, or integrated circuits because no two exporters produce the exact same good. Thus, we conjecture that countries have more market power in differentiated goods than commodities.

James E. Rauch (1999) classified goods into three categories—commodities, reference priced goods, and differentiated goods—based on whether they were traded on organized exchanges, listed as having a reference price, or could not be priced by either of these means. Table 5 uses this classification and confirms the prediction by testing the differences of the median and mean market power across these categories. The ranking is exactly as expected with the highest market power in differentiated goods followed by reference priced and then commodities. The most striking feature of the table is that both the median and the mean market power are significantly higher for differentiated products—its median value is 2.4, which is about three times larger than reference goods and five times the value for commodities. This pattern is also clear when we look at the median in each category for individual countries, as shown in Figure 2.

We find a similar pattern if we look at specific goods. For example, among the set of goods with the largest import shares in this sample, the three goods with the least market power are

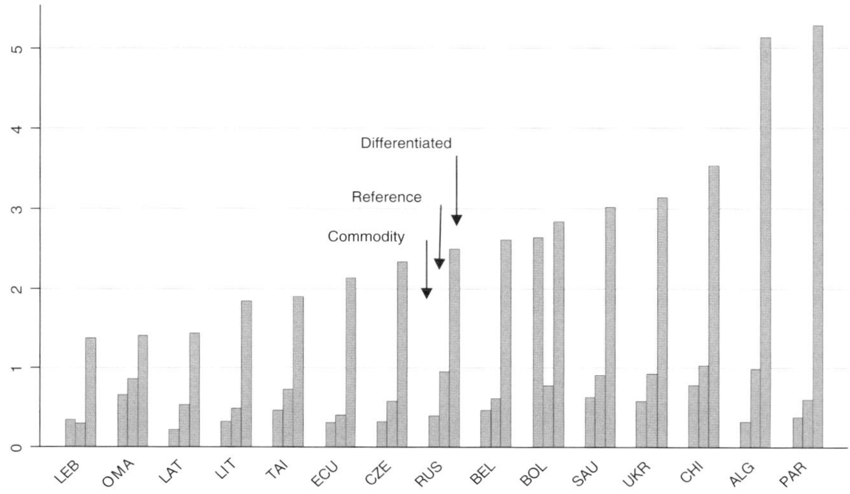

FIGURE 2. MEDIAN INVERSE ELASTICITIES BY PRODUCT TYPE
(*Goods classified by Rauch into commodities, reference priced products, and differentiated products*)

soybeans, barley, and natural gas, all with inverse elasticities below 0.1. All of these are commodities for which it is reasonable to expect that a single importer would have a small impact on world prices. In contrast, the median market power in goods such as locomotives and integrated circuits is more than double the sample median. These are all differentiated goods for which it is more likely that even a single importer can have market power. Thus, our methodology generates a reasonable ordering for major import categories.

As a third check for the reasonableness of the elasticities, we examine whether they reflect the common intuition that market power increases with country size. Since the subsample of products for which we can compute elasticities differs somewhat across countries, computing simple means and medians across different sets of goods may be misleading. Thus, we include HS four-digit dummies in the regression so as to compare market power for different countries within each import good. The first column in Table 6 reports the results from the regression of log inverse export elasticities on log GDP. There is a positive relationship, which supports the notion that market power rises as GDP rises.[18] Although GDP is often strongly positively correlated with import shares, the latter are more appropriate for the current purpose, as noted in equation (12). We also obtain a positive relationship when we use an importer's market share in each good instead of GDP. Moreover, this remains true even if we drop China. Hence, our estimated elasticities also pass our third reasonableness check—larger countries have more market power.[19]

[18] This is consistent with the results in James R. Markusen and Randall M. Wigle (1989) who use a CGE model to calculate the welfare effects of scaling up all baseline tariffs and find a larger optimal tariff for the United States than for Canada.

[19] When we include both the GDP and import share measure we obtain positive coefficients for both, but the import share variable is not significant. Although this is partly due to their correlation, the small amount of variation explained by the import share (shown by the R-square within) implies that one must be careful about using it as a proxy for market power. The within R-square for GDP is also small, which explains why tariffs and GDP in our sample do not have a

TABLE 6—INVERSE EXPORT SUPPLY ELASTICITIES, GDP, REMOTENESS, AND IMPORT SHARES

Dependent variable	Log inverse export supply		
Log GDP	0.17 (0.04)	0.18 (0.03)	
Log remoteness		0.40 (0.15)	
Share of world HS4 imports			7.19 (1.48)
Observations	12,343	12,343	12,343
R^2	0.26	0.26	0.25
R^2 within	0.01	0.02	0.00

Notes: All regressions include four-digit HS fixed effects (1,201 categories). Robust standard errors in parentheses. In the log GDP regressions, standard errors are clustered by country. GDP is for 1996. Remoteness for country i is defined as $1/(\Sigma_j \text{GDP}_j/\text{distance}_{ij})$. The share of world imports is calculated in 2000.

Empirically, we know that trade volume falls off quite rapidly with distance.[20] This implies that some goods are traded only regionally so that even countries that are small from the world's perspective may have considerable amounts of *regional* market power. For example, Ecuador may represent a large share of demand for certain regionally traded goods, such as Chilean cement, and it is this elasticity that we estimate. This suggests that for any given GDP, a country in a more remote region would be expected to have higher market power, as it accounts for a larger fraction of the region's demand, i.e., it has a larger value for m^*_{igv}/m^*_{gv} in (12). We confirm this in the second column of Table 6 by including a standard measure of remoteness—the inverse of the distance weighted GDPs of other countries in the world.

Finally, consider the magnitudes of the elasticity estimates. Given the absence of alternative estimates, it is difficult to make definitive statements about the reasonableness of the magnitudes we find. One of our interesting findings is that even small countries have market power. This may seem surprising if one assumes the world is composed of homogeneous goods that are traded at no cost. However, this may not be the right framework for thinking about trade. First, as noted above, there are still large trade costs segmenting markets. Second, although we do find that countries have almost no market power in homogenous goods (those that Rauch (1999) defines as commodities), those goods make up only about 10 percent of the tariff lines in the sample. About 60 percent of the HS4 goods in the sample are differentiated with the remaining 30 percent classified as reference priced.

In sum, the analysis above suggests that our elasticity estimates are reasonable by a number of criteria. We now ask if they are an important determinant in setting tariffs.

robust positive correlation (e.g., it disappears once we drop China), but tariffs and inverse elasticities do, as we show in the next section.

[20] According to James E. Anderson and Eric van Wincoop's review of the literature, "the tax equivalent of 'representative' trade costs for industrialized countries is 170 percent" (2004, 692). Estimates from gravity equations imply that trade with a partner who shares a border is typically over 14 times larger than with an identically sized nonbordering country if one considers the decay due to distance alone (c.f. Limão and Anthony J. Venables 2001).

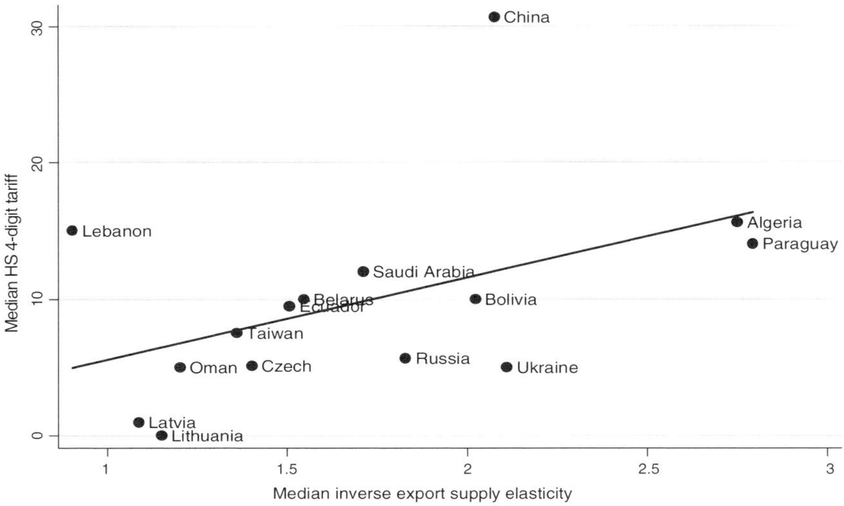

FIGURE 3. MEDIAN TARIFFS AND MARKET POWER ACROSS COUNTRIES

IV. Estimating the Impact of Market Power on Tariffs

A. *Cross-Country Evidence*

Before turning to the regression evidence, we will examine a crude cross-country version of the theory. Figure 3 shows that there is a strong positive relationship between the median tariff in a country and market power in the typical good, as measured by its median inverse elasticity. The pattern does not seem to be driven by any one country or even set of countries on a particular continent or with a particular income level. The positive relationship between median tariffs and median elasticities is also statistically significant.[21] Of course, there are many reasons to be wary of this relationship, starting with the small number of observations. Fortunately, the vast quantity of country-good data underlying this plot can be used to examine the relationship more carefully, and we do so in our original working paper where we confirm its robustness.

The result we have presented thus far is suggestive but still far from convincing. Expressing the tariff purely in terms of an aggregate country's characteristic, such as size and resulting market power, may be natural in a two-good model, but is not very useful from an empirical perspective because of the many cross-country differences that may affect average tariff levels. Furthermore, as we have seen, the theory also provides important predictions for tariff variation within a country. Since there is considerable variation in tariffs and elasticities within countries and fewer potential omitted variables, our main results, in the next section, follow this route.

[21] If we regress the median tariff on the median inverse elasticity, we obtain a positive slope (b = 5.9; s.e. = 2.9; R^2 = 0.21). The positive relationship is still present if we exclude China (b = 4.2; s.e. = 2.36).

B. *Baseline Results*

In this section, we provide baseline results from specifications where the inverse export supply elasticity is the key determinant of protection, and we include country and industry effects to control for tariff motives highlighted by various political economy models. In the subsequent subsections we provide a variety of robustness checks and further augment the model to include two specific prominent motives for protection: tariff revenue and lobbying.

The general econometric model we employ can be written as follows:

$$\tau_{ig} = \beta_i f(\omega_{ig}) + \boldsymbol{\eta}_{iG} + \mathbf{x}_{ig}\boldsymbol{\gamma} + u_{ig}, \tag{13}$$

where the ad valorem tariff, τ, varies by country i and HS four-digit good, g, as does the market power variable, ω. Although the basic theory yields a linear relationship, we have discussed theoretical reasons to expect the true effect to diminish at higher levels of market power. Because of this and of econometric reasons, we also consider alternative functional forms for $f(\cdot)$. Since our main objective is to establish whether market power is a significant determinant of tariffs rather than to establish in which countries the marginal effect is stronger, the baseline results focus on the case where $\beta_i = \beta$ for all countries. However, we also present country-specific regressions.

As we discuss in the theory section, the tariff may depend on various other factors. Some are country specific, e.g., country location, level of development, expected WTO accession, formerly Communist, etc. Several others depend on political economy factors that are not easily observable. Many of the latter factors, however, are channeled by lobbies organized at the sector or industry level, where each industry, G, includes a different subset of goods, g. A flexible way to capture the impact of such determinants on tariffs is to include country and/or industry effects.[22] Therefore, we consider three alternatives. First, estimating only the country effects and treating any industry-country factors, v_{iG}, as part of the error term, so that in (13) we have $\boldsymbol{\eta}_{iG} = \boldsymbol{\eta}_i + v_{iG}$. Second, including country and common industry effects, i.e., $\boldsymbol{\eta}_{iG} = \boldsymbol{\eta}_G + \boldsymbol{\eta}_i + v_{iG}$ for all i. This controls for the fact that there is considerable variation in trade protection across industries. Any given industry can, however, have very different levels of protection across countries and, therefore, the most general case is one where $\boldsymbol{\eta}_{iG}$ represents a set of industry-by-country effects. The latter is the case we focus on primarily since it controls for a considerable amount of unobserved industry heterogeneity and allows us to identify the effect of market power on tariffs by exploring product variation within countries and industries.

Most trade policy models focus on industry-level determinants for which we can control. In any given country, however, there may exist certain product characteristics that are correlated with market power and affect the tariff set in that product. There is little empirical guidance on what these other relevant characteristics are (since most studies are conducted at the industry level), and it is therefore impossible to ensure that we control for all relevant ones. Thus, our main strategy for addressing omitted product variables in this section is to use instrumental variables. Subsequently, we test if the IV results are robust to controlling for some key determinants of tariffs represented by the vector $\mathbf{x}_{ig}$ in (13).

Table 7 presents OLS and Tobit estimates for the pooled sample. The first three columns include country effects. The next six columns also include industry effects. Since the results in columns 1–3 are qualitatively similar to the ones in columns 4–6, we discuss the latter.[23] The

[22] The industry that contains the good is defined to be one of the 21 sections of the Harmonized Tariff Schedule, e.g., textiles, chemicals, plastics, etc.

[23] The comparable three specifications with industry-by-country effects are also similar and available upon request.

TABLE 7— TARIFFS AND MARKET POWER ACROSS GOODS (WITHIN COUNTRIES): OLS AND TOBIT ESTIMATES

Dependent variable	Average tariff at four-digit HS (%)								
Fixed effects	Country			Country and industry					
Estimation method	OLS	OLS	OLS	OLS	OLS	OLS	Tobit	OLS[a]	OLS
	(1)	(2)	(3)	(4)	(5)	(6)	(7)	(8)	(9)
Inverse exp. elast.	0.0003			0.0004					
	(0.0001)			(0.0004)					
Mid and high inv exp elast		1.24			1.46			1.86	
		(0.25)			(0.24)			(0.31)	
Log(1/export elasticity)			0.12			0.17	0.17		
			(0.04)			(0.04)	(0.05)		
(Inv. exp. elast) × (1 − med hi)								1.45	
								(0.31)	
(Inv. exp. elast) × med hi								0.0003	
								(0.0001)	
Mid inv. exp. elast.									1.56
									(0.28)
High inv. exp. elast.									1.37
									(0.28)
Algeria	23.8	23.0	23.6	24.6	23.6	24.3	24.3	23.1	23.6
	(0.64)	(0.65)	(0.64)	(0.95)	(0.96)	(0.95)	(0.93)	(0.97)	(0.96)
Belarus	12.3	11.5	12.2	12.6	11.6	12.5	12.4	11.3	11.7
	(0.29)	(0.33)	(0.29)	(0.76)	(0.78)	(0.76)	(0.94)	(0.79)	(0.78)
Bolivia	9.8	9.0	9.7	10.1	9.2	10.0	10.0	8.8	9.2
	(0.03)	(0.17)	(0.06)	(0.73)	(0.75)	(0.73)	(0.95)	(0.77)	(0.75)
China	37.8	37.0	37.7	38.2	37.2	38.0	37.9	36.6	37.2
	(0.77)	(0.79)	(0.77)	(0.98)	(1.01)	(0.99)	(0.89)	(1.03)	(1.01)
Czech Republic	9.5	8.7	9.4	9.7	8.7	9.6	8.8	8.3	8.7
	(0.53)	(0.53)	(0.53)	(0.85)	(0.86)	(0.85)	(0.89)	(0.87)	(0.86)
Ecuador	9.8	9.0	9.7	10.3	9.4	10.2	10.1	9.0	9.4
	(0.19)	(0.26)	(0.20)	(0.73)	(0.74)	(0.73)	(0.93)	(0.76)	(0.74)
Latvia	7.3	6.4	7.2	7.3	6.3	7.2	6.9	6.0	6.3
	(0.35)	(0.40)	(0.35)	(0.76)	(0.78)	(0.76)	(0.91)	(0.79)	(0.78)
Lebanon	17.1	16.2	17.0	17.1	16.1	17.0	17.0	15.9	16.1
	(0.53)	(0.56)	(0.53)	(0.84)	(0.86)	(0.84)	(0.92)	(0.86)	(0.86)
Lithuania	3.6	2.8	3.6	3.6	2.6	3.5	−6.0	2.3	2.6
	(0.26)	(0.31)	(0.26)	(0.74)	(0.76)	(0.74)	(0.98)	(0.77)	(0.76)
Oman	5.6	4.9	5.6	5.7	4.8	5.6	4.9	4.4	4.8
	(0.34)	(0.37)	(0.34)	(0.77)	(0.79)	(0.77)	(0.94)	(0.79)	(0.79)
Paraguay	16.0	15.3	15.9	16.3	15.4	16.1	15.9	14.9	15.4
	(0.49)	(0.52)	(0.50)	(0.84)	(0.85)	(0.84)	(0.99)	(0.86)	(0.85)
Russia	10.6	9.8	10.5	10.8	9.9	10.7	10.0	9.4	9.9
	(0.34)	(0.38)	(0.34)	(0.77)	(0.79)	(0.77)	(0.89)	(0.82)	(0.79)
Saudi Arabia	12.1	11.3	12.0	12.4	11.4	12.2	12.1	10.9	11.4
	(0.08)	(0.18)	(0.09)	(0.71)	(0.74)	(0.72)	(0.89)	(0.76)	(0.74)
Taiwan	9.7	8.9	9.6	10.3	9.3	10.1	9.7	9.0	9.3
	(0.28)	(0.33)	(0.28)	(0.74)	(0.76)	(0.75)	(0.91)	(0.77)	(0.76)
Ukraine	7.4	6.6	7.2	8.1	7.1	7.9	6.8	6.6	7.1
	(0.28)	(0.33)	(0.29)	(0.74)	(0.76)	(0.74)	(0.93)	(0.78)	(0.76)
Observations	12,333	12,333	12,333	12,333	12,333	12,333	12,333	12,333	12,333
Number of parameters	16	16	16	36	35	36	35	38	36
Adj. R^2	0.61	0.61	0.61	0.66	0.66	0.66			0.66

Notes: Standard errors in parentheses (all heteroskedasticity robust except Tobit). Industry dummies defined by section according to Harmonized Standard tariff schedule.

[a] Optimal threshold regression based on minimum RSS found using a grid search over 50 points of the distribution of inverse exp. elast. (from first to ninety-ninth percentile in intervals of two). Optimal threshold is fifty-third percentile. Accordingly, med hi equals one above the fifty-third percentile and zero otherwise. Bruce E. Hansen (2000) shows that the dependence of the parameters on the threshold estimate is not of "first-order" asymptotic importance, so inference on them can be done as if the threshold estimate were the true value.

linear market power measure, in column 4, has a positive and significant effect on tariffs. The coefficient is small because of a few large outliers in the inverse elasticity, as we previously discussed. Moreover, the effect represents an average of increases in the market power at low and high levels. When market power is high, the tariff is closer to being prohibitive and the marginal effect of further increases in market power is expected to be small. This is confirmed in column 8 by a regression where the knot for the different slopes is endogenously determined by the data. Despite the lower marginal effect at high market power, those goods do have significantly higher average tariffs.[24]

A parsimonious way to address the skewness of market power and its nonlinear impact on tariffs is a semi-log specification, i.e., to use $f(\omega) = \ln(\omega)$ in (13). The OLS estimate in column 6 shows that market power also has a positive and significant effect on tariffs under this specification. The result is identical for the Tobit specification in column 7 where the tariff censoring point is zero.

In column 5 we address the measurement error and, to some extent, the functional form issue, by sorting each country's data by the inverse export elasticity and creating a dummy equal to one if it is above the thirty-third percentile. The estimate shows that goods with higher inverse elasticities have higher tariffs. In column 9 we find that this difference in tariffs relative to goods with low market power is similar for goods where market power is high (above sixty-sixth percentile of inverse export elasticity) or medium (between thirty-third and sixty-sixth). This confirms the diminishing marginal effect we found and further supports the use of a flexible functional form such as the semi-log or dummy.

The OLS estimates are potentially biased because of attenuation caused by measurement error and omitted variables. Since our objective is to determine causality and provide a quantification of the effect of market power on tariffs, we now turn to estimates that employ instrumental variables.

The main instrument we employ for a given country's market power in a good is the average market power in that good in the other countries. The basic motivation is simple: to minimize the country-product specific portion of market power that may be correlated with other determinants for the tariff on that good in a particular country. In the semi-log specification, we could use as an instrument the average of other countries' log inverse elasticities, since the variables are strongly correlated, as shown in Table 4. This procedure addresses endogeneity concerns. When we employ the continuous measures, however, this procedure alone does not necessarily eliminate the measurement error, since if there are at least a couple of countries with large measurement error in any given good, the instrument itself will have error. When assessing the elasticities, we showed that our estimates clearly distinguish between goods where a country has low versus medium or high market power. Thus in equation (13) we instrument $f(\omega_{ig})$ with the average of the categorical variable for all countries other than i. This instrument is also strongly positively correlated with $f(\omega_{ig})$.

Table 8 presents the IV results for the pooled sample of 15 countries. The results contain three specifications: level, dummy, and semi-log. We estimate each including country effects (columns 1–3), country and industry effects (4–6), and industry-by-country effects (7–9). The last specification best isolates the impact of market power, but comparing it to the other specifications also provides useful insights.

The first point that stands out is that the estimated market power effect on tariffs is positive for all specifications and considerably larger than with OLS. In the semi-log specification, for

[24] It estimates a slope of 1.9 when market power is below the estimated threshold (fifty-third percentile), which is considerably larger than the slope above it. The threshold in a similar specification without industry effects is at the thirty-third percentile.

TABLE 8—TARIFFS AND MARKET POWER ACROSS GOODS (WITHIN COUNTRIES): IV ESTIMATES

Dependent variable	Average tariff at four-digit HS (%)								
Fixed effects	Country			Country and industry			Industry by country		
Estimation method	IV GMM (1)	IV GMM (2)	IV GMM (3)	IV GMM (4)	IV GMM (5)	IV GMM (6)	IV GMM (7)	IV GMM (8)	IV GMM (9)
Inverse exp. elast.	0.040			0.089			0.075		
	(0.027)			(0.055)			(0.028)		
Mid and high inv. exp. elast.		3.96			8.88			9.07	
		(0.76)			(1.18)			(1.08)	
Log(1/export elasticity)			0.75			1.71			1.73
			(0.15)			(0.23)			(0.21)
Observations	12,258	12,258	12,258	12,258	12,258	12,258	12,258	12,258	12,258
No. of parameters	16	16	16	35	35	35	284	282	283
1st stage F	5	1649	1335	2	653	517	3	691	544

Notes: Standard errors in parentheses (heteroskedasticity robust). Industry dummies defined by section according to the Harmonized Standard tariff schedule.

example, the coefficient is 1.7 when we control for industry or industry-by-country effects in columns (6) and (9), respectively. This estimate is ten times larger than the OLS one and significant at the 1 percent level. The dummy estimates in columns 5 and 8 illustrate a similar point. Products in which countries have medium or high market power have tariffs about 9 percentage points higher, a result that is both economically and statistically significant. Since the dummy is less prone to measurement error, these results suggest there was a downward bias due to omitted variables that is addressed by the IV. We will thoroughly discuss the magnitude of these effects in Section IVF.[25]

A third point worth noting is the importance of accounting for unobserved industry heterogeneity when we employ a parsimonious specification. The estimated market power coefficients in columns 1–3 generally double after we account for such heterogeneity in columns 4–6 and 7–9.

The linear version is unlikely to be the correct functional form, as both the data and basic extensions of the theory strongly suggest. Given its prominence in the basic theoretical prediction, however, we also present baseline results for it. The more general specification in column 7 confirms the results obtained with the semi-log and dummy: a positive and significant effect that is considerably larger than the OLS estimate.[26]

C. *Individual Country Results*

To carefully establish the tariff determinants of any given country requires its own paper. We want to determine, however, whether the baseline results represent trade policy setting in the typical country. We remain as close as possible to the framework we have used so far. Yet we cannot ignore obvious issues such as the bunching of tariffs in Bolivia, Oman, and Saudi Arabia.

[25] There is also indirect evidence that our IV approach addresses the measurement error in ω satisfactorily. Recall that this was most important for estimates above the ninetieth percentile in each country. However, when we reestimate the IV without those observations, we obtain very similar estimates for β.

[26] Bolivia, Oman, and Saudi Arabia had little variation in their tariffs, with most grouped in two or three value bins. A linear regression approach is generally not the most appropriate way to treat these observations. If we drop these countries, the estimates become more precise and increase in magnitude in the dummy and semi-log specifications.

For the other 12 countries, we still employ the IV approach with industry effects and estimate the unrestricted version of (13) for each country.[27]

Table 9 presents the IV results by country using the semi-log specification. The first two columns reproduce the pooled results from Table 8 for comparison. The estimate is positive for each and every one of the 15 countries. It is also statistically significant at the 5 percent or 1 percent level for all but two.[28] The estimate for the typical country is 1.75 and the mean is 2.15. These are very close to the pooled estimates, which were 1.73 for the full sample and 2.11 for the subsample of 12 countries.[29]

A measure that is more directly comparable across countries is the implied elasticity of tariffs with respect to market power. We obtain it by dividing the coefficient by the mean tariff and show it in the last row. This value ranges from 0.13 to 0.15 in the pooled estimates, which is close to the mean over the country estimates, 0.17, as well as the value obtained for the typical country, 0.16. The range of elasticity estimates across countries is fairly narrow for 13 of the countries, and it does not have an obvious pattern. So the pooled estimates capture an effect that is typical of the countries in the sample.

The pattern of heterogeneity in the point estimates across countries in Table 9 provides some additional support for the theory. Countries are sorted in decreasing order of their 1996 GDP. The largest, China, has the highest coefficient. More generally, the larger economies tend to have larger estimates. When we test this directly, we find that the difference in the estimate is large and significant.[30] As we pointed out in the previous paragraph, however, there is no such pattern in the *elasticity* of tariffs with respect to market power, that is, after we divide the estimated coefficient by the average tariff. The reason is that in this sample average tariffs are higher for larger countries, as the theory would predict.

D. *Other Robustness Tests*

By construction, much of the variation in our instrument is across goods. This is one key reason to focus the analysis within countries and across goods. In the pooled regressions, the fact that the instrument varies mostly across goods could induce a correlation in the error term for any given good across countries. Clustering the standard errors by HS4 addresses this concern, and we verified that it does not change the significance of the results.[31]

[27] Tariffs in those three countries have little variation and almost none within industries. So it is doubtful that we can find a strong relationship for them and it is clear that we require a different econometric approach to address the fact that a large fraction of their tariffs appear to be censored below and/or above. Thus for these three countries we run censored regressions where we also instrument for the market power variables.

[28] One of them is Saudi Arabia, where we did not expect a precise estimate anyway. The other is the Czech Republic which, as we note in Table 1, set its tariffs in 1992 as a federation with Slovakia. Since this federation was a member of GATT its tariffs are less likely to reflect a terms-of-trade motive, possibly explaining our finding here. Note also that the pooled results in Tables 7, 8, and 10 are robust to dropping the Czech observations (available upon request).

[29] Table 9, panel B, of Broda, Limão, and Weinstein (2006) presents the analog using the categorical variable. They are qualitatively similar to those presented in the semi-log specification in terms of sign and significance. The typical country sets tariffs that are 9 percentage points higher in goods with medium or high market power relative to those where it has low power.

[30] That is, in the general specification we model $\beta_i = \beta + \beta^L \times 1(\text{Size}_i)$, where the indicator variable 1(Size) is one if country i is above the sixty-sixth percentile in terms of size. We defined size as either GDP in 1996 or GDP adjusted by "regional market size," i.e., divided by an inverse distance weighted average of other countries' GDPs. Both measures identified the same six countries as the largest. The additional instrument required is simply the original instrument interacted with $1(\text{Size}_i)$. The estimates for β remain positive and significant and the extra effect for the larger countries was 2.6 for the semilog (s.e. 0.5) and 12 for the dummy (s.e. 2.3).

[31] We also analyzed an alternative instrument with more variation over countries. The theory and our initial regressions of the determinants of market power suggest using a measure of country size to help predict market power in the first stage. Since the regression already includes country effects, we interact a measure of country size with our original

TABLE 9A—TARIFFS AND MARKET POWER ACROSS GOODS BY COUNTRY: IV ESTIMATES

Dependent variable	Average tariff at four-digit HS (%)									
Fixed effects	Ind. by Country	Ind. by Country	Ind.	Ind.	Ind.		Ind.	Ind.	Ind.	Ind.
Estimation method	IV GMM	IV GMM	IV GMM	IV GMM	IV GMM	IV Tobit	IV GMM	IV GMM	IV GMM	IV GMM
Sample	All	Exc. Bol., Om., Sau.	China	Russia	Taiwan	Saudi Arabia	Ukraine	Czech.	Algeria	Belarus
Log(1/export elasticity)	1.73	2.11	7.60	2.42	1.98	1.75	0.71	0.16	5.40	2.28
	(0.21)	(0.25)	(1.78)	(0.61)	(0.78)	(2.55)	(0.26)	(0.24)	(0.97)	(0.52)
Observations	12,258	9,952	1,089	1,021	841	1,031	685	1,000	739	703
No. of parameters	283	227	20	18	20		18	20	18	18
First stage F	544	477	45	44	12	7.6[a]	48	61	60	40
Mean tariff (%)	13.4	14.2	38.2	10.3	8.9	12.2	5.8	5.5	23.8	12.4
Elasticity (at mean)	0.13	0.15	0.20	0.23	0.22	0.14	0.12	0.03	0.23	0.18

TABLE 9B— TARIFFS AND MARKET POWER ACROSS GOODS BY COUNTRY: IV ESTIMATES

Dependent variable	Average tariff at four-digit HS (%)								
Fixed effects	Ind.		Ind.	Ind.	Ind.		Ind.		
Estimation method	IV GMM	IV Tobit	IV GMM	IV GMM	IV GMM	IV Tobit	IV GMM		
Sample	Ecuador	Oman	Paraguay	Lithuania	Lebanon	Bolivia	Latvia	Mean	Median
Log(1/export elasticity)	1.55	0.60	2.44	0.83	2.41	0.79	1.41	2.15	1.75
	(0.34)	(0.18)	(0.67)	(0.27)	(0.54)	(0.36)	(0.60)		
Observations	753	628	510	768	754	647	868		
No. of parameters	19		17	19	20		19		
First stage F	45	3.7[a]	33	35	52	8.96[a]	37		
Mean tariff (%)	9.8	5.7	16.0	2.3	15.0	9.8	7.0		
Elasticity (at mean)	0.16	0.11	0.15	0.36	0.16	0.08	0.20	0.17	0.16

Notes: Standard errors in parentheses (heteroskedasticity robust). Industry dummies defined by section according to the Harmonized Standard tariff schedule. Extreme tariff outliers were dropped. This affects the sample of only five countries, and even then only slightly since the criteria drop only 3–7 percent of their observations (those with tariff values more than three times the interquartile range above the seventy-fifth percentile or below the twenty-fifth). Bolivia, Oman, and Saudi Arabia are estimated via an IV Tobit procedure to account for the fact that a large fraction of their observations is censored from above and/or below. Given the lack of variation in their tariff within industries, their estimation does not include industry dummies.

[a] z-stat of the instrument in the first stage of IV Tobit.

We can relax the assumption of common elasticities across sets of exporters of a given good to country i. This is costly, however, since it reduces both the number of elasticities we can estimate and their precision. It also raises the question of how we should aggregate the elasticities over exporters of the same good to estimate the tariff equation, since the tariff data we use for i do not vary by exporter. Nonetheless, we test if the results are sensitive to the sample of exporters used. Effectively, we calculate two estimates for *each* ω_{ig}, each using a different set of exporters. For

instrument. The magnitude and significance of the results for the three baseline specifications in columns 7, 8, and 9 of Table 8 are quite similar when we employ this alternative instrument that varies over both countries and goods.

each importer i we rank exporters by their total export value in *all* goods shipped to i in the entire period. The even sample includes exporters with even ranking and the odd includes the remaining. We then rerun the baseline results in columns 7–9 of Table 8 with each set of estimates. Both sets yield a positive and significant effect of market power on tariffs. Moreover, the quantitative result is nearly identical across the sets. So the precise selection of exporters in estimating the elasticity does not change the key finding.

E. *Augmented Models: Revenue and Lobbying*

The preceding analysis established that these countries set higher tariffs in goods in which they have more market power. However, trade policy can also be strongly influenced by revenue considerations and domestic political interests. It is hard to see why there might be a systematic correlation between our estimates of export supply elasticities and political economy variables because all importer-industry-time variation has been purged from the elasticity data before estimation. Moreover, lobbies tend to form at the industry level and, as we reported above, our results are stronger when we include industry effects that account for unobserved heterogeneity. Finally, the IV estimates indicate that the results are strengthened when we address potential endogeneity problems such as the one that could result from omitted variable bias.

Nonetheless, we want to further test if our baseline results are biased due to omitted variables. As noted before, much of the theory and empirical evidence on trade protection focuses on industry-level determinants, so it is difficult to know for which *product* characteristics we should control. Thus, we focus on two prominent motives for protection that may also have implications for cross-product variation in protection: revenue and lobbying. This also allows us to determine the importance of market power relative to these prominent alternative explanations for tariff setting.

Consider first the use of tariffs to collect revenue. To the extent that this motive is correlated with the level of development, it is captured by country effects. It is simple to show, however, that if governments use tariffs to raise revenues they would impose higher tariffs on goods with lower import demand elasticities, σ_{ig}. This occurs because governments obtain more revenue and impose lower consumption distortions when they impose a given tariff on a good with a lower import elasticity. If the import elasticity were correlated with the foreign export supply elasticity, our results could simply be picking up the tariff revenue motive.

The results in Table 10 address this question. We obtain the inverse import demand elasticity, $1/\sigma_{ig}$, using the procedure described earlier, and instrument it using the same approach as the market power variable. That is, we create a categorical variable for each country that is zero for product g if its value of $1/\sigma_{ig}$ is in the bottom tercile in country i, and one otherwise. We then use its average for that product over the other countries as the instrument.

In columns 3 and 4 of Table 10, we include the tariff revenue variable to augment the baseline model with industry-by-country effects. The coefficient on the dummy variable for market power is 9—identical to the baseline reproduced in the first column. This indicates that these countries apply tariffs that are 9 percentage points higher in sectors in which they have market power. The estimate for the semi-log is also statistically identical to the baseline. So, once we have accounted for industry-by-country effects and instrumented the market power variable, our baseline estimates do not reflect an omitted variable bias arising from a tariff revenue motive for tariffs.

The specific political economy factors that are relevant for the tariff structure can also differ across these countries. So, we include a political economy variable that is central to an important model, Grossman and Helpman (1995), and that also plays a role in alternative political economy models. When all sectors are politically organized, the Grossman-Helpman model provides a parsimonious characterization of the effects of both market power and domestic lobbying. In this

TABLE 10—MARKET POWER VERSUS TARIFF REVENUE OR LOBBYING AS A SOURCE OF PROTECTION

Dependent variable	Average tariff at four-digit HS (%)					
Fixed effects	Industry by country					
Estimation method	IV GMM					
Sample	Pooled (all)		Pooled (all)		Pooled (7)	
Theory	Market power		Market power and tariff revenue		Market power and lobbying	
Mid and high inv. exp. elast.	9.07 (1.08)		9.04 (1.24)		10.20 (1.79)	
Mid and high inv. imp. elast.			−0.20 (2.08)			
Mid and hi inv. imp. pen/imp. elast.					6.28 (1.97)	
Log(1/export elasticity)		1.73 (0.21)		1.81 (0.23)		1.94 (0.38)
Log(1/import elasticity)				−0.90 (0.81)		
Log(inv. imp. pen/imp. elas.)						1.59 (0.55)
Observations	12,258	12,258	12,258	12,258	5,178	5,178
No. of parameters	282	283	283	284	132	133
First stage F (market power)	691	544	370	312	171	129
First stage F (other)	na	na	102	144	131	188

Notes: Standard errors in parentheses (heteroskedasticity robust). Industry dummies defined by section according to the Harmonized Standard tariff schedule. The countries with available data for the lobbying specifications are Bolivia, China, Ecuador, Latvia, Lithuania, Taiwan, and Ukraine. These data are not available for mining and agricultural products.

model, tariffs are given by the sum of the inverse elasticity and what we refer to as the lobbying variable, z_{ig}/σ_{ig}, as defined in equation (7) with $I_{ig} = 1$.

Recall that the variable z_{ig} is the ratio of domestic production value to import value, where the latter excludes tariffs. Thus, it requires production data, which we could obtain for 7 of the 15 countries in our sample for years close to the tariff data. This is available for all these countries only at the ISIC three-digit data from the United Nations Industrial Development Organization (UNIDO) industrial database. So z_{ig} can be interpreted as country i's average penetration for the goods in that ISIC three-digit category. Since we divide this by the import demand elasticity, which varies by HS4, the lobbying variable also varies at the HS four-digit level.

In the regressions, we treat the lobbying variable similarly to market power. More specifically, we employ either its log or a categorical variable that takes the value of zero for the lower tercile of z_g/σ_g in that country, and one otherwise. We instrument the variable, since production and imports depend on tariff levels. The instrument is constructed by taking the average of the categorical lobbying variable over the remaining countries for each good. As indicated by the partial F-statistics for the first stage in Table 10, the instrument used is strongly correlated with the lobbying variable.

The last two columns of Table 10 present the estimates when we augment our baseline estimates with industry-by-country effects using the lobbying variable above. The market power effect in the dummy specification is statistically indistinguishable from the baseline results. The same conclusion holds if we consider the semi-log specification. Note also that the reason the results are similar is *not* because we are adding an irrelevant variable. Several studies found that a similar variable is empirically important for other countries, and we find that it is significant for this sample as well. Below we quantify the importance of market power in tariff setting not only by itself, but also relative to this important alternative explanation.

TABLE 11—MARKET POWER AND LOBBYING: IV ESTIMATES BY COUNTRY

Panel A: Semilog										
Dependent variable	Average tariff at four-digit HS (%)									
Fixed effects	Ind. by country	Ind.	Ind.	Ind.	Ind.	Ind.		Ind.		
Estimation method	IV GMM	IV GMM	IV GMM	IV GMM	IV GMM	IV GMM	IV Tobit	IV GMM		
Sample	Pooled (7)	China	Taiwan	Ukraine	Ecuador	Lithuania	Bolivia	Latvia	Mean	Median
Log(1/export elasticity)	1.94	4.69	2.39	0.91	1.81	0.84	0.97	1.52	1.87	1.5
	(0.38)	(2.12)	(1.32)	(0.25)	(0.45)	(0.27)	(0.16)	(0.67)		
Log(inv. imp. pen./imp. elas.)	1.59	6.21	0.43	0.97	0.27	1.64	0.21	1.89	1.66	1.0
	(0.55)	(4.31)	(1.18)	(0.75)	(0.57)	(0.40)	(0.19)	(1.33)		
Observations	5,178	861	780	616	712	706	618	788		
No. of parameters	133	21	20	19	20	20		20		
1st stage F: log(1/exp. el)	129	39	6	25	24	18	9	18		
1st st. F: log(Imp. pen/imp. el)	188	37	32	7	47.2	28.5	18.4	24.9		
Mean tariff (%)	12.8	37.0	8.8	5.7	10.0	2.4	9.8	6.9		
Elasticity (at mean)	0.15	0.13	0.27	0.16	0.18	0.35	0.10	0.22	0.20	0.18
Panel B: Dummy										
Dependent variable	Average tariff at four-digit HS (%)									
Fixed effects	Ind. by country	Ind.	Ind.	Ind.	Ind.	Ind.		Ind.		
Estimation method	IV GMM	IV GMM	IV GMM	IV GMM	IV GMM	IV GMM	IV Tobit	IV GMM		
Sample	Pooled (7)	China	Taiwan	Ukraine	Ecuador	Lithuania	Bolivia	Latvia	Mean	Median
Mid and high inv. exp. elast.	10.2	22.9	13.3	4.2	10.3	3.4	8.0	6.7	9.83	8.0
	(1.79)	(9.18)	(4.61)	(1.17)	(2.87)	(1.43)	(0.92)	(2.86)		
Mid and high inv. imp. pen./imp. elast	6.28	16.1	0.9	1.4	1.5	6.4	2.5	6.4	5.01	2.5
	(1.97)	(10.07)	(3.52)	(1.84)	(3.35)	(1.84)	(1.36)	(3.54)		
Observations	5,178	861	780	616	712	706	618	788		
No. of parameters	132	21	20	19	20	20		20		
1st-stage F: log(1/exp. el)	171	48	10	36	27	24	9	29		
1st-stage F: log(imp. pen/imp. el)	131	37	19	11	23.9	14.0	17.8	19.7		
Mean tariff (%)	12.8	37.0	8.8	5.7	10.0	2.4	9.8	6.9		
Mid-hi inv. exp. elast. /mean (%)	80	62	151	73	103	140	82	97	101	97

Notes: Standard errors in parentheses (heteroskedasticity robust). Constant and industry dummies included but not reported. Industry dummies defined by section according to the Harmonized Standard tariff schedule. Observations with extreme outliers in terms of tariffs were dropped. This affects the sample for Taiwan, Lithuania, and Ukraine, but only slightly since the criteria drops fewer than 36 observations in any of these countries (those with tariff values more than three times the interquartile range above the seventy-fifth percentile or below the twenty-fifth). Bolivia is estimated via an IV Tobit procedure to account for the fact that a large fraction of their observations are censored from above and/or below. Given the lack of variation in its tariffs within industries, the estimation for Bolivia does not include industry dummies. The first-stage statistic in this case refers to the z-statistic of the relevant instrument.

Table 11 shows that these results are not driven by a single country. In all countries for which we have production data, market power has a positive effect on tariffs, which is statistically and economically significant.

F. *Quantification*

We now quantify the impact of market power in explaining tariffs and the implication of removing this motive for tariff setting on prices received by exporters.

TABLE 12—ECONOMIC AND STATISTICAL IMPORTANCE OF MARKET POWER IN TARIFF SETTING: SUMMARY MEASURES

		Specification				
		Market power			Market power and lobbying	
Variable	Measure	Pooled (Table 8)	Subsample[a] (Table 8)	Typical country[b] (Table 9)	Pooled (Table 10)	Typical country (Table 11)
Log(1/export elasticity)	β	1.7 pp	2.1 pp	1.8 pp	1.9 pp	1.5 pp
	Elasticity (β/mean tariff)	0.13	0.15	0.16	0.15	0.18
	$\beta\times$s.d.	5 pp	6 pp	5 pp	5 pp	4 pp
	Elasticity relative to PE (β/γ)	.	.	.	1.2	0.9
	Impact relative to PE ($\beta\times$s.d.$(\ln\omega)/\gamma\times$s.d.$(\ln z/\sigma)$)	.	.	.	1.6	1.5
Mid and high inv. exp. elast.	β	9 pp	11 pp	9 pp	10 pp	8 pp
	β/mean tariff (%)	68%	77%	92%	80%	97%
	Impact relative to PE (β/γ)	.	.	.	1.6	3.1

Note: β and γ correspond to the coefficients on market power and the lobbying variable respectively; "pp" stands for percentage points.

[a] Equivalent of specifications in columns 8 and 9 of Table 8 excluding Bolivia, Oman, and Saudi Arabia.

[b] Estimates for bottom rows are obtained from the equivalent of specifications in Table 9 using the categorical variable.

Table 12 provides summary statistics for the key parameters estimated and computes simple counterfactuals that illustrate the economic and statistical importance of market power in tariff setting. The columns correspond to the main specifications in the baseline and lobbying augmented models. The results are fairly similar across specifications, so we focus on the pooled results with the lobbying variable in which we can assess the relative importance of the terms-of-trade motive.

The first row reproduces the coefficient for the semi-log specification. The pooled regression in Table 10 indicates that a one-log-point increase in market power increases tariffs by 1.9 percentage points. Thus, one standard deviation in market power leads to a 5 percentage point increase in tariffs, which is large if we recall that the median tariff in this sample is 10 percentage points. The market power effect is also important relative to the lobbying variable. Since their coefficients are similar, so is the elasticity of tariffs with respect to these two important determinants.

Alternatively, we can ask how important market power is in explaining tariff variation. We will do so with respect to a natural benchmark: the importance of political economy. To do this, we compute the impact of a one-standard-deviation change on each of those variables on tariffs. This effect is about 1.6 times larger for market power, indicating that it is more important in explaining tariff variation in these countries than the lobbying variable. We obtain a similar value if we use the dummy variable, as shown in the last row.

To gauge the economic importance of the terms-of-trade motive relative to all tariff setting motives, we can compare the average effect due to market power to the average tariff. The effect ranges from 8 to 11 percentage points, depending on the specification. For the typical country, this terms-of-trade motive is about the same magnitude as their average tariff: 92 percent of the average in the baseline case and 97 percent in the lobbying augmented model. Given that the effect applies to two-thirds of the tariff lines, the estimates imply that if these countries did not exert their market power, the implied tariff reductions would be around 60 percent of existing levels. This is much larger than the Uruguay Round's 25 percent tariff reduction target for developing countries.

If countries possess and exert market power, then their tariffs should depress the price received by foreign exporters. Thus, reducing tariffs increases those prices. Our estimates allow us to calculate the exporter's price increase that results when an importer, *i*, reduces its tariffs. This is an interesting counterfactual because this type of beggar-thy-neighbor trade policy is believed to have been central in the trade war of the 1930s and, arguably, one of the key motives behind the creation of the GATT. In fact, Bagwell and Staiger (1999) suggest that when a country enters a trade agreement such as the GATT/WTO, its tariffs no longer reflect its market power, or reflect it only partially. The counterfactual also provides an estimate of the impact of a country leaving the agreement and reexerting its market power, which is obtained by reversing the direction of the exporter price effects.

The price received by exporting variety v of good g to country i can be written as $p^*_{igv} = p^*_{igv}(\tau_{ig}(\omega_{ig}), .)$, i.e., a function of the tariff it faces and other parameters that are omitted. The percent increase in that price if an importer were to start treating a given good with medium or high market power as if it had low market power would then be

$$(14)\qquad d\ln p^*_{igv} = \frac{d\ln p^*_{igv}}{d\ln(1+\tau_{ig})|_{\omega^{med\_hi}_{ig}}} \times [\ln(1+\tau_{ig})|_{\omega^{low}_{ig}} - \ln(1+\tau_{ig})|_{\omega^{med\_hi}_{ig}}] \times 100,$$

$$\approx -(\zeta_{ig} - 1)^* \beta_i,$$

where ζ_{ig} is simply the domestic pass-through, i.e., the effect on the domestic price of good g in country i of a 1 percent increase in country i's tariff factor. Since $p_{igv} = (1 + \tau_{ig})p^*_{igv}$, we have $\zeta_{ig} = 1 + (d\ln p^*_{igv}/ d\ln(1+\tau_{ig}))$, so $\zeta_{ig} - 1$ is the effect of the tariff factor on exporter prices. In equation (13), β_i measures how much higher tariffs are in a good with medium or high market power relative to low.[32]

In the appendix of our working paper, we show that $\zeta_{ig} = 1/(1 + \omega_{ig})$ in our framework. The typical good in the middle tercile in terms of market power has an inverse elasticity of 1.6, implying a domestic pass-through of 0.4, which is similar to the values in that literature. Therefore, the impact on exporter prices, $\zeta_{ig} - 1$, equals $-0.6 (= 0.4 - 1)$. Multiplying this by the estimated tariff reduction due to treating those goods as low market power goods (9 percentage points in Table 8, column 8), we obtain a 5 percent increase in the price received by the exporters. By construction, this applies to a third of goods in each country. For the typical good in the high market power bin, we have $\omega_{ig} = 54$ (Table 3A), and thus any given tariff reduction has a larger effect on export prices. In this case the change in exporter prices for these goods is close to 9 percent.

Finally, for the three largest countries, the effect is stronger than the average. Using the country-specific estimates in our working paper, the effect for Russia and Taiwan is 6–10 percent and for China it is particularly large, 17–25 percent. Thus, if entry into the WTO leads these countries to remove the portion of their tariffs driven by a terms-of-trade motive, exporters into these markets will enjoy a large benefit from this direct price effect. Conversely, if these countries

[32] The approximation arises because in equation (13) we use tariffs rather than ln $(1 + \tau_{ig})$, but these are identical for most tariffs in the sample. When they differ, e.g., China, we report the results with the tariff factor. Note also that the estimate for $\zeta_{ig} - 1$ assumes that all exporters of good g face similar tariffs. In the WTO interpretation of the counterfactual, this implies they would all be in the WTO. Otherwise, the effect would be larger since the tariff reduction on exporter v alone would lead to an additional import demand for v due to substitution away from exporters of other varieties of g not in the WTO.

were to abandon an agreement and reexert their market power, this would be quite costly for the foreign exporters facing the higher tariffs.

In sum, the terms-of-trade motive is economically and statistically important for tariff setting in these countries. It is more important in explaining tariff variation than a key political economy variable used in previous studies. Moreover, it causes significant changes to prices received by foreign exporters, particularly as they try to sell in the larger countries such as China, Russia, and Taiwan.

V. Market Power and Trade Barriers in a Large Developed WTO Member

Our focus on non-WTO members is motivated by the theory that predicts that a country's tariffs will reflect its market power when it acts noncooperatively. Since the terms-of-trade gain for the importer is lower than the corresponding cost to the exporter, cooperation between the two, e.g., as they become WTO members, could attenuate or eliminate this motive for tariffs. However, a reasonable question is whether the forces we identify in this paper are present for any instruments of protection used by WTO members. Obviously, we cannot simply analyze if market power affects the most favored nation (MFN) tariffs of WTO members, because a failure to find such a relationship could simply be due to the effectiveness of this agreement in eliminating the terms-of-trade externality (c.f. Bagwell and Staiger 1999; Grossman and Helpman 1995). Thus we need to consider alternative experiments.

We consider instruments of protection whose levels are not negotiated within the GATT/WTO, or are only partially so. While this experiment may not be as clean as our earlier one, it does allow us to explore this question further. Moreover, it can provide insights about how the negotiated trade policies of current members would change if they were not subject to WTO constraints.

We focus on two such instruments for the United States, both because it has good data and because it is the world's largest economy. First, we follow most empirical studies of US protection and use nontariff barriers (NTBs) as the measure of its noncooperative trade policy (e.g., Goldberg and Maggi 1999; Kishore Gawande and Ursee Bandyopadhyay 2000). Several of these NTBs—e.g., antidumping duties, countervailing duties, and some forms of quotas—generate higher welfare for the importing country if they are implemented in goods where it has market power. Thus the prediction is that NTBs are more prevalent in goods with higher market power. Until recently, there were no tariff equivalents of NTBs for a large set of goods. Thus we use the standard measure of NTB strength in the literature: the coverage ratio, i.e., the share of six-digit goods within each four-digit classification that contain an NTB. We complement this by using the ad valorem equivalent recently estimated by Hiau L. Kee, Alessandro Nicita, and Marcelo Olarreaga (forthcoming).

Second, we examine "statutory rates"—the tariffs the United States applies to countries to which it does not grant MFN status. Statutory tariffs are set noncooperatively, which is apparent from their high levels and the targeted countries.[33] Successive rounds of trade negotiations opened a large gap between these rates and the MFN rates the United States negotiates with and applies to WTO members. The average US statutory rate in 1999 was about 30 percent—almost ten times larger than the MFN rate in our sample. Although statutory rates currently apply to a small number of countries, understanding their determinants provides an interesting and unique

[33] In 1989, the countries subject to these tariffs were Afghanistan, Albania, Bulgaria, Cuba, Czechoslovakia, Estonia, German Democratic Republic, Kampuchea, Laos, Latvia, Lithuania, Mongolia, North Korea, Romania, USSR, and Vietnam. Before 1980, China was also subject to this set of tariffs.

TABLE 13— MARKET POWER AND LOBBYING AS A SOURCE OF PROTECTION IN THE US

Panel A: Nontariff barriers

Theory	*Market power*				*Market power and lobbying*			
Fixed effects	Industry				Industry			
Estimation method	IV Tobit				IV Tobit[b]			
Dependent variable	Coverage ratio (HS4)[a]		Advalorem equiv. (HS4, %)		Coverage ratio (HS4)		Advalorem equiv. (HS4, %)	
	(1)	(2)	(3)	(4)	(5)	(6)	(7)	(8)
Mid and high inv. exp. elast.	0.90		38.8		4.93		70.8	
	(0.31)		(15.73)		(1.52)		(21.99)	
Mid and hi inv. imp. pen./imp. elast					−0.08		3.99	
					(0.86)		(13.14)	
Log(1/export elasticity)		0.22		9.71		1.16		16.0
		(0.08)		(4.00)		(0.39)		(5.47)
Log(inv. imp. pen./imp. elas.)						0.19		4.74
						(0.34)		(4.94)
Observations[c]	804	804	804	804	708	708	708	708
Number of parameters	17	17	17	17	17	17	17	17
First stage z-stat (market power)	7.1	6.6	7.1	6.6	6.2	5.3	6.2	5.3
First stage z-stat (other)	na	na	na	na	10.1	11.4	10.1	11.4

Panel B: Tariff barriers

Theory	*Market power*				*Market power and lobbying*			
Fixed effects	Industry				Industry			
Estimation method	IV Tobit				IV Tobit[b]			
Dependent variable	Non-WTO (HS4, %)		WTO (HS4, %)		Non-WTO (HS4, %)		WTO (HS4, %)	
	(1)	(2)	(3)	(4)	(5)	(6)	(7)	(8)
Mid and high inv. exp. elast.	21.2		1.52		26.9		1.89	
	(5.53)		(1.18)		(8.05)		(1.58)	
Mid and hi inv. imp. pen./imp. elast					10.8		−0.63	
					(4.91)		(0.96)	
Log(1/export elasticity)		5.07		0.36		5.58		0.45
		(1.36)		(0.28)		(1.86)		(0.38)
Log(inv. imp. pen./imp. elas.)						4.76		−0.18
						(1.69)		(0.34)
Observations[c]	870	870	869	869	775	775	774	774
Number of parameters	20	20	20	20	21	21	21	21
First stage z-stat (market power)	7.3	7.1	7.3	7.1	6.0	5.3	6.0	5.3
First stage z-stat (other)	na	na	na	na	10.0	11.6	10.0	11.6
Mean	30.6	30.6	3.4	3.4	33.0	33.0	3.7	3.7
Mid-hi inv. exp. elast. /mean (%)	69		45		81		51	
Elasticity (at mean)		0.17		0.11		0.17		0.12

Notes: Standard errors in parentheses. Industry dummies defined by section according to the Harmonized Standard tariff schedule.

[a] Coverage ratio is defined as the fraction of HS6 tariff lines in a given HS4 category that had an NTB. Since it varies between zero and one we use a two-limit IV Tobit. For the remaining variables we use a lower limit Tobit that accounts for censoring at zero. There is a lower share of censored observations in panel B, and we confirmed that these results are very similar if we use IV-GMM instead.

[b] We employ the Newey two-step estimator in the specifications with more than one endogenous variables since it is well known that in these cases the maximum likelihood estimator has difficulty in converging.

[c] The difference in the number of observations across specifications is due to missing production data for mining and agricultural products. The difference between tariff and nontariff barriers is due to the lack of variation of NTBs within certain industries, which must therefore be dropped. The tariff results in panel B based on a comparable sample to the NTB are identical.

insight into how the United States sets tariffs noncooperatively. Thus they are a useful complement to US NTBs, which apply to many countries.

Our estimation strategy is similar to the one used thus far. We estimate the relevant elasticities for the US using the same procedure, and use them to estimate equation (13), including industry dummies and instrumenting for the remaining variables. The structure of US production, trade, and demand differs in important ways from those of the developing countries we analyzed. Thus, we construct instruments for US elasticities and import penetration ratios as before, but use data from large developed countries: Canada, France, Germany, Japan, and the United Kingdom.[34]

In Table 13 we report the results for the United States. The results in panel A show that the United States sets significantly higher NTBs in products where it has more market power. This is true if we measure NTBs by the coverage ratio (columns 1, 2, 5, and 6) or the ad valorem equivalent (columns 3, 4, 7, and 8). The magnitudes for the ad valorem specification are large since products with NTBs have large tariff equivalents—about 18 percent for the typical HS4 with an NTB. These NTBs affect a large number of products—a quarter of the HS4 lines in the sample.[35] The results are robust to including the lobbying variable, which has a smaller impact on tariffs than market power, as we previously found for other countries.

Panel B focuses on tariff barriers. Market power has a strong and significant positive effect on statutory tariffs, which the United States sets noncooperatively. These rates are between 21 and 27 percentage points higher in goods with medium or high market power (columns 1 and 5). Interestingly, the elasticity at the mean is 0.17, very similar to the typical value we found for the non-WTO countries.

Finally, when we use the US MFN rates (columns 3, 4, 7, and 8), we find a much weaker relationship with market power. In fact, although the effect is positive, it is not significant at the conventional levels. Even if we take into account the lower mean of MFN rates, we still find a lower elasticity for them than for statutory rates. In sum, the evidence on NTBs, statutory tariffs, and MFN tariffs indicates that market power matters for US trade policy in areas not covered by the WTO. In other words, when the US can set trade barriers noncooperatively, it takes market power into account. This strongly suggests that market power would play an important role for *all* US trade policy if it were set noncooperatively, e.g., in the absence of the WTO.

VI. Conclusion

The idea that a country can improve its terms of trade and welfare through the imposition of tariffs has been in the economics literature for over a century. This motive continues to play a key role in most theoretical models of trade policy, but there has been considerable disagreement about its practical importance as an empirical determinant of tariffs. Despite this, no one had thus far tested whether countries set higher tariffs in goods in which they have more market power.

Part of the reason for the absence of such tests was that many economists simply assumed that most countries are small, i.e., do not have market power in trade. One of the contributions of this work is to demonstrate that this assumption is not correct. This is likely to have important implications in areas like computable general equilibrium modeling where small country assumptions are often the rule. One additional area that deserves further research surrounds how the

[34] The US elasticity estimates are reasonable when we use the criteria previously applied. For example, they are strongly correlated with those of these five countries. Moreover, the typical inverse elasticity is highest for differentiated (1.6) than reference priced goods (0.55) or commodities (0.41).

[35] We control for the censoring at zero by using an IV-Tobit. For the coverage ratio, we also control for censoring at one.

elasticities we estimate change over time. Our elasticities are computed over a one-year horizon, and it is possible that one might obtain different elasticity values over longer time horizons. As long as the ranking across goods remained unchanged, however, our main tariff results would hold.

Our paper is the first to provide evidence that when countries are not subject to constraints such as those imposed in the WTO, they set higher tariffs on goods with lower export supply elasticities. This result is present when looking at tariffs across countries, across goods within countries and industries, and even after controlling for tariff revenue and various political economy motivations.

The results also show that the impact of market power on tariffs is economically significant. It is of the same magnitude as the average tariffs of the countries we examine, and at least as important as the lobbying motive that has attracted much attention in previous work. Thus, removing the terms-of-trade motive for tariff setting would lead to increases in the prices received by foreign exporters to these markets. These increases are significant for the several goods in which we estimate that importers have considerable market power and suggest potentially large gains from *reciprocal* tariff liberalization agreements such as the WTO.

We also find that market power strongly affects the noncooperative trade policies of a large developed country, the United States. Its statutory tariffs, for example, are 27 percentage points higher in goods in which it has significant market power. Thus the importance of the terms-of-trade motive extends to WTO members, and understanding its implications for trade policy is essential. One such implication arises from our finding that market power significantly affects trade policies not subject to WTO constraints, but not those policies where such constraints are present (at least for the United States). This indicates that the WTO plays a quantitatively important role in reducing protection, unlike what is suggested by recent research.[36]

REFERENCES

Alvarez, Fernando, and Robert E. Lucas, Jr. 2007. "General Equilibrium Analysis of the Eaton-Kortum Model of International Trade." *Journal of Monetary Economics*, 54(6): 1726–68.

Anderson, James E., and Eric van Wincoop. 2004. "Trade Costs." *Journal of Economic Literature*, 42(3): 691–751.

Bagwell, Kyle, and Robert W. Staiger. 1999. "An Economic Theory of GATT." *American Economic Review*, 89(1): 215–48.

Bagwell, Kyle, and Robert W. Staiger. 2006. "What Do Trade Negotiators Negotiate About?" *Empirical Evidence from the World Trade Organization.* National Bureau of Economic Research Working Paper 12727.

Bickerdike, Charles F. 1907. "Review of A. C. Pigou's Protective and Preferential Import Duties." *Economic Journal,* 17: 98–108.

Broda, Christian, Nuno Limão, and David Weinstein. 2006. "Optimal Tariffs: The Evidence" National Bureau of Economic Research Working Paper 12033.

Broda, Christian, and David E. Weinstein. 2006. "Globalization and the Gains from Variety." *Quarterly Journal of Economics*, 121(2): 541–85.

Chang, Won, and L. Alan Winters. 2002. "How Regional Blocs Affect Excluded Countries: The Price Effects of Mercosur." *American Economic Review*, 92(4): 889–904.

Edgeworth, Francis Y. 1894. "The Theory of International Values." *Economic Journal*, 4: 35–50.

Efron, Bradley. 1981. "Non-parametric Standard Errors and Confidence Intervals." *Canadian Journal of Statistics*, 9(2): 139–172.

Feenstra, Robert C. 1989. "Symmetric Pass-through of Tariffs and Exchange Rates under Imperfect Competition: An Empirical Test." *Journal of International Economics*, 27(1–2): 25–45.

[36] Andrew K. Rose (2004) uses 68 measures of aggregate trade policy and finds that GATT/WTO accession leads to no significant reduction of protection.

Feenstra, Robert C. 1994. "New Product Varieties and the Measurement of International Prices." *American Economic Review*, 84(1): 157–77.

Gawande, Kishore, and Usree Bandyopadhyay. 2000. "Is Protection for Sale? Evidence on the Grossman-Helpman Theory of Endogenous Protection." *Review of Economics and Statistics*, 82(1): 139–52.

Goldberg, Pinelopi Koujianou, and Giovanni Maggi. 1999. "Protection for Sale: An Empirical Investigation." *American Economic Review*, 89(5): 1135–55.

Graaf, Jan de V. 1949–1950. "On Optimum Tariff Structures," *The Review of Economic Studies*, 17(1): 47–59.

Gros, Daniel. 1987. "A Note on the Optimal Tariff, Retaliation and the Welfare Loss from Tariff Wars in a Framework with Intra-Industry Trade." *Journal of International Economics*, 23(3/4): 357–67.

Grossman, Gene M., and Elhanan Helpman. 1994. "Protection for Sale." *American Economic Review*, 84(4): 833–50.

Grossman, Gene M., and Elhanan Helpman. 1995. "Trade Wars and Trade Talks." *Journal of Political Economy*, 103(4): 675–708.

Hansen, Bruce E. 2000. "Sample Splitting and Threshold Estimation." *Econometrica*, 68(3): 575–603.

Helpman, Elhanan. 1997. "Politics and Trade Policy." In *Advances in Economics and Econometrics: Theory and Applications: Seventh World Congress Volume 1*, ed. D. M. Kreps and K. F. Wallis, 19–45. Cambridge: Cambridge University Press.

Irwin, Douglas A. 1988. "Welfare Effects of British Free Trade: Debate and Evidence from the 1840s." *Journal of Political Economy*, 96(6): 1142–64.

Irwin, Douglas A. 1996. *Against the Tide: An Intellectual History of Free Trade*. Princeton: Princeton University Press.

Johnson, Harry G. 1953–54."Optimum Tariffs and Retaliation." *Review of Economic Studies*, 21(2): 142–53.

Kee, Hiau L., Alessandro Nicita, and Marcelo Olarreaga. Forthcoming. "Estimating Trade Restrictiveness. *Economic Journal*.

Kreinin, Mordechai E. 1961. "Effect of Tariff Changes on the Prices and Volume of Imports." *American Economic Review*, 51(3): 310–24.

Krugman, Paul R. and Obstfeld, Maurice. 1997. *International Economics: Theory and Policy*. 4th edition. New York: Addison-Weslley.

Limão, Nuno, and Anthony J. Venables. 2001. "Infrastructure, Geographical Disadvantage, Transport Costs, and Trade." *World Bank Economic Review*, 15(3): 451–79.

Markusen, James R., and Randall M. Wigle. 1989. "Nash Equilibrium Tariffs for the United States and Canada: The Roles of Country Size, Scale Economies, and Capital Mobility." *Journal of Political Economy*, 97(2): 368–86.

Mill, John Stuart. 1844. *Essays on Some Unsettled Questions of Political Economy*. London: Parker.

Rauch, James E. 1999. "Networks versus Markets in International Trade." *Journal of International Economics*, 48(1): 7–35.

Romalis, John. 2007. "NAFTA's and CUSTFA's Impact on International Trade." *Review of Economics and Statistics*, 89(3): 416–35.

Rose, Andrew K. 2004. "Do WTO Members Have More Liberal Trade Policy?" *Journal of International Economics*, 63(2): 209–35.

Scitovsky, Tibor. 1942. "A Reconsideration of the Theory of Tariffs." *Review of Economic Studies*, 9(2), 89–110.

Torrens, Robert. 1833. *Letters on Commercial Policy*. London: Longman.

Chapter 3

Uncertainty and Trade Agreements†

By NUNO LIMÃO AND GIOVANNI MAGGI*

We explore conditions under which trade agreements can provide gains by reducing trade policy uncertainty. Given the degree of income risk aversion, this is more likely when economies are more open, export supply elasticities are lower, and economies more specialized. Governments have stronger incentives to sign trade agreements when the trading environment is more uncertain. As exogenous trade costs decline, the gains from reducing tariff uncertainty become more important relative to reducing average tariff levels. We also develop a simple "sufficient statistic" approach to quantify the gains from managing trade policy uncertainty, and examine the impact of ex ante investments on such gains. (*JEL* D81, F13)

Policy practitioners often argue that a central benefit of trade agreements (TAs) is to reduce trade policy uncertainty. Indeed, the World Trade Organization (WTO) and many other TAs explicitly state that one of their goals is to increase the predictability of the trade policy environment.[1] But in spite of the importance that policy makers and international institutions attribute to the notion of an uncertainty-reducing role of TAs, we know little about its theoretical underpinnings. A large body of theory has explored the possible roles of TAs as means to correct international policy externalities (e.g., Grossman and Helpman 1995; Bagwell and Staiger 1999; and Ossa 2011) and to allow governments to commit vis-à-vis domestic actors (e.g., Maggi and Rodríguez-Clare 1998, and Limão and Tovar 2011). But this research focuses on the role of TAs in managing the *level* of trade barriers, not their uncertainty.

The main objective of our paper is to explore the conditions under which there is an uncertainty-reducing motive for a TA, and examine the potential gains that a

* Limão: Economics Department, University of Maryland, College Park, MD 20817 and National Bureau of Economic Research (NBER) (e-mail: limao@econ.umd.edu); Maggi: Yale University, 30 Hillhouse Avenue, New Haven, CT 06520, FGV/EPGE, and NBER (e-mail: giovanni.maggi@yale.edu). We thank the reviewers for useful suggestions. We also thank Kyle Bagwell, Mostafa Beshkar, Paola Conconi, Swati Dhingra, Avinash Dixit, and Robert Staiger for helpful comments as well as participants in the 2012 AEA meetings, the 2012 Venice CAGE/CEP Workshop, the 2012 Princeton IES Summer Workshop, the Australasian Econometric Society, and seminars at Stanford University, University of Wisconsin, Oxford University, London School of Economics, University of Warwick, University of Nottingham, and Universidade de Sao Paulo.

† Go to http://dx.doi.org/10.1257/mic.20130163 to visit the article page for additional materials and author disclosure statement(s) or to comment in the online discussion forum.

[1] For example, the WTO's website states that "Just as important as freer trade—perhaps more important—are other principles of the WTO system. For example non-discrimination, and making sure the conditions for trade are stable, predictable and transparent." Several preferential trade agreements such as some of those entered into by the United States, the European Union, and by developing countries often claim that they aim to "reduce distortions to trade" *and* "ensure a predictable environment for business planning and investment."

Originally Published in *American Economic Journal* 7(4), pp. 1–42.

TA can provide by regulating trade policy uncertainty, above and beyond the more standard gains from reducing the levels of trade barriers.

We focus on a scenario without frictions in contracting between governments, so that the TA is a complete contingent contract. Since we are focusing on the potential gains from a TA, rather than its design, focusing on a setting without transaction costs is a natural first step. To isolate the uncertainty-managing motive for a TA we focus on the following thought experiment: we consider the optimal "mean preserving agreement," that is the optimal TA among all agreements that keep the average trade barrier at the same level as in the noncooperative equilibrium; if such agreement leads to a policy distribution that is different from the noncooperative one, we say that there is an "uncertainty-managing motive" (or simply an "uncertainty motive") for a TA, and if it reduces policy uncertainty relative to the noncooperative equilibrium, we say that there is an "uncertainty-reducing motive."[2]

Our first step is to examine a simple framework in which government objectives are specified in reduced form as functions of a trade policy and an underlying shock. Starting from a reduced-form framework with relatively little structure is useful for several reasons. First, the framework delivers general formulas for the direction of the uncertainty motive and the gains from regulating policy uncertainty, which admit intuitive interpretations and make the logic of our results quite transparent. Second, these formulas can be readily applied to a specific trade model to examine how the direction of the uncertainty motive and the associated gains depend on the underlying economic environment. And third, the framework can in principle also apply to other types of international agreements, such as environmental or investment agreements.

Initially we focus on a setting where only one country (Home) chooses a trade barrier, which exerts a negative externality on a policy-passive country (Foreign); later we extend the model to allow for two policy-active countries. We identify two key effects that determine whether there is an uncertainty motive for a TA, and if so, in what direction it goes. The first one is what we label the *policy-risk preference* effect, determined by the concavity/convexity of Foreign's payoff with respect to Home's policy: when the Foreign country is policy-risk averse, this effect works in favor of an uncertainty-reducing motive. Intuition might suggest that this effect is all that matters for determining whether there is "too much" or "too little" risk in the noncooperative policy. And indeed this is the case when the shock affects the Foreign country only through Home's policy (a "political economy" shock). However, when the shock affects the Foreign country also in a direct manner (an "economic" shock), there is an additional effect that we label the *externality-shifting* effect. A positive shock is defined as one that increases the noncooperative trade barrier. If a positive shock strengthens the marginal international policy externality holding the policy level constant, this effect works in favor of the uncertainty-reducing motive for a

[2] We also consider an alternative thought experiment, which focuses on the tariff schedule that a government would unilaterally choose if it were constrained to deliver the same mean as the optimal agreement. If such "mean-preserving unilateral" choice exhibits more uncertainty than the optimal trade agreement, we say that there is an uncertainty-reducing motive. In Section I, we discuss the similarities and differences between the results under the two thought experiments, and the reasons why we focus the analysis on the mean-preserving-agreement thought experiment.

TA, otherwise it works against it, and the uncertainty motive need not go in the same direction as the Foreign country's policy-risk preference.

Our next step is to apply these general conditions and formulas to a standard competitive trade model with two countries and two sectors. Focusing on a perfectly competitive setting—rather than one that emphasizes the role of firms—seems like a natural choice, given that this is a first step in exploring the uncertainty motive for TAs.[3] For simplicity, we assume that the Foreign country is small relative to the Home country and maximizes welfare. We allow individuals to be risk averse. In the basic model we consider shocks of the political-economy type, and later extend the model to allow for more general shocks.

It is natural to start with the benchmark case of risk-neutral individuals. In this case we find that there tends to be an uncertainty-*increasing* motive for a TA. The reason is that, given the political-economy nature of the shock, all that matters for the uncertainty motive is the Foreign country's policy-risk preference (as mentioned above), and in the presence of income-risk neutrality the Foreign country tends to be policy-risk *loving*. This is due to the convexity of the indirect utility function and of the revenue function in prices, reflecting the ability of firms and consumers to make decisions after observing prices. Interestingly, then, the standard trade model with risk neutrality seems at odds with the often-heard informal argument that TAs can provide gains by reducing trade policy uncertainty.

When we allow individuals to be risk averse, we find that the uncertainty-managing motive for a TA is determined by a trade-off between risk aversion and flexibility: on the one hand, the degree of risk aversion, in interaction with the degree of openness, pushes toward an uncertainty-reducing motive; on the other hand, the degree of flexibility of the economy, which in turn is determined by the export supply elasticity and the degree of specialization, pushes toward an uncertainty-increasing motive. We note that, empirically, lower-income countries tend to have lower export supply elasticities and a lower degree of diversification, thus at a broad level our model suggests that the uncertainty-reducing motive for a TA should be more important for lower income countries than for higher income countries.

The uncertainty motive for a TA is affected in interesting ways by changes in exogenous trade costs (e.g., transport costs). We show that if individuals are sufficiently risk averse, as the trade cost declines from its prohibitive level, initially there is an uncertainty-increasing motive for a TA, but this turns into an uncertainty-reducing motive as the trade cost continues to fall. Thus, the model suggests that uncertainty-reducing motives for TAs are increasingly likely to emerge as trade costs decline over time, and are more likely to be present for countries within a region.

Next we examine the gains from regulating trade policy uncertainty relative to the gains from regulating the tariff mean. We isolate the latter by focusing on "uncertainty preserving" agreements,[4] while we capture the former (as explained above)

[3] It is also important to note that, as we discuss in footnote 25, a key effect highlighted by our model also would operate in models with imperfect competition and sunk investments, namely the feature that in the presence of risk neutrality the model tends to predict an uncertainty-*increasing* motive for a TA.

[4] Specifically, an uncertainty-preserving agreement is an agreement that shifts the tariff schedule in a way that changes the mean but preserves all the higher central moments (variance, skewness, kurtosis, etc.).

by focusing on mean-preserving agreements. We find that, if individuals are sufficiently risk averse, the relative gains from regulating trade policy uncertainty are non-monotonic in the trade cost: as the trade cost falls, these relative gains initially decrease, but eventually grow in magnitude. Another implication of the model concerns the impact of the underlying degree of uncertainty, as captured by the variance of the political economy shock: an increase in this variance leads to larger overall gains from a TA, thus suggesting that governments should have a higher propensity to sign TAs when the trading environment is more uncertain.

Next we extend the model to allow for more general economic shocks. As mentioned above, economic shocks may amplify or reduce the impact of Home's protection on Foreign, thereby introducing a policy-externality-shifting effect, in addition to the policy-risk-preference effect. The externality-shifting effect operates through two possible channels: first, to the extent that the shock affects domestic economic conditions in the Home country, it will affect the Foreign country through the terms-of-trade; and second, to the extent that the shock affects domestic economic conditions in the Foreign country, it will have a further impact on this country. We discuss conditions under which the externality-shifting effect strengthens the uncertainty-reducing motive for a TA.

Our model suggests a simple "sufficient statistic" approach to empirically determine the direction of the uncertainty motive for a TA and to quantify the relative gains from regulating trade policy uncertainty. We start from the observation that the international externality exerted by Home's tariff is given by an adjusted measure of Foreign's openness (where the adjustment factor is related to the marginal utility of income), and show that there is an uncertainty-reducing motive for a TA if and only if the adjusted openness co-varies with the noncooperative tariff level as a result of the underlying shocks. Furthermore, the covariance between the tariff and the adjusted openness can be used, in conjunction with the tariff mean, to approximate the relative gains from regulating trade policy uncertainty.

We then illustrate how our "sufficient statistic" approach can be taken to the data. We focus on the trading relationship between a small and a large country, Cuba and the United States, respectively, during a period of noncooperative trade policies, namely before the 1934 agreement between these two countries. We find a positive correlation between US tariffs and Cuban-adjusted openness when calculated at reasonable levels of risk aversion, which suggests there was an uncertainty-reducing motive for a TA between these two countries, and we find that the relative gains from reducing trade policy uncertainty were significant. Our model is extremely stylized, so this exercise should be interpreted with caution, but it suggests that the model can be taken to the data in a meaningful way, and it points to a potential direction for future research: developing richer versions of the model and taking them to richer datasets.

In our baseline model, factors can be allocated only after uncertainty is resolved. In Section V, we extend the model to allow for ex ante investments. We show that the condition determining the direction of the uncertainty motive for a TA in the presence of ex ante investments is analogous to the one derived in the static model, provided the market allocation of capital is efficient given Home's trade policy. Even though the TA can change the allocation of capital, this change has no first-order welfare effect in the Foreign country, due to the initial efficiency of the factor allocation. We interpret this result as suggesting that there is no separate uncertainty motive associated with ex ante investment. Next, we examine the direction in which a TA affects investment and trade *via* changes in policy uncertainty. We show that, if risk aversion is sufficiently strong, the support of the shock is sufficiently small and the export supply elasticity does not increase too steeply with the price, then (i) there is an uncertainty-reducing motive for a TA and (ii) a reduction in policy uncertainty leads to more investment in the export sector and a higher expected trade volume. Overall, our analysis of ex ante investments suggests an important caveat to the statements made by the WTO and other TAs that an important goal is to reduce policy uncertainty in order to increase investment in export markets: even though a reduction in policy uncertainty does (under some conditions) have this effect, this in itself is not sufficient to ensure a first-order increase in welfare.

Finally, we extend the analysis to allow for two (symmetric) policy-active countries. The general condition that determines the direction of the uncertainty motive for a TA in this case still includes the policy-risk-preference and externality-shifting effects, but now there is an additional effect, which works in favor of an uncertainty-reducing motive if tariffs are strategic substitutes, and against it if they are strategic complements.

Before proceeding, it is natural to ask: empirically, is there significant uncertainty in trade policies? At a broad level one can distinguish between two types of trade policy uncertainty. A first type is the risk of major protectionist events, such as trade wars, which are very infrequent and thus not typically observed in a specific period of time. A second type is the presence of frequent, small-magnitude changes in trade policy (we will refer to this as trade policy "volatility"), which can be more easily observed in the data.[5]

Regarding the first type of trade policy uncertainty, it is difficult to measure it empirically, but there seems to be a definite belief among policy makers and businesses that this risk is real, and such belief seems reflected in the stated goals of TAs mentioned above. A recent example of this perceived risk was the widespread fear of a tariff war during the 2008 financial crisis, which lead to the implementation of monitoring systems described in Bown (2011) and pledges by G-20 countries not to "repeat the historic mistakes of protectionism of previous eras." Ex post the worst fears have not be realized, perhaps because there was a network of TAs in place, but what matters more is the perceived ex ante risk of protectionist spikes.[6]

Focusing on the second type of trade policy uncertainty, it is easier to examine empirically its significance. Since the relevance of our theory rests more on the presence of uncertainty in *noncooperative* trade policies, it seems natural to focus on volatility in trade policy before the inception of GATT. One of the few available measures that are comparable over time and countries in this period is the import-weighted tariff. Figure 1 presents the distribution of this measure for

[5] Note that our model can accommodate both types of policy uncertainty: the high-frequency/small-magnitude type would be captured by significant probability weight on policy levels relatively close to the mean, while the infrequent/large-magnitude type would be captured by a small probability weight on policy levels that are much higher than the mean level (and of course the two types of risk can co-exist in the same distribution).

[6] This point is made in Handley and Limão (forthcoming). More on this paper below.

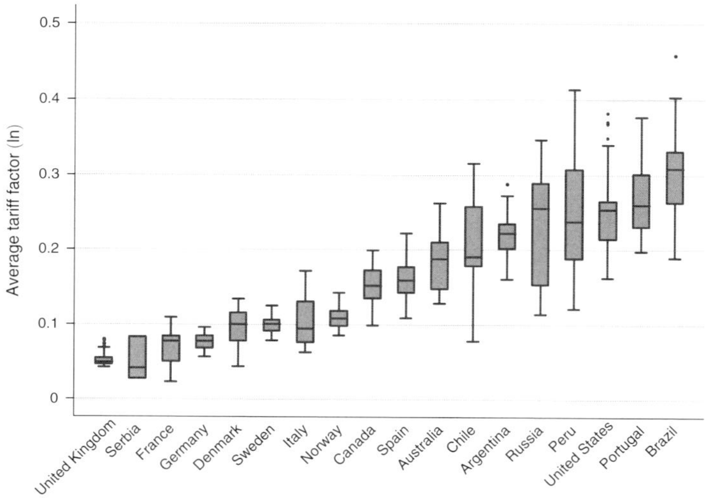

FIGURE 1. AVERAGE TARIFF DISTRIBUTIONS: 1865–1913

Note: Import weighted tariff τ, modified to $t = \ln(1 + \tau)$.
Source: Schularick and Solomou (2011)

several countries in 1865–1913. The figure visually suggests a considerable amount of volatility in most of these countries.[7] To place this trade policy volatility into perspective, we can compare it to that of the (log) terms-of-trade. The typical standard deviation for the (log) tariff across countries is 0.026, which is about one-fourth the magnitude of the typical standard deviation for the (log) terms-of-trade. This is a reasonably large value given that the terms-of-trade of two thirds of the countries in this sample reflect commodity export prices, which are known to be very volatile.[8]

[7] In particular, we note that a number of countries have large inter-quartile ranges (represented by the edges of the boxes), up to about 14 percentage points (Russia), and several countries have unusually high periods of protection relative to their typical levels (e.g., the United Kingdom, United States, Argentina, and Brazil had tariffs exceeding their third quartile by more than 1.5 times the inter-quartile range). A legitimate question is whether the measured volatility of the average tariff for a country over time reflects volatility at the tariff-line level or might instead be driven by volatility in the import weights used to construct average tariffs. It seems unlikely to us that the volatility in average tariffs is driven mainly by changes in import weights for a country over time, for a couple of reasons. First, to replicate the observed volatility in average tariffs, one would need large shifts in import weights within short time periods, and this would be counterfactual because a country's import basket is typically diversified and adjusts slowly over time. Second, at the anecdotal level, in the period we consider, some of the changes in tariffs are clearly due to statutory changes in policy. For example, the US average tariff in the pre-GATT era reflected changes in statutory tariffs, some of which were due to switches in the party in control of Congress (as discussed by Irwin 1998).

[8] Our calculation of the terms-of-trade volatility is based on data from Blattman, Hwang, and Williamson (2007). They measure short-term volatility using the standard deviation of the detrended terms-of-trade. If we do the same (i.e., apply a Hodrick-Prescott filter), we find that the relative short run volatility of the tariff to terms-of-trade is one-fourth, which is similar to the one using the underlying series.

FIGURE 2. US AVERAGE TARIFF: 1867–1961

Note: Import weighted tariff τ, modified to $t = \ln(1 + \tau)$.
Source: Irwin (2007)

There is also some evidence that trade policy volatility decreases after countries sign TAs. For example, Figure 2 plots the US average tariffs until 1961. The standard deviation of the policy before 1934 is at least twice as high as during 1934–1961—a period marked by the Reciprocal Trade Agreement Act (1934) and the signing of GATT (1948).[9] At the anecdotal level, the higher volatility of US trade policy before 1934 is a reflection not only of the well-known Smoot-Hawley tariff hike of 1930, but also of several major changes in the tariff code (see Irwin 1998, for a detailed account of these episodes).[10] To be clear, the fact that noncooperative tariffs are more volatile than cooperative tariffs does not necessarily imply that there is an uncertainty-reducing *motive* for TAs in the sense defined in this paper. This is because our notion of uncertainty-reducing motive is based on a counterfactual agreement (the mean-preserving agreement) that is fully contingent and preserves the noncooperative tariff mean, while real-world TAs do not preserve tariff means, and moreover the low volatility of a cooperative tariff may simply reflect contracting frictions that cause rigidity in the agreement.

Next, we discuss the related literature. One strand of literature that is related to our paper focuses on how uncertainty, in conjunction with contracting imperfections,

[9]Even if some of the trends of protection and liberalization were anticipated, and thus not uncertain, we are still left with short-term volatility. Using a standard Hodrick-Prescott filter, the short-term volatility prior to 1934 is 2.4 times higher than in the 1934–1961 period.

[10]We are not aware of studies that investigate more systematically whether trade agreements reduce policy volatility. Cadot, Olarreaga, and Tschopp (2013) focus on the volatility of agricultural policies, presenting evidence that it was significantly reduced by regional trade agreements. Rose (2004) and Mansfield and Reinhardt (2008) examine the effect of trade agreements on the volatility of trade flows.

affects the optimal design of TAs. For example, Horn, Maggi, and Staiger (2010); Amador and Bagwell (2013); and Beshkar and Bond (2012) show that the presence of uncertainty and contracting imperfections can explain the use of rigid tariff bindings.[11] In contrast to these papers, we focus on the uncertainty-managing motive for a TA and the gains that a TA can provide by regulating policy uncertainty.

Also related is the work by Handley and Limão (2015) and Handley (2014). These papers examine theoretically and empirically the impact that TAs have on trade flows specifically through the channel of removing the risk of future increases in protection. Handley and Limão (2015) find evidence that Portugal's accession to the EC eliminated the risk of exporters losing preexisting preferences and facing MFN tariffs in the EC. Handley (2014) examines the impact that the imposition of WTO tariff bindings had on exports to Australia, finding evidence that a significant portion of the impact of such bindings on export growth is due to the reduction in the risk of tariff hikes. The contribution of our paper is very distinct. These two papers examine how trade flows are impacted by exogenous reductions in the risk of protection increases, whereas our paper focuses on the endogenous formation of trade policy in noncooperative and cooperative scenarios, and in particular it examines under what conditions there is "too much" uncertainty in noncooperative policies, and what are the gains from "correcting" the degree of policy uncertainty through a TA.

The paper is organized as follows. Section I presents our basic reduced-form framework. Section II examines the standard trade model with political economy shocks. Section III extends the model by allowing for more general economic shocks. Section IV presents our "sufficient statistic" approach. Section V extends the analysis to allow for ex ante investments. In Section VI we consider a setting with two symmetric policy-active countries. Section VII concludes. The Appendix contains the proofs of our results.

I. Basic Framework

To make our points transparent, we start by focusing on a two country setting where only one country is policy-active, hence—there is a one-way international policy externality. In this section, we model government objectives in reduced form, as functions of a trade policy and an underlying shock; in the next section, we will "open up" the black box of government objectives in the context of a standard trade model.

There are two countries, Home and Foreign. The Home government chooses a trade barrier t, while the Foreign government is passive. We let $G(t, \lambda)$ denote the Home government's objective function, where λ is interpreted as an exogenous shock to this government's policy preferences; this could represent, for example, a politically adjusted welfare function, with λ a political-economy parameter (e.g., the extra weight attached to a special interest group) or an economic parameter. We let $F(\lambda)$ denote the cumulative distribution function of λ. We assume that G is concave in t and

[11] These contracting imperfections take the form of contracting costs in Horn, Maggi, and Staiger (2010); of private information in Amador and Bagwell (2013); and of costly state verification in Beshkar and Bond (2012).

satisfies the single crossing property $G_{t\lambda} > 0$. The Foreign government's objective is $G^*(t, \lambda)$. We assume that an increase in the trade barrier hurts Foreign: $G_t^* < 0$. The governments' joint payoff is denoted by $G^W(t, \lambda) = G(t, \lambda) + G^*(t, \lambda)$. We assume G^W is concave in t and satisfies the single crossing property $G_{t\lambda}^W > 0$. The role of the single crossing properties will be apparent shortly.

As we will discuss in the next section, this reduced-form framework can be interpreted as capturing a two-sector, perfectly competitive world in which a large country trades with a small welfare-maximizing country, and in which a TA is motivated by a terms-of-trade externality.[12] But we note that this framework could also be applied to settings where TAs are motivated by externalities unrelated to terms-of-trade as emphasized by "new trade" models of agreements (e.g., Ossa 2011; Bagwell and Staiger 2012; Mrázova 2011).

We start by describing the noncooperative policy choice. We assume the Home government observes λ before choosing its trade policy, hence, the noncooperative policy is given by:

$$t^N(\lambda) = \arg\max_t G(t, \lambda).$$

The single crossing property $G_{t\lambda} > 0$ implies that $t^N(\lambda)$ is increasing. The distribution of the shock $F(\lambda)$ and the shape of the $t^N(\cdot)$ schedule induce a distribution for the noncooperative policy t^N.

We now describe our assumptions regarding the TA. The agreement is signed, ex ante, before λ is realized, so the timing is the following: (0) the TA is signed; (1) λ is realized and observed by both countries; (2) t is implemented and payoffs are realized. We assume that λ is verifiable and there are no costs of contracting, so the agreement can be contingent on λ. As we mentioned at the beginning of this paper, given that our main focus is on the *potential* gains from regulating policy uncertainty relative to the noncooperative equilibrium, abstracting from contracting imperfections is a natural first step.[13]

We assume that the TA maximizes the governments' expected joint payoff EG^W,[14] so the (unconstrained) optimal TA is given by

$$t^A(\lambda) = \arg\max EG^W(t, \lambda).$$

[12] In the literature on trade agreements there is a small tradition of models with a small country and a large country, a prominent example being McLaren (1997).

[13] While our assumption of frictionless contracting serves to focus more sharply on the questions we are addressing, we note that the GATT-WTO does include a number of contingent clauses, for example, the "escape clauses" in GATT Articles XIX and XXVIII. For a model that endogenizes the degree to which a trade agreement is contingent, based on the presence of contracting costs, see Horn, Maggi, and Staiger (2010).

[14] This implicitly assumes that international transfers are available and that transfers enter governments' payoffs linearly, so that Home's payoff is given by $G + T$ and Foreign's payoff by $G^* - T$, where T is a transfer from Foreign to Home. The transfer can be interpreted, for example, as a non-trade policy concession that serves as a form of compensation between governments. Focusing on a transferrable-utility setting seems like a natural choice given that we are abstracting from any form of international transaction costs. We also note that the need for government-to-government transfers would be reduced or even eliminated in a more symmetric setting where both countries are policy-active. In Section VI, we consider a fully symmetric setting, and in such a setting governments select the optimal symmetric agreement, which maximizes the sum of their expected payoffs.

The single crossing property $G^W_{t\lambda} > 0$ implies that $t^A(\lambda)$ is increasing.

What motivates governments to sign a TA in this setting is the presence of an international policy externality, which causes the noncooperative policy choice to be inefficient. When we introduce an explicit trade structure in the next section, this externality will operate via terms-of-trade, but for now this can be interpreted as a more general international policy externality.

The international policy externality is transmitted through the whole *distribution* of t. For example, if Home's policy schedule $t(\lambda)$ is changed in such a way that the mean of t remains unchanged but the degree of uncertainty in t changes, this will have an impact on Foreign's expected welfare EG^*. In order to isolate the "uncertainty motive" for a TA from the "mean motive," we consider the following thought experiment: if we constrain the TA to keep the average t at the noncooperative level, is there any role left for a TA? This is the idea behind our notion of "mean preserving agreement" (MPA). If the optimal MPA changes the riskiness of t relative to the noncooperative policy $t^N(\lambda)$, we say that there is an uncertainty-*managing* motive for a TA. And in this case, if the optimal MPA decreases (increases) the riskiness of t relative to $t^N(\lambda)$, we say that there is an uncertainty-*reducing* (-increasing) motive for a TA.

Formally, the optimal MPA is defined as

$$t^{MPA}(\lambda) = \arg\max_{t(\lambda)} EG^W(t(\lambda), \lambda) \text{ s.t. } Et(\lambda) = Et^N(\lambda), \tag{1}$$

where the operator E denotes an expectation over λ.

Before we study the optimal MPA, we can build intuition by considering a local argument for the simplest possible case. Consider the case where λ affects Foreign only through the policy t, so that its payoff is simply $G^*(t)$. This can be interpreted as a scenario in which λ represents a domestic political economy shock in the Home country.

Let us start from the noncooperative policy $t^N(\lambda)$ and ask: how can we change the policy schedule locally to achieve an increase in $EG^W = EG + EG^*$, while preserving the mean of the policy? Since $t^N(\lambda)$ maximizes EG, a small change from $t^N(\lambda)$ will have a second-order effect on EG and a first-order effect on EG^*. Clearly, then, to achieve an increase in EG^W we must increase EG^*. Suppose G^* is convex in t, then if we change the policy schedule (slightly) in such a way that the new policy is a mean-preserving spread of $t^N(\lambda)$, this will increase EG^* (by the well-known Rotschild-Stiglitz 1970, equivalence result) and thus EG^W will also increase. Likewise, if G^* is concave in t, we can achieve an increase in EG^W by making a (slight) mean-preserving compression of $t^N(\lambda)$. Therefore this argument suggests that the key condition determining whether the optimal MPA increases or decreases policy uncertainty is the concavity/convexity of Foreign's objective with respect to t.

Of course, the argument above suggests only a sufficient condition for local improvement over the noncooperative outcome; in particular, one can improve over the noncooperative outcome in many other ways, including by changing the policy schedule in ways that are neither a mean-preserving compression nor spread of $t^N(\lambda)$. But as we show below, this intuition does carry over to the globally optimal

MPA in the case of political economy shocks (when the single-crossing properties are satisfied).

Importantly, however, the Rotschild-Stiglitz type argument no longer applies if the shock λ affects the Foreign payoff G^* directly as well as through the policy t. In this case, it is not enough to know whether Foreign's objective is concave or convex in t to determine how the optimal MPA will change policy uncertainty, as we now show.

To derive the FOCs for the optimal MPA problem in (1) we set up the Lagrangian:

$$L = EG^W(t,\lambda) + \psi\big(Et^N(\lambda) - Et(\lambda)\big). \tag{2}$$

Since the multiplier ψ is constant with respect to λ, we can rewrite the Lagrangian as follows

$$L = \int \big[G^W(t,\lambda) + \psi\big(t^N(\lambda) - t(\lambda)\big)\big]\, dF(\lambda), \tag{3}$$

and since we can maximize this pointwise we obtain the following FOCs

$$G_t^W(t(\lambda),\lambda) = \psi \text{ for all } \lambda$$

$$Et^N(\lambda) = Et(\lambda).$$

Note that the FOC requires the marginal contribution of t to joint surplus, G_t^W, to be equalized across states (realizations of λ), and in particular G_t^W should be equal to the multiplier ψ, which is easily shown to be negative. Also note that the FOC for the unconstrained optimal agreement is given by $G_t^W(t,\lambda) = 0$, so both for the unconstrained optimum and for the optimal MPA, G_t^W is equalized across states, but in the former case it is equalized at zero, while in the MPA case it is equalized at some negative constant.

Using the FOC we can prove:

LEMMA 1:

(*i*) *If* $\frac{d}{d\lambda}G_t^*(t^N(\lambda),\lambda) < 0$ (> 0) *for all* λ, *then* $t^{MPA}(\lambda)$ *intersects* $t^N(\lambda)$ *once and from above (below).*

(*ii*) *If* $\frac{d}{d\lambda}G_t^*(t^N(\lambda),\lambda) = 0$ *for all* λ, *then* $t^{MPA}(\lambda) = t^N(\lambda)$ *for all* λ.

Figure 3 illustrates Lemma 1 graphically for the case $\frac{d}{d\lambda}G_t^*(t^N(\lambda),\lambda) < 0$. The basic intuition for the result can be conveyed by focusing on the case in which λ can take only two values, say λ^H and λ^L. Let us start from $t^N(\lambda)$ and ask: how can we improve the ex ante joint payoff? Given the mean-preservation constraint, there are only two ways to modify the schedule $t^N(\lambda)$: decreasing t for $\lambda = \lambda^H$

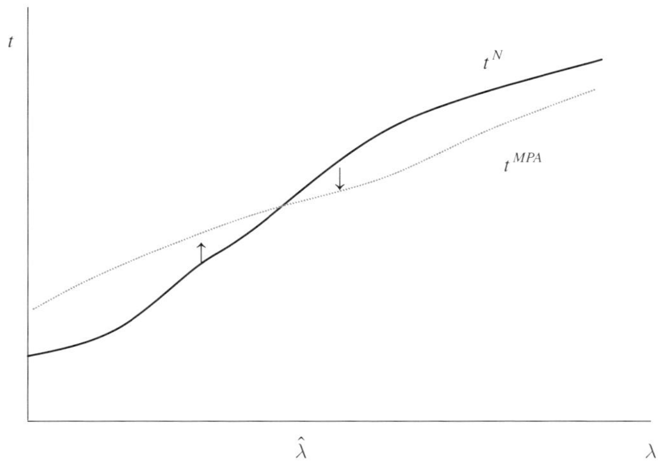

FIGURE 3. NONCOOPERATIVE POLICY VERSUS MEAN PRESERVING AGREEMENT

and increasing t for $\lambda = \lambda^L$ (that is, flattening the schedule), or vice-versa (that is, steepening the schedule). Intuitively it is preferable to reduce t in the state where it is more important to do so, that is where the international externality is stronger (more negative). If $\frac{d}{d\lambda} G_t^*(t^N(\lambda), \lambda) < 0$, then the international externality is stronger in the high-λ state, so it is preferable to flatten the policy schedule relative to $t^N(\lambda)$. Similarly, if $\frac{d}{d\lambda} G_t^*(t^N(\lambda), \lambda) > 0$ the objective can be improved by making the opposite change, that is, steepening the schedule relative to $t^N(\lambda)$. The proof of Lemma 1 (in Appendix) extends this basic logic to the case of continuous λ. Notice that Lemma 1 does not rely on the single crossing properties we assumed for G and G^W, while the next result does.

Lemma 1 leads directly to our first proposition. In the proposition, we say that there is an uncertainty-reducing (-increasing) motive for a TA if $t^{MPA}(\lambda)$ is a mean preserving compression (spread) of $t^N(\lambda)$.

PROPOSITION 1:

(*i*) *If* $\frac{d}{d\lambda} G_t^*(t^N(\lambda), \lambda) < 0$ (> 0) *for all* λ, *there is an uncertainty-reducing (-increasing) motive for a TA.*

(*ii*) *If* $\frac{d}{d\lambda} G_t^*(t^N(\lambda), \lambda) = 0$ *for all* λ, *then* $t^{MPA}(\lambda) = t^N(\lambda)$, *hence there is no uncertainty-managing motive for a TA.*

Proposition 1 states that the *direction* of the uncertainty-managing motive for a TA, if any, is determined by how the shock λ affects the marginal international externality G_t^* at the noncooperative equilibrium, taking into account its direct effect and its indirect effect through the policy. In particular, if $G_t^*(t^N(\lambda), \lambda)$ is decreasing (increasing) in λ, then there is an uncertainty-reducing (-increasing) motive for a TA. Writing $G_t^*(t^N(\lambda), \lambda) = G_{tt}^{*N} \cdot \frac{dt^N}{d\lambda} + G_{t\lambda}^{*N}$ (where we use a superscript N to indicate that a function is evaluated at $t^N(\lambda)$), the uncertainty motive for a TA can be traced to two key determinants: (i) Foreign's *policy-risk preference* $\left(\text{captured by } G_{tt}^* \text{ and weighted by } \frac{dt^N}{d\lambda}\right)$, and (ii) the direct impact of the shock λ on the marginal international externality holding t constant (as captured by $G_{t\lambda}^*$), which we refer to as the *externality-shifting* effect.

Proposition 1 makes clear that the source of uncertainty matters. In particular, we can distinguish between two types of shock: (i) a "political economy" shock, which affects the Foreign country only through the policy t (in which case $G^* = G^*(t)$); and (ii) an "economic" shock, which affects the Foreign country not only indirectly through the policy t but also directly (in which case $G^* = G^*(t, \lambda)$).

In the case of "political economy" shocks, Proposition 1 says that the uncertainty motive for a TA is determined solely by Foreign's preference for policy risk, as captured by the sign of G_{tt}^*. This confirms our initial intuition based on Rotschild and Stiglitz's (1970) result: when Foreign's objective is concave in t, a MPS in t reduces EG^*, so there is a negative "policy-risk externality," hence the noncooperative policy is "too risky" (with the reverse logic holding if Foreign's objective is convex in t).[15] In the case of "economic" shocks, on the other hand, Proposition 1 states that Foreign's policy-risk preference (the sign of G_{tt}^{*N}) is no longer sufficient to determine whether there is "too much" or "too little" risk in the noncooperative policy, because the externality-shifting effect ($G_{t\lambda}^*$) comes into play. In this case, the direction of the uncertainty motive for a TA is determined by whether the international policy externality G_t^* is increasing or decreasing in λ at the noncooperative equilibrium.

Before concluding this section, we mention an alternative thought experiment that one could consider to isolate the uncertainty motive for a TA. Suppose the Home government can choose a contingent policy $t(\lambda)$ subject to the constraint that this policy have the same mean as the optimal agreement policy $t^A(\lambda)$. If such "mean-preserving unilateral" policy is more risky than $t^A(\lambda)$, then we say that the noncooperative policy is "too risky," and so there is an uncertainty-reducing motive for a TA. One can show that, under this alternative thought experiment, the direction of the uncertainty motive is again determined by the sign of $\frac{d}{d\lambda}G_t^*$, but this time evaluated at $t^A(\lambda)$ rather than at $t^N(\lambda)$.[16] As a consequence, if λ is a "political economy" shock, the two thought experiments yield the same answer (there is an uncertainty-reducing motive for a TA if and only if $G_{tt}^* < 0$). If λ is an "economic" shock, on the other

[15] We highlight, however, that, even in this case where the result is intuitive, it is far from self-evident: a priori the optimal MPA could have entailed any mean-preserving change in t relative to $t^N(\lambda)$, and since the MPS risk criterion is a partial ordering, it was not a priori obvious that the distribution of $t^{MPA}(\lambda)$ could be ranked in a MPS sense relative to that of $t^N(\lambda)$. We also note here that if $G_{tt}^* < 0$ (> 0), then the optimal MPA policy is a "simple" mean preserving spread (compression) of the noncooperative policy, meaning that the respective cumulative distribution functions cross only once (as shown in the proof of Proposition 1).

[16] The proof of this statement is available upon request.

hand, both thought experiments indicate that the uncertainty motive depends on Foreign's policy-risk preference (G^*_{tt}) and on the externality-shifting effect ($G^*_{t\lambda}$), but the relative weight of these two terms differs (in one case G^*_{tt} is weighted by $t^{N'}(\lambda)$, in the other case it is weighted by $t^{A'}(\lambda)$). In what follows we base our analysis on the MPA thought experiment. The main reason is that, as we will show later, focusing on the MPA allows us to characterize the gains from regulating trade policy uncertainty and trade policy mean in terms of quantities that can, in principle, be observed or estimated, while the alternative thought experiment does not share this property.[17]

A. *Gains from Regulating Policy Uncertainty and Policy Mean*

In this section, we develop a simple formula for the gains from regulating policy uncertainty relative to the more standard gains from regulating the policy mean. We will later apply this formula in the context of our trade model, in order to analyze how the relative gains from regulating policy uncertainty depend on economic fundamentals, and to illustrate how they can potentially be quantified with data.

Ideally one would focus on the gain from the optimal MPA, that is the increase in EG^W associated with a move from $t^N(\lambda)$ to $t^{MPA}(\lambda)$. Here, we focus on a simpler task, namely, evaluating the gain from a *small* improvement in policy uncertainty. In particular, we consider a small mean-preserving change in the policy schedule starting from $t^N(\lambda)$ and evaluate the effect of this change on EG^W. We will then evaluate the gain from a small reduction in the policy mean, and finally derive an expression for the ratio between the two gains. Our approach of focusing on small policy changes is similar in spirit to the analysis of "piecemeal" policy reforms commonly applied in second-best theory.

Consider moving from $t^N(\lambda)$ to $t^N(\lambda) - \delta(t^N(\lambda) - \overline{t}^N)$, where δ is a small constant and $\overline{t}^N$ is the mean of $t^N(\lambda)$. Clearly, if $\delta > 0$ ($\delta < 0$), this represents a small mean-preserving compression (spread) of $t^N(\lambda)$. The resulting change in EG^W can be approximated as follows:

$$(4)\quad \left.\frac{\partial EG^W(t^N(\lambda) - \delta(t^N(\lambda) - \overline{t}^N), \lambda)}{\partial \delta}\right|_{\delta=0} = -E[G^*_t(t^N, \lambda(t^N))(t^N - \overline{t}^N)]$$

$$\approx -E\left[\left(G^*_t(\overline{t}^N, \lambda(\overline{t}^N)) + \left.\frac{dG^*_t(t^N, \lambda(t^N))}{dt^N}\right|_{t^N=\overline{t}^N} \cdot (t^N - \overline{t}^N)\right)(t^N - \overline{t}^N)\right]$$

$$= -\left.\frac{dG^*_t(t^N, \lambda(t^N))}{dt^N}\right|_{t^N=\overline{t}^N} \cdot \sigma^2_{t^N}.$$

[17] To be more specific, with our MPA thought experiment we approximate the gains from regulating trade policy uncertainty starting from the noncooperative tariff, which is in principle observable. Under the alternative thought experiment the starting point for the approximation would be the "mean-preserving unilateral" tariff choice (defined above), which is unobservable.

In the first line of (4) we use the fact that $G_t = 0$ at the noncooperative policy, and employ a change of variables from λ to t^N, letting $\lambda(t^N)$ denote the inverse of $t^N(\lambda)$ (with the expectation now taken with respect to t^N). In the second line we use a first-order Taylor approximation of $G_t^*(t^N, \lambda(t^N))$ around $\bar{t}^N$.

The last line of (4) states that the effect of a small change in policy uncertainty on EG^W is the product of two components. The first one is analogous to the derivative $\frac{dG_t^*(t^N(\lambda), \lambda)}{d\lambda}$, except for the change of variable from λ to t^N. Recall from Proposition 1 that the sign of this derivative determines the direction of the uncertainty-managing motive: if the international externality G_t^* is stronger when the noncooperative policy is higher, there is value to reducing policy uncertainty. The second component is the variance of t^N, which intuitively magnifies the value of managing policy uncertainty.

Since the sign of δ can be chosen to ensure a positive gain, we can write the approximate value of a small change in policy uncertainty as

$$\tilde{V}^{MPA} \equiv \left| \frac{dG_t^*(t^N, \lambda(t^N))}{dt^N} \right|_{t^N = \bar{t}^N} \cdot \sigma_{t^N}^2. \tag{5}$$

Next we focus on the gains from regulating the mean level of the policy. A natural approach is to define an "uncertainty-preserving agreement" (UPA) in the following way. Consider a parallel downward shift of the $t^N(\lambda)$ schedule, $t^N(\lambda) - \kappa \bar{t}^N$, where κ is a positive constant. This shift reduces the mean of the policy by a factor κ, but preserves all its central higher moments (variance, skewness, kurtosis), so it is natural to interpret such a shift as one that changes the policy mean while preserving policy uncertainty.

Following similar steps as above, we can approximate the value of a "small" UPA as

$$\begin{aligned} \left. \frac{\partial EG^W(t^N(\lambda) - \kappa \bar{t}^N, \lambda)}{\partial \kappa} \right|_{\kappa=0} &= -EG_t^*(t^N, \lambda(t^N)) \cdot \bar{t}^N \\ &\approx -E\left(G_t^*(\bar{t}^N, \lambda(\bar{t}^N)) + \left. \frac{dG_t^*(t^N, \lambda(t^N))}{dt^N} \right|_{t^N = \bar{t}^N} \cdot (t^N - \bar{t}^N) \right) \cdot \bar{t}^N \\ &= -G_t^*(\bar{t}^N, \lambda(\bar{t}^N)) \cdot \bar{t}^N \equiv \tilde{V}^{UPA}. \end{aligned} \tag{6}$$

Intuitively, the gain from reducing the mean policy level is approximately equal to the marginal international externality from the policy $(G_t^*(\cdot))$ evaluated at certainty and scaled up by the mean policy level.

Next, we write down the gains from a small change in policy uncertainty versus a small change in policy mean:

$$\frac{\tilde{V}^{MPA}}{\tilde{V}^{UPA}} = \left|\frac{d \ln G_t^*(t^N, \lambda(t^N))}{dt^N}\right|_{t^N=\bar{t}^N} \cdot \frac{\sigma_{t^N}^2}{\bar{t}^N}. \tag{7}$$

Notice that $\frac{\tilde{V}^{MPA}}{\tilde{V}^{UPA}}$ can be interpreted as the value of a 1 percent change in the standard deviation of t relative to a 1 percent reduction in the level of t, starting from the noncooperative equilibrium.[18] Later on, when we apply this framework to a simple competitive trade model, we will examine how the ratio $\frac{\tilde{V}^{MPA}}{\tilde{V}^{UPA}}$ depends on underlying model parameters. Before proceeding though, it is important to be clear on the limitations of this approach: this ratio captures the gains from a "small" MPA relative to a "small" UPA, rather than the gains from the optimal MPA relative to the optimal UPA. At the same time, intuitively the former ratio should be informative about the latter. In particular, when we examine how $\frac{\tilde{V}^{MPA}}{\tilde{V}^{UPA}}$ depends on model parameters, a reasonable conjecture is that the qualitative results would not be overturned if one were to consider the "ideal" measure of relative gains. In what follows, with a slight abuse of terminology, we will refer to $\frac{\tilde{V}^{MPA}}{\tilde{V}^{UPA}}$ as the "relative gains from regulating policy uncertainty."

Finally, one can consider the value of a small joint improvement in policy mean and policy uncertainty starting from the noncooperative equilibrium. Clearly, this value is given by a weighted average of expressions (4) and (6) above, with the weights determined by the relative change in policy mean and uncertainty. Below we will apply this observation in the context of our economic structure.

II. The Uncertainty Motive for a TA in a Competitive Trade Model

A. *Setup*

We now impose more structure on the model in order to examine how the uncertainty motive for a TA depends on economic fundamentals. We consider a standard two-country, two-good trade model with competitive markets. We assume Home is the natural exporter of the numeraire good, indexed by 0, while Foreign (the small country) is the natural exporter of the other good, which has no index.

Let p (resp. p^*) denote the price of the non-numeraire good in Home (resp. Foreign). We will often use the logarithms of prices, letting $\pi \equiv \ln p$ and $\pi^* \equiv \ln p^*$. The Home country can choose an ad-valorem tariff on imports of the non-numeraire good. Let $t \equiv \ln \tau$, where τ is the ad-valorem tariff factor. We also

[18] To understand this, note that the standard deviation of $t^N - \delta(t^N - \bar{t}^N)$ is equal to $(1 - \delta)$ times the standard deviation of t^N.

allow for an exogenous iceberg trade cost and denote the logarithm of this cost factor by γ. The reason we allow for trade costs is not only that such costs are important empirically, but because they will play an important role in determining the gains from regulating policy uncertainty, as will become clear below. By the usual arbitrage condition, if the tariff is not prohibitive, then we must have $\pi^* = \pi - t - \gamma$. Since Foreign has no policy of its own, we can refer to π^* as Foreign's "terms-of-trade" (TOT). Since Foreign is small, π is determined entirely in the Home country, so we can leave the market clearing condition that determines π in the background.

The reason we use the logarithms of relative prices is the following. In general equilibrium settings with uncertainty about relative prices, the standard notion of arithmetic mean preserving spread leads to results that are sensitive to the choice of numeraire, as pointed out by a number of papers, for example, Flemming, Turnovsky, and Kemp (1977). These papers have argued that a more robust approach is to define an increase in relative price risk as a *geometric* mean preserving spread (GMPS) of the relative price, that is an arithmetic mean preserving spread of the log of the relative price. For this reason, we will follow the mainstream literature and consider arithmetic mean preserving changes in $\ln \tau$ (and hence in $\ln p^*$), so our results are not sensitive to the choice of numeraire.[19]

We next impose some standard assumptions on preferences and technology. To make the key points we only need to specify the economic structure in the Foreign country. On the technology side, we assume constant returns to scale with a strictly concave PPF, so that supply functions are strictly increasing. This allows us to describe the supply side through a GDP (or revenue) function. Letting p^* be the domestic relative price and (q_0^*, q^*) the outputs, we define $R^*(p^*) \equiv \max_{q_0^*, q^*}\{q_0^* + p^*q^*\}$ s.t. $(q_0^*, q^*) \in Q^*$, where Q^* is the set of feasible outputs.

On the preference side, we assume that all citizens have identical and homothetic preferences. This implies that indirect utility takes the form $U\left(\frac{y^*}{\phi^*(p^*)}\right)$, where y^* is income in terms of numeraire and $\phi^*(p^*)$ a price index. It is natural to refer to $\frac{y^*}{\phi^*(p^*)}$ as the representative individual's "real income." For the purposes of comparative statics it is convenient to parametrize the degree of risk aversion, so we assume that $U(\cdot)$ exhibits constant relative risk aversion (CRRA), indexed by the parameter θ.

[19]To elaborate on this point, the way one defines a change in risk is an axiomatic choice: there is no single, "correct" way to define a change in risk, so it seems reasonable to choose a definition that satisfies certain desirable properties (axioms) in the relevant context of analysis. In a general equilibrium model such as ours, the GMPS notion is a reasonable choice for the reason discussed in the text. The same approach is followed by Eaton (1979), which we discuss below.

All citizens have identical factor endowments, and the population measure is normalized to one. There are no international risk-sharing markets, so that the Foreign country cannot diversify away its income risk.[20] The Foreign government maximizes social welfare, so we can write[21]

$$G^* = \frac{1}{\theta}\left(\frac{R^*(p^*)}{\phi^*(p^*)}\right)^{\theta}.$$

We first focus on the case in which shocks are of the "political economy" type, that is, shocks originate in Home and affect Foreign only through t. Subsequently, we extend the analysis to the case of more general "economic" shocks.

Given this simple structure, we do not have to be explicit about Home's technology and preferences, so we will keep them in the background. All that matters for our purposes is Home's noncooperative tariff schedule $t^N(\lambda)$. Finally, we assume that the trade pattern cannot switch as a result of the shock, that is, Foreign exports the nonnumeraire good for all values of λ in its support.

The analysis of Section I shows that the key to gauge the uncertainty motive for a TA is to consider how the marginal international externality exerted by the Home tariff, G_t^*, responds to the shock λ. In our model, Home's tariff exerts only a TOT externality on Foreign welfare, which is given by

$$G_t^* = -v^{*\theta} \cdot \Omega^*, \tag{8}$$

where $v^* = \frac{R^*}{\phi^*}$ is Foreign's real income and $\Omega^* \equiv \frac{p^*x^*}{R^*}$ is Foreign's degree of openness (export share of GDP). Intuitively, the degree of openness Ω^* captures the impact of an increase in t on Foreign's real income through TOT, and the factor $v^{*\theta}$ is related to the marginal utility of income: with $\theta < 0$, the externality is stronger when real income (v^*) is lower (for a given level of openness), because the marginal utility of income is higher. In what follows we will refer to $v^{*\theta}\Omega^*$ as the "adjusted" degree of openness.[22]

[20] International risk sharing is arguably very incomplete in reality, and our assumption captures this incompleteness in an extreme way, but even if it had perfect risk-sharing markets in the model, in general there would still be an uncertainty motive for a TA: in this case, the model would be equivalent to one where agents are income-risk neutral, and as we show below, there would typically be an uncertainty-increasing motive for a TA.

[21] We note that the assumption of risk-averse citizens is not in contradiction with the assumption—discussed in footnote 14—that the government's utility is transferrable. Recall that the Foreign government's payoff is assumed to be $G^* - T$, where G^* is the utility of the representative citizen and T the transfer made to the Home government (e.g., in the form of a non-trade policy concession). We view the assumption of transferrable government utility as a convenient modeling device that allows us to focus on the TA that maximizes the governments' joint payoff. A more restrictive assumption that is implicit in our setting, on the other hand, is that the TA cannot specify contingent transfers that can in turn be used to provide insurance to citizens: if this were the case, a TA could be used as an international risk-sharing mechanism, thus making risk aversion irrelevant. Contingent transfers between governments can be allowed in our model only if they take a non-monetary form so that they cannot be used to provide insurance to citizens.

[22] As stated earlier, in this model the underlying motive for a TA is the presence of a TOT externality. To be more precise, the reason why the noncooperative equilibrium is inefficient is not the presence of a TOT externality per se, but the fact that the Home country has monopoly power over TOT. To confirm this point, consider an alternative version of this model where the Home country is replaced by a continuum of symmetric small countries (all

B. *Income-Risk Neutrality*

Since we are adopting the GMPS notion of risk, it is natural to define risk neutrality as indifference with respect to a GMPS of real income, which corresponds to the case: $U(\cdot) = \ln(\cdot)$, or $\theta \to 0$ in the CRRA specification. Thus, the government's objective is $G^* = \ln\left(\frac{R^*(p^*)}{\phi^*(p^*)}\right)$, and the international externality is simply $G_t^* = -\Omega^*$.

The key step to apply Proposition 1, given that λ is a political economy shock, is to examine the Foreign country's attitude toward policy risk, as captured by G_{tt}^*. This is given by the impact of t on openness, which is easily shown to be

$$G_{tt}^*|_{\theta \to 0} = \Omega^*(\varepsilon_x^* + D^*),$$

where ε_x^* is the export supply elasticity and $D^* \equiv 1 - \frac{p^*q^*}{R^*}$ is the import-competing sector share of GDP, which can be interpreted as the degree of income diversification.[23]

We will assume throughout that ε_x^* is nonnegative.[24] Given this assumption, it follows that $G_{tt}^*|_{\theta \to 0} > 0$: thus, in the case of income-risk neutrality, the Foreign country benefits from an increase in policy risk. The intuition for this result is that, since production and consumption can be optimized after observing prices, both the producers' revenue function and the consumers' indirect utility functions (given income) are convex in prices.[25] The insight that a small country may gain from TOT risk in itself is not new to our model, and was pointed out, for example, by Eaton (1979);[26] what is new is that in light of Proposition 1, the convexity of G^* with respect to t, implies that the optimal MPA increases trade policy uncertainty.

To summarize the discussion thus far, *if individuals are income-risk neutral, there is an uncertainty-managing motive for a TA, but this calls for an increase—rather than a decrease—in trade policy uncertainty.*

Evidently, then, if one wants to make economic sense of the WTO-type informal arguments discussed in the introduction, which state that one of the goals of TAs is to reduce trade policy uncertainty, one must depart from the benchmark case of income-risk neutrality in this standard model and focus on the case of income-risk aversion, which is what we do next.

---

affected by a common λ shock): in such a setting it can be verified that the noncooperative equilibrium would be efficient for all λ.

[23] Note that $D^* = 0$ when the country is completely specialized, and $D^* = 1/2$ when the two sectors have equal GDP shares. In interpreting D^* as an index of diversification we are implicitly assuming that the GDP share of the export sector is at least $1/2$, so that D^* cannot exceed $1/2$.

[24] There is considerable empirical evidence that this is the case in reality for most sectors and most countries (see, for example, Tokarick 2010).

[25] It is important to note that this feature extends well beyond the simple perfectly competitive setting we are considering here. In particular, one might wonder whether the presence of imperfect competition or irreversible investments might make exporting firms' profit functions concave in prices, but even in these circumstances profit functions can be convex in prices. The intuitive reason is that profit functions are convex whenever firms can make *any* ex post adjustment in their production decisions after observing prices, and this feature is extremely general.

[26] See also Anderson and Riley (1976), who examine how the degree of specialization of a small economy affects its gains from TOT fluctuations.

C. *Income-Risk Aversion*

Let us now re-examine the Foreign country's preference for trade policy risk allowing for income-risk aversion ($\theta < 0$).[27] Recalling that the international externality from the tariff is given by $G_t^* = -v^{*\theta} \cdot \Omega^*$ and differentiating this expression with respect to t, we obtain

$$G_{tt}^* = v^{*\theta}\Omega^*(\theta\Omega^* + \varepsilon_x^* + D^*). \tag{9}$$

This expression (derived in the Appendix within the Proof of Proposition 2), together with the result of Proposition 1, leads to:

PROPOSITION 2: *There is an uncertainty-reducing (-increasing) motive for a TA if* $\theta\Omega^* + \varepsilon_x^* + D^* < 0\ (> 0)$ *at the noncooperative equilibrium.*

There are several aspects of Proposition 2 that are worth highlighting. First, if income-risk aversion is sufficiently strong relative to the other parameters of the model $\left(\text{namely if } \theta < -\frac{\varepsilon_x^* + D^*}{\Omega^*}\right)$, then there is an uncertainty-reducing motive for a TA. While the role of risk aversion is quite intuitive, the impact of the other variables—which we focus on next—is more subtle.

Proposition 2 states that, for a given degree of risk-aversion $\theta < 0$, the uncertainty motive for a TA is more likely to be in the direction of reducing policy uncertainty when: (i) the economy is more open (Ω^* is higher); (ii) the export supply elasticity ε_x^* is lower; and (iii) the economy is more specialized (D^* is lower).[28]

Focus first on the degree of openness Ω^*. This variable affects the uncertainty motive through its interaction with the income-risk preference parameter θ, so the role of openness is in essence to magnify the impact of the citizens' income-risk preference.

[27] Note that, even with income risk aversion, in the foreign country there is still no motive for trade protection, so our assumption that this country practices free trade continues to be without loss of generality given the representative-citizen assumption. As Eaton and Grossman (1985) made clear, in a small country an insurance motive for trade protection can arise only if citizens have heterogenous incomes, at least ex post. In our setting, foreign citizens are always homogenous, even ex post. Here we also mention the paper by Young and Anderson (1982), who compare the effects of quotas and tariffs for a small economy where individuals are risk averse and the government faces political-economy constraints (in the form of a minimum expected output level). We note that the focus of this paper is very different from ours, since it focuses on optimal policies for a small country, while in our setting the optimal policy for the small country is free trade, and our focus is on the externality that the large country's policy fluctuations exert on the small country, and how a TA can correct such externality.

[28] Here we can make the statements in the text a bit more precise. First, when we say that the uncertainty motive is "more likely" to be in the direction of reducing policy uncertainty when a variable x is higher, we mean that as x increases the sign of G_{tt}^{*N} can switch from negative to positive, but not vice-versa. Second, in the text we talk about changes in Ω^*, D^*, and ε_x^* as if these variables were exogenous, but of course they are not. To make our statements more precise, let $\boldsymbol{\xi}$ denote the vector of all technology and preference parameters (excluding θ). We can think of the key endogenous variables Ω^*, D^*, and ε_x^* as functions of $\boldsymbol{\xi}$. Note that θ does not affect these variables. Next note that $\Omega^* \in [0, 1]$ and $D^* \in [0, 1]$, while $\varepsilon_x^* \geq 0$ by assumption. In the text, when we refer to a change in an endogenous variable, we mean that the parameter vector $\boldsymbol{\xi}$ is being changed in such a way that the variable of interest changes while the others do not. If we include in $\boldsymbol{\xi}$ the whole technology and preference structure, by varying $\boldsymbol{\xi}$ we can span the whole feasible range of Ω^*, D^*, and ε_x^*, so this "all else equal" thought experiment can be performed.

Next, consider the role of the export supply elasticity ε_x^*. Intuitively, a country that can easily adjust production and consumption as a result of the shocks (that is, a country with a higher ε_x^*) is more likely to have a welfare function that is convex in the foreign tariff, and hence is less likely to benefit from a decrease in tariff uncertainty. This in turn suggests an interesting implication. At the empirical level, lower income countries tend to have lower export supply elasticities, and this in turn implies that the uncertainty-reducing motive for a TA should be more important for lower income countries than for higher income countries.[29]

Focus next on the degree of diversification, D^*. Proposition 2 indicates that, other things equal, the uncertainty motive for a TA is more likely to be in the direction of reducing policy uncertainty if the Foreign country is less diversified. A related remark is the following: assuming that preferences are Cobb-Douglas and the supply function $q^*(p^*)$ is differentiable, if the economy is sufficiently specialized (D^* is sufficiently close to zero), then there is an uncertainty-reducing motive for any $\theta < 0$.[30] Interestingly, these twin observations go in the same direction as the one we made above about ε_x^*: to the extent that lower income countries are more likely to be specialized, our model predicts that the uncertainty-reducing motive for a TA should tend to be more important for lower income countries.

One way to summarize the discussion above is that the direction of the uncertainty motive for a TA is determined by an overall tradeoff between risk aversion, which operates through the term $\theta\Omega^*$ and pushes toward an uncertainty-reducing motive, and the degree of flexibility of the economy, which is captured by $(\varepsilon_x^* + D^*)$ and pushes toward an uncertainty-increasing motive.

Finally, it is interesting to consider the impact of the exogenous trade cost γ. We consider the following thought experiment: letting γ^{prohib} denote the level of γ for which there is no trade ($\Omega^* = 0$), we examine the effect of decreasing γ from γ^{prohib} to zero.

Suppose risk aversion is sufficiently strong that in the absence of trade costs ($\gamma = 0$) there is an uncertainty-reducing motive for a TA, that is $\theta < \left(-\frac{\varepsilon_x^* + D^*}{\Omega^*}\right)_{\gamma=0}$.[31] Clearly, as γ drops below γ^{prohib}, initially the uncertainty

[29] See, for example, Tokarick (2014), who estimates that the median export supply elasticity is 0.52 for low income countries, 0.77 for low/medium income countries, 0.83 for medium/high income countries, 0.92 for high income non-OECD countries, and 1.14 for high income OECD countries. These estimates are based on a standard trade model for a small economy with one export, one import, and one non-traded good, with no own consumption of the export good.

[30] To see this, recall that there is an uncertainty-reducing motive if $\theta < -\frac{\varepsilon_x^* + D^*}{\Omega^*}$. In the limit as the country becomes fully specialized, $\frac{p^*q^*}{R^*} \to 1$, hence $D^* \to 0$. Next note that $\varepsilon_x^* = \frac{q^*}{x^*}\varepsilon_q^* - \frac{c^*}{x^*}\varepsilon_c^*$, where ε_q^* is the elasticity of $q^*(p^*)$ and ε_c^* is the elasticity of $c^*(p^*)$. Cobb-Douglas preferences imply $c^* = \frac{\alpha R^*}{p^*}$, where α is the consumption share of the non-numeraire good, hence, $\varepsilon_c^* = \frac{d \ln R^*}{d \ln p^*} - 1$; but $\frac{d \ln R^*}{d \ln p^*} = \frac{p^*q^*}{R^*} \to 1$, hence, $\varepsilon_c^* \to 0$. Given the assumption that $q^*(p^*)$ is smooth, in the limit as the economy becomes fully specialized clearly $q^{*\prime}(p^*)$ must approach zero (because of the resource constraint), hence $\varepsilon_q^* \to 0$, which implies $\varepsilon_x^* \to 0$. And since $\Omega^* > 0$, then $\frac{\varepsilon_x^* + D^*}{\Omega^*} \to 0$. So we can conclude that for any fixed $\theta < 0$ the condition $\theta < -\frac{\varepsilon_x^* + D^*}{\Omega^*}$ is satisfied if the economy is sufficiently specialized.

[31] It may be interesting to note that in our quantification exercise for the US-Cuba case (see Section IV) this condition seems to be largely satisfied. In that context we find that, at the factual level of trade cost γ, there is an

motive for a TA goes in the direction of increasing policy uncertainty (because $\theta\Omega^*$ is negligible and hence dominated by $\varepsilon_x^* + D^*$), but as γ drops further, the direction of the uncertainty motive will at some point reverse and call for a reduction in policy uncertainty. Thus, we can state:

REMARK 1. *Assume risk aversion is sufficiently strong, in the sense that* $\theta < \left(-\frac{\varepsilon_x^* + D^*}{\Omega^*}\right)_{\gamma=0}$. *If the trade cost* γ *is close enough to its prohibitive level, there is an uncertainty-increasing motive for a TA* ($\theta\Omega^* + \varepsilon_x^* + D^* > 0$), *while if* γ *is close enough to zero there is an uncertainty-reducing motive for a TA* ($\theta\Omega^* + \varepsilon_x^* + D^* < 0$).

Remark 1 suggests two broad implications of the model, one concerning the evolution of the uncertainty motive for TAs over time and one of a cross-sectional nature. First, as trade costs fall over time, the model suggests that uncertainty-reducing motives for TAs are increasingly likely to emerge, provided citizens are sufficiently risk-averse. And second, since trade costs tend to increase with geographical distance, the model suggests that uncertainty-reducing motives for TAs are more likely to be present (other things equal) for countries within a region.

D. *Gains from Regulating Trade Policy Uncertainty*

In this section, we apply the formulas developed in Section IA to examine the gains from regulating trade policy uncertainty relative to its mean.

Given that the political economy shock λ affects Foreign welfare only through Home's tariff t, we have $\frac{dG_t^*(t^N, \lambda(t^N))}{dt^N} = G_{tt}^*(t^N)$. Plugging the expressions for G_t^* and G_{tt}^* in the formulas of Section IA, we obtain:

PROPOSITION 3:

(*i*) *The value of a small change in tariff uncertainty is* $\tilde{V}^{MPA} = |\theta\Omega^* + \varepsilon_x^* + D^*| \cdot \left(v^{*\theta}\Omega^*\right) \cdot \sigma_{t^N}^2$;

(*ii*) *the value of a small reduction in the tariff mean is* $\tilde{V}^{UPA} = v^{*\theta}\Omega^* \cdot \bar{t}^N$; *and*

(*iii*) *the relative value of regulating tariff uncertainty is* $\tilde{V}^{MPA}/\tilde{V}^{UPA} = |\theta\Omega^* + \varepsilon_x^* + D^*| \cdot \frac{\sigma_{t^N}^2}{\bar{t}^N}$, *where all expressions are evaluated at the noncooperative equilibrium.*

It is worth highlighting the role of two key determinants of $\tilde{V}^{MPA}$ and $\tilde{V}^{UPA}$: the variance of the noncooperative tariff, $\sigma_{t^N}^2$, which can be interpreted as capturing the

uncertainty-reducing motive for a TA, given the available estimates of θ. The condition should then be satisfied a fortiori at the counterfactual level $\gamma = 0$, since lowering γ increases openness Ω^*.

degree of uncertainty in the trade policy environment, and the exogenous trade cost γ.

Focus first on the role of $\sigma^2_{t^N}$. Other things equal, an increase in $\sigma^2_{t^N}$ leads to an increase in $\tilde{V}^{MPA}$, while leaving $\tilde{V}^{UPA}$ unaffected. Thus, the gain from a joint improvement in tariff uncertainty and tariff mean—which is given by a weighted average of $\tilde{V}^{MPA}$ and $\tilde{V}^{UPA}$, as discussed in Section IA—is increasing in $\sigma^2_{t^N}$. Thus, our model suggests that governments should have stronger incentives to sign trade agreements when the trading environment is more uncertain.[32]

Next, we focus on the impact of the trade cost γ, and in particular on how it affects the relative gains from regulating policy uncertainty $(\tilde{V}^{MPA}/\tilde{V}^{UPA})$. We continue to assume $\theta < \left(-\frac{\varepsilon_x^* + D^*}{\Omega^*}\right)_{\gamma=0}$, as in the previous section. As we observed above, there exists a critical level of γ, say $\hat{\gamma}$, for which $\theta\Omega^* + \varepsilon_x^* + D^* = 0$. To simplify, we assume that $\hat{\gamma}$ is unique. Under this assumption, the ratio $\tilde{V}^{MPA}/\tilde{V}^{UPA}$ is non-monotonic in γ, with a minimum value of zero at $\gamma = \hat{\gamma}$. To see this, note that when γ is close to γ^{prohib}, the relative gain is strictly positive (with the gains from the MPA coming from an increase in uncertainty); when γ is equal to $\hat{\gamma}$ the ratio $\tilde{V}^{MPA}/\tilde{V}^{UPA}$ reaches zero; and if γ is lower than $\hat{\gamma}$, this ratio is strictly positive again, but this time the gains from the MPA come from a decrease in uncertainty. Thus, we can state:

REMARK 2: *Assume that* $\theta < \left(-\frac{\varepsilon_x^* + D^*}{\Omega^*}\right)_{\gamma=0}$ *and* $\hat{\gamma}$ *is unique. Then* $\tilde{V}^{MPA}/\tilde{V}^{UPA}$ *is non-monotonic in* γ, *with a minimum value of zero at* $\gamma = \hat{\gamma}$.

This result, which can be seen as complementing the result in Remark 1, suggests that, if trade costs fall over time, the relative gains from regulating trade policy uncertainty may initially decrease, but should eventually grow in magnitude, provided citizens are sufficiently risk averse.

E. *Impact of Policy Uncertainty on Trade Volume*

The next question we address is, what is the impact of the optimal MPA on the expected volume of trade? To fix ideas, suppose that the optimal MPA leads to a mean preserving compression in t. Writing trade volume as $x^*(\pi^*)$, the change in expected log trade due to the MPA is $\int \ln x^*(\pi^*)\, d\big(F_{MPA}(\pi^*) - F_N(\pi^*)\big)$, where $F_N(\pi^*)$ (resp. $F_{MPA}(\pi^*)$) is the distribution of π^* induced by $t^N(\lambda)$ (resp. $t^{MPA}(\lambda)$). Noting that a mean preserving compression in t leads to a mean preserving

[32] While $\tilde{V}^{MPA}$ and $\tilde{V}^{UPA}$ capture only the gains from small policy changes, we can make a similar point by focusing on the gains from the optimal TA, if we take quadratic approximations of the payoff functions. The value of the optimal TA is given by $E[G^W(t^A(\lambda),\lambda) - G^W(t^N(\lambda),\lambda)]$. Consider a mean preserving spread of λ, which captures an increase in underlying uncertainty. This will increase the value of the TA if and only if $G^W(t^A(\lambda),\lambda) - G^W(t^N(\lambda),\lambda)$ is convex in λ. Assuming that all third derivatives of G and G^W are zero, this is the case if $G^W_{tt}(t^{A'})^2 + 2G^W_{t\lambda}t^{A'} - \left(G^W_{tt}(t^{N'})^2 + 2G^W_{t\lambda}t^{N'}\right) > 0$. Using $t^{A'} = \frac{G^W_{t\lambda}}{-G^W_{tt}}$ and simplifying, this condition becomes $\left(t^{A'} - t^{N'}\right)^2 > 0$, which is always satisfied if $t^{A'} \neq t^{N'}$.

compression in π^*, by standard Rotschild-Stiglitz logic it is immediate to conclude that expected log trade increases if and only if Foreign's export supply elasticity ε_x^* is decreasing in π^*. Also note that the same conclusion applies to the (log) trade value $\pi^* + \ln x^*(\pi^*)$, since an MPA keeps $E(t)$ and thus $E(\pi^*)$ unchanged.

In general the export supply function can have increasing or decreasing elasticity, so this is ultimately an empirical question. It is interesting to relate this analysis with a central result of the TOT theory of trade agreements, highlighted by Bagwell and Staiger (1999) and other papers by the same authors, namely that a mutually beneficial TA always expands trade relative to the noncooperative equilibrium. Recast in our framework, the analog of Bagwell and Staiger's result is that the *mean motive* for a TA has an unambiguous expanding impact on trade. In contrast, the *uncertainty motive* for a TA may impact trade volume in either direction.[33]

There is a special but interesting case where the model yields a more definite prediction about the impact of a decrease in trade policy uncertainty on expected trade. This is the same case we considered above when highlighting that an uncertainty-reducing motive is more likely to be present for lower income countries. We showed above that, if preferences are Cobb-Douglas and Foreign is sufficiently specialized, then the optimal MPA reduces policy uncertainty for any $\theta < 0$. In this case, the export supply elasticity ε_x^* must be decreasing in π^* around the point of full specialization, since it is zero if the country is fully specialized (and we assumed $\varepsilon_x^* \geq 0$). As a consequence, a decrease in policy uncertainty increases expected trade. This suggests that heavily specialized countries are not only more likely to benefit from a reduction in policy uncertainty, as we argued above, but also more likely to experience an increase in expected trade volume if policy uncertainty decreases.

III. More General Economic Shocks

Thus far we have focused on shocks of the political-economy kind, which affect Foreign welfare only through Home's tariff t. We now extend the analysis to the case of more general economic shocks, allowing λ to affect Foreign welfare not just through the policy but also directly; conventional demand or supply shocks in Home and/or in Foreign in general will have this feature. This extension is important for two reasons. First, empirically there is evidence that trade policy responds to a variety of economic shocks, such as aggregate downturns (see Bown and Crowley 2013). Second, economic shocks may magnify or dampen the impact of Home's trade protection on Foreign, that is, they may have a policy-externality-shifting effect, in addition to the policy-risk-preference effect.

To apply the condition derived in the reduced-form analysis of Section I, start by recalling that Foreign's terms-of-trade are given (in logarithmic form) by

[33] One can also ask how the optimal MPA affects trade volatility. It is easy to show that in the "neutral" case of constant export supply elasticity, an MPA that reduces policy uncertainty also reduces trade volatility. Thus, there is a tendency for the optimal MPA to impact policy uncertainty and trade (volume and value) uncertainty in the same direction. But if the export supply elasticity is not constant, the impact of a change in policy uncertainty on trade volatility is ambiguous.

$\pi^*(t,\lambda) = \pi(\lambda) - t - \gamma$. This notation emphasizes that the shock may affect Foreign's TOT, holding the policy t constant, through Home's domestic price; this will be the case if the domestic shock affects economic conditions at Home. In addition to affecting Foreign welfare through the TOT channel just highlighted, the shock may also affect Foreign welfare *directly* (that is, holding the TOT constant); this will be the case, for example, if λ represents a global demand or supply shock.

We extend our notation to reflect the more general nature of the shock. To this end, we write Foreign welfare as a function of TOT and the shock as $u^*(\pi^*(\cdot),\lambda)$. Recalling that the Foreign government maximizes national welfare, we can then write $G^*(t,\lambda) = u^*(\pi(\lambda) - t - \gamma, \lambda)$.

Recall from Section I that there is an uncertainty-reducing motive for a TA if $G_{tt}^{*N} \cdot \frac{dt^N}{d\lambda} + G_{t\lambda}^{*N} < 0$, and recall our interpretation of the term $G_{tt}^{*N} \cdot \frac{dt^N}{d\lambda}$ as capturing the effect of policy-risk preference, while we interpreted the term $G_{t\lambda}^{*N}$ as capturing a policy-externality-shifting effect.

In what follows it is convenient to interpret λ as the log of the underlying shock, so that $\varepsilon_\lambda^\tau \equiv t^{N'}(\lambda)$ can be interpreted as the elasticity of the tariff factor with respect to the shock.

Using $G_t^{*N} = v^{*\theta}\Omega^*$, plugging in the expression (9) for G_{tt}^{*N} and simplifying, we find that there is an uncertainty-reducing motive for a TA if

$$(10)\qquad \left(\theta\Omega^* + \varepsilon_x^* + D^*\right)\left(\varepsilon_\lambda^\tau - \varepsilon_\lambda^\pi\right) - \frac{\partial \ln\left(v^{*\theta}\Omega^*\right)}{\partial\lambda} < 0,$$

where $\frac{\partial \ln\left(v^{*\theta}\Omega^*\right)}{\partial\lambda}$ denotes the elasticity of adjusted openness with respect to the shock holding π^* constant, $\varepsilon_\lambda^\pi \equiv \pi'(\lambda)$ is the elasticity of Home's domestic price with respect to the shock, and (10) is evaluated at the noncooperative tariff.

To interpret (10), start by recalling that the sign of Foreign's preference for trade policy risk is given by the sign of $\left(\theta\Omega^* + \varepsilon_x^* + D^*\right)$. Thus, the term $\left(\theta\Omega^* + \varepsilon_x^* + D^*\right)\varepsilon_\lambda^\tau$ in (10) is related to the policy-risk preference effect. This term is analogous to the case of political economy shocks considered in the previous section.

The new feature with more general shocks is the presence of a policy-externality-shifting effect. Recall our discussion above of the two possible channels through which λ can affect Foreign welfare holding t constant. Similarly, λ can affect the marginal international externality through two possible channels: the term $\left(\theta\Omega^* + \varepsilon_x^* + D^*\right)\varepsilon_\lambda^\pi$ in (10) captures the impact of λ on the policy externality through Home's domestic price π, and the term $\frac{\partial \ln\left(v^{*\theta}\Omega^*\right)}{\partial\lambda}$ captures the direct impact of λ on the policy externality holding the TOT, π^*, constant.

First focus on the case in which the shock λ is *importer specific*, in the sense that it originates in the Home country and affects Foreign welfare only through the TOT. In this case only the first of the two channels highlighted above is operative, so $\frac{\partial \ln\left(v^{*\theta}\Omega^*\right)}{\partial\lambda} = 0$ and condition (10) boils down to $\left(\theta\Omega^* + \varepsilon_x^* + D^*\right)\left(\varepsilon_\lambda^\tau - \varepsilon_\lambda^\pi\right)$

< 0. To highlight the implications of this type of shock, suppose that Foreign is averse to TOT risk (or equivalently to trade policy risk), that is $\theta\Omega^* + \varepsilon_x^* + D^* < 0$. Note that the total impact of λ on TOT is given by $\frac{d\pi^*}{d\lambda} = \varepsilon_\lambda^\pi - \varepsilon_\lambda^\tau$, so there are two different sources of TOT risk: a "policy" risk (captured by $\varepsilon_\lambda^\tau > 0$) and an "economic" risk (captured by ε_λ^π). Without economic risk (e.g., in the case of a pure political economy shock), a mean preserving compression in t clearly reduces TOT risk. And the same is true whenever policy risk is not offset by economic risk, so that $\frac{d\pi^*}{d\lambda} < 0$. But if the economic risk offsets the policy risk (ε_λ^π is positive and dominates ε_λ^τ), then TOT risk is reduced by *increasing* policy risk, so in this case the optimal MPA will increase policy risk.[34]

Next focus on the case in which the shock λ is *global*, in the sense that it affects domestic conditions in both countries (or equivalently, suppose that the two countries experience perfectly correlated domestic shocks). In this case both channels of the policy-externality-shifting effect that we described above will be operative. The second effect $\left(\text{through } \frac{\partial \ln\left(v^{*\theta}\Omega^*\right)}{\partial\lambda}\right)$ can be interpreted as follows: if shocks that increase the noncooperative tariff also increase the adjusted degree of openness for a fixed tariff, this strengthens the uncertainty-reducing motive.

It is worth emphasizing that, unlike in the case of political economy shocks considered in the previous section, here the direction of the uncertainty motive for a TA may go in a different direction than Foreign's preference for policy risk. So, for example, it is *possible* that even if individuals are risk-neutral ($\theta \to 0$) and hence the Foreign country is policy-risk loving, there may be an uncertainty-reducing motive for a TA.

The sign of the externality-shifting effect in general depends on the exact nature of the shock and of the economic structure, but we highlight an interesting case in which the externality-shifting effect pushes toward an uncertainty-reducing motive. Suppose that λ is a global productivity shock that strengthens comparative advantage, so that Foreign's openness Ω^* is higher (for given TOT) when λ is higher. Further suppose that Home's noncooperative tariff t^N increases with trade volume; this is compatible with our model if TOT manipulation motives are important for Home's choice of tariff. In this case t^N is increasing in λ, as assumed in our model. Then, if the effect of the shock via $v^{*\theta}$ is not too strong, the sign of $\frac{\partial\left(v^{*\theta}\Omega^*\right)}{\partial\lambda}$ will be positive, thus contributing toward an uncertainty-reducing motive.

[34] In the case of importer-specific shocks we can show a further result: under a regularity condition that we specify below, the optimal MPA reduces *terms-of-trade* risk if foreign is averse to TOT risk (or equivalently to trade policy risk), that is if $\theta\Omega^* + \varepsilon_x^* + D^* < 0$. Thus, the impact of the optimal MPA on TOT risk is determined solely by the foreign country's preference for TOT/policy risk, and follows the same intuitive pattern as in the case of political economy shocks. The regularity assumption we need is the following: if we define home's choice variable as π^* rather than t (which is clearly equivalent), we need home's noncooperative choice of π^* to be monotonic in λ, which is ensured if $\frac{d^2G}{d\pi^* d\lambda}$ does not change sign over the relevant range of (π^*, λ).

IV. A Sufficient Statistic for the Uncertainty Motive

If one is willing to assume that the model is true, one can in principle use the model to determine empirically the direction of the uncertainty motive for a TA between two countries and quantify the relative gains from regulating policy uncertainty. In this section, we illustrate with a simple example how this could be done with actual data.

As we observed above, there is an uncertainty-reducing motive for a TA if the (negative) international externality from the tariff at the noncooperative equilibrium is stronger when λ is higher, that is if $\frac{d}{d\lambda}(-v^{*\theta}\Omega^*)^N < 0$. Since $t^N(\lambda)$ is increasing, this condition can be equivalently written as

$$\frac{d(v^{*\theta}\Omega^*)^N}{dt^N} > 0. \tag{11}$$

Note that this condition is valid not only in the case of political-economy shocks considered in Section II, but also in the case of more general economic shocks considered in Section III.

In principle, condition (11) can be implemented empirically, if one has data on a small country facing noncooperative tariffs from the rest of the world. Suppose one has information on this country's openness (Ω^*), real income per capita (v^*), and estimates of θ to construct a measure of the adjusted degree of openness, as well as the average tariff faced by this country (t^N). Our model then suggests that, *if the adjusted measure of openness co-varies with the tariff, then there is an uncertainty-reducing motive for a TA.*

This sufficient-statistic approach can also be used to approximate the relative gains from regulating policy uncertainty. Applying formula (7), we can write

$$\frac{\tilde{V}^{MPA}}{\tilde{V}^{UPA}} = \left|\frac{d\ln(v^{*\theta}\Omega^*)^N}{dt^N}\right| \cdot \frac{\sigma^2_{t^N}}{\overline{t}^N}.$$

This suggests quantifying $\tilde{V}^{MPA}/\tilde{V}^{UPA}$ by taking a measure of correlation between $\ln(v^{*\theta}\Omega^*)^N$ and t^N, for example, the estimated coefficient of a simple OLS regression, and multiplying it by $\sigma^2_{t^N}/\overline{t}^N$. In what follows we will adopt this approach and quantify $\tilde{V}^{MPA}/\tilde{V}^{UPA}$ as $|\beta^{ols}| \cdot \frac{\sigma^2_{t^N}}{\overline{t}^N} = \frac{|\mathrm{Cov}(\ln(v^{*\theta}\Omega^*)^N, t^N)|}{\overline{t}^N}$, where β^{ols} is the estimated OLS coefficient.[35]

We now illustrate how this approach can be implemented with actual data by focusing on a simple empirical example, namely the trade relationship between United States and Cuba in the period before 1934. As already mentioned in the introduction, this was a period of noncooperative trade relations, which ended with

[35] As we discussed in Section IA, the ratio $\tilde{V}^{MPA}/\tilde{V}^{UPA}$ involves gains from small policy changes, rather than gains from optimal policy changes, so it is not the ideal measure, but we see no reason to believe that $\tilde{V}^{MPA}/\tilde{V}^{UPA}$ would systematically overstate or understate the relative gains from optimal policy changes.

the Reciprocal Trade Agreement Act (RTAA). The first agreement signed by the United States under the RTAA was the agreement with Cuba in 1934. This, together with the fact that Cuba was a small open country (its export share of GDP in this period was on average 0.32) that exported mostly to the United States, makes these countries a good fit to illustrate our approach.

Our model is static in nature, but it seems natural to use the time variation in noncooperative tariffs and adjusted openness to measure their covariation. We focus on the annual US average tariff prior to 1934. More specifically, we use $t = \ln(1 + \tau)$, where τ is the US import-weighted average tariff starting in 1867 calculated by Irwin (2007). Figure 2 plots t from 1867 to 1960, showing considerable variation prior to 1934.[36] We use data available for Cuba on openness and income per capita in the period 1903–1933 to calculate a measure of adjusted openness at alternative levels of risk aversion.[37]

The first point we note is that, if citizens were income-risk neutral ($\theta = 0$), to evaluate the direction of the uncertainty motive we would only need to look at the sign of the covariance between Cuban openness and the US tariff. We find this covariance to be negative, which is plausible, since higher US tariffs tend to reduce the Cuban share of exports in GDP, and is consistent with the model, recalling the result that if $\theta = 0$ there should be an uncertainty-increasing motive for a TA (see Section II).[38]

If, as is more reasonable, citizens are risk averse, then we need to consider the covariance between Cuba's *adjusted* openness and the US tariff. We compute this covariance at alternative levels of θ, and find that it is positive for $\theta < -1.1$. So our analysis indicates that there is an uncertainty-reducing motive for a TA for $\theta < -1.1$. We do not have estimates of risk aversion for Cuba, but we note that Kimbal, Sahm, and Shapiro (2008) estimate CRRA coefficients for US households (by using their preferences over different gambles), finding that about 90 percent of the distribution lies below -1.5.

We obtain a similar result if instead of the aggregate US tariff we use the US tariff on Cuban sugar. The latter may be a better proxy of the US trade barriers that affected Cuba directly, since Cuban exports of sugar to the US accounted for

[36] Part of this variation is simply a downward trend, but there is also considerable variation around the trend. This trend is probably due to the fact that the revenue motives for imposing tariffs (which were arguably important before the civil war) declined over time for various reasons, including the introduction of the income tax in 1916. Another part of the variation is caused by price changes since the United States had many specific tariffs. However, statutory rates also oscillated considerably prior to 1934 depending on whether Congress was controlled by Republicans (protectionist) or Democrats. The RTAA lowered the ability of Congress to engage in such policy reversals.

[37] The start date is dictated by income data availability from the Montevideo-Oxford Latin American Economic History Database, available at <http://oxlad.qeh.ox.ac.uk/results.php>. We note that 1903 also coincided with an initial US-Cuba trade agreement whereby the United States granted a 20 percent preferential reduction to Cuban sugar and tobacco. However, as Cuba scholars such as Dye and Sicotte (1999) point out, there was no legal commitment to those lower tariffs so the "regime was not risk-free—exporters in both countries faced the possibility that tariff modifications could reduce or even eliminate the benefits conveyed by the treaty" (Dye and Sicotte 1999, 22). This was in fact what happened starting in 1921 when the US increased tariffs on several goods including Cuban sugar. In fact, some argue that the subsequent US tariff increases in the Smoot Hawley act caused the sharp decline of Cuban Sugar exports in 1930–1933 and contributed to the Revolt of 1933.

[38] We find a negative covariance between $\ln \Omega^*$ and t whether or not we control for a linear time-trend.

TABLE 1—RELATIVE GAINS FROM REDUCING TARIFF UNCERTAINTY

	θ	US average tariff (t)	US sugar tariff (t)
log Cuban adjusted openness ($\theta \ln v^* + \ln \Omega^*$)	0	−0.046	−0.079
	−1	−0.004	0.000
	−2	0.04	0.08
	−3	0.08	0.16
	−4	0.12	0.24
	−5	0.16	0.32
	−6	0.20	0.40
	−7	0.25	0.48
	−8	0.29	0.56
	−9	0.33	0.64
	−10	0.37	0.72

Notes: $\mathrm{Cov}(y^*, t)/E(t)$ for 1903–1933, where y^* is log(Cuban adjusted openness) and t is either $\ln(1 + \text{tariff})$ averaged over all products for United States or only its tariff on Cuban sugar. See text for data sources. The relative gain is the absolute value of $\mathrm{Cov}(y^*, t)/E(t)$.

Source: Authors' calculations

25–30 percent of Cuban national income (Dye 2005, 193). Using the sugar tariff, we find that there is an uncertainty-reducing motive for $\theta < -1$.

Finally, using the approach developed above, we can quantify the relative gains from regulating policy uncertainty $(\tilde{V}^{MPA}/\tilde{V}^{UPA})$ by computing the adjusted covariance measure $|\mathrm{Cov}(\ln(v^{*\theta}\Omega^*)^N, t^N)|/\overline{t}^N$ at alternative levels of θ. Table 1 reports the results of this quantification. Note from the last column of Table 1 that, even at moderate levels of risk aversion, the estimate of $\tilde{V}^{MPA}/\tilde{V}^{UPA}$ is not negligible, and it is close to $1/3$ if $\theta = -5$ (the median value in the study by Kimbal, Sahm, and Shapiro 2008).

In sum, this section illustrates how the model can be used to evaluate the direction of the uncertainty motive for a TA between two countries and to quantify the relative gains from regulating trade policy uncertainty. The positive correlation between US tariffs and Cuban adjusted openness at reasonable levels of risk aversion suggests that there was indeed an uncertainty-reducing motive for a TA between these two countries before 1934, and we find the relative gains from reducing policy uncertainty to be significant. It is important to emphasize, however, that this exercise is not a test of the model, but rather it assumes that the model is true and so it must be taken with a grain of caution, since the model is very stylized. The message we want to convey is that it is feasible to take our model to the data in a meaningful way, and it might be desirable to develop richer and more realistic versions of our model in order to quantify the uncertainty-related gains from TAs.

V. Ex Ante Investments

Our basic model assumes that allocation decisions occur ex post, after the shock is realized. But in reality there are a variety of production factors that cannot be flexibly shifted in response to policy and economic shocks. In this section we extend our analysis to allow for allocation decisions that must be made ex ante, before the shock is realized, or "ex ante investments." As we noted in the introduction, the often-heard informal arguments about the motives for TAs claim that they should increase investment and trade by reducing uncertainty. Allowing for ex ante investments in our model seems compelling if one wants to formally examine this issue.

Recall that the standard model allows for an arbitrary number of factors that are mobile ex post. We now assume that one of these, "capital," is mobile ex ante but fixed ex post.[39] We normalize the endowment of capital to one and let k^* denote the fraction of capital allocated to the export sector. To simplify the analysis we assume that all factors in the Home country are perfectly flexible so they can be allocated after the shock λ is realized. This allows us to keep the economic structure for Home in the background, as we did in the static model.

We assume the following timing: (0) The tariff schedule is selected (cooperatively or noncooperatively); (1) capital is allocated; (2) λ is realized; (3) the trade policy is implemented and markets clear.

Both in the cooperative and noncooperative scenarios, we allow the tariff schedule to be contingent on λ. Note that we keep the timing constant across the cooperative and noncooperative scenarios. The reason for this choice is to abstract from domestic-commitment motives for a TA. And of course, if we want a TA to be able to affect investment decisions by managing policy uncertainty, we need policy choices to be made before investment decisions, and this explains our choice of timing.[40]

The first step of the analysis is to extend Proposition 1 from the previous static setting to the present dynamic environment. We write Foreign welfare as $G^*(t, \lambda, k^*)$, and we continue to write Home's objective as $G(t, \lambda)$, which reflects the assumption that Foreign is a small country.[41]

In keeping with our assumption that there is no role for trade policy intervention in Foreign, we assume that capital is perfectly divisible, so that the citizens of the small country are not only identical ex ante, but also ex post, and thus there is no redistribution motive for a tariff. This in turn implies that, given Home's (cooperative or noncooperative) tariff schedule $t(\lambda)$, capital in Foreign is efficiently allocated, and hence k^* maximizes $EG^*(t(\lambda), \lambda, k^*)$.[42] To simplify the arguments below, we assume that G^* is strictly concave in k^*.

[39] We could allow for a higher number of factors that are mobile ex ante but fixed ex post, but the notation would get more cumbersome. And of course, the model also allows for factors that are fully fixed (immobile both ex ante and ex post).

[40] While the assumption is made to provide a clean thought experiment, we note that in some cases countries are able to unilaterally choose contingent protection programs in ways that represent long-term commitments. For example the United States and the European Union have contingent protection laws that apply in the absence of trade agreements.

[41] If Home's objective G is some weighted social welfare function, then for a given Home tariff t the level of k^* can affect G only through the Home country's terms of trade π, but since Foreign is small π is not affected by k^*. On the other hand, k^* can in general affect the noncooperative tariff t^N, for example because it can affect the Foreign country's export supply elasticity. In our notation we suppress the dependence of t^N on k^*, as this should not cause any confusion.

[42] If capital is divisible, all citizens have identical incomes ex post, and as a consequence there is no idiosyncratic risk, which implies that the competitive allocation is efficient, conditional on Home's trade policy. Note that there is aggregate risk in this economy, but it cannot be diversified away (since there are no international insurance markets in our model).

As in the previous static setting, we characterize the optimal MPA, that is the tariff schedule that maximizes expected joint welfare subject to the constraint $Et(\lambda) = Et^N(\lambda)$.

We now argue that Proposition 1 extends to this setting, in the sense that we only need to determine the sign of $\frac{d}{d\lambda}G_t^*(t^N(\lambda), \lambda, k^*)$ to know if there is an uncertainty-reducing role for a TA. The following local argument provides some intuition for the result. Starting at $t^N(\lambda)$, a small mean-preserving compression has no first order effect on EG since this objective is maximized by $t^N(\lambda)$. Therefore, the new schedule will only increase EG^W if it increases EG^*. Since, as noted above, k^* maximizes $EG^*(t(\lambda), \lambda, k^*)$, this policy change has no first-order effect on EG^* via k^*. So any impact of the policy change on EG^* must be due to the "static" effect, i.e., to $\frac{d}{d\lambda}G_t^{*N} \neq 0$.

We now consider the full MPA program. Recalling that, for a given $t(\lambda)$, the level of k^* maximizes $EG^*(t(\lambda), \lambda, k^*)$ and has no effect on EG, then k^* maximizes $EG^W(t(\lambda), \lambda; k^*)$. Thus, we can write the MPA program as if the governments were choosing k^* directly:

$$\max_{t(\lambda), k^*} EG^W(t(\lambda), \lambda, k^*) \tag{12}$$

$$\text{s.t. } Et(\lambda) = Et^N(\lambda).$$

Assuming an interior optimum, we obtain the following FOCs:

$$G_t^W(t, \lambda, k^*) = \psi \text{ for all } \lambda \tag{13}$$

$$Et(\lambda) = Et^N(\lambda)$$

$$EG_{k^*}^W(t(\lambda), \lambda, k^*) = 0. \tag{14}$$

We can now apply an argument similar to the static model, using the first two of the FOC above. The only difference is that the derivative $\frac{d}{d\lambda}G_t^{*N}$ is evaluated at the optimal level of k^*, but as long as the sign of this derivative does not change with k^*, Proposition 1 extends to this setting. In the Appendix, we prove the following:

PROPOSITION 4: *If* $\frac{d}{d\lambda}G_t^*(t^N(\lambda), \lambda, k^*) < 0\ (> 0)$ *for all* (k^*, λ), *then there is an uncertainty-reducing (-increasing) motive for a TA.*

Proposition 4 highlights that the uncertainty motive for the TA is driven by the static effect, i.e., the impact of the shock on the policy externality conditional on the capital level. In a broad sense, we can interpret this result as indicating that the presence of ex ante investments does not generate a *separate* uncertainty motive for a TA.

This conclusion, as we highlighted, relies on the competitive allocation of capital being socially efficient given Home's trade policy, which is ensured in our setting by the assumption of perfectly divisible capital. While this assumption is somewhat restrictive, we note that the same result would obtain in a setting where capital is not divisible, provided that an efficient domestic insurance market is present, or alternatively that the government can use an entry subsidy/tax to control the allocation of capital.[43]

Of course one could consider reasonable alternative scenarios where capital allocation is not efficient, and in such scenarios there could be an "investment motive" for an MPA, or in other words, there could be scope for a TA to "correct" the capital allocation through changes in policy uncertainty, but we note that this would be a second-best argument for a TA, as the first-best way to address such inefficiency would be the use of more targeted policies.

Given that the condition for an uncertainty-reducing motive for a TA is similar as in the static model, the results of the previous sections all extend to the present setting, with the only difference that the relevant expressions are evaluated at a given capital allocation. Moreover, the expressions for the approximate values of an MPA and a UPA are also unchanged, since there is no first order effect on Foreign welfare due to capital reallocation. But even if there is no separate "investment motive" for an MPA, such an agreement in general does affect equilibrium investment levels relative to the noncooperative equilibrium, as we show next.

A. *Impact of Policy Uncertainty on Investment and Trade*

We start by asking how the optimal MPA affects ex ante investments. We focus on the case in which $\frac{d}{d\lambda}G_t^{*N} < 0$, so that the optimal MPA reduces policy risk. To simplify the exposition we assume that the trade pattern does not switch as k^* changes, that is, Foreign exports the nonnumeraire good for all $k^* \geq 0$. Also, for simplicity we focus here on the case of political economy shocks, as in the basic model of Section II.

Recall that efficient capital allocation implies $\frac{\partial EG^*}{\partial k^*} = 0$. By standard results (Rotschild and Stiglitz 1971), the equilibrium k^* increases as a result of a mean-preserving compression in t if $\frac{\partial}{\partial k^*}G_{tt}^*(t, k^*) < 0$ for all t in its support. Thus, the effect depends on the impact of k^* on Foreign's policy-risk preference. In general this effect can go in either direction, but we now highlight a set of sufficient conditions under which it is negative.[44]

Note that the result of Proposition 3 extends directly to this dynamic setting, in the sense that the expression for G_{tt}^* is just the same as in (9), provided its various

[43] If capital is indivisible, so that each citizen must choose ex ante whether to allocate her capital to the export sector or the import-competing sector, then ex post agents fare differently in different states of the world. In this situation, the competitive equilibrium is efficient (given Home's trade policy) only if a domestic insurance market is present, or if the government can use policies to correct the allocation of capital, such as an entry subsidy/tax.

[44] The general ambiguity of the impact of mean-preserving changes in prices on investment decisions is well known. In the literature this ambiguity is resolved in different ways, e.g., assuming decreasing absolute risk aversion, positing a specific shock distribution, restricting the economic environment or, as we do, considering cases with small uncertainty. But we emphasize that our result is novel: we are not aware of any existing result that expresses a similar set of sufficient conditions for a similar economic environment. We also note that we could prove the result under the alternative assumption that the probability mass is sufficiently concentrated, rather than the support being sufficiently small, but in this case the notation and the analysis would be more cumbersome.

components are re-interpreted as *conditional on the capital allocation* k^*. Subject to this re-interpretation, we have

$$\frac{\partial}{\partial k^*}G_{tt}^*(t,k^*) = \frac{\partial}{\partial k^*}\left[v^{*\theta}\Omega^*(\theta\Omega^* + \varepsilon_x^* + D^*)\right] \tag{15}$$

In the Appendix we prove that, if θ is sufficiently negative and the support of λ sufficiently small, then $\frac{\partial}{\partial k^*}G_{tt}^*(t,k^*) < 0$ for all t in its support, which leads to the following:

PROPOSITION 5: *Suppose λ is a political economy shock. If there is sufficient income risk aversion and the support of λ is sufficiently small, then the optimal MPA increases investment in the export sector.*

Broadly interpreted, this proposition suggests that under the condition that generates an uncertainty-reducing motive for a TA, namely a strong degree of income-risk aversion, the optimal MPA leads to higher investment in the export sector, provided the underlying uncertainty in the environment is small enough. We also note that the same result would hold if we replaced the condition that θ is sufficiently negative with the alternative condition that the export supply elasticity ε_x^* is sufficiently close to constant, as we show in Appendix.

Finally we examine the impact of the optimal MPA on expected trade volume in the presence of ex ante investments.

Recall first that, in the absence of ex ante investment, if the MPA reduces policy uncertainty, expected trade increases if and only if the export supply elasticity $\varepsilon_x^*(\pi^*)$ is decreasing in π^*. In the presence of ex ante investment, we can write trade volume as $x^*(\pi^*, k^*)$, thus the MPA increases expected log trade if and only if the following is positive

$$\int \ln x^*(\pi^*, k^{*MPA})\, dF_{MPA}^k(\pi^*) - \int \ln x^*(\pi^*, k^{*N})\, dF_N^k(\pi^*)$$

$$= \int \ln x^*(\pi^*, k^{*N})\, d\big(F_{MPA}^k(\pi^*) - F_N^k(\pi^*)\big) + \int \ln \frac{x^*(\pi^*, k^{*MPA})}{x^*(\pi^*, k^{*N})}\, dF_{MPA}^k(\pi^*),$$

where k^{*MPA} and k^{*N} are, respectively, the equilibrium capital levels at the optimal MPA and at the noncooperative equilibrium; and F_N^k and F_{MPA}^k are the respective distributions of π^*. The first term in the expression above is analogous to the one in the static model, so it depends on whether $\varepsilon_x^*(\pi^*, k^{*N}) \equiv \partial \ln x^*(\pi^*, k^{*N})/\partial\pi^*$ is increasing or decreasing in π^*. The second term captures the expected growth in exports due to the change in investment. If k^* increases, this effect will be positive if the support of the shock is sufficiently small and the economy is not completely specialized.[45]

[45] To see this, note that $\frac{\partial x^*(\pi^*, k^*)}{\partial k^*} = \frac{\partial(q^* - c^*)}{\partial k^*} = \frac{\partial q^*}{\partial k^*} - \frac{\partial c^*}{\partial R^*}\cdot\frac{\partial R^*}{\partial k^*}$, where $\frac{\partial R^*}{\partial k^*}$ is the ex post differential in the rate of return to capital across sectors. This differential is zero in expectation under risk neutrality, while it can differ from zero with risk aversion, but if the shock has small support it is close to zero at the optimal ex ante

Summarizing the discussion above, if risk aversion is sufficiently strong and uncertainty is sufficiently small, the optimal MPA reduces uncertainty in trade policy and increases investment in the export sector. Moreover, under these conditions, expected trade increases provided the export supply elasticity does not increase too rapidly with the price.

We conclude this section with a final point regarding the statement made by the WTO that one of its key goals is to reduce policy uncertainty for the purposes of increasing investment in export sectors. Our analysis suggests that, even though under some conditions a reduction in policy uncertainty does lead to more investment in the export sector, this by itself does not imply a first-order welfare increase: if capital markets are efficient, the only first-order welfare change from a (small) reduction in policy uncertainty is of a "static" nature, that is, it comes from the correction of the international policy-risk externality, conditional on the initial allocation of capital.

VI. Two Policy-Active Countries

In this section, we extend our analysis by considering a setting with two policy-active countries. We focus on the reduced-form framework of Section I and abstract from ex ante investments for simplicity.

We represent the reduced-form payoff functions as $G(t, t^*, \lambda)$ and $G^*(t^*, t, \lambda^*)$, where t is Home's policy and t^* is Foreign's policy. For tractability, we assume that countries are mirror-image symmetric, and we continue to assume a single dimension of uncertainty, that is $\lambda^* = \lambda$; the interpretation is that there is a global shock that affects the two countries symmetrically, or equivalently, two domestic shocks that are perfectly correlated. We assume that each payoff function is concave in its first argument $(G_{tt} < 0, G^*_{t^*t^*} < 0)$, that the single-crossing property is satisfied $(G_{t\lambda} > 0, G^*_{t^*\lambda} > 0)$ and that reaction functions are stable $(|G_{tt}| > G_{tt^*})$.

We denote the common payoff given a symmetric tariff t as $\tilde{G}(t, \lambda) \equiv G(t, t, \lambda)$. We assume that $\tilde{G}$ is concave in t and satisfies the single crossing property $(\tilde{G}_{t\lambda} > 0)$.

Given that countries are symmetric, we look for a symmetric noncooperative equilibrium tariff, which is implicitly defined by the following FOC:

$$G_t(t^N, t^N, \lambda) = 0.$$

Let $t^N(\lambda)$ denote the noncooperative tariff schedule. Given our assumptions, $t^N(\lambda)$ is increasing, as can be verified by implicitly differentiating the FOC:

$$\frac{dt^N}{d\lambda} = \frac{G^N_{t\lambda}}{-(G^N_{tt} + G^N_{tt^*})} > 0,$$

allocation. Thus, if the support of λ is sufficiently small then $\frac{\partial x^*}{\partial k^*} > 0$, provided that $\frac{\partial q^*}{\partial k^*} > 0$, which is the case if the economy is not completely specialized.

One may also ask how an MPA affects the volatility of trade flows. When ε^*_x is not constant, this impact is ambiguous, but it is direct to show that in the "neutral" case where ε^*_x is constant, an MPA that decreases trade policy uncertainty decreases uncertainty in trade volume, i.e., $\ln x^*(\pi^{*N})$ is a MPS of $\ln x^*(\pi^{*MPA})$.

where the numerator is positive by the single crossing property and the denominator is positive by the stability assumption.

Given the symmetry of the problem, it is natural to focus on the optimal symmetric MPA,[46] which is given by:

$$t^{MPA}(\lambda) = \underset{t(\lambda)}{\arg\max}\ E\tilde{G}(t(\lambda), \lambda) \text{ s.t. } Et(\lambda) = Et^N(\lambda). \tag{16}$$

We can write the Lagrangian for this problem as

$$L = \int \left[\tilde{G}(t, \lambda) + \psi\left(t^N(\lambda) - t(\lambda)\right)\right] dF(\lambda) \tag{17}$$

Maximizing this Lagrangian pointwise yields the FOCs

$$\tilde{G}_t(t(\lambda), \lambda) = \psi \text{ for all } \lambda$$

$$Et(\lambda) = Et^N(\lambda).$$

We can then prove the following:

PROPOSITION 6: *If* $\left(G_{tt}^{*N} + G_{tt^*}^{*N}\right) \cdot \frac{dt^N}{d\lambda} + G_{t\lambda}^{*N} < 0\ (> 0)$ *for all* λ, *then there is an uncertainty-reducing (-increasing) motive for a TA. If* $\left(G_{tt}^{*N} + G_{tt^*}^{*N}\right) \cdot \frac{dt^N}{d\lambda} + G_{t\lambda}^{*N} = 0$ *for all* λ, *then there is no uncertainty motive for a TA.*

We can now contrast the result of Proposition 6 with the corresponding result for the small-large country setting. The general condition for an uncertainty-reducing motive, $\frac{d}{d\lambda}G_t^{*N} < 0$, is similar as in the small-large country setting, but in the large-large country setting this expression includes an additional term, namely $G_{tt^*}^{*N}$. We label this the "strategic interaction" effect, which is positive if tariffs are strategic complements and negative if they are strategic substitutes. Thus, an interesting new insight that emerges is that the strategic-interaction effect works in favor of the uncertainty-reducing motive if tariffs are strategic substitutes, and vice-versa if tariffs are strategic complements. Whether tariffs are strategic substitutes or complements depends on the specifics of the trade structure (see, for example, Syropoulos 2002), so the direction of this effect is ultimately an empirical question.

Note also that, while the other terms are similar as in the small-large country setting, they will reflect additional effects when one applies the general formula to a specific trade structure. In particular, the policy-risk-preference effect G_{tt}^{*N} and the externality-shifting effect $G_{t\lambda}^{*N}$ will include tariff-revenue and pass-through elasticity effects that were absent in the small-large country setting.

[46] Given the concavity of the payoff functions, we conjecture that the global maximum is indeed symmetric.

Finally, it can be shown that the expressions derived in Section IA for the gains from regulating policy uncertainty and policy mean extend directly to the large-large country setting considered in this section.

VII. Conclusion

The objective of this paper is to conduct a rigorous examination of the often-heard informal argument that an important motive for TAs is to reduce uncertainty in trade barriers. Focusing on a standard competitive trade model with political/economic shocks, we find that if citizens are risk-neutral there tends to be an uncertainty-increasing motive for a TA. If citizens are risk-averse, an uncertainty-reducing motive for a TA is more likely to be present, other things equal, when the economy is more open, the export supply elasticity is lower, the economy is more specialized, and citizens are more risk-averse. The model suggests that, as the world becomes more integrated, the gains from decreasing trade policy uncertainty should tend to become more important relative to the gains from reducing the levels of trade barriers. Furthermore, governments have more to gain by joining a TA when the trading environment is more uncertain. We develop a simple "sufficient statistic" approach to determine the direction of the uncertainty motive for a TA and quantify the associated gains, and illustrate how it can be taken to the data. Finally, we examine how the uncertainty motive for a TA is affected by the presence of ex ante investments, and examine conditions under which an uncertainty-reducing TA will increase investment in the export sector and raise expected trade volume.

There are several potentially interesting avenues for future research. First, in this paper we have abstracted from contracting frictions. As mentioned in the introduction, we believe this is a natural first step given that our main focus is the potential gains from regulating policy uncertainty, but it would be interesting to examine how results would change in the presence of contracting frictions. Second, it would be desirable to examine the potential uncertainty-managing role of trade agreements in settings where the underlying reason for the agreement is not the classic TOT externality: in particular, one might consider settings in which agreements are motivated by the governments' need for domestic commitment, or by the presence of non-TOT international externalities. Finally, a challenging but potentially fruitful direction of research would be to develop a richer version of our model with the objective of taking it to a comprehensive dataset: this would probably require, among other things, allowing for multiple countries, multiple goods, and imperfectly correlated shocks across countries.

Appendix

PROOF OF LEMMA 1:

We start by proving part (iii). The schedules $t^{MPA}(\lambda)$ and $t^{N}(\lambda)$ are clearly continuous. The mean constraint and the continuity of $t^{MPA}(\lambda)$ and $t^{N}(\lambda)$ ensure the existence of at least one intersection. Consider one such intersection $\hat{\lambda}$, so that $t^{MPA}(\hat{\lambda}) = t^{N}(\hat{\lambda})$. By the FOC, $G_t^W(t^N(\hat{\lambda}), \hat{\lambda}) = \psi$. Since $G_t(t^N(\hat{\lambda}), \hat{\lambda}) = 0$ this implies $G_t^*(t^N(\hat{\lambda}), \hat{\lambda}) = \psi$. Now if $\frac{d}{d\lambda}G_t^*(t^N(\lambda), \lambda) = 0$, then $G_t^*(t^N(\lambda), \lambda) = \psi$ for all λ, which in turn implies $G_t^W(t^N(\lambda), \lambda) = \psi$ for all λ. Therefore the schedule $t^N(\lambda)$ satisfies the FOC, hence $t^{MPA}(\lambda) = t^N(\lambda)$ for all λ.

We next prove part (i), focusing on the case $\frac{d}{d\lambda}G_t^*(t^N(\lambda), \lambda) < 0$. Again, $t^{MPA}(\lambda)$ and $t^N(\lambda)$ must intersect at least once. We now argue that $t^{MPA}(\lambda)$ can only intersect $t^N(\lambda)$ from above. This, together with continuity, will also ensure the uniqueness of the intersection.

We argue by contradiction. Suppose $t^{MPA}(\lambda)$ intersects $t^N(\lambda)$ at some point $\hat{\lambda}$ from below. Consider two values of λ on opposite sides of this intersection, $\lambda_1 < \hat{\lambda} < \lambda_2$, such that $t^{MPA}(\lambda_1) < t^N(\lambda_1)$ and $t^{MPA}(\lambda_2) > t^N(\lambda_2)$.

Recalling that $G_t(t^N(\lambda), \lambda) = 0$ and $\frac{d}{d\lambda}G_t^*(t^N(\lambda), \lambda) < 0$ for all λ, then

$$G_t^W(t^N(\lambda_2), \lambda_2) = G_t^*(t^N(\lambda_2), \lambda_2) < G_t^*(t^N(\lambda_1), \lambda_1) = G_t^W(t^N(\lambda_1), \lambda_1)$$

These inequalities and the concavity of G^W in t imply

$$G_t^W(t^{MPA}(\lambda_2), \lambda_2) < G_t^W(t^N(\lambda_2), \lambda_2) < G_t^W(t^N(\lambda_1), \lambda_1) < G_t^W(t^{MPA}(\lambda_1), \lambda_1)$$

This contradicts the FOC, which requires G_t^W to be equalized across states.

Part (ii) can be similarly proved. ■

PROOF OF PROPOSITION 1:

First observe that $G_{t\lambda} > 0$ implies $t^N(\lambda)$ is increasing, and $G_{t\lambda}^W > 0$ implies $t^{MPA}(\lambda)$ is increasing (this can be proved by implicitly differentiating the FOC for the MPA problem and recalling that ψ is independent of λ).

Part (i). Focus on the case $\frac{d}{d\lambda}G_t^*(t^N(\lambda), \lambda) < 0$. By Lemma 1, in this case $t^{MPA}(\lambda)$ intersects $t^N(\lambda)$ once and from above. We show that the random variable $t^N(\lambda)$ is a second-order stochastic shift of the random variable $t^{MPA}(\lambda)$, which together with the fact that these two random variables have the same mean implies that the former is a MPS of the latter. Let $\lambda^N(t)$ denote the inverse of $t^N(\lambda)$ and $\lambda^{MPA}(t)$ the inverse of $t^{MPA}(\lambda)$; these inverse functions exist because $t^N(\lambda)$ and $t^{MPA}(\lambda)$ are both increasing. Also, let $\hat{t}$ be the value of t for which the two curves intersect.

The cumulative distribution function of t^N is given by $F_N(t) = \Pr(t^N(\lambda) \leq t) = \Pr(\lambda \leq \lambda^N(t))$ and the cumulative distribution function of t^{MPA} is given by $F_{MPA}(t) = \Pr(t^{MPA}(\lambda) \leq t) = \Pr(\lambda \leq \lambda^{MPA}(t))$. Lemma 1 implies that $\lambda^{MPA}(t) < \lambda^N(t)$ for all $t < \hat{t}$ and $\lambda^{MPA}(t) > \lambda^N(t)$ for all $t > \hat{t}$, which in turn implies that $F_{MPA}(t) < F_N(t)$ for all $t < \hat{t}$ and $F_{MPA}(t) > F_N(t)$ for all $t > \hat{t}$. This implies that $t^N(\lambda)$ is a second-order stochastic shift of $t^{MPA}(\lambda)$, as claimed.

Part (ii) can be similarly proved.

Part (iii) was already proved in Lemma 1. ■

PROOF OF PROPOSITION 2:

Start by noting that $G_{tt}^* = \frac{\partial^2 G^*}{\partial(\ln p^*)^2}$. It is straightforward to derive

$$\frac{\partial^2 G^*}{\partial(\ln p^*)^2} = \left(v^{*\theta}\right)\left[\theta\left(\frac{\partial \ln v^*}{\partial \ln p^*}\right)^2 + \frac{\partial^2 \ln v^*}{\partial(\ln p^*)^2}\right],$$

where $\ln v^* = \ln R^* - \ln \phi^*$. Next note that $\frac{\partial \ln R^*}{\partial \ln p^*} = \frac{p^* q^*}{R^*}$. Differentiating this elasticity with respect to $\ln p^*$ and simplifying, we obtain

$$\frac{\partial^2 \ln R^*}{\partial(\ln p^*)^2} = \frac{p^* q^*}{R^*} \cdot \left(1 - \frac{p^* q^*}{R^*}\right) + \frac{p^{*2} q^{*\prime}}{R^*}.$$

Next note that employing Roy's identity we obtain $\frac{c^*}{R^*} = \frac{\phi^{*\prime}}{\phi^*}$, hence $\frac{\partial \ln \phi^*}{\partial \ln p^*} = \frac{p^* c^*}{R^*}$. It follows that

$$\frac{\partial^2 \ln \phi^*}{\partial(\ln p^*)^2} = \frac{\partial\left(\frac{p^* c^*}{R^*}\right)}{\partial p^*} \cdot p^*.$$

Adding things up and simplifying, we find $G_{tt}^* = v^{*\theta}\Omega^*(\theta\Omega^* + \varepsilon_x^* + D^*)$. ∎

PROOF OF PROPOSITION 4:

We start by proving part (ii). The schedules $t^{MPA}(\lambda)$ and $t^N(\lambda)$ are clearly continuous. The mean constraint and the continuity of $t^{MPA}(\lambda)$ and $t^N(\lambda)$ ensure the existence of at least one intersection. Consider one such intersection $\hat{\lambda}$, so that $t^{MPA}(\hat{\lambda}) = t^N(\hat{\lambda})$. By the FOC, $G_t^W(t^N(\hat{\lambda}), \hat{\lambda}, k^{*MPA}) = \psi$. Since $G_t(t^N(\hat{\lambda}), \hat{\lambda}) = 0$, this implies $G_t^*(t^N(\hat{\lambda}), \hat{\lambda}, k^{*MPA}) = \psi$. Now if $\frac{d}{d\lambda}G_t^*(t^N(\lambda), \lambda, k^{*MPA}) = 0$, then $G_t^*(t^N(\lambda), \lambda, k^{*MPA}) = \psi$ for all λ, which in turn implies $G_t^W(t^N(\lambda), \lambda, k^{*MPA}) = \psi$ for all λ. Therefore the schedule $t^N(\lambda)$ satisfies the FOC, hence $t^{MPA}(\lambda) = t^N(\lambda)$ for all λ and $k^{*MPA} = k^{*N}$.

We next prove part (i). Again, $t^{MPA}(\lambda)$ and $t^N(\lambda)$ must intersect at least once. We now argue that if $\frac{d}{d\lambda}G_t^*(t^N(\lambda), \lambda, k^{*MPA}) < 0$ for all λ, then $t^{MPA}(\lambda)$ can only intersect $t^N(\lambda)$ from above. This, together with continuity, will also ensure the uniqueness of the intersection.

We argue by contradiction. Suppose $t^{MPA}(\lambda)$ intersects $t^N(\lambda)$ at some point $\hat{\lambda}$ from below. Consider two values of λ on the opposite sides of this intersection, $\lambda_1 < \hat{\lambda} < \lambda_2$, such that $t^{MPA}(\lambda_1) < t^N(\lambda_1)$ and $t^{MPA}(\lambda_2) > t^N(\lambda_2)$.

Recalling that $G_t(t^N(\lambda), \lambda) = 0$ for all k^* and assuming $\frac{d}{d\lambda} G_t^*(t^N(\lambda), \lambda, k^{*MPA}) < 0$ for all λ, then

$$G_t^W(t^N(\lambda_2), \lambda_2, k^{*MPA}) = G_t^*(t^N(\lambda_2), \lambda_2, k^{*MPA})$$

$$< G_t^*(t^N(\lambda_1), \lambda_1, k^{*MPA}) = G_t^W(t^N(\lambda_1), \lambda_1, k^{*MPA}).$$

These inequalities and the concavity of G^W in t imply

$$G_t^W(t^{MPA}(\lambda_2), \lambda_2, k^{*MPA}) < G_t^W(t^N(\lambda_2), \lambda_2, k^{*MPA})$$

$$< G_t^W(t^N(\lambda_1), \lambda_1, k^{*MPA}) < G_t^W(t^{MPA}(\lambda_1), \lambda_1, k^{*MPA}).$$

The claim follows. ∎

PROOF OF PROPOSITION 5:

As a first step, we argue that an increase in k^* leads to a decrease in the degree of diversification D^*. We can write $D^* = 1 - \frac{p^*q^*}{p^*q^* + q_0^*} = 1 - \frac{1}{1 + \frac{q_0^*}{p^*q^*}}$. An increase in k^* (holding $\pi^* = \ln p^*$ constant) leads to an increase in q^* and a decrease in q_0^*, hence D^* falls.

Next, focus on Ω^*. We have $\Omega^* = \frac{p^*x^*}{R^*} = \frac{p^*q^* - p^*c^*}{R^*} = \frac{1}{1 + \frac{q_0^*}{p^*q^*}} - \frac{p^*c^*}{R^*}$. As k^* increases, the first term in the above expression increases, as we argued above. Next note that k^* affects the consumption share $\frac{p^*c^*}{R^*}$ only through R^*. In principle $\frac{\partial R^*}{\partial k^*}$ has an ambiguous sign, but note that under certainty k^* maximizes R^*, hence $\frac{\partial R^*}{\partial k^*} = 0$ under certainty. If p^* is uncertain but has a small support, $\frac{\partial R^*}{\partial k^*}$ will be small in absolute value, and hence $\frac{\partial}{\partial k^*}\left(\frac{p^*c^*}{R^*}\right)$ will also be small in absolute value. This ensures that if the support is small enough, Ω^* is increasing in k^*.

Next note that a change in k^* in general has an ambiguous effect on the export supply elasticity ε_x^*, so in general the effect of k^* on $\Omega^*(\theta\Omega^* + \varepsilon_x^* + D^*)$ is ambiguous, however, if risk aversion is sufficiently strong, i.e., if θ is sufficiently negative, then clearly the effect is negative. If ε_x^* is approximately constant we do not require θ to be sufficiently negative.

Finally, consider the sign of the whole expression (15). Letting $\Omega^*(\theta\Omega^* + \varepsilon_x^* + D^*) \equiv h(p^*, k^*)$, we can rewrite (15) as

$$(18) \quad \frac{\partial}{\partial k^*}\left[v^{*\theta}(p^*, k^*)h(p^*, k^*)\right] = \frac{\partial v^{*\theta}}{\partial k^*} \cdot h + v^{*\theta} \cdot \frac{\partial h}{\partial k^*} = \left(\theta\frac{v_{k^*}^*}{v^*} + \frac{h_{k^*}}{h}\right) \cdot h \cdot v^{*\theta}.$$

Note that the term $\frac{v_{k^*}^*}{v^*}$ is the relative change in real income due to a capital re-allocation. This is zero under certainty, and under uncertainty it necessarily changes sign over the range of k^*, since if it was always positive or negative there would be an incentive to re-allocate capital. We now argue that if θ is sufficiently negative and the support of p^* is small enough, the expression above is negative. Fix θ at some level $\hat{\theta}$ such that $h < 0$ and $\frac{h_{k^*}}{h} > A > 0$ under certainty (where A is some positive constant). The arguments above ensure that such $\hat{\theta}$ must exist. Next recall that k^* satisfies $v_{k^*}^* = 0$ under certainty. Then, as the support of p^* shrinks to zero, $\hat{\theta}\frac{v_{k^*}^*}{v^*}$ goes to zero for all p^* in the support, while $\frac{h_{k^*}}{h}$ approaches $A > 0$, therefore $\frac{\partial}{\partial k^*}\left[v^{*\theta}(p^*, k^*)h(p^*, k^*)\right] < 0.$ ∎

PROOF OF PROPOSITION 6:

Focus on the case $(G_{tt}^{*N} + G_{tt^*}^{*N})\frac{dt^N}{d\lambda} + G_{t\lambda}^{*N} < 0$, or equivalently $\frac{d}{d\lambda}G_t^*(t^N(\lambda), t^N(\lambda), \lambda) < 0$. The key is to prove the analog of Lemma 1, namely that $t^{MPA}(\lambda)$ intersects $t^N(\lambda)$ once and from above.

We argue by contradiction. Suppose $t^{MPA}(\lambda)$ intersects $t^N(\lambda)$ at some point $\hat{\lambda}$ from below. Consider two values of λ on the opposite sides of this intersection, $\lambda_1 < \hat{\lambda} < \lambda_2$, such that $t^{MPA}(\lambda_1) > t^N(\lambda_1)$ and $t^{MPA}(\lambda_2) > t^N(\lambda_2)$.

Recalling that $G_t(t^N(\lambda), t^N(\lambda), \lambda) = 0$ and $\frac{d}{d\lambda}G_t^*(t^N(\lambda), t^N(\lambda), \lambda) < 0$ for all λ, then

$$\tilde{G}_t(t^N(\lambda_2), \lambda_2) = G_t^*(t^N(\lambda_2), t^N(\lambda_2), \lambda_2) < G_t^*(t^N(\lambda_1), t^N(\lambda_1), \lambda_1) = \tilde{G}_t(t^N(\lambda_1), \lambda_1)$$

These inequalities and the concavity of $\tilde{G}$ in t imply

$$\tilde{G}_t(t^{MPA}(\lambda_2), \lambda_2) < \tilde{G}_t(t^N(\lambda_2), \lambda_2) < \tilde{G}_t(t^N(\lambda_1), \lambda_1) < \tilde{G}_t(t^{MPA}(\lambda_1), \lambda_1)$$

This contradicts the FOC, which requires that $\tilde{G}_t(t^{MPA}(\lambda), \lambda)$ be equalized across states.

Having proved the analog of Lemma 1, the claim of the proposition follows immediately: just observe that the assumed single crossing properties imply $t^N(\lambda)$ and $t^{MPA}(\lambda)$ are increasing, and apply a similar argument to that in the proof of Proposition 1. ∎

REFERENCES

►**Amador, Manuel, and Kyle Bagwell.** 2013. "The Theory of Optimal Delegation with an Application to Tariff Caps." *Econometrica* 81 (4): 1541–99.

►**Anderson, James E., and John G. Riley.** 1976. "International Trade with Fluctuating Prices." *International Economic Review* 17 (1): 76–97.

►**Bagwell, Kyle, and Robert W. Staiger.** 1999. "An Economic Theory of GATT." *American Economic Review* 89 (1): 215–48.

►**Bagwell, Kyle, and Robert W. Staiger.** 2012. "Profit Shifting and Trade Agreements in Imperfectly Competitive Markets." *International Economic Review* 53 (4): 1067–1104.

Beshkar, Mostafa, and Eric W. Bond. 2012. "Cap and Escape in Trade Agreements." http://mypage.iu.edu/~mbeshkar/papers/Cap-Escape.pdf.

Blattman, Christopher, Jason Hwang, and Jeffrey G. Williamson. 2007. "Winners and losers in the commodity lottery: The impact of terms of trade growth and volatility in the Periphery 1870–1939." *Journal of Economic Development* 82 (1): 156–79.

Bown, Chad P., ed. 2011. *The Great Recession and Import Protection: The Role of Temporary Trade Barriers*. Washington, DC: Centre for Economic Policy Research.

Bown, Chad P., and Meredith A. Crowley. 2013. "Import protection, business cycles, and exchange rates: Evidence from the Great Recession." *Journal of International Economics* 90 (1): 50–64.

Cadot, O., M. Olarreaga, and J. Tschopp. 2013. "Do Trade Agreements Reduce the Volatility of Agricultural Distortions?" In *The Political Economy of Agricultural Trade Distortions*, edited by Kym Anderson, 332–57. Cambridge: Cambridge University Press.

Dye, Alan D. 2005. "Cuba and the Origins of the US Sugar Quota." *Revista de Indias* 65 (233): 193–218.

Dye, Alan, and Richard Sicotte. 1999. "US-Cuban Trade Cooperation and its Unraveling." *Business and Economic History* 28 (2): 19–31.

Eaton, Jonathan. 1979. "The Allocation of Resources in an Open Economy with Uncertain Terms of Trade." *International Economic Review* 20 (2): 391–403.

Eaton, Jonathan, and Gene M. Grossman. 1985. "Tariffs as Insurance: Optimal Commercial Policy when Domestic Markets are Incomplete." *Canadian Journal of Economics* 18 (2): 258–72.

Flemming, John S., Stephen J. Turnovsky, and Murray C. Kemp. 1977. "On the Choice of Numeraire and Certainty Price in General Equilibrium Models of Price Uncertainty." *Review of Economic Studies* 44 (3): 573–83.

Grossman, Gene M., and Elhanan Helpman. 1995. "Trade Wars and Trade Talks." *Journal of Political Economy* 103 (4): 675–708.

Handley, Kyle. 2014. "Exporting under trade policy uncertainty: Theory and evidence." *Journal of International Economics* 94 (1): 50–66.

Horn, Henrik, Giovanni Maggi, and Robert W. Staiger. 2010. "Trade Agreements as Endogenously Incomplete Contracts." *American Economic Review* 100 (1): 394–419.

Irwin, Douglas A. 1998. "From Smoot-Hawley to Reciprocal Trade Agreements: Changing the Course of U.S. Trade Policy in the 1930s." In *The Defining Moment: The Great Depression and the American Economy in the Twentieth Century*, edited by Michael D. Bordo, Claudia Goldin, and Eugene N. White, 325–52. Chicago: University of Chicago Press.

Irwin, Douglas A. 2007. "Trade Restrictiveness and Deadweight Losses from U.S. Tariffs, 1859–1961." National Bureau of Economic Research (NBER) Working Paper 13450.

Kimball, Miles S., Claudia R. Sahm, and Matthew D. Shapiro. 2008. "Imputing Risk Tolerance from Survey Responses." *Journal of the American Statistical Association* 103 (483): 1028–38.

Limão, Nuno, and Tovar, Patricia. 2011. "Policy Choice: Theory and evidence from commitment via international trade agreements." *Journal of International Economics* 85 (2): 186–205.

Maggi, Giovanni, and Andres Rodríguez-Clare. 1998. "The Value of Trade Agreements in the Presence of Political Pressures." *Journal of Political Economy* 106 (3): 574–601.

Mansfield, Edward D., and Eric Reinhardt. 2008. "International Institutions and the Volatility of International Trade." *International Organization* 62 (4): 621–52.

McLaren, John. 1997. "Size, Sunk Costs, and Judge Bowker's Objection to Free Trade." *American Economic Review* 87 (3): 400–420.

Mrázova, Monika. 2011. "Trade agreements when profits matter." http://www.monikamrazova.com/TradeAg.pdf.

Newbery, David M. G., and Joseph E. Stiglitz. 1981. *The Theory of Commodity Price Stabilization: A Study in the Economics of Risk*. Oxford: Oxford University Press.

Ossa, Ralph. 2011. "A New Trade Theory of GATT/WTO Negotiations." *Journal of Political Economy* 119 (1): 122–52.

Rose, Andrew K. 2004. "Do WTO members have more liberal trade policy?" *Journal of International Economics* 63 (2): 209–35.

Rothschild, Michael, and Joseph E. Stiglitz. 1970. "Increasing risk I: A definition." *Journal of Economic Theory* 2 (3): 225–43.

Rothschild, Michael, and Joseph E. Stiglitz. 1971. "Increasing risk II: Its economic consequences." *Journal of Economic Theory* 3 (1): 66–84.

Schularick, Moritz, and Solomos Solomou. 2011. "Tariffs and economic growth in the first era of globalization." *Journal of Economic Growth* 16 (1): 33–70.

Staiger, Robert W., and Guido Tabellini. 1987. "Discretionary Trade Policy and Excessive Protection." *American Economic Review* 77 (5): 823–37.

►**Syropoulos, Constantinos.** 2002. "Optimum Tariffs and Retaliation Revisited: How Country Size Matters." *Review of Economic Studies* 69 (3): 707–27.

►**Tokarick, Stephen.** 2014. "A Method for Calculating Export Supply and Import Demand Elasticities." *Journal of International Trade and Economic Development* 23 (7): 1059–87.

►**Young, Leslie, and James E. Anderson.** 1982. "Risk Aversion and Optimal Trade Restrictions." *Review of Economic Studies* 49 (2): 291–305.

Chapter 4

Trade and Investment under Policy Uncertainty: Theory and Firm Evidence†

By Kyle Handley and Nuno Limão*

In a dynamic model with sunk export costs, a firm's export investment is lower under trade policy uncertainty, and credible preferential trade agreements (PTAs) increase trade even if current tariffs are low. Exploring Portugal's accession to the European Community as a policy uncertainty shock we find that the trade reform accounted for a large fraction of Portuguese exporting firms' entry and sales; the accession removed uncertainty about future EC trade policies; and this uncertainty channel accounted for a large fraction of the predicted growth. Our approach can be applied to other PTAs and sources of policy uncertainty. (*JEL* D22, F12, F14, F15, G31, L11)

Firms face considerable uncertainty about future conditions, which can arise from purely economic shocks—e.g., to productivity or tastes—or from policy shocks—e.g., monetary or fiscal reforms. The role of future conditions is particularly important when firms must decide on costly irreversible investments. We examine the impact of policy uncertainty on a firm's decision to invest and export to new markets, which is an interesting setting for several reasons. First, global integration has considerably increased firms' exposure to foreign policy uncertainty. Second, while most trade analysis assumes policy is deterministic, we argue that it can be quite uncertain. Trade policy shocks are not frequent but when they happen they can be large and persistent, as witnessed in the 1930's trade war.[1] Third, there is growing evidence that firms must incur sunk costs to start exporting (cf. Roberts and Tybout

*Handley: Ross School of Business, University of Michigan, 701 Tappan St. R3390, Ann Arbor, MI 48109 (e-mail: handleyk@umich.edu); Limão: Department of Economics, University of Maryland, College Park, MD 20742, (e-mail: limao@econ.umd.edu). I thank the Bank of Portugal for financial and research support to prepare the empirical application of this paper for its 2010 Annual Conference on Portuguese Development. The Bank of Portugal Research Group, the Portuguese Census (INE) and Mario Centeno provided valuable help with the firm level data. I also thank Yale University's Leitner Program, which hosted me during part of this project and the University of Maryland (UMD) Economics Department for funding to digitize data. We thank two anonymous referees for helpful comments as well as seminar and conference participants at Pennsylvania State University, the World Trade Organization (WHO), the Bank of Portugal, University of Notre Dame, University of Virginia, the Stanford Institute for Theoretical Economics, Washington Area International Trade Symposium (WAITS), European Trade Study Group (ETSG), and Becker-Friedman Institute Policy Uncertainty conferences and National Bureau of Economic Reseach (NBER) Spring Trade meeting. Jeronimo Carballo provided valuable research assistance. The usual disclaimer applies. We acknowledge financial support from the National Science Foundation (NSF) under grants SES-1360738 (Handley) and SES-1360780 (Limão).

†Go to http://dx.doi.org/10.1257/pol.20140068 to visit the article page for additional materials and author disclosure statement(s) or to comment in the online discussion forum.

[1] Fears of a similar war during the Great Recession of 2008–2009 prompted leaders of the G-20 to repeatedly pledge that "We will not repeat the historic mistakes of protectionism of previous eras." http://www.londonsummit.gov.uk/en/summit-aims/summit-communique/. While a trade war did not break out, the initial fears were not unfounded since nontariff barriers have often been used during downturns (Bown and Crowley 2013). Other

Originally Published in *American Economic Journal* 7(4), pp. 189–222.

1997). To capture these elements we develop a tractable dynamic heterogeneous firms' model under policy uncertainty. We derive, estimate, and quantify the impacts of current and future trade policy on investment and export decisions by combining novel firm-level and trade policy data in the context of preferential trade agreements.

A broader motive to focus on trade is the rich policy and firm data available, which has the potential to inform us about the firm impacts of other types of policy uncertainty. The basic theoretical impacts of uncertainty on investment are understood (cf. Bernanke 1983), and recent evidence links aggregate uncertainty shocks to investment.[2] However, there is scant empirical evidence of the importance of policy uncertainty for firms, even though thousands of firms worldwide rank it as "one of the most important constraints in doing business" (World Bank Development Report 2005). The scant evidence is likely due to the inherent conceptual and empirical challenges surrounding this question. These include the difficulty in measuring policy uncertainty and clearly identifying its causal impact on specific investment decisions.[3] The international trade setting can help address these issues. First, it allows us to construct detailed measures of policy uncertainty that are easy-to-interpret and vary across countries, products, and time. Second, we can trace the effects of these measures to specific firm investment and sales decisions that also vary along all these dimensions and can thus help address endogeneity concerns.

We build on the option value insights in Dixit (1989) and Rodrik (1991) and extend them to a context with trade policy uncertainty (TPU) and heterogenous firms. We characterize policy by using a stochastic process that generates closed form solutions and clearly guides the empirical estimation and quantification. The theoretical framework can be applied to alternative sources of TPU including the timing and credibility of large trade policy reforms, be they unilateral (e.g., China, India, and Brazil's liberalizations), multilateral (e.g., completion or implementation of trade rounds) or bilateral (e.g., passage of the North American Free Trade Agreement (NAFTA)).[4]

In order to identify the effect of *changes* in policy uncertainty we focus on whether and how trade agreements reduce TPU and thus affect export investments. Our empirical analysis focuses on preferential trade agreements (PTAs)—the most important source of trade policy reform in the last 20 years.[5] Importantly, many such agreements claim to "reduce distortions to trade" *and* "ensure a predictable environment for business planning and investment."[6] As we will show, a key determinant for whether PTAs spur export investment is whether the tariff reductions they generate are credible or face some probability of reversal. This concern is pervasive for

sources of potentially large and permanent changes in protection include import bans due to safety concerns; and threats of tariffs to counter exchange rate manipulation or carbon emissions in production.

[2] Bloom, Bond, and Reenen (2007) and Bloom (2009) provide evidence that shocks to stock market volatility delay firm-level investment and attenuate its response to demand shocks.

[3] As Rodrik (1991) notes "the idea that policy instability can be detrimental to private investment is easy to accept (…). However, it is hard to deploy serious econometrics in support of the proposition."

[4] US trade agreements are subject to congressional modification if the president does not have "fast-track" authority (Conconi, Facchini, and Zanardi 2012), which can generate TPU.

[5] In 2014, there were 377 PTAs in force and 583 notified to the WTO. www.wto.org.

[6] For examples see the Global PTA Database at wits.worldbank.org/GPTAD. The WTO also aims to generate "Predictability through bindings and transparency [to] promote investment (…)" www.wto.org.

the many developing countries that obtain unilateral preferences from the United States or Europe.[7]

The empirical application focuses on Portugal's accession to the European Community (EC). This is a good setting to study the trade and investment effects of TPU for several reasons. First, the focus on a specific country and policy event allows us to cleanly identify the effect and carefully control for a number of factors. Second, the effects of TPU should be important for small, developing, open economies where trade is central both to consumers and firms.[8] So, this episode can be relevant for many developing countries currently seeking secure access to the United States and European markets.[9] Third, Portuguese trade increased dramatically after 1986 and that increase was largest towards the EC partners, *suggesting* that it was caused by the accession. Finally, the export expansion upon accession was characterized by considerable entry of Portuguese firms exporting into EC markets even in industries where applied tariffs did not change and we find this cannot be explained by standard determinants such as income or exchange rates, which indicates a potential role for the agreement in reducing TPU.

Our model shows how to measure, test, and quantify the impact of TPU on firm entry and trade. We estimate a structural equation where export entry depends on current policy and a measure of TPU: the percent loss in profits due to a negative tariff shock that reverts tariffs to their nonpreferential levels, which we observe. We find supporting evidence for several of the model's predictions by exploring variation in firm entry and policy across different export markets (EC-10 and Spain), industries, and time. The estimates indicate that Portuguese exporters believed that the probability of losing preferences was zero after EC accession but positive before. So the agreement eliminated that source of TPU.

Using the estimated structural parameters, we then quantify the impact of alternative policies. The trade policy changes due to accession accounted for 61 percent of the growth in entry and 87 percent of the growth in export value. If the accession had only reduced applied tariffs, but not TPU, it would have achieved only 20 percent of the total predicted firm entry and less than 30 percent for total exports. So, a substantial fraction of the growth was generated by the elimination of TPU. Moreover, about 65 percent of the growth in entry is due to securing previous tariff reductions, and more than half of this is accounted for by a mean preserving reduction in tariff risk.

Our work is related to research in different fields. We build on Dixit (1989) who shows that price uncertainty creates an option value of waiting before making sunk cost entry investments. These insights have mainly been used to analyze the impact of exchange rate uncertainty on exports (cf. Baldwin and Krugman 1989; and Das,

[7] US preferences to several developing countries are often conditional on a variety of criteria that can and have triggered nonrenewal for periods up to fourteen months.

[8] A large fraction of Portuguese firms are engaged in some form of international trade—about 24 percent—and account for a large fraction of private sector nonagricultural employment—58 percent or 46 percent if we focus only on exporters. These figures for 1987 are based on merged information from Quadros de Pessoal and Portuguese Trade statistics.

[9] For example, Peru and Colombia received US preferences subject to periodic renewal and subsequently agreed to lower barriers on US products to permanently secure those preferences and spur investment (cf. United States International Trade Commission (USITC) 2008). Similarly, several countries that seek (or sought) PTAs with the EC previously received some form of preference.

Roberts, and Tybout 2007); FDI (Russ 2007); or both (Fillat and Garetto 2014).[10] We, too, develop a dynamic model of trade with sunk costs, but we focus on TPU and provide closed form solutions that guide the estimation.

The impact of trade and tax policy uncertainty when there are sunk costs of investment, has received far less attention. For example, Rodrik (1991) develops a model of capital investment when firms believe an investment tax credit may be reversed in the future. If the probability or cost of a policy reversal is high, a reform to promote investment may produce the opposite outcome. The scant empirical evidence has mostly focused on aggregate outcomes; Baker, Bloom, and Davis (2013) find that increases in a news-based index of policy uncertainty are negatively correlated with aggregate employment, output, and investment in the United States. Our approach is different and our trade focus aims to identify the effects of policy uncertainty shocks as cleanly as possible.

We also contribute to the debate regarding the value of trade agreements. Early empirical work on the trade impacts of PTAs delivered mixed results, e.g., Frankel (1997) reports small and sometimes negative effects of EC membership on trade between members in the 1960s and 1970s but positive ones in the 1980s and 1990s. Our approach highlights that whether PTAs increase bilateral trade depends on whether their policies are credible.[11] The role of TPU is also explored by Handley (2014), who provides evidence that WTO tariff bindings reduce TPU and thus promote export entry.[12] Limão and Maggi (2015) theoretically examine the value of endogenous trade agreements under uncertainty in a perfectly competitive setting with risk averse individuals.

In Section I we derive the structural relationship between TPU and firm investment decisions. In Section II we describe the empirical approach, provide estimates and quantify the policy impacts. In the final section we summarize our results and discuss implications and possible extensions.

I. Theory

To determine the impact of TPU on export entry investments we first determine operating profits for each firm conditional on exporting. Second, we examine a firm's decision to invest to enter that market and how it is affected by policy uncertainty.

A. *Demand and Operating Profits*

The operating profit for a firm that exports a differentiated good, v, to country i is determined as follows. At the start of each period a firm can observe the policy and demand that it will face in each market before it produces, which allows us to

[10] There is stronger evidence for a negative effect of exchange rate volatility on FDI (cf. Campa 1993, and Russ 2012) than exports (cf. Das, Roberts, and Tybout 2007; and Alessandria and Choi 2007). Impulliti, Irarrazabal, and O'Promolla (2013) show that firm productivity uncertainty can generate hysteresis in firms' export decisions.

[11] This can help explain why even though PTAs increase trade substantially on average (cf. Baier and Bergstrand 2007) not all PTAs do so (Baier, Bergstrand, and Vidal 2007). Egger et al. (2011) address the endogeneity of PTAs and zero bilateral flows in a unified way. Ruhl (2008) argues that PTAs can generate export entry by permanently lowering trade frictions, which strengthens response to future macro variable shocks.

[12] Sala, Schröder, and Yalcin (2010) study the impact of WTO bindings on exports theoretically.

focus on the export entry investment as the sole decision made under uncertainty. This timing, and the absence of any adjustment costs, implies that, after entry, firms simply maximize operating profits period by period and those profits can be derived similarly to standard deterministic monopolistic competition models.

One industry produces a homogeneous, freely traded good—the numeraire—and each of the remaining V industries produce differentiated goods. Each industry V has a fixed exogenous fraction μ_V of each country's total expenditure on goods and the rest is spent on the numeraire. Consumers have constant elasticity of substitution preferences over goods in each V with $\sigma = 1/(1-\rho) > 1$. Therefore, a firm v faces the standard optimal demand, $q_{iv} = \tilde{A}_{iV} p_{iv}^{-\sigma}$, where $\tilde{A}_{iV}$ is an industry demand parameter, which is exogenous from the perspective of any given firm.[13] The consumer price, p_{iv}, includes trade costs. We focus on ad valorem import tariffs and note that they are product or industry specific. We denote the tariff factor that i sets on V by $\tau_{iV} \geq 1$, so free trade is represented by $\tau_{iV} = 1$. Therefore, producers of any $v \in V$ exporting to i receive p_{iv}/τ_{iV}.

The supply side is standard. There is a single factor, labor, which has constant marginal productivity in the numeraire sector, so the wage is normalized to unity. Differentiated goods are produced with a constant marginal cost, characterized by a labor coefficient of c_v, which is heterogenous across firms. The firm chooses prices to maximize operating profits in each period, $(p_{iv}/\tau_{iV} - c_v)\, q_{iv}$, leading to the standard mark-up rule over cost, $p_v = c_v/\rho$. Consumers in i face this price augmented by the tariff, that is $p_{iv} = (c_v/\rho)\,\tau_{iV}$. Using the optimal price and demand we obtain, respectively, the export revenue received by the firm and the associated operating profit:

$$p_{iv} q_{iv}/\tau_{iV} = (\tau_{iV})^{-\sigma}\, \tilde{A}_{iV}(c_v/\rho)^{1-\sigma} \tag{1}$$

$$\pi(c_v, \tau_{iV}) = (\tau_{iV})^{-\sigma}\, A_{iV} c_v^{1-\sigma}, \tag{2}$$

where $A_{iV} \equiv \tilde{A}_{iV}(1-\rho)\,\rho^{\sigma-1}$ summarizes industry demand conditions in the foreign market.

B. *Firm Value, Investment, and Export Entry Setup*

In each industry V there is an exogenous constant mass of firms that produce for their home market and an endogenous subset of them that exports.[14] Firms face no uncertainty about their productivity when deciding whether to export (they already produce domestically). To focus on foreign demand uncertainty due to policy we assume the following. First, the single underlying source of uncertainty is the future

[13] Under this structure $\tilde{A}_{iV} = \mu_V Y_i (P_{iV})^{\sigma-1}$, where P_{iV} is the standard CES price aggregator over varieties in each V sold in i, and Y_i is the aggregate expenditure on goods. The standard assumption is that each firm is sufficiently small relative to the total number in industry V and country i to take into account any effect that they may have on the price index or aggregate goods' expenditure.

[14] To focus on firms' foreign market entry decisions we assume there are no fixed costs to enter the domestic market. This simplification does not affect our basic empirical results since our identification approach controls for industry-time effects, and thus accounts for domestic entry into any particular industry.

tariff policy in the foreign market. Second, the exporting country is sufficiently small that changes in the policy it faces when selling to i have no impact on the foreign aggregate demand term, A_{iV}.[15] Given these assumptions and the constant mass of domestic producers in i, we will treat A_{iV} as constant in the theory when analyzing firms' decisions to export to this market. We can allow for unanticipated shocks to A_{iV} and will control for them empirically.

Let us first consider a benchmark case where the policy is deterministic. A firm enters a new export market if the present discounted value of its profit exceeds the sunk investment cost of entry, i.e., $\pi(c_v, \tau_{iV}) \geq K_{iV}(1 - \beta)$. The discount factor $1 - \beta$ reflects the exogenous probability of a death shock to exporting.[16] Each industry has a continuum of firms with heterogenous marginal cost drawn from a distribution function $G_V(c)$. Thus, we can use the condition above to determine the marginal entrant without policy uncertainty.

$$c_{iV}^D = \left[\frac{(\tau_{iV})^{-\sigma}}{1 - \beta} \frac{A_{iV}}{K_{iV}}\right]^{1/(\sigma-1)} \tag{3}$$

The cutoff is common to all firms that face a similar tariff and sunk cost, so for $v \in V$ all firms with $c_v < c_{iV}^D$ enter. Reductions in tariffs increase demand and thus induce entry.

Trade policy is rarely deterministic and potential exporters can choose when to invest so TPU can generate an option value of waiting. The analysis below applies for each firm v considering the decision to export to a given market i so we drop these subscripts for simplicity. We model the entry decision as an optimal stopping problem. Firms can be divided into exporters and nonexporters. The expected value of being an exporter is denoted by Π_e; such a firm exits only when hit by a "death" shock since it has no other fixed costs after it enters.[17] Nonexporters decide to enter only when the value of exporting net of the sunk entry costs exceeds the expected value of waiting, Π_w. The investment and entry decision rule for a firm with cost c can be defined as a function of the threshold tariff $\overline{\tau}$ that makes it indifferent between entering today or waiting.

$$\Pi_e(c, \overline{\tau}) - K = \Pi_w(c, \overline{\tau}) \tag{4}$$

So, any tariff below $\overline{\tau}(c)$ triggers entry by firms with cost c or lower. To characterize the impact of uncertainty on this entry cutoff we describe the policy process and derive these value functions.

[15] This assumption is reasonable in the setting we examine empirically—a small country (Portugal) exporting to the EC—but should be relaxed in other settings. In Handley and Limão (2013), we extend this model and allow for general equilibrium effects of the policy, via impacts on the price index, in order to analyze the impact of China's entry into the WTO on its exports to the United States. Doing so introduces a price index adjustment, which attenuates the direct effects of tariff policy on entry decisions but does not overturn them.

[16] Similar qualitative results hold if we allow firms to place less weight on future profits due to an exogenous pure time preference factor.

[17] While the assumption of no per period fixed costs of exporting may seem extreme, Das, Roberts, and Tybout (2007) find these per period fixed costs are negligible, on average, across all sectors analyzed in their structural model of Colombian exporters. When we incorporate endogenous exit, the analysis is more complex but does not change the central results nor does it add much additional insight for the empirical application we pursue.

C. *Trade Policy Regimes*

We model trade policy as an exogenous stochastic process that is tractable and rich enough to span alternative trade policy regimes. Each period there is some probability γ of a policy shock (e.g., a new agreement, a new government, a macroeconomic shock, etc.). If the shock occurs, then a policymaker reconsiders the current policy and sets a new one denoted by τ', otherwise the policy is unchanged. Firms form expectations over future policies based on their belief of γ and a probability measure of tariff outcomes, $H(\tau')$, with support $\tau' \in [\tau^L, \tau^H]$, where τ^H is the worst-case scenario. We assume that both γ and H are similar across firms within a given industry V so that entry decisions depend only on a firms' productivity relative to the industry cutoff.

The stochastic path of the policy is characterized by the current tariff, τ_t, and the "policy regime" described by the pair $\{\gamma, H\}$. Firms believe that the *regime* is time-invariant and take it as given. Our results will then apply to any given exogenous γ and H and will allow us to compare equilibrium firm behavior across different regimes. This characterization encompasses alternative regimes. When $\gamma \in (0, 1)$, we have a setting with imperfectly anticipated shocks of uncertain magnitude. Alternatively, if $\gamma = 1$ and H is degenerate at some τ', then a reform is perfectly anticipated and the government credibly committed to τ' in the following period. When $\gamma = 0$, the government has committed to the current tariff, τ_t. The setup can also be used to capture staged tariff reductions—typical in trade agreements—provided that their implementation is uncertain.

D. *Value of Credible versus Noncredible Policies*

We now derive the entry decisions and the impact of policy changes within a credible regime ($\gamma = 0$) versus a noncredible one ($\gamma > 0$, so a policy change is expected).

The expected value of a firm that exports at time t conditional on it observing τ_t is given by

$$\Pi_e(c, \tau_t) = \pi(c, \tau_t) + \beta[\underbrace{(1 - \gamma)\Pi_e(c, \tau_t)}_{\text{No Shock}} + \underbrace{\gamma E \Pi_e(c, \tau')}_{\text{Shock}}], \tag{5}$$

which includes current operating profits in the *export market* and the discounted future value.[18] With probability $1 - \gamma$, there is no policy shock and the expected firm value is unchanged. With probability γ, there is a policy shock. So the third term on the right-hand side (RHS) of (5) is the ex ante expected value of exporting following a shock and E denotes the expectation over the H distribution.

[18] We do not explicitly include profits from domestic sales because in our setting they are independent of export conditions and constant over time. We can include them by adding the same constant term to the value of exporting and to the value of waiting, which will change none of the subsequent results.

The expected value of a firm waiting to export is given by

$$(6) \quad \Pi_w(c) = 0 + \beta\Big[\underbrace{(1-\gamma)\Pi_w(c)}_{\text{No Shock}} + \underbrace{\gamma(1-H(\bar{\tau}))\Pi_w(c)}_{\text{Shock above Trigger}} + \underbrace{\gamma H(\bar{\tau})(E[\Pi_e(c,\tau')|\ \tau' \leq \bar{\tau}] - K)}_{\text{Shock below Trigger}}\Big].$$

A nonexporter receives zero profits from that activity today; the continuation value stays at Π_w if there is no shock or the shock entails a tariff above the trigger. If a policy shock arrives, it will be below $\bar{\tau}$ with probability $H(\bar{\tau})$ and the firm will choose to pay K and start exporting.

To obtain the equilibrium values of exporting, $\Pi_e(c,\tau_t)$, and waiting, $\Pi_w(\tau_t)$, we solve the linear system given by (5), (6), $E\Pi_e(c,\tau')$ and $E[\Pi_e(c,\tau')\,|\ \tau' \leq \bar{\tau}]$ (given in Appendix A) and obtain

$$(7) \quad \Pi_e(c,\tau_t) = \frac{\pi(c,\tau_t)}{1-\beta(1-\gamma)} + \frac{\beta\gamma}{1-\beta}\frac{E\pi(c,\tau')}{1-\beta(1-\gamma)}$$

$$(8) \quad \Pi_w(c) = \frac{\beta\gamma H(\bar{\tau}(c))}{1-\beta(1-\gamma H\bar{\tau}(c))}\left\{\frac{E[\pi(c,\tau')|\ \tau' \leq \bar{\tau}(c)]}{1-\beta(1-\gamma)} + \frac{\beta\gamma}{1-\beta}\frac{E\pi(c,\tau')}{1-\beta(1-\gamma)} - K\right\} \quad \text{if } \tau_t \geq \bar{\tau}(c).$$

The interpretation of (7) is straightforward: after investment, the firm value from exporting conditional on τ_t equals the discounted value of expected profits. If γ were zero this would be the deterministic value. But the policy changes with probability γ and the ensuing per period expected profits are $E\pi(c,\tau')$. If the current tariff is above a given firm's trigger, $\tau_t > \bar{\tau}(c)$, then it does not export today and its value, $\Pi_w(c)$, would be zero if the tariff remained above that trigger, but with probability $\gamma H(\bar{\tau})$, the tariff will fall below the trigger leading the firm to incur K and export. The expected value of exporting is then captured by the remaining terms in brackets.

Using (7) we see that reductions in the current tariff, τ_t, increase the firm value, Π_e, at any γ. Moreover, that impact is higher under a credible policy regime ($\gamma = 0$) then when the policy is expected to change ($\gamma > 0$). This complementarity between reductions in current tariffs and uncertainty is one possible reason why countries that obtain temporary preferential tariffs spend considerable resources trying to eliminate any uncertainty about their future reversal.

E. *Policy Impacts on Investment and Entry*

We now derive the impact of different policy changes on entry. Using (7), (8), and (4) we determine the threshold tariff $\bar{\tau}(c)$ such that a firm with cost c is indifferent between waiting or exporting. Assuming $G(c)$ is strictly increasing, we can invert the threshold function $\bar{\tau}(c_t^U) = \tau_t$ to uniquely determine the cutoff cost for any given current tariff. In Appendix A, we show that c_t^U equals the product of an uncertainty factor and the deterministic cutoff

$$c_t^U = U_t \times c_t^D \tag{9}$$

$$U_t \equiv \left[\frac{1 - \beta(1 - \gamma\omega(\tau_t))}{1 - \beta(1 - \gamma)}\right]^{\frac{1}{\sigma - 1}} \leq 1. \tag{10}$$

We highlight two properties of the uncertainty factor U_t, which captures the frequency of policy shock arrivals and expectations about future tariffs. First, if $\gamma = 0$ then $U_t = 1$, and we are back to the deterministic cutoff, c_t^D. Second, if $\gamma > 0$ then there is lower entry whenever the current tariff is below the maximum, i.e., $\tau_t < \tau^{\max}$. To see this, note that when $\gamma > 0$, we obtain $c_t^U < c_t^D$ if and only if $\omega(\tau_t) < 1$. In Appendix A, we show that $\omega(\tau_t) - 1$ is the expected growth in operating profits conditional on a shock that increases tariffs, which is negative if and only if $\tau_t < \tau^{\max}$. This expected profit loss term will be central in the empirical application so we record it here:

$$\omega(\tau_t) - 1 = -(1 - H(\tau_t))\frac{\tau_t^{-\sigma} - E(\tau^{-\sigma} \mid \tau \geq \tau_t)}{\tau_t^{-\sigma}} \leq 0. \tag{11}$$

We make three observations First, because this is a proportional loss of operating profits, it is independent of a firm's productivity. Second, when tariffs are the only source of uncertainty, we can use information on the current tariff and a measure of the expectation of future tariffs *above* τ_t to construct ω. So, even though the policy shock can trigger a lower or higher tariff, it is only the possibility of higher tariffs that affects entry.[19] Third, this term varies with tariffs across different industries, which will prove useful to identify the impact of uncertainty.

We conclude this section by noting that for any $\tau_t < \tau^{\max}$ entry is monotonically decreasing over all values of γ. This has two implications for the empirical analysis. First, we can test if any given event, e.g., an agreement, impacts entry via uncertainty without assumptions on whether γ was zero before or after that event.[20] Second, if the current tariff is at the long-run mean, then reductions in γ can be interpreted as mean risk compressions of the tariff (see Appendix A). This insight will allow us to decompose the quantitative effects of moving to a more credible policy regime into two components: pure risk and long-run mean changes of the policy.[21]

[19] This is an example of the "bad news" principle first identified by Bernanke (1983).

[20] More specifically, $d\ln c_t^U/d\gamma < 0$ if $\tau_t < \tau^{\max}$ as derived in Appendix A.

[21] In online Appendix A we also show that for *any* τ_t above the minimum there exist mean preserving compressions in the H distribution that increase entry.

II. Evidence

We explore the theoretical framework to address two questions. What are the effects of current policy and uncertainty on export entry? Do trade agreements reduce uncertainty?

A. *Policy and Institutional Setting*

We focus on Portugal's accession to the European Community (EC) in 1986. One reason for doing so is that this agreement reduced some tariffs that Portuguese exports faced *and* secured preexisting preferences to the EC markets and Spain, which joined the EC in 1986.

Portugal's EC accession was signed on June 1985 and implemented on March 1, 1986. EC tariffs on Portuguese industrial goods did *not* change in 1986, they remained duty-free, as they had been since 1977. So the trade policy impact of the 1986 accession on such products will *not* be due to changes in applied tariffs. We will test if the impact of accession on those products was to make those preexisting preferences more credible, i.e., whether the accession lowered the probability that Portugal lost its EC preferences and faced the 8 percent average tariffs that other countries—those without preferential access to the EC—faced.[22]

Spain also joined the EC in 1986 and was required to liberalize its industrial tariffs against Portugal. Spanish tariffs on Portuguese goods prior to the agreement were 7.9 percent. So the impact of accession on Portuguese exports towards Spain will reflect a reduction in applied tariffs, but it will also reflect an uncertainty reduction component related to securing preexisting preferences. In 1980 Spain signed an agreement that began a partial liberalization of its tariffs towards certain countries including Portugal. But this agreement contained no definite timetable or scheduled reductions and was potentially incompatible with General Agreements on Tariff and Trade's (GATT) requirement that PTAs implement zero tariffs on substantially all trade.[23] Thus, before 1986, Portuguese exporters faced considerable uncertainty about whether they would maintain preferential access to Spain. Had they ever lost those preferences, Portuguese exports would face an average tariff of 14 percent.

B. *Macro Evidence*

Following the 1986 accession, Portugal experienced a trade boom. Between 1985 and 1992 *total* Portuguese real exports grew by 90 percent and imports by about 300 percent.[24] Figure 1 shows that the share of Portugal's trade with Spain and the EC-10 rose rapidly from 52 percent in 1985 to 72 percent by 1992. Remarkably, the

[22] The accession did reduce applied protection on agricultural goods. This is why the average preferential tariff faced by Portuguese exporters in the EC was about 2.5 percent before 1986.

[23] This uncertainty about the elimination of tariffs is clear from a GATT report where one of its members noted that Spain's agreement with the European Free Trade Association (EFTA) "provided only an expectation that at some point in time the duties and other regulations of commerce would be eliminated, but no specific provisions existed in this respect. There was a great difference between an expectation and a specific plan and schedule." "Agreement between the EFTA countries and Spain," Report of the Working Party, L/5045, October 24, 1980, p.3.

[24] Authors' calculations based on data from Pinheiro (1997).

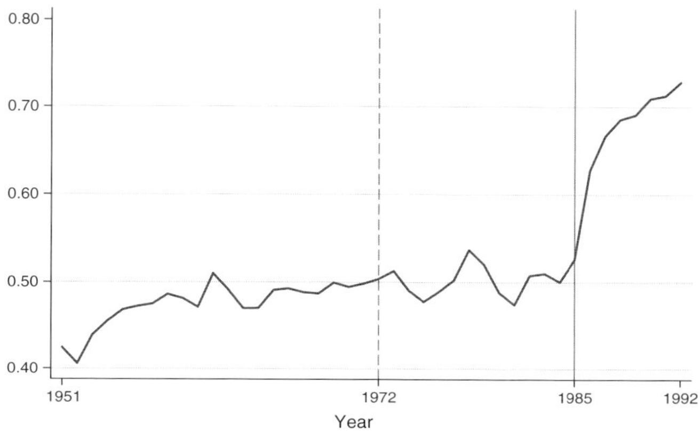

FIGURE 1. PORTUGUESE TRADE SHARES WITH EC-10 AND SPAIN

Notes: 1972: EC industrial preferences agreed. 1985: Accession signed.

initial preferential agreement between the EC-10 and Portugal (agreed in 1972 and implemented by 1977) and Spain and Portugal (early 1980s), which reduced applied tariffs, left their trade share nearly unchanged at about 50 percent between 1972 and 1985.[25] This is consistent with the model if exporters believed that those preferences could be reversed before 1986 but became confident they were secure after accession. Starting in 1981 we have access to firm-level trade data from the Portuguese census. As a first pass, we check whether the growth in Portuguese exports towards the EC-10 and Spain is also accompanied by a growth in the number of exporting firms and whether either of these can simply be explained by standard trade gravity determinants. More specifically, we test if Portuguese exports to Spain or the EC-10 grew differentially relative to the rest of the world by interacting an EC accession time dummy (= 1 for 1986 and subsequent years) with EC-10 and Spain country dummies, and control for standard determinants of trade.[26] The first column of Table 1 shows an increase of 23 log points towards the EC-10 and 115 toward Spain following the accession. In column 2 we use the (ln) number of exporting firms to each market as the dependent variable and find it was significantly higher for EC-10 and Spain after accession.

We also note that the typical new Portuguese exporter to a given market (defined as a firm exporting to a country at t but not $t-1$) is smaller than a continuing

[25] We can detect more of an effect during this period if we focus on Portuguese export shares alone, which go from 50 to 62 percent in this 13 year period. But export growth is faster after the 1986 accession, and the EC share in Portugal exports goes up to 73 percent in only seven years. The strong increase in trade shares with the EC after 1985 was not merely a switch away from exporting to other markets. There is strong evidence of trade creation: total real exports in 1993 were almost twice as high as in 1985 (Pinheiro 1997).

[26] We also include bilateral fixed effects to address PTA endogeneity following Baier and Bergstrand (2007). These reduce to importer fixed effects since the only exporter is Portugal. Year effects control for Portuguese productivity and price changes.

Table 1—Portuguese Export Growth Margins 1981–1990

Dependent variable (ln):	Exports (1)	Number of firms (2)	Exports/firm (3)
EC10 × Post_86	0.232***	0.451***	−0.219***
	[0.0829]	[0.0411]	[0.0710]
Spain × Post_86	1.146***	1.159***	−0.0129
	[0.199]	[0.132]	[0.113]
Real importer GDP (ln)	1.045***	0.598***	0.447*
	[0.306]	[0.137]	[0.258]
Importer price index (ln)	0.167**	0.0185	0.148**
	[0.0776]	[0.0374]	[0.0655]
Exchange rate (ln)	0.211***	−0.00118	0.212***
	[0.0763]	[0.0365]	[0.0653]
Observations	1,305	1,305	1,305
Adjusted R^2	0.92	0.97	0.75

Notes: Includes dummies for country and year. Robust standard errors are in brackets. The sample is aggregate values to each country of destination. Column 3 is the logarithm of total exports over number of firms. For variable definitions and sources see Appendix C. See online Appendix, Table D4 for summary statistics.

***Significant at the 1 percent level.
**Significant at the 5 percent level.
*Significant at the 10 percent level.

firm (about 6 times smaller for Spain and 20 times for the EC-10), which is consistent with our model of heterogenous firms with export entry costs. Moreover, size heterogeneity implies that *if* accession increased the number of entrants but not the average sales of continuing firms, then we should observe a reduction in average sales per firm as we do for the EC-10 in column 3 of Table 1. In the online Appendix D, we provide further evidence that a large share of the increase in the number of exporters and export volume is due to new entrants (as opposed to fewer exits), and is thus likely to have required considerable entry investments. We also find that even though individual entrants are smaller, they had a significant impact on aggregate exports in subsequent years.

C. *Micro Evidence: Empirical Approach*

The macro evidence is suggestive but by itself it does *not* allow us to determine what *caused* the accession effect, whether TPU was reduced and if so how important this was relative to any changes in applied policies. First, factors other than trade policy may have affected exports and firm entry over the long period used in the gravity estimate.[27] Therefore, to minimize the role of other confounding factors we will subsequently focus on the growth between 1985–1987, and note that even over

[27] Even in the gravity estimate, the accession effect is *not* due to two alternative explanations: monetary integration and infrastructure investments. First, the sample we use for the gravity estimate ends in 1990—two years before the signing of the Maastricht Treaty setting out the *timetable* for the Euro and nine years before the exchange rates were irrevocably fixed. Second, even if accession affected exchange rates, these effects are controlled for by including its level and its volatility (see Handley and Limão 2012). Portugal received substantial EC support for transport infrastructure, but this *funding* only began in 1989. At best it could have started to reduce trade costs in 1990 and can't explain the large prior trade increases.

this short period the net growth in the number of exporting firms was on average 25 and 91 log points toward the EC-10 and Spain, respectively. Second, to identify a causal effect and estimate the relative importance of applied policies and TPU we must explore the model predictions using firm-level data and theory-consistent policy measures that vary across countries, products and time.

Measuring Policy Uncertainty.—We construct the profit loss measure in (11) by assuming a discrete tariff distribution H. We choose a tractable distribution that covers the main cases present in our data. After a policy shock, exporters consider three potential values for the random variable, τ_i: the tariff faced in destination $i = \{\text{EC-10, Spain}\}$. The realized tariff values can (and do) vary over goods but for simplicity we omit those subscripts.

$$\tau_i = \tau_{si}, \quad \Pr(\tau_{si}) = p_{si} \text{ for } s = \{l, m, h\}$$

We take τ_{li} to be 1 for all goods and destinations, i.e., free trade. This captures the industrial goods that Portugal exported to the EC free of ad valorem tariffs both after the accession *and* before it. It also captures the lowest possible tariffs observed at any point. The high tariff, τ_{hi}, is the potential worst-case tariff that the Portuguese exporters feared if they lost preferences. In the data we assume this is the MFN rate that the EC (or Spain) applied to GATT members before 1986. Note that τ_{hi} is different for the EC and Spain before 1986, so that will be one source of variation in the uncertainty measure.[28] The intermediate tariff, τ_{mi}, captures *transitional* preferences granted to Portugal before 1986 by Spain in several types of goods and the EC-10 in agricultural goods. The latter preferences were transitional and *not* GATT legal in the absence of a permanent trade agreement. Therefore, although we did observe "medium" tariffs during the mid 1980's, the Portuguese exporters likely placed a negligible probability ($p_{mi} \approx 0$) on the event that conditional on a policy shock these would remain since either an agreement would be signed and tariffs would transition to the low state or negotiations would fail and no preferences would remain.

In online Appendix B, we show that if the tariff was initially high or medium then we can use (11) to derive

$$\omega(\tau_{ti}) - 1 = -p_{hi}\left[1 - (\tau_{ti}/\tau_{hi})^{\sigma}\right]. \tag{12}$$

The term in square brackets is the percentage profit reduction conditional on a shock that increases tariffs from τ_{ti} to τ_{hi}, which happens with probability p_{hi}. The same term applies to cases when the initial tariff is low and p_{mi} is negligible.[29] Moreover,

[28] This may somewhat underestimate the degree of uncertainty in these goods but seems a reasonable approximation of what the Portuguese exporters may have feared as the worst-case scenario before the agreement.

[29] Alternatively, if we consider only a two state world, $s = h, l$, the expression above applies to tariffs with either history. Note that the tariffs are different across markets and industries. In online Appendix B, we show that if p_m were large then there would be an *additional* term where the high probability and tariff are replaced by the medium ones. We ignore this extra term since there is no obvious empirical counterpart for the medium probability term; it would be highly correlated with the high value; and we have good reasons to believe $p_m \approx 0$ given these were transitional tariffs that could not be sustained under GATT rules.

the applied tariff may change over time but the worst-case tariff, τ_{hi}, is constant in the data over the short period of time we analyze. If there is no preferential tariff, as is the case for some goods, then the GATT rate and the applied rate are the same, $\tau_{ti} = \tau_{hi}$, and potential profit reductions are zero. In Section D we further describe how we use information on tariffs and the elasticity of substitution to construct this measure.

We cannot observe the probabilities that exporters place on a worst-case scenario, $\gamma_i p_{hi}$. However, we can estimate this as part of the entry equation, provided we assume it is roughly common across industries and countries. The similarity across countries in our application is more reasonable if we restrict our attention to i = Spain, EC-10, the markets to which Portugal secured access. One of our goals is therefore to test if there was a regime change, i.e., if the probability of reversal to the worst-case scenario, $r \equiv \gamma p_h$, fell after accession.

Unobserved Cutoffs and Firm Export Entry.—We do not directly observe if firms have costs below the cutoff but we do observe the number of firms and their export status at the country-product level. Our model focuses on variation in policies over time and across products, and the cutoffs we derived are common across some sets of firms. In particular, producers exporting to i face a tariff that does not discriminate by firm but rather by product or industry classification, denoted by V. So, in the model, producers of $v \in V$ face the *same* critical cutoff, denoted by c_{tiV}^U. Hence, we examine the fraction of exporters in an "industry" V to each country pair. This approach has another advantage: it does not require us to be able to follow specific firms over time, which is important since we are unable to do this between 1985 and 1986 (see Appendix C).

The number of firms exporting in V to market i is at least equal to the mass of domestic producers in V, n_{tV}, times the fraction of those firms with costs below the cutoff, $G_V(c_{tiV}^U)$. Therefore the observed number of firms, n_{tiV}, can be written as

$$\ln n_{tiV} = \ln G_V(c_{tiV}^U) + \ln n_{tV} + u_{tiV}, \tag{13}$$

where u_{tiV} is a random disturbance due to measurement error.[30]

Baseline Model.—We obtain an estimation equation that identifies key structural parameters as follows. We use a linear Taylor approximation of the cutoff in (9) *around* no uncertainty and use the definitions for the uncertainty factor, U, and the profit loss term, $\omega(\tau_{tiV})$, from (12). We substitute the resulting expression for c_{tiV}^U on the RHS of (13). Finally, we assume that productivity follows a Pareto distribution

[30]The term can also capture the potential for "legacy" firms: those that survive until period t even though they have costs above c_{tiV}^U. This cannot occur if current conditions are better than in the past, so a sufficient condition to rule out legacy firms is that $c_{tiV}^U \geq \max\{c_{TiV}^U \; \forall \; T < t\}$. In the mid-1980's, the conditions for Portuguese exporters were improving, as is clear from the observed high entry rates into EC countries. Therefore, we do not think legacy firms pose a significant issue in this particular setting. Furthermore, in Handley and Limão (2012) we argue that our approach and results are robust to certain instances where legacy firms are present.

with shape k and minimum value of $1/c_V$, so $G_V(c_{tiV}^U) = (c_{tiV}^U/c_V)^k$. We then obtain the following for each t, i, and V

$$\ln n_{tiV} = k\left[-r_T \frac{\beta}{1-\beta} \frac{1-(\tau_{tiV}/\tau_{hiV})^{\sigma}}{\sigma-1} - \frac{\sigma}{\sigma-1} \ln \tau_{tiV}\right] + k\left[\frac{1}{\sigma-1} \ln \frac{A_{iV}}{K_{iV}(1-\beta)} - \ln c_V\right] + \ln n_{tV} + \tilde{u}_{tiV}. \tag{14}$$

The term $r_T \equiv \gamma_T p_{Th}$ represents the probability of reversal to the worst-case tariff, and $\tilde{u}$ captures the random disturbance term and higher order terms from the cutoff's approximation. Recall that at any point in time firms treat the regime as time invariant. In the estimation we want to test if the regime changed after accession, so we include a T subscript in r_T, where $T = 0$ denotes parameter values for years pre-accession and $T = 1$ post-accession. We discuss relaxing this and some of the identifying assumptions in the robustness section.[31]

Rewriting (14) in terms of parameters and observables, we obtain

$$\ln n_{tiV} = b_{\gamma T} \tilde{\omega}_{tiV} + b_{\tau} \ln \tau_{tiV} + a_{ti} + a_{iV} + a_{tV} + \tilde{u}_{tiV} \quad \text{for each } t,\ i, V, \tag{15}$$

where $\tilde{\omega}_{tiV} \equiv \frac{1-(\tau_{tiV}/\tau_{hiV})^{\sigma}}{\sigma-1}$ captures the uncertainty measure and its impact on entry is estimated by $b_{\gamma T} = -r_T k\beta/(1-\beta)$. The coefficient on the applied tariff is $b_{\tau} = -k\sigma/(\sigma-1)$. To identify the parameters of interest we must be able to control for certain key variables in the model, which we do using various fixed effects. The a_{iV} and a_{tV} terms represent country-industry and industry-time effects that absorb the foreign demand conditions in A_{iV}, the investment cost K_{iV}, and other time invariant costs of exporting (e.g., transport or other nontariff barriers we abstracted from in the theory), the productivity distribution heterogeneity across industries c_V, and industry time-varying effects, such as the domestic mass of producers, n_{tV}. The term a_{ti} captures country-year effects that control for any unanticipated log-separable aggregate shocks, e.g., to aggregate expenditure.[32]

We estimate (15) in differences taking a period before and one after the accession.

$$\Delta_t \ln n_{tiV} = b_{\gamma 1} \tilde{\omega}_{1iV} - b_{\gamma 0} \tilde{\omega}_{0iV} + b_{\tau} \Delta_t \ln \tau_{tiV} + a_i + a_V + \Delta_t \tilde{u}_{iV} \quad \text{for each } i, V \tag{16}$$

[31] The baseline estimation relies on three assumptions to identify the effect of uncertainty: k is common across V (but c_V need not be); σ is common across V; and r is common across V and i.

[32] Recall from Section I that A_{iV} is log-separable in importer aggregate expenditure, Y_i. So any unanticipated shocks to Y_i are captured by a_{ti}. In the robustness section we also address the possibility of shocks to the price index.

We focus on $i = \{\text{EC-10, Spain}\}$ and first address two basic questions:

- Did the agreement generate more entry in industries with higher initial potential loss, $-b_{\gamma 0} > 0$?
- Did the agreement reduce the probability of a worst-case scenario: $-b_{\gamma 0} > -b_{\gamma 1}$, which implies $r_1 < r_0$; or even eliminate it: $b_{\gamma 1} = 0$, which implies exporters expect preferences not to be reversed, i.e., $r_1 = 0$?

In order to control for destination and industry shocks, our identification relies on differential tariffs and uncertainty that Portuguese exporters in each industry faced in the EC versus the Spanish market and focus on a short period: 1985–1987. Doing so required us to compile a rich dataset.

D. *Data*

To estimate (16) we collected and digitized detailed data on trade policy for Spain and the original EC-10 countries before and after the agreement, as described in online Appendix B. The uncertainty measure we compute varies across industries and members of the agreement. For some industries the policy data are *recorded* at a fine level of disaggregation, so they could potentially be matched to six-digit classifications for the trade data, which includes over 5,000 products (using the classification that preceeded the Harmonized System). We do not test the model at this disaggregated level for a few reasons. First, the model suggests that we define industries according to a set of characteristics (such as productivity distribution) that is common across a set of firms and broader than the six-digit level. Second, most of the variation in the policy in this data occurs across industries, rather than within them.[33] Third, an exporter's perception of the worst-case tariff scenario is likely to be broader than what is implied by the worst case for a *single* six-digit good, since he may either export multiple goods and/or fear tariff changes simply because they are reclassified. Thus, our measure will reflect the uncertainty of other six-digit products in the same two-digit category.[34]

We construct the profit loss uncertainty term as described in Section C, i.e., taking τ_{hi} for a six-digit product to be the ad valorem GATT tariff that country i = EC-10 or Spain, had before the agreement.[35] We take τ_{0i} to be the tariff that i actually applied to Portuguese exports in that product before the agreement, namely the preexisting preferential tariffs they provided to Portugal.[36] To construct the measure in (12), we use an elasticity consistent with the data for these countries

[33] About 80 percent of the variation in applied tariffs and 75 percent of variation in the uncertainty measure in exporting to the EC-10 before the agreement are accounted for by differences across two-digit industries (of which there are 99). Those fractions are lower for Spain but still more than half of the variation is accounted for by cross-industry differences.

[34] If we were to run the model at the six-digit level there would be a large number of zeroes. Since our estimation equation is in logs we would eventually have to drop those categories, which could be where uncertainty was most important.

[35] If that tariff was not bound in the GATT, then we use the autonomous ad valorem tariff that i applied.

[36] For the EC-10 countries there is no cross-country variation in the policy measures because they have a common trade policy. There is, however, variation in applied tariffs for the EC-10 over time and variation between the EC-10 and Spain in policy within each industry.

TABLE 2—SUMMARY STATISTICS FOR FIRM-LEVEL BASELINE REGRESSIONS

	Total	Spain	EC-10
Change in number of firms[a]	33.0	91.1	24.7
	(55.1)	(62.6)	(48.7)
Change in number of varieties[a]	35.7	101	26.4
	(60.7)	(69.1)	(53.3)
Change in exports[a]	55.3	135	43.9
	(157)	(150)	(155)
Pre-tariff[b] (faced by Portugal)	3.13	7.89	2.45
	(5.66)	(5.10)	(5.40)
Pre-tariff[b] (faced by GATT countries)	9.14	14.07	8.44
	(5.29)	(7.75)	(4.43)
Post-tariff[b] (faced by Portugal)	1.74	1.33	1.79
	(3.91)	(3.51)	(3.96)
Tariff change[b] (faced by Portugal)	−1.39	−6.56	−0.66
	(2.90)	(4.78)	(1.44)
Applied tariff standard deviation change[c]	−0.64	−2.86	−0.33
	(1.25)	(1.86)	(0.69)
Price index proxy change[c]	−0.19	−1.52	0.00
	(0.88)	(2.06)	(0.00)
NTM share change[c]	−2.32	−18.66	0.00
	(10.9)	(25.4)	(0.00)
Specific tariff share change[c]	−0.37	−3.01	0.00
	(2.80)	(7.45)	(0.00)
Proportion of profits lost if preference reversed			
Initial uncertainty (at pre-tariffs)	15.5	16.0	15.4
	(10.9)	(9.52)	(11.1)
Post uncertainty (at post-tariffs)	18.8	29.4	17.3
	(10.8)	(15.0)	(9.08)
Observations	731	91	640

Note: Sample means and standard deviations in parentheses.

[a] $100 \times \Delta\ln(x)$, where $x = \{\text{firms, varieties, exports}\}$.

[b] $100 \times \ln(1 + t)$, where t is the ad valorem rate; "Pre-tariff" is evaluated in 1985 (pre-accession); "Post-tariff" is the 1987 tariff faced by Portugal; "Tariff change" is a simple difference.

[c] See Appendix C for sources and details. Profit loss term is $1 - (\tau_{0V}/\tau_{hV})^{\sigma}$ $(\sigma = 3)$. Loss measures in regressions divided by $\sigma - 1$ to normalize.

$(\sigma = 3)$. We then aggregate the ω measure and the applied tariff by taking the simple average over all six-digit products in each two-digit industry.

Our firm level data is from the Portuguese census (INE) and we describe it in online Appendix C. The dependent variable in (16) is the log growth in the number of firms exporting to each country i in each two-digit industry. Since some firms export more than one product in a two-digit industry to some markets, one of our specifications will use this measure of varieties.

Table 2 provides summary statistics for the tariffs that Portuguese firms faced in Spain in both 1985 and 1987. The average industry in Portugal enjoyed preferential tariffs that were nearly 50 percent below the tariff Spain levied on the rest of the world. Moreover, this difference is not driven by any one set of goods or industries. Using the measure of profits lost we calculate that if Portugal lost these preferences, the typical exporter would see profits reduced by over 16 percent per annum. There

TABLE 3—FIRM-VARIETY ENTRY GROWTH INTO EC-10 AND SPAIN
(*By industry*)

	Change in (ln) number of firm varieties					
Dependent variable:	(1)	(2)	(3)	(4)	(5)	(6)
Initial uncertainty ($-b_{\gamma 0} > 0$)	4.399** [1.772]	5.626** [2.756]	4.301** [1.810]	4.431** [1.788]	4.351** [1.839]	4.752** [1.854]
Applied tariff change ($b_\tau < 0$)	−3.006** [1.260]	−4.273* [2.271]	−3.072** [1.266]	−2.919** [1.247]	−3.113** [1.291]	−3.520*** [1.260]
Post uncertainty ($b_{\gamma 1} \leq 0$)		−1.51 [3.277]				
NTM share change			−0.166 [0.256]			
Specific tariff share change				−0.579 [1.034]		
Applied tariff SD change					0.468 [4.144]	
Price index Proxy change						1.946 [2.066]
Observations	731	731	731	731	731	731
R^2	0.471	0.471	0.472	0.472	0.471	0.471
Number of parameters	101	102	102	102	102	102
AIC	1,083	1,085	1,084	1,084	1,085	1,084
BIC	1,551	1,558	1,557	1,557	1,558	1,558

Notes: Structural parameters and expected sign in parentheses below regressor names. All specifications include country and industry effects. Clustered standard errors are in brackets (industry × EC-10). The sample is Spain and EC 10 countries, 1987–1985. All regressions assume that $\sigma = 3$. AIC and BIC denote Akaike and Bayes Information Criterion. See Table 2 for summary statistics.
***Significant at the 1 percent level.
**Significant at the 5 percent level.
*Significant at the 10 percent level.

is also scope for export increases due to a reduction in Spain's applied tariffs, which stood at 8 percent before 1986. Portugal enjoyed lower preferential tariffs from the EC-10 before the agreement, but the potential loss in profits measure was high—15 percent on average. Table 2 also shows that the EC average tariff reduction was small since tariffs in industrial products were zero before accession.

E. *Baseline Estimates*

Table 3 provides estimates of the parameters in (16). Entry is negatively affected by applied tariffs, as predicted by the theory. The coefficient on the uncertainty measure, $-b_{\gamma 0}$, is positive, implying that entry was strongest in the industries that initially faced higher potential profit lost in the worst-case scenario.[37] If protection measures other than tariffs were reduced and this reduction was correlated with the uncertainty measure, then the results in column 1 would suffer from omitted variable bias. We address this by controlling for changes in "nontariff barriers" and

[37] The policy measures vary across industry and for Spain versus the EC-10. But they do not vary across the EC-10 so we cluster the standard errors to allow for arbitrary correlation across EC-10 countries within each industry.

specific tariffs in columns 3 and 4, respectively. Both have the predicted negative sign but they are insignificant. Neither affects the baseline results for uncertainty and applied ad valorem tariffs. The results are also robust to including other policy measures (in columns 5 and 6), which we discuss below.

The results thus far exclude any uncertainty measure *after* the agreement. This reflects an implicit assumption that the coefficient on that variable is insignificant, i.e., that the agreement was credible and eliminated the preference reversal, $b_{\gamma 1} = 0$. We test this hypothesis in column 2 by including the potential profit loss term evaluated at the post agreement tariffs, $\tilde{\omega}_{1iV}$. We find that this variable has no significant effect, i.e., we can't reject that $r_1 = p_{h1}\gamma_1 = 0$, nor can we reject that the probability of a reversal has fallen, i.e., $r_1 < r_0$. The insignificance of uncertainty *after* the agreement and the fact that the restricted version is preferred by standard information criteria (in the last two rows), leads us to focus on column 1 as the baseline estimates.[38]

What is the relative impact of uncertainty and applied policy changes on entry? One simple measure of this impact is how much variation in entry each of the variables explains. For the full sample, we find that a one standard deviation reduction in applied tariffs leads to a 0.14 standard deviation increase in entry compared with an increase of 0.4 for uncertainty, which is almost three times larger. Using the model structure in the next section we will go considerably beyond this in quantifying the impact of each policy and their complementarity. But before doing so we discuss additional potential threats to identification and robustness.

F. *Identification and Robustness*

The baseline estimates address several identification concerns, and we summarize the main ones here. We differenced out time invariant country-by-industry effects and explored variation over time and within industry across countries. One potential concern is preexisting growth trends in specific destination markets or industries (either European demand or Portuguese supply trends in specific industries). To ensure that any such trends do not bias our results we included industry and country effects in the baseline specification in *changes*. These industry and country effects also address other potential sources of bias.[39]

We also examine the robustness of the results along different dimensions, which we summarize here and discuss in detail in Handley and Limão (2012).

Alternative Policy Uncertainty Measure.—Suppose the relevant measure of uncertainty for exporters is different so our model is misspecified. One alternative

[38] The results that we discuss subsequently will be qualitatively unchanged if we included the post uncertainty variable. Moreover, while the magnitude of the tariff and initial uncertainty are somewhat different, their ratio is fairly similar with or without post uncertainty, and as we will see it is that ratio that is key to the quantification.

[39] First, they control for possible changes in fixed or sunk costs provided they are industry or destination market specific (e.g., accession could have lowered fixed or sunk costs of entry through streamlining of customs procedures or raised them through additional rules of origin). Second, the accession may have changed the share of intermediates used in Portugal's exports; even if this was differential across industries it would be captured by the industry effects. Third, the accession could have affected exchange rates, but this aggregate shock is addressed by the destination effects.

policy uncertainty measure is the standard deviation of the tariff faced by Portugal in each industry, i.e., $\Delta(stdev \ln \tau_{tiv})$ where $v \in V$. In column 5 of Table 3, we find this variable is insignificant and does not change the value or significance of the theoretically based uncertainty measure.

Omitted Variable Bias.—The theory allows the aggregate foreign demand shifter for any given industry to vary across countries, A_{iV}, but not over time. The model can be extended to allow for unanticipated shocks such that $A_{tiV} \equiv Y_{ti}(P_{tiV})^{\sigma-1}\mu_V(1-\rho)\rho^{\sigma-1}$. Such shocks are most plausible in the aggregate expenditure, $Y_{ti,}$ and price index terms. Our differenced estimation equation and country and industries dummies control for shocks to Y_{ti} and some of the potential shocks to P_{tiV}. Thus, we are only left with the residual variation in $\Delta \ln P_{tiV}$ at both the country *and* industry level. Portugal is small and therefore not likely to affect the price indices of destination markets. But during this period Spain liberalized against many other countries, which could have affected Spain's price index. If Spain's tariff reductions relative to the rest of the world were correlated with those it made towards Portugal then the baseline estimates would suffer from an omitted variable bias. To test this we collected additional data on changes in Spain's tariffs to the rest of the world to proxy for any residual variation in the price index.[40] In column 6 of Table 3, we find that this variable is not significant and does not change the baseline effects of either the uncertainty or applied tariff variables. The same is true if we also include all the other applied policy controls in columns 2, 3, and 4.

Agriculture.—Agricultural products are subject to more nontariff barriers than others. To some extent these are captured in the baseline by the industry effects. Moreover, including the change in one type of nontariff barrier does not affect the baseline results (column 3). If there was an unobserved change in agricultural product barriers *and* it was different across Spain and the EC-10, we would not be able to control for it. But our results are robust to dropping agricultural goods altogether.

Elasticity of Substitution.—The baseline assumes that the *typical* elasticity within any given industry V is three. This value is consistent with median estimates (across sub industries in each V) calculated using the data in Broda, Limão, and Weinstein (2008) for Spain and the other EC-10 countries. Moreover, the median elasticity across two-digit industries (i.e., across V) does not exhibit substantial variation in these countries. There are three industries with somewhat higher elasticities, so we verified the baseline results are unchanged if we drop these industries. In addition, if we instead use $\sigma = 2$ or 4 we find results similar to the baseline (Table 4).

Firm and Variety Growth.—The dependent variable in the baseline is the growth in the number of varieties in an industry to a particular destination. So a firm exporting a single good in an industry V to a market is counted as one variety, and if it

[40] No such tariff changes were made by the EC-10 against the rest of the world so this variable is zero for the EC-10.

TABLE 4—REVERSAL, ATTENUATION, AND ENTRY ESTIMATES

Value of σ =	2	3	4
Probability of reversal	0.36	0.39	0.42
(standard error)	(0.16)	(0.17)	(0.18)
Tariff elasticity attenuation factor	0.56	0.56	0.55
Entry growth, uncertainty removal (mean ω)	0.08	0.08	0.08
Entry growth, uncertainty removal (min. ω)	0.24	0.24	0.24

Notes: We use the initial uncertainty estimate from Table 3 in calculations. Probability of reversal $= \frac{\hat{b}_{\gamma 0}}{\hat{b}_{\tau}} \frac{\sigma}{\sigma - 1} \frac{1-\beta}{\beta}$ with standard error obtained using delta method ($\beta = 0.85$). Conditional on some p_h, the attenuation and theoretical uncertainty term U can be derived using regression estimates independently of β assumptions. We take p_h = (Pr. reversal)$^{0.5}$ and compute attenuation and entry growth at mean ω. The attenuation factor is the ratio of the entry elasticity to tariff changes at initial uncertainty relative to no uncertainty; see equation (24). We compute entry due to uncertainty removal as the log difference in the number of entrants at post-uncertainty versus initial uncertainty using $k \times [\ln(U_1) - \ln(U_0)]$ and assume post-uncertainty is removed, $U_1 = 1$.

exports two goods in that industry this will be counted as two. If most firms are single good or each good a firm exports entails a separate sunk cost, then this is reasonable. Otherwise we may want to measure entry by the number of firms exporting in an industry instead of varieties. In Table 2, we see a similar average growth of entry using either the variety or firm definition. Moreover, using the firm definition of entry leads to estimates very similar to those in the baseline, as we show below.

Alternative Pre-Accession Period.—The baseline results are robust to alternative definitions of the pre-accession period. We verify this by reestimating the baseline using the growth in varieties between 1987 and the *average* in three years prior to the accession (1983–1985). So the baseline results that use only 1985 as the preperiod are not driven by a "pretreatment" dip. A similar result holds if we use the firm entry definition. This will be reflected in similar reversal probabilities, as we show below.

In sum, the baseline estimates already address several identification concerns and are robust to other potential concerns.

G. *Quantification and Counterfactuals*

Since the parsimonious baseline specification in Table 3 is closest to the theory and preferred by standard information criteria, we focus on it to estimate the probability of reversal and quantify the importance of uncertainty on entry.

Policy Reversal Estimates.—The coefficients for initial uncertainty and tariffs in column 1 of Table 3 map to the following structural parameters: $-b_{\gamma 0} = r_0 k\beta/(1-\beta)$ and $b_\tau = -k\sigma/(\sigma - 1)$. So the estimated probability of reversal before the agreement is

$$\hat{r}_0 = \frac{\hat{b}_{\gamma 0}}{\hat{b}_{\tau}} \frac{\sigma}{\sigma - 1} \frac{1-\beta}{\beta}. \tag{17}$$

TABLE 5—PROBABILITY OF REVERSAL ROBUSTNESS

Sample	1987–1985		1987–pre-mean	
Dependent variable (ln), number of:	Varieties	Firms	Varieties	Firms
Value of $\sigma = 2$	0.36	0.36	0.27	0.26
3	0.39	0.39	0.29	0.28
4	0.42	0.41	0.31	0.30

Notes: We assume $\beta = 0.85$, for any other value of β, simply divide by $0.15/0.85$ and multiply by the new $(1 - \beta)/\beta$. The 1987–1985 sample uses the growth between 1987 and 1985, which is the baseline. The 1987–pre-mean sample uses the growth between 1987 and the average of the three years before the agreement: 83, 84, 85.

The first row of Table 4 shows that for the baseline estimate $\hat{r}_0 = 0.39$ when $\beta = 0.85$.[41] Even though we did not constrain this parameter, its estimate falls in the theoretically feasible range between zero and one. Moreover, its standard error allows us to reject that it is zero. Recall that $r_0 \equiv p_{h0}\gamma_0$ so the estimate indicates that exporters in 1985 believed that the policy was neither fixed, i.e., $\gamma_0 \neq 0$, nor certain to improve, i.e., $p_{h0} \neq 0$, so the reform was not fully anticipated. The reversal probability is similar if we estimate it using $\sigma = 2$ or 4 as seen in the first column of Table 5.[42]

Given that $p_h\gamma$ captures the ex ante belief of exporters, we can't definitively argue that a particular estimate is too high or low. In order to provide additional quantification, it is useful to ask what reform scenarios the estimates are compatible with and whether any seem unreasonable. The baseline reversal estimate of $p_{h0}\gamma_0 = 0.39$ is consistent with two extreme beliefs before the agreement. Either the policy shock is fully anticipated, $\gamma_0 = 1$, and preferences are lost with probability $p_{h0} = 0.39$, or preferences will surely be lost, $p_{h0} = 1$, but the timing of the policy change is uncertain and has probability $\gamma_0 = 0.39$. We can bracket our subsequent quantification using these extremes but will focus on describing the intermediate case that seems more reasonable and where $\hat{\gamma}_0 = 0.62 = \widehat{p_{h0}\gamma_0}^{0.5}$ so the policy shock was likely but not certain, i.e., $\gamma \in (0.5, 1)$.

Policy Impacts on Export Entry.—We now quantify the policy impact on entry and decompose it into three effects:

$$(18)\quad \ln\frac{n(\tau_1, r_1)}{n(\tau_0, r_0)} = \underbrace{\ln\frac{n(\tau_0, r_1)}{n(\tau_0, r_0)}}_{\text{Credibility Effect}} + \underbrace{\ln\frac{n(\tau_1, r_0)}{n(\tau_0, r_0)}}_{\text{Noncredible } \Delta\tau} + \underbrace{\left[\ln\frac{n(\tau_1, r_1)}{n(\tau_1, r_0)} - \ln\frac{n(\tau_0, r_1)}{n(\tau_0, r_0)}\right]}_{\text{Complementarity}}.$$

[41] Taking the model literally this implies an annual exogenous death shock probability of 0.15. Other authors have assumed this parameter to be 0.125 (Constantini and Melitz 2008, 24) and Portuguese annual firm exit rates from production is about 0.17 (calculated from Quadros de Pessoal), which is an upper bound for the exogenous death shock probability since it includes endogenous exit decisions. If more realistically we model firms discount factor to allow for a positive real interest rate, R, then the discount factor is $\beta = (1 - \delta)/(1 + R)$, where δ is the annual probability of death, and $\beta = 0.85$ is equivalent to alternative reasonable combinations such as using the average real interest rate for Portugal in 1983–1995, $R = 0.03$, and an annual death shock probability $\delta = 0.125$.

[42] The second column of Table 5 shows that the firm entry definition generates reversal estimates similar to those of the variety entry specifications for each σ.

TABLE 6—ENTRY COUNTERFACTUALS AND QUANTIFICATION

	Total	Spain	EC
Predicted entry effect of tariff and uncertainty reductions	0.12	0.28	0.10
Share of predicted effect due to:			
Uncertainty removal (at initial tariffs)	0.65	0.28	0.80
Tariff reduction (at initial uncertainty)	0.19	0.40	0.11
Complementarity	0.16	0.32	0.09
Share of predicted entry probability explained by policy	0.61	0.33	1.03

Notes: We use the initial uncertainty estimate from Table 3 in calculations (but results are similar if $\sigma = 2, 4$). Predicted average entry probability is the sum tariffs reductions, $b_\tau \Delta \ln \tau$, and removal of uncertainty at initial tariffs. See Appendix B for further details. Entry growth from uncertainty removal is the log difference in the number of entrants at post-uncertainty versus initial uncertainty using $k \times [\ln(U_1) - \ln(U_0)]$ (we assume post-uncertainty is removed, $U_1 = 1$). Counterfactual shares of predicted entry hold initial tariffs and uncertainty fixed, respectively. The complementarity share captures the remaining entry growth from simultaneously reducing tariffs and uncertainty. The share of predicted entry probability explained by policy is the ratio of policy predictions relative to the one observed in the data.

The *credibility* effect measures the growth in entry from eliminating policy uncertainty at the initial tariffs; so it captures the effect from making prior tariff concessions by the EC and Spain permanent. The second term measures growth from a counterfactual noncredible agreement that reduced tariffs to τ_1 but left the initial regime unchanged. The complementarity terms measures the effect of tariff reductions made credible in the agreement.

Table 6 shows that noncredible tariff changes have relatively small effects on entry (for computation details see Appendix A). Overall, the tariff policy impacts led to an increase in entry of 12 log points. Credibility accounts for 65 percent and complementarity for 16 percent of the policy impacts. Therefore, if tariffs had been reduced in a noncredible way (i.e., leaving initial uncertainty unchanged) entry would have grown by only about 2.3 log points.[43]

Our structural estimates also allow us to determine what fraction of the credibility effect can be attributed to a pure reduction in risk. To do so we rewrite the credibility effect as follows

$$\text{(19)} \quad \underbrace{\ln \frac{n(\tau_0, r_1)}{n(\tau_0, r_0)}}_{\text{Credibility Effect}} = \underbrace{\ln \frac{n(E(\tau'), r_1)}{n(E(\tau'), r_0)}}_{\text{Pure Risk Reduction}} + \left[\ln \frac{n(\tau_0, r_1)}{n(E(\tau'), r_1)} - \ln \frac{n(\tau_0, r_0)}{n(E(\tau'), r_0)} \right].$$

The first term is the growth in entry due to credibly setting tariffs permanently at their long-run mean, $E(\tau')$, so it represents a mean preserving compression in tariffs, as argued in the theory section. If the initial tariff was at the long-run mean, i.e., $\tau_0 = E(\tau')$, then all of the credibility effect would be accounted for by risk reduction. If the initial tariffs are below the long-run mean, as is the case here, then the agreement will have an additional effect of locking in lower mean tariffs. The

[43] These results are for the overall sample. In the remaining columns we see that a noncredible tariff reduction would have generated only about 40 percent of the predicted entry for Spain and 11 percent for the EC.

TABLE 7—CREDIBILITY EFFECT FROM SECURING PREEXISTING REFORMS

	Total	Spain	EC
Entry growth:			
Total effect (ln points)	8.4	8.6	8.3
Share from risk reduction (at long-run mean)	0.57	0.83	0.53
Export growth:			
Total effect (ln points)	21.2	21.8	21.1
Share from risk reduction (at long-run mean)	0.50	0.73	0.47

Notes: Calculations use an initial uncertainty estimate from the entry or total export regressions where $\sigma = 3$ and the probability of reversal is estimated at $r_0 = 0.39$ and $r_0 = 0.45$, respectively. Total growth from uncertainty removal is the log difference in entry or exports at post versus initial uncertainty using k or $(k - \sigma + 1)$ times $[\ln(U_1) - \ln(U_0)]$ evaluated at the preperiod applied (τ_0) and GATT tariff (τ_h) means from Table 2 (we assume post-uncertainty is removed, $U_1 = 1$). The counterfactual shares from risk reduction evaluate $\ln(U_0)$ while holding applied tariffs at $\tau_0 = E(\tau)$ to obtain a mean preserving compression of the tariff distribution. We compute $E(\tau)$ from our estimates of $\gamma_0 p_h$ (results are similar if $\sigma = 2, 4$).

latter effect is captured by the term in brackets and is positive because more permanent reductions in tariffs relative to the mean—the first term in brackets—have larger effect on entry than temporary ones (the second term).[44] In Table 7, we see that the credibility effect is about 8 log points and 57 percent of that is due to a pure risk reduction. For the EC, where most tariffs were already at zero, the pure risk reduction still accounted for more than half of the credibility effect; for Spain, where initial tariffs were closer to the estimated mean, it accounted for 83 percent.

One final point regarding quantification is the fraction of entry *observed* in the data that the trade policy changes implied by the theory predict. As we see in Table 2, varieties increased by 36 log points in this period so the model accounts for about one-third of this. There was a substantial increase in the number of Portuguese producers in this period, 16 log points between 1985–1987 (authors calculations from Quadros de Pessoal). Recall that this is exogenous in our model. Thus, we can also ask what is the share of predicted entry probability explained by policy, $\Delta \ln(n_{iV}/n_V)$; we show in Table 6 that trade policy changes explain 61 percent of this value.[45]

Policy Impacts on Export Value.—Our focus thus far has been on entry but we can also employ our framework to analyze export values.[46] Industry V exports to country i are given by $R_{tiV} = n_{tV} G(c^U_{tiV}) \times \overline{R}_{tiV}$, where $\overline{R}_{tiV}$ is the average over firm sales in equation (1). Using the equilibrium cutoff, c^U_{tiV}, we obtain a gravity equation at the industry level, which we estimate in first differences—between 1987 and 1985—as done for entry.

[44] We estimate the pure risk reduction component using the credibility effect formula (25) in Appendix A, evaluated at $E(\tau'_{iV}) \approx (1 - \hat{p}_{h0})\tau_{liV} + \hat{p}_{h0}\tau_{hiV}$. We employ the assumptions about the tariff process described in Section C (namely $\tau_l = 1$ and $p_m \approx 0$).

[45] The model explains almost all of this increase in the data for the EC and one-third in Spain indicating that for the latter other factors were also important, e.g., Spain's high income growth.

[46] Understanding the determinants of the extensive margin is important for several reasons. First, the extensive margin may dominate the response of trade flows to reductions in trade barriers (Chaney 2008). Second, conditional on survival, small export market entrants grow over time and make up a significant fraction of export growth, as we show is the case for Portugal in online Appendix D.

Table 8—Total Exports Counterfactuals and Quantification

	Total	Spain	EC
Predicted export effect of tariff and uncertainty reductions	0.34	0.85	0.26
Share of predicted total exports due to:			
Uncertainty removal (at initial tariffs)	0.59	0.23	0.75
Tariff reduction (at initial uncertainty)	0.28	0.53	0.17
Complementarity	0.13	0.24	0.08
Share of predicted total exports explained by policy	0.87	0.72	0.96

Notes: Calculations use an initial uncertainty estimate from the total export regression where $\sigma = 3$ and the probability of reversal is estimated at 0.45; see Appendix B for details (results are similar if $\sigma = 2, 4$). Average predicted total exports are the sum of the tariff reduction, $B_\tau \Delta \ln \tau$, and the effect of uncertainty removal at initial tariffs. Total export growth from uncertainty removal is the log difference in exports at post-uncertainty versus initial uncertainty using $(k - \sigma + 1) \times [\ln(U_1) - \ln(U_0)]$ (we assume post-uncertainty is removed, $U_1 = 1$). Counterfactual shares of predicted exports hold initial tariffs and uncertainty fixed, respectively. The complementarity share captures the remaining export value growth from simultaneously reducing tariffs and uncertainty. The share of total export growth explained by policy is the ratio of policy predictions relative to exports observed in the data net of the aggregate growth in number of Portuguese firms.

$$\Delta_t \ln R_{tiV} = B_{\gamma 1}\tilde{\omega}_{1iV} - B_{\gamma 0}\tilde{\omega}_{0iV} + B_\tau \Delta_t \ln \tau_{tiV} + a_i + a_V + \Delta_t \tilde{u}_{iV} \quad \text{for each } i, V \tag{20}$$

In Appendix B, we derive this interpretation for the coefficients: $B_{\gamma t} = -r_t \frac{\beta}{1-\beta}\left(k - (\sigma - 1)\right)$ and $B_\tau = -\frac{k\sigma}{\sigma - 1}$. The estimation confirms the entry results. Both policy variables have the expected sign and are statistically significant; moreover, uncertainty has no effect *after* the agreement. The exact parameter estimates for $B_{\gamma t}$ and B_τ themselves are not as interesting as the quantification exercises that they allow us to perform, so we focus on the latter. We derive the implied probability of reversal when $\sigma = 3$ to be $\hat{r}_0 = 0.45$—statistically identical to the estimate obtained using the entry equation. We then use this reversal estimate, assuming $\gamma = \sqrt{0.45}$, and the structure of the model to predict the impact of policy on exports.

Tables 7 and 8 quantify and decompose the policy impacts analogously to what we did for entry (see Appendix B for computation details). The total predicted export growth due to policy is given by the sum of the uncertainty removal at initial tariffs, $\ln\left[R_{iV}(r_1)/R_{iV}(r_0)\right]$, and the tariff reduction in the absence of uncertainty. This sum is 34 log points for the EC and Spain combined and accounts for 87 percent of the export growth in 1985–1987 (net of the increase in the number of portuguese firms, last row of Table 8).[47] The first column of Table 8 shows that credibility accounts for 59 percent of the predicted 34 log points, which is a large effect. To

[47] In Table 2 we see the average export growth is 55 log points, so if we net out 16 log points (the growth in the mass of Portuguese firms, which is exogenous in the model) we obtain 39 log points. The predicted export growth is higher than the growth due to entry, suggesting that the policy changes also affected average exports. Such an effect would arise naturally if firms could make technology upgrading or capacity building investments after entry. Such upgrading is likely given the large increase in export values for existing firms, that we derived previously. Handley and Limão (2013) extend this model to allow for technology upgrading and show that in this case there is an additional effect of reducing uncertainty on export values.

see this, notice that Portugal's exports to the EC-10 and Spain were 14.7 percent of its gross domestic product (GDP) in 1987 but would have only been 11.5 percent if uncertainty had remained at its 1985 level. We also calculate that about half of the credibility effect is attributable to a pure-risk reduction (Table 7, column 1).

One final point to note is that if the agreement had taken the form of a noncredible tariff reduction it would have increased exports by less than ten log points overall. The effect is weaker for the EC-10 (because its tariffs were already low) than for Spain. But even a noncredible reduction in Spain's high tariffs would have only lead to about half of the predicted growth to that market because Portuguese exporters would not have entered as strongly.[48] This contrast in the sources of growth of exports provides another interesting motive to consider both the EC-10 and Spanish case since some recent PTAs may look more like the EC-10 case (e.g., Colombia securing preexisting preferences received in the US market) and others like Spain's (e.g., Korea obtaining US tariff reductions and securing them).

III. Conclusion

Credibility is an important component of a policy reform; our approach and results show it is possible to measure and quantify the impact of trade policy credibility on firm investment and export decisions. The model delivers clear predictions for how to empirically compute policy uncertainty and estimate its impact. Applying our framework to a particular type of trade agreement we find that, before accession to the EC, Portuguese exporters believed there was a positive probability of losing preexisting preferences in the EC and Spanish markets, but the 1986 accession eliminated this TPU; the overall trade policy changes account for a considerable share of firm entry and export value in the data; and if the agreement had only reduced the applied tariffs, but not TPU, it would have achieved only 20 percent of the total predicted growth for entry and less than 30 percent for total exports. So a substantial fraction of the growth was generated by the elimination of TPU. Moreover, about 65 percent of the growth in entry is due to securing previous tariff reductions, and more than half of this is attributable to a mean preserving reduction in risk.

These results have several implications. First, they point to one reason why unilateral preferences provided to developing countries by the United States and European Union are not always successful in promoting trade and investment—they are subject to uncertain renewal—and this may change if those preferences are secured through formal PTAs. Second, ex post analysis of PTAs often find large trade effects even if applied policies are low. From this it is often inferred that either those applied policies are correlated with other unmeasured but *applied* trade costs that were also reduced, or that their trade elasticity is very high. Our results suggest an alternative explanation: the reduction of TPU. This uncertainty may also help explain the border puzzle: why trade across an international border is considerably smaller than within a country even when trade costs appear similar.

[48] The tariff elasticity of exports values under uncertainty is 0.69 of its deterministic counterpart (see Appendix B).

Our framework can be extended and address other important questions. Interesting extensions include the effects of TPU on pricing (under variable markups) and the intensive margin (via technology upgrading). Handley and Limão (2013) incorporate technology upgrading in a two-country model to identify and quantify the role of the US threat to impose Smoot-Hawley tariffs on China.[49]

Appendix

A. Theory Appendix

Value Function Solution.—To obtain the equilibrium values of exporting, $\Pi_e(c, \tau_t)$, and waiting, $\Pi_w(\tau_t)$ in (7) and (8) we solve the linear system given by (5), (6) and the following two equations

$$E\Pi_e(c,\tau') = E\pi(c,\tau') + \beta E\Pi_e(c,\tau')$$

$$E[\Pi_e(c,\tau')\,|\,\tau' \le \bar{\tau}] = E[\pi(c,\tau')\mid \tau' \le \bar{\tau}] + \beta[(1-\gamma)E[\Pi_e(c,\tau')\mid \tau' \le \bar{\tau}] + \gamma E\Pi_e(c,\tau')].$$

Cutoff Expression (c_t^U).—We use (7), (8), and (4) to solve for c_t^U as a function of the current tariff

$$c_t^U = \left\{\frac{A}{K}\left[\frac{\tau_t^{-\sigma}}{1-\beta(1-\gamma)} + \frac{\beta\gamma E(\tau^{-\sigma})}{(1-\beta)[1-\beta(1-\gamma)]} + \frac{\beta\gamma H(\tau_t)[\tau_t^{-\sigma} - E(\tau^{-\sigma}\mid \tau \le \tau_t)]}{(1-\beta)[1-\beta(1-\gamma)]}\right]\right\}^{\frac{1}{\sigma-1}}. \tag{21}$$

Using this and the definition below for $\omega(\tau_t)$, we obtain (9) in the text.

Profit Loss Expression and Bound.— $(\omega(\tau_t) \le 1)$

$$\begin{aligned}\omega(\tau_t) &\equiv \{E(\tau^{-\sigma}) + H(\tau_t)[\tau_t^{-\sigma} - E(\tau^{-\sigma}\mid\tau\le\tau_t)]\}/\tau_t^{-\sigma}\\ &= [H(\tau_t)E(\tau^{-\sigma}\mid\tau\le\tau_t) + (1-H(\tau_t))E(\tau^{-\sigma}\mid\tau\ge\tau_t) + H(\tau_t)\tau_t^{-\sigma}\\ &\quad - H(\tau_t)E(\tau^{-\sigma}\mid\tau\le\tau_t)]/\tau_t^{-\sigma}\\ &= [(1-H(\tau_t))E(\tau^{-\sigma}\mid\tau\ge\tau_t) + H(\tau_t)\tau_t^{-\sigma}]/\tau_t^{-\sigma} \le 1,\end{aligned}$$

[49] Another interesting extension is to examine the interaction of uncertainty between trade policy and demand conditions, to analyze the role of TPU during the great trade collapse (Carballo, Handley, and Limão 2014).

where the last inequality follows from $(1 - H(\tau_t))E(\tau^{-\sigma} \mid \tau \geq \tau_t) + H(\tau_t)\tau_t^{-\sigma} \leq \tau_t^{-\sigma}$, and the fact that the LHS is a weighted average of two terms, one equal to $\tau_t^{-\sigma}$ and the other equal to $E(\tau^{-\sigma} \mid \tau > \tau_t)$, which is less than $\tau_t^{-\sigma}$. When the current tariff is at the maximum of the support of $H(\tau)$ such that $\tau_t = \tau_h$, then the difference in brackets and the term $(1 - H(\tau_t))$ are both zero.

Entry Monotonically Decreasing in γ.—To show this we simply take the derivative of (21) to obtain

$$-\frac{d \ln c_t^U}{d\gamma}\bigg|_{\tau_t} = -\frac{\beta}{1 - \beta(1-\gamma)} \frac{1-\beta}{1-\beta(1-\gamma\omega(\tau_t))} \frac{\omega(\tau_t) - 1}{\sigma - 1} \geq 0, \tag{22}$$

which is nonnegative given $\omega(\tau_t) \leq 1$.

Equivalence of γ Increase and Mean Preserving Spread if $\tau_t = E(\tau')$.—In Section IE we note that if $\tau_t = E(\tau')$ then increases in γ induce a mean preserving *spread* of the tariff, so they correspond to a pure increase in risk. To see this, denote the tariff distribution conditional on the current tariff and policy regime by $F(\tau_{t+1} | \tau_t, \gamma)$, and note that if $\tau_t = E(\tau')$, then $E_t(\tau_{t+n} | \tau_t) = E(\tau')$ for any γ since $E_t(\tau_{t+n} | \tau_t) = (1-\gamma)^n \tau_t + (1 - (1-\gamma)^n) E(\tau')$. So changes in γ leave any n period ahead mean unchanged. To show the mean preserving spread result of increasing γ, we derive $F(\tau_{t+1} | \tau_t, \gamma)$ as a function of the current tariff τ_t and the unconditional distribution $H(\tau)$, after a shock γ, as follows

$$F(\tau_{t+1} | \tau_t, \gamma) = \Pr(\tau_{t+1} < \tau) = \begin{cases} \gamma H(\tau) \text{ if } \tau < \tau_t \\ 1 - \gamma + \gamma H(\tau) \text{ if } \tau \geq \tau_t \end{cases}.$$

When $\tau_t = E(\tau')$ $(\equiv \int_{\tau_l}^{\tau_h} \tau dH(\tau))$ then an increase in γ to γ^{hi} induces a new distribution $F(\tau_{t+1} | \tau_t, \gamma^{hi})$ with the same mean, as shown above. We now show that $\int_{\tau_l}^{\tau} F(\tau_{t+1} | \tau_t, \gamma^{hi})\, d\tau \geq \int_{\tau_l}^{\tau} F(\tau_{t+1} | \tau_t, \gamma)\, d\tau$ for any $\tau \leq \tau_h$ so $F(\tau_{t+1} | \tau_t, \gamma)$ second order stochastically dominates $F(\tau_{t+1} | \tau_t, \gamma^{hi})$. This clearly holds when $\tau < \tau_t$ since $\int_{\tau_l}^{\tau} \gamma^{hi} H(\tau) d\tau \geq \int_{\tau_l}^{\tau} \gamma H(\tau) d\tau$. To prove the condition, for $\tau \geq \tau_t$ we note that $\int_{\tau_l}^{\tau} F(\tau_{t+1} | \tau_t, \gamma)\, d\tau = (1-\gamma)[\tau - \tau_l] + \int_{\tau_l}^{\tau} \gamma H(\tau) d\tau$ is increasing in γ when $\tau_\tau = E(\tau')$

$$\begin{aligned} \frac{\partial}{\partial \gamma}\left[\int_{\tau_l}^{\tau} F(\tau_{t+1} | \tau_t, \gamma)\, d\tau\right] &= -[\tau - E(\tau')] + \int_{\tau_l}^{\tau} H(x) d\tau \\ &= -\tau + E(\tau') + [H(\tau)\tau - H(\tau_l)\tau_l] - \int_{\tau_l}^{\tau} \tau dH(x) \\ &= -\tau(1 - H(\tau)) + E(\tau') - H(\tau_l)\tau_l \\ &\quad - (H(\tau) - H(\tau_l))E(\tau_{t+1} \mid \tau_l < \tau_{t+1} < \tau) \\ &= (1 - H(\tau))[E(\tau_{t+1} \mid \tau_{t+1} > \tau) - \tau] \geq 0. \end{aligned}$$

The second line uses integration by parts. The third simplifies and uses the definition of conditional mean. The last line follows by writing the unconditional mean as a weighted average of the conditional means $E(\tau') = H(\tau_l)\tau_l + (H(\tau) - H(\tau_l)) \times E(\tau_{t+1} \mid \tau_l < \tau_{t+1} < \tau) + (1 - H(\tau))(E(\tau_{t+1} \mid \tau_{t+1} > \tau)$, where we allow for H to be continuous or discrete at the end points, and canceling terms.

Current Tariff Impact on Profit Loss ($d\omega(\tau_t)/d\tau_t \geq 0$).—As τ_t increases, the profit lost from being hit with a shock to a higher tariff is reduced so $\frac{d\omega_t}{d\tau_t} > 0$

$$\begin{aligned}
\frac{d\omega(\tau_t)}{d\tau_t} &= \left[-\tau_t^{-\sigma}h(\tau_t) + h(\tau_t)\tau_t^{-\sigma} - \sigma H(\tau_t)\tau_t^{-\sigma-1}\right]/\tau_t^{-\sigma} \\
&\quad + [(1 - H(\tau_t))E(\tau^{-\sigma} \mid \tau \geq \tau_t) + H(\tau_t)\tau_t^{-\sigma}](\sigma\tau^{\sigma-1}) \\
&= \left[-\sigma H(\tau_t)\tau_t^{-1}\right] + \sigma\tau^{\sigma-1}[(1 - H(\tau_t))E(\tau^{-\sigma} \mid \tau \geq \tau_t) + H(\tau_t)\tau_t^{-\sigma}] \\
&= \sigma\tau^{\sigma-1}[-H(\tau_t)\tau_t^{-\sigma} + (1 - H(\tau_t))E(\tau^{-\sigma} \mid \tau \geq \tau_t) + H(\tau_t)\tau_t^{-\sigma}] \\
&= \sigma[(1 - H(\tau_t))E(\tau^{-\sigma} \mid \tau \geq \tau_t)]/\tau^{1-\sigma} \geq 0.
\end{aligned}$$

In semi-elasticity terms, this becomes

$$\frac{d\omega(\tau_t)}{d\ln\tau_t} = \frac{\sigma[(1 - H(\tau_t))E(\tau^{-\sigma} \mid \tau \geq \tau_t)]}{\tau^{-\sigma}} \in [0, \sigma]. \tag{23}$$

This implies that as the current tariff τ_t increases, the proportional gap between the deterministic and uncertain cutoff narrows. We can see that if $\tau_t = \tau_h$, the derivative goes to zero. Then $\frac{d\ln c_t^U}{d\ln\tau_t} = -\frac{\sigma}{\sigma - 1}$, and the elasticity of the cutoff under uncertainty evaluated at the tariff maximum equals the elasticity at the deterministic cutoff.

Attenuated Tariff Impact on Entry under Uncertainty.—$\frac{d\ln c_t^U}{d\ln\tau_t} / \frac{d\ln c_t^D}{d\ln\tau_t} \in [0, 1]$ Using the expression for c_t^U from the text, we log differentiate and derive

$$\begin{aligned}
\frac{d\ln c_t^U}{d\ln\tau_t} &= \frac{d\ln c_t^D}{d\ln\tau_t} + \frac{d\ln U_t}{d\ln\tau_t} \\
\frac{d\ln c_t^U}{d\ln\tau_t} &= -\frac{\sigma}{\sigma - 1} + \frac{1}{\sigma - 1}\frac{\beta\gamma}{1 - \beta(1 - \gamma\omega)}\frac{d\omega_t}{d\ln\tau_t} \\
\frac{d\ln c_t^U}{d\ln\tau_t} / \frac{d\ln c_t^D}{d\ln\tau_t} &= 1 - \frac{\beta\gamma}{1 - \beta(1 - \gamma\omega)}\frac{d\omega_t}{d\ln\tau_t}\frac{1}{\sigma}
\end{aligned} \tag{24}$$

As we show in (23) $\frac{d\omega_t}{d\ln\tau_t}\frac{1}{\sigma} \in [0, 1]$, so entry is less responsive to tariff changes under uncertainty except at the two limiting cases when $\gamma = 0$ (deterministic τ) and when τ_t is at the maximum.

B. *Estimation and Quantification*

In this Appendix, we describe how to implement the decomposition of the policy effects in Tables 6, 7, and 8 and derive the estimating equation for total exports presented in the text.

Decomposing and Quantifying the Policy Impacts on Entry.—To estimate the average credibility effect component of equation (18), we use the relationship between n and the cutoff in (13) and the equilibrium cutoff in (9) to obtain

$$\text{(25)} \qquad \ln\frac{n(\tau_{0iV}, r_1)}{n(\tau_{0iV}, r_0)} = k\left[\ln U(\tau_{0iV}, r_1) - \ln U(\tau_{0iV}, r_0)\right]$$

$$= -\frac{k}{\sigma - 1}\ln\left[\frac{1 - \beta(1 - \gamma_0\omega(\tau_{0iV}))}{1 - \beta(1 - \gamma_0)}\right],$$

where the second line uses $U(\tau_{0iV}, r_1 = 0) = 1$, as suggested by the baseline estimates. The expression in brackets can be rewritten in terms of the estimated parameters, $-b_{\gamma 0}$ and b_τ, the data $\tilde{\omega}_{0iV}$ and a given γ, such as $\hat{\gamma}_0 = 0.62$, which we can then average over the observations. Doing so, we obtain the credibility effect of about 8 log points in Table 4. Given there were about 40,428 country × (firm-product) pairs in total in the sample this predicts an additional 3,167 pairs by 1987.

We also compute the counterfactual effect of a noncredible agreement that reduced only applied tariffs. First, because τ also affects the uncertainty term, U, we must determine how attenuated the entry elasticity is under uncertainty relative to no uncertainty, i.e., $\frac{d\ln n(\tau_0, r_0)}{d\ln\tau}\Big/\frac{d\ln n(\tau_0, r = 0)}{d\ln\tau}$. From (13) we see that this is equal to the ratio of the cutoff elasticities, $\frac{d\ln c^U}{d\ln\tau}\Big/\frac{d\ln c^D}{d\ln\tau}$, in equation (24) derived above. Using the definition of ω in (12), in (24) we obtain $\frac{d\omega_0}{d\ln\tau}\frac{1}{\sigma} = p_{h0}\left(\frac{\tau_{0iV}}{\tau_{hVi}}\right)^{\sigma}$, which we combine with estimated parameters and data. In Table 4, we show that this factor is 0.56, so under the initial uncertainty the same tariff reductions would have generated only about half as much entry than if uncertainty was absent (so only slightly over two log points overall, 1 for EC and 11 for Spain).[50]

The impact of applied policy on entry in the absence of uncertainty, the term $\ln\frac{n(\tau_1, r_1)}{n(\tau_0, r_1)}$ in (18), is given by multiplying the deterministic entry elasticity, b_τ, and

[50] The result is not sensitive to the choice of σ. The magnitude of the attenuation does depend on how much of the reversal, $p\gamma$, is due to the arrival shock. The effect is bounded by the extremes: if the arrival shock is very likely ($\gamma = 1$), the attenuation is 0.71, if it is unlikely ($\gamma = 0.39$), then the attenuation is 0.35.

the change in applied tariffs. This yields an overall entry growth of about 4 log points (2 for the EC-10 and 20 for Spain since the latter had larger tariff reductions). Therefore the total predicted entry due to removal of applied tariffs and uncertainty is about 12 log points (4+8), slightly lower for EC-10 (10) and higher for Spain (28), as we report in Table 5.

Aggregation to Industry Exports.—The total export value to a given country in an industry V is

$$R_{tiV} = \left[n_{tV}G_V\left(c_{tiV}^U\right)\right] \times \overline{R}_{tiV}, \tag{26}$$

where average sales $\overline{R}_{tiV} \equiv A_{iV}\sigma\tau_{tiV}^{-\sigma}\tilde{c}$ are obtained by averaging (1) over all exporting firms and when $G_V\left(c_{tiV}^U\right) = \left(c_{tiV}^U/c_V\right)^k$, we have $\tilde{c} = \frac{k}{k-(\sigma-1)}\left(c_{tiV}^U\right)^{1-\sigma}$. Using the cutoff expression and simplifying we obtain

$$\begin{aligned}\ln R_{tiV} &= (k-\sigma+1)\ln c_{tiV}^U - k\ln c_V + \ln n_{tV} + \ln\frac{k}{k-(\sigma-1)} - \sigma\ln\tau_{tiV} \\ &\quad + \ln A_{iV} + \ln\sigma \\ &= \frac{k-\sigma+1}{\sigma-1}\ln\left[\frac{1-\beta(1-\gamma\omega(\tau_{tiv}))}{1-\beta(1-\gamma)}\right] - \frac{k\sigma}{\sigma-1}\ln\tau_{tiV} + \alpha_{tiV},\end{aligned} \tag{27}$$

where $\alpha_{tiV} = \frac{k-\sigma+1}{\sigma-1}\ln\frac{A_{iV}}{K_{iV}(1-\beta)} + \ln n_{tV} - k\ln c_V + \ln\frac{k}{k-(\sigma-1)} + \ln A_{iV} + \ln\sigma$. We take a first order approximation of the uncertainty term around $\gamma = 0$ and substitute that and the constructed measure $\tilde{\omega}_{tiV}$ in (27) to obtain

$$\ln R_{tiV} = B_{\gamma T}\tilde{\omega}_{tiV} + B_\tau \ln\tau_{tiV} + a_{ti} + a_{iV} + a_{tV} + \tilde{u}_{tiV} \qquad \text{for each } t,\ i,\ V \tag{28}$$

where $B_{\gamma T} = -r_T\frac{\beta}{1-\beta}(k-(\sigma-1))$, $B_\tau = -\frac{k\sigma}{\sigma-1}$ and the a_x terms capture all the terms in α_{tiV} defined above. If we then difference this equation, we obtain (20).

Decomposing and Quantifying the Policy Impacts on Industry Exports.—The impact of removing uncertainty at initial tariffs on exports used in Table 7 is

$$\ln R_{tiV}|_{\gamma_1} - \ln R_{tiV}|_{\gamma_0} = -\frac{k-\sigma+1}{\sigma-1}\ln\left[\frac{1-\beta(1-\gamma_0\omega(\tau_{0iV}))}{1-\beta(1-\gamma_0)}\right]. \tag{29}$$

The total impact of applied tariff changes under uncertainty is

$$\frac{\partial\ln R}{\partial\ln\tau} = -\frac{k\sigma}{\sigma-1}\left[1-\frac{k-\sigma+1}{k}\frac{\beta\gamma}{1-\beta(1-\gamma\omega)}\frac{\partial\omega_t}{\partial\ln\tau_t}\frac{1}{\sigma}\right]. \tag{30}$$

The leading term is the full elasticity of total exports to tariff changes and the term in brackets is the attenuation factor, which is equal to $\frac{\partial\ln R}{\partial\ln\tau}|_{\gamma_0>0}/\frac{\partial\ln R}{\partial\ln\tau}|_{\gamma_1=0}$, and is reported in Table 8. As above for the entry equation, we can compute the attenuation factor from estimated parameters of the export equation and data. We compute the effect of the tariff reduction at initial uncertainty in Table 8 by multiplying the attenuation factor by the change in tariffs, as if uncertainty remained high.

C. *Data Appendix*

Data Appendix Table

Variable	Description	Source
Aggregate regressions (Table 1, 1981–1990):		
Exports (ln)	Nominal value of exports in euro of all goods to country i in year t	a
Number of firms exporting (ln)	Number of uniquely identified shippers with positive exports to i in year t	a
Exports per firm (ln)	ln (Exports$_{it}$/Number of firms$_{it}$)	a
Real importer GDP (ln)	Country i, year t in billions of importer currency	b
Importer price index (ln)	ln (nominal GDP) − ln (real GDP) in local currency	b
Annual exchange rate	Simple average of ln monthly rate, where latter is defined as ln ((escudo/importer currency)/200.482). The fixed conversion factor from escudo to euro is 200.482 and plays no role in the regressions	b
Firm and policy data in estimates of Tables 2–8:		
Change in number of firms(ln)	ln (number firms exporting to i in V, 1987) − ln (number firms exporting to i in V, 1985) where i is an EC-11 country and V corresponds to a NIMEXE 2-digit industry	a
Change in number of firm-varieties(ln)	ln (number varieties exported to i in V, 1987) − ln (number varieties exported to i in V, 1985), "varieties" defined as distinct 8-digit NIMEXE products exported by each firm	a
Change in exports(ln)	ln (export value to i in V, 1987) − ln (export value to i in V, 1985)	a
Pre-tariff (GATT)	ln τ where τ is 1 + ad valorem rate at product level that GATT members faced in Spain or EC-10, which is then averaged to NIMEXE 2-digit industry	c,d
Pre-tariff (Portugal)	ln τ where τ is 1 + ad valorem rate at product level Portugal faced in Spain or EC-10, which is then averaged to NIMEXE 2-digit industry	c,d
Post-tariff (Portugal)	ln τ for immediate post-agreement period that Portugal faced in Spain or EC-10, constructed as described in previous section	c,d
Applied tariff standard deviation change	Δstd (ln τ) where the standard deviation is over tariffs Portugal faced in each NIMEXE 2-digit industry; the change is between the pre- and post-tariff	f
Uncertainty	$1-(\tau_{tiV}/\tau_{hiV})^{\sigma}$ Proportional reduction in per period profits if the tariff faced by an exporter reverts from the preferential tariff received prior to accession (pre-tariff above) to the tariff received by all nonpreferential partners (i.e., the GATT member tariff)	g
NTM share change	Change in coverage ratio measured by fraction of products in 2-digit industry subject to a specific tariff or other NTB	c,d
Specific tariff share change	Difference in the share of lines in 2-digit industry with specific tariffs between post and pre-agreement period	f

(*Continued*)

DATA APPENDIX TABLE (*Continued*)

Variable	Description	Source
Price index proxy change	Difference in Spain's external tariff, ln(1 + ad valorem rate), between post- and pre-agreement period	f
Other data (figures and text):		
Import and export to GDP ratios	Referenced in text	h
Trade shares	Figure 1, IMF direction of trade statistics	
Export price index (ln)	1985 base chain price index for exports	h
Employment	Number of employees	i
Firm identifier (*NPC*)	Unique code to match firms between 1981–1985. Portuguese customs changed this code in 1986 and it is consistent for 1986 onwards but not between 1985 and 1986	INE
New exporter in year t	Firm exporting to a market at t but not in $t-1$ for $t < 1986$ and $t > 1986$, used in online Appendix	i
Gross entry rate in year t	(Total number new exporters in t)/(Number exporters $t-1$).	i
Gross exit rate in year t	(Number exporters with positive exports in $t-1$ and none in t)/(Number exporters with positive exports in t)	i

Notes: Additional details are in the supplementary Appendix.
[a] Authors' calculations based on INE data.
[b] IMF International Financial Statistics (IFS), volatility uses monthly data.
[c] Spain: International Customs Journal, Spain, No. 24, 16th Edition, 1984.
[d] EC: Official Journal, L342, 31.12.1979, p. 1–382.
[e] Articles of Accession, Official Journal L 302, 15/11/1985.
[f] Calculations based on tariff schedules.
[g] Authors' calculations using equation (12) with $\sigma = 3$ in the baseline regressions.
[h] Authors' calculations from Pinheiro (1997). Indices are yearly price deflators of export goods to all destinations.
[i] Authors' calculations using trade data matched to firm employment data (Quadros Pessoal) by INE.

REFERENCES

▶**Alessandria, George, and Horag Choi.** 2007. "Do Sunk Costs of Exporting Matter for Net Export Dynamics?" *Quarterly Journal of Economics* 122 (1): 289–336.

▶**Baier, Scott L., and Jeffrey H. Bergstrand.** 2007. "Do Free Trade Agreements Actually Increase Members' International Trade?" *Journal of International Economics* 71 (1): 72–95.

▶**Baier, Scott L., Jeffrey H. Bergstrand, and Erika Vidal.** 2007. "Free Trade Agreements *In* the Americas: Are the Trade Effects Larger than Anticipated?" *World Economy* 30 (9): 1347–77.

Baker, Scott R., Nicholas Bloom, and Steven J. Davis. 2013. "Measuring Economic Policy Uncertainty." http://www.policyuncertainty.com/media/BakerBloomDavis.pdf.

▶**Baldwin, Richard, and Paul Krugman.** 1989. "Persistent Trade Effects of Large Exchange Rate Shocks." *Quarterly Journal of Economics* 104 (4): 635–54.

▶**Bernanke, Ben S.** 1983. "Irreversibility, Uncertainty, and Cyclical Investment." *Quarterly Journal of Economics* 98 (1): 85–106.

▶**Bloom, Nicholas.** 2009. "The Impact of Uncertainty Shocks." *Econometrica* 77 (3): 623–85.

▶**Bloom, Nick, Stephen Bond, and John Van Reenen.** 2007. "Uncertainty and Investment Dynamics." *Review of Economic Studies* 74 (2): 391–415.

▶**Bown, Chad P., and Meredith A. Crowley.** 2013. "Import protection, business cycles, and exchange rates: Evidence from the Great Recession." *Journal of International Economics* 90 (1): 50–64.

▶**Broda, Christian, Nuno Limão, and David E. Weinstein.** 2008. "Optimal Tariffs and Market Power: The Evidence." *American Economic Review* 98 (5): 2032–65.

▶**Campa, José Manuel.** 1993. "Entry by Foreign Firms in the United States under Exchange Rate Uncertainty." *Review of Economics and Statistics* 75 (4): 614–22.

Carballo, Jerónimo, Kyle Handley, and Nuno Limão. 2014. "Trade Collapses: The Role of Economic and Policy Uncertainty in the Great Recession." Unpublished.

▶**Chaney, Thomas.** 2008. "Distorted Gravity: The Intensive and Extensive Margins of International Trade." *American Economic Review* 98 (4): 1707–21.

►**Conconi, Paola, Giovanni Facchini, and Maurizio Zanardi.** 2012. "Fast-Track Authority and International Trade Negotiations." *American Economic Journal: Economic Policy* 4 (3): 146–89.

Costantini, James A., and Marc J. Melitz. 2008. "The Dynamics of Firm-Level Adjustment to Trade Liberalization." In *The Organization of Firms in a Global Economy,* edited by Elhanan Helpman, Dalia Marin, and Thierry Verdier, 107–41. Cambridge: Harvard University Press.

►**Das, Sanghamitra, Mark J. Roberts, and James R. Tybout.** 2007. "Market Entry Costs, Producer Heterogeneity, and Export Dynamics." *Econometrica* 75 (3): 837–73.

►**Dixit, Avinash.** 1989. "Entry and Exit Decisions under Uncertainty." *Journal of Political Economy* 97 (3): 620–38.

►**Egger, Peter, Mario Larch, Kevin E. Staub, and Rainer Winkelmann.** 2011. "The Trade Effects of Endogenous Preferential Trade Agreements." *American Economic Journal: Economic Policy* 3 (3): 113–43.

Fillat, José L., and Stefania Garetto. 2014. "Risk, Returns, and Multinational Production." http://people.bu.edu/garettos/jlfsg_11_2014.pdf.

Frankel, Jeffrey A. 1997. *Regional Trading Blocs.* Washington, DC: Institute for International Economics.

General Agreement on Tariffs and Trade. 1980. "Agreement between the EFTA countries and Spain." Working Party Report GATT L/5045.

►**Handley, Kyle.** 2014. "Exporting under trade policy uncertainty: Theory and evidence." *Journal of International Economics* 94 (1): 50–66.

Handley, Kyle, and Nuno Limão. 2012. "Trade and Investment under Policy Uncertainty: Theory and Firm Evidence." National Bureau of Economic Research (NBER) Working Paper 17790.

Handley, Kyle, and Nuno Limão. 2013. "Policy Uncertainty, Trade and Welfare: Theory and Evidence for China and the U.S." National Bureau of Economic Research (NBER) Working Paper 19376.

Handley, Kyle, and Nuno Limão. 2015. "Trade and Investment under Policy Uncertainty: Theory and Firm Evidence: Dataset." *American Economic Journal: Economic Policy.* http://dx.doi.org/10.1257/pol.20140068.

►**Impullitti, Giammario, Alfonso A. Irarrazabal, and Luca David Opromolla.** 2013. "A theory of entry into and exit from export markets." *Journal of International Economics* 90 (1): 75–90.

►**Limão, Nuno, and Giovanni Maggi.** 2015. "Uncertainty and Trade Agreements." *American Economic Journal: Microeconomics* 7 (4): 1–42.

Pinheiro, Maximiano. 1997. "Séries Longas para a Economia Portuguesa pós II Guerra Mundial." In *Séries Estatísticas Banco de Portugal I.* Lisbon: Banco de Portugal.

Roberts, Mark J., and James R. Tybout. 1997. "The Decision to Export in Colombia: An Empirical Model of Entry with Sunk Costs." *American Economic Review* 87 (4): 545–64.

►**Rodrik, Dani.** 1991. "Policy uncertainty and private investment in developing countries." *Journal of Development Economics* 36 (2): 229–42.

Ruhl, Kim J. 2008. "The International Elasticity Puzzle." http://www.kimjruhl.com/research-papers/ElasticityMarch08.pdf.

►**Russ, Katheryn Niles.** 2007. "The endogeneity of the exchange rate as a determinant of FDI: A model of entry and multinational firms." *Journal of International Economics* 71 (2): 344–72.

►**Russ, Katheryn Niles.** 2012. "Exchange rate volatility and first-time entry by multinational firms." *Review of World Economics* 148 (2): 269–95.

►**Sala, Davide, Philipp J. H. Schröder, and Erdal Yalcin.** 2010. "Market Access Through Bound Tariffs." *Scottish Journal of Political Economy* 57 (3): 272–89.

United States International Trade Commission. 2008. "Andean Trade Preference Act: Impact on U.S. Industries and Consumers and on Drug Crop Eradication and Crop Substitution." United States International Trade Commission (USITC) Technical Publication 4037.

World Bank. 2005. *World Development Report 2005: A Better Investment Climate for Everyone.* Washington, DC: The World Bank.

Chapter 5

Policy Uncertainty, Trade, and Welfare: Theory and Evidence for China and the United States[†]

By KYLE HANDLEY AND NUNO LIMÃO*

We examine the impact of policy uncertainty on trade, prices, and real income through firm entry investments in general equilibrium. We estimate and quantify the impact of trade policy on China's export boom to the United States following its 2001 WTO accession. We find the accession reduced the US threat of a trade war, which can account for over one-third of that export growth in the period 2000–2005. Reduced policy uncertainty lowered US prices and increased its consumers' income by the equivalent of a 13-percentage-point permanent tariff decrease. These findings provide evidence of large effects of policy uncertainty on economic activity and the importance of agreements for reducing it. (*JEL* D72, F13, F14, O19, P33)

One of the most important economic developments of the last 20 years is China's integration into the global trading system. The world's share of imports from China between 1990 and 2010 rose from 2 to 11 percent. For the United States, that increase was even larger, rising from 3 to 19 percent. This has translated into more than a tenfold increase in the share of US manufacturing expenditure on Chinese goods and there is evidence that this has contributed to declines in both US prices (cf. Auer and Fischer 2010) as well as manufacturing employment and local wages (cf. Autor, Dorn, and Hanson 2013). Figure 1 shows that most of this trade boom occurred after China's accession to the World Trade Organization (WTO), which has led some authors to argue that the accession may have reduced trade costs faced

* Handley: Ross School of Business, University of Michigan, 701 Tappan Street, R3390, Ann Arbor, MI 48109 (email: handleyk@umich.edu); Limão: Department of Economics, University of Maryland, Tydings Hall, College Park, MD 20742, and NBER (email: limao@econ.umd.edu). We thank Nick Bloom, Helia Costa, Steve Davis, Rafael Dix-Carneiro, Robert Dekle, Brian Kovak, Justin Pierce, Gisela Rua, Tim Schmidt-Eisenlohr, Jagadeesh Sivadasan, Robert Staiger, and Shang-Jin Wei for useful comments. We are also thankful for comments from participants at several seminars (Dartmouth College, London School of Economics, University of Chicago, University of Michigan, Western Michigan University, World Bank Research Group, Yale University) and conferences (Empirical Investigations in International Trade, FRB Atlanta Trade Workshop, Hitotsubashi Conference on International Trade and FDI, Lisbon meeting on Institutions and Political Economy, NBER China Group, Policy Uncertainty Conference at Princeton University, Washington Area Trade Conference). We acknowledge financial support from the NSF under grants SES-1360738 (Handley) and SES-1360780 (Limão). We are also grateful for comments on preliminary results from participants at the Economic Policy Uncertainty Conference (Chicago University 2012). Jeronimo Carballo, Frank Li, and Alejandro Graziano provided excellent research assistance. The authors declare that they have no relevant or material financial interests that relate to the research described in this paper.

[†]Go to https://doi.org/10.1257/aer.20141419 to visit the article page for additional materials and author disclosure statement(s).

Originally Published in *American Economic Review* 107(9), pp. 2731–2783.

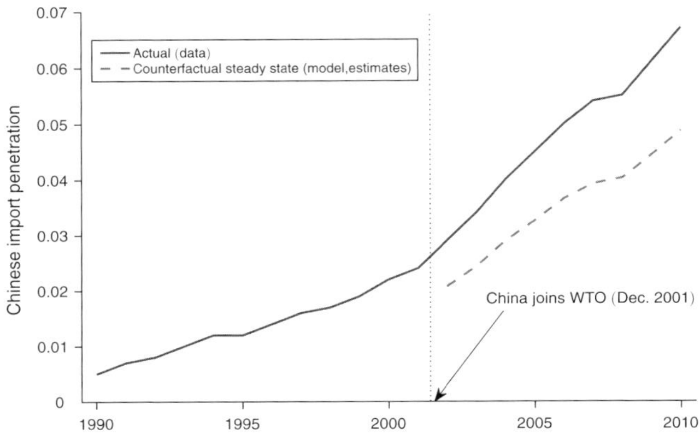

Figure 1. Chinese Import Penetration in United States: Actual versus Counterfactual under Policy Uncertainty

Notes: Import penetration ratio defined as manufacturing imports from China as share of total US expenditure on manufacturing (total shipments − net exports). Counterfactual line adjusts Chinese imports as if uncertainty reintroduced in any year after 2001. See Appendix B for further details.

by Chinese exporters.[1] But US-applied trade barriers toward China remained largely unchanged at that time.

We argue that China's WTO accession significantly contributed to its export boom to the United States through a reduction in US trade policy uncertainty. Specifically, China obtained permanent most favored nation (MFN) status with accession, which ended the annual US threat to impose high tariffs. China obtained temporary MFN in 1980 and never lost it, but it came close. In the 1990s, after the Tiananmen Square protests, Congress voted on a bill to revoke MFN status every year and the House passed it three times. Had MFN status been revoked, the United States would have reverted to Smoot-Hawley tariff levels and a trade war may have ensued. In 2000, for example, the average US MFN tariff was 4 percent, but if China had lost its MFN status it would have faced an average tariff of 31 percent. After WTO accession, the Chinese Foreign Trade Minister pointed out that by establishing "the permanent normal trade relationship with China, [the United States] eliminated the major long-standing obstacle to the improvement of Sino-US... economic relations and trade."[2]

To examine this argument, we build a model that allows us to interpret, measure, and quantify the effects of trade policy uncertainty (TPU). We obtain structural estimates of key policy uncertainty parameters and use them to quantify the implications for aggregate prices, the welfare of US consumers, and other outcomes. We focus on the role of TPU for investment and prices in part because of their importance in

[1] Autor, Dorn, and Hanson (2013) make this point and also cite other motives for this export growth. China's income has risen, driven by internal reforms (many in the 1990s) with a subset targeted to exports (Hsieh and Klenow 2009; Blonigen and Ma 2010).

[2] "China-US Trade Volume Increases 32 times in 23 years—Xinhua Reports." *BBC Summary of World Broadcasts,* February 18, 2002.

the context of the MFN debate. For example, the US decision to delink MFN from China's human rights record was described as having "removed a major issue of uncertainty" and MFN renewal would have an impact on investment and reexports that "will remove the threat of potential losses that would have arisen as a result of revocation." US business leaders argued that "... the imposition of conditions upon the renewal of MFN [was] virtually synonymous with outright revocation. Conditionality means uncertainty."[3] They lobbied Congress to make MFN permanent (Zeng 2003). At the same time, congressional research reports highlighted the higher consumer prices that would result if MFN was ever revoked (Pregelj 2001). We will argue that our approach and results have broader important implications and contribute to the growing literature on the impact of economic policy uncertainty and the role of trade agreements.

Our model captures the interaction between uncertainty and investment by modeling the latter as sunk costs and thus generating an option value of waiting. This basic theoretical mechanism is well understood (see Bernanke 1983; Dixit 1989), and there is some evidence that economic uncertainty, as proxied by stock market volatility, leads firms to delay investments (Bloom, Bond, and van Reenen 2007). In the international trade context, there is evidence of sunk costs to export market entry (see Roberts and Tybout 1997), but most empirical research on uncertainty's impact on export dynamics has focused on exchange rate uncertainty and finds small or negligible impacts (IMF 2010). In a general equilibrium setting, Impullitti, Irarrazabal, and Opromolla (2013) find a sunk cost model with heterogeneous firms and uncertain efficiency fits observed aggregate trade dynamics well.

Much less is known about the implications of economic policy uncertainty. Early theoretical contributions to this issue, such as Rodrik (1991), recognized the difficulty in measuring, identifying, and quantifying the causal effects of policy uncertainty. Recent work is tackling these difficult issues. For example, Baker, Bloom, and Davis (2016) construct a news-based index of policy uncertainty and find it helps predicting declines in aggregate output and employment. Our focus and empirical approach are considerably different. We use applied policy and counterfactual policy measures, both of which are observable in our setting, to directly estimate the effects of policy uncertainty on economic activity. In order to identify the effects of TPU, we explore both variation over time and countries (capturing the differential reduction in the probability of a trade war after WTO accession) and across industries (since they would face different tariffs if a trade war broke out and differ in their sunk costs).

To guide the estimation and quantification we develop a dynamic heterogeneous firms model with TPU. We build on Handley and Limão (2015) and extend it in three ways. First, firms can invest not only to enter foreign markets but also to upgrade their export technology. This allows changes in uncertainty to affect the extensive margin (new exporters) and the intensive margin (continuing exporters with upgraded technology).[4] Second, the exporting country is allowed to be large

[3] Quotes from, respectively, "HK Business Leaders Laud US Decision," *South China Morning Post*, May 28, 1994 and Tyco Toys CEO, "China MFN Status," Hearing before the Committee on Finance, US Senate, June 1996, p. 97.

[4] Evidence for both margins in China's export boom is documented by Amiti and Freund (2010) and Manova and Zhang (2009). Other evidence indicates that applied tariff changes can trigger within firm productivity increases

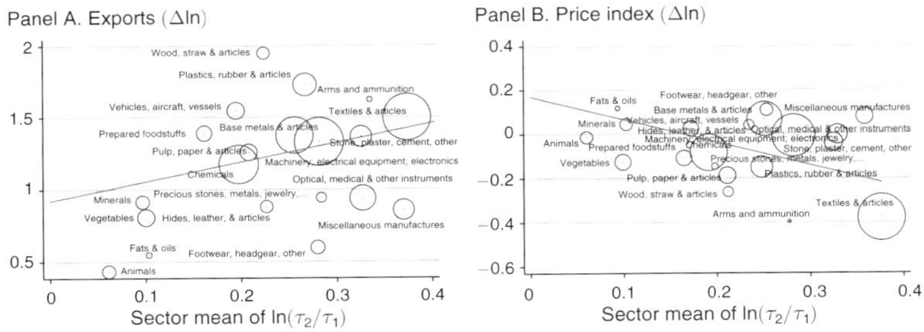

FIGURE 2. SECTOR-LEVEL CHINESE EXPORT AND PRICE INDEX GROWTH VERSUS INITIAL UNCERTAINTY

Notes: Simple means within sector of export and price index change versus means of initial uncertainty measured by $\ln(\tau_{2V}/\tau_{1V})$, where τ_{2V} and τ_{1V} are the column 2 and MFN tariff factors in 2000 in HS-6 industry V. Circles are proportional to the number of observations used as weights in the linear fit represented.

enough to affect the importer's aggregate outcomes. Otherwise, TPU has no significant impact on the importer. Third, entry into production is endogenous and subject to sunk entry costs such that TPU affects the formation and reallocation of firms. The model provides a number of insights. We highlight that TPU has both a direct and indirect effect on firm outcomes. The direct effect of TPU is to lower entry through an option value of waiting for exporters (fear of higher protection) and domestic firms (fear of low protection). The effect of these entry reductions is to increase the price index of the importer, which is central to the welfare gains from reforms that lower TPU. This price index increase has an indirect positive effect on exporter and domestic entry that can dominate for exporters (if initial protection is high) or for domestic firms (if initial protection is low).

As preliminary evidence and motivation for why we require a theoretical framework, consider Figure 2. In panel A we plot Chinese average export growth to the United States between 2000 and 2005 by sector against the (log) difference of the column 2 and MFN tariffs in 2000. On average, those sectors facing a relatively higher initial tariff threat in the case of MFN revocation experienced faster export growth and larger declines in prices, as shown in panel B. The exercise is suggestive, but also raises questions regarding the identification of partial effects and the quantification of the general equilibrium effects, both of which the model helps to address. First, what is a theory-consistent measure of uncertainty? The model shows it is the proportion of profits that Chinese exporters would lose if China ever lost its MFN status. We map this to observable tariff measures and then find evidence that our measure is relevant to exporters. Second, what are the necessary controls and assumptions required to identify the TPU effect and what structural parameters can we estimate? The model generates a tractable TPU-augmented gravity equation that allows us to consistently aggregate individual firm decisions to the industry level and identify the change in the probability of MFN being revoked. Moreover, the

(cf. Lileeva and Trefler 2010) so it is plausible that the same may happen due to reductions in TPU. This could account for the evidence of substantial firm-level TFP growth increases in China since 2001 (Brandt, Van Biesebroeck, and Zhang 2012).

model generates a relationship between ideal import price indices and TPU that we also estimate. Third, the model predicts these effects should only apply to trading partners where TPU changed and in industries with sunk costs of exporting.

We use variation in policies, export values, and prices across thousands of products to estimate the effects of TPU. We find nonparametric and parametric evidence that Chinese export growth in the period 2000–2005 was higher in industries with higher initial TPU. The effect is robust to controlling for applied tariff and nontariff barriers, transport costs, and sector-specific growth trends. The effect is only present in industries with export sunk costs, which we identify by exploring persistence in export behavior. Moreover, the effect is also robust to allowing for a broader set of shocks than those present in the theoretical model: namely, unobserved shocks to import demand (TPU has no direct effect on other US imports) and export supply (US TPU toward China has no direct effect on Chinese exports to non-US destinations), which rules out a large set of potential confounding factors.

We also construct industry-level ideal import price indices following Feenstra (1994) and find larger reductions in industries with initially higher TPU. This is the effect the model predicts due to new imported varieties (for which we find direct evidence) and technology upgrading. The price effect is also robust to controlling for alternative variables and unobserved import demand shocks and it is only present in high sunk cost industries. The partial effect of reducing TPU was to lower the average US industry price indices for Chinese imports by at least 15 log points and the corresponding aggregate index by slightly more.

The significant partial effects of TPU on import prices leads us to quantify its aggregate effects. In Section III we characterize the general equilibrium effects of TPU by solving for the model in changes. We derive the impacts on firm entry, sales, and prices (foreign and domestic) and how they depend on key features of the policy regime: current and future tariffs and the probability of transitioning between them. Combining this framework with a nonlinear estimate of the TPU-augmented gravity equation, we identify the reduction in the probability of MFN revocation. To isolate and quantify the aggregate effects of reducing TPU we then evaluate the impacts of the estimated shock to this structural parameter. The counterfactual implies an aggregate Chinese export increase of 32 log points, which is about one-third of the observed growth in this period. The predicted changes in the US import price index, domestic manufacturing firm sales, employment, and entry are also consistent with the observed changes during this period. The counterfactual import penetration if TPU had remained in place between 2002 and 2010 would have been substantially lower, as shown by the dashed line in Figure 1.

We also contribute to the long-standing question of the aggregate gains from trade. Recent work by Arkolakis, Costinot, and Rodríguez-Clare (2012) shows that import penetration and trade cost elasticities are sufficient statistics to compute those gains in a class of models. That is also the case for the deterministic version of our model, and so the gains from trade, or autarky cost, provides a useful benchmark. However, under TPU those are no longer sufficient statistics and we require the change in the ideal price index. We estimate that TPU increased that US price index (for tradables) by one-half as much as fully eliminating trade with China, or the equivalent of a permanent tariff increase of 13 percentage points. So the consumer welfare cost from TPU was about one-half of the cost of prohibiting all Chinese imports.

TPU plays a key role in evaluating the impacts of international trade agreements more broadly. Promoting trade is a central goal of the WTO, but Rose (2004) argues this institution has not succeeded whereas others argue it has (cf. Subramanian and Wei 2007). Our work highlights a trade promotion channel that, until recently, was largely missing from the analysis of trade agreements. The theoretical literature has emphasized that the central role of the General Agreement on Tariffs and Trade (GATT)/WTO is to internalize terms-of-trade effects (Bagwell and Staiger 1999). There is now evidence that countries possess market power, so their tariffs can affect their terms-of-trade, and exploit it before an agreement but less so afterward (Broda, Limão, and Weinstein 2008; Bagwell and Staiger 2011; Ludema and Mayda 2013). Moreover, the welfare cost of trade wars in the absence of such agreements are potentially large (cf. Ossa 2014). Recent theoretical work has focused on TPU. Limão and Maggi (2015) examine the role of risk aversion in the design and impact of agreements that target TPU; Horn, Maggi, and Staiger (2010) and Amador and Bagwell (2013) rely on TPU and imperfect contracting to explain a specific feature of such agreements—the use of tariff ceilings or bindings. Handley (2014) provides empirical evidence that reducing bindings increases foreign product entry. Our framework allows for a quantification of reducing such bindings; we also provide direct evidence of the welfare gains from reducing TPU and offer qualitatively new predictions. Specifically, agreements that allow a country to commit to a more stable and predictable trade policy, as the WTO claims to, can lower the probability of large swings in protection and thus increase entry not only by foreign firms but also by domestic ones in the import competing sector (and can also increase their domestic sales and employment). This outcome for domestic firms is possible when tariffs are sufficiently high, as they were when GATT 1947 was signed, which points to one of GATT's potential benefits.

The framework can also be applied ex ante to evaluate potential TPU shocks. We illustrate this through a range of counterfactual exercises where the United States unilaterally threatens to abandon or renegotiate all its trade agreements, which is extreme but plausible under the forty-fifth US president's administration. An increase in the US threat of higher tariffs on all its partners would generate considerable consumer welfare costs even if no tariffs were actually changed. If the threat was raised to a level similar to what China faced then the resulting loss in US consumer welfare would be equivalent to one-third of the cost of trade autarky.

Our research also complements the recent empirical work on the impact of Chinese exports on developed countries. Bloom, Draca, and van Reenen (2016) assess the impact of Chinese exports on wages and employment in the European Union while Acemoglu et al. (2016) and Caliendo, Dvorkin, and Parro (2015) focus on the United States. Pierce and Schott (2016) study the effects of Chinese exports on US manufacturing employment and, as an intermediate step, they estimate the reduced-form effect of column 2 tariffs on exports.[5] Our papers differ in important ways. First, our focus is on the trade, price, and consumer welfare effects. Second, we provide evidence for the central mechanism: sunk costs of exporting. Third,

[5] Therefore, independently from us, they too follow the proposal in Handley and Limão (2012, p. 44) to estimate the importance of "the US threat of nonrenewal of China's MFN status and whether its elimination in 2001 (upon China's WTO entry) can explain the subsequent export boom to the United States."

we develop a theoretical framework that contributes to the literature on agreements and gains from trade while allowing for the structural identification of parameters. Among other things, we explore the counterfactual exercises to isolate and quantify the aggregate effects of TPU on several outcomes and decompose them: e.g., we find that a large fraction of the trade and price changes is explained by a mean-preserving compression of the tariff and the rest is due to locking in tariffs below the mean.

We present the basic framework and derive the TPU-augmented gravity equation in Section I, followed by the empirical analysis in Section II. The general equilibrium solution in Section III is used for the structural estimation and quantification in Section IV. The appendices contain information on extensions, derivations, data, and robustness tests.

I. Framework and Partial Equilibrium Effects

We first describe the basic framework and firm entry decision problems, which apply throughout the paper. We then derive the effect of TPU on these decisions from the perspective of a small exporting country, one that takes foreign aggregate variables as given. We initially focus on a single industry and, in Section IE, we model multiple industries and technology upgrading, which we use to derive the TPU-augmented gravity equation. This partial equilibrium structure is sufficient to derive and empirically identify any effect of TPU on exports. But in order to quantify its effects on exporter and importer outcomes, we allow for a large exporter and endogenous domestic entry in Section III.

A. *Demand, Supply, and Pricing*

Consumers spend a fixed share of income on a homogeneous good and the remaining on a constant elasticity of substitution (CES) aggregate of differentiated goods, both tradable. Each period consumers observe current economic conditions and choose the optimal quantity of each differentiated good, q_v, to maximize utility subject to their budget constraint. The resulting CES aggregate demand is $q_v = EP^{\sigma-1}p_v^{-\sigma}$ where $\sigma > 1$ is the constant elasticity of substitution across varieties v and p_v is the consumer price. The aggregate demand shifter, E, is the total expenditure in the differentiated sector in that country and $P = \left[\int_{v\in\Omega}(p_v)^{1-\sigma}\right]^{\frac{1}{1-\sigma}}$ is the CES price index for the set of available varieties, Ω.

The supply side is also standard. There is a single factor (labor) with constant marginal productivity normalized to unity in the homogeneous good; the latter is taken as the numéraire so the equilibrium wage is unity in a diversified equilibrium. In the differentiated sector, there is a continuum of monopolistically competitive firms each producing a variety, v, with heterogeneous productivity $1/c_v$. Firms know their underlying productivity and the distribution of other firms in each market.

The consumer price, p_v, includes an ad valorem tariff, $\tau \geq 1$, so exporters receive p_v/τ per unit; domestic producers face no taxes in their market. The tariff is common to all firms in the differentiated industry. After observing τ, each firm chooses p_v to maximize operating profits taking aggregate conditions as given and correctly anticipating their equilibrium value. We allow for an ad valorem export cost, $d \geq 1$, so operating profits from exporting are $(p_v/\tau - dc_v)\,q_v$. This yields the standard markup rule over cost, $p_v = \tau d c_v \sigma/(\sigma - 1)$, and equilibrium operating profit equal to

$$\pi(a, c_v) = a c_v^{1-\sigma}, \tag{1}$$

where the *economic conditions* faced by any exporter are summarized by $a \equiv (\tau\sigma)^{-\sigma}((\sigma - 1)P/d)^{\sigma-1}E$.

B. *Policy Uncertainty and Entry*

Export Entry.—The timing and information relevant for export entry are the following. At the start of each period, surviving firms observe the state, denoted by s, that includes information about (i) the set of firms active in the previous period; (ii) the current realization of the policy; and (iii) all model parameters in the start of the period. This information permits each firm to correctly infer market conditions in that state, a_s, and form rational expectations about future profits. If entry in a state maximizes the firm's expected profits net of a sunk entry cost, K, then it will enter and continue to export in the following period with probability $\beta < 1$, the exogenous probability of survival. There are no period fixed costs and thus no endogenous exit. Since the sunk and marginal costs are known and constant, the only source of uncertainty is the future value of market conditions and the timing of death.

The expected value from exporting for any firm v after entry is

$$\Pi_e(a_s, c) = \pi(a_s, c) + \mathbb{E}_s \sum_{t=1}^{\infty} \beta^t \pi(a_s', c), \tag{2}$$

where we omit the variety subscript for simplicity; $\mathbb{E}_s$ denotes the expectation over possible future states conditional on the current state's information set.

If the firm does not expect the state to change, there is no uncertainty about economic conditions and no option value of waiting to enter. In this case the firm enters if its cost is below a threshold value, c_s^D. This benchmark threshold is obtained by equating the present discounted value of profits to the sunk cost:

$$\frac{\pi(a_s, c_s^D)}{1 - \beta} = K \Leftrightarrow c_s^D = \left[\frac{a_s}{(1 - \beta)K}\right]^{\frac{1}{\sigma-1}}. \tag{3}$$

If future conditions are uncertain then a nonexporter must decide whether to enter today or wait until conditions improve. The optimal entry decision of a firm in state s maximizes its expected value, given by the Bellman equation

$$\Pi(a_s, c) = \max\{\Pi_e(a_s, c) - K, \beta\mathbb{E}_s\Pi(a_s', c)\}. \tag{4}$$

The solution to this optimal stopping problem takes the form of intervals of a over which a firm will enter. Under reasonable assumptions on the persistence of policy we can show that a firm will enter if economic conditions are sufficiently good. Therefore, when a is decreasing in tariffs the solution is to enter when current tariffs are below a firm-specific threshold tariff. For any given a_s, there is a marginal firm with cost equal to the threshold value, c_s^U, given by the entry indifference condition,

$$\Pi(a_s, c_s^U) = \Pi_e(a_s, c_s^U) - K, \tag{5}$$

and any firms with lower costs will enter in state s.

Production Entry.—Our estimation strategy for the partial effect of TPU on exports is valid under alternative assumptions regarding entry into production. However, the general equilibrium effects of TPU will depend on production entry decisions. We model the latter similarly to export entry: to start production, a firm requires a sunk cost, K_h, in order to activate a known technology. The firms make this decision after observing the current realization of the policy. Thus, firms with a cost below a certain threshold enter and continue to produce the following period with a fixed probability, their survival rate (there are no production fixed costs). The domestic operating profit of a home firm is $\pi_h = a_h c_v^{1-\sigma}$ where $a_h = (\sigma)^{-\sigma}((\sigma-1)P)^{\sigma-1}E$ and we assume that $K_h \geq 0$ is sufficiently small that the marginal home entrant does not export. Therefore the domestic entry thresholds for home market firms can be obtained using the expressions we derived above when evaluated at K_h, $a_{s,h}$, and β_h; specifically by using (3) if there is no uncertainty to obtain $c_{s,h}^D$ and (5) to determine $c_{s,h}^U$.

C. *Policy Regime*

To characterize the effects of TPU, we propose an exogenous policy process that captures three key states of trade policy, denoted $m = 0, 1, 2$. Standard models of trade policy consider permanently high or low protection states, where $\tau_2 > \tau_0$. These extremes can capture outcomes under no cooperation (e.g., US tariffs on Cuba or North Korea) or under a credible agreement (e.g., US tariffs on Canada or certain WTO members). To analyze the effect of TPU we add an intermediate protection state characterized by a temporary tariff $\tau_1 \in [\tau_0, \tau_2]$ that changes with probability γ. Formally, the *trade policy regime* is characterized by a Markov process with time-invariant distribution, denoted by $\Lambda(\tau_m, \gamma)$.

By allowing for three states, we can capture a rich set of situations.[6] To address the central questions, we can focus on a simple transition matrix where policy is uncertain only in the intermediate state, so $\gamma > 0$, and the extreme states are absorbing.[7] The exact interpretation of each state depends on the setting. In our empirical application the intermediate state captures China's pre-WTO period when its temporary MFN status in the United States could change with probability γ and give way to either high protection (column 2 tariffs) with probability λ_2, or low protection with probability $1 - \lambda_2$. So we can interpret WTO accession as a switch to the low state in this application. Alternatively, we can interpret the WTO accession

[6]These include any setting where there is some probability of (i) cooperation with negligible probability of increases in protection (e.g., under credible agreements); (ii) partial cooperation (e.g., when protection may increase but a credible agreement is also possible); and (iii) higher protection levels (including a trade war or even autarky).

[7]This holds if $\Lambda(\tau_{m+1}, \gamma)$ first-order stochastically dominates $\Lambda(\tau_m, \gamma)$ for $m = 0, 1$, which is what we use in Appendix AA to establish the key entry results and how they generalize if the high state is not absorbing.

as an exogenous change in policy regime, if it lead to an unanticipated change in γ (or τ_m). Thus, we derive the effects of transitions across policy states within a regime and transitions across regimes.

The three state process has two other benefits when considering countries starting in the intermediate protection state. First, it captures the two key effects of agreements: reducing applied protection and/or TPU. Second, it allows for the possibility that policy worsens for either foreign firms (higher protection state) or domestic ones (lower protection state); this generates an option value of waiting for both types of firms. These benefits will become clearer in Section III when we decompose and quantify the applied and TPU effects and account for the general equilibrium responses of domestic firms.

D. *Partial Equilibrium*

To estimate the impact of trade policy on entry and exports, we derive the effects on cutoffs from switching regimes or switching states and decompose the latter into a change in applied policy and policy uncertainty.

Tariffs are the only underlying source of uncertainty and we initially focus on a small exporting country such that changes in its exports have a negligible effect on the importer's aggregate variables, *E* and *P*.

The small country assumption implies that tariffs worsen export business conditions only via a direct effect, and there is one distinct value of a_s for each τ_m for any given value of $EP^{\sigma-1}$. Moreover, tariffs leave exporter wages unchanged at unity in any diversified equilibrium. So we do not require additional general equilibrium structure to derive the basic cutoff expressions. In Appendix AA we use this to show that the solution to the Bellman equation (4) is a single value of economic conditions above which a firm enters. Therefore, the condition in (5) implies a distinct cutoff, c_s^U, for each τ_m. The cutoff for the intermediate state, c_1^U, is proportional to its deterministic counterpart in (3) by an *uncertainty factor*, $U(\omega,\gamma)$:

$$c_1^U / c_1^D = U(\omega,\gamma); \tag{6}$$

$$U(\omega,\gamma) \equiv \left[\frac{1+u(\gamma)\,\omega}{1+u(\gamma)}\right]^{\frac{1}{\sigma-1}}. \tag{7}$$

If U is less than 1, then entry is reduced under uncertainty. To interpret this factor, note that $\omega \equiv (\tau_2/\tau_1)^{-\sigma} < 1$ is the ratio of operating profits under the worst-case scenario relative to the intermediate state (given no other conditions changed). The term $u(\gamma) \equiv \gamma\lambda_2\beta/(1-\beta)$ is the average spell that a firm starting at the intermediate state expects to spend under τ_2. This spell is increasing in the probabilities of exiting the intermediate policy state, γ, and then facing a higher tariff, λ_2, and surviving, β. Note that if $\gamma = 0$ then policy is fixed in all states, thus we say that there is *policy uncertainty* if $\gamma > 0$. Moreover, any increase in γ implies a higher probability of a policy change but does not change the odds of the worst- or best-case scenario. We interpret this as an increase in policy uncertainty.

From these expressions we can see that entry in the intermediate state is lower under uncertainty if and only if tariff increases are possible, i.e., $c_1^U < c_1^D$ if and only if $\tau_2 > \tau_1$ and $u(\gamma) > 0$. Note that while TPU can lead to lower or higher tariffs, it is only the possibility of high tariffs that affects export entry; if there is uncertainty but tariff increases are not possible, $\lambda_2 = 0$, then uncertainty has no impact on entry.

The entry result in (6) reflects a specific switch in policy regime: an unanticipated introduction of TPU at a given tariff. We note two simple extensions that are relevant for the empirical analysis. First, the effect of TPU on entry is monotonic $(dc_1^U/d\gamma < 0$ for all $\gamma)$ so we can also test for marginal changes in TPU, e.g., whether before WTO accession Chinese exporters faced higher TPU in years when an MFN revocation seemed more likely. Second, we also want to understand the effect of agreements that are anticipated with some probability, i.e., switches to state 0, and compare them to unanticipated changes in TPU. In Appendix AA we show the cutoff in the intermediate state relative to any deterministic baseline state with tariffs τ_b is

$$c_1^U/c_b^D = U(\omega,\gamma) \times (\tau_1/\tau_b)^{-\frac{\sigma}{\sigma-1}}. \tag{8}$$

If $\tau_b = \tau_0$ this expression captures the reduction in applied policy and uncertainty from entering state 0 since, when there is no uncertainty in that state, the cutoff is equal to the deterministic value, $c_0^U = c_0^D$. Switching from the intermediate to the low state increases entry by reducing applied tariffs by τ_1/τ_0 and/or TPU. Thus, even if an agreement is anticipated with some probability, entering it can be used to identify an unanticipated elimination of TPU after we control for applied tariff changes.

The impact of eliminating TPU, as we have defined it, can be decomposed into a pure risk and expected mean effect. To understand each of these, consider the regime switch described above when we start in the intermediate state and uncertainty is eliminated. If τ_1 was at the long-run mean of the original tariff process then this uncertainty reduction is exactly a mean-preserving compression of tariffs, or a *pure risk* reduction.[8] However, if τ_1 was below its long-run mean, as will be the case in our application, then the reduction in γ has the additional effect of locking in tariffs below their expected value under uncertainty. Thus, the model will help us quantify each of these effects.

In sum, the explicit solution for the entry cutoff in equation (6) allows us to derive its elasticity with respect to γ, and the appropriate measure to capture the potential losses under the worst-case scenario, ω. Next, we show how to explore variation in this measure over industries to identify the effect of TPU.

[8] In this three state process, if state 1 has a policy τ_1 equal to the long-run mean then a decrease in γ induces a mean-preserving compression of the initial conditional policy distribution, $\Lambda(\tau_1,\gamma)$. This is one motive to use a 3-state process.

E. *TPU-Augmented Gravity*

We derive a TPU-augmented gravity equation to estimate how changes in policy uncertainty translate into export growth. This requires extending the baseline model in two dimensions. First, we model the effect of uncertainty on the intensive margin of a firm's exports. Second, we allow for industry variation in policies, which is necessary for our identification strategy.

Technology Upgrade.—We will focus on estimating the effect of changes in TPU on export growth. This growth can reflect extensive and intensive margin effects and we now show how the TPU-augmented gravity can capture both. We believe this extends the applicability of the framework to situations where both margins are potentially important. For example, most Chinese export growth to the United States in the period 2000–2005 took place in HS-10 goods that were already being exported in 2000. Some of the growth in existing products is due to new exporters but it is also plausible that existing ones grew by investing in export activities due to reduced TPU in the United States. We model one potential channel, irreversible investments by incumbent exporters to upgrade their technologies. This is consistent with the large increases in TFP growth of Chinese firms since WTO accession.[9]

To illustrate the main points in the simplest setting, consider upgrades that are specific to an export market. In particular, suppose that exporters can incur an additional sunk cost, K_z, to reduce the marginal export cost to a fraction $z < 1$ of the baseline cost d. The operating profits are then $\pi_v = a_s(zc_v)^{1-\sigma}$. In Appendix AB we show that the upgrading decision is similar to the entry decision in that it also takes the form of a cutoff cost. The upgrade cutoff is $c_{sz}^U = \phi c_s^U$. It is proportional to the entry cutoff by a constant *upgrading parameter*, $\phi \equiv \left[(z^{1-\sigma} - 1)(K/K_z)\right]^{\frac{1}{\sigma-1}}$. The upgrade cutoff is lower than the entry one if the marginal cost reduction from upgrading is sufficiently low relative to its sunk cost. This implies that the marginal entrant does not upgrade. The export entry cutoff solutions will be similar to those we derived, but only the more productive exporters will upgrade. Since ϕ is independent of tariffs, the elasticity of the upgrade and entry cutoff are exactly the same with respect to tariffs and uncertainty.

Multi-Industry Aggregation.—We define an industry V as the set of firms that draw their productivity from a similar distribution, $G_V(c)$, and face similar trade barriers. The basic structure of the model is otherwise unchanged. Namely, the policy regime is still described by a Markov process, $\Lambda(\tau_{mV}, \gamma)$ with $m = 0, 1, 2$ and it applies to each V. It thus captures our empirical setting such that if any industry V moved to the agreement state (or the high protection state) then all industries would face the same policy state.

[9] We are not aware of any direct evidence of the impact of foreign tariffs on Chinese productivity but Brandt, Van Biesebroeck, and Zhang (2012) find that firm-level TFP growth in manufacturing between 2001 and 2007 is about three times higher than prior to WTO accession, 1998–2001. Moreover, the TFP growth in the WTO period is higher for larger firms, which is consistent with our model's prediction that those are the most likely to upgrade. In future work we plan to directly estimate if there is a causal effect of TPU on Chinese firm TFP.

The export revenue in state s for firm $v \in V$ is $p_{sv} q_{sv} / \tau_{sV} = a_{sV} \sigma (z_V c_v)^{1-\sigma}$ once we plug in the optimal price and quantity from Section IA, where $z_V < 1$ for the upgraders and unity otherwise. The economic conditions variable, a_{sV}, still reflects aggregate income and price index effects but it now reflects industry-specific tariffs (and export costs). The export entry cutoff in (6) is industry-specific but otherwise the previous cutoff results are unchanged.

The mass of exporting firms in any stationary equilibrium, characterized by a constant mass of active firms, is equal to $N_V \times G_V(c_s^U)$, the total number of potential firms in industry V in the export country times the fraction of these with costs below the cutoff. Export revenue in industry V is obtained by aggregating over firms that upgrade and those that do not as follows:[10]

$$R_{sV} = a_{sV} d_V^{1-\sigma} \sigma N_V \left[\int_0^{\phi_V c_{sV}^U} (z_V c)^{1-\sigma} dG_V(c) + \int_{\phi_V c_{sV}^U}^{c_{sV}^U} c^{1-\sigma} dG_V(c) \right]. \tag{9}$$

We assume that productivity in each industry is drawn from a Pareto distribution bounded below at $1/c_V$, so $G_V(c) = (c/c_V)^k$ and $k > \sigma - 1$. Under this assumption we can obtain sharper predictions, nest a standard gravity model in our framework, and provide precise conditions under which we can identify the impact of uncertainty on exports. We integrate the cost terms in (9), use the definition of a_{sV}, and c_{sV}^U, and take logs to obtain an uncertainty-augmented gravity equation,

$$\ln R_{sV} = (k - \sigma + 1) \ln U_{sV} - \frac{\sigma}{\sigma - 1} k \ln \tau_{sV} - k \ln d_V + k \ln P + \frac{k}{\sigma - 1} \ln E + \ln \zeta_V + \ln \tilde{\alpha}_V. \tag{10}$$

Without either policy uncertainty, $U_{sV} = 1$, or upgrading, $\zeta_V = 1$, (10) reduces to a standard industry-level gravity equation conditional on aggregate expenditure on differentiated goods, E, and the price, P (cf. Chaney 2008). The terms $\tilde{\alpha}_V$ and ζ_V are combinations of industry parameters that are time invariant.[11] Finally, all else equal, upgrading increases export levels, as reflected in ζ_V, but not the *elasticity* of industry exports with respect to U_{sV}. Thus, we can aggregate sales from all firms to estimate the impact of uncertainty on their industry exports without requiring additional information on which firms upgrade.

II. Estimation and Identification

We use the model to examine how China's WTO accession, which eliminated the annual MFN renewal debate in the United States, contributed to its export boom to the United States. We focus on industry exports, which will reflect both entry and upgrading effects. The objective of this section is to identify a causal effect of TPU

[10] We use the relationship $c_{sz}^U = \phi c_s^U$ and allow industry variation in the upgrade technology and sunk costs. Away from stationary equilibria there are additional exporters who entered in previous periods under better conditions.

[11] $\tilde{\alpha}_V \equiv \frac{N_V \sigma}{c_V^k} \frac{k}{k - \sigma + 1} \left(\frac{1}{(1-\beta) K_V} \right)^{\frac{k-\sigma+1}{\sigma-1}} \sigma^{\frac{-\sigma k}{\sigma - 1}} (\sigma - 1)^k$ and $\zeta_V \equiv 1 + \frac{K_{zV}}{K_V} (\phi_V)^k$.

on exports and test if the data is consistent with some of the model's assumptions. We use the TPU-augmented gravity equation in (10). As we show in Section III, this same equation holds even when the exporter is large enough to affect the aggregate variables. If we control for those variables, then we can identify whether TPU affected exports regardless of exporter size.

A. *Approach*

We estimate the export equation in changes for two reasons. First, it allows us to difference out unobserved industry characteristics such as entry costs, the productivity and mass of Chinese producers in V and the technology parameters in ζ_V. In the robustness tests we address the possibility that they vary over time and are correlated with TPU. Second, we are interested in the impact of the *change* in uncertainty after the United States removed the threat of column 2 tariffs due to China's WTO entry. So our baseline uses the time-difference of (10),

$$\Delta \ln R_V = f\left(\frac{\tau_{2V}}{\tau_{1V}}, \gamma\right) + b_\tau \Delta \ln \tau_V + b_d \Delta \ln D_V + b + e_V, \tag{11}$$

where Δ ln represents the difference between post- and pre-WTO periods. The coefficient $b_\tau = -k\sigma/(\sigma - 1) < 0$ is the effect of applied tariffs (conditional on the uncertainty factor). We model ad valorem export costs, d_V, as a function of observable shocks given by the ad valorem equivalent of insurance and freight, $\Delta \ln D_V$, and an i.i.d. error term contained in e_V. The changes in transport costs allow us to identify the Pareto shape parameter, $b_d = -k$. Any changes in *aggregate* expenditure on differentiated goods or its price index are captured in the constant term, b. The null hypothesis under the model is that prior to WTO accession there is a positive probability of column 2 tariffs, i.e., $\gamma\lambda_2 > 0$, and thus f is increasing in τ_{2V}/τ_{1V} if the accession reduced γ. If the accession eliminated uncertainty then $f = -(k - \sigma + 1)\ln U(\tau_{2V}/\tau_{1V}, \gamma)$. Under the regime switch interpretation, the model allows for $\gamma > 0$ even after entry. In that case $f = (k - \sigma + 1)\,\Delta \ln U(\tau_{2V}/\tau_{1V}, \gamma)$ where changes in U reflect either changes in tariffs or γ. In the period we consider τ_{2V}/τ_{1V} is nearly constant within industries, so f captures changes in γ. So in this case f is also increasing in τ_2/τ_1.

Standard trade models with a gravity structure yield a restricted version of (11) with $f = 0$ that is nested in our model. Even if uncertainty is important, our functional form assumptions may not be satisfied by the data. We address this as follows. First, we provide nonparametric estimates of the impact of τ_{2V}/τ_{1V} on export growth. Second, we control for observed changes in policies and trade costs and provide semiparametric estimates of the impact of policy uncertainty—imposing only the gravity structure that is common in trade models without uncertainty. Third, we test the model's functional form for f and perform numerous robustness checks (e.g., the possibility of industry-specific growth trends and unobserved demand and supply shocks). Fourth, after introducing the general equilibrium structure we provide a nonlinear structural estimate of the corresponding term for f that we then use to quantify the impact of TPU.

We also test if the uncertainty effect is predominant in high sunk cost industries, as the model predicts.

B. *Data and Policy Background*

We combine trade and policy data from several sources. US import trade data at the HS-10 level for several years is obtained from the NBER Harmonized System Imports by Commodity and Country. These data are concorded over time and used to compute ideal price indices and aggregated to the HS-6 level for the price and export growth regressions. We obtained US tariff schedules via the World Bank's WITS. The source of other policy measures we use are described in Appendix B. The cost of insurance and freight is reflected in the import data. We convert all tariff and transport cost data to their iceberg form (e.g., from 10 percent to $\ln\tau = \ln 1.1$).

There are 5,113 HS-6 industries in the 1996 classification; China exported in 3,617 of these in both 2000 and 2005 to the United States. The baseline analysis focuses on the industries traded in both years so that a log growth rate exists. These industries account for 99.8 percent of all export growth from China to the United States in this period.[12]

The following policy background is useful for understanding the timing choice for our baseline estimates. Uncertainty remained about both China's accession to the WTO and its permanent normal trade relations (PNTR) as late as 2000 due to tense foreign and economic relations. In October 2000, Congress passed the US-China Relations Act granting PNTR but its enactment was contingent on China's accession to the WTO. Protracted accession negotiations and a jet fighter collision meant that in the summer of 2001 Congress again voted on whether to revoke MFN. China joined the WTO on December 11, 2001 and the United States effectively enacted PNTR on January 1, 2002. This strongly suggests that uncertainty about column 2 tariffs remained at least until 2000 and that it was not reduced until 2002. We will focus on the growth between 2000 and 2005 but show that the basic effect is present for other relevant periods.

C. *Partial Effect Estimates of TPU on Exports*

Table 1 provides summary statistics for our baseline sample. Export growth from 2000 to 2005 averaged 128 log points (lp) across HS-6 industries, with substantial variation across them; the standard deviation is 168 lp. This industry variation suggests that the boom can't simply be explained by aggregate shocks. Table 1 also shows substantial variation in column 2 tariffs across the industries.

All else equal, the model predicts lower initial export levels in the pre-WTO period for industries with higher potential profit losses if there was a possibility of tariff increases. If WTO accession reduces or eliminates this probability, we should observe relatively higher export growth in those industries. For any given value of σ the industry ranking of potential profit loss is determined by τ_{2V}/τ_{1V} so we use this ratio to partition the sample into the columns in Table 1 labeled Low (bottom tercile of τ_{2V}/τ_{1V}) and High TPU industries. Export growth in high uncertainty industries is 19 lp higher, a mean difference that is statistically significant. The export

[12] Our baseline sample is smaller because it focuses on the 94 percent of HS-6 lines where tariffs are levied on an ad valorem basis, other HS-6 lines have only specific tariffs. We show the results are robust to this and the zero trade flow industries in Section IID.

TABLE 1—SUMMARY STATISTICS BY PRE-WTO POLICY UNCERTAINTY

	Uncertainty		
	Low	High	Total
Chinese export value growth (Δln, 2005 − 2000)[a]	1.16	1.35	1.28
	[1.77]	[1.62]	[1.68]
Chinese export price index growth (Δln, 2005 − 2000)[a]	−0.07	−0.14	−0.11
	[0.70]	[0.69]	[0.69]
Chinese export variety growth (Δln, 2005 − 2000)[a]	0.27	0.35	0.32
	[0.46]	[0.41]	[0.43]
MFN tariff (ln), 2000	0.03	0.04	0.04
	[0.04]	[0.05]	[0.05]
Column 2 tariff (ln), 2000	0.16	0.39	0.31
	[0.10]	[0.12]	[0.16]
Ratio of column 2 to MFN tariff	1.14	1.42	1.33
	[0.09]	[0.14]	[0.18]
Uncertainty (pre-WTO)[b]	0.30	0.64	0.52
	[0.18]	[0.09]	[0.20]
Change in MFN tariff (Δln, 2005 − 2000)	−0.002	−0.004	−0.003
	[0.01]	[0.01]	[0.01]
Change in transport costs (Δln, 2005 − 2000)	−0.01	−0.002	−0.005
	[0.10]	[0.08]	[0.09]
Observations[c]	1,124	2,087	3,211

Notes: Simple means with standard deviations in brackets. Low: subsample of industries in the bottom tercile of pre-WTO uncertainty (ranked by τ_2/τ_1); High refers to the rest of the sample. Total includes the full sample used in baseline Table 2.

[a] Test of mean difference across samples significant at least at the 5 percent level.

[b] Potential profit loss measure if MFN revoked pre-WTO: $1-(\tau_1/\tau_2)^{\sigma}$, using $\sigma = 3$.

[c] Total observations for price index change: 2,579 HS-6 industries used in baseline Table 4. Total observations for variety growth (number of traded HS-10 varieties with an HS-6 industry): 1,051 and exclude industries with censored varieties (traded in both 2000 and 2005). High and low bins for price and variety are defined on the baseline sample.

growth distribution for high TPU industries first-order stochastically dominates the one for low TPU industries, as shown by the respective kernel densities in panel A of Figure 3 and confirmed via a Kolmogorov-Smirnov test. Panel A of Figure 4 provides further nonparametric evidence of this relationship by estimating a local polynomial regression of export growth on $\ln(\tau_{2V}/\tau_{1V})$. We confirm the higher growth in high initial uncertainty industries, via a mean test, and a nonnegative relationship over the domain.

Semiparametric Evidence and Functional Form.—Using a semiparametric approach, we can control for other determinants of export growth and test for specific functional forms of the uncertainty term. Several trade models yield a gravity equation that is a special case of (11) with the implicit restriction that $f = 0$. We use the residuals from that restricted estimation to determine how τ_{2V}/τ_{1V} affects f without imposing functional forms. Using a double residual semiparametric regression (Robinson 1988) we find that τ_{2V}/τ_{1V} has a significant effect on subsequent export growth net of tariff or transport cost changes. This result is robust to including 21 sector dummies in the restricted regression to net out any heterogeneous growth trends in Machinery, Textiles, Footwear, and the remaining 18 other sectors that the UN defines as coherent groups of HS-2 categories.

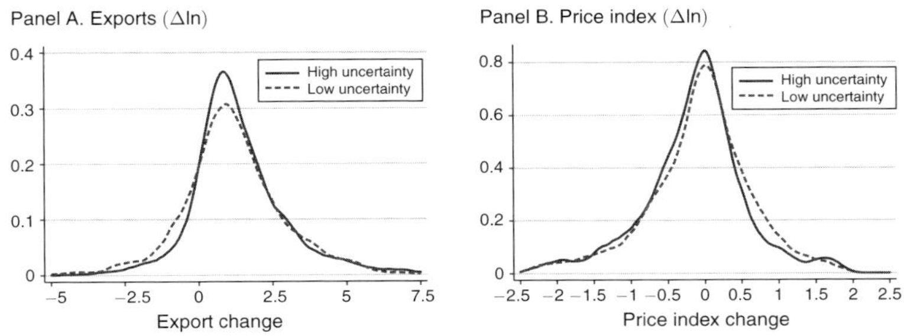

FIGURE 3. CHINESE EXPORT AND PRICE INDEX GROWTH IN HIGH VERSUS LOW UNCERTAINTY INDUSTRIES

Notes: Epanechnikov kernel density estimates. High uncertainty defined as the top two terciles of ratio of US column 2 to MFN tariff in HS-6 industry V. Low uncertainty is the bottom tercile. Equality of distributions rejected with p-value of 0.001 (panel A) and 0.009 (panel B) in Kolmogorov-Smirnov tests. See text for details of price index calculation.

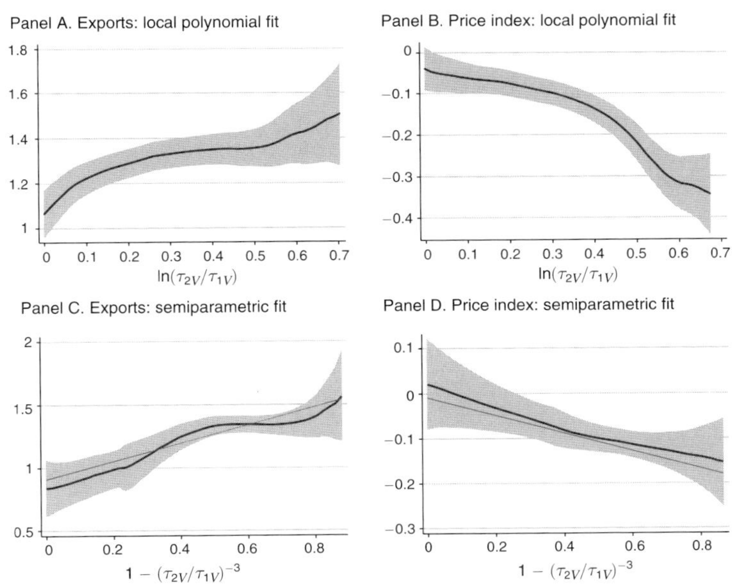

FIGURE 4. CHINESE EXPORT AND PRICE INDEX GROWTH ($\Delta \ln$) VERSUS INITIAL POLICY UNCERTAINTY

Notes: Panels A and B are a local polynomial fit on $\ln(\tau_{2V}/\tau_{1V})$, where τ_{2V} and τ_{1V} are the column 2 and MFN tariff factors in 2000 in HS-6 industry V. Panels C and D regress log export and log price index growth on changes in transport costs, tariffs, and on sector dummies. The linear fit uses OLS and also includes $-(\tau_{2V}/\tau_{1V})^{-3}$, which the semiparametric uses as an argument of the local polynomial estimated using the Robinson (1988) semiparametric estimator. We plot the fit against $1 - (\tau_{2V}/\tau_{1V})^{-3}$ for ease of comparison with the uncertainty variable used in the baseline OLS regressions.

Table 2—Chinese Export Growth (US, $\Delta\ln$): Baseline Estimates, 2000–2005

	(1)	(2)	(3)	(4)
Uncertainty pre-WTO	0.743	0.791	0.716	0.734
[+]	[0.154]	[0.150]	[0.186]	[0.184]
Change in tariff ($\Delta\ln$)	−9.967	−4.34	−7.356	−4.25
[−]	[4.478]	[0.676]	[5.060]	[0.677]
Change in transport costs ($\Delta\ln$)	−2.806	−2.893	−2.795	−2.833
[−]	[0.455]	[0.450]	[0.456]	[0.451]
Constant	0.851	0.843		
	[0.0853]	[0.0850]		
Observations	3,211	3,211	3,211	3,211
R^2	0.03	NA	0.05	NA
Sector fixed effects	No	No	Yes	Yes
Restriction p-value (F-test)	0.204	1	0.536	1

Notes: Robust standard errors in brackets. Predicted sign of coefficient in brackets under variable. Uncertainty measure uses US MFN and column 2 Tariffs to construct profit loss measure at $\sigma = 3$. All specifications employ OLS and 2 and 4 impose theoretical constraint on tariffs and transport cost coefficients: $b_\tau = b_d(\sigma/(\sigma-1))$. Sectors defined by the 21 HS sections.

In panel C of Figure 4, we plot the resulting semiparametric fit and see it is increasing in $1-(\tau_{2V}/\tau_{1V})^{-3}$, the potential profit loss measure when $\sigma = 3$. The figure also shows the partial effect of this measure obtained from OLS estimation of (11), so controlling for tariffs, transport costs, and sector trends. We see the parametric estimate lies everywhere within the shaded area representing the semiparametric 95 percent confidence interval. Because we can't reject their equality, we will use the OLS specifications with $\sigma = 3$ as a baseline from which to perform robustness tests. We also test if the semiparametric fit is equal to alternative parametric fits that are linear or log-linear in τ_{2V}/τ_{1V} and find they are rejected by the data. This suggests that reduced-form measures of column 2 tariffs should not be used for quantitative predictions. Partially because the nonlinearity implies a smaller effect of τ_{2V} at high tariffs where trade would be negligible.

Parametric OLS Estimates.—The semiparametric evidence supports approximating the uncertainty term using $b_\gamma \times \left(1-(\tau_{2V}/\tau_{1V})^{-3}\right)$ in (11). When we approximate U_V linearly around $\gamma = 0$ and use (7) we have the following structural interpretation of $b_\gamma^{OLS} = [(k-\sigma+1)/(\sigma-1)]u(\gamma)\,g \geq 0$. We first present parametric estimates of b_γ and check their robustness to two potentially important sources of omitted variable bias.

Baseline.—The ordinary least squares (OLS) results in Table 2 are consistent with the structural interpretation of the parameters. In column 1 we see that b_γ is positive and significant. As predicted, this implies that industries with higher initial potential losses grew faster after WTO accession. The coefficients on tariffs and transport costs are negative and significant. The estimation equation contains an over identifying restriction, $b_\tau = b_d\sigma/(\sigma-1)$, that we cannot reject. We therefore reestimate the model in column 2 with this restriction, which increases the precision of the estimates. One reason for the increase in precision for the tariff coefficient is the small variation for this variable in this period.

Sector-Level Growth Trends and Unobserved Heterogeneity.—The preliminary evidence in panel A of Figure 2 showed a positive relationship between the average export growth and the mean of $\ln(\tau_{2V}/\tau_{1V})$ by sector. If most of the variation in TPU or export growth was across sectors then we would worry their relationship would be proxying for an omitted sector effect. To explicitly control for this possibility, we reestimate the baseline including a set of 21 sector dummies. The results in columns 3 and 4 of Table 2 are similar to the baseline and show the robustness to potential sources of omitted variable bias, such as differential changes across sectors in productivity, sunk costs, upgrading parameters, FDI, and Chinese barriers on intermediates.

D. *Robustness*

The baseline results are robust to several potential issues, which we outline below. The online Appendix includes the associated tables and a detailed discussion of each issue.

Nontariff Barriers.—In Table A2 we control for changes in HS-6-level nontariff barriers, including the removal of the Multi-fiber quotas, which does not affect the baseline estimates.

Elasticity of Substitution, Outliers and Sample Selection.—In Table A3 we find that the qualitative impact of TPU is robust to (i) alternative assumptions regarding the elasticity of substitution used to construct this variable; (ii) downweighting outliers using a robust regression procedure; and (iii) extending the sample to incorporate zero trade flows (by calculating midpoint growth rates) and HS-6 industries that do not have ad valorem but have specific tariffs.

Processing Trade.—In Table A3 we drop the HS-6 industries where processing trade is most prevalent (Kee and Tang 2016) and continue to find a significant impact of TPU. This specification controls for several potential omitted variables (e.g., Chinese policy toward the input purchase, transformation, and resale of output to a foreign firm) and indicates TPU affected a broad set of industries.

Capital/Labor Intensity.—In Table A4 we find the TPU effect is robust to controlling for capital/labor intensity and marginally stronger for industries where that intensity is highest.

Unobserved Export Supply Shocks.—We addressed omitted variable bias thus far by controlling for specific variables at the HS-6 level and for unobserved contemporaneous sector shocks. In Table A5 we control for unobserved HS-6 industry Chinese export supply shocks common across destinations. First, we provide a placebo test and find no effect from regressing Chinese export growth to the European Union and Japan on the US TPU measure. Second, we pool these observations with the US sample and include HS-6 effects and identify a positive differential growth effect of US TPU on Chinese exports to the United States (relative to other markets in the same industry). Thus, the baseline estimates are robust to controlling for narrowly defined Chinese supply shocks common across destinations, including any Chinese policy changes induced by WTO accession and Chinese technology changes.

Unobserved Import Demand Shocks.—If US import demand increased in industries with higher uncertainty, then the baseline estimates could be biased upward. Such shocks would also increase US imports from other countries and cause them to be correlated with the TPU measure. However, in Table A6 we find no evidence of this. US import growth from nonpreferential trade partners was not significantly affected. Pooling these imports and those from China allows us to control for HS-6 effects and thus any unobserved US import demand shocks. The differential effect of TPU on Chinese imports is positive and significant. We perform a similar test focusing on a specific control, Taiwan. This country also acceded to the WTO in January 2002 but unlike China it never faced an annual renewal process for its MFN status so the model would predict little or no effect of TPU. The results in Table A6 support this prediction.

Pre-Accession Growth Trends.—The baseline focuses on export growth over the period 2000–2005. Any pre-accession growth trends correlated with TPU could bias these estimates. In Table A7 we find no significant effect of the uncertainty measure in 1996 on Chinese export growth to the United States in the years 1996–1999. We then extend the baseline sample to include the pre-accession period and perform a difference-in-differences estimation—we find the baseline estimates are robust to controlling for HS-6 specific growth trends.

Timing of TPU Shocks.—In Table A8 we provide estimates from a yearly panel in levels between 1996 and 2006 and find a similar effect to the baseline. Moreover, the timing of the effect matches the WTO accession. The increased growth in higher TPU industries only becomes significant in 2002. We find lower import *levels* in the period 1996–2001 in industries with higher TPU but that effect is similar across those years suggesting that, prior to WTO accession, minor changes in the legislation or in the relations between the United States and China did not significantly affect Chinese firms' beliefs about losing the MFN status.[13]

E. *Additional Evidence: Sunk Cost Channel*

The baseline provides an average elasticity of exports to TPU across all industries. We now test if that elasticity is only present in industries with sunk costs of exporting, as predicted by the model. Doing so requires a measure of those costs and, since none is readily available, we estimate it by exploiting variation in the persistence of exporting over time. A standard approach (Roberts and Tybout 1997) is to use firm-level data to estimate a probability model where, after conditioning

[13] These insignificant changes in γ during the period 1996–2001 are also consistent with the lack of variability in the vote share to revoke MFN status in the House of Representatives. According to the Congressional Quarterly Almanac, that share increased slightly from 33 percent in 1996 to 40 percent in 1997 and remained around that level (except for 2000, 34 percent). We also constructed and found that a news index of US TPU did not fall significantly during the period 1996–2002 but did so between 2002 and 2006, both of which are consistent with the panel estimates of changes in γ. We thank two referees for these suggestions.

on firm characteristics to capture their current incentive to participate, any correlation with lagged participation provides evidence of sunk costs. We apply a similar approach but use HS-10 product data and estimate export persistence parameters, b_V^{sunk}, industry-by-industry.

In online Appendix C4 we argue that the estimates appear reasonable and provide additional details on the estimation and identification.[14] We classify industries as having relatively higher sunk costs if their t-statistic for b_V^{sunk} is higher, which indicates we can be more confident of rejecting $b_V^{sunk} = 0$. More specifically, the top two terciles of the regression sample with higher t-statistics are classified as higher sunk cost relative to those in the bottom tercile.

In panel A of Table 3 we find no effect of TPU on Chinese exports in low sunk cost industries (column 1). In contrast we find a positive and significant effect for the high sunk cost subsample (column 2). This provides strong evidence for the model's option value of waiting uncertainty channel.

The heterogeneity of TPU due to sunk costs is not driven by its correlation with import demand shocks. US imports from Taiwan are not significantly affected by TPU either on average (Table A6) or in either sunk cost subsample (Table 3, columns 3 and 4). Moreover, in the last two columns of Table 3, we pool Taiwan and China and include HS-6 effects to control for the possibility that sunk costs have some unobserved correlation with the uncertainty measure. We find a positive and significant differential effect of TPU on Chinese trade (relative to Taiwan) in high sunk cost industries but not in low.[15]

The heterogeneity of TPU due to sunk costs is also not driven by its correlation with export supply shocks. Recall that we found no average effect of US TPU on Chinese exports to the European Union. In panel B of Table 3 we also find no differential effect of TPU on Chinese exports to the European Union between high and low sunk costs (columns 3 and 4). When we pool Chinese exports to the United States and European Union in columns 5 and 6 and include sector-country and HS-6 industry dummies, we find a positive and significant differential effect on China's export growth to the United States in the high sunk cost industries and none in the low, as the model predicts.[16]

In sum, there is strong support for the sunk cost channel and the effect is robust to controlling for unobserved demand and supply shocks.

F. *Partial Effect Estimates of TPU on Prices and Entry*

Prices.—The model predicts that a reduction in TPU lowers the ideal consumer import price index due to the entry of new varieties and a reduction in the prices of existing ones if there is technology upgrading. For industry V in state s this index for

[14] To minimize the impact of the episode we study on the persistence estimates, we use data for the pre-accession period, 1996–2000, and focus on the effect of lagged export participation on current export participation for each HS-10 product-country variety for all US nonpreferential trade partners, excluding China.

[15] These estimates also include a full set of sector-country dummies with standard errors clustered on industry. The significance is similar when using 500 bootstrap replications to account for the generated regressor.

[16] We employ the same sunk cost measure as in panel A, which requires only a similar industry ranking of these costs when exporting to the United States or the European Union.

TABLE 3—US IMPORT AND CHINESE EXPORT GROWTH: SUNK COST HETEROGENEITY AND UNOBSERVED SHOCKS, 2000–2005

	China		Taiwan		Pooled	
US imports from:	Low	High	Low	High	Low	High
Sunk cost sample:	(1)	(2)	(3)	(4)	(5)	(6)
Panel A. US import growth (Δln)*: robustness to unobserved HS-6 import demand shocks in high versus low sunk cost industries*						
Uncertainty pre-WTO (US)	−0.611	1.105	−0.593	0.0486		
	[0.393]	[0.280]	[0.414]	[0.297]		
Uncertainty pre-WTO (US) × **1**(China)					0.0663	1.026
					[0.517]	[0.383]
Change in tariff (Δln)	−9.59	−12.0	−6.699	−19.3		
	[13.30]	[7.107]	[11.91]	[6.484]		
Change in transport costs (Δln)	−2.28	−4.51	−3.21	−5.18	−1.12	−4.67
	[1.200]	[0.743]	[0.892]	[0.724]	[0.880]	[0.797]
Observations	759	1,519	759	1,519	1,518	3,038
R^2	0.08	0.09	0.13	0.11	0.32	0.43
Sector × country fixed effects	Yes	Yes	Yes	Yes	Yes	Yes
HS-6 fixed effects	No	No	No	No	Yes	Yes

	US		EU−15		Pooled	
Chinese exports to:	Low	High	Low	High	Low	High
Sunk cost sample:	(1)	(2)	(3)	(4)	(5)	(6)
Panel B. Chinese export growth (Δln)*: robustness to unobserved HS-6 export supply shocks in high versus low sunk cost industries*						
Uncertainty pre-WTO (US)	0.0363	0.816	0.492	−0.336		
	[0.313]	[0.263]	[0.302]	[0.241]		
Uncertainty pre-WTO (US) × **1**(China)					−0.444	1.144
					[0.409]	[0.315]
Change in tariff (Δln)	−2.659	−7.703	5.845	−12.43	−1.15	−9.563
	[11.49]	[5.805]	[6.075]	[3.166]	[5.881]	[3.876]
Observations	975	1,945	975	1,945	1,950	3,890
R^2	0.047	0.037	0.066	0.05	0.03	0.04
Sector × country fixed effects	Yes	Yes	Yes	Yes	Yes	Yes
HS-6 fixed effects	No	No	No	No	Yes	Yes

Notes: Robust standard errors in brackets clustered on HS-6 industry in columns 5 and 6. Uncertainty pre-WTO is defined as in the baseline US sample. Total sample in columns 1 and 2 reduced relative to Table 2 because sunk cost estimates not available for all HS-6 industries. The change in the US MFN tariff does not vary across nonpreferential partners and is not identified in panel A when HS-6 industry effects are included. The uncertainty coefficient is also not separately identified for non-Chinese imports in panel A or non-US exports in panel B. For panel A, the sample is the subset of HS-6 products with trade in 2000 and 2005 for US imports from both Taiwan and China. For panel B, the sample is the subset all HS-6 products with trade in 2000 and 2005 exported by China to the United States and European Union.

an exporter x is defined by $P_{sV,x} \equiv \left[\int_{\Omega_{sV}^{x}} (p_{Vs})^{1-\sigma}\right]^{1/1-\sigma}$.[17] In online Appendix C5, we establish that changes in this index between 2005 and 2000 have an exact log-linear representation in terms of uncertainty and trade costs, yielding

$$(12) \quad \Delta \ln P_{V,x} = -\left(\frac{k}{\sigma-1} - 1\right)(-\ln U_V) + b_\tau^P \Delta \ln \tau_V + b_d^P \Delta \ln D_V + b^P + e_V,$$

[17] These reflect the consumer prices inclusive of any tariffs and transport costs. A change in this price index could still be consistent with a negligible change in the aggregate US price index if the expenditure share on those goods is negligible.

TABLE 4—CHINESE PRICE INDEX AND VARIETY GROWTH (*US*, Δln), 2000–2005

	Price index				Variety			
	(1)	(2)	(3)	(4)	(5)	(6)	(7)	(8)
Uncertainty pre-WTO	−0.284	−0.217	−0.418	−0.483	0.0736	0.0606	0.243	0.200
	[0.0689]	[0.0828]	[0.173]	[0.223]	[0.0309]	[0.0380]	[0.0722]	[0.0907]
MFN tariff (Δln)	5.137	0.560	9.839	6.829	−5.170	−4.066	−3.196	−2.792
	[1.608]	[1.682]	[4.313]	[4.497]	[0.957]	[1.024]	[1.179]	[1.185]
Transport cost (Δln)	−0.435	−0.460	−0.477	−0.465	−0.227	−0.200	−0.514	−0.504
	[0.254]	[0.248]	[0.626]	[0.620]	[0.0909]	[0.0897]	[0.165]	[0.160]
Observations	2,579	2,579	907	907	2,579	2,579	1,051	1,051
Industry sample	HS6	HS6	HS4	HS4	HS6	HS6	HS6, uncensored	HS6, uncensored
R^2	0.02	0.06	0.02	0.06	0.03	0.06	0.03	0.07
Sector fixed effects	No	Yes	No	Yes	No	Yes	No	Yes
Uncertainty price impact (Δln)[a]								
Average price	−0.15	−0.11	−0.22	−0.25				
Aggregate price	−0.17	−0.13	−0.25	−0.28				

Notes: Robust standard errors in brackets. All specifications employ OLS. Constant or sector fixed effects included but not reported. The dependent variable is the ln change in the ideal price index of Chinese varieties sold in the United States between 2000 and 2005 calculated at the industry level; see online Appendix C for details. Sample: we use the subset of industries where value and quantity data are available and price changes are defined for at least one HS-10 variety in 2000 and 2005 for the industry (HS-6 in columns 1–2 or HS-4 in columns 3–4). The HS-6 sample trims outliers in the 2.5 percent tails of the dependent variable. Columns 7 and 8 exclude censored HS-6 industries, i.e., those where all their HS-10 categories had positive trade in both periods (these observations contain no information about whether the number of firms exporting in that industry changed).

[a]Uncertainty impacts are weighted effects of all industries. For average effect the weight is the mean of the uncertainty variable. For the aggregate we weight the uncertainty by the ideal CES price index relative weight of each industry as described in online Appendix C.

where b^P contains the aggregate terms and e_V is an error term. Higher initial uncertainty, i.e., lower U, generates lower price changes because $k > \sigma - 1$ (for a finite first moment of exports). We use the same linear approximation of $\ln U_V$ as the OLS gravity estimates of equation (11).[18]

We compute the change in the price indices for each industry using the approach in Feenstra (1994), which captures the new varieties and changes in the price of existing ones. We define varieties at the HS-10 product-country level, as in Broda and Weinstein (2006). We continue to assume a common σ so any correlation between the price change and our measure of TPU does not reflect variation in the elasticity.

Similarly to export growth, we first provide nonparametric and semiparametric evidence. First, the distribution of price changes is lower for high TPU industries and present across the full range of TPU, as seen in panel B of Figures 3 and 4. Second, in panel D of Figure 4, we show the result is also present in the semiparametric estimates after controlling for tariffs, transport costs, and sector effects.

Table 4 presents the estimates for equation (12) showing that industries with higher initial TPU indeed had larger price reductions. In column 1 we see the uncertainty effect estimated at the same level as export growth, HS-6, is significant and robust to controlling for sector effects (column 2).[19] The partial effects of uncertainty

[18]Thus, $\ln U_V \approx -\frac{ug}{\sigma - 1}\left(1 - \left(\tau_{2V}/\tau_{1V}\right)^{-3}\right)$ and the estimated OLS coefficient is $b_\gamma^P = -ug\frac{k - (\sigma - 1)}{(\sigma - 1)^2}$.

[19]The number of observations is lower than the gravity regressions because quantity is not always consistently observed and because the price index is only defined for HS-6 industries where at least one variety is traded in both periods, which may introduce a sample selection bias. Any such bias should be mitigated by recomputing the price

on prices are the following. First, using column 1, the average reduction in the price index is 15 log points at the mean of initial TPU. Second, the aggregate import price index change is a weighted average of the industry-level changes; applying those same weights to the estimates of TPU in each industry we obtain its impact on the aggregate import price index: 17 log points.

The baseline price index results are also robust to controlling for HS-6 industry-specific shocks, e.g., to tastes and quality. We apply the approach used to control for import demand shocks in Table A9. For each HS-6 we compute an additional aggregate import price index, which reflects all nonpreferential partners trading with the United States and pool them with the Chinese observations to estimate the differential effect of TPU. The first column of Table A9 shows that industries where Chinese exporters faced higher initial TPU had larger price reductions if the good was imported from China but that same measure of TPU had no significant effect on the price index measure from the remaining countries. In column 2 we find a significant differential effect of TPU on the Chinese goods prices even after controlling for HS-6 effects. We find similar results in columns 3 and 4 when we restrict the control group to Taiwan. All the results control for sector-country growth shocks and cluster standard errors at the HS-6 level.

Evidence on Channels: Entry, Upgrading, and Sunk Costs.—The price index effects are the relevant ones for consumer welfare. But we can provide some additional evidence for the entry and upgrading channels and the role of sunk costs highlighted by the model.

The model predicts that at least a fraction $G(c_{sV}^{U})$ of Chinese firms in industry V export to the United States. In Section IB, we derive an exact log-linear representation of entry in terms of uncertainty and trade costs that yields the following estimation equation:

$$(13) \qquad \Delta \ln n_V = k(-\ln U_V) + b_\tau^n \Delta \ln \tau_V + b_d^n \Delta \ln D_V + b + e_V,$$

where b captures aggregate changes and e_V is an error term. The predicted signs match those for the export equation. Using the changes in the number of traded HS-10 products as a proxy for entry, we find TPU reductions lead to entry in the same sample where we found it reduced the price index. Moreover, all other variables are significant and have the predicted sign (Table 4).[20]

Directly testing the effect of TPU on upgrading requires data on export technology expenditures, which are not available. Nevertheless, we can provide indirect evidence. In the absence of upgrading, the model predicts no effect of uncertainty

change at a higher level of aggregation. In column 3 we do so and regress it on the HS-4 average of the TPU and trade cost measures, which yields a stronger effect of TPU. We focus the quantification and robustness on the more conservative HS-6 estimates.

[20] The magnitude of the uncertainty coefficient in column 5 of Table 4 is attenuated toward zero because entry is measured with error when we use product data. The attenuation reflects measurement error whenever a *true* variety is defined at a level finer than the HS-10, thus we do not use these estimates for quantification. This issue is potentially important in industries where all HS-10 categories within an industry already had positive trade in both periods, so the growth in the number of measured variety is zero but true variety may have increased or decreased. We address this in column 7 by dropping those industries; the sign and significance are similar to those in the full sample but the impact of uncertainty triples.

TABLE 5—CHINESE PRICE INDEX AND VARIETY GROWTH: SUNK COST HETEROGENEITY (US, $\Delta\ln$), 2000–2005

	Price index		Variety	
	(1)	(2)	(3)	(4)
Uncertainty pre-WTO				
× High sunk cost indicator	−0.449	−0.320	0.096	0.082
	[0.0816]	[0.0923]	[0.0423]	[0.0485]
× Low sunk cost indicator [~0]	−0.009	−0.062	0.019	0.030
	[0.118]	[0.130]	[0.0396]	[0.0471]
MFN tariff ($\Delta\ln$)	4.429	0.332	−4.710	−3.788
	[1.610]	[1.687]	[0.950]	[1.012]
Transport cost ($\Delta\ln$)	−0.446	−0.465	−0.217	−0.196
	[0.253]	[0.248]	[0.0896]	[0.0888]
High sunk cost indicator	0.165	0.103	0.029	0.029
	[0.0793]	[0.0810]	[0.0324]	[0.0345]
Constant	−0.047		0.055	
	[0.0658]		[0.0230]	
Observations	2,579	2,579	2,579	2,579
R^2	0.02	0.06	0.04	0.07
Sector fixed effects	No	Yes	No	Yes

Notes: Robust standard errors in brackets. All specifications employ OLS. Dependent variables and sample described in notes to Table 4. High sunk cost indicator is 1 for industries in top two terciles of export sunk cost estimates ranked by t-statistic, as described in text.

on the prices of continuing varieties. The ideal price index for Chinese imports in industry V is composed of a weighted average of changes in unit values of HS-10 varieties traded in 2000 and 2005 plus a variety growth term. If a reduction in TPU only operated by inducing export entry, then the model predicts an increase in the continuing variety component for industries with higher initial TPU, i.e., an increase in average prices since the entrants would be less productive. In online Appendix Figure A2 we find the opposite.[21] This evidence that continuing varieties have substantially lower prices in industries with higher TPU is not consistent with a basic version of our model where TPU only affects entry (nor one with quality upgrading); the finding requires a channel whereby reductions in TPU lower the prices of continuing varieties. One such channel is export technology upgrading.

In Table 5 we examine whether the baseline price and entry effects are stronger in high sunk cost industries. We interact the TPU measure with indicators for high and low sunk cost industries, defined as before. We find significant effects of TPU on prices and entry for high sunk cost industries but no significant effects for low, as the model predicts.

In sum, we have documented a strong and robust relationship of TPU on export values and prices of Chinese goods sold in the United States and provided evidence for the channels highlighted by the model. The nonnegligible share of expenditure on those goods suggests this episode affected aggregate outcomes in the United States. To quantify these we model the general equilibrium effects of TPU.

[21] The local polynomial fit in Figure A2 of the continuing variety component against TPU shows a significant negative relationship, which is also robust to controlling for changes in tariffs, transport costs, and sector effects in a parametric setting similar to the one used for the full price index in Table 4.

III. General Equilibrium Effects of Policy Uncertainty

To quantify and decompose the GE effects of TPU, we now allow countries to be large enough to affect aggregate outcomes in their export market. We examine consumer welfare and firm outcomes such as entry investments and sales. The exposition focuses on the key equilibrium conditions and the intuition for these in a single industry setting. In online Appendix D we provide details on the derivation of certain expressions and the multi-industry extension. We show that with limited information the model can be used to examine counterfactuals beyond the Chinese episode such as the impact of US TPU against all its trade partners. In Section IV we employ this structure and the estimated structural parameters to examine the implications for China's WTO accession.

A. *Setup*

These extra assumptions allow us to determine aggregate expenditure, E_s, and the price index, P_s:

A1. There is no borrowing technology available across periods.
A2. Individuals are either workers or entrepreneurs, with mass L and N, respectively. Entrepreneurs are endowed with a blueprint embodied in the marginal cost, c_v, and receive the profits of their variety and any lump-sum rebates of tariff revenues.
A3. The period utility reflects a constant expenditure share on differentiated goods equal to $\mu > 0$ for workers and zero for entrepreneurs.
A4. There are two countries with identical preferences.

Under these assumptions, TPU does not affect aggregate expenditures, which allows us to focus on the effects via the price index; the latter are important in our empirical setting and in understanding welfare effects for consumers. To see this we highlight the following implications. (i) A1 implies that current expenditures must equal current income each period for each individual. (ii) A2 implies that the only source of worker income is the wage, which is pinned down at unity—by the marginal product of labor in the numéraire—provided the population in each country is sufficiently large for the numéraire to be produced in equilibrium. (iii) The constant equilibrium wage and A1–A3 together imply that expenditure on differentiated goods is constant: $E_s = \mu L$ for all s; so the price index is the only aggregate endogenous variable that is uncertain in each country. (iv) The indirect utility for workers is $\tilde{\mu} P_s^{-\mu}$ in each state.[22] (v) A3 implies that entrepreneurs have linear utility so the entry decision of risk-neutral entrepreneurs is obtained by solving the Bellman

[22]The constant is $\tilde{\mu} \equiv w\ell\mu^{\mu}(1-\mu)^{(1-\mu)}$ where ℓ is the labor endowment and $w = 1$ in equilibrium.

equation defined in Section IB.[23] (vi) A4 rules out third country effects, mostly for expositional reasons.[24]

The price index for differentiated goods in state s depends on imported and home varieties, $\Omega_s = \Omega_{s,x} \cup \Omega_{s,h}$:

$$(14) \quad P_s^{1-\sigma} = \int_{\Omega_s} (p_{vs})^{1-\sigma} \, dv = \int_{\Omega_{s,x}} (\tau_m d c_v / \rho)^{1-\sigma} \, dv + \int_{\Omega_{s,h}} (c_v/\rho)^{1-\sigma} \, dv,$$

where $\rho \equiv (\sigma - 1)/\sigma$. Before deciding to enter, firms form rational expectations about the expected price index, P_s^e. In equilibrium $P_s^e = P_s$ given the following information structure. At the start of each period t a surviving firm knows its cost, c_v, and there is a common knowledge information set, denoted by $\mathbf{i}_s$, that includes: (i) the fixed exogenous parameters of the model including the survival rate and the time invariant set of potential varieties in each country, Ω; (ii) the structure of the model including the entry decision rules; (iii) the current realization of the policy; and (iv) the equilibrium set of varieties sold in each market in the previous period, denoted by Ω_{t-1}. The state, s, is defined by the combination of the realized policy at t and Ω_{t-1}.

We define the equilibrium as the following set of prices and quantities in each country and state s: (a) a demand vector for the differentiated and numéraire good, $\mathbf{q}_s$; (b) a market entry decision for each differentiated firm v and a distribution of active firms, Ω_s, with prices, $\mathbf{p}_s$; (c) an expected and actual price index, P_s^e and P_s; and (d) labor demands for the differentiated and numéraire goods and a wage, that satisfy the following conditions: (i) the numéraire good market clears; (ii) workers maximize utility subject to their budget constraint taking their factor endowments and all prices as given; (iii) entrepreneurs maximize utility subject to their budget constraint taking as given their factor endowment, technology, wage, P_s^e, the policy regime (Λ) and its lump-sum revenue, and all other information in $\mathbf{i}_s$; (iv) $P_s = P_s^e$ due to rational expectations (see online Appendix D); and (v) the labor market clears.

Since TPU now affects the price index there will be aggregate uncertainty and transition dynamics after policy shocks. We derive key analytical results for cutoffs, to compare with the partial effects, and for the price index, to compare with the literature on the aggregate gains from trade. We then provide a numerical solution for the model using exact changes.

B. *Equilibrium Entry, Prices, and Welfare*

We focus on exact changes, $\hat{y}_s \equiv y_s / y_b$—the ratio of some outcome y in state s and its baseline value. To fix ideas we choose a baseline with a deterministic

[23] Namely, equation (4) evaluated at a, K, β for the export decision to the home market and the same equation evaluated at a_{sh}, K_h, β_h for domestic production entry. We can interpret the exogenous discount factor in the Bellman equation as the survival probability of the entrepreneur or more generally the product of that probability and the probability of survival of the invested entry capital. We rule out the possibility that entrepreneurs are credit constrained by assuming that their endowment ℓ is always at least as high as the sunk entry investment so they can always self-finance this cost in a single period even if it exceeds that period's operating profits.

[24] If third countries don't face tariff shocks themselves in this market then they can be included since any shocks to their competitors' tariffs affect third-country firms only via the price index and so they react similarly to domestic firms.

policy $\tau = \tau_b$, so $y_b \equiv y(\tau_b, \gamma = 0)$. Using the demand expressions and (14) we rewrite the aggregate price change as a function of the price changes in imports, $P_{s,x}$, and domestic varieties $P_{s,h}$ —where $P_{s,i} \equiv \left[\int_{\Omega_{s,i}} (p_{vs})^{1-\sigma} dv\right]^{1/(1-\sigma)}$ for $i = x, h$, as follows:

$$(15) \qquad \left(\hat{P}_s\right)^{1-\sigma} = I\left(\hat{P}_{s,x}\right)^{1-\sigma} + (1 - I)\left(\hat{P}_{s,h}\right)^{1-\sigma} \quad \text{for all } s.$$

The weight, $I \equiv \tau_b R_b / E_b$, is the share of expenditure on imports in the baseline, i.e., the import penetration ratio (online Appendix D.1.2).

Any firm with costs below the relevant cutoff in state s serves the market as do other surviving firms that previously entered under better conditions. Therefore, the varieties that determine each $P_{s,i}$ can reflect the entry cutoffs in that state and prior ones. The expression in (15) reflects this hysteresis due to sunk costs as does the quantification. The latter focuses mainly on comparing stationary equilibria and so does the exposition below. Stationary equilibria are characterized by a constant mass of active domestic and foreign firms in each market and thus constant price indices for any given τ_m. The stationary price index is then $P_m = P(c_m, c_m^h, \tau_m)$, which evaluates (14) at the cutoffs for each state.[25] Similarly, the domestic component of the price index is $P_{m,h} = P_h(c_m^h)$ so its change, $\hat{P}_{m,h}$, depends on changes in the domestic entry cutoff, $\hat{c}_{m,h}$. The import price index is $P_{m,x} = P_x(c_m, \tau_m)$ and therefore $\hat{P}_{m,x}$ depends on the change in the cutoff and also in tariffs if $\tau_m \neq \tau_b$.

The key analytical results do not rely on a specific productivity distribution but the estimation and quantification uses a Pareto, and in this case we obtain

$$(16) \qquad \left(\hat{P}_m\right)^{1-\sigma} = I(\hat{\tau}_m)^{1-\sigma}(\hat{c}_m)^{k-(\sigma-1)} + (1 - I)\left(\hat{c}_{m,h}\right)^{k-(\sigma-1)} \quad \text{for all } m.$$

The equilibrium price change depends on entry changes for which we now solve.

Deterministic Policy Baseline.—If the policy is expected to remain at τ_m then the price index is $P_m^D \equiv P\left(c_m^D, c_{m,h}^D, \tau_m\right)$, which evaluates (14) using the available varieties. An exporting firm serves this market if its cost is below $c^D\left(P_m^D, \tau_m\right)$, as given in (3). A domestic firm serves the market if its cost is below $c_h^D\left(P_m^D\right) = \left[a_{mh}/((1 - \beta_h) K_h)\right]^{\frac{1}{\sigma-1}}$.

Each firm's investment to serve a country is independent of the price index in another country.[26] We can then solve for the price, production, and export cutoffs by finding the unique solution to the three equations defining the equilibrium value of these variables in each country. In online Appendix D.1 we show that higher tariffs increase the equilibrium price index, $dP^D/d\tau > 0$, reduce export entry, $dc^D/d\tau < 0$, and increase domestic entry, $dc_h^D/d\tau > 0$. Replacing the equilibrium

[25] If $T \geq 0$ periods ago the tariff changed to τ_m then the stationary equilibrium is given by the value of $y_{T\to\infty}(\tau_m)$. In a stationary equilibrium there is still exogenous death but it is exactly offset by entry thus leaving the firm mass unchanged.

[26] The separability arises because the equilibrium wage is constant and the marginal domestic entrant pays the sunk cost after knowing its productivity and is assumed to be unproductive enough that it never exports.

cutoff changes into (16) we obtain the following price index change in any state m as a function of policy changes and baseline import penetration:

$$\hat{P}_m^D = \left[I(\hat{\tau}_m)^{1-\frac{\sigma k}{\sigma-1}} + (1-I)\right]^{-1/k} \quad \text{for all } m. \tag{17}$$

Consumer welfare changes in this model are given by $\left(\hat{P}_m^D\right)^{-\mu}$ and we can compare them to the cost of autarky, which is $\left[\hat{W}_m = \left(\hat{P}_m^D\right)^{-\mu}\right]_{\hat{\tau}_m\to\infty} = (1-I)^{\mu/k}$. Autarky is costlier, or equivalently the gains from trade with a given country larger, the higher the initial import share from that country, I, and the lower the trade cost elasticity, k. Thus, the expression for deterministic welfare gains from trade for consumers in our model is similar to those obtained in a broader class of static trade models (cf. Arkolakis et al. 2012).[27]

Uncertain Policy.—We now allow for three policy states. Switching out of the intermediate state occurs with probability γ and can worsen conditions for foreign firms (higher protection) or domestic ones (lower protection). Either switch leads to gradual exit and transition dynamics as the price index adjusts up toward its stationary value. So entry decisions will depend on the expected transition paths for economic conditions.

The export entry cutoff relative to the deterministic baseline, τ_b is $\hat{c}_1 \equiv c_1^U / c_b^D$, is still obtained by solving the optimal stopping problem in Section IB but now tariffs also affect the price index, P (online Appendix D.1.3):

$$\hat{c}_1 = U(\omega g, \gamma) \times \hat{P}_1 \times (\hat{\tau}_1)^{-\frac{\sigma}{\sigma-1}}; \tag{18}$$

$$U(\omega g, \gamma) \equiv \left[\frac{1 + u(\gamma)\,\omega g}{1 + u(\gamma)}\right]^{\frac{1}{\sigma-1}}. \tag{19}$$

The effect of uncertainty if we hold tariffs fixed is obtained by setting $\hat{\tau}_1 = 1$. We note two differences relative to the small exporter. First, there is a price change, captured by $\hat{P}_1$. Second, the average operating profits under the worst-case scenario relative to state 1 are now $\omega g = (\tau_2/\tau_1)^{-\sigma} g$, where

$$g \equiv (1-\beta)\sum_{T=0}^{\infty}\beta^T\left(\frac{P_{2,T}}{P_1}\right)^{\sigma-1}, \tag{20}$$

and $P_{2,T}/P_1$ is the relative price index T periods after switching to high protection. So g is the average change in profits due to aggregate price changes after a transition to high protection. With a small exporter $g = 1$, whereas now it will typically differ from unity. Our solution will show that this does not overturn the direct tariff effect, i.e., we continue to have $(\tau_2/\tau_1)^{-\sigma} g < 1$ and thus $U < 1$.[28]

[27] Equation (17) also applies to a model with multiple exporters to this market if they face deterministic tariffs and have the same distribution parameter, k. We use I equal to either the aggregate import share (complete autarky) or the import share of a specific country (partial autarky).

[28] So, conditional on the price index change, we continue to obtain the TPU-augmented gravity equation (10); the main difference is that the coefficient on τ_2/τ_1 reflects $u \times g$, whereas it reflected only u in the small exporter case.

Next we solve for the change in domestic entry. With sunk costs of domestic entry, $K_h > 0$, the domestic cutoff change, $\hat{c}_{1,h} \equiv c_{1,h}^{U}/c_{b,h}^{D}$ is

$$\hat{c}_{1,h} = U_h(g_h, \gamma) \times \hat{P}_1; \tag{21}$$

$$U_h(g_h, \gamma) \equiv \left[\frac{1 + u_h(\gamma)\, g_h}{1 + u_h(\gamma)}\right]^{\frac{1}{\sigma-1}}; \tag{22}$$

$$g_h \equiv (1 - \beta_h) \sum_{T=0}^{\infty} (\beta_h)^T \left(\frac{P_{0,T}}{P_1}\right)^{\sigma-1}. \tag{23}$$

The relevant domestic TPU factor is now U_h, which depresses domestic entry. The intuition is similar to export entry, except that the worst-case scenario for domestic firms is the low protection state. Starting in the intermediate state the expected duration of low protection is $u_h(\gamma) \equiv \gamma(1 - \lambda_2)\, \beta_h / (1 - \beta_h)$ and the expected change in profits after that transition, g_h. After a transition to low protection the domestic price index falls and thus so do domestic profits, hence $g_h < 1$.

Sunk costs generate transition dynamics after moving from the intermediate state. A switch to the low protection state triggers immediate entry of exporters and a lower price index; over time domestic firms die and fewer reenter due to the lower price index. Thus, the price index overshoots: it jumps down on impact and then increases along the transition (Figure A4). The switch to high protection increases the price index both on impact and gradually over the transition, as fewer exporters enter.

Replacing the export and domestic entry cutoffs into (16) we obtain the change in the stationary price index in the intermediate TPU state relative to the deterministic baseline:

$$\hat{P}_1 = \left[I(\hat{\tau}_1)^{1-\frac{\sigma k}{\sigma-1}}(U)^{k-(\sigma-1)} + (1 - I)\,(U_h)^{k-(\sigma-1)}\right]^{-1/k}. \tag{24}$$

When $U = U_h = 1$ we obtain the deterministic expression in (17). The price change due to TPU alone, if $\hat{\tau}_1 = 1$, increases the price index due to its effect on foreign firms, $U < 1$, and domestic ones, $U_h < 1$. Therefore, the intermediate TPU equilibrium must contain fewer foreign firms, fewer domestic firms, or both.

The general equilibrium entry effects are perhaps less obvious. TPU has a direct negative effect on foreign and domestic entry, which pushes up the price index; so the net impact of TPU is to lower entry if the direct uncertainty effect is sufficiently strong. These opposing effects may imply that foreign and domestic entry move in opposite directions. If the intermediate tariff, τ_1, is very close to its low protection value, τ_0, then TPU increases domestic and lowers foreign entry. This will be the case in our application to China and occurs because the domestic firms were already close to their worst-case scenario of low protection. Conversely, if τ_1 were close to τ_2, then there would be more foreign entry under TPU and less domestic entry.

In sum, the general equilibrium analysis will allow us to quantify key effects and highlights qualitatively novel implications of TPU. Notably, TPU can reduce domestic entry, which is not possible in a similar setting with a deterministic tariff.

Moreover, when this domestic entry reduction is sufficiently large it implies that consumer welfare is below the permanent autarky level, as one of our counterfactual exercises shows.

C. *Solution*

To characterize and quantify the effects of TPU, we solve a multi-industry version of the model for the complete sequence of prices and entry decisions. We describe the key elements and solution approach here.

Inputs: The model and its solution require:
- a set of exogenous parameters: $\Theta \equiv \{k, \sigma, \Lambda(\tau_m, \gamma), \beta, \beta_h\}$;
- baseline equilibrium import shares: $\mathbf{I} \equiv \{I_V(\tau_b, \gamma = 0)\}$, where $I(\tau_b, \gamma = 0) = \Sigma_V I_V(\tau_b, \gamma = 0)$.

Equilibrium: The entry conditions (18) and (21) and U, U_h yield a system of equations for:
- the relative stationary price index in the intermediate state, $\hat{P}_1(g, g_h, \Theta, \mathbf{I})$ in (24);
- the sequence of relative prices after a switch to low or high protection, respectively $\hat{P}_{0,T}(g_h, \hat{P}_1, \Theta, \mathbf{I})$, in (20) and $\hat{P}_{2,T}(g, \hat{P}_1, \Theta, \mathbf{I})$, (45) in online Appendix D.1.2;
- the average profit change due to prices after a switch to high or low protection, respectively $g(\hat{P}_{2,T}/\hat{P}_1, \Theta)$ in (20) and $g_h(\hat{P}_{0,T}/\hat{P}_1, \Theta)$ in (23), where $\hat{P}_.$ denotes a price index relative to the baseline, e.g., $\hat{P}_{2,T} \equiv P_{2,T}/P_b$.

Solution: $\Upsilon(\Theta, \mathbf{I}) \equiv \{\hat{P}_1; g; g_h; (\hat{P}_{2,T}; \hat{P}_{0,T})_{T=0}^{\infty}\}$ is found by:
- fixing a set Θ consistent with our estimation and data I;
- iterating n times until we obtain a fixed point such that $\Upsilon^{(n)}(\Theta, \mathbf{I}) = \Upsilon^{(n-1)}(\Theta, \mathbf{I})$.

To understand the approach, recall that entry requires firms to incorporate expected changes in profits caused by tariffs and prices. To solve for prices starting in state 1, the solution algorithm uses the upper bounds $g^{(0)} = (P_2^D/P_1^D)^{\sigma-1}$ and $g_h^{(0)} = (P_0^D/P_1^D)^{\sigma-1}$, which we compute using the deterministic equation in (17). Using these we compute the initial values for $\hat{P}_1$ and the paths $(\hat{P}_{2,T}; \hat{P}_{0,T})_{T=0}^{\infty}$, which are then used to update g and g_h. We iterate until the g's and thus the other elements of the solution converge.

We use the following inputs. First, we choose 2005, a post-agreement year, as the baseline and use it to measure the import expenditure shares, I_V, and tariffs, τ_{0V}. Second, we require values for Θ; the elasticities can be estimated (as we show below); β and β_h are obtained from annual export and domestic firm survival rates data. The tariffs for each of the three states are observable in the China episode (τ_{1V} is the 2000 MFN and τ_{2V} the column 2); we use these unless stated otherwise for specific counterfactual exercises.

To solve the model we also require the expected durations embodied in u and u_h. One contribution of this paper is to identify these parameters and quantify the role of TPU in China's WTO accession, which we do in Section IV. But first we analyze the model's behavior under alternative parameters.

D. *Outcomes and Policy Experiments*

We solve the model under alternative policy regimes to explain its key mechanisms and illustrate its applicability to a range of trade policy questions. The main counterfactual is one where the United States unilaterally abandons its trade agreement commitments against all its trading partners and adopts a regime similar to the one it used for China prior to 2002. This is a potentially useful benchmark to illustrate the qualitative effects of TPU and is also not implausible under the forty-fifth US president.[29]

We allow for alternative policy regimes as follows. Recall that $u \equiv \gamma\lambda_2\beta/(1-\beta)$ and $u_h \equiv \gamma(1-\lambda_2)\beta_h/(1-\beta_h)$. To focus on the uncertainty parameter we use $\lambda_2 = 1/2$, so high and low protection are equally likely and then solve the model under all possible $\gamma \in [0,1]$. The policies τ_{0V}, τ_{1V}, and τ_{2V} are set equal to their simple means when computing $\hat{\tau}_1$ and $\hat{\tau}_2$, which implies we only require aggregate import penetration.[30] The remaining parameters are given in Table A11. We proceed in three steps:

(i) Evaluate the effects of switching policy states within a regime, e.g., a transition to the low protection state, and decomposing them into a TPU and an applied policy component.

(ii) Perform counterfactual analysis of switching policy regimes, e.g., the effects of introducing TPU under different applied or threat policies.

(iii) Calculate gains from trade under TPU and draw implications for trade agreements.

Effects of Switching Policy States.—The total change in the stationary price index between state 1 and 0, where we interpret the latter as an agreement, can be decomposed into a TPU and applied policy change as follows:

$$\hat{P}_1 \equiv \frac{P_1}{P_0^D} = \underbrace{\left(\frac{P_1}{P_1^D}\right)}_{\text{TPU}} \times \underbrace{\left(\frac{P_1^D}{P_0^D}\right)}_{\text{Applied } \hat{\tau}_1}. \tag{25}$$

To obtain the TPU component we solve the model for $\hat{P}_1$, at each possible γ, and then divide it by the applied policy component, $P_1^D/P_0^D = \hat{P}_1^D$ computed from (17).

[29] For any given set of parameters, the qualitative impacts of TPU are similar to those we later obtain for China alone. But since aggregate import penetration is larger when introducing TPU on all partners (0.25 in 2005), it typically generates stronger aggregate impacts on the United States.

[30] In the application to China (Section IV) we use: (i) specific parameters implied by the estimation; (ii) $\hat{\tau}_{1V}$ and $\hat{\tau}_{2V}$ as the ratio of the 2000 MFN and column 2 tariffs, respectively, to the 2005 MFN tariffs in each industry V; and (iii) Chinese import penetration in each industry V.

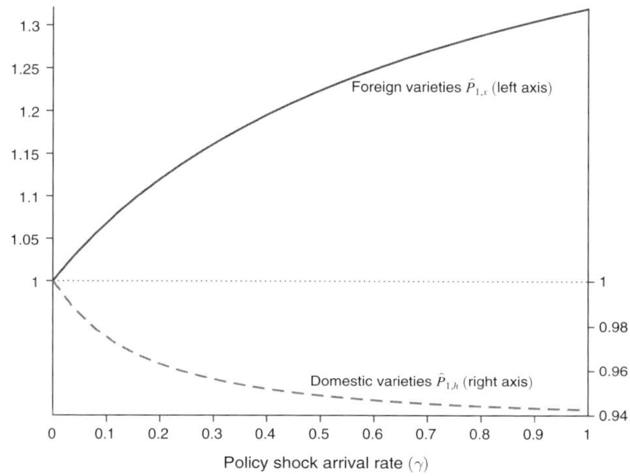

FIGURE 5. DOMESTIC AND FOREIGN VARIETY PRICE INDICES (*Counterfactual Introduction of US TPU on All Partners*)

Notes: General equilibrium solution of the model for each variable's growth relative to deterministic baseline if the United States introduces TPU in 2005. Solutions computed from estimated and other parameters in Table A11.

We can decompose the impact of TPU on entry and all other variables similarly. The tariffs in 2005 and 2000 were very similar so $\hat{\tau}_1$ and thus $\hat{P}_1^D$ are close to 1. Therefore, in Figures 5 and in the first column of Figure 6 we graph the TPU component for different outcomes against all possible γ.

Aggregate price index increases by as much as 5 percent if $\gamma = 1$ with almost one-half occurring even at moderate uncertainty, $\gamma = 0.25$ (panel A).

Foreign sales and entry fall by as much as 35 percent (sales) and 60 percent (entry) if $\gamma = 1$. Even moderate uncertainty generates a considerable reduction in entry, 40 percent (panel D).

Domestic sales and entry sales increase by up to 12 percent if $\gamma = 1$. Entry is only initially increasing in TPU but at sufficiently high γ the direct effect of TPU, U_h, starts to offset the indirect price effect (panel G).

We break the price index change into its foreign and domestic components in Figure 5. The decline in foreign variety entry due to TPU causes the foreign component to increase by as much as 30 percent. This large change is partly offset in the aggregate price index by the decline in the price index of domestic varieties.

Effects of Switching Policy Regimes.—Different events can trigger a change in γ without any change in a state or tariff values. For example, in the years leading up to WTO accession Chinese exporters may have changed their assessment about the probability of that outcome. Alternatively, if the United States abandoned its trade agreements but left its tariffs unchanged then we could examine it as a change in γ. The graphs just described also allow us to evaluate such counterfactuals by simply taking the ratio of the outcomes at different γ since $\hat{P}_1(\gamma')/\hat{P}_1(\gamma) = P_1(\gamma')/P_1(\gamma)$.

An alternative counterfactual regime is one with different threat tariffs. To examine this we continue to fix $\tau_1 = 1.04$ and now also fix $\gamma = 0.25$ and then compute $\hat{P}_1$ and $\hat{P}_1^D$ by solving the model at all alternative counterfactual values of τ_2. We allow $\tau_2 \in [1.04, 1.38]$ so it ranges from τ_1 to the maximum value of τ_2 in our sample. We obtain the TPU component for prices using (25) and do the same for the other outcomes.

The middle column of Figure 6 shows that TPU has the strongest effects on entry and sales at the highest threat tariff. Reductions in τ_2 have opposing effects on domestic and foreign entry and thus on their respective price indices. But the import price index effect always dominates; as reflected in the monotonically increasing effect of TPU on the aggregate price as we raise τ_2. At the highest τ_2 introducing TPU implies an increase in the price index that is about one-third of what would result if the United States reverted to autarky. The autarky cost is shown by the straight line and is computed using (17).

Finally, we consider the impact of TPU under alternative applied tariffs, e.g., if the United States did abandon its trade commitments and reverted to a temporary tariff above the 2000 MFN level. We fix τ_2 and γ and solve the model for $\tau_1 \in [\tau_0, \tau_2]$. The results in the last column of Figure 6 reflect two effects of increasing τ_1. First, at higher τ_1 the import penetration on which TPU acts is lower. Second, higher τ_1 implies a relative decrease in the threat for foreign varieties and the opposite for domestic varieties. Introducing TPU can reduce both foreign and domestic entry at high enough tariffs, as shown in the last column of Figure 6 and summarized here.

Aggregate price index is higher under TPU at all τ_1 (panel C).

Foreign sales and entry both fall with TPU when τ_1 is close to τ_0 (as seen before) since the possibility of high protection implies a substantial tariff increase. This negative effect of TPU is reversed when τ_1 approaches τ_2. At that point foreign exporters have little to lose if the policy switches to τ_2 and thus the direct price effect (due to lower entry of domestic firms) dominates (panel F).

Domestic sales and entry both increase with TPU when τ_1 is close to τ_0 (as seen before). But if τ_1 is above 1.1 then TPU reduces entry because the direct effect, from lower U_h, eventually offsets the indirect price effect. At high enough τ_1, TPU reduces domestic sales (panel I).

In this exercise, the long-run mean is $\overline{\tau}_1 = \lambda_2\tau_2 + (1-\lambda_2)\tau_0 = 1.21$ so introducing TPU at that point is a mean-preserving spread of the policy. Therefore the outcomes in the last column of Figure 6 evaluated at that tariff level show the pure risk effect of TPU, which leads to lower entry: both foreign and domestic. In Section IVA we extend this approach to decompose the effects of TPU on China into a pure risk and mean effect.

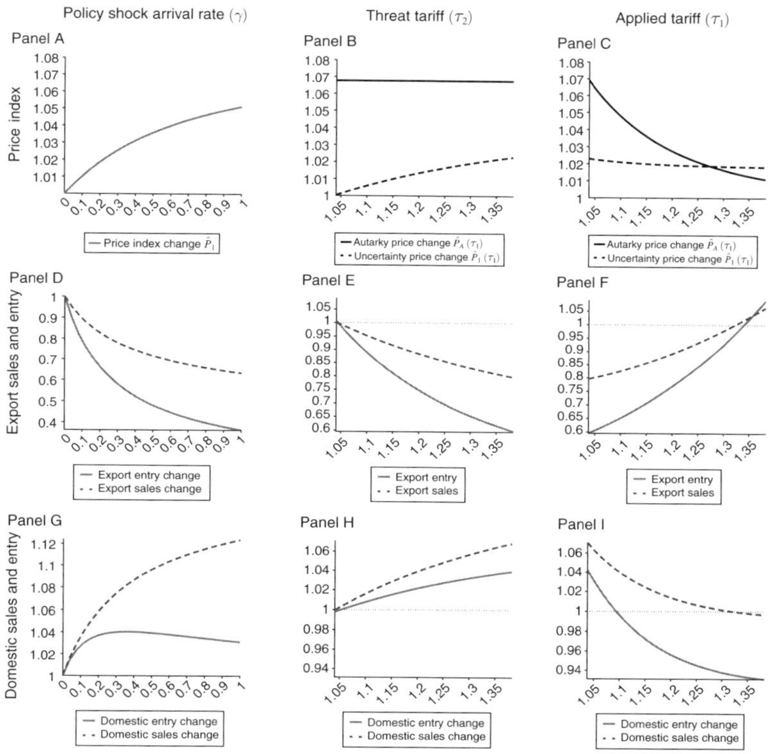

FIGURE 6. AGGREGATE PRICE, SALES, ENTRY (*Counterfactual Introduction of US TPU on All Partners*)

Notes: Model solution for a variable's growth relative to deterministic baseline if the United States introduces TPU in 2005 using parameters in Table A11. For panels B, E, and H, the threat tariff (τ_2) ranges from the mean observed MFN tariff of 1.041 to the column 2 tariffs of 1.38, both in 2000. For panels C, F, and I, the applied tariff (τ_1) ranges from the simple mean of the observed MFN tariff in 2005 of 1.038 to the column 2 tariffs in 2000 of 1.38. Aggregate import weights and import penetration are adjusted for the counterfactual τ_1 relative to observed values in 2005. For B the price change from increasing uncertainty or autarky is computed relative to a fixed applied $\tau_1 = 1.041$. For C the autarky price change is computed over $\tau_1 \in [1.038; 1.38]$.

Gains from Trade, Value of Agreements, and Tariff Bindings.—What are the implications of these results for the value of trade agreements and some of their key features?

An immediate implication is that if agreements reduce TPU then they increase consumer welfare via aggregate price reductions. How important are these price effects of TPU relative to say imposing prohibitive tariffs? This depends on the policy regime. At the baseline value of τ_1 autarky generates a price increase of about 6.8 percent; the effect of TPU is one-third of that when $\gamma = 0.25$ and two-thirds if

$\gamma = 1$ (panel A of Figure 6). This suggests an important value of agreements that eliminate such uncertainty.[31]

Can the cost of TPU ever exceed that of autarky? In the last column of Figure 6 we see that it may, depending on the initial tariff. The price effect of autarky, $(\hat{P}_m^D)_{\hat{\tau}_m \to \infty} = (1 - I_{\tau_1})^{-1/k}$, is decreasing in τ_1 because at higher tariffs there is lower import penetration and thus a lower cost of eliminating trade. At high enough τ_1 the cost of TPU is higher than that of autarky because TPU reduces domestic entry by so much that it eventually leads to less entry than autarky.

The possibility that TPU is costlier than autarky relies on TPU reducing domestic entry. In this exercise that occurs above $\tau_1 = 1.1$. During most of the GATT era the US simple average tariff has been below 1.1, but it was around 1.22 immediately preceding GATT, in 1947 (Bown and Irwin 2015). So if GATT 1947 reduced the probability of a trade war, which was one of its objectives, then the model suggests it may have increased both foreign and domestic entry investments and realized a large fraction of the possible gains from trade (since at $\tau_1 = 1.22$ the price effect of TPU is close to that of autarky).

Our counterfactual results can also provide support for the central role of tariff bindings in the WTO. Countries negotiate maximum tariffs in the WTO and commit not to exceed those bindings but are otherwise free to set their applied tariffs. We can reinterpret γ as the probability of changing tariffs anywhere below the binding and τ_2 as the potential maximum levels and examine the effect of changes in the latter.[32] By 2005 the US applied and tariff bindings were almost the same, so this would match the outcome when $\tau_2 = \tau_1$ in the middle column of Figure 6, where we see that increasing that binding decreases welfare and trade.

In sum, this section illustrates how the model works qualitatively, how it can be applied more broadly and indicates there is an important role for trade agreements. We now turn to a specific episode where we can estimate the uncertainty parameters and quantify the effect of an agreement.

IV. Structural Estimates and Quantification

NLLS Structural Estimates.—We identify the key structural parameters to quantify the effects of TPU via nonlinear estimation. This approach differs from Section II in two ways. First, the gravity equation is still (10) but the uncertainty factor, $U(\omega_V g, \gamma)$, now reflects a general equilibrium factor common to all industries. Second, we now use $f(\cdot) = -(k - \sigma + 1)\ln U(\omega_V g, \gamma)$ and the exact definition of U instead of an approximation around no uncertainty to rewrite (11) and obtain

$$(26) \quad \Delta \ln R_V = b_{d\sigma} \ln \left[\frac{1 + \tilde{b}_\gamma \left(\frac{\tau_{2V}}{\tau_{1V}} \right)^{-b_\sigma}}{1 + \tilde{b}_\gamma / g} \right] + b_\tau \Delta \ln \tau_V + b_d \Delta \ln D_V + b + e_V.$$

[31] In our setting, the welfare effects for US consumers would be similar if other countries retaliated and introduced uncertainty on US exporters (the latter would then have lower profits). This is due to the separability of markets, fixed wage and the assumption that the marginal domestic entrant knows its productivity and is not an exporter.

[32] We can reinterpret the model as corresponding to three different states between members of the WTO: in state 1 countries have discretion to set tariffs anywhere at or below the binding, τ_2, and a probability $\gamma\lambda_2$ they will use the discretion and set τ_2; state 0 corresponds to giving up any such discretion.

TABLE 6—CHINESE EXPORT GROWTH: NONLINEAR AND LINEAR ESTIMATES (US, $\Delta\ln$), 2000–2005

	NLLS (1)	OLS (2)	NLLS (3)	OLS (4)
Uncertainty (pre-WTO)	0.903	0.686	0.712	0.567
[+]	[0.324]	[0.150]	[0.345]	[0.185]
MFN tariff ($\Delta\ln$)	−6.678	−6.464	−6.446	−6.34
[−]	[1.26]	[1.266]	[1.268]	[1.270]
Transport cost ($\Delta\ln$)	−4.452	−4.309	−4.298	−4.227
[−]	[0.84]	[0.844]	[0.845]	[0.847]
Constant	1.598	0.877		
	[0.109]	[0.0845]		
Observations	3,043	3,043	3,043	3,043
R^2	0.02	.	0.04	.
Sector fixed effects	No	No	Yes	Yes
Number of coefficients estimated	3	3	23	23
Restriction test $\sigma = 3$ (p-value)	0.11	NA	0.98	NA
Restriction test $b_\tau = b_d \times \sigma/(\sigma - 1)$ (p-value)	0.335	0.373	0.72	0.818

Notes: Standard errors in brackets. Columns 1 and 3 use nonlinear least squares and columns 2 and 4 use ordinary least squares. Predicted sign of coefficient in brackets under variable. Sample: all specifications exclude transport cost outliers, as measured by changes in costs that exceed the top or bottom quartile by more than three times the value of the interquartile range. Uncertainty measure uses US MFN (τ_1) and column 2 tariffs (τ_2) to construct the profit loss measure. This is approximated by $1 - (\tau_1/\tau_2)^\sigma$ under OLS. For NLLS we do not approximate and use instead the general function $\ln(1 + b_\gamma \times (\tau_1/\tau_2)^\sigma)$ where b_γ is estimated as described in the text. The four specifications in the columns restrict $\sigma = 3$. We test this by relaxing the restriction in two additional NLLS specifications; we report the p-values in the second to last line at which we can't reject the restriction. We also impose the restriction that $b_\tau = b_d \times \sigma/(\sigma - 1)$. The last row reports p-values from the test of this restriction.

The parameters have the following structural interpretation: $b_d = -k$ and $b_\tau = -k\sigma/(\sigma - 1)$, $\tilde{b}_\gamma = u(\gamma)\, g$, $b_\sigma = \sigma$, and $b_{d\sigma} = -(k - \sigma + 1)/(\sigma - 1)$. One component of U, $1 + \tilde{b}_\gamma/g = 1 + u$, is log-separable and does not vary by industry so we cannot identify it separately from the constant, b. The nonlinear least squares (NLLS) regression yields estimates for $\tilde{b}_\gamma$, b_d, and b. We impose two theoretical restrictions: $b_{d\sigma} = \left((b_d + b_\sigma - 1)\right)/(b_\sigma - 1)$ and $b_\tau = b_d b_\sigma/(b_\sigma - 1)$; as before we impose $b_\sigma = 3$ but we will now test it.

Column 1 of Table 6 provides the NLLS estimates. For comparison with earlier results, we transform the estimate for $\tilde{b}_\gamma = 0.736$ into its OLS regression counterpart, $b_\gamma^{nlls} = \tilde{b}_\gamma(-b_d - b_\sigma + 1)/(b_\sigma - 1) = 0.90$. The point estimates are comparable to the OLS counterpart (column 2) and similar when we control for sector effects (columns 3 and 4). But below we show the partial equilibrium OLS estimates overestimate the trade effects.[33]

[33] Given that the NLLS estimation relies on the model structure and the variation in the transport cost variable to identify k, we minimize the potential influence of outliers by focusing on the subsample without transport cost outliers, as measured by changes in costs more than three times the interquartile range value beyond the top or bottom quartile value of the baseline sample. The estimate for k in this subsample is higher (under NLLS or OLS) than the baseline, which suggests that the transport cost for some products contained measurement error and generated attenuation bias.

Consistency with Model and Other Evidence.—Before using these estimates, we ask whether they are consistent with the model and other evidence. The signs of all estimated parameters are those predicted by the model. We also run the NLLS baseline specifications by individually relaxing $b_\tau = b_d\sigma/(\sigma - 1)$ or $b_\sigma = 3$. We fail to reject either of these restrictions and report p-values in the last two rows of Table 6. Our choice of $\sigma = 3$ is typical in trade estimates and the partial elasticity of exports to tariffs in the absence of uncertainty, -6.6, is close to previous estimates that use similarly disaggregated US trade and tariff data (cf. Romalis 2007).

Under a Pareto productivity distribution with shape parameter k, export sales without uncertainty are also Pareto but with shape $k/(\sigma - 1)$. The 95 percent confidence interval for our estimate of the sales distribution parameter is $b_d/(\sigma - 1)$ is $[1.4, 3.1]$. The estimate is larger than 1 and it satisfies the model's requirement for a finite first moment of sales, which we did not impose. The magnitude is similar to that in other studies using firm-level data.[34]

The other parameter central to the quantification is u: a Chinese exporter's expected duration of a spell under column 2 prior to WTO accession. This reflects the exporters' beliefs for an event that never occurred so we can't defend any particular value. Nevertheless, the bounds on our estimate are reasonable and consistent with the model. To fix ideas, consider a Chinese firm that starts exporting in 2000. Since firm-level studies suggest an expected export duration of between 6 and 7 years, our estimate implies that those firms expected to spend at least 10 percent of their exporting spell under column 2.[35]

We also estimate the probability of transitioning from state 1 to 2, given by $\lambda_{12} = \gamma\lambda_2$. Using the definition of $\tilde{b}_\gamma$ and u we obtain the estimate $\hat{\lambda}_{12} = \hat{u}(1 - \beta)/\beta$. The estimation does not restrict this parameter and yet we still find that it is bounded in the unit interval for reasonable annual probabilities of firm survival, β. The point estimate using the value for β employed in the general equilibrium derivation, is $\hat{\lambda}_{12} = 0.13$.[36]

In the presence of endogenous domestic firm entry we require those firms' beliefs of the expected duration of an agreement, u_h, for quantification. We are unable to identify this parameter empirically using US firm entry or sales data because the relevant uncertainty factor, U_h, does not vary across industries (all the tariff effects work through the price index). Therefore, we parametrize u_h by defining $\alpha \equiv u_h/u$. We choose $\alpha = 4$ as the central value, which implies that before the agreement, a US firm expected to spend 4 times as long under the WTO state than a Chinese exporter expected to spend under column 2. In Section IVA, we show that the quantification results are not very sensitive to alternative feasible values of α.[37,38]

[34] Eaton, Kortum, and Kramarz (2011) obtain an aggregate estimate of 2.46 using French exports; Hsieh and Ossa (2016) obtain a range from 1 to 1.44 over industries using Chinese firm data.

[35] The exit rate for new Chinese exporters is 0.16, implying a survival of 6.25 years (Ma, Tang, and Zhang 2014); our quantification employs $1 - \beta = 0.15$.

[36] When $\hat{u} = 0.73$ then $\hat{\lambda}_{12} = 0.73\frac{1-\beta}{\beta} \in (0, 1]$ if $\beta \in [0.42, 1)$.

[37] Our estimate of $\gamma\lambda_2 = 0.13$ implies that $\lambda_2 \in [0.13, 1]$ and so, after applying the discount factor values, the range consistent with the estimates is $\alpha \in [0, 12]$, for which we report sensitivity. For the central case, $\alpha = 4$, we obtain $\lambda_2 = 0.28$.

[38] We also solved a special case of the model without domestic entry costs, so there is a constant mass of active domestic producers, which is independent of u_h. We find similar export value effects, and the effects for the

A final cross-validation of the NLLS estimates is to ask if the implied uncertainty measure, $\hat{U}_V$, can predict the observed industry price index changes exactly as predicted by (12) in Section IIF. Recall that we found larger price reductions in industries with higher initial TPU by using a linear approximation to U_V. Our objective here is to test a more specific structural implication of the model. We regress the observed changes in prices on tariff and trade cost changes and on $(k/(\sigma-1)-1)(-\ln U_V)$, where the latter is constructed using the NLLS estimates obtained using the export data. The uncertainty measure thus constructed is predicted to have a coefficient of -1 on price changes and we estimate it to be -0.96 (SE 0.21). Thus, the estimates from the export equation predict the effect of TPU on prices well.

A. *Quantification: Exports*

We quantify the effects of TPU changes, decompose them into a pure risk and mean effect, perform different counterfactual experiments and provide an ad valorem tariff equivalent cost of TPU. Table A11 summarizes the parameters we use based on our estimates and auxiliary data.

We quantify the effect of reintroducing uncertainty in 2005 on Chinese exporters. Qualitatively, the outcomes for Chinese varieties are similar to Section IIID but there are two differences worth noting. First, export entry and sales reflect the response of Chinese varieties whereas the *domestic entry* and sales reflect both US and other non-Chinese varieties.[39] Second, we now account for variation in policy across industries. The main quantitative difference is that in Section IIID we did not have the uncertainty parameters and so described a range of TPU impacts. We can now use our estimates for China to pinpoint a particular value for each outcome. We now contrast these GE point estimates to the partial effect estimates and place them into perspective relative to the observed changes during this period.

In the discussion that follows, we quantify the effect of reintroducing TPU in 2005, e.g., R_1/R_1^D for exports, and interpret its inverse as the impact of TPU reduction. We present all results using log changes.

Average Effects: General versus Partial.—The average log change from increasing TPU is given by

$$\mathbb{E}_V \ln R_{1V}/R_{1V}^D = \mathbb{E}_V \ln (U_V)^{k-(\sigma-1)} + k \ln P_1/P_1^D. \tag{27}$$

aggregate price index are only somewhat stronger than under endogenous domestic entry (because the absence of a domestic extensive margin is partially offset by a larger intensive margin impact).

[39] The US firms respond to the general equilibrium price index changes, as they did in the two-country model, but so do any other non-Chinese firms that face constant trade barriers in the United States. It is simple to show that, because we are solving for changes, this is the outcome from extending the model to multiple countries as long as all non-Chinese firms face a common σ and k, as is typical in this type of model, and a similar expectation of the duration of the low protection state, u_h.

TABLE 7—IMPACT OF TPU REDUCTION ON CHINESE EXPORT VALUE AND PRICE (US, $100 \times \Delta\ln$), 2000–2005

	Policy uncertainty reduction estimates					
	Partial effect		General equilibrium effect		Data equivalent	
	Average	Aggregate	Average	Aggregate	Average	Aggregate
Export value	36	40	28	32	112	73.0
Export price	−15.2	−17.2	−14.8	−17	−26	−13

Notes: The first four columns are the model estimates for the growth in Chinese export value (or price) due to TPU reduction. The general equilibrium employs the coefficients from NLLS export estimates in column 1 of Table 6 and uses the model to incorporate the price index effects. The partial effect estimates ignore the price index effect and use OLS estimates for exports (column 2 of Table 6) and prices (column 1 of Table 4). The data equivalents for exports use the observed Chinese export growth (average or aggregate) and subtract nominal growth in the aggregate US expenditure on manufactures to account for nominal effects and aggregate expenditure shocks, which are held constant in the model prediction. The price growth data equivalent uses the average from Table 1 (or its aggregate using ideal weights) and subtracts the corresponding average (or aggregate) for non-Chinese varieties (used in Table A9) to account for common nominal shocks. The difference in the price data equivalent is mostly driven by the Chinese differential average and aggregate price growth.

The direct effect is −30 log points and the price index effect is 2 log points. Therefore the model implies that the reduction in TPU in the period 2000–2005 led to an average export increase of 28 log points, as shown in Table 7.[40]

We can contrast this with the partial effect from the linear estimation. The latter assumes no price effects and a linear approximation to U so the estimated partial effect counterpart to (27) is simply $-b_{\gamma}^{OLS} \times \mathbb{E}_V\big(1 - (\tau_{2V}/\tau_{1V})^{-3}\big) = -36$ log points. Thus, the implied partial effect on exports due to a TPU reduction is more than 20 percent higher than the GE effect. All subsequent exercises focus on the GE nonlinear estimates.

Aggregate Effects.—We now turn to aggregate effects of TPU for exports. The direct uncertainty effect, $-\ln(U_V)^{k-(\sigma-1)}$, ranges from about 0 to 57 log points and there is also considerable dispersion in export shares. So we weight each uncertainty factor by the relevant expenditure share to compute the growth of total expenditure on Chinese goods due to TPU. The aggregate effect is 32 log points, so higher than the average one;[41]

$$(28)\qquad \ln R_1/R_1^D = \ln \sum_V r_{1V}^D (U_V)^{k-(\sigma-1)} + k \ln P_1/P_1^D.$$

The quantification implies that TPU can account for over one-third of observed changes on expenditure in Chinese goods. The counterfactual holds income and

[40] We compute $(U_V)^{k-(\sigma-1)}$ using the estimates in column 1 of Table 6, the implied $\hat{u} = 0.73$, and each τ_{1V}/τ_{2V}. The price effect term uses the multi-industry version of (24) at fixed tariffs and the decomposition given in (25). The effect is not sensitive to alternative values of α, it ranges from 29 to 30 log points if $\alpha = 6$ or 0 respectively.

[41] The appropriate weight to evaluate the TPU component is the import share at τ_1 that would have been observed if $\gamma = 0$, $r_{1V}^D \equiv \tau_{1V} R_{1V}^D / \Sigma \tau_{1V} R_{1V}^D$. Since these are not observed we compute them by using the observed initial equilibrium imports, R_{0V}^D, the model implied deterministic change due to tariff changes, $\hat{\tau}_{1V}$, and the estimated tariff elasticity, b_τ. Thus, we obtain $r_{1V}^D = \tau_{1V} R_{0V}^D (\hat{\tau}_{1V})^{b_\tau} / \Sigma \tau_{1V} R_{0V}^D (\hat{\tau}_{1V})^{b_\tau}$ since the aggregate effects cancel out.

aggregate US expenditure on differentiated goods constant, so it also applies to the growth in the share of US tradables expenditure on Chinese goods, i.e., the growth in Chinese import penetration. In Table 7 we report this share increased by 73 log points so TPU can account for over one-third of that growth.

For any given level of aggregate expenditure, the effect of TPU on import penetration growth is the same as its effect on imports. So introducing TPU in 2005 would reduce penetration from 4.5 percent to 3.3 percent. The effect of TPU can depend on the baseline year's expenditure share, which may vary for exogenous reasons. Thus, we calculate the TPU effect on import penetration for each year after the agreement as the baseline and plot them in Figure 1. The solid line shows the observed import penetration, which tripled between 2000 and 2010. The dashed line is the GE counterfactual showing that penetration would only have doubled if TPU had remained.

Mean-Risk Decomposition.—In Section IIID, we describe how to decompose the effect of an agreement into a change in applied policies and TPU. The latter TPU effect can be further decomposed into changes in the mean versus changes in risk. To show this, we rewrite the impact of a change in γ evaluated at the pre-agreement applied tariff level, τ_{1V} as

$$(29)\quad \ln\frac{R_V(\gamma_0,\tau_{1V})}{R_V(\gamma_1,\tau_{1V})} = \ln\frac{R_V(\gamma_0,\overline{\tau}_V)}{R_V(\gamma_1,\overline{\tau}_V)} + \left[\ln\frac{R_V(\gamma_0,\tau_{1V})}{R_V(\gamma_0,\overline{\tau}_V)} - \ln\frac{R_V(\gamma_1,\tau_{1V})}{R_V(\gamma_1,\overline{\tau}_V)}\right].$$

The first term on the right is the growth in exports due to credibly securing tariffs at their long-run expected value, denoted by $\overline{\tau}_V$, a reduction in γ will then work as a mean-preserving compression in tariffs, which we label the risk effect. If $\tau_{1V} < \overline{\tau}_V$ then eliminating uncertainty reduces the expected value of tariffs and this lock-in effect is captured by the term in brackets, which is positive when the initial tariffs are below the long-run mean, as is the case in our application.

To quantify the risk effect we require the counterfactual long-run tariffs, $\overline{\tau}_V$. Prior to the agreement these are $\overline{\tau}_V = \lambda_2\tau_{2V} + (1-\lambda_2)\,\tau_{0V}$ and can be computed using an estimate of λ_2 and the observed values for τ_{2V} and τ_{0V}. In Section IIID, we showed that the TPU effect can be computed at any counterfactual τ_1, so setting $\tau_1 = \overline{\tau}_V$ we compute $\ln[R_V(\gamma_0,\overline{\tau}_V)/R_V(\gamma_1,\overline{\tau}_V)]$ by industry. We then aggregate these changes, using the expenditure weights evaluated at $\overline{\tau}_V$. This yields a risk effect of TPU for exports equal to 23 log points, which is 71 percent of the total. The substantial share due to risk arises because even if we start at the higher mean tariffs the threat of moving to τ_2 entails a doubling of tariffs on average.

Ad Valorem Equivalents: TPU versus Applied Policies.—To compare the effects of TPU with other policies, we calculate ad valorem tariff equivalents (AVE) of TPU on exports and other outcomes. The AVE is defined as the deterministic log change in the uniform tariff factor, $\ln\Delta_y$, that generates the same change in an outcome y as TPU. Formally, Δ_y solves

$$(30)\qquad y(\tau_1\Delta_y,\gamma = 0) = y(\tau_1,\gamma > 0).$$

Table 8—Impact on Chinese and US Outcomes of TPU Reduction and Corresponding Tariff Ad Valorem Equivalent ($100 \times \Delta\ln$), 2000–2005

	AVE (tariff equivalent)	Aggregate change
Chinese (real) export value [−]	5.0	32.4
Chinese export entry and investment [−]	9.4	61.2
Chinese export price index [+]	6.1	−16.9
US price index (manufacturing) [+]	13	−0.5
US consumer welfare [−]	13	−0.4
US (real) domestic sales (manufacturing) [+]	5.9	−1.3
US domestic employment (manufacturing) [+]	7.3	−1.2
US firm entry and investment (manufacturing) [+]	1.8	−0.4

Notes: Quantification uses NLLS estimates (column 1, Table 6). AVE (ad valorem equivalent) refers to the equivalent tariff reduction that would induce the same change in outcome x in the deterministic model with no uncertainty as the TPU reduction does. See text for details of calculation. Equivalents for outcome x in any period after uncertainty changes but applied policies remain unchanged. Reported values reflect differences in steady-state outcomes between policy states. [−/+] denotes sign of derivative of column variables with regard to tariff.

If we divide both sides by the baseline value for exports $R(\tau_1, \gamma = 0)$ then the expression on the right-hand side yields the 32 log point change previously derived. The left-hand side will then reflect the change in exports due to a deterministic tariff change, both the direct and indirect effect via prices. Solving for the AVE we obtain $\ln \Delta_R = 5$ log points (Table 8). So the export AVE was higher than the US applied average tariff in 2000.

B. *Quantification: Entry, Prices, and Welfare*

We now quantify the aggregate effects of TPU on entry, US price indices, and additional domestic outcomes. We then compare their magnitude with other pieces of evidence.

Aggregate Price and Welfare.—The overall price index increase from reintroducing TPU in 2005, $\ln P_1 / P_1^D$, is 0.52 log points.[42] In Table 8 we show this is equivalent to a deterministic tariff increase of 13 log points using (17) and the AVE definition in (30). This is roughly one-half of the price index increase predicted by the model if there was no TPU and the United States stopped all imports from China in 2005.

Increasing TPU from an initial equilibrium with a (counterfactual) long-run mean tariff increases the price index by 0.515 log points—almost the same as increasing it at the lower MFN tariffs. This implies the lock-in effect defined in (29) from eliminating TPU on the price index is close to zero because it generates an increase in foreign varieties that is offset by fewer domestic varieties.[43] Thus, the pure risk cost of TPU on the price index is large.

[42] We compute it using the multi-industry version of (24) at fixed tariffs and the decomposition given in (25).

[43] This does not mean that changes in tariffs have little effect on the price index. In fact, the price impact of increasing tariffs to their mean in the absence of uncertainty is 0.43 log points. However, if we lower those tariffs back down under uncertainty the price index will fall by almost as much so the net lock-in effect is close to zero.

These price index effects also apply to the (stationary) effect of TPU on consumer welfare because it is simply $-\mu \ln P_1 / P_1^D$. Namely, the welfare cost of TPU in 2005 is almost one-half that of going to autarky with China. The price index AVE also applies to consumer welfare. Thus, the effect of a TPU increase on the price index and welfare is equivalent to permanently raising the average tariff factor on Chinese goods in 2005 from 4 to 17 log points.

The AVE and autarky comparisons for welfare are relative magnitudes and so independent of the US expenditure share on manufacturing, μ. To provide an absolute effect and place it in context of other large trade shocks, we use the 2005 US expenditure on manufacturing as a share of tradables expenditure and obtain a welfare cost of TPU of 0.45 log points. This is over one-half the cost that Costinot and Rodríguez-Clare (2014) calculate for North America under a worldwide trade war with a uniform tariff of 40 percent. The TPU effect is also substantial when compared to another reference point for the magnitude of gains from trade: Broda and Weinstein (2006) estimate the real income gain from all new imported varieties in the United States between 1990 and 2001 to be 0.8 percent. Neither incorporates the role of uncertainty.[44]

Other Outcomes.—In our setting, the price AVE also applies to various outcomes of incumbent US firms in the differentiated sector, namely their domestic profits, sales, and employment, which are affected by uncertainty and tariffs only indirectly via the price index. The aggregate effects of TPU on domestic firm outcomes also reflect changes in entry decisions. The latter depend directly on uncertainty so their AVE is different from the one for the price index, as shown in Table 8. Reintroducing TPU in 2005 would increase US firm entry by 0.44 log points: equivalent to a 1.8 log point increase in tariffs. The effect on aggregate domestic sales is about 1.3, equivalent to a tariff increase of 5.9. Finally, TPU increases domestic quantities and employment in the differentiated sector by 1.2 log points, equivalent to a 7.3 log point tariff increase on Chinese goods, a sizable permanent tariff change in the context of recent US agreements.

How do these outcomes relate to observed changes in the period 2000–2005? To answer this we identify the differentiated sector with manufacturing, and the numéraire with the remaining tradable sectors (agriculture and mining), as is standard. In this period, we observed a reduction in both gross and net entry of manufacturing establishments. According to the Business Dynamics Statistics Database (US Census) the manufacturing gross entry rate was 7.9 percent and gross exit was 8.7 on average between 2002–2006. We also observed an expansion outside of the manufacturing sector, both in terms of establishments and employment. The sign of these observed changes is predicted by the model after a reduction in TPU.

The quantification can also account for a nontrivial fraction of US manufacturing employment and domestic sales reallocation. Our counterfactuals hold total employment, L, constant and therefore we should interpret the model's prediction

[44] Over 98 percent of Chinese exports to the United States are manufactures. As is standard in most trade models, neither our quantification nor the other ones discussed here take services into account. However, the model and calculations do take into account the large fraction of nontraded goods since many of the differentiated goods are produced by firms that are not productive enough to export. This is reflected in the relatively low values of US imports/consumption captured by the import penetration.

as applying to the manufacturing employment *share* in the tradable sector. Our estimates imply the reduction in TPU in the period 2000–2005 caused this employment share to fall by 1.2 log points (Table 8) and the observed reduction was 3.3 log points. The US sales counterfactual holds total manufacturing expenditure, $E = \mu w L$, constant and implies a 1.3 log point reduction in the US firms' share of manufacturing expenditure; the corresponding observed reduction was 3.3 log points. Thus, the reduction in TPU can account for at least one-third of the reallocation of domestic manufacturing sales and a similar fraction of its employment share in tradables.[45]

Export Entry and Price Index.—We conclude by comparing the quantitative implications for export entry and prices with other information.

The model predicts that at least a fraction $G(c_{sV}^U)$ of Chinese firms in V export to the United States under state s. The growth in this cutoff is given by (18) and its TPU component is obtained by holding tariffs fixed. Therefore, under a Pareto distribution, the growth in the number of exporters is simply k times that expression. Thus, we can compute the average entry effect of TPU as

$$\mathbb{E}_V \ln n_{1V}/n_{1V}^D = k\left(\mathbb{E}_V \ln U_V + \ln P_1/P_1^D\right). \tag{31}$$

On average TPU had reduced entry by 54 log points. This is also the change in the number of firms that upgrade since the fraction of exporters that do so is independent of uncertainty in this setting.

The aggregate entry and upgrading effect is 61 log points, which is sizable relative to the growth in the number of Chinese firms exporting to the world over the period 2000–2005 (83 log points, Ma et al. 2014).[46] The AVE for entry is nearly twice as large as for exports (Table 8). Moreover, when we apply the decomposition in (29) to entry we find that most of the TPU effect on entry is attributable to a risk reduction.

The negative effects of TPU on entry and upgrading imply increases in the price index for Chinese varieties. Comparing (15) and (16), the change in the import index for each industry when holding tariffs fixed is $\hat{P}_{1V,x} = \left(\hat{c}_{1V}\right)^{1-\frac{k}{\sigma-1}}$. Thus, the average effect of TPU across industries is

$$\mathbb{E}_V \ln P_{1V,x}/P_{1V,x}^D = \left(1 - \frac{k}{\sigma - 1}\right)\left(\mathbb{E}_V \ln U_V + \ln P_1/P_1^D\right), \tag{32}$$

which is simply a rescaling of the entry effect in (31). Using the NLLS estimates obtained with export data we compute the terms on the right-hand side and find an average price effect of 15 log points. The aggregate price effect is 17 log points and is obtained by aggregating the computed industry effects using the theoretically consistent weights in (28). These average and aggregate effects are reported in Table 7

[45] A more complete analysis of the effects of TPU on US firm entry and employment requires extending the model to account for features such as the input-output linkages analyzed by Acemoglu et al. (2016).

[46] The aggregate entry effect recomputes the expression in (28) using the entry elasticity for U. The expenditure weights used are the relevant ones to obtain the effect of changes in entry on prices.

and are similar to the estimates in Section IIF when using the empirical counterpart to this price index.

To compare the price effects to a relevant data counterpart, we control for nominal and other shocks common across varieties by focusing on relative prices. The quantification implies a reduction of 17 log points for the price index of Chinese varieties in 2000 to 2005 and a negligible impact for non-Chinese varieties. This is close to the relative ideal price index reduction we measure in that period.[47]

V. Conclusion

We assess the impact of trade policy uncertainty in a tractable general equilibrium framework with heterogeneous firms. Increased TPU reduces investment in export entry and technology upgrading, which in turn reduces trade flows and real income for consumers. We apply the model to China's WTO accession and use it to estimate and quantify the impacts of reducing the TPU faced by Chinese exporters when the United States ended its annual threat to revert to Smoot-Hawley tariffs.

We derive observable, theory-consistent measures of TPU and estimate its effect on trade flows, prices, and welfare. We find a large and robust effect of reducing TPU on China's export growth to the United States. The same measure of TPU does not predict China's exports to other major industrial countries or US import growth from its other nonpreferential trade partners. The reduction in TPU lowered Chinese industry export price indices, as the model predicts. Both the export and price effects of TPU are strongest in industries with high sunk costs of exporting.

Using the estimates of the structural parameters we compute the exact changes in price indices and the effect on entry and sales of domestic and foreign firms. Had the MFN status been revoked, the typical Chinese exporter would have faced an average tariff of 31 percent. The removal of this threat had large effects on Chinese export entry, about 60 log points, and export growth, 32 log points. The quantification indicates the reduction in TPU decreased US manufacturing sales and employment by more than one percent, but also lowered the price index and thus improved consumer welfare by the equivalent of a permanent tariff decrease of 13 percentage points on Chinese goods—a substantial amount of effective protection.

Our findings also point to a broader role of agreements in reducing TPU and generating aggregate welfare gains. For example, if the United States unilaterally threatens to abandon or renegotiate all its trade agreements and raises the tariff threat to a level similar to what China faced, then the US consumer cost would be equivalent to one-third of the cost of trade autarky. Moreover, for a range of applied tariffs an increase in TPU may leave consumers worse off than autarky. Therefore, events such as Brexit and threats to renegotiate agreements can undermine their value even if they lead to no applied policy change.

Future work could explicitly model, quantify, and decompose the relative importance of alternative channels through which TPU may operate (e.g., intermediates and offshoring) as well as its impact relative to that of alternative sources of Chinese

[47] We measure the latter using the industry price index changes in Section IIF and aggregating them for $i = \text{China}$ or US nonpreferential trading partners using their respective log change ideal weights, $\Delta \ln P_i \equiv \sum_V w_{V,i} \Delta \ln P_{V,i}$. We obtain $\Delta \ln P_{china} - \Delta \ln P_{non-pref} = -0.6 - 12$.

export changes in own trade policy or the partial dismantling of central planning. It could also be useful to structurally quantify the labor market effects of TPU in the presence of frictions. More generally, our research points to the value of specific data-rich settings to identify the effects of policy uncertainty on economic activity and shows these potentially substantial effects should not be ignored.

Appendix A. Theory Appendix

A. *Entry under Partial Equilibrium*

Proposition 1 derives the equilibrium entry expressions and related results in Section ID. We employ a more general policy transition matrix and show the special case in the text is obtained when $\lambda_{22} = 1$:

$$M = \begin{bmatrix} \lambda_{22} & \lambda_{21} & 0 \\ \lambda_{12} & \lambda_{11} = 1-\gamma & \lambda_{10} \\ 0 & 0 & 1 \end{bmatrix}. \tag{33}$$

PROPOSITION 1 (Policy Uncertainty and Export Entry, Small Exporter): *Under a regime $\Lambda(\tau_m, \gamma)$ with policy uncertainty and where tariff increases are possible, $\tau_2 > \tau_1$ and $u(\gamma) > 0$, the entry cutoff in the intermediate state, c_1^U, is*

(*A*) *unique and $c_1^U = c_1^D U(\omega, \gamma)$, and U is given by (7);*

(*B*) *lower than the deterministic, $c_1^U < c_1^D$, and decreasing in policy uncertainty, $dc_1^U / d\gamma = dU/d\gamma < 0$;*

(*C*) *lower than the cutoff in the low state, $c_1^U < c_0^U = c_0^D$ and $c_1^U / c_0^U = c_1^U / c_0^D = U(\omega, \gamma) \times (\tau_1 / \tau_0)^{-\frac{\sigma}{\sigma-1}}$.*

To prove the uniqueness of the industry cutoff in (i), we first establish sufficient conditions for a unique tariff below which each firm enters. We say $\Lambda(\tau_m, \gamma)$ exhibits uncertainty persistence if $\Lambda(\tau_{m+1}, \gamma)$ first order stochastically dominates $\Lambda(\tau_m, \gamma)$ for $m = 0, 1$, which is satisfied by (33).

LEMMA 1 (Entry Threshold): *For any given policy regime $\Lambda(\tau_m, \gamma)$ that exhibits uncertainty persistence, and each firm c from a small exporting country, there is a unique threshold tariff per state, $\tau_s^U(\gamma, c)$, below which a firm enters into exporting.*

PROOF OF LEMMA 1:

Rewriting (2) recursively we have $\Pi_e(a_s, c, \gamma) = \pi(a_s, c) + \beta \mathbb{E}_s \Pi_e(a_s', c, \gamma)$. Substitute in (4) to obtain

$$\Pi(a_s, c, \gamma) - \Pi_e(a_s, c, \gamma) + K = \max\{0, \beta \mathbb{E}_s[\Pi(a_s', c, \gamma) - \Pi_e(a_s', c, \gamma)] - \pi(a_s, c) + K\}; \tag{34}$$

$$V_s = \max\{0, \beta \mathbb{E}_s V_s' - \pi(a_s, c) + K(1-\beta)\}, \tag{35}$$

where the option value of waiting is $V_s \equiv \Pi(a_s, c, \gamma) - \Pi_e(a_s, c, \gamma) + K$ and $\mathbb{E}_s V_s' \equiv \mathbb{E}_s[\Pi(a_s', c, \gamma) - \Pi_e(a_s', c, \gamma) + K]$.

(i) Entry by firms from small exporting countries have no effect on the importer aggregates. Thus, for given E and P we have $a_s \equiv EP^{\sigma-1}\tau_s^{-\sigma}\sigma^{-\sigma}(\sigma-1)^{\sigma-1}$ so $\mathbb{E}_s V_s' = \int V_s \, d\Lambda(\gamma, \tau' | \tau)$.

(ii) Because $-\pi(a_s, c)$ is increasing in τ, it is more attractive to wait at higher tariffs because the second element of (35) and therefore V_s would be higher, all else equal.

(iii) Since Λ exhibits uncertainty persistence we have $\int V_s \, d\Lambda(\gamma, \tau' | \tau + \varepsilon) > \int V_s \, d\Lambda(\gamma, \tau' | \tau)$ if V_s is increasing in τ.

Given (iii), if we start with an increasing V_s the fixed point to this iteration is also increasing in τ. By properties (ii) and (iii), $\beta \mathbb{E}_s V_s' - \pi(a_s, c)$ is increasing in τ, so there is some $\tau_s^U(\gamma, c)$ below which the firm value is higher if exporting and above which the opposite is true. ∎

PROOF OF PROPOSITION 1(A):

Lemma 1 shows that each firm v has a single tariff entry cutoff $\tau_s^U(\gamma, c_v)$. All firms have different cost but face the same τ and γ in the industry so there is a unique entry cutoff for any given τ_m, $c_1^U(\tau_m, \gamma)$, and only those with cost below this enter into exporting.

To show $c_1^U = c_1^D U(\omega, \gamma)$ we first derive $\Pi(a_s, c \leq c_s^U, \gamma)$ if $s = 1$. Starting with (35) and taking the expectation over the possible states we have

$$\text{(36)} \quad \mathbb{E}_s V_s' = \lambda_{s,s+1}[\beta \mathbb{E}_{s+1} V_s' - \pi(a_{s+1}, c) + K(1-\beta)] \quad \text{if } c \leq c_s^U$$

$$= \lambda_{s,s+1}\left[\beta\left(\frac{\lambda_{s+1,s+1}}{1-\beta\lambda_{s+1,s+1}}[K(1-\beta) - \pi(a_{s+1}, c)]\right) - \pi(a_{s+1}, c) + K(1-\beta)\right]$$

$$= \frac{\lambda_{s,s+1}}{1-\beta\lambda_{s+1,s+1}}[K(1-\beta) - \pi(a_{s+1}, c)],$$

where the second line uses (35) and takes the conditional expectation starting at $s+1$:

$$\text{(37)} \quad \mathbb{E}_{s+1} V_s' = \lambda_{s+1,s+1}[\beta \mathbb{E}_{s+1} V_s' - \pi(a_{s+1}, c) + K(1-\beta)] \quad \text{if } c \leq c_s^U$$

$$= \frac{\lambda_{s+1,s+1}}{1-\beta\lambda_{s+1,s+1}}[K(1-\beta) - \pi(a_{s+1}, c)].$$

We can then show by contradiction that $c_s^U < c_s^D$. Suppose instead that $c_s^U \geq c_s^D$ so the marginal deterministic firm has nonpositive option value of waiting at s

under uncertainty, i.e., $V_s(c_s^D) \le 0$. By definition $\pi(a_s, c_s^D) = K(1-\beta)$ and so $V_s(c_s^D) = \max\{0, \beta \mathbb{E}_s V_s'(c_s^D)\}$. Moreover, $\pi(a_{s+1}, c_s^D) < K(1-\beta)$ when $\tau_s < \tau_{s+1}$, which implies that $\mathbb{E}_s V_s' > 0$ and therefore $V_s(c_s^D) > 0$. This contradiction implies that $c_s^U < c_s^D$.

The marginal firm at s under uncertainty has

$$V_s(c_s^U) = 0 = \max\left\{0, \beta \mathbb{E}_s\left[V_s'(c_s^U)\right] - \pi(a_s, c_s^U) + K(1-\beta)\right\} \tag{38}$$

and we can solve for c_s^U by equating the second term in curly brackets to zero and simplifying to obtain

$$\pi(a_s, c_s^U) + \beta\lambda_{s,s+1}\frac{\pi(a_{s+1}, c_s^U)}{1-\beta\lambda_{s+1,s+1}} = K(1-\beta)\left(1+\frac{\beta\lambda_{s,s+1}}{1-\beta\lambda_{s+1,s+1}}\right). \tag{39}$$

Starting at $s = 1$, replacing π using (1) and simplifying we obtain the cutoff expression (6) in the text

$$a_1\left(c_1^U\right)^{1-\sigma}\left[1+\frac{\beta\lambda_{12}}{1-\beta\lambda_{22}}\frac{a_2}{a_1}\right] = K(1-\beta)\left(1+\frac{\beta\lambda_{12}}{1-\beta\lambda_{22}}\right)$$

$$a_1\left(c_1^U\right)^{1-\sigma}\left[1+u(\gamma)\frac{a_2}{a_1}\right] = K(1-\beta)\left(1+u(\gamma)\right)$$

$$c_1^U = \left(\frac{a_1}{K(1-\beta)}\right)^{\frac{1}{\sigma-1}} \times \left(\frac{1+u(\gamma)\omega}{1+u(\gamma)}\right)^{\frac{1}{\sigma-1}}. \tag{40}$$

The last line uses the expressions given in the main text: $\omega \equiv a_2/a_1 = (\tau_2/\tau_1)^{-\sigma}$, $\gamma \equiv 1-\lambda_{11}$, $\gamma\lambda_2 = \lambda_{12}$, and $u(\gamma) \equiv \frac{\beta\gamma\lambda_2}{1-\beta\lambda_{22}}$ where in the text we assumed $\lambda_{22} = 1$.∎

PROOF OF PROPOSITION 1(B):

Since $c_1^U/c_1^D = U$ we must show $U < 1$ if and only if tariff increases are possible. From the definition in (7) we obtain $U < 1$ if and only if $u(\gamma)\omega < u(\gamma)$, which is true if and only if $\tau_2 > \tau_1$ and $\gamma\lambda_2 > 0$ so that $u(\gamma) > 0$. Since $c_1^U = c_1^D U(\omega, \gamma)$ (part A) we can use (7) to obtain

$$\gamma\frac{d\ln c_1^U}{d\gamma} = \gamma\frac{d\ln U_1(\omega,\gamma)}{d\gamma} = \frac{1}{\sigma-1}\frac{u}{1+u}\frac{\omega-1}{1+u\omega} < 0, \tag{41}$$

where the inequality holds only if $\omega < 1 \Leftrightarrow \tau_2 > \tau_1$ and $u(\gamma) > 0$. ∎

PROOF OF PROPOSITION 1(C):

If $\tau_2 > \tau_1$ *and* $u > 0$ then $c_1^U < c_1^D$, (part B). Since $\lambda_{00} = 1$ we have $c_0^D = c_0^U$. If $\tau_0 \le \tau_1$ then $c_1^D \le c_0^D$ (from (3)) and therefore $c_1^U < c_1^D \le c_0^D = c_0^U$. Using c_1^U from part (A) $c_1^U/c_0^D = U(\omega,\gamma)\times(c_1^D/c_0^D) = U(\omega,\gamma)\times(\tau_1/\tau_0)^{-\frac{\sigma}{\sigma-1}}$, where the last equality uses (3), and the definition of a_s for fixed E and P. ∎

B. *Upgrading Cutoffs*

After paying the initial export entry cost, K, the firm can incur an additional K_z to lower its marginal export cost by a fraction $z < 1$ of the industry's baseline variable export cost d. Its operating export profits become $\pi_v = a_s(zc_v)^{1-\sigma}$, so they grow by a factor $z^{1-\sigma} - 1$. If policy is deterministic, a firm will be indifferent between upgrading or not if its marginal cost of production is c_{sz}^D, which is defined by $\pi(a_s, zc_{sz}^D) - \pi(a_s, c_{sz}^D) = K_z(1-\beta)$:

$$c_{sz}^D = \left[\frac{a_s(z^{1-\sigma} - 1)}{K_z(1-\beta)}\right]^{\frac{1}{\sigma-1}}. \tag{42}$$

We consider a sufficiently high fixed cost of upgrading such that only the most productive and thus only a fraction of exporters upgrade. This implies that the marginal entrant into exporting will not upgrade and therefore the entry cutoff, c_s^D, is still given by (3). In this case the upgrade cutoff is proportional to the entry cutoff by an upgrading parameter, ϕ, which is independent of the policy. Thus, we have

$$\frac{c_{sz}^D}{c_s^D} = \phi \equiv \left[(z^{1-\sigma} - 1)\frac{K}{K_z}\right]^{\frac{1}{\sigma-1}} < 1. \tag{43}$$

Below we show that if only a fraction of exporters upgrade then under uncertainty we also obtain an upgrade to entry cutoff ratio equal to ϕ. This is a result we use in the aggregation and estimation. Given the similarities with the entry decision, here we just outline the main steps and modifications to incorporate upgrading.

In order to use the entry cutoffs derived in the text we must ensure that ϕ is sufficiently low to ensure that even the most productive marginal entrant would never upgrade, i.e., even a firm that is indifferent about entering under the worst policy state would never upgrade when conditions improved. Formally, the condition for the upgrading parameter to be sufficiently low if $\phi < \overline{\phi}$ and $\overline{\phi}$ is defined by $c_{0z}^U(\overline{\phi}) = c_2^U$, where c_2^U is the entry cutoff under column 2 tariffs previously derived and $c_{0z}^U(\phi)$ is the upgrade cutoff under the agreement state.

At a given state s a firm will be just indifferent between upgrading if it has cost c_{sz}^U, which is implicitly defined by the equality of the expected value of exporting using the upgraded technology net of the sunk cost and the expected value of waiting while using the old technology:

$$\Pi_e(a_s, c) = \max\{\Pi_{ez}(a_s, zc) - K_z, \beta \mathbb{E}_s \Pi_e(a_s', c)\}. \tag{44}$$

The upgrade factor z multiplies the cost in the expression of operating profits for each period after upgrading. The key differences relative to the entry decision are that a firm that has not upgraded makes positive export profit today. Moreover, in the following period the firm either transitions to the same state or to column 2 tariffs, in which case it continues to use the initial technology, or transitions to the agreement state, where it will upgrade. Since z is state independent it is straightforward to show that the expected value of exporting under the new technology is

$$\Pi_{ez}(a_s, z c_{sz}) = z^{1-\sigma}\Pi_e(a_s, c_{sz}) \quad \text{for each } s. \tag{45}$$

When a is decreasing in tariffs (τ) the solution is to enter when current tariffs are below a firm-specific threshold tariff. The cutoff at any particular a must satisfy the following upgrade indifference condition:

$$\Pi_{ez}(a_s, z c_{sz}^U) - K_z = \Pi_e(a_s, c_{sz}^U) \quad \text{for each } s. \tag{46}$$

Solving this yields $c_{1z}^U = U(\omega, \gamma)\, c_{1z}^D$ and thus the elasticity with regard to the uncertainty factor is the same as the entry cutoff's. Moreover, the relationship between the cutoffs is $\frac{c_{1z}^U}{c_1^U} = \frac{c_{1z}^D U(\omega,\gamma)}{c_1^D U(\omega,\gamma)} = \phi$. Since the upgrade cutoff is proportional to the entry one by a fixed factor that is independent of policy, we can replace it to derive the structural industry gravity equation that aggregates without requiring knowledge of which firms actually upgrade in the industry.

Appendix B. Data Appendix

- *Change in Ad Valorem Tariffs* $\Delta \ln \tau_V$: Log change in 1 plus the statutory ad valorem MFN tariff rate aggregated to the HS-6 level between 2005 and 2000. Source: TRAINS via WITS
- *Change in AVE Tariffs* $\Delta \ln \tau_V$: Log change in 1 plus the ad valorem equivalent (AVE) of the MFN tariff rate at the HS-6 level between 2005 and 2000. For specific tariffs, the AVE is given by the ratio of unit duty to the average 1996 import unit value. Source: TRAINS for tariff rates and COMTRADE for unit values via WITS
- *Column 2 Tariff* τ_{2V}: Log of 1 plus the column 2 tariff rate at the HS-6 level. For specific tariffs at the HS-8, base year unit values from 1996 used for all years to compute the AVE tariff and then average at the HS-6 level. Source: TRAINS for tariff rates and COMTRADE for unit values via WITS
- *Uncertainty Pre-WTO:* Measure of uncertainty from the model $1 - (\tau_{2V}/\tau_{1V})^{-\sigma}$ computed using year 2000 column 2 and MFN tariff rates.
- *Change in NTBs:* Indicators for temporary trade barriers in-force including anti-dumping duties, countervailing duties, special safeguards, and China-specific special safeguards. Data are aggregated up to HS-6 level. Source: Bown (2015)
- *Change in MFA:* Indicators for in-force Multi-Fiber Agreement on Textiles and Clothing (MFA/ATC) quotas aggregated to the HS-6 level and concorded through time. Source: Brambilla, Khandelwal, and Schott (2010)
- *Change in Transport Costs* $\Delta \ln D_V$: Log change in the ratio of trade values inclusive of costs, insurance, and freight (CIF) to free on board value (FOB). Source: CIF/FOB ratios constructed at HS-6 level using disaggregated data from NBER

- *US Import Growth:* Change in log US imports by HS-6 industry between 2000 and 2005. Source: NBER
- *Chinese Export Growth (Non-US Destinations):* Change in log Chinese exports by HS-6 industry between 2000 and 2005 to Japan or EU-15 (members of EU by 1995). Source: COMTRADE
- *Chinese Variety Growth:* Change in log count of HS-10 products exported to United States within each HS-6 industry from 2000 to 2005. Source: NBER
- *Chinese Price Index Growth:* Change in log ideal price index of exports to the United States by HS-6 industry from 2000 to 2005. Source: Authors calculations described in online Appendix C.5
- *Sunk Cost Classification:* Indicator for top two terciles of industries according to their export sunk cost estimate. Source: Authors calculations described in online Appendix C.4
- *Import Penetration in Manufacturing:* US manufacturing imports over US expenditure on manufacturing, $R_{Ch,t}/E_t$, where E_t is total manufacturing shipments (US Census Bureau) less net manufacturing exports (USITC).

We use the published UN Statistics Division concordances to map the HS 2002 codes into the HS 1996 to match the policy data with the trade data over time. To compute price indices we also match the ten-digit level import flows over time, for which we use the method in Pierce and Schott (2012). We then aggregate up to the six-digit level of HS 1996 when constructing price indices or product variety counts as needed and described in online Appendix C.5. A small fraction of HS-10 codes are reassigned across multiple HS-6 and can't be tracked longitudinally without arbitrary aggregation in which case we drop them for all years.

REFERENCES

Acemoglu, Daron, David Autor, David Dorn, Gordon H. Hanson, and Brendan Price. 2016. "Import Competition and the Great US Employment Sag of the 2000s." *Journal of Labor Economics* 34 (S1): S141–98.

Amador, Manuel, and Kyle Bagwell. 2013. "The Theory of Optimal Delegation with an Application to Tariff Caps." *Econometrica* 81 (4): 1541–99.

Amiti, Mary, and Caroline Freund. 2010. "The Anatomy of China's Export Growth." In *China's Growing Role in World Trade*, edited by Robert C. Feenstra and Shang-Jin Wei, 35–56. Chicago: University of Chicago Press.

Arkolakis, Costas, Arnaud Costinot, and Andrés Rodríguez-Clare. 2012. "New Trade Models, Same Old Gains?" *American Economic Review* 102 (1): 94–130.

Auer, Raphael, and Andreas M. Fischer. 2010. "The Effect of Low-Wage Import Competition on U.S. Inflationary Pressure." *Journal of Monetary Economics* 57 (4): 491–503.

Autor, David H., David Dorn, and Gordon H. Hanson. 2013. "The China Syndrome: Local Labor Market Effects of Import Competition in the United States." *American Economic Review* 103 (6): 2121–68.

Bagwell, Kyle, and Robert W. Staiger. 1999. "An Economic Theory of GATT." *American Economic Review* 89 (1): 215–48.

Bagwell, Kyle, and Robert W. Staiger. 2011. "What Do Trade Negotiators Negotiate About? Empirical Evidence from the World Trade Organization." *American Economic Review* 101 (4): 1238–73.

Baker, Scott R., Nicholas Bloom, and Steven J. Davis. 2016. "Measuring Economic Policy Uncertainty." *Quarterly Journal of Economics* 131 (4): 1593–636.

Bernanke, Ben S. 1983. "Irreversibility, Uncertainty, and Cyclical Investment." *Quarterly Journal of Economics* 98 (1): 85–106.

Blonigen, Bruce A., and Alyson C. Ma. 2010. "Please Pass the Catch-Up: The Relative Performance of Foreign Firms in Chinese Exports." In *China's Growing Role in World Trade*, edited by Robert C. Feenstra and Shang-Jin Wei, 475–509. Chicago: University of Chicago Press.

▶**Bloom, Nicholas, Stephen Bond, and John van Reenen.** 2007. "Uncertainty and Investment Dynamics." *Review of Economic Studies* 74 (2): 391–415.

▶**Bloom, Nicholas, Mirko Draca, and John van Reenen.** 2016. "Trade Induced Technical Change? The Impact of Chinese Imports on Innovation, IT and Productivity." *Review of Economic Studies* 83 (1): 87–117.

Bown, Chad P. 2015. *Temporary Trade Barriers Database*. http://econ.worldbank.org/ttbd/ (accessed April 2012).

Bown, Chad P., and Douglas A. Irwin. 2015. "The GATT's Starting Point: Tariff Levels circa 1947." National Bureau of Economic Research Working Paper 21782.

Brambilla, Irene, Amit K. Khandelwal, and Peter K. Schott. 2010. "China's Experience under the Multi-Fiber Arrangement (MFA) and the Agreement on Textiles and Clothing (ATC). In *China's Growing Role in World Trade*, edited by Robert C. Feenstra and Shang-Jin Wei, 345–87. Chicago: University of Chicago Press.

Brandt, Loren, Johannes Van Biesebroeck, and Yifan Zhang. 2012. "Creative Accounting or Creative Destruction? Firm-Level Productivity Growth in Chinese Manufacturing." *Journal of Development Economics* 97 (2): 339–51.

Broda, Christian, Nuno Limão, and David E. Weinstein. 2008. "Optimal Tariffs and Market Power: The Evidence." *American Economic Review* 98 (5): 2032–65.

Broda, Christian, and David E. Weinstein. 2006. "Globalization and the Gains from Variety." *Quarterly Journal of Economics* 121 (2): 541–85.

Caliendo, Lorenzo, Maximiliano Dvorkin, and Fernando Parro. 2015. "The Impact of Trade on Labor Market Dynamics." National Bureau of Economic Research Working Paper 21146.

Chaney, Thomas. 2008. "Distorted Gravity: The Intensive and Extensive Margins of International Trade." *American Economic Review* 98 (4): 1707–21.

Costinot, Arnaud, and Andrés Rodríguez-Clare. 2014. "Trade Theory with Numbers: Quantifying the Consequences of Globalization." In *Handbook of International Economics*, Volume 4, edited by Gita Gopinath, Elhanan Helpman, and Kenneth Rogoff, 197–261. Amsterdam: Elsevier.

Dixit, Avinash K. 1989. "Entry and Exit Decisions under Uncertainty." *Journal of Political Economy* 97 (3): 620–38.

Eaton, Jonathan, Samuel Kortum, and Francis Kramarz. 2011. "An Anatomy of International Trade: Evidence from French Firms." *Econometrica* 79 (5): 1453–98.

Feenstra, Robert C. 1994. "New Product Varieties and the Measurement of International Prices." *American Economic Review* 84 (1): 157–77.

Handley, Kyle. 2014. "Exporting under Trade Policy Uncertainty: Theory and Evidence." *Journal of International Economics* 94 (1): 50–66.

Handley, Kyle, and Nuno Limão. 2012. "Trade and Investment under Policy Uncertainty: Theory and Firm Evidence." National Bureau of Economic Research Working Paper 17790.

Handley, Kyle, and Nuno Limão. 2015. "Trade and Investment under Policy Uncertainty: Theory and Firm Evidence." *American Economic Journal: Economic Policy* 7 (4): 189–222.

Handley, Kyle, and Nuno Limão. 2017. "Policy Uncertainty, Trade, and Welfare: Theory and Evidence for China and the United States: Dataset." *American Economic Review*. https://doi.org/10.1257/aer.20141419.

Horn, Henrik, Giovanni Maggi, and Robert W. Staiger. 2010. "Trade Agreements as Endogenously Incomplete Contracts." *American Economic Review* 100 (1): 394–419.

Hsieh, Chang-Tai, and Peter J. Klenow. 2009. "Misallocation and Manufacturing TFP in China and India." *Quarterly Journal of Economics* 124 (4): 1403–48.

Hsieh, Chang-Tai, and Ralph Ossa. 2016. "A Global View of Productivity Growth in China." *Journal of International Economics* 102 (1): 209–24.

Impullitti, Giammario, Alfonso A. Irarrazabal, and Luca David Opromolla. 2013. "A Theory of Entry into and Exit from Export Markets." *Journal of International Economics* 90 (1): 75–90.

International Monetary Fund. 2010. "Getting the Balance Right: Transitioning out of Sustained Current Account Surpluses." In *World Economic Outlook*. Washington, DC: International Monetary Fund.

Kee, Hiau Looi, and Heiwai Tang. 2016. "Domestic Value Added in Exports: Theory and Firm Evidence from China." *American Economic Review* 106 (6): 1402–36.

Lileeva, Alla, and Daniel Trefler. 2010. "Improved Access to Foreign Markets Raises Plant-Level Productivity… For Some Plants." *Quarterly Journal of Economics* 125 (3): 1051–99.

Limão, Nuno, and Giovanni Maggi. 2015. "Uncertainty and Trade Agreements." *American Economic Journal: Microeconomics* 7 (4): 1–42.

Ludema, Rodney D., and Anna Maria Mayda. 2013. "Do Terms-of-Trade Effects Matter for Trade Agreements? Theory and Evidence from WTO Countries." *Quarterly Journal of Economics* 128 (4): 1837–93.

Ma, Yue, Heiwai Tang, and Yifan Zhang. 2014. "Factor Intensity, Product Switching, and Productivity: Evidence from Chinese Exporters." *Journal of International Economics* 92 (2): 349–62.

Manova, Kalina, and Zhiwei Zhang. 2009. "China's Exporters and Importers: Firms, Products and Trade Partners." National Bureau of Economic Research Working Paper: 15249.

Ossa, Ralph. 2014. "Trade Wars and Trade Talks with Data." *American Economic Review* 104 (12): 4104–46.

Pierce, Justin R., and Peter K. Schott. 2012. "A Concordance between Ten-Digit U.S. Harmonized System Codes and SIC/NAICS Product Classes and Industries." *Journal of Economic and Social Measurement* 37 (1–2): 61–96.

Pierce, Justin R., and Peter K. Schott. 2016. "The Surprisingly Swift Decline of US Manufacturing Employment." *American Economic Review* 106 (7): 1632–62.

Pregelj, Vladimir N. 2001. *Most-Favored-Nation Status of the People's Republic of China.* CRS Report for Congress. Washington, DC: Library of Congress.

Roberts, Mark J., and James R. Tybout. 1997. "The Decision to Export in Colombia: An Empirical Model of Entry with Sunk Costs." *American Economic Review* 87 (4): 545–64.

Robinson, Peter M. 1988. "Root-N-Consistent Semiparametric Regression." *Econometrica* 56 (4): 931–54.

Rodrik, Dani. 1991. "Policy Uncertainty and Private Investment in Developing Countries." *Journal of Development Economics* 36 (2): 229–42.

Romalis, John. 2007. "NAFTA's and CUSFTA's Impact on International Trade." *Review of Economics and Statistics* 89 (3): 416–35.

Rose, Andrew K. 2004. "Do We Really Know That the WTO Increases Trade?" *American Economic Review* 94 (1): 98–114.

Subramanian, Arvind, and Shang-Jin Wei. 2007. "The WTO Promotes Trade, Strongly But Unevenly." *Journal of International Economics* 72 (1): 151–75.

Trefler, Daniel. 2004. "The Long and Short of the Canada-U.S. Free Trade Agreement." *American Economic Review* 94 (4): 870–95.

Zeng, Ka. 2003. *Trade Threats, Trade Wars: Bargaining, Retaliation, and American Coercive Diplomacy.* Ann Arbor, MI: University of Michigan Press.

Part II
Domestic Externalities and the Role of International Trade Agreements

Chapter 6

Policy choice: Theory and evidence from commitment via international trade agreements☆

Nuno Limão [a,*], Patricia Tovar [b]

[a] University of Maryland, NBER and CEPR, United States
[b] Brandeis University, United States

ARTICLE INFO

Article history:
Received 28 September 2009
Received in revised form 22 April 2011
Accepted 16 June 2011
Available online 24 June 2011

JEL classification:
C7
D7
F13
F5
H2

Keywords:
Commitment
International agreements
Trade
Tariff
Non-tariff barrier
Political economy

ABSTRACT

Why do governments employ inefficient policies when more efficient ones are available for the same purpose? We address this puzzle in the context of redistribution toward special interest groups (SIGs) by focusing on a set of important policies: tariffs and non-tariff barriers (NTBs). In our policy choice model a government can gain by committing to constrain tariffs through international agreements even if this leads to the use of less efficient NTBs; commitment has political value because it improves the bargaining position of a government that is weak relative to domestic SIGs. Using detailed data we find support for several of the model's predictions including: (i) tariff commitments in trade agreements increase the likelihood and restrictiveness of NTBs but not enough to offset the original tariff reductions; (ii) tariff commitments are more likely to be adopted and more stringent when the government is weaker relative to a SIG. Thus, the results can explain the use of inefficient policies for redistribution and suggest that the bargaining motive is an important source of the political value of commitment in international agreements.

1. Introduction

Governments can use multiple policies to achieve a given objective, which raises basic questions such as how do policies interact and how is their mix chosen. These questions have been addressed in important specific cases such as the differential impact of tax cuts versus government spending in stimulating aggregate demand. However, many models still assume that a single policy is available and ignore why and how it is actually chosen, so they generally cannot provide positive predictions. Moreover, this type of partial policy equilibrium analysis can generate erroneous normative prescriptions given two basic features of policymaking. First, governments choose policies to maximize their own utility rather than social welfare. Second, some policies are much less efficient than others in achieving an objective, as stressed by the optimal targeting literature (c.f. Bhagwati and Ramaswami, 1963). Therefore, in order to predict and assess the full impact of government actions in any given issue we must explain their policy composition, both theoretically and empirically.

We analyze policy choice and interaction in the context of redistribution toward special interest groups (SIGs). There is considerable public concern and research about the amount of redistribution that SIGs obtain in exchange for lobbying politicians (c.f. Grossman and Helpman, 2001). It is crucial to understand the composition of redistribution to SIGs because governments frequently use policies that are apparently inefficient for this purpose, i.e. policies that reduce the surplus that governments and SIGs can bargain over. There is a growing *theoretical* literature that addresses this inefficient redistribution puzzle and provides interesting motives for why a particular group may prefer redistribution via a "bridge to nowhere" instead of a lump-sum transfer, or via a complex trade regulation instead of a tariff. However, as we describe in Section 2, these papers do *not*

☆ Limão gratefully acknowledges the research assistance of Antoine Gervais and Shrayes Ramesh as well as the hospitality of the Kiel Institute for World Economy and Yale University's Leitner program where part of this research was conducted. We thank two referees and the editor for very useful comments and suggestions. We also thank Stephanie Aaronson, Chad Bown, Peter Debaere, Allan Drazen, Andrei Levchenko, Giovanni Maggi, Horst Raff, Ken Scheve, Robert Staiger, Alan Sykes and participants at the American Economic Association Meetings, Stanford Law and Economics seminar, the George Washington University Seminar on Regionalism, Kiel University, International Economic Institutions Workshop in Seoul, Brandeis WTO Trade Conference and Yale University Leitner seminar for useful comments and discussions. Any remaining errors are ours.

* Corresponding author.
E-mail addresses: Limao@econ.umd.edu (N. Limão), tovar@brandeis.edu (P. Tovar).

0022-1996/$ – see front matter © 2011 Elsevier B.V. All rights reserved.
doi:10.1016/j.jinteco.2011.06.002

Originally Published in *Journal of International Economics* 85, pp. 186–205.

typically model the policy choice mechanism and thus fail to predict which policies are adopted and their resulting composition. This may explain the lack of empirical work on such an important issue.

Our main contribution is to derive and test specific predictions about the choice of policies used for redistribution toward SIGs and their composition, i.e. relative levels. Our theory builds on Drazen and Limão (2008) who argue that a government can benefit from constraints on efficient policies. This can occur because, although the constraints reduce the *total* surplus available to the government and SIGs it bargains with, they actually increase the government's share of that surplus. We develop and test a model where the government has a bargaining motive for commitment and it explicitly decides whether to commit to certain rules and constraints via international agreements.[1]

To tightly link the theory and estimation we must focus on a specific set of policies. Two key requirements for this choice are data availability and a reasonable efficiency ranking. These requirements are often satisfied by trade policies and this is also a setting where the inefficiency puzzle is prominent (c.f. Rodrik, 1995). Moreover, our theory requires an institution via which countries can credibly commit to policy constraints, which many argue is a central role of the World Trade Organization (c.f. Staiger and Tabellini, 1987). The policy constraints are also quite interesting in this setting. The WTO forbids most production subsidies – a relatively more efficient redistribution policy than tariffs – but allows its members to negotiate and bind tariffs, and it has fewer or no constraints in some non-tariff barriers (NTBs).[2] Many of these NTBs are highly trade restrictive; they include technical regulations and many other measures that are often less efficient than a (trade equivalent) tariff.[3] In sum, the setting we explore is a useful one for analyzing policy choice in general and to address other important questions such as (i) the value of trade agreements and (ii) whether tariff constraints increase protection via NTBs, as often claimed (c.f. Hillman, 1989, p. 76).

We show that a self-interested government can benefit from an international commitment to constrain its relatively more efficient policies (e.g. production subsidies and/or tariffs). The constraint improves the bargaining position of the government relative to the domestic SIG by limiting the maximum redistribution it can offer for a given "payment" made by that SIG. However, as we noted above, in practice these agreements do not constrain *all* policies, so SIGs can generally find some alternative one (e.g. some NTB) that is less efficient but still allows SIGs to exploit any political gains from trade with the government.[4] Despite this increase in the use of inefficient policies the government can still benefit from the constraints. The model also predicts that tariff constraints increase the likelihood of NTBs and that there is imperfect policy substitution, i.e. tighter tariff constraints increase the restrictiveness of NTBs but not enough to offset the tariff reduction. By deriving the structural relationship between the policies we can also provide estimates of the average inefficiency of NTBs.

We then show that weak governments adopt policy constraints but strong ones do not. Briefly, a strong government, i.e. one with high (Nash) bargaining power relative to a domestic industry's SIG, already captures most of the total surplus, so reductions in that surplus due to the constraints cannot be offset by an increase in the share the government captures. Moreover, the model predicts that if a government commits then it chooses less stringent tariff constraints on products where it is stronger relative to a SIG.

We find support for several of the model's predictions by using tariff and NTB data for about 5000 products. To exploit the adoption and impact of tariff constraints using detailed data we focus on a single country, Turkey. We discuss several reasons for this choice in Section 4; one of them is that it allows us to analyze two of the most common types of commitment in tariffs: those imposed via multilateral agreements such as the WTO and via preferential trade agreements (PTAs). We find that tariff constraints adopted by Turkey through the WTO and its PTA with the European Union increase the probability and restrictiveness of NTBs in this country. Moreover, the effects of the WTO constraints are related to their actual implementation *dates*, suggesting that they are not simply a proxy for other product characteristics. The results are robust to alternative NTB measures and various other issues, including endogeneity concerns.

To analyze the policy choice predictions we construct a novel measure of government bargaining power relative to SIGs: their relative probability of survival—a measure directly suggested by theory. We find that Turkey is less likely to constrain tariffs in the WTO in industries where its government is relatively stronger. Moreover, we present parametric and nonparametric evidence that tariff constraints were less stringent in industries where the government was stronger. This result is significant only for industries where SIGs are organized, as the theory predicts, and it is robust to endogeneity concerns.

The estimated effects are also economically significant. For example, tariff constraints are about 20 percentage points tighter in industries against which the government is weaker. We estimate that this causes NTB ad valorem equivalents to rise but not by enough to offset the tariff declines implied by the constraint. This suggests there is imperfect policy substitution, which is interesting for two reasons. First, it is a prediction of the model assuming that the NTB is inefficient; and we do provide an estimate that indicates this assumption is correct. Second, imperfect substitution is a necessary condition for tariff commitment to have an important *side* benefit: increase social welfare.

In sum, the results support key assumptions and predictions of the model. This, and the fact that the key theoretical insights apply to other policies that can be ranked in terms of efficiency, suggests that the model may be a useful lens to analyze similar issues in other settings. The structure of the paper is the following. In Section 2, we discuss the related literature. In Section 3, we introduce the model and derive the predictions that we test in Section 4. We conclude in Section 5.

2. Literature

We first briefly discuss the literature on the inefficient policy puzzle and the value of commitment via international trade agreements.

One argument for the use of relatively inefficient policies is that they make redistribution toward SIGs costlier and thus act like "sand in the wheels" of the redistributive process. This sand causes a reduction in the equilibrium amount of redistribution and thus may increase social welfare (c.f. Rodrik, 1986; Wilson, 1990). These papers do not model the policy choice process whereas we do; thus we can provide a positive theory of inefficient policies. This is particularly important given that our main goal is to test the model. Another prominent argument is the "disguised" transfer idea put forward by Tullock (1983) and formalized by Coate and Morris (1995). Their model

[1] Therefore, we also contribute to the general literature on why governments commit to rules by analyzing a motivation that is conceptually distinct from standard ones such as the time inconsistency of policy (c.f. Kydland and Prescott, 1977).

[2] As a referee pointed out tariffs may be more restricted than NTBs in the WTO because the latter have larger contracting frictions. Our focus is on the impact of existing policy restrictions in trade agreements for small countries rather than on explaining why those precise restrictions are the ones available in the WTO. However, in Appendix A we discuss some insights of the model for the optimal design of restrictions and compare the predictions to what is currently observed in the WTO and early attempts in the GATT to curb quotas and certain subsidies.

[3] According to the estimates in Kee et al. (2009), if we ignore NTBs then the trade restrictiveness index for the typical country in the world is equivalent to a tariff of 14% on all goods, but this jumps to 27% when NTBs are included.

[4] There may be different reasons for this, one recently emphasized by Horn et al. (2010) is that it is costly to agree on every single policy and thus trade agreements remain incomplete contracts in order to save on such costs.

specifies the policy choice mechanism but it is best suited to explain public projects rather than policies such as tariffs and subsidies, as the authors themselves explain (p. 1228).[5]

Some authors argue that this redistribution "puzzle" is simply due to an incorrect *economic* ranking of policy inefficiency. In our setting the tariff is generally at least as efficient as an NTB; but in less standard economic settings NTBs can be more economically efficient (c.f. Young and Anderson, 1982, and Kaempfer et al., 1989). Some NTBs may also be more politically efficient than tariffs, e.g. voluntary export restraints can help redistribute income toward foreign exporters lobbying the domestic government. Such ranking reversals are certainly possible but unlikely to be the norm for most goods. Ultimately this ranking is an empirical question and our model provides an estimation equation to test if NTBs are inefficient on average.

As we note in the Introduction we build on Drazen and Limão (2008). The key differences in terms of the theoretical *approach* are that (i) we model tariffs and NTBs whereas they focus on a lump-sum transfer and a production subsidy and (ii) we analyze trade agreements as the policy choice mechanism. This allows us to extend their results to a trade setting, which is interesting in of itself and also more amenable to testing since there is more systematic data on tariff caps and NTBs than lump-sum caps and subsidies.[6] We also derive welfare implications of policy commitments and explicit expressions for the equilibrium policies. This is central given our interest in estimating the extent of policy substitution and several other predictions of the model. The empirical focus of our paper distinguishes it not only from Drazen and Limão (2008) but also from nearly all other papers in this topic, which are purely theoretical.[7]

There is a long standing view that trade agreements are valuable because they provide governments with a commitment mechanism to better withstand or mitigate import competing pressures.[8] This view has been formalized almost exclusively by appealing to specific time-inconsistency problems related to some form of investment (Staiger and Tabellini, 1987; Maggi and Rodriguez-Clare, 1998; Mitra, 2002). In our model, the source of the gain from commitment is a government's improvement in its bargaining position relative to the lobbies rather than a standard time inconsistency problem. The underlying bargaining mechanism we exploit is thought to be important in negotiations.[9] Moreover, none of the papers above models the *choice* of policy and, with the exception of Staiger and Tabellini (1987), they do not even consider the possibility of alternative policies. This is important because no international agreement allows commitment in all policies, so to evaluate the value of such agreements we need to move away from partial political equilibrium models. Finally, all the papers above focus on the theoretical commitment value of agreements whereas we also provide evidence.[10]

[5] A broader argument for the use of inefficient transfers is that they can give additional political benefits to the government or SIG (e.g. Weingast et al., 1981; Dixit and Londregan, 1996).

[6] Drazen and Limão (2008) provide some examples of caps on lump-sum transfers, e.g. in U.S. farm programs.

[7] An exception is Ederington and Minier (2006), who examine the aggregate determinants of tariffs as a share of tariff plus production subsidy protection for a panel of countries. They note that (at that time) "none of the theoretical models proposed a fully specified equation for the proper ratio of tariffs to other policy instruments". Their approach is to test broad implications and "none of the results should be interpreted as an outright rejection of any model." We tackle these issues by specifically deriving such equations from a fully specified model and testing them using detailed product data.

[8] Another argument is that trade agreements allow countries to reduce tariffs and internalize terms-of-trade effects (Bagwell and Staiger, 1999). Maggi and Rodriguez-Clare (2007) combine the terms-of-trade and commitment motives.

[9] Schelling (1960) states that "The power of a negotiator often rests on a manifest inability to make concessions and meet demands."

[10] Staiger and Tabellini (1999) provide indirect evidence that GATT rules helped U.S. domestic trade policy commitments.

3. Theory

3.1. Setup

We consider a small competitive economy that takes world prices as given. Our *economic* structure is closely related to Grossman and Helpman (1994) but we model an additional policy. Each individual's factor endowments may differ but they have identical quasilinear preferences described by $u = x_0 + \sum_{i=1}^{n} u_i(x_i)$, where x_0 is consumption of the numeraire good; x_i denotes consumption of good i and the sub-utility functions $u_i(\cdot)$ are differentiable, increasing and strictly concave. An individual with income E consumes $d_i(p_i) = [u_i'(p_i)]^{-1}$ of each x_i, and $E - \sum_i p_i d_i(p_i)$ units of the numeraire. The indirect utility is thus given by $v(\mathbf{p}, E) = E + s(\mathbf{p})$, where $\mathbf{p}$ is the vector of domestic prices, and the consumer surplus derived from the non-numeraire goods is given by $s(\mathbf{p}) = \sum_i u_i(d_i(p_i)) - \sum_i p_i d_i(p_i)$.

The numeraire is produced using only labor with a marginal product equal to one. Assuming a sufficiently large labor supply ensures that in equilibrium this good is always produced and thus the wage equals unity. Each of the non-numeraire goods is produced using labor and a sector-specific factor, with constant returns to scale. The supply of the specific factors is fixed. Since the wage is constant, we can denote the return to the specific factors as $\Pi_i(p_i)$. By Hotelling's lemma, output is then given by $y_i = \Pi_i'(p_i)$.

The government has tariffs and NTBs at its disposal.[11] We model NTBs that generate a wedge between the domestic and foreign price, as a tariff does, and can also generate rents. The NTBs here are less efficient than tariffs in a single dimension: a fraction ϕ of those rents is dissipated whereas in the tariff case they are available in the form of tariff revenues that can be consumed in the importing country. By allowing ϕ to range between zero and one we can capture different degrees of the inefficiency in a simple but clear way.[12]

The per capita rents from using an NTB with ad valorem equivalent of τ and a tariff t is then given by

$$r(\mathbf{p}) = \sum_i [t_i p_i^* + (1-\phi)\tau_i p_i^*][d_i(p_i) - y_i(p_i)/N]$$

where p_i^* is the world price and $t_i p_i^*$ measures the increase in the domestic price due to the tariff whereas $\tau_i p_i^*$ is the equivalent wedge due to the NTB. The domestic price is thus given by $p_i = (1 + t_i + \tau_i)p_i^*$. The second term in brackets represents import quantity (N measures the total population). All the tariff rents (i.e., its revenue) are available for domestic consumption, but for the NTB that is the case for only a fraction $1-\phi \in [0, 1]$. We make the standard assumption that the government rebates *these* rents uniformly to all individuals, but the results would be similar if the government consumed them directly.

The policies also generate rents for the set of sectors, L, where the specific factors organize into SIGs that lobby the government. The joint gross welfare of lobby i is $W_i = \Pi_i(p_i) + \alpha_i N[1 + r(\mathbf{p}) + s(\mathbf{p})]$, where α_i is the fraction of the population that owns some of the specific factor in this industry and the terms in brackets are respectively those owners' wage, rebated rents, and consumer surplus. We analyze the case of highly concentrated factor ownership, i.e. $\alpha_i \to 0$, so each industry lobbies only for its own product. This allows us to focus on the interaction between the government and each SIG and abstract from lobby competition. Each SIG offers the government a "lobby good", represented by C_i and described below, in

[11] This policy set is determined by the data available to test the model. If we instead included production subsidies and tariffs then the mechanism we explore predicts that the government gains by restricting subsidies and using tariffs.

[12] A specific example of such NTBs is quantitative restrictions where some of the licenses are given to foreigners. The key insight of the model applies to other NTBs that generate a wedge between the domestic and world price and are less efficient than the tariff in maximizing the political surplus, as defined below.

order to obtain an increase in the level of protection it receives. Thus, we denote the net welfare of the members of lobby i by $V_i = W_i - C_i$.

The government maximizes a weighted sum of lobby goods and social welfare:

$$G = \sum_{i \in L} \Psi_i(C_i) + aW(\mathbf{p}), \qquad a \geq 0 \tag{1}$$

where social welfare is given by the sum of indirect utilities over all individuals gross of contributions:

$$W(\mathbf{p}) = N + \sum_{i=1}^{n} \Pi_i(p_i) + N[r(\mathbf{p}) + s(\mathbf{p})].$$

Several models of SIGs, e.g. Grossman and Helpman (1994), assume that the lobby good is equally valued by the government and the lobby, i.e. that Ψ_i is linear and thus utility is transferable. This is a useful simplifying assumption that may be reasonable if, for example, C_i is cash and there are no contribution limits. However, in several countries – including the one we analyze in the empirical section – there are strict constraints on such contributions. Thus, SIGs can and do resort to other goods and services, which are not necessarily perfect substitutes. Moreover, as Drazen and Limão (2008) argue, politicians may have diminishing marginal utility for lobby goods such as getting out the vote in a district where a lobby's membership is concentrated; providing information about an issue; lending jets for campaigning or vacationing; etc. In sum, we think it is reasonable to assume, as we do, that Ψ_i is strictly concave. The resulting non-transferability of utility between government and lobbies will be key in generating the use of inefficient policies.[13]

There are two stages in the game. In the first, the government decides whether to commit to policy constraints via an international agreement. In the second stage, the government (Nash) bargains with each SIG over the level of lobby goods, C, and policies, (t,τ). We derive the subgame perfect Nash equilibrium for C, t and τ for given policy constraints and then which first stage constraints emerge.

3.2. Absence of commitment and the use of the most efficient available policy

We first show that, in the absence of policy constraints, the most efficient available policy is the only one used in equilibrium. This is a useful baseline for two reasons. First, it starkly illustrates the importance of having access to a commitment technology to generate inefficient policies. Second, as we subsequently show, the government does not always choose constraints even if it has access to a commitment technology; the policy values derived below also apply to the latter case.[14]

In the absence of constraints we observe only the tariff because it is the politically efficient policy, i.e. it maximizes the joint payoff to the government and lobby for any given level of the lobby good. To see this note that for a given contribution, the lobby payoff, V, is identical under a given level of protection whether implemented via tariffs or NTBs. But the government payoff is lower under the NTB since it generates only a fraction of the rents. Thus in equilibrium it is costlier for the lobby to compensate the government for an increase in τ that leads to the same change in imports as an equivalent change in t, and hence only the tariff is used.

To analyze the specific case of no commitment we employ the general Nash bargaining problem solved in the second stage but assume the first-stage tariff constraint is absent or not binding. In the following section we relax this. Formally, we write the problem as follows:

$$\max_{t,\tau,C} \quad U = \left(G(t,\tau,C) - G^0\right)^{\gamma}\left(V(t,\tau,C) - V^0\right)^{1-\gamma} \quad \text{s.t.}\ t \leq t^c;\ G \geq G^0;\ V \geq V^0. \tag{2}$$

Subsequently, we will determine the optimal constraint and whether it binds relative to the unconstrained, so it is useful to derive the (implicit) value of the unconstrained tariff as (see Appendix A for the derivation):

$$t_i^u = \frac{y_i(p_i)}{-ap_i^* m_i'(p_i)} \Psi_i'(C_i). \tag{3}$$

If C entered the government's objective linearly then Eq. (3) would be similar to the expression in Grossman and Helpman (1994) for an organized industry under concentrated factor ownership. It is also straightforward to show (as we do explicitly in the working paper) that without commitment $\tau = 0$. This occurs by design and the intuition is simple: both policies have a similar effect on the domestic price and thus profits but the NTB is more costly for the government since it generates fewer rents than the tariff and thus only the latter is used.

3.3. Commitment tariff caps in the absence of NTBs

We now allow government access to commitment so it can *choose* whether it prefers to set a maximum cap on the tariff prior to negotiating with each SIG. To clearly illustrate the government's incentive to do so we first assume that no other redistribution policies can be used. In the next section we show the government's incentive is still present when less efficient policies are available.

The government sets the cap, t^c, in the first stage by maximizing its objective, in Eq. (1), taking into account the effect on the equilibrium tariff and contributions, which are found by solving the Nash problem previously defined but with $\tau = 0$ as an additional *constraint*.[15] The first order condition for t^c is

$$\Psi_i'(C_i)\frac{\partial C_i}{\partial t_i} + a\frac{\partial W}{\partial t_i} = 0 \quad \Rightarrow \quad t_i^c = \frac{\partial C_i / \partial t_i}{-a(p_i^*)^2 m_i'} \Psi_i'(C_i). \tag{4}$$

If $t_i^c \geq t_i^u$ then the constraint does not bind; otherwise it binds and this would prove the government's benefit from constraining tariffs ex-ante. In Appendix A we show that the government prefers to constrain tariffs if and only if it does not have all the bargaining power and lobby goods have diminishing marginal utility. The intuition is the following: if the constraint binds then relaxing it, i.e. increasing the tariff, increases the payoff to lobbies with no first order cost to the government (since it is optimally setting t). The resulting increase in joint surplus could be collected via the bargaining in the second stage if the government had all the bargaining power. Alternatively, this increase would also be collected if contributions entered linearly so that they are used to share the joint surplus. But if contributions have diminishing marginal utility and the government cannot obtain the entire joint surplus then the increase in joint surplus from relaxing

[13] An additional, or alternative, motive for non-transferability would be for C to be produced by each lobby using the numeraire as the input into a diminishing returns production process.

[14] In our empirical work the goods where such constraints are absent will therefore be used as the counterfactual to test the model's prediction that constraints on a policy lead to the use of relatively less efficient ones.

[15] Note that the government is able to extract contributions from the lobby under a tariff cap even in the absence of NTBs as long as it can credibly threaten to set a zero tariff. This is the case with WTO tariff bindings, which have downward flexibility, so the analysis applies directly to this case. However, in a customs union the government threat of a zero tariff is less credible since the customs union partner may not allow it to fulfill it. In practice, customs unions probably allow some flexibility for members to threaten to deviate down from the exact external tariff. However, in the extreme case where they do not, the only threat governments can use in bargaining with SIGs is the cap itself, in which case the government can only extract contributions if additional unconstrained policies are available, as we analyze next.

the cap is offset by a smaller government share of it. This decrease in the share is due to the deterioration in the government's political terms-of-trade.

In other words, a binding cap improves the government's bargaining position and thus its share of the surplus, which can leave it better off even as the *joint* surplus falls. One way to understand the intuition behind the increase in the government's share of the surplus is that the binding constraint implies lower equilibrium contributions and thus a higher marginal benefit of contributions for the government. This means it is now relatively more efficient (in terms of the Nash product being maximized) to increase the government share.

3.4. Commitment and the co-existence of efficient and inefficient policies

In Sections 3.2 and 3.3 we showed that, in the absence of a commitment technology, only the relatively efficient policy is used and commitment generates a benefit for the government. Thus, we expect governments to seek access to commitment mechanisms, such as trade agreements, that constrain those policies, and any of their close substitutes. But SIGs are notoriously creative in finding alternative redistribution policies and the government is not able to constrain all of them. For example, the WTO provides countries with a potential commitment mechanism to constrain subsidies and tariffs but not all types of NTBs.[16] Therefore, we now show how constraints on tariffs lead to the emergence of less efficient policies. We first take these constraints as given, as they would be in the second stage, and derive their impact on NTBs.

Let us first explain how tariff caps, $\bar{t}^c$, can lead to NTB use in the second stage. Clearly if that cap is equal to zero and the NTB were also set to zero there would be gains from trade between the lobby and government. This occurs since when $t=\tau=0$ the lobby offers $C=0$ and the marginal benefit of increasing C is sufficiently large to the government—as is simple to verify using the FOCs in the appendix, Eqs. (A2) and (A3). Given the large gains from political trading at $t=\tau=0$, it is also straightforward to show that an NTB will also be used for some strictly positive cap level. However, as the cap increases the NTB value must eventually decline since, as we have shown earlier, when $\bar{t}^c = t^u$ we have $\tau=0$. So our model predicts that:

(i) a good with a sufficiently low tariff cap implies an NTB will be used and
(ii) the likelihood and the value of the NTB are eventually decreasing in the value of that cap, or more precisely the difference between that cap and the unconstrained tariff value.

Alternative models could predict similar relationships between tariffs and NTBs in *all* goods. One specific feature of our model, and one we will test, is that it predicts these relationships only in goods where a binding tariff cap exists. Before generating any additional predictions, we derive the precise NTB expression to show the results above and guide the estimation more precisely (see Appendix A).

$$\tau_i^c = \frac{1}{1-\phi}\left[\frac{y_i(p_i)}{-ap_i^* m_i'}\Psi'(C_i)-\bar{t}_i^c\right]-\frac{\phi}{1-\phi}\frac{1}{\varepsilon_i} \tag{5}$$

where $\varepsilon_i = -m'_i(p_i)(p_i^*/m_i(p_i))$ is a measure of the absolute value of import demand elasticity. We immediately see that if the tariff constraint was zero and the NTB was almost as efficient as the tariff, i.e. $\phi \to 0$, then the NTB level would equal the first term in the brackets, which is exactly the unconstrained tariff level in Eq. (3), t^u. More generally, the NTB level is increasing in the gap between the

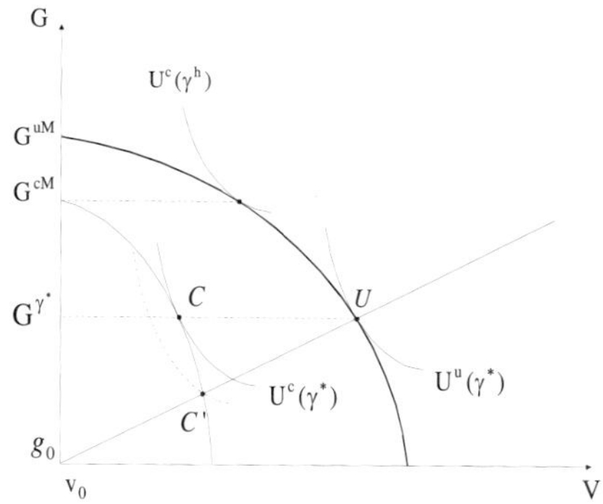

Fig. 1. Impact of policy constraint on payoffs.

"unconstrained level" and the cap. This is one of the central predictions we will test.

3.5. Commitment decision

We now derive the set of goods and the extent of policy commitment the government chooses. At the end we also discuss the impact of allowing SIGs to *directly* influence those commitments.

The government commitment decision in the first period can be modeled in two ways: (a) allow it to choose whether to commit to an exogenously given cap or (b) allow it to choose whether to commit *and* the optimal level of the cap that maximizes its objective in the first stage. It is important to show the result for the first alternative – commitment to an exogenous cap – since it may be the only available one. One example is when a country must adopt another's common external tariff and it can at most decide if a given good is subject to an exogenous cap level. Another example is if the government has *some* influence over the cap level but is unable to choose it to exactly maximize its objective as we represented it (e.g. if there are other constraints unobservable to us). Thus, we first derive sufficient conditions such that a government can benefit from a commitment to a cap even if it is not necessarily able to set its level optimally.

In the first stage, the government chooses to commit to an exogenously *given* cap in a product i if its payoff evaluated at the constrained equilibrium exceeds the unconstrained[17]:

$$G(\bar{t}_i^c, \tau_i^c(\bar{t}_i^c, \gamma_i), C_i^c(\bar{t}_i^c, \gamma_i), .) \geq G(t_i^u(\gamma_i), \tau_i^u(\gamma_i), C_i^u(\gamma_i), .) \tag{6}$$

If Eq. (6) holds then the government chooses to commit even if it cannot choose the optimal cap, thus it would also commit if it could choose $\bar{t}^c$ to maximize the left-hand side of Eq. (6). This means that a sufficient condition for Eq. (6) to hold is also sufficient to ensure that a government commits to an optimal cap level of its choosing.

We illustrate the result in Fig. 1. The bold line represents the Pareto frontier of payoffs for the government and each SIG in the absence of commitment. No commitment yields a higher joint payoff than the alternative where the tariff is constrained and the NTB used. Note first

[16] In Appendix A we discuss why this unavailability of commitment technology for some NTBs is present and potential insights of the model into the optimal design of policy restriction rules in the WTO.

[17] Given the separability of G over goods i, we can treat the choice over *each* good independently of each other. If the government had to choose between entering an agreement with an exogenous cap on a *set* of goods and could not opt out of any given one then we would need to consider the aggregate effect and Eq. (6) would not necessarily hold for each i. In the WTO and in some PTAs the government has some discretion to opt out, which is why we focus on this formulation.

that for a large enough bargaining power Eq. (6) never holds, that is the government always chooses *not* to commit to a cap. This is obvious for $\gamma=1$, since then the government obtains the entire surplus and never wants it reduced. It is also simple to illustrate that the same is true for other sufficiently high γ that are still lower than 1 provided the cap is sufficiently low that the maximum *possible* government payoff is strictly lower than with no constraint. We can thus define γ^h such that $G^u(\gamma=\gamma^h)=G^{cM}(\gamma=\gamma^h)$, as shown in Fig. 1. Therefore, governments with sufficiently high bargaining power do not commit to a stringent cap.

Governments with no bargaining power are indifferent between policies. When γ is zero, Eq. (6) must hold with equality since the government obtains its reservation payoff – the free trade equilibrium in good i – and thus it is identical with or without commitment. Therefore, Eq. (6) holds with a strict inequality if as we increase γ from zero the government payoff increases faster under commitment than in its absence. When this is the case the government has a strictly higher payoff under commitment for some $\gamma\in(0,\gamma^*)$, where γ^* is defined as the lowest positive γ at which Eq. (6) holds with equality. More formally, the sufficient condition for this is

$$\lim_{\gamma_i\to 0}\frac{d}{d\gamma_i}G(\bar{t}_i^c,\tau_i^c(\bar{t}_i^c,\gamma_i),C_i^c(\bar{t}_i^c,\gamma_i),..)>\lim_{\gamma_i\to 0}\frac{d}{d\gamma_i}G(t_i^u(\gamma_i),\tau_i^u(\gamma_i),C_i^u(\gamma_i),..) \quad (7)$$

This condition can be simplified and interpreted in an intuitive way: it requires the improvement in the government's bargaining position from committing to a tariff cap to exceed the loss arising from the reduction in bargaining surplus due to the constraint and subsequent use of the NTB. Drazen and Limão (2008) show this for different policies and note that this condition need not always hold and must be checked in each policy setting. Thus in Appendix A we provide a numerical simulation showing this condition holds in our model if the cap is not too stringent relative to the unconstrained value. Very stringent caps make the *sufficient* condition less likely to hold because they destroy too much surplus, which cannot be offset by the government's increased share in it.

Fig. 1 illustrates the role of bargaining power in the government's decision to commit. Consider a $\gamma\in(0,\gamma^*)$ so that point U is the solution under no commitment. Consider the ray from the origin that maintains the same ratio of payoffs at C' as at U. The dotted Nash iso-value line at C' has the same slope as U^U at U (since the Nash product is log linear) indicating an unchanged marginal rate of substitution of payoffs. But the Pareto frontier under commitment is steeper due to the inefficiency of the NTB and the fact that the government has diminishing marginal utility for lobby goods. Thus the equilibrium under commitment entails a value of G above C', which at the critical value γ^* is equal to the unconstrained level. For lower γ the government payoff is higher when it commits to a constraint.

In sum, if a government can commit to a cap in the first stage, then, all else equal, it is less likely to do so in products from an industry I than J if its bargaining power in the second stage is higher against I, i.e. if $\gamma_I>\gamma_J$. If the government benefits from committing to an exogenous cap for some $\gamma\in(0,\gamma^*)$ then it benefits even more if it can optimally choose the cap *level*. Moreover, if γ is sufficiently high then it has no incentive to commit so if it were to ever commit to a cap it would be to one that is not binding, i.e. at or above the unconstrained level. We already explained why this is so for the case of an exogenous cap in Fig. 1 whenever $\gamma>\gamma^h$. If the government could choose the cap optimally then its incentive to commit below the unconstrained tariff is also reduced at high bargaining power and fully disappears but only in the limit when $\gamma=1$.[18]

In the empirical section we examine if the government is more likely to set a tariff cap in goods where it has less bargaining power. However, our main focus will be to test a related prediction, namely whether tariff commitments are more stringent at lower levels of bargaining power. This prediction follows from the discussion above since at low levels of γ we have $t^{c^*}(\gamma)<t^u(\gamma)$ but at sufficiently high levels of γ the desired cap is not below the unconstrained.

To sharpen the model's predictions we have thus far assumed that SIGs have a negligible ability to influence the first stage constraints. This absence of ex-ante lobbying is also used by others in the context of trade agreements, c.f. Maggi and Rodriguez-Clare (1998), and it would be satisfied for example in industries that are expected to organize but have not yet done so at the commitment stage (so they cannot lobby against constraints). It may also be a reasonable assumption for organized industries provided that the government is somewhat insulated from their pressure during the international negotiation stage. It is also important to note that we can relax this simplifying assumption. For example, we can show that policy constraints can emerge in equilibrium even if we allow the government and SIG to bargain over them during the first stage; this would occur provided the government has higher bargaining power during the first stage than the second.[19]

3.6. Social welfare value of commitment

Before testing any predictions, we clarify a key normative implication of the model. The government joins an agreement if it improves its objective in Eq. (1) so, as shown, the agreement provides a *political* commitment value. We now ask if there is also a social welfare value of commitment.

A necessary condition for social welfare to increase with commitment is for total protection to fall. In the absence of NTBs, this reduction is both necessary *and* sufficient; so in this case the agreement has both a political *and* a social welfare commitment values since the new protection level is simply $t^c<t^u$, as shown in Section 3.3. However, if we allow for NTBs to substitute for the constrained tariffs we must also determine if total protection falls by enough to offset the inefficiency of the NTB.

Total protection under commitment is τ^c+t^c, for a given $t^c<t^u$. If the NTB is as efficient as the tariff, and thus a perfect substitute for it, then total protection should be unchanged, i.e. if $\phi=0$ then $\tau^c+t^c=t^u$. Therefore, if an increase in ϕ reduces τ then total protection will be lower under commitment. In Appendix A we describe how to employ the parameterized model to show this effect. As we report in the working paper, when $\phi=0$ there is full substitution and so no change in total protection; but inefficient NTBs do lower total protection, e.g. we find that commitment causes total protection to fall by more than 5% if $\phi=0.3$–a value close to our subsequent inefficiency estimate. The exact magnitudes depend on other parameter values but the key point is that it is simple to find cases

[18] Note that the government is indifferent between no cap and a cap that is not binding (i.e. equal to or higher than the unconstrained tariff). But this indifference is easily broken if we include plausible costs of introducing a cap, e.g. a fixed cost of deciding, negotiating and implementing the cap or some uncertainty about the future unconstrained tariff. One implication of including such costs would be that the government caps only if the bargaining benefit is large enough; thus even if it could optimally choose the cap level it would not cap either at $\gamma=1$ (where the bargaining benefit is zero) or (by a continuity argument) at values sufficiently close to it.

[19] This result is presented in Drazen and Limão (2008) in the context of lump-sum transfers and production subsidies and a similar logic applies here. Thus, an additional prediction of the model is that, all else equal, the government is more likely to commit in industries where its bargaining power in the first stage, b_i, is higher than in the second than in industries where it is lower. Testing this in future work may be interesting but challenging since it requires choosing a specific first stage mechanism and then empirically measuring the *difference* in bargaining power for each industry between the stages, i.e. $b_i-\gamma_i$. When $b_i=1$, as in the basic model, it is simple to see this prediction is similar to the one we test since all the variation is in γ_i. Our test can also apply to cases where $b_i<1$ provided that (i) b_i is similar across industries and (ii) $b_i>\gamma_i$ for at least some industries. Possible reasons for (ii) include the fact that a government has direct participation and control over the negotiations in an international trade agreement and the possibility that some lobbies may have not yet formed. If the maintained assumptions in (i) and (ii) fail we should find little support for the commitment prediction of the model. For example, if import-competing SIGs had full control over any tariff constraints via agreements in the first stage, then the model would predict no tariff commitments. Ultimately, whether such commitments occur and are affected by bargaining power is an empirical question, which we address in Section 4.

where the government chooses to commit and total protection falls by a non-trivial amount.

Even if total protection falls, a part of it is now done via a less efficient policy, which generates fewer rents. If the rents are rebated to the citizens then we need to factor in this change, which may decrease welfare, but we can show that if total protection fell sufficiently then the net effect of commitment on social welfare would be positive. The parameterized model in Appendix A, for example, yields a 1.5% increase in social welfare if the government chooses to commit in a good where the degree of NTB inefficiency is $\phi = 0.3$.

To summarize, agreements that restrict tariffs lead to less efficient policies that partially offset it. This imperfect policy substitution throws "sand-in-the-wheels" of the redistribution process and tends to improve social welfare to the extent that it reduces total protection. Thus in the empirical section we will try to estimate if there is policy substitution and it is imperfect. Finally, it is important to note that the social welfare effect is a positive side benefit rather than a sufficient or necessary motive for the government to enter such agreements.[20]

4. Evidence

We now investigate several predictions of the model. First, we examine the impact of tariff constraints on the use of the typically less efficient NTBs. We then estimate the impact of bargaining power on governments' commitment choices in trade agreements. Next, we quantify each of these effects and the impact of bargaining power via tariff commitments on NTBs and provide structural estimates of how inefficient these NTBs are.

4.1. Commitment and the use of less efficient policies: data and empirical strategy

We exploit variation in tariff constraints generated by the two most common types of commitment in these policies: those in multilateral and preferential trade agreements. WTO members negotiate tariff "bindings" in certain products, which are essentially ceilings on *applied tariffs*. If countries set their applied tariffs above that binding, they may be subject to costly dispute from foreign exporters.[21] When those costs are sufficiently high, the government can credibly constrain its maximum tariff and, according to the model, if that tariff constraint binds there is a higher likelihood of an NTB. Moreover, all else equal, the lower the tariff binding level relative to the unconstrained the higher the NTB ad valorem equivalent. Given this, we exploit the cross-product variation in tariff binding status and binding level in the WTO to examine their effect on the use of NTBs.

In PTAs, countries agree to preferential tariffs between themselves and, in customs unions, to set a common external tariff. Non-enforcement of those tariffs can generate retaliation by other PTA members—a cost that provides an additional source of commitment. Moreover, when there is a large asymmetry in the size of members the common external tariff is determined by the tariffs of the larger partner. This can generate a large change in tariffs for the smaller partner that is likely to be "exogenous" in the sense that it is independent of other determinants of its trade policy. For example, the WTO's Trade Policy report for Turkey notes it had to adopt pre-existing EU tariffs, except in a few products temporarily excluded. If the common EU tariff constrains Turkey to lower its tariffs then the model predicts additional Turkish protection via NTBs on non-EU exporters.

Several of the predictions of the model are better tested by exploring cross-product rather than cross-country variation since the latter would contain considerable unobserved heterogeneity. Given this and the detailed data required for some variables, we focus on a single country. Our country choice was guided by data and theoretical considerations. First, we require a country with NTB data and with variation in binding status in the WTO. Since the implementation of the Uruguay Round commitments many developed countries have bound most of their tariff lines. Thus we focus on Turkey, which has bound only about half. Second, the NTB data for this country is available for the year immediately after an important customs union with the EU that led to a substantial cut in Turkey's external tariff. Third, Turkey has strict laws on cash contributions to politicians, which suggests that industries must reward them using "lobby goods". These goods are more likely to be subject to diminishing returns than cash and thus Turkey fits our model better than a country where unlimited cash contributions are possible.[22] Moreover, the theory focuses on a small open economy, which rules out several alternative countries.

Below we discuss the different variables we employ. Tables A1 and A2 in the appendix provide more detailed information about their source and summary statistics, respectively. To place the analysis in context, we note some facts. Turkey implemented a major trade liberalization in the 1980s that reduced tariffs and removed NTBs, such as quotas (Togan, 1995). Therefore, by 1994 only about 2% of all HS-6 lines were subject to any NTB, which implies there is little variation to exploit that year. Moreover, there is no data on NTB ad valorem equivalents that most closely match the theory's predictions; such data is only available for 1997.

In 1997 Turkey had considerably more NTBs than in 1994. They covered about 9% of all HS-6 products spread through about a third of 97 different HS-2 industry classifications. The NTBs were almost exclusively classified as authorization for imports, e.g. requiring a product to satisfy specific criteria before being imported.[23] This increase in NTBs since 1994 could have been due to new tariff commitments, as our model predicts. In fact, by 1997, there had been two recent changes to Turkey's tariff constraints that may have caused the increase in NTBs. First, it had started to implement additional WTO bindings, increasing the share of goods covered from 30% to about 47%, and reducing binding levels from about 41 to 30% on average. Second, the 1996 customs union led Turkey to adopt the EU external tariffs and thus generated a large reduction in the tariffs it applied to non-EU countries, from about 27% in 1993 to 13% in 1998.

A preliminary analysis of variance of the Turkish data reveals an interesting feature. A considerable fraction of the variation is across industry, which has two main implications. First, it accords well with our model and several other models of trade policy that emphasize the role of *industry* level lobbies. A second related implication is that we should not discard this information in our estimation. For example, if we focused only on within HS-2 variation we would ignore two thirds of industries and we would be exploring less than 30% of the variation in key variables such as the EU bindings and the WTO tariff.

[20] We can see it is not sufficient since the government chooses not to commit if it has sufficient bargaining power even though commitment can increase social welfare. It is not necessary since the government would commit even if it placed no value on social welfare, e.g. if W in Eq. (1) represented only the policy rents and these were consumed by the government.

[21] These can range from the costs of legal defense to the loss of market access if the exporter retaliates by increasing tariffs.

[22] In the last election, the elected party's revenue share from private contributions was less than 0.1% whereas 92.5% was from state funding. Accessed at <http://www.akparti.org.tr/gelir_gider/haziran.htm>.

[23] There were no safeguard measures or countervailing duties in Turkey in 1997. But there were a few anti-dumping barriers, which we do not account for in our main analysis because (i) they applied to specific countries whereas our theoretical model focuses on NTBs that apply equally to all exporters and (ii) the NTB ad valorem equivalent measure available to us did not include anti-dumping. Incorporating these measures should not affect our main results since they apply to only 31 products, which is less than 1% of the products in our sample. As a robustness test we redefine the NTB indicator to reflect anti-dumping (from the *Global Antidumping Database* by Bown, 2009) and find that the results that use this new indicator as a dependent variable are identical to the ones that ignore anti-dumping in those 31 products.

Table 1
Impact of tariff commitments on NTB probability.

	(1)	(2)	(3)	(4)	(5)	(6)	(7)[a]	(8)[b]
WTO BIND	0.060***	0.127***	0.088***	0.013	0.112***	0.097***	0.092***	0.108***
(β>0)	[0.008]	[0.009]	[0.007]	[0.021]	[0.010]	[0.008]	[0.009]	[0.009]
WTO 1997 implement				0.051**				
(β>0)				[0.022]				
WTO BIND TARIFF		−0.369***			−0.236***			
(β_c<0)		[0.029]			[0.040]			
WTO BIND TARIFF ADJ.			−0.406***			−0.249***	−0.282***	−0.280***
(β_c<0)			[0.028]			[0.038]	[0.047]	[0.042]
EU BIND					0.076***	0.044***	0.061***	0.029*
(β >0)					[0.006]	[0.010]	[0.012]	[0.016]
EU BIND TARIFF					−0.758***			
(β_c<0)					[0.121]			
EU BIND TARIFF ADJ.						−0.831***	−0.853***	−0.912***
(β_c<0)						[0.081]	[0.100]	[0.089]
Observations	5112	5112	5112	5112	4930	4930	4110	4553
Log-pseudolikelihood	−1472	−1396	−1384	−1470	−1348	−1304	−1259	−1289
Pseudo R2	0.02	0.07	0.08	0.02	0.09	0.12	0.10	0.11

Notes: Marginal Probit effects with standard errors in brackets. *,**,*** respectively significant at 10%, 5% and 1%.
[a] Excludes textiles and clothing products (ISIC 321 and 322).
[b] Includes ISIC-1 sector effects. The difference in sample size relative to the baseline is due to Probit estimation dropping observations in ISIC-1 groups without NTB variation.

An interesting question is to what extent these Turkish NTBs were intended to protect the consumer and the environment – as Turkey claimed in a 1998 WTO report – or a relatively inefficient way of protecting importers, as required by our model. It is impossible to answer this for each product, but in our working paper we provide evidence that on average the NTBs were not used for consumer and environmental protection but rather for import protection motives. One piece of evidence that is worth mentioning is that *none* of Turkey's NTBs actually covered products that are widely considered worthy of consumer and environmental protection by WTO members. Furthermore, our model can provide estimates that, as we will see, indicate NTBs are less efficient than tariffs, particularly in organized industries where NTBs are most likely used for protection.

4.2. Impact of commitment on NTBs

We write the NTB econometric model for the population of products i in a given year as

$$NTB_i^* = \beta BIND_i + \beta_c BIND\_TARIFF_i + \beta_\varepsilon (BIND_i / \varepsilon_i) + \alpha + \theta z_i + e_i \quad \text{(E1)}$$

where NTB_i^* represents a latent variable capturing the NTB, which maps into the observed NTB variable in different ways depending upon whether we estimate the likelihood of an NTB or its ad valorem equivalent (AVE). The first three terms in Eq. (E1) capture the determinants of the NTB AVE highlighted in Eq. (5) of the theory. Thus the model predicts that $\beta>0$, that is higher NTBs for products where a binding tariff commitment is present, i.e. goods where $BIND_i = 1$. For these goods, an increase in the commitment tariff, denoted by $BIND\_TARIFF_i$, should lower the NTB; so $\beta_c<0$.

We identify a product as having a tariff commitment, and set $BIND_i = 1$, if it has a formal constraint in the WTO. We refer to such products as having tariff bindings, which is their common designation in the WTO.[24] We measure the level of tariff commitment, $BIND\_TARIFF_i$, in two alternative ways. We first employ the official binding level in the WTO, which corresponds to t^c in our model. We then augment this to capture the difference relative to the unconstrained tariff, i.e. $t^c - t^u$ (recall that the first term in the brackets in Eq. (5) is the unconstrained tariff, t^u). The model suggests we construct t^u as the applied tariff in the absence of a commitment in that product. This counterfactual is calculated as the average applied tariff over the products with no commitment. We do this using values for 1993 (thus pre-determined relative to the 1997 NTB) and averaging separately for each industry (to ensure that the counterfactual for each product i better matches the incentives for the unconstrained tariff in the industry it belongs to). We also include analogous variables capturing EU tariff commitments separately, which we describe further below.

In Tables 1 and 2 we provide results that focus on the binding variables. To follow the theory more closely we then extend the model to reflect the inverse import elasticity measure and test if $\beta_\varepsilon<0$. We also test the robustness of the results to endogeneity concerns by including additional determinants for NTBs, e.g. sector effects reflected in z_i, and by using an instrumental variable approach.[25]

Table 1 presents Probit estimates based on Eq. (E1) where the dependent variable is equal to 1 if good i was subject to an NTB in 1997 and zero otherwise. In column 1 we find that a WTO tariff commitment increases the probability of an NTB, as the model predicts. In column 2, we also include the level of the tariff commitment and confirm that the higher it is the lower the probability of NTBs. Column 3 shows the result is similar if we instead use the difference between the constrained and unconstrained tariffs ($t^c - t^u$), as suggested by the theory.

One potential concern is that the binding status proxies for an omitted variable that affects NTBs. Here, we address this in two ways. First, we confirmed that the results in columns 1–3 are robust to unobserved heterogeneity by including sector dummies defined at the 1-digit ISIC level (results are available on request). Second, we test if a more specific variable – the timing of tariff commitments – is insignificant; if that were the case and binding status on other goods remained highly significant this would be evidence that the latter simply captures an omitted variable. We find evidence *against* this hypothesis in column 4, where we include a dummy for the subset of products with new tariff commitments already being implemented by 1997. The probability of an NTB is higher for those products and in fact binding status for the remaining products is statistically insignificant. This suggests that the variable is capturing the intended effect rather than an omitted factor.

We then test if the EU tariff constraints affected Turkish NTBs. We exploit the fact that, in 1997, only 85% of Turkish tariffs in our sample

[24] This correctly captures the goods for which there is no commitment as also not having a cap that binds but may misclassify some with a non-binding commitment. Any resulting measurement error should cause attenuation bias and thus make it less likely for us to find significant support for the model's predictions.

[25] Initially we implicitly assume that all products are in organized industries because there is no such data at the product level. Subsequently, we analyze the effects of commitment for a subsample of *industries* more likely to be organized.

Table 2
Impact of tariff commitments on NTB ad-valorem equivalent.

	(1)	(2)	(3)	(4)	(5)	(6)	(7) [a]	(8)[b]
WTO BIND	0.495***	1.05***	0.793***	−0.014	0.876***	0.794***	0.679***	0.773***
(β>0)	[0.072]	[0.102]	[0.079]	[0.200]	[0.101]	[0.079]	[0.078]	[0.079]
WTO 1997 implementation				0.540***				
(β>0)				[0.199]				
WTO BIND TARIFF		−3.08***			−1.89***			
(β_c<0)		[0.419]			[0.438]			
WTO BIND TARIFF ADJ.			−3.50***			−1.982**	−1.86***	−1.97[illegible]***
(β_c<0)			[0.434]			[0.427]	[0.431]	[0.423
EU BIND					0.935***	0.350**	0.421***	0.099
(β>0)					[0.173]	[0.160]	[0.160]	[0.169
EU BIND TARIFF					−5.69***			
(β_c<0)					[1.144]			
EU BIND TARIFF ADJ.						−6.89***	−5.89***	−6.7[illegible]***
(β_c<0)						[0.838]	[0.829]	[0.83[illegible]]
Constant	−2.14***	−2.06***	−2.05***	−2.13***	−2.65***	−2.72***	−2.58***	−2.4[illegible]***
	[0.124]	[0.118]	[0.118]	[0.123]	[0.211]	[0.211]	[0.207]	[0.20[illegible]]
Observations	5080	5080	5080	5080	4898	4898	4078	4414
Log-likelihood	−1207	−1155	−1147	−1203	−1128	−1096	−1066	−12[illegible]3
Pseudo R2	0.02	0.06	0.07	0.03	0.08	0.11	0.09	0.12

Notes: Tobit estimates with standard errors in brackets. *significant at 10%; **significant at 5%; ***significant at 1%.
[a] Excludes textiles and clothing products (ISIC 321 and 322).
[b] Includes ISIC-1 sector effects. The difference in sample size relative to the baseline is due to dropping observations in ISIC-1 groups without NTB variation, as in the Probit. The coefficients are identical if we include them.

were constrained by the EU external tariff while the other 15% were phased in later. Thus, EU BIND equals one for those constrained products and, in columns 5 and 6, we find it increases the NTB likelihood, similarly to WTO BIND. In addition, the level of the constraint for the bound products is given by the EU external tariff, which is expected to have a negative effect on NTBs; this is what we find in columns 5 and 6 (where the latter is adjusted by the Turkish unconstrained tariff, t^u, measured as before). The results for the WTO variables remain unchanged so both types of commitment have similar qualitative effects.

In order to quantify the impact of tariff commitments it is necessary to know how restrictive an NTB is. Moreover, the structural Eq. (5) gives us specific guidance about the functional form and determinants of the NTB AVE.[26] Estimates based on that structural equation will be our baseline estimate but before that we provide a set of specifications focusing on the binding variables. These are analogous to those in Table 1 but use the NTB AVE as a dependent variable and so employ a Tobit rather than a Probit and appear in Table 2. We find very similar results: (i) Binding the tariff of a product via the WTO or a customs union significantly increases the AVE; (ii) Tighter tariff constraints also increase the AVE significantly. This holds whether we use the tariff bindings (column 5) or, as Eq. (5) suggests, we adjust them with the unconstrained Turkish tariff (column 6).

The similarity to the Probit results is partly explained by the large share of censored observations, which imply the binary effect of bindings on using an NTB is strong. But it is important to note that the constraints on tariffs also affect the restrictiveness of existing NTBs. Using column 6, for example, we calculate the effect of binding a product in the WTO *if it already has an NTB* and find it is about 10 percentage points (i.e. E(NTB|**x**, NTB>0, WTO BIND = 1)-E(NTB|**x**, NTB>0, WTO BIND = 0)). Similarly, the NTB AVE is higher for tighter WTO tariffs. The effects for the EU are also significant and of the expected signs. We discuss their magnitudes and implication for imperfect policy substitution in Section 4.8.

[26] The ad valorem equivalents are estimated by Kee et al. (2009) at the HS6 level for several countries. In Appendix A we briefly describe their estimation and the adjustment we make to use this data.

4.3. Impact of commitment on NTBs: IV estimates and other robustness tests

We follow the theory closely and so are parsimonious in the inclusion of regressors. This raises the possibility that an omitted variable may influence both Turkey's binding decisions and NTB levels. This concern can be addressed in different ways depending on its source, as we now describe.

First, we address events in specific industries or sectors that may have generated a correlation between Turkish NTBs and the binding variables. As part of the customs union, Turkey was required to also harmonize its NTBs in the textile sector with those of the EU, and thus if the EU NTBs were correlated with its own tariffs there would be a correlation between the EU *tariff* and Turkish NTB that is not caused by the commitment mechanism in our model. To test this we exclude textile and clothing products from the sample in column 7 of Tables 1 and 2 and find it does not affect the results.[27]

More importantly perhaps, there may exist omitted sector level variables that affect the Turkish NTBs and the binding variables. In particular, the single undertaking in the WTO required countries to accept certain restrictions, one of which was binding tariffs on agricultural products. These were typically bound at very high levels and at the same time the WTO tried to curb NTBs in those goods. This can generate a negative relationship in our data between bindings and NTBs due to agriculture, which may not have come about because of Turkish choice of policy substitution. Moreover, the EU binding exceptions were focused on agriculture, so the identification of the EU binding *status* relies heavily on the cross-sectoral variation. To test if the results are robust to this (or other) source of unobserved sector heterogeneity we include ISIC-1 sector dummies. In column 8 of Tables 1 and 2 we find the EU binding status effect is now less than half the original effect and only marginally significant in the Probit. However, the effects for the EU tariff and both WTO variables are qualitatively and quantitatively unchanged.

[27] Turkey was also required to incorporate EU legislation on technical barriers to trade by 2001. However, progress on this was rather slow and limited even by 2005 so they are not an issue for our 1997 sample (see Togan, 2005, and the EU reports at http://europa.eu/legislation_summaries/enlargement/ongoing_enlargement/community_acquis_turkey/e07113_en.htm).

Table 3
Impact of tariff commitments on NTB (IV estimates).

	(1)[a]	(2)[b]	(3)[c]	(4)[c]	(5)	(6)	(7)
Dependent variable	NTB AVE	NTB AVE	NTB 0/1	NTB 0/1	WTO BIND × 1/elasticity	WTO BIND	WTO BIND TARIFF ADJ
Estimation stage	Second				First		
WTO BIND	1.08***	0.779*	0.127***	0.130**			
($\beta>0$)	[0.258]	[0.437]	[0.021]	[0.052]			
WTO BIND TARIFF ADJ.	−1.50***	−2.04*	−0.074***	−0.277**			
($\beta_c<0$)	[0.394]	[1.111]	[0.024]	[0.132]			
EU BIND	0.186	−0.096	0.039***	−0.020	−0.699***	−0.433***	−0.203***
($\beta>0$)	[0.136]	[0.372]	[0.015]	[0.044]	[0.095]	[0.030]	[0.011]
EU BIND TARIFF ADJ.	−5.99***	−5.68***	−1.27***	−1.19***	−0.474	−0.050	0.315***
($\beta_c<0$)	[0.748]	[0.863]	[0.101]	[0.115]	[0.571]	[0.178]	[0.069]
WTO BIND × 1/elasticity	−0.319*	−0.316*	−0.020	−0.021			
($\beta_\varepsilon<0$)	[0.178]	[0.179]	[0.014]	[0.014]			
IV WTO BIND × 1/elasticity					0.298***	0.007	−0.001
					[0.022]	[0.007]	[0.003]
IV WTO BIND					0.554***	0.364***	0.000
					[0.091]	[0.028]	[0.011]
IV WTO BIND TARIFF ADJ					0.238	−0.089	0.241***
					[0.178]	[0.056]	[0.022]
Constant	−2.16***	−1.73***	−0.039***	0.029	0.482***	0.596***	0.188***
	[0.179]	[0.491]	[0.015]	[0.059]	[0.143]	[0.045]	[0.017]
Observations	4478	4478	4478	4478	4478	4478	4478
F-stat joint IV[d]	n/a	n/a	n/a	n/a	74	56	44

Notes: Standard errors in brackets. *significant at 10%; **significant at 5%; ***significant at 1%.

[a] Employs a two-step IVTOBIT where the elasticity variable is instrumented by using the average of inverse elasticity for five other WTO members: India, Malaysia, Philippines, Thailand and Tunisia. The lower number of observations relative to the baseline in columns 6 of Tables 2 and 3 is due to unavailable elasticity data. Imputing the missing elasticities using the mean leads to very similar results. We report two-step results for comparability (see note (b) below) but similar coefficients obtained using a ML IVTOBIT. A Wald test rejects exogeneity at the 5% level. We exclude 15 outlier observations with NTB AVE > 170%, which also have abnormal elasticity values (Kee et al., 2009, use the elasticity to back out the NTB AVE thus if the former is measured with error so is the latter). Including the outliers does not affect these estimates qualitatively as we show in the working paper.

[b] This specification treats as endogenous both the elasticity and the WTO variables and instruments the latter two using the mean (in each given good) of WTO binding status and tariff across the same 5 WTO members used to calculate the instrument for the elasticity. Given the multiple endogenous regressors we employ a two-step IVTOBIT (Newey's minimum chi-squared estimator). There are three missing observations for these instruments. Despite the fact that one of the endogenous regressors is a dummy we can still use a Wald test of exogeneity and fail to reject it at a p-level of 0.88.

[c] Specification 3 instruments for the elasticity and 4 also instruments the WTO variables using the variables described above. Both employ two-stage least squares so the first stage OLS regressions (columns 5, 6, and 7) are exactly the same as for specifications 1 and 2.

[d] F-statistic for the joint significance of the three excluded instruments. The first stage R-squares for Eqs. (5), (6) and (7) are respectively 0.08, 0.14, 0.26.

An alternative piece of evidence suggests that the commitment effect is not simply capturing an omitted variable that generates a correlation between all tariffs (bound and unbound) and NTBs. When we add the Turkish applied tariff for unbound products to a specification otherwise similar to column 5 or 6 in Table 2 we find that unbound tariffs are positively correlated with NTBs. But the tariff effect via bound products remains negative and significant (results available upon request).[28]

As we see from Eq. (5), one missing variable from the NTB AVE estimation is the elasticity. We have excluded it thus far because it requires estimates that are not available for all products – thus it may introduce sample selection bias – and because it depends on the AVE—so we must to instrument for it. We use the average elasticity in each product over five other countries (their selection is described below) and find this instrument is strongly correlated with the endogenous elasticity—with a first stage t-statistic of 14.5. The second stage results in column 1 of Table 3 confirm the predicted negative effect of the elasticity on the AVE. Moreover, the effects of the commitment variables are qualitatively similar to the baseline in Table 2, which excluded the elasticity.

[28] Our estimates of policy substitution are consistent with our model but also with other alternative theories, c.f. Copeland (1990). This is one reason why in the next section we focus on the commitment predictions that are specific to our model. Nonetheless, the substitution evidence is still interesting since there may exist plausible alternative models that predict the opposite. In fact, the scant empirical evidence on this issue indicates that in 1970 U.S. NTBs were more likely in industries with higher tariffs (Ray, 1981) and those where applied tariff cuts had been smallest (Marvel and Ray, 1983). The difference in results highlights the importance of carefully modeling and estimating the relationship between policies.

Turkey had to take EU tariffs as given but it did have the ability to choose its WTO bindings. It did so before 1995, which was at least two years before implementing the NTBs we are measuring. Nonetheless, we cannot rule out the possibility that some Turkish industries or producers tried to influence both the bindings and the NTBs; therefore, we also instrument for the WTO binding and tariff. As instruments we employ the mean of WTO BIND and WTO BIND TARIFF in each product over five WTO members that do not trade much with Turkey but are broadly similar to it, particularly in their overall fraction of bound products. The first stage results in columns 6 and 7 of Table 3 indicate these variables have a strong positive correlation with their Turkish counterparts, with individual t-statistics in excess of 11 and joint F-statistics in excess of 40. Moreover, these instruments pick up motives that are similar across countries for binding tariffs but minimize any Turkish-specific reasons for why it sets a particularly high (or low) binding in a given good, i.e. the instrument avoids the variation in Turkish bindings most likely to be correlated with how it sets its NTBs.

Column 2 of Table 3 presents the AVE estimates when the WTO variables are also treated as endogenous. The instrumented variables have the same sign as the baseline in column 1 and remain significant. The most important point is that we fail to reject exogeneity at a very high probability – 0.88 – and therefore our baseline for quantification is the more efficient estimates in column 1. We report a similar exogeneity statistic for subsequent AVE specifications (Table 4), which is derived from running the specification in its respective column *but* instrumenting the WTO variables.

We also test whether our binding variables are simply proxying for omitted determinants of NTBs but find little evidence for this. We do so by controlling for determinants that previous empirical work has

Table 4
Impact of tariff commitments on NTB AVE (lobby organization and sector effects).

	(1)	(2)	(3)	(4)	(5)	(6)
Sample	Full[a]	Organized[b]	Unorganized	Full	Organized[b]	Unorganized
WTO BIND	1.08***	1.05***	0.664***	1.10***	1.10***	0.672***
(β>0)	[0.258]	[0.369]	[0.210]	[0.263]	[0.387]	[0.211]
WTO BIND TARIFF ADJ.	−1.50***	−1.53***	−1.25**	−1.45***	−1.49***	−1.14**
(β_τ<0)	[0.394]	[0.508]	[0.576]	[0.389]	[0.504]	[0.571]
EU BIND	0.186	−0.049	0.185	0.002	−0.205	0.097
(β>0)	[0.136]	[0.151]	[0.279]	[0.143]	[0.158]	[0.286]
EU BIND TARIFF ADJ.	−5.99***	−6.36***	−4.45***	−5.88***	−6.19***	−4.52***
(β_τ<0)	[0.748]	[0.916]	[1.266]	[0.741]	[0.901]	[1.266]
WTO BIND × 1/elasticity	−0.319*	−0.382	−0.097	−0.350*	−0.427	−0.102
(β_ε<0)	[0.178]	[0.258]	[0.127]	[0.181]	[0.271]	[0.128]
Constant	−2.16***	−1.94***	−1.74***	−1.92***	−1.73***	−1.65***
	[0.179]	[0.215]	[0.300]	[0.177]	[0.210]	[0.301]
Observations	4478	3287	1176	4027	2872	1155
ISIC-1 sector effects	No	No	No	Yes	Yes	Yes
Wald test exog. (P-value)[c]	0.88	0.77	0.83	0.83	0.71	0.83

Notes: Standard errors in brackets. *significant at 10%; **significant at 5%; ***significant at 1%. All specifications employ a two-step IVTOBIT where WTO BIND × 1/elasticity is instrumented as described in Table 3. The difference in sample in 4–6 relative to 1–3 is due to dropping observations in ISIC-1 groups without NTB variation. The coefficients are identical if we include them.

[a] Baseline specification identical to Table 3 column (1) for ease of comparison.

[b] An industry is classified as organized if it lists an organization for Turkey in the 4th edition of the World Guide to Trade Associations. Raw electronic data generously provided by Bonnie Wilson and Dennis Coates. Authors matched the description of organization entries to ISIC 3 industries. Fifteen HS6 codes in the baseline sample could not be matched to a well defined ISIC-3 code so the organization status is not determined. Thus the sum of organized and unorganized does not add up to the full sample.

[c] Probability at which we reject the null of exogeneity for the equivalent regression where WTO BIND and WTO BIND TARIFF ADJ. are also treated as endogenous and instrumented as in Table 3.

emphasized such as import values as well as industry employment, value added, output, wages, gross fixed capital formation and number of establishments (c.f. Lee and Swagel, 1997). We find that the baseline results in Table 3 are also robust to including these variables.[29]

Our model's predictions are derived for industries that are organized to lobby for trade protection. In practice it is difficult to identify these precisely, as is well known (c.f. Goldberg and Maggi, 1999). Nonetheless, using a reasonable proxy we can ask if the effects in the full sample mainly reflect those of the organized industries and whether they are stronger than for industries less likely to be organized. We do so in Table 4 by using a standard measure of organization: if an industry in Turkey lists an organization in the World Guide to Trade Associations. We find that the coefficients for the statistically significant variables are very similar for the full sample (column 1) and the organized (column 2) and that the marginal effects for the latter are somewhat stronger than for those industries less likely to be organized, in column 3. Those effects are even more pronounced if we calculate elasticities.[30] These results are robust to the inclusion of sector effects, as shown in columns 4 to 6. We also test and fail to reject the exogeneity of the WTO variables for all specifications.[31]

The theory suggests that the relationship between bindings and NTBs should reflect variation across industries, but one question is at what industry level lobbying actually occurs. Our organization variable is defined at the ISIC-3 level but it is possible that some sub-industries within each ISIC-3 are negotiating with the government and others are not. While we can't observe this directly we can examine how the results change if we control for finer industry effects. We do so in Appendix A where we describe that there is much less variation in our binding variables within rather than across industries. But three of them (WTO binding, WTO tariff and EU Tariff) do have some remaining variation within industries and we find that these variables retain their predicted sign in the baseline specifications in Table 3 augmented with industry effects (at ISIC-3 or HS-2 level).[32] However, both the magnitude and significance of their effect on NTBs tends to decrease. These findings are consistent with our model as long as several, but not all, SIGs lobby at the broader industry level.

In sum, the results in Tables 1 through 4 indicate that international constraints on tariffs increase the probability and restrictiveness of NTBs. These effects are dampened if the tariffs are constrained at higher levels, as the theory predicts. In addition, the effects appear to be related to the actual implementation dates of caps, present only for bound tariffs and somewhat stronger in industries likely to be organized. Therefore, these results support several key predictions of the model.

4.4. Impact of bargaining power on policy commitment: data and empirical approach

The model also predicts which goods a government prefers to constrain tariffs in and the level of that constraint. We think the results from testing these predictions can provide stronger empirical support for our theory since they are more specific to our model. We analyze the WTO commitments since in the EU case the Turkish government had little or no choice over the tariff levels. The basic econometric model is now given by

$$COMMIT_i = \alpha + \beta_\gamma g(BARG_I) + \mathbf{x}_I\boldsymbol{\theta} + e_i \tag{E2}$$

where $\mathbf{x}$ is a set of control variables and $COMMIT_i$ captures how restrictive the desired commitment tariffs are. We focus on estimating if β_γ is positive, i.e. if the government prefers a less restrictive commitment when it has higher bargaining power relative to a SIG, which is captured by $BARG_I$.

[29] We lag each of these variables 3 years to minimize the potential for reverse causation.

[30] In our working paper we show the results are similar if we use an alternative measure of NTB intensity: the NTB coverage ratio, i.e. the fraction of HS-8 lines with NTBs within each HS-6 product.

[31] We also obtain similar results for the WTO variables if we exclude the EU variables from all specifications in Table 4.

[32] This further suggests that our earlier results are not simply capturing industry omitted variables.

Table 5
Impact of bargaining power on WTO commitments (product binding probabilities).

Sample	All	Organized	Unorganized
Low bargaining power	0.59	0.60	0.58
Medium-high bargaining power	0.41	0.38	0.49
Difference	0.18*	0.22*	0.09
	[0.10]	[0.13]	[0.11]
Observations	4598	3255	1343

Notes: Standard errors in brackets clustered at isic 3 based on a maximum likelihood Probit using the medium-high bargaining power dummy for each relevant sample.
* significant at 10%.

We only observe commitment tariffs, t^c_i, for products that are bound. According to the theory this is not a random sample, which is something we will confirm in the data. Therefore, we need to account for the selection effect. The theory provides specific guidance on how to econometrically model it. First, the binding decision and its level depend on similar factors. Second, if we do not observe the commitment tariff it is because it would not bind, i.e. the desired commitment would have been higher than t^u_i. This strongly suggests a model with right censoring for t^c_i equal to t^u_i for the products that are not bound.

Many variables could potentially proxy for bargaining power and if we searched enough for the "appropriate" measure, we could certainly confirm any theoretical prediction. To avoid this pitfall we constrain ourselves to measuring bargaining power in a way that captures the Nash parameter γ as closely as possible to the theory. Binmore et al. (1986) show that Nash bargaining can be interpreted as a bilateral game of alternating offers, where the parameter γ reflects the relative discount factors of agents. Thus if we denote the discount factors of the government and the SIG in industry I by δ_g and δ_I respectively, then bargaining power should be measured as $BARG_I = \delta_g/(\delta_g + \delta_I)$.

The parameter δ_g (or δ_I) can be thought of as the product of the probability that the government (or industry) survives another period and the weight it places on next period's payoffs if it survives. In several contexts, the latter component is simply captured by a measure of the inverse interest rate that the government or industry have access to. We assume that all industries in a given country have access to the same rate and so the only relevant industry variation affecting $BARG_I$ is due to differences in their probability of survival; the lower the probability of survival of an industry, the higher the bargaining power of the *government* ($BARG_I$).[33] We use (1-exit rate$_I$) to capture the probability of survival of firms in industry I, calculated over the period 1994–1997. Given the potential for measurement error we use g($BARG_I$) where g(.) transforms $BARG_I$ into categorical variables that divide industries into terciles.[34]

4.5. Bargaining power and commitment: baseline results

The model predicts that a government is more likely to constrain tariffs in products where it has low bargaining power (henceforth low BP). The results in Table 5 confirm this: 59% of products in such industries are bound versus only 41% in industries relative to which the government has higher BP. The selection effect is stronger for the subset of organized industries where the probability of binding is 22 percentage points higher under low than high BP, a difference that is statistically and quantitatively significant. Moreover, for unorganized industries that difference is statistically equal to zero. Thus we only find a significant effect for the organized industries—exactly as the model predicts.

The results described above are robust to controlling for other regressors such as the number of exporters and exporter value concentration indices. As we noted in the theoretical section, a government can bind a product and then choose a high tariff, which effectively invalidates the impact of the commitment. Hence, rather than focusing on the probability of commitment separately we will consider it jointly with the restrictiveness of the commitment. Thus, in Table 6 we estimate the impact of BP on the desired WTO tariff commitment using the censoring procedure described above.

The first column of Table 6 shows that the government sets higher tariff bindings in industries where it has medium or high BP. The model predicts this relationship to be present in industries that are organized (columns 2 and 3) but not in unorganized ones (column 4), which is exactly what we find. To focus, as the theory does, on how restrictive the commitment is we also analyze $t^c - t^u$. The right censoring point suggested by the model is now zero, i.e. if we do not observe the commitment tariff it is because it would not bind. In the last columns of Table 6 we confirm that using this measure yields similar results.[35]

The theory assumes that Turkey is small in order to isolate the commitment channel. However, recent evidence by Broda et al. (2008) suggests that even if the country is not large on aggregate its tariffs in *some* goods may still affect the prices received by foreign exporters. This generates an incentive for foreigners to lobby Turkey for lower commitments. We control for this incentive in our baseline results by including two additional regressors that are outside this model but featured in the tariff negotiation literature: the number of exporters and a Herfindahl index of export value in a given good. Ludema and Mayda (2009) for example show that if the export sources of a good are highly concentrated then any given exporter is more likely to negotiate a tariff reduction; thus we expect Turkey's tariff binding to be decreasing in the export Herfindahl index. Holding this concentration measure fixed, an increase in foreign exporters implies a larger pressure for Turkey to bind at lower levels. The results in Table 6 confirm the sign and significance of these effects.

To further address the possibility of omitted variable bias, we extend the baseline estimates to control for plausible industry characteristics potentially correlated with our BP measure and bindings. One potential concern is that industries with higher exit rates (where the government has higher BP) also have more volatile employment or value-added. Governments can try to minimize such volatility for welfare reasons via relatively high tariff bindings so they can adjust up their *applied* tariffs. To tackle this, we use variation in employment between 1990 and 96 to construct a measure of volatility in each industry. Second, an important determinant of protection in Grossman and Helpman (1994) and other models is the output to import ratio divided by import demand elasticity. We construct this ratio for 1990–93, i.e. prior to the setting of the bindings. We include this and the volatility measure in columns 3 and 7 of Table 6 and find that they do not change the BP effect at all.[36]

[33] Since we consider a cross section for a single country, the government's probability of survival simply scales the variable equally for all industries and can thus be ignored in constructing the bargaining variable.

[34] To see why this is may be a reasonable proxy, consider a case where member firms of a SIG vote on whether to accept a government's proposal and realize the payoff or make a counter offer and wait another period. The fraction of firms that expect to die before the next period accept immediately, thus, all else equal, the lower the probability of survival of firms in the industry, the more likely it is to accept the government's offer and so the higher the government's bargaining power is.

[35] Moreover, we test and find that the BP coefficient for the organized industries is statistically different from that of the unorganized. We find evidence for this when testing equality across specifications and also if instead of splitting the sample according to organization we employ interactions with the organization indicator. We also obtain similar results using a Heckman selection model, which also shows that bargaining power lowers the probability to bind but only in organized industries. These results are available on request.

[36] The results using the variation in value added instead of employment are similar. Including these extra controls does not affect the baseline results for the unorganized industries either.

Table 6
Impact of bargaining power on desired WTO commitment tariffs (organized vs. unorganized industries).

Dependent variable	Tariff binding level[a]				Tariff binding–unconstrained[b]			
Estimation method	Censor.	Censor.	Censor.	Censor.	Censor.	Censor.	Censor.	Censor.
Sample	All	Organized	Organized	Unorganized	All	Organized	Organized	Unorganized
Medium-high bargaining ($\beta_\gamma > 0$)	0.147*	0.230***	0.209**	−0.046	0.127	0.199**	0.181**	−0.043
	[0.084]	[0.084]	[0.085]	[0.070]	[0.083]	[0.087]	[0.089]	[0.065]
Number of exporters	−0.015**	−0.016**	−0.016**	−0.005**	−0.016**	−0.017***	−0.017**	−0.005*
	[0.006]	[0.007]	[0.007]	[0.003]	[0.006]	[0.007]	[0.007]	[0.002]
Herfindahl of export value	−0.168*	−0.232**	−0.231**	0.051	−0.169*	−0.234**	−0.234**	0.054
	[0.094]	[0.098]	[0.101]	[0.047]	[0.099]	[0.102]	[0.105]	[0.047]
Variance log employment			−0.321				−0.136	
			[3.047]				[3.284]	
(Output/import)/(imp. dem. Elast.)			0.001***				0.001**	
			[0.000]				[0.000]	
Constant	0.498***	0.523***	0.519***	0.308***	0.418***	0.456***	0.450***	0.204***
	[0.135]	[0.140]	[0.127]	[0.078]	[0.138]	[0.145]	[0.131]	[0.070]
Observations	4546	3210	3210	1336	4546	3210	3210	1336

Notes: Standard errors in brackets clustered at isic 3 (the level of variation of the bargaining variable). *,**,*** respectively significant at 10%, 5% and 1%.
[a] Right censored at $t^c_i > t^u_i$ for goods not bound.
[b] Right censored at $t^c_i - t^u_i > 0$ for goods not bound.

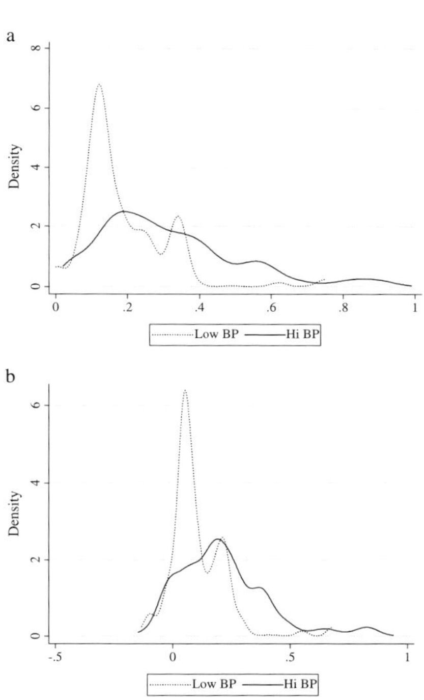

Fig. 2. a: Kernel density of WTO tariff commitments, t^c: low vs. high bargaining power. b: Kernel density of WTO commitments, $t^c - t^u$: low vs. high bargaining power.

4.6. Bargaining power and commitment: non-parametric evidence and robustness tests

We now provide additional robustness checks and evidence for the model's predictions.

In the working paper we show that the results in Table 6 are robust to alternative censoring points. Furthermore, the model predicts that the difference in tariff commitments should be strongest when contrasting industries where the government has high BP versus those with low. We confirm this by including separate variables for high and medium BP and finding tariff bindings for high BP larger than both medium and low BP; the difference between high and low BP is at least 20 percentage points.

The evidence that high BP industries have higher commitment tariffs goes beyond the conditional means just discussed. Fig. 2a presents a kernel density estimate of the observed WTO tariff commitments. The dark line represents the subset of goods where BP is high and it is clearly shifted to the right of the dashed one that represents the low BP goods. Thus high BP goods not only have higher mean commitment tariffs but also higher median, 75th percentile, etc.

To provide additional non-parametric evidence we ask if the bindings are more restrictive when BP is low. We confirm this is so in Fig. 2b, which plots the kernel density estimates for $t^c - t^u$. When BP is low there is a large share of goods (dashed line) centered around zero, indicating commitments that actually bind. For high BP the median is over 20%, indicating that a large share of these goods does not have binding commitments. In sum, there is evidence for the main prediction of the model across the whole distribution, not just the mean, and even if we focus only on the subsample of bound products, i.e. even if we ignore the selection effect.

4.7. Bargaining power and commitment: addressing endogeneity concerns

The specifications follow the model closely and are therefore parsimonious. Including the regressors described and controlling for organization mitigates the potential for omitted variable bias. Nonetheless, in this section we further address this possibility in two ways: (i) by providing some additional evidence that our measure captures bargaining power; and (ii) by employing instrumental variables to directly address whether there is omitted variable bias or reverse causality from bindings to exit rates.

Table 7
Impact of bargaining power on desired WTO commitment tariffs (instrumental variables).

Dependent variable	Tariff binding level			Tariff binding–unconstrained		
Estimation method	IV Tobit	IV Tobit	IV Tobit	IV Tobit	IV Tobit	IV Tobit
Sample	All (2)	Organized (3)	Unorganized (4)	All (6)	Organized (7)	Unorganized (8)
Medium-high bargaining ($\beta_\gamma>0$)	0.203***	0.261***	0.088	0.214***	0.259***	0.052
	[0.071]	[0.098]	[0.248]	[0.072]	[0.089]	[0.186]
Number of exporters	−0.016**	−0.017**	−0.005	−0.016***	−0.017***	−0.005
	[0.007]	[0.007]	[0.005]	[0.006]	[0.007]	[0.004]
Herfindahl of export value	−0.167*	−0.232**	0.051	−0.167*	−0.232**	0.053
	[0.095]	[0.099]	[0.049]	[0.097]	[0.101]	[0.046]
Constant	0.432***	0.476***	0.189**	0.363**	0.417***	0.144**
	[0.150]	[0.120]	[0.088]	[0.142]	[0.118]	[0.074]
Observations	4461	3183	1278	4461	3183	1278
Wald test exog. (P-value)	0.38	0.33	0.37	0.24	0.21	0.43

Notes: Standard errors in brackets clustered at isic 3 (the level of variation of the bargaining variable). *,**,*** respectively significant at 10%, 5% and 1%. Bargaining power instrumented using labor share of value added, gross fixed capital formation, the inverse of the # of establishments, and a Herfindahl index of that #, all between 1990 and 93 via a maximum likelihood IV Tobit. The reduction in observations is due to missing data for the # of establishments.

To evaluate if the measure we employ generates a plausible bargaining power ranking we searched for industry redistribution outcomes unrelated to trade policy. Such data is rare, which is the reason we focused on trade policies in the first place. However, Mitra et al. (2002) provide government subsidy data for some Turkish industries. If our measure of government bargaining power captures what it is meant to then we should find that when it is low the industry can obtain higher subsidies than when it is high. That is what we find for the industries that we can match to their data. The average subsidy for industries in which the government has low BP is 22%, while it is 14% in industries where the government's BP is high. This further suggests that our BP ranking is reasonable.

Next, we instrument for BP using a combination of industry level variables: gross fixed capital formation, the labor share of value added and measures of concentration (e.g. the inverse of the number of establishments and a Herfindahl index). There are plausible economic arguments why each of these should be correlated with BP.[37] These variables can also be thought of as affecting the subsequent probability of survival of firms in an industry (or 1-exit rate$_l$), which we used to construct BARG and they are indeed reasonably correlated with it. In the first stage, three out of the four instruments are individually significant and they are jointly significant. According to our model there is no obvious reason why these instruments should directly determine the tariff binding. But, to further justify their exclusion from the second stage, we construct the instruments for the period prior to the bargaining period, i.e. prior to 1994, so they were not affected by the tariff commitments we analyze, which were adopted *after* that date. Moreover, the overidentification allows us to provide some evidence for this exclusion: each of the instruments is insignificant when separately included in the second stage.

Table 7 shows that the IV results are qualitatively similar to the baseline in Table 6. The magnitudes are similar, but we do not place much emphasis on this since we cannot reject exogeneity for any specification. The exogeneity and the fact that we are instrumenting for a dummy in a censored regression setting leads us to focus on the more efficient estimates where we do not instrument.

[37] Some studies of the determinants of a firm's bargaining power relative to its workers have related it to variables such as capital intensity (Doiron, 1992), industry concentration (Veugelers, 1989) and asset liquidity. Some of these should also be correlated with firms' bargaining power relative to the government. Industries with lower gross fixed capital formation have more flexibility in shifting resources to alternative uses and thus more bargaining power. More concentrated industries may have more bargaining power due to either larger profits and/or lower cost to organize and cooperate.

Table 8
NTB inefficiency and imperfect substitution estimates.

	(1)	(2)	(3)	(4)
Sample	Full	Organized	Full	Organized
WTO BIND ($\beta>0$)	0.12***	0.13***	0.12***	0.11***
WTO BIND TARIFF ($\beta_c<0$)	−0.16***	−0.11*		
WTO BIND TARIFF ADJ. ($\beta_c<0$)			−0.20***	−0.19***
EU BIND ($\beta>0$)	0.086***	0.065***	0.02	−0.01
EU BIND TARIFF ($\beta_c<0$)	−0.78***	−0.49***		
EU BIND TARIFF ADJ. ($\beta_c<0$)			−0.79***	−0.80***
WTO BIND × 1/elasticity ($\beta_\varepsilon<0$)	−0.048*	−0.059	−0.04	−0.05
Observations	4481	3288	4481	3288
NTB Inefficiency: $\hat{\phi}=\hat{\beta}_\varepsilon/\hat{\beta}_c\in(0,1]$	0.30	0.54	0.21	0.25
Imperfect policy substitution: $d\tau/dt^c\approx\hat{\beta}_c\in(-1,0)$	−0.16	−0.11	−0.20	−0.19

Notes: (a) All specifications employ a ML IVTOBIT where we instrument for the elasticity measure as in Table 4. (b) The reported marginal effect for each variable x_j is calculated as $\partial E(y|\mathbf{x},y>0)/\partial x_j$ and equals $\beta_j\ \mu(\mathbf{x}\beta/\sigma)$ where β_j is the structural parameter in E(1) and $\mu(\mathbf{x}\beta/\sigma)$ is the common Tobit factor evaluated at WTO BIND = EU BIND = 1, EU tariff = WTO tariff = unconstrained and at mean of 1/elasticity. (c) *significant at 10%; **significant at 5%; ***significant at 1%. (d) All specifications exclude outliers as defined before.

4.8. Policy inefficiency, imperfect substitution and quantification of estimates

We conclude by tying the theory and evidence as follows. First, we estimate if NTBs are inefficient relative to tariffs—an assumption of our theory. Second, we examine if NTBs are imperfect substitutes for tariffs—an outcome of our theory. Third, we quantify the role of BP on tariff commitments and, via this channel, on NTBs.

Recall that the structural Eq. (5) is only defined for non-negative NTB AVEs and thus, for the purposes of quantification, we should focus on those marginal effects, i.e. on $\partial E(y|\mathbf{x},y>0)/\partial\mathbf{x}$. We report these in Table 8 for the full sample and for organized industries based on the specifications in columns 1 and 2 of Table 4.

As we can see from Eq. (5) the ratio of the parameters that multiply the elasticity and the tariff constraint terms yields ϕ, the average inefficiency of NTBs relative to tariffs. Thus we can estimate it as $\hat{\phi}=\hat{\beta}_\varepsilon/\hat{\beta}_c$ where $\hat{\beta}_\varepsilon$ and $\hat{\beta}_c$ are the estimated coefficients for the elasticity and tariff constraint variables respectively.[38] The

[38] Note that in Table 8 we report $\partial E(y|\mathbf{x},y>0)/\partial x_j$, which with Tobit yields $\beta_j\ \mu(\mathbf{x}\beta/\sigma)$, where β_j is the estimate of the structural parameter in Eq. (E1) and $\mu(\mathbf{x}\beta/\sigma)$ is the standard Tobit factor (between 0 and 1). Thus, we cannot use the estimate for any individual variable in Table 8 to back out ϕ. However, since $\mu(\mathbf{x}\beta/\sigma)$ is common to all variables we eliminate it by using the ratio $\partial E(y|\mathbf{x},y>0)/\partial x_T/\partial E(y|\mathbf{x},y>0)/\partial x_\varepsilon=\hat{\beta}_\varepsilon/\hat{\beta}_c$.

estimates for ϕ, shown at the bottom of Table 8, are in the predicted range – between zero and one – even though we did not restrict the estimation to ensure this. The value for the specification closest to the theory is 0.25 (organized industries in column 4), which indicates that, on average, a quarter of NTB rents, as defined in Section 3.1, are lost relative to an equivalent tariff. Interestingly, we also find a similar estimate if we use the coverage ratio as the NTB measure.

As we discuss in Section 3.6, when the NTB is relatively inefficient it should be an imperfect substitute for tariffs, i.e. $d\tau/dt^c \in (-1,0)$. Our findings in Table 8 do suggest there is imperfect substitution. For example, tightening a WTO tariff constraint by about 20 percentage points (p.p.) increases the NTB AVE by 4 p.p. in organized industries (column 4). A similar tightening of the EU constraint generates a larger increase in the NTB but one that is still not enough to offset the initial decrease in protection. One may argue that to capture the total rather than partial effect we should instead estimate a reduced form where we do not control for the unconstrained tariff level. We do so in columns 1 and 2 and find even less policy substitution. Moreover, when we calculate 95% confidence intervals for all these estimates they lie precisely in the imperfect substitution range. This finding suggests that tariff commitments lead to a reduction in total protection—an important prediction of the model and a necessary condition for commitment to raise social welfare.

Given this evidence supporting a key theoretical assumption – the NTB inefficiency – and prediction – the imperfect policy substitution – it is important to also quantify the impact of the bargaining mechanism, both on tariff commitments directly and on NTBs. Table 6 shows that tariff constraints are stricter by about 20 p.p. in low BP industries. This is a significant amount, equivalent to the effect of adding pressure to liberalize from about 12 extra exporters – almost a two standard deviation increase in that variable – or an increase of almost three standard deviations in the export concentration index emphasized by other tariff theories.

Clearly, BP has a strong effect on tariff commitments. To estimate how it translates into higher NTBs we employ the following counterfactual: what is the change in the average NTB if the government treated all goods where it has medium or high BP as if it had low BP instead. To employ our existing estimates we approximate this effect by decomposing the impact of BP into two channels: tighter tariffs for goods with existing commitments and new tariff commitments. We summarize how BP affects NTBs via this intensive and extensive margin of commitment below and explain their calculation in more detail in Table 9.

As we noted, the tariff commitment is 20 p.p. tighter in organized industries where government BP is low. Because of the imperfect substitution shown in Table 8 this tariff commitment increases NTBs by about 4 p.p. for each medium-hi BP product already bound. But there is an extra effect on NTBs since under low BP an additional fraction of products would be bound. If these products were bound at the average level of $t^c - t^u$ predicted for low BP, then the NTB on them increases by 7 p.p.

We can weigh the intensive margin effect by the fraction of products with medium-hi BP that are already bound (0.38) and the extensive effect by the fraction of newly bound goods (0.22 from Table 5). This procedure yields an average increase of 3 p.p. for the NTB AVE caused by the bargaining power channel. This effect is significant relative to the average AVE over all the goods in the data, (about 3 p.p.), but it is modest relative to the average over the subset of products that already have a positive NTB AVE.

In sum, we find that bargaining power affects tariff commitments significantly and in that way increases the use of inefficient policies. However, NTBs are relatively inefficient and imperfectly substitute for tariffs so their increase is unlikely to offset the decrease in tariff protection, particularly if the good's tariff was already bound.

Table 9
Impact of Bargaining Power on NTB AVE via WTO Tariff Commitments.

Sample:	All	Organized
Channel (affected goods)		
Existing tariff commitment	3 p.p.	4 p.p.
New tariff commitment	7 p.p.	7 p.p.
Average	2 p.p.	3 p.p.

Notes: Values represent the percentage point increase in the NTB ad valorem equivalent if the government had low bargaining power instead of medium or high and changed tariff commitments as predicted by the model. The effect via existing commitments for organized industries is approximately $100^*.04 = 100*(-0.2)*(-.19)$ where -0.2 is the predicted tariff effect from switching to low (estimated from Table 6), -0.19 is the effect of that tariff commitment change on the NTB from Table 8 column 4. This affects the fraction of bound products with medium-hi BP, which is 0.38 (Table 6). The new tariff commitment effect is approximately $100^*0.07 = 100*(0.11 - 0.19^*0.22)$ where the marginal coefficients 0.11 and -0.19 are from Table 8 and 0.22 is the average level of $t^c - t^u$ for low BP (estimated from Table 6). This applies to 0.22 of goods that would be newly bound where this extra probability of binding is from Table 6. The average change over all goods assumes the only NTB changes occur on the 0.38 of bound and 0.22 of newly bound so it equals $.38^*4 + .22^*7$.

5. Conclusion

Governments can use multiple policies to achieve a given objective. Moreover, in important cases, such as redistribution to SIGs, the observed policy composition includes policies that appear relatively inefficient for the purpose. This theoretical puzzle can have important implications, e.g. alternative policy mixes can lead to different welfare costs for a given amount of redistribution and alter the equilibrium level of redistribution itself. To tightly link the theory and estimation we focus on a specific model and a set of policies that are ubiquitous and economically important: tariffs vs. NTBs.

The model shows that a government bargaining with its domestic SIGs can gain by committing to limit its tariffs through international trade agreements. Moreover, we show that the NTB increases with the stringency of those tariff commitments. We also show how the decision to commit depends on the government's strength relative to SIGs. We test and find support for the main predictions of the model using detailed data for Turkey. Tariff commitments imposed via the WTO and the PTA with the European Union increase the likelihood and restrictiveness of Turkish NTBs. Moreover, we construct a measure of bargaining power and find that tariff commitments are less likely and less stringent in industries where the government is stronger. The results are robust to a variety of concerns, e.g. endogeneity, and particularly strong for organized industries, as predicted.

The evidence is also economically significant in terms of its implications for partial versus general policy equilibrium approaches. We estimate that on average NTBs are less efficient than tariffs in organized industries. The model predicts imperfect policy substitution in this case and we find evidence supporting it. Policy substitution implies that the actual reduction in total protection due to tariff commitments was not as large as a partial policy equilibrium analysis would predict since some of it was offset by higher NTBs. However, since this substitution was imperfect the commitments may have still reduced total protection and thus improved social welfare. This suggests that (i) tariff commitments are not just politically but also socially valuable and (ii) that recent concerns with rising NTBs around the world are mitigated once we model them in a general policy equilibrium framework.

Future research could apply our approach to examine if similar results apply to other countries' policies, both in trade and possibly in other areas. More broadly, it is important to model and carefully test alternative motives for policy choice in order to better understand its composition and impacts.

Appendix A

Derivation of unconstrained tariff in Eq. (3)

For the problem given by Eq. (2), the FOC for t, τ and C are respectively

$$\frac{\gamma}{G-G^0}G_t + \frac{1-\gamma}{V-V_0}V_t - \lambda = 0 \quad \text{(A1)}$$

$$\frac{\gamma}{G-G^0}G_\tau + \frac{1-\gamma}{V-V_0}V_\tau \leq 0 \quad \text{(A2)}$$

$$\frac{\gamma}{G-G^0}G_C + \frac{1-\gamma}{V-V^0}V_C = 0 \quad \text{(A3)}$$

$$t - t^c \leq 0 \quad \text{(A4)}$$

along with the (omitted) complementary slackness conditions for Eqs. (A2) and (A4). Here a subscript denotes a partial derivative and to ensure an interior solution we assume throughout that $\Psi'(0) \to \infty$. If the tariff cap is absent or not binding then its multiplier, λ, equals 0 and then from Eqs. (A1) and (A3) we obtain:

$$\frac{G_t}{G_c} = \frac{V_t}{V_c} \Longleftrightarrow \frac{a t_i (p_i^*)^2 m_i'}{\Psi_i'(C_i)} = \frac{y_i(p_i)p_i^*}{-1} \quad \text{(A5)}$$

which can be rewritten as Eq. (3) in the text.

Condition for tariff constraint in the absence of NTBs

Given the independence of irrelevant alternatives in Nash bargaining, the government would be indifferent between $t_i^c = t_i^u$ and any higher constraint, so we can focus on determining if Eq. (4) in the text is equal to Eq. (3) or lower. Omitting the product subscripts the condition for a non-binding constraint is

$$\frac{\partial C / \partial t}{-a(p^*)^2 m'(t^c)} \Psi'(C(t^c)) = \frac{y(t^u)}{-ap^* m'(t^u)} \Psi'(C(t^u)).$$

If $t_i^c = t_i^u$ then the equilibrium values of C, p, and thus y and m' would be identical in Eqs. (3) and (4). Replacing these above we should then obtain $\partial C/\partial t = \partial \Pi/\partial t$. We now show that $t^c < t^u$ when the NTB is unavailable. Proof by contradiction: if $t^u = t^c$ then C, p and m' are identical under both equilibria. Using this we show that the RHS of the constrained tariff, t^c, in Eq. (4) is actually lower than the RHS of the unconstrained tariff expression in Eq. (3) and hence the constraint binds.

$$-\frac{C_t \Psi'}{a(p^*)^2 m'} < -\frac{y\Psi'}{ap^* m'}$$
$$C_t < p^* y$$
$$C_t < \Pi_t.$$

If they are equal then we should use C_t from the unconstrained problem, which we obtain from implicitly differentiating the FOC for C in Eq. (A3)

$$C_t = -\frac{\gamma V_t \Psi' - (1-\gamma)G_t}{\gamma\left(-\Psi' + [V-V_0]\Psi''\right) - (1-\gamma)\Psi'}.$$

If the tariff is the same than under the unconstrained equilibrium then $G_t/G_C = V_t/V_C$, and therefore $G_t = -\Psi' V_t$. Replacing and simplifying

$$C_t = \frac{\gamma V_t \Psi' - (1-\gamma)(-\Psi' V_t)}{\Psi' - \gamma\left([V-V_0]\Psi''\right)} = \frac{\Psi' V_t}{\Psi' - \gamma\left([V-V_0]\Psi''\right)}$$

So the condition $C_t < \Pi_t$ $(= V_t)$ is

$$\frac{\Psi' V_t}{\Psi' - \gamma\left([V-V_0]\Psi''\right)} < V_t$$
$$\Psi' < \Psi' - \gamma\left([V-V_0]\Psi''\right)$$
$$0 > \gamma[V-V_0]\Psi''$$

which must hold because: (a) $\Psi'' < 0$ and (b) $V > V_0$ for all $\gamma < 1$. This makes it clear that as long as the government has some but not all the bargaining power and lobby goods have diminishing marginal utility so utility is not transferable at a constant rate, the government prefers to commit to a binding tariff constraint. If $\gamma = 0$ the government would be indifferent about setting a cap since it would receive the reservation payoff either way. If the constraint binds then instead of $\partial C/\partial t = \partial \Pi/\partial t$ we have $\partial(\Pi - C)/\partial t > 0$, which means that relaxing the constraint, i.e. increasing the tariff, would increase the payoff to lobbies with no first order cost to the government, as explained in the text.

Derivation of NTB expression in Eq. (5)

The interior NTB solution under a tariff cap equalizes the marginal rates of substitution across policies for the government and lobbies, as we can see from solving Eqs. (A2) and (A3) to obtain:

$$\frac{G_\tau}{G_c} = \frac{V_\tau}{V_c} \Longleftrightarrow \frac{a\left[(\tau_i(1-\phi) + \bar{t}_i^c)(p_i^*)^2 m_i' - \phi p_i^* m_i\right]}{\Psi_i'(C_i)} = \frac{y_i(p_i)p_i^*}{-1} \quad \text{(A6)}$$

which we can re-arrange to obtain Eq. (5) in the text.

Simulation

The following simulation shows that the condition in Section 3.5 can be satisfied so the government commits to a tariff constraint in this good if the cap is not too stringent.

Assumptions:

$$y \equiv k^{1-\alpha} l^\alpha \Rightarrow \pi(p) = (1-\alpha)pk(p\alpha)^{\frac{\alpha}{1-\alpha}}$$
$$u(x) = Bx - \frac{b}{2}x^2 \Rightarrow d(p) = \frac{1}{b}(B-p)$$
$$\Psi \equiv C^n, p^* = k = b = a = N = 1, n = \alpha = 0.5, \gamma = 0, B = 3.$$

The value of B was chosen to ensure positive import levels in equilibrium; the value of γ because we are evaluating a limit condition; and the remaining mostly for computational simplicity and to match the requirements of the model.

Slope condition for tariff

The unconstrained tariff level t^u is implicitly defined by the efficiency condition $G_t/G_C = V_t/V_C$ for a given contribution level

$$\Psi'\left(C^{mt}\right) = -a\frac{t^u(p^*)^2 m'(p^*(1+t^u))}{p^* y(p^*(1+t^u))}$$

202 N. Limão, P. Tovar / Journal of International Economics 85 (2011) 186–205

where C^{mt} is the minimum level of the good provided by the lobby required to maintain the government at the reservation utility.

We can define the Pareto frontier when t is used as $V^t - v^0 = \Omega^t(G^t - g^0)$. The condition we describe in the text can then be written as

$$\lim_{\gamma \to 0} -\Omega^t / \Omega'^t = \lim_{\gamma \to 0} \left(V^t - v^0\right) \Psi'\left(C^t\right)$$
$$= \left[\left(\pi(.) - \pi(p^*) - C^{mt}\right)\left(-a\frac{t^u (p^*)^2 m'(.)}{p^* y(.)}\right)\right]_{\gamma=0}$$

where $\pi(.) \equiv \pi(p^*(1+t^u))$, similarly for $m'(.)$ and $y(.)$. The first equality is due to the definition of Ω, and the fact that the slope of the Pareto frontier in G–V space is $-1/\Omega'^t$. It equals $\Psi'(C^t)$ at any given equilibrium as this is the ratio at which utility is traded as contributions are used, i.e. G_C/V_C. The expression for $\Psi'(C^t)$ in the second equality is derived from the efficiency condition given above. Using the definition of V we obtain $\lim_{\gamma \to 0}(V^t - v^0) = \pi(p^*(1 + t^u(\gamma=0))) - C^{mt} - \pi(p^*)$. Using the definition of G and the condition $G(t=0, \tau=0, C=0) = G(t=t^u(\gamma=0), \tau=0, C^{mt})$ (recalling that in the unconstrained equilibrium $\tau=0$), we can write C^{mt} as:

$$C^{mt} = \lim_{\gamma \to 0} \Psi^{-1}\left(a[\pi(p^*) + Ns(p^*) - \{\pi(.) + Ns(.) + t^u p^* m(.)\}]\right).$$

Using the expressions derived above for $\lim_{\gamma \to 0} - \Omega^t/\Omega'^t$ and C^{mt}, and using the functional forms for $\pi(p)$, $d(p)$ and $\Psi(.)$ as well as the parameter values listed we obtain:

$$\lim_{\gamma \to 0} -\Omega^t / \Omega'^t = 0.1875(t^u)^2 \frac{8 + 4t^u - 9(t^u)^3}{1 + t^u}.$$

To evaluate this expression we require the equilibrium t^u, which is calculated by plugging in the expression for C^{mt} above and the functional form assumptions into the efficiency condition $G_t/G_C = V_t/V_C$ previously defined.

Slope condition for NTB

The equilibrium condition for the NTB is the one in Eq. (A6):

$$\Psi'\left(C^{mt}\right) = -a\frac{(\tau(1-\phi) + t^c)(p^*)^2 m'(.) - \phi p^* m(.)}{p^* y(.)} \tag{A7}$$

where the domestic price is $p = p^*(1 + \tau + t^c)$ so $m'(.) \equiv m'(p^*(1 + \tau + t^c))$ and similarly for m and y.

The ratio for the NTB is

$$\lim_{\gamma \to 0} -\Omega^\tau / \Omega'^\tau = \lim_{\gamma \to 0} \left(V - v^0\right) \Psi'(C^\tau)$$
$$= \left[\left(\pi(.) - \pi(p^*) - C^{mt}\right)\left(-a\frac{(\tau(1-\phi) + t^c)(p^*)^2 m'(.) - \phi p^* m(.)}{p^* y(.)}\right)\right]_{\gamma=0}.$$

If the cap were zero and $\phi = 0$ then the expression is identical to the tariff's, as expected. We also have:

$$C^{mt} = \lim_{\gamma \to 0} \Psi^{-1}\left(a[\pi(p^*) + Ns(p^*) - \{\pi(.) + Ns(.) + (\tau(1-\phi) + t^c) p^* m(.)\}]\right).$$

Using the expressions derived for $\lim_{\gamma \to 0} - \Omega^\tau/\Omega'^\tau$ and C^{mt}, and for $\pi(p)$, $d(p)$ and $\Psi(.)$ as well as the parameter values we obtain:

$$\lim_{\gamma \to 0} -\Omega^\tau / \Omega'^\tau = \Big\{-\frac{1}{4}\left(1 - (1 + \tau + t^c)^2\right)$$
$$-\left(\left(\left(\frac{1}{4}\right)\left(1 - (1 + \tau + t^c)^2\right) + \frac{1}{2}((t^c + \tau)(4 - \tau - t^c))\right.\right.$$
$$\left.\left.-\left(\frac{1}{2}(\tau(1-\phi) + t^c)(3 - 3(\tau + t^c))\right)\right)\right)^2\Big\} \times \frac{3(t^c - \phi t^c + \tau + \phi - 2\tau\phi)}{1 + \tau + t^c}.$$

Using $\phi = 0.3$ and a given value for t^c we solve for the equilibrium τ using Eq. (A6) and replace it above to obtain the values in the table. The first row corresponds to a case in which the cap is half the equilibrium value of the unconstrained tariff under this set of parameters. The second row is for $t^c = 0.85t^u$.

Model insights for "optimal" vs. observed commitment rules in trade agreements

In Section 3.4 we took the commitment mechanism as given and assumed it allows the government to set positive caps on tariffs but not on all NTBs, which captures the available restrictions in the WTO. A deeper question is whether our model provides any insight into whether the set of available restrictions in the WTO are "optimal". Fully answering this question would require extending the model to include an institution design stage (possibly with contracting costs) and large countries (to account for terms-of-trade motives), which is beyond the scope of this paper. Even though the model was not specifically designed to answer this question we now conjecture that such an extension may generate policy restrictions that are consistent with some of those observed in the WTO (and GATT). In particular, with the following facts

(i) There are constraints on the relatively efficient policies (subsidies, tariffs).
(ii) There are lax or no constraints on many NTBs.
(iii) There is a small set of NTBs subject to tight restrictions and efforts to curb a subset of these (namely, quotas) dates back to the GATT.

Suppose the government can choose the set of policies in which commitment is available at some fixed cost per policy (e.g. a contracting cost at the rule design stage and/or an enforcement cost). It will then choose a commitment rule for a policy if the bargaining benefit exceeds that fixed cost. Since the efficient policies are the ones used in the absence of commitment, they present the largest benefit suggesting the constraints in point (i) above would emerge. If the alternative NTBs are sufficiently inefficient then in equilibrium they will be insignificant even if there are constraints on the other policies (as shown by Eq. (5)) thus there is no benefit to paying the fixed cost to restrict them, which can explain (ii). Now, if the available NTB is relatively efficient then it will easily substitute the tariff (e.g. some quotas) and thus there is a large benefit from constraining such NTBs.

A slightly more subtle issue is why the restrictions sometimes take the form of bans (e.g. quotas or subsidies) or positive caps (tariffs). The ban on quotas is consistent with the simple version of the model where if the government can choose a tariff cap level optimally then it wants to prevent that gain from being undone by a policy that is very similar, so it bans the quota. A similar logic suggests a ban of tariffs if a positive cap on the more efficient production subsidies could be enforced. In practice, there are other motives why governments would not want to ban tariffs (e.g. to deal with import surges) but the model suggests governments would favor tighter constraints on tariffs than subsidies. This was actually the case under GATT, but it proved very difficult to define and enforce subsidy commitments. Therefore, it is possible that the only enforceable commitment on

Table 1
Simulation result for the choice of tariff versus NTBs.

	$\lim_{\gamma \to 0} - \frac{\Omega^x}{\Omega'^x}$		
t^c	$x = \tau$		$x = t$
$0.5t^u$	0.37	<	0.43
$0.85t^u$	0.44	>	0.43
Parameters			
$p^* = k = b = a = N = 1, n = \alpha = 0.5, \gamma = 0, B = 3, \phi = 0.3$			
Functions			
$\Psi = C^n; q = k^{1-\alpha} l^\alpha, u(x) = Bx - \frac{b}{2}x^2$			

Notes: Similar inequalities for $t^c = 0.85t^u$ also hold for $\phi = 0.1, 0.2, 0.4$.

Table A1
data sources and construction details.

Description	Source	Construction notes
NTB indicator	TRAINS	= 1 if the HS-6 product had an NTB in 1997
NTB coverage ratio	TRAINS	Fraction of sub-lines in each HS-6 product with an NTB in 1997
NTB ad-valorem equivalent (AVE)	Kee et al. (2009)	Based on the trade value impact of an NTB indicator, converted into a price equivalent using a product specific import demand elasticity. We use their estimated AVE if NTB = 1 in the TRAINS 1997 data and set it to 0 otherwise
WTO BIND (B)	WTO database[a]	= 1 if HS-6 tariff is bound by a WTO commitment, 0 otherwise
WTO 1997 implementation	WTO database[a]	= 1 if WTO commitment for this HS-6 product was scheduled for implementation by 1997, 0 otherwise
WTO TARIFF (t^c)	WTO database[a]	Binding tariff level
WTO BIND TARIFF	Authors	$= t^c$ if B = 1 and 0 otherwise
WTO BIND TARIFF ADJ.	Authors	$= (t^c - t^u)$ if B = 1 and 0 otherwise where t^u is calculated as 1993 average applied TRAINS tariff over the unbound products in the HS-2 industry to which the HS-6 line belongs to.
EU BIND	TRAINS	= 1 if HS-6 tariff is bound by a EU commitment, 0 otherwise
EU BIND TARIFF	Authors	= EU tariff if EU BIND = 1, 0 otherwise
EU BIND TARIFF ADJ.	Authors	$=$ (EU tariff $- t^u$) if EU BIND = 1 and 0 otherwise where t^u is calculated as above
Import demand elasticity	Kee et al. (2009)	We divide their measure by $1 + t + \tau$ (the tariff and AVE in that HS-6) to obtain ε, as required by the model. We instrument this variable using their (unadjusted) import demand elasticity in each good averaged over 5 other countries[b]
Bargaining power of government relative to industry; (Medium bargaining, High bargaining, and Medium-high bargaining)	Various	Construction of bargaining power is described in text. Industry survival rates = 1-exit rate. The exit rates are averaged to ISIC-3 level from ISIC-4 level census data on firms by Kaya and Üçdoğruk (2002), to minimize measurement error. Medium/high bargaining = 1 if bargaining power is in the middle/upper tercile, 0 otherwise; medium-high bargaining = 1 if in either tercile, 0 otherwise
Organization	WGTA	An industry is classified as organized if it contains an organization listed for Turkey in the 4th edition of the World Guide to Trade Associations. Raw electronic data provided by Bonnie Wilson and Dennis Coates. We matched the description of organization entries to ISIC 3 industries
Number of exporters	TRAINS	Number of exporters per HS-6 to Turkey in 1997
Herfindahl of export value	TRAINS	Herfindahl index of exporter shares per HS-6 to Turkey in 1997
Herfindahl of number of establishments	Authors	Herfindahl of number of establishments in each subline of ISIC-3 industries (1990–1993 data from Kaya and Üçdoğruk, 2002)
Gross fixed capital formation	World Bank TPP[c]	Average over 1990–1993 of gross-fixed capital formation at the ISIC-3 level
Labor share of value added	World Bank TPP[c]	Ratio of the wage bill to value added (average over 1990–1993) at the ISIC-3 level
Inverse of number of establishments	World Bank TPP[c]	Average over 1990–1993 of the inverse of the number of establishments at the ISIC-3 level

[a] Accessed via WITS (World Integrated Trade Solution).
[b] India, Malaysia, Philippines, Thailand and Tunisia, which are also used to construct instruments for WTO BIND and WTO BIND TARIFF by taking the average across them in each HS6 product.
[c] World Bank Trade, Production and Protection database.

production subsidies was the ban, which was effectively adopted by the WTO. It is possible to show that in our model a government may prefer such a ban on subsidies and the use of tariffs if it has low bargaining power (see Drazen and Limão, 2008, for a proof in the context of different policies).

Calculation of total protection and welfare effects of commitment in Section 3.6

- Percent change in total protection. Defined as $(\tau(\phi) + t^c)/t^u$ where t^u and $\tau(\phi)$ are calculated as described above, we calculate $\tau(\phi)$ for $\phi = 0,.1,.2,.3,.4$; t^u is independent of ϕ. We use $t^c = 0.85t^u$ to satisfy the government sufficient condition to commit shown above.
- Percent change in welfare. Defined as $(W_i^c - W_i^u)/W_i^u$ where W_i^x measures welfare under commitment (x = c) or in its absence (x = u) as $W_i(p_i) \equiv \pi_i(p_i) + N[r_i(p_i, \phi) + S_i(p_i)]$. for a good i that is imported. We can map this standard measure of trade gains to the aggregate social welfare defined in Section 3.1 since the latter can be written as $W(p) = N + \sum W_i(p_i)$, $i \in imp \cup exp$ We calculate this for $t = t^u$ and $\tau = 0$ for the unconstrained case and $\tau(\phi) + t^c$ for the constrained. We employ the percentage change in this measure of welfare for a good i that is imported since the aggregate wage bill and

Table A2
Summary statistics.

Variable	Obs.	Mean	Std. Dev.	Min	Max
NTB indicator	5112	0.086	0.281	0	1
NTB coverage ratio	5112	0.059	0.213	0	1
NTB Ad-valorem equivalent (AVE)	5080	0.029	0.175	0	2.286
WTO BIND	5112	0.473	0.499	0	1
WTO 1997 implementation	5112	0.433	0.496	0	1
WTO TARIFF (t^c)	2420	0.294	0.368	0	2.250
WTO BIND TARIFF	5112	0.139	0.293	0	2.250
WTO BIND TARIFF ADJ.	5112	0.095	0.272	−0.146	2.200
EU BIND	5112	0.853	0.354	0	1
EU BIND TARIFF	4930	0.046	0.038	0	0.250
EU BIND TARIFF ADJ.	4930	−0.038	0.042	−0.250	0.118
WTO BIND × 1/import elasticity	4632	0.718	1.684	0	47.340
Mean binding status for 5 other WTO members	5112	0.712	0.267	0	1
Mean binding tariff for 5 other WTO members	5035	0.325	0.186	0	1.650
Mean inverse elasticity for 5 other WTO members	4665	1.063	0.980	0.082	36.999
Medium-high bargaining	4598	0.700	0.458	0	1
Medium bargaining	4598	0.335	0.472	0	1
High bargaining	4598	0.364	0.481	0	1
Organization	5089	0.731	0.443	0	1
Number of exporters	5042	7.713	6.648	0	66
Herfindahl of export value	5042	0.437	0.294	0	1
Herfindahl of number of establishments	4513	0.496	0.283	0.173	1
Gross fixed capital formation	4598	238,180	201,374	4870	671,517
Labor share of value added	4598	0.268	0.055	0.020	0.430
Inverse of number of establishments	4598	0.007	0.015	0.001	0.200

Table A3
Impact of tariff commitments on NTB AVE: across vs. within industry variation.

	(1)	(2)	(3)	(4)	(5)	(6)	(7)	(8)	(9)	(10)
Dependent variable	*NTB*	*NTB*	*NTB*	*NTB*	*NTB*	*NTB*	*NTB*	*NTB*	*NTB*	*NTB*
	AVE[a]	*AVE*[a]	*AVE*	*AVE*[a]	*AVE*[a]	*0/1*[b]	*0/1*[b]	*0/1*[b]	*0/1*[b]	*0/1*[b]
WTO BIND	1.08***	1.10***	0.74***	0.510***	0.348***	0.127***	0.136***	0.111***	0.169***	0.129***
(β>0)	[0.258]	[0.263]	[.249]	[0.123]	[0.120]	[0.021]	[0.024]	[0.034]	[0.032]	[0.032]
WTO BIND TAR. ADJ.	−1.50***	−1.45***	−0.20	−0.829**	−0.06	−0.074***	−0.097***	−0.133	−0.342***	−0.09
(β_c<0)	[0.394]	[0.389]	[0.425]	[0.412]	[0.457]	[0.024]	[0.028]	[0.089]	[0.127]	[0.139]
EU BIND	0.186	0.002	−0.59**	−0.627***	−0.482	0.039***	0.014	−0.138**	−0.207***	−0.286**
(β>0)	[0.136]	[0.143]	[0.236]	[0.199]	[0.307]	[0.015]	[0.018]	[0.060]	[0.069]	[0.112]
EU BIND TARIFF ADJ.	−5.99***	−5.88***	−2.60***	−3.00***	−2.169	−1.27***	−1.32***	−0.754***	−1.117***	−0.925**
(β_c<0)	[0.748]	[0.741]	[0.836]	[0.711]	[1.432]	[0.101]	[0.110]	[0.188]	[0.215]	[0.400]
WTO BIND × 1/elasticity	−0.319*	−0.350*	−0.342**	−0.117*	−0.091	−0.020	−0.024	−0.032	−0.033**	−0.032**
(β_ε<0)	[0.178]	[0.181]	[0.163]	[0.069]	[0.064]	[0.014]	[0.016]	[0.021]	[0.017]	[0.016]
Observations	4478	4027	2573	1855	1855	4478	4027	2573	1855	1855
Sector effects	No	ISIC-1	ISIC-3	No	HS-2	No	ISIC-1	ISIC-3	No	HS-2

Notes: Standard errors in brackets. *significant at 10%; **significant at 5%; ***significant at 1%.
[a] Specifications in columns 1–5 employ a two-step IVTOBIT where WTO BIND × 1/elasticity is instrumented as described in Table 3.
[b] Specifications 6–10 employ two-stage least squares where WTO BIND × 1/elasticity is instrumented as described in Table 3. Constants included but not reported.

surplus in export goods in $W(p)$ are independent of commitment. The functional form for $\pi_i(p_i)$ was provided above. It is straightforward to derive per capita measures of surplus, $S_i(p) = (B - p)^2/2b$, and rents, $(\tau(1-\phi)+t)p^*(d_i(.)-\pi'_i(.)/N)$.

Robustness: impact of tariff commitments on NTB AVE: across vs. within industry

The theory suggests that the impact of bindings on NTBs should be strongest across rather than within industries since SIGs often organize at the industry level. This appendix explores the extent to which that is the case and whether there is any within industry variation in the variables we use. The results in Table A3 indicate that the baseline NTB results are strongly, but not exclusively, driven by variation across industries within a broad sector. To see this note that the results without sector effects (column 1 for NTB AVE and column 6 for NTB indicator) are similar in magnitude and significance to those with sector effects (columns 2 and 7 respectively) with one exception: the EU binding dummy.[39] The remaining three binding variables retain their predicted sign when we include ISIC-3 effects (columns 3 and 8) or HS-2 industry effects (columns 5 and 10), suggesting that in some cases the government bargains with sub-industries. However, their magnitude and significance tends to decrease, suggesting that the cross-industry variation is an important component of the baseline results. To better understand why this happens and the implications for our baseline results we must unbundle two effects of the within industry estimation. The fact that it:

1. drops any "extreme" industries, in this sample this amounts to those where no products have NTBs since there are none where all products have NTBs and
2. explores within industry variation in the remaining industries.

To isolate the impact of the first effect we re-ran the basic specification but using the subsample that excludes the "extreme" HS-2 industries, i.e. those with no NTBs. As we can see the subsample results without industry effects (columns 4 and 9) are not qualitatively different from those in the basic specification (columns 1 and 5 respectively) with the same exception as before, the EU dummy. Therefore, although more than half of our sample is composed of these extreme industries our results are robust to excluding them. This further reduces our concern with any industry level omitted variables that could generate these extreme protection cases.

To isolate the effect in point Eq. (2) above, we compare the results just described with those on the same sample that include industry effects. We find that the EU tariff level and both WTO binding variables have the expected sign but their magnitudes are smaller and, in the AVE case, only the WTO binding indicator is significant. Thus it is the second effect (the focus on within industry variation of remaining industries) rather than the elimination of extreme industries that is responsible for the change in results. This occurs because there is not much variation left in our explanatory variables within industries. If we take the baseline IV sample and regress the EU dummy or the WTO tariff on HS-2 dummies we can account for at least 84% of the variation in these variables and at least 74% for EU tariff. The WTO binding dummy has significant variation that is cross-industry (60%) but still enough remains to identify some effect within. The fact that more of the variation is across industries and that the results are stronger in that case is fully consistent with the model where organization for lobbying occurs along industry lines.

[39] This variable becomes insignificant since it captures temporary exceptions and most of its variation is across sectors. In the sample with sector effects most products have a EU binding so there is not much variation left to explore.

References

Bagwell, Kyle, Staiger, Robert W., 1999. An Economic Theory of GATT. American Economic Review 89 (1), 215–248.
Bhagwati, Jagdish, Ramaswami, V.K., 1963. Domestic distortions, tariffs and the theory of optimum subsidy. Journal of Political Economy 71, 44–50.
Binmore, Ken, Rubinstein, Ariel, Wolinsky, Asher, 1986. The Nash bargaining solution in economic modeling. The RAND Journal of Economics 17 (2), 176–188.
Broda, Christian, Limão, Nuno, Weinstein, David E., 2008. Optimal tariffs and market power: the evidence. American Economic Review 98 (5), 2032–2065.
Coate, Stephen, Morris, Stephen, 1995. On the form of transfers to special interests. Journal of Political Economy 103 (6), 1210–1235.
Copeland, Brian R., 1990. Strategic interaction among nations: negotiable and non-negotiable trade barriers. Canadian Journal of Economics 23 (1), 84–108.
Dixit, Avinash, Londregan, John, 1996. The determinants of success of special interests in redistributive politics. Journal of Politics 58, 1132–1155.
Doiron, Denise, 1992. Bargaining power and wage-employment contracts in a unionized industry. International Economic Review 33 (3), 583–606.
Drazen, Allan, Limão, Nuno, 2008. A bargaining theory of inefficient redistribution. International Economic Review 49 (2), 621–657.
Ederington, Josh, Minier, Jenny A., 2006. Why tariffs, not subsidies? a search for stylized facts. Contributions to Economic Analysis & Policy 5 (1) Article 31.
Goldberg, Pinelopi K., Maggi, Giovanni, 1999. Protection for sale: an empirical investigation. American Economic Review 89 (5), 1135–1155.
Grossman, Gene, Helpman, Elhanan, 1994. Protection for sale. American Economic Review 84, 833–850.
Grossman, Gene, Helpman, Elhanan, 2001. Special Interest Politics. MIT Press, Cambridge, MA.
Hillman, Arye L., 1989. The Political Economy of Protection. Hardwood Academic, New York.
Horn, Henrik, Maggi, Giovanni, Staiger, Robert W., 2010. Trade agreements as endogenously incomplete contracts. American Economic Review 100 (1), 394–419.
Kaempfer, William H., McClure, Harold J., Willet, Thomas D., 1989. Incremental protection and efficient political choice between tariffs and quotas. Canadian Journal of Economics 22 (2), 228–236.

Kaya, Seçil, Üçdoğruk, Yeşim, 2002. The dynamics of entry and exit in the Turkish manufacturing industry. ERC Working Papers in Economics.
Kee, Hiao, Nicita, Alessandro, Olarreaga, Marcelo, 2009. Estimating trade restrictiveness. Economic Journal 119 (534), 172–199.
Kydland, Finn E., Prescott, Edward C., 1977. Rules rather than discretion: the inconsistency of optimal plans. Journal of Political Economy 85 (3), 473–491.
Lee, Jong-Wha, Swagel, Phillip, 1997. Trade barriers and trade flows across countries and industries. Review of Economics and Statistics 79 (3), 372–382.
Ludema, Rodney D., Mayda, Anna Maria, 2009. Do countries free ride on MFN? Journal of International Economics 77 (2), 137–150.
Maggi, Giovanni, Rodriguez-Clare, Andres, 1998. The value of trade agreements in the presence of political pressures. Journal of Political Economy 106 (3), 574–601.
Maggi, Giovanni, Rodriguez-Clare, Andres, 2007. A political economy theory of trade agreements. American Economic Review 97 (4), 1374–1406.
Marvel, Howard, Ray, Edward, 1983. The Kennedy Round: evidence on the regulation of international trade in the United States. American Economic Review 73 (1), 190–197.
Mitra, Devashish, 2002. Endogenous political organization and the value of trade agreements. Journal of International Economics 57, 473–485.
Mitra, Devashish, Thomakos, Dimitrios, Mehmet, Ulubasoglu, 2002. Protection for sale' in a developing country: democracy vs. dictatorship. Review of Economics and Statistics 84 (3), 497–508.
Ray, Edward J., 1981. The determinants of tariff and nontariff trade restrictions in the United States. Journal of Political Economy 89 (1), 105–121.
Rodrik, Dani, 1986. Taxes, subsidies, and welfare with endogenous policy. Journal of International Economics 21, 285–299.
Rodrik, Dani, 1995. Political economy of trade policy. In: Grossman, Gene M., Rogoff, Kenneth (Eds.), Handbook of International Economics, vol. 3. North-Holland, Amsterdam, pp. 1457–1494.
Schelling, Thomas C., 1960. The Strategy of Conflict. Harvard University Press, Cambridge, MA.
Staiger, Robert W., Tabellini, Guido, 1987. Discretionary trade policy and excessive protection. American Economic Review 77 (5), 823–837.
Staiger, Robert W., Tabellini, Guido, 1999. Do GATT rules help governments make domestic commitments? Economics and Politics 11 (2), 109–144.
Togan, Sübidey, 1995. Trade policy review of the Republic of Turkey. World Economy 18 (5), 107–120.
Tullock, G., 1983. Economics of Income Redistribution. Kluwer-Nijhoff, Boston MA.
Veugelers, Reinhilde, 1989. Wage premia, price-cost margins and bargaining power in Belgian manufacturing. European Economic Review 33, 169–180.
Weingast, Barry, Shepsle, Kenneth, Johnsen, Christopher, 1981. The political economy of benefits and costs: a neoclassical approach to distributive politics. Journal of Political Economy 89, 642–664.
Wilson, John, 1990. Are efficiency improvements in government transfer policies self-defeating in political equilibrium? Economics and Politics 2 (3), 241–258.
Young, Leslie, Anderson, James E., 1982. Risk aversion and optimal trade restrictions. Review of Economic Studies 49 (2), 291–305.

Chapter 7

A BARGAINING THEORY OF INEFFICIENT REDISTRIBUTION POLICIES*

BY ALLAN DRAZEN AND NUNO LIMÃO[1]

University of Maryland, NBER, and CEPR, U.S.A.

When two policies are available to achieve the same goal why is the relatively inefficient one often observed? We address this question in the context of policies used to redistribute income towards special interest groups (SIGs) where in the first stage the constraints on policy instruments are chosen and in the second the government bargains with SIGs over the level of the available policies. Restrictions on the use of efficient policies and the use of inefficient ones reduce the surplus over which SIGs and governments can bargain but it also improves the government's bargaining position thus increasing its share of the surplus. The positive effect for the government dominates under plausible conditions. Inefficient policies are the equilibrium outcome under alternative policy selection mechanisms, e.g., election of policymakers and bargaining between SIGs and the government. The model also explains the coexistence of transfer policies. Moreover, we show why a weak government is more likely to choose the inefficient transfer and discuss how this result may be tested.

1. INTRODUCTION

Policy analysis often focuses on a single policy instrument and provides positive and normative predictions about its level in the context of a specific model. However, the question of whether that instrument would actually be the one used by the government to achieve its aim is generally ignored. This is an important question because frequently there are more efficient policies available for the same purpose.[2] Models that fail to explain why apparently more efficient polices are not used are incomplete and likely to generate incorrect predictions.

*Manuscript received June 2006; revised April 2007.

[1]We thank Stephanie Aaronson, Daron Acemoglu, David Austen-Smith, Elhanan Helpman, Helen Milner, Peter Murrell, Robert Schwab, and seminar participants at Harvard's Political Institutions and Economic Policy Conference (December 2003), Syracuse University, and University of Maryland for useful comments. The usual disclaimer applies. Piyush Chandra provided excellent research assistance. AD wishes to thank the Jack and Lisa Yael Chair in Comparative Economics, Tel Aviv University for financial support. NL gratefully acknowledges the financial support of the International Monetary Fund Research Group, which hosted him during part of this research. The views expressed in this paper are those of the authors. Please address correspondence to: Nuno Limão, Economics Department, University of Maryland, College Park, MD 20742, USA. Phone: 301-405-7842. E-mail: *Limao@wam.umd.edu.*

[2] For example, in reviewing the literature on the political economy of trade policy Rodrik (1995) states: "Of course trade policy is not the only, or even the most important, mechanism of redistribution used by governments. But practically all governments apparently use it for that purpose. A sufficiently general and convincing explanation for this phenomenon has yet to be formulated" (p. 1476).

Originally Published in *International Economic Review* 49(2), pp. 621–657.

In this article we address the policy-choice question in the context of an important specific case—the use of inefficient policies to redistribute income. In particular, we ask why do governments redistribute income towards different special interest groups (SIGs), via targeted projects, production subsidies, or tariffs when, in the absence of specific externalities, lump-sum payments would be more efficient? Despite how important and puzzling this question is, only a few papers, which we discuss below, attempt to address it. The puzzle is not that the transfers take place—after all governments are not pure social welfare maximizers—but that they are done in a way that reduces the surplus that governments and SIGs can bargain over.

Two key elements must be explicit if a model is to predict which policies are used: how the set of policies is chosen and the preferences of *all* agents who influence that choice. For example, in our model if identical citizens could directly determine the rules or institutions governing transfers the outcome would be simple: no transfers would be allowed. However, direct democracy is an uncommon method of choosing rules or institutions. In fact, as North (1994, p. 360) puts it, "Institutions are not necessarily or even usually created to be socially efficient; rather they, or at least the formal rules, are created to serve the interests of those with the bargaining power to create new rules."[3] This implies that self-interested politicians or governments play a key role in determining the available policies and so we focus on a theory that highlights their incentive to restrict efficient policies and use inefficient ones.

We model policymaking as a two-stage process. In the first stage the set of constraints on policy instruments is chosen. This corresponds to a "constitutional" stage in which the rules of policymaking are decided.[4] We describe each of the three first-stage choice mechanisms we consider below. In the second stage the incumbent government bargains with the SIGs over the level of the available transfer policies that it provides; in exchange it demands "lobby goods" because transfers are costly to the government.

We provide the conditions under which a government benefits from restrictions on efficient transfers and from using inefficient ones in addition to, or instead of, the efficient ones. Constraining the use of efficient transfer policies reduces the overall surplus that the SIGs and government can bargain over, which *by itself* leaves both worse off. This is a well-known effect and the source of the aforementioned puzzle. However, what has not been previously explored in explaining the use of inefficient transfer policies is that the switch can also increase the government's share of the surplus, that is, it can improve its bargaining position. This is the key effect behind the use of inefficient policies in our model.

[3] Beard (1913) is a classic reference on how the writing of the U.S. Constitution reflected the economic interests of the framers rather than an abstract notion of social welfare.

[4] Positive constitutional analysis often uses a two-stage analysis, where the first stage seeks to explain why one constitution rather than another is adopted, often through competition among groups who recognize how a constitution will later affect their interests. See, for example, Buchanan and Tullock (1962) or Beard (1913). In our article the "constitutional" stage can also be interpreted as, for example, a stage where a country can enter into an international treaty or one in which voters choose between policymakers who will themselves choose the rules and constraints.

By carefully modelling the interaction between the government and SIGs we can identify the causes for the improvement in the bargaining position. There are two necessary conditions for this improvement. First, the government must have some (but not all) bargaining power during the second stage negotiations with SIGs. Second, utility between them must not be transferable; otherwise any reduction in the total surplus would necessarily leave *both* worse off in equilibrium since they could exchange utility at a constant rate. As we will argue, these two conditions are likely in practice, even though they are often ignored in theory for tractability reasons, as we point out in the literature section. When they are satisfied, the type of transfer policy determines not only the available surplus but the rate at which it can be transferred across the parties. More specifically, a given increase in the SIG's payoff is costlier to the government when it cannot be achieved through the more efficient transfer policy. This generates an improvement in the government's bargaining position since it allows it to credibly offer a smaller transfer for any given level of the lobby good; that is, ex ante restrictions on the use of the efficient transfer improve the government's political terms-of-trade.

The interesting question then becomes whether the improvement in bargaining position we identify ever dominates the loss of surplus effect thus increasing the government's payoff. We show this occurs when the government can choose any binding cap on the efficient transfer policy in the first stage. In the second stage, when such restrictions are in place, some relatively less efficient transfer policy is used instead of, or in addition to, the more efficient one. Hence, our model can explain why governments may use inefficient policies and also why different policies aimed at achieving the same goal may be used simultaneously.

The model also provides an interesting prediction about the government's optimal redistribution policy when it is restricted to use only one policy. In this case we show that the improvement in bargaining position dominates when the government is relatively weak since when the SIG has most of the bargaining power it also bears most of the loss in surplus from switching to the inefficient policy. In Section 5, we discuss how to measure these policies and bargaining power to test this prediction.

We then consider alternative first-stage institutions and ask which ones yield restrictions on efficient transfers and the use of inefficient ones. A natural benchmark is to allow the government to choose the set of available policies. In this case, it chooses to restrict the use of efficient policies under the conditions described above. We are also interested in deriving predictions when the other affected parties play an active role in the first stage. When governments and SIGs bargain in the first stage we show that the outcome is still a binding cap on efficient policies and the use of inefficient ones if the government's bargaining power is higher in the first stage than in the second. We argue that this condition is plausible but not universally satisfied and discuss when it is likely to hold. We also explain why inefficient forms of transfer can arise even if the government and lobby interact repeatedly.

Finally, we analyze the outcome under a general election for policymakers that, once elected, can choose restrictions on transfers and then bargain with SIGs in the second stage. We show that transfers occur in equilibrium and, more interestingly, that voters may elect the candidate with lower bargaining power, who prefers to use the inefficient transfer. This occurs even though voters are rational, fully informed, and vote solely on the basis of the effect of the redistribution policy. The sharp contrast of this outcome under representative democracy with the outcome obtained under a direct democracy (where transfers would generally be prohibited) further highlights the importance of considering the self-interested policymaker and the first stage mechanism.

In this article the only role of economic policy is to redistribute income towards SIGs. However, the basic insight that the government faces a trade-off between the improvement in bargaining position and the reduction in bargaining surplus applies to any pair of policies that can be ranked according to their transfer efficiency. This includes models where one of the policies can address an economic externality (as we discuss in our working paper). Thus it would be interesting to apply our insight to other models and analyze how normative and positive predictions change when the policy set itself is endogenous.

The article is organized as follows. In the remainder of this section, we discuss the literature. In Section 2, we set up the model. In Section 3, we show under what conditions the government gains from restricting the efficient transfer and using the inefficient one. In Section 4, we model alternative first-stage choice mechanisms and derive their equilibrium policy. In Section 5, we discuss some examples of policy use that are broadly consistent with the model and also how to econometrically test its specific predictions. In the final section we summarize our results. All proofs are in the Appendix.

1.1. *Literature.* Three main arguments stand out in explaining the use of inefficient rather than efficient policies to redistribute income toward SIGs. One is the "disguised transfer" argument put forward by Tullock (1983). When a project is not ostensibly aimed at redistribution, those who bear the costs may be ignorant of the redistribution and thus less likely to oppose it if the policy also has some social benefit. Coate and Morris (1995) elegantly formalize this idea and clarify when exactly it works. A "bad" politician values the utility of the SIG directly but wants to be re-elected and chooses the inefficient transfer—a project that benefits the SIG—instead of a lump-sum transfer if voters believe the project could be motivated by social welfare concerns. The argument requires that voters have asymmetric information both about the value of the project *and* the aims of politicians. In the absence of such asymmetric information, transfers to SIGs could not be disguised as being social-welfare enhancing and politicians would not use them.

The key difference in our approach is that asymmetric information plays *no* role in the argument. We focus on a setting where the policies have no social benefit and show that inefficient transfers can arise even if voters are fully informed about this and about the government's objective. In fact, in our electoral framework, full information by voters about politicians may be seen as integral to inefficient policies being used in equilibrium. Our model also delivers additional interesting predictions about the coexistence of policies and the effect of choice mechanisms other than elections on the adoption of inefficient policies.

Another motive why our argument is an important complement to the disguised transfer one is that ours applies to a broader set of transfers, including ones that can be easily reversed and are known to have little or no social welfare benefit beyond redistribution, e.g., tariffs, subsidies and certain regulations. As Coate and Morris themselves note, the requirements that the transfer be socially beneficial in some states of nature and that voters have imperfect information about its effect (ex ante and ex post) imply that their model is best suited to explain public projects rather than tariffs, subsidies, etc. This is an important distinguishing point, particularly if one were to try testing the predictions of our models.[5]

A second argument is that specific types of transfers, even if fully observed, give political benefits that lump-sum transfers do not. For example, Shepsle and Weingast (1981) and Weingast et al. (1981) argue that geographically concentrated projects may give political in addition to economic benefits. The legislative process may then lead to an oversupply of such projects.[6] Dixit and Londregan (1996) consider a model where two parties compete for votes by giving transfers to different population groups. Parties have differential effectiveness in influencing voters by different types of transfers or expenditures, perhaps because each party has a better sense of what its "core" supporters want. It may also be the case, as in Dixit and Londregan (1995), that parties can make post-electoral commitments to inefficient transfers (such as continuation of investment projects) more credible than lump-sum transfers. In all of these models, differences in the electoral value of different groups and how this is related to the value they put on types of transfers is crucial to the use of non-lump-sum transfers. In contrast, in our approach the "political" characteristics of the group receiving the transfers plays no role; the mechanism we present would be operative even with a single SIG.

A third argument is that inefficient policies act like "sand in the wheels" of the redistributive process by making it costlier to redistribute. This mechanism causes a reduction in the equilibrium amount of redistribution, which can explain why inefficient policies may be preferred from a social welfare perspective (Rodrik, 1986; Wilson, 1990; Becker and Mulligan, 2003). Our argument may at first seem similar to this one but it is crucially different in a number of respects. First of all, these papers provide a normative rather than a positive theory of inefficient transfers since they leave the government in the background and do not model the first stage of policymaking, in which the constraints on policymaking (the "sand") are themselves chosen.[7] In contrast, in our approach the government is an active

[5] More specifically, Coate and Morris (1995) state that "A certain amount of care is warranted in applying the model to the analysis of subsidies and regulations. Imposing such a policy, unlike undertaking a public project, is not a one off decision. A decision to impose or withdraw the same policy can be taken each period [i.e., they have low reversal costs]. As a consequence citizens can learn about its effects over time" (p. 1228, footnote 19). They then note that "The class of policies to which our argument applies does not include two of the most commonly cited examples of inefficient transfers, namely the farm program and tariffs" (p. 1228, footnote 20).

[6] The implications of the institutional details of the legislative process by which transfers are chosen is also considered by Fiorina (1981) and Baron (1991).

[7] For example, in Becker and Mulligan (2003, pp. 305–6), "Government redistribution in this approach might be modeled as a two-staged 'game,' where in the first stage tax and spending systems are

player and self-interested agents choose or bargain over rules. Modelling the first-stage of policymaking allows us to provide a positive theory of inefficient transfers by showing when such policies are actually adopted. Moreover, in our model governments prefer the inefficient policies because they improve its bargaining position relative to SIGs, even though they reduce the surplus to be divided. The decrease in bargaining surplus from using the inefficient policy is costly for the government, so such policies are preferred by the government in spite of acting like "sand in the wheels" *not* because of it.

Grossman and Helpman (1994) and Dixit et al. (1997) focus on bargaining between government and SIGs. Although their main focus is not on the choice of redistribution policy they do show that competition among SIGs for government transfers will imply that more distortionary instruments improve the outcome for SIGs. However, like the papers discussed in the previous paragraph, these papers do not model the crucial first-stage process. There are other key differences as well. Competition among lobbies is not the driving force in our model, so in our setting the SIGs generally prefer efficient policies whereas the government may prefer the opposite. Another key distinction is that two basic modelling assumptions in those papers—the SIGs have all the bargaining power and utility is transferable—actually imply that inefficient policies would not be adopted in our setting.

2. THE MODEL

We illustrate our arguments in a model with no economic externalities such that the only role of economic policy is to redistribute income towards SIGs. We do so both because many policies have redistributive motives and because our argument is especially clear when applied to redistribution via lump-sum transfers versus less efficient redistribution policies, for example, production subsidies. We choose a basic economic framework similar to Grossman and Helpman (1994) in order to clearly contrast the results. However, the central insights also hold in more general environments, as will be clear below.

Each individual's utility function is

$$u \equiv x_n + \sum_i u_i(x_i), \tag{1}$$

where the subutility for good x_i is u_i, which is twice differentiable and concave. The consumer price of each good, p_i, is exogenously given, as in a small open economy without import restrictions that takes world prices as given. The term x_n represents the consumption of the numeraire. The numeraire is produced using only labor with a marginal product normalized to unity, which implies the wage is equal to one.[8] For given prices an individual who owns the specific factor used to produce i has income E_i and chooses consumption to maximize utility subject

chosen, while in the second stage, groups try to maximize their political surplus, taking these systems as given. A more complete analysis of the first-stage problem is beyond the scope of this paper..."

[8] This requires a sufficiently large labor force such that n is produced in this country and a fixed world price at unity.

to a budget constraint, $x_n + \sum_i p_i x_i \leq E_i$. It is then straightforward to show that this constraint is satisfied with equality and indirect utility is the sum of income and consumer surplus—denoted by $s(\mathbf{p})$.[9]

The production of each good i exhibits constant returns in the two factors it uses: labor and a specific factor. Since the wage is unity the return to the specific factor depends only on the supplier price of the good, p_i^s. The specific factor owner receives the quasi-rent $\pi_i(p_i^s)$, i.e., revenue inclusive of any production subsidy minus labor costs, and thus equilibrium output is $\pi_i'(p_i^s)$. In the absence of any government intervention we have $p_i^s = p_i$.

To redistribute income to lobbies of specific factor owners in sector i the government may use a lump-sum transfer, T_i, or other types of transfer, which we summarize by a unit production subsidy, t_i. Transfers to lobbies are financed by lump-sum taxes charged on the voting population of N individuals. We allow for a unit collection cost of $\beta \in (0, 1)$ and assume that the government balances its budget, so that a total transfer of τ requires the government to collect $\tau/(1 - \beta)$. Total transfers are given by $\tau = \sum_i T_i + \sum_i t_i \pi_i'$.

Production subsidies in this economy are a less efficient transfer policy because they distort the use of productive factors. The producer supplies as if he faced a price $p + t$ and thus draws more labor into its sector than what is optimal at the prevailing world prices (recall there are diminishing returns to labor in the nonnumeraire sectors because the specific capital in each of those sectors is fixed). Thus the subsidy increases the return to the specific factor owners at a higher cost than a given lump-sum transfer.[10]

An exogenously given set of sectors L is organized into SIG and their gross welfare is[11]

$$W_i = l_i + \pi(p_i + t_i) + T_i + \alpha_i N[s(\mathbf{p}) - \tau/(1-\beta)N] \quad \text{if } i \in L, \tag{2}$$

where α_i is the share of the voting population that owns factor i and l_i is their labor income. Each lobby can also use the numeraire to linearly produce some amount, C_i, of a good that it offers to the politician in exchange for an increase in a transfer in the form of T_i or t_i. We assume that factor ownership in any one sector is sufficiently concentrated, i.e., α_i is sufficiently small, such that each SIG takes the size of the budget as given when bargaining over its own transfer. Thus the lobby maximizes its gross welfare net of its expenditure on lobby goods, which is given by

$$V_i \equiv W_i - C_i. \tag{3}$$

[9] An individual's demand for x_i is $d_i(p_i) = u_i'(p_i)^{-1}$ and consumer surplus is $s(\mathbf{p}) = \sum_i u_i(d_i(p_i)) - p_i d_i(p_i)$.

[10] Note that in this economy the production subsidy does not generate a demand distortion for two reasons. First, it does not affect consumer prices since it is a small open economy that takes world prices as given. Second, the nonnumeraire goods depend only on their prices and so income effects are ruled out. However, production subsidies do increase domestic supply and lower aggregate income; but this will only result in lower consumption of the numeraire. This increase in domestic supply leads to a reduction in net imports since domestic demand remains unchanged.

[11] Extending the model to allow for endogenous formation of lobbies could be done by applying the insights from Mitra (1999).

Social welfare gross of lobby goods expenditure is the sum of indirect utility over all individuals. It is equal to total income net of taxes, which is spent on the numeraire and given by the terms in parenthesis, and surplus from consuming the nonnumeraire goods.[12]

$$W \equiv \left[l + \sum_i \pi(p_i + t_i) + \sum_i T_i - \tau/(1-\beta) \right] + Ns(\mathbf{p}). \tag{4}$$

The policymaker's preferences are represented by a weighted sum of social welfare and the lobby goods he receives in exchange for transfers:

$$G \equiv aW + \sum_{i \in L} \Psi_i(C_i). \tag{5}$$

We assume a is positive but finite because our interest is on a policymaker with preferences that are not identified with social welfare but reflect at least some social cost transfers to the SIGs. However, the results showing the policymaker's preference for restricting the efficient policies can be derived even if the cost to the policymaker arises from a source other than social welfare (e.g., if he incurs a direct cost to supply the policies to the SIGs such as paying a fraction of the taxes required to fund them).

If the SIGs could compensate the politician with the numeraire good, e.g., if any SIG could make unlimited cash contributions, and the politician valued these equally and additively then utility would be transferable (as in Grossman and Helpman, 1994). As will be clear below, in that case any reduction in the bargaining surplus would always lower the utility of the politician and thus he would never choose to switch to inefficient policies. However, we think that it is not realistic to assume that politicians can (a) perfectly substitute a lobby's good for another and (b) obtain a constant marginal utility from any level of any lobby good (even if they are cash contributions). Therefore we assume that the lobby good is valued according to $\Psi_i(.)$, which can vary across lobby goods and is concave. Examples of lobby goods that are not perfectly substitutable and are likely to exhibit diminishing utility for the politician include getting out the vote in a district where a lobby's membership is concentrated; providing information about an issue; lending jets for campaigning or vacationing; etc. So we think the assumption is reasonable. Alternatively, we could model nontransferability by allowing C_i to enter linearly

[12] We follow the literature in considering social welfare gross of lobby goods expenditure (e.g., Grossman and Helpman, 1994, assume the same for cash contributions). One way to justify the exclusion of C from the definition is that the income term in brackets is the expenditure on the numeraire good whereas C is simply the amount of that numeraire that lobbies spend on producing lobby goods. Nonetheless, we could consider an alternative measure, $\tilde{W}$, net of C, and change the government's objective accordingly. We don't believe this would change the insight that the government gains from restricting the efficient transfer since it places a finite weight on social welfare and this change would not change the key properties of the government objective.

in G but requiring the lobby to produce it using the numeraire as the input into a diminishing returns process.[13]

Finally, by modelling lobby goods as additively separable in G and assuming concentrated ownership (i.e., $\alpha_i \to 0$ for each i) we ensure no economic interaction among lobbies and thus are able to focus on their bilateral interaction with the government. Lobby competition is an interesting issue, but we want to look for important effects elsewhere. Concavity in each of the lobby goods is consistent with it being a "good" that can be supplied primarily by that lobby. Moreover, in several instances SIGs lobby for policies only in their own sector so the absence of lobby competition may be a plausible representation.

The timing is as follows. In the first stage the restrictions on the use of policies are determined; we consider alternative mechanisms in Sections 3 and 4. In the second stage each lobby bargains with the government over a level of the lobby good and government transfers to it taking other lobbies actions as given. We model the outcome in the second stage as the solution to a Nash bargaining problem, which can be interpreted as a bilateral game of alternating offers with an exogenous, constant risk of breakdown of negotiations in each round or if players discount the future (Binmore et al., 1986). We do not specify the institutional structure, which might imply a game of alternating offers, but argue that the "give-and-take" that such a game is meant to represent is a key feature of the interaction of politicians and lobbyists.[14]

3. GOVERNMENT GAINS FROM CAPS AND THE USE OF INEFFICIENT POLICIES

In this section, we allow the government to unilaterally choose first-stage restrictions on the use of redistribution policies. This gives the government a determinant role, which is precisely what we want to highlight. We begin with a benchmark case where only lump-sum transfers are available and show that the government gains from setting a cap on them below the unconstrained solution. Once the mechanism is clear we introduce a production subsidy as the alternative, relatively inefficient, transfer and show when it will be used. We conclude by providing a general condition that allows one to determine the government's preferred redistribution policy from *any* two policies that can be ranked in terms of their relative efficiency. As we point out in the previous section our assumptions allow us to focus on the interaction of the government and each SIG separately so in this section we drop the lobby subscript i.

[13] If the government makes lump-sum transfers, T, then allowing C to also enter linearly in both G and V generates an unrealistic outcome. The marginal rate of substitution of the policies in both G and V are then constant so either (a) the government never wants to bargain since the marginal benefit of the lobby good it gets never exceeds the marginal cost of the transfer it makes or (b) the government always wants to transfer. Outcome (a) is both unrealistic and uninteresting since there are no transfers in equilibrium. Outcome (b) is also unrealistic since it implies that the government would want to tax all of the economy's income to transfer it to the SIGs.

[14] In our working paper, we show that proposition 1 also holds under the Kalai–Smorodinsky bargaining solution. It is possible that alternative more complex bargaining setups could lead to different results.

3.1. *Benchmark Case: The Government Caps Efficient Transfers.* We begin with the case in which only lump-sum transfers are available. As background, suppose first that the government sets no constraint on the use of transfers. The bargaining solution is easy to calculate. Substituting (4) into (5) and maximizing the expression subject to the SIG receiving a given level of utility yields the first-order condition

$$\frac{G_T}{G_C} = \frac{V_T}{V_C}, \tag{6}$$

where G_T, etc. are partial derivatives.[15] This is the contract curve, which uniquely determines the C_i as we can see by using the definitions of G and V to rewrite (6) as

$$\Psi_i'(C_i) = \frac{a\beta}{1-\beta}. \tag{7}$$

To determine the equilibrium level of the lump-sum transfer we must consider the division of the surplus that arises from the Nash bargaining solution, which may be represented by the solution to

$$\text{(8)}\quad \text{Max}_{G \geq g^0, V \geq v^0}\ U = (G - g^0)^{\gamma}(V - v^0)^{1-\gamma} \quad \text{s.t. } G = g^m - \frac{a\beta}{1-\beta}(V - v^0),$$

where v^0 represents the SIG's reservation utility, and g^0 the government's reservation utility, corresponding to no bargaining so that C and T both equal to zero. The constraint in (8) represents the Pareto frontier in utilities G and V. The government's maximum attainable utility in the bargain is g^m, which is achieved when the SIGs utility is at its reservation level, v^0. Any increase in the interest group's utility above v^0 requires a reduction in the government's utility in the form of a lower transfer.

Since the marginal utility of the lump-sum transfer is constant for both, the unconstrained Pareto frontier is linear and the Nash utility level, denoted by superscript N, can be written as a function of the reservation and maximum utilities, denoted by superscripts 0 and m, respectively,

$$g^N - g^0 = \gamma(g^m - g^0); \quad v^N - v^0 = (1-\gamma)(v^m - v^0). \tag{9}$$

The government receives a share of the bargaining surplus that is proportional to its bargaining power, γ. Similarly for the lobby. We can then solve for the level of the efficient transfer, T^N, which in this case is used to divide the surplus as shown in Figure 1.

[15] This interior solution exists if the marginal rate of substitution of lobby goods for transfers is lower for the government then the lobby at the origin, i.e., if lobbying is "politically efficient." This is satisfied if $\Psi'(0) > a\beta/(1-\beta)$, which we assume holds.

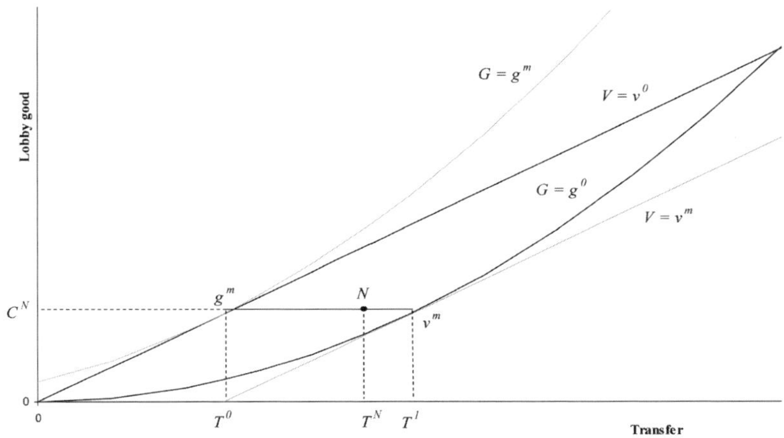

FIGURE 1

EFFICIENT TRANSFER

This equilibrium is illustrated in Figure 1. The vertical axis denotes lobby goods to the politician, the horizontal axis represents transfers, T, to the lobby. The line $V = v^0$ represents the lobby's reservation utility and is found by allowing the lobby to choose C to maximize V in (3) taking T as given. Similarly for the government's reservation, g^0. The outcome with no bargaining yields C and T equal to zero so both v^0 and g^0 go through the origin. The lobby is indifferent between providing C to the government and receiving an efficient transfer of the same amount so the slope of V is unity (as is clear from (2) and (3) when $\alpha \to 0$). Any movements towards the southeast leave the lobby better off. The government's indifference curve is upward sloping because the negative effect of a transfer paid to the lobby (due to the cost of raising tax revenues) must be compensated by an increase in C. The slope is increasing since $\Psi(C)$ is concave. Movements to the northwest improve the government's welfare. The segment $g^m v^m$ represents the contract curve in (7) and it is horizontal because G and V are linear in T.

We now allow the government to cap the efficient transfer in the first stage. No alternative transfer policies are yet available—an assumption which we relax in the next section. The government chooses a cap T^c in the first stage to maximize its objective in (5) taking into account its effect on the second stage equilibrium values C^{Nc} and $T^{Nc} \leq T^c$. Our objective is to show that there exists a cap that benefits the government, i.e., that the subgame perfect equilibrium level of the cap, T^c, chosen by the government is lower than the unconstrained transfer, T^N.

Solving backwards, suppose that the cap is given by T^c in Figure 2. The contract curve is now defined by the kinked segment $g^{mc} v^{mc}$. Note that if the cap is not lower than T^0 then the government's maximum utility, g^m, is still feasible as is v^0.

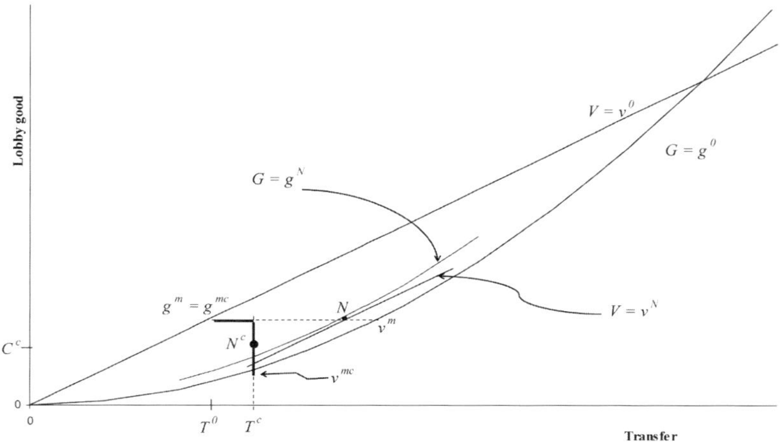

FIGURE 2

CAP ON EFFICIENT TRANSFER

But for the cap to be binding it must be strictly less than T^N and therefore the maximum utility for the lobby is v^{mc}, which is lower than v^m. If the equilibrium under the cap is at a point such as N^c in Figure 2, above $G = g^N$, then we can see the government is better off. Proposition 1 shows under what conditions such caps exist and would therefore be selected by the government in the first stage.

PROPOSITION 1 (Government cap on efficient transfers). *In the absence of alternative transfer policies the government chooses a cap on the efficient transfer that is strictly binding at* (C^N, T^N) *if neither the government nor the SIG have all the bargaining power.*

The basic intuition is best understood if we recall that the Nash bargaining solution can be interpreted as the limit of an alternating offers game. By setting a binding cap the government credibly commits to transferring less than T^N in exchange for C^N. This improves the government's bargaining position and explains the resulting increase in its utility. That is, by constraining its supply of transfers that are to be traded for the lobby good the government improves its political terms-of-trade.

This improvement in the government's bargaining position can be illustrated in Figure 3 where we graph G against V. The dashed straight line represents the Pareto frontier in the unconstrained case, with N as the respective solution. The constrained frontier coincides with the original one until the cap binds, after which point the lobby can only be made better off by offering less of C. Reductions in C come at an increasing cost for the government given the concavity of $\Psi(.)$,

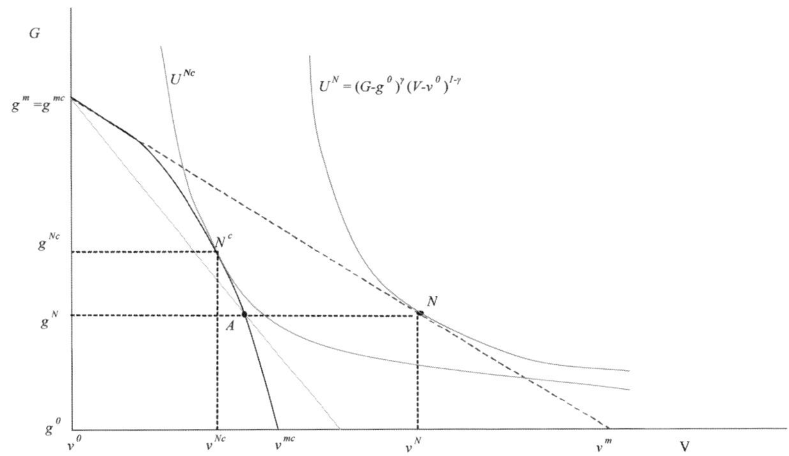

FIGURE 3

BARGAINING SOLUTION WITH CAP ON EFFICIENT TRANSFER

hence the concave Pareto frontier. We refer to an increase in the steepness of the Pareto frontier as an improvement in the government's bargaining position. Such an improvement is irrelevant if the government obtains all or none of the surplus, but when $\gamma \in (0, 1)$ the government can always find a binding cap that leaves it *strictly* better off; such a solution is illustrated by N^c. In a model with transferable utility the slope of the Pareto frontier is constant and so a cap would not change the government's bargaining position; it would only reduce the bargaining surplus and thus the government would not restrict T.

The cap also raises social welfare, W, because it reduces transfers and thus the taxes used to finance them (recall there is a unit cost of tax collection, $\beta > 0$). Note however that Proposition 1 would hold even if the cap had no effect on social welfare provided that the policymaker faced some cost of making transfers.[16] Thus our mechanism differs from those in other explanations that require social welfare to be higher under the inefficient policy (e.g., Rodrik, 1986).

Finally, Proposition 1 also makes clear the importance of allowing for a more general distribution of bargaining power between the government and SIGs. The strict gain for the government from setting a cap occurs only when $\gamma \in (0, 1)$. This is important because several leading political economy models focus on the extreme cases where the government has either no bargaining power (Grossman and Helpman, 1994; Dixit et al., 1997) or all of it (cf. the veto player model in Tsebelis, 2002).

[16] To see this consider the case when $\beta = 0$ so that social welfare is independent of lump-sum transfers. If we now postulate $G = \sum_i [\phi T_i + \Psi_i(C_i)]$ and $\phi < 0$ we still obtain Proposition 1 despite the fact that social welfare is unaffected by the cap.

3.2. *Inefficient and Efficient Transfers.* We now allow for transfers that are not lump-sum. We show that if the government can determine policy restrictions in the first stage, then it continues to set a cap on the efficient transfer and, more importantly, the equilibrium will feature redistribution that uses the relatively inefficient policy.

Inefficient transfers to producers can occur through various instruments of industrial policy such as loan guarantees, tax breaks, unit production or export subsidies, price supports, etc. In practice, it is not possible for the government to anticipate and prohibit *every* type of inefficient transfer. Moreover, even in the absence of lobbying for transfers, a welfare-maximizing government may want to use a production subsidy, for example, as a way to correct a production externality. Hence, a government may choose not to cap or outright prohibit the use of a production subsidy, even if it could commit to do so in the first stage.[17] Therefore, either because the government cannot or does not want to prohibit all possible policies with redistributive implications, it leaves itself open to credible offers of lobby goods in exchange for further, potentially less efficient, transfers.[18]

For concreteness, we consider the case of a production subsidy. We deliberately rule out any social benefit from the subsidy in the second stage so that if subsidies are used it is *known* that they are used for redistribution. This rules out any benefits for politicians to use them as disguised transfers.

When government and lobbies can gain from exchanging lobby goods for transfers, we may ask what it means to say that a transfer policy is "inefficient"? And, how does it relate to any social welfare benefit (or lack of it) of the policy use? The following definition (and related Lemma 1 in the Appendix) addresses these questions.

Definition 1. Policy t is an inefficient transfer policy relative to T if there are no joint political gains from trade between the government and lobby by lowering T and increasing t above the social welfare maximizing level of $t \equiv t^{ext}$. That is $t^* = t^{ext}$ *where* $\{T^*, t^*\} \equiv argmax_{T,t}(G((., \bar{C}) + V(., \bar{C}))$.

The social welfare maximizing value for t is zero in the absence of externalities. This definition then requires that joint gains to the government and lobby are not possible from using t as a transfer to partially replace T for any given value of the lobby good $\bar{C}$.

The timing of the two-stage game is the same as before. In the first stage, the government commits to a maximum level of the lump-sum transfer T^c chosen to maximize its objective. In the second stage, the government and lobby bargain

[17] Evidence for this is found in the WTO agreement on subsidies, which rules out the use of production subsidies targeted at firms or industries but it allows subsidies aimed at correcting market failures, e.g., if they are aimed at education, infrastructure, or R&D.

[18] In our working paper, we address the case where the government can restrict both policies in the first stage. We show that it chooses a strictly positive cap for the inefficient transfer t when it addresses a time-varying production externality. We also show that t is used for redistribution even if in the second stage, when policies are implemented, there is no externality, i.e., even when t is inefficient.

over the levels of C, T, and t taking the cap as given. In the Appendix we present a more formal definition of the equilibrium.

We start by analyzing the second stage. If no inefficient transfers took place after a cap was set then the Pareto frontier and solution would be exactly identical to the one in the benchmark case in Figure 3. However, the following proposition shows that is not the case and that t is used.

PROPOSITION 2 (Government cap on efficient transfers and use of inefficient transfers). *When the government can set a cap on the efficient transfer,* T^c :

a. *that cap is strictly binding (i.e.,* $T^c < T^N$*) iff neither the government nor the SIG have all the bargaining power;*
b. *the relatively inefficient transfer policy, t, is used; and*
c. *there always exist governments that are not too weak (i.e.* $\gamma \in [\gamma^l, 1)$*) for which the optimal binding cap is positive (*$T^c > 0$*) so that efficient and inefficient policies are simultaneously used.*

According to this proposition if the government can cap the efficient policy it will do so even in the presence of alternative policies that are less efficient. The basic intuition is identical to Proposition 1: The cap allows the government to credibly commit to a lower offer. However, the presence of inefficient transfers introduces some additional complexity to the problem, which we now explain.

The result from Proposition 1 applies directly to part (a) of Proposition 2 once we show that the constrained Pareto frontier for some binding cap $T^c < T^N$ is concave when t is used, at least for small values of t. Intuitively this property of the frontier holds due to the following reasons. First, because the subsidy is inefficient relative to the lump-sum transfer the Pareto frontier when t is used (not depicted) lies below the unconstrained frontier. The unconstrained frontier when t is available is the same as when it is not, i.e., the dashed line in Figure 3, since in either unconstrained solution only the efficient transfer is used. Second, there is always some binding cap $T^c \in [T^0, T^N)$ that allows government payoffs up to the maximum unconstrained level, g^m, so for caps in this range the unconstrained frontier in Figure 3 coincides with the constrained one (not depicted) up to the point where the cap binds. Third, the relative inefficiency of t disappears when t is exactly zero and thus the slope of the two frontiers is identical at that point. Therefore, since the constrained frontier lies below the unconstrained one it must be steeper, at least for small values of t.[19]

The second part of the proposition is less obvious. Why does the government set a cap when it *knows* that it will use the inefficient transfer policy in equilibrium? Why not simply relax the cap and replace t with a similar value transfer using the efficient policy? Doesn't that leave the lobby better off and thus willing to provide more lobby goods, which in turn would leave the government better off?

[19] In the appendix to our working paper we show that a sufficient condition for the constrained frontier to be concave for all t is for the contract curve in $C - t$ space to be downward sloping, which is assured if the production function is not too concave or convex. However, this global concavity condition is not necessary for proving Proposition 2.

This argument captures only the increase in the Pareto set from relaxing the cap. However, this will not cause an increase in government welfare because relaxing the cap worsens its bargaining position, as shown in Proposition 1. The inefficiency of the second transfer relative to T partially "protects" the gain in the bargaining position and loosening the cap erodes that gain.

The equilibrium production subsidy is strictly positive and thus that policy is strictly less efficient than the lump-sum transfer. To understand this note that in the second stage with a binding cap on T there are joint gains to be made by exchanging higher T for C and, since at $t = 0$ the two transfer policies are equally efficient, t will be used. This sufficient condition is satisfied without requiring any further assumptions in the case of a production subsidy relative to a lump-sum transfer; we conjecture that we would also see a positive use of the more inefficient policy if we used other pairs of interesting policies, e.g., production subsidies and tariffs. However, the basic insight of Proposition 2 can be generalized to a case when we consider *any* pair of policies that can be ranked in terms of efficiency, as we show in the following section.

Whereas the first part of the proposition provides the conditions for the cap to bind, the last part provides a sufficient condition for the optimal cap to be positive. This condition along with the result in part (b) implies that efficient and inefficient policies are simultaneously used. The intuition for this is based on the trade-off that the constraint generates between loss of surplus and improvement in bargaining position. The government sets $T^c > 0$ when it is not too weak because when $\gamma \geq \gamma^l$ it receives a large enough share of the aggregate surplus that the reduction in that surplus from further restrictions in T offsets the gains from any improvement in the share of that surplus from a better bargaining position. The simplest way to understand why such $\gamma^l < 1$ must exist is to consider the limit case when γ is close to 1. If γ were exactly equal to 1 the government would capture all the aggregate bargaining surplus and would therefore prefer the efficient policy since, by definition, T maximizes that surplus. Therefore there must also exist some γ^l sufficiently close to 1 such that the government still strictly prefers the unrestricted use of T instead of t. That is some governments that are not too weak prefer the unconstrained efficient policy to setting a constraint of $T = 0$ and using only the inefficient, as we analyze in more detail in the next section. But when $\gamma <$ 1 the government can further improve on this by constraining the efficient policy (as seen in part (a) of this proposition) even if it uses some of the inefficient policy (part (b)); so the optimal cap in that case is $\hat{T}^c(\gamma) > 0$ and we obtain a coexistence of redistribution policies.[20]

3.3. *The Government's Optimal Redistribution Policy.* Thus far we have allowed the government to set optimal caps on the relatively efficient policy. Doing so permitted us to clearly identify the government's incentives and also to explain the simultaneous use of two transfer policies. However, it may be easier for

[20] Note that this is a sufficient but not a necessary condition for the coexistence of policies. Moreover, as will be clear in the next section, and shown in the proof, γ^l need not be the limit case of γ close to 1. Therefore the coexistence outcome is not as unlikely as it may seem at first.

governments to rule out the use of a policy altogether than to commit to a positive cap (e.g., if the commitment device requires a third party to enforce it and there is imperfect information on the exact level of the policy but not on whether it is used). We therefore ask: Under what conditions would the government choose to forgo the efficient transfer completely and instead use a less efficient transfer policy?

Below we refer to the policies as T and t. However, the general condition we derive applies to *any* two policies that redistribute towards SIGs and can be ranked in terms of their relative efficiency in the way we previously defined. The condition we derive reflects the basic trade-off underlying Propositions 1 and 2—a switch to the inefficient policy causes a reduction in bargaining surplus but improves the government's bargaining position. The difference is that now if a cap is chosen it must be zero, i.e., the policy is ruled out, and thus the government may not always want to restrict the relatively efficient transfer. We show that this depends critically on the government's bargaining power, γ.

In the first stage the government now chooses whether to use T or t as a transfer, where the chosen policy cannot be capped. In the second stage, the government bargains with the lobby. We could also allow the government to choose no transfer policy but it is simple to show that it would never strictly prefer this option since it yields only the reservation utility, g^0. Thus we focus on the choice between two policies. A government with bargaining power γ chooses the inefficient policy if

$$G(T=0, t^{Nt}(\gamma), C^{Nt}(\gamma)) > G(T=T^N(\gamma), t=0, C^N). \tag{10}$$

Figure 4 illustrates why this condition may hold in the case of lump-sum transfers and some inefficient policy t. The line $g^m v^m$ on the right-hand panel represents

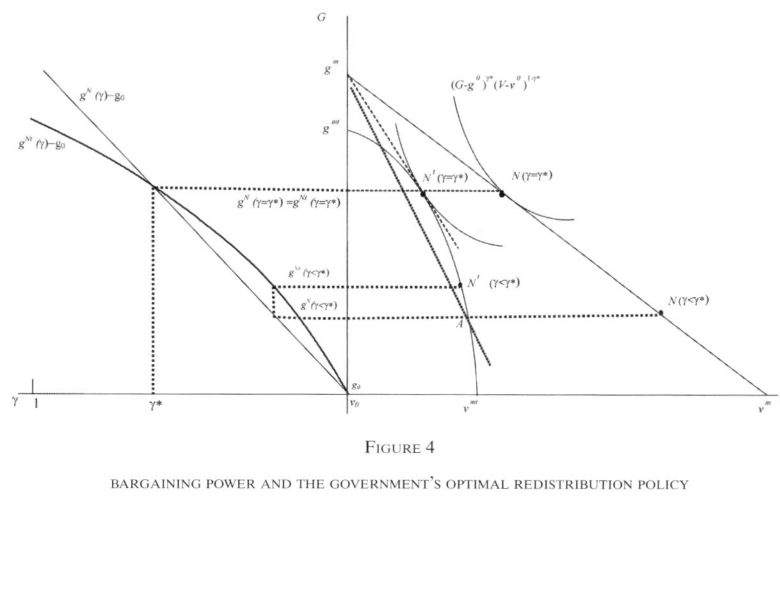

FIGURE 4

BARGAINING POWER AND THE GOVERNMENT'S OPTIMAL REDISTRIBUTION POLICY the Pareto frontier when the lump-sum is used. The curve $g^{mt}v^{mt}$ represents the frontier when an inefficient policy t is used, which is interior to $g^{m}v^{m}$ because t is inefficient.

Suppose that a critical bargaining power, γ^*, exists at which the government is indifferent between the policies. This value is implicitly defined by

$$G(0, t^{Nt}(\gamma^*), C^{Nt}(\gamma^*)) = G(T^N(\gamma^*), 0, C^N). \tag{11}$$

We represent such an equilibrium in Figure 4 by the points $N(\gamma = \gamma^*)$ and $N^t(\gamma = \gamma^*)$ for T and t, respectively. We can then define a *weak government* as one with a low bargaining power, $\gamma \in (0, \gamma^*)$. What we show next is that if γ^* exists then a weak government chooses the inefficient policy since it yields a higher payoff, as shown by the equilibrium labelled $N^t(\gamma < \gamma^*)$ relative to $N(\gamma < \gamma^*)$. To understand why consider the left panel of Figure 4 where we graph the government's maximized utility against γ. When $\gamma = 0$ the government receives its reservation utility, which is identical under T and t. But when the government has all the bargaining power it *always* chooses T since this is the policy that maximizes surplus, which the government fully appropriates when $\gamma = 1$. Therefore, if at $\gamma = 0$ the government's marginal gain from an increase in γ is higher under t than T then (10) is satisfied for sufficiently low γ since the government's maximized objective is continuous in γ. So, a sufficient condition for the government to choose the inefficient policy when γ is sufficiently low is

$$\lim_{\gamma \to 0} \frac{d}{d\gamma} G(0, t^{Nt}(\gamma), C^{Nt}(\gamma)) > \lim_{\gamma \to 0} \frac{d}{d\gamma} G(T^N(\gamma), 0, C^N). \tag{12}$$

When this condition holds there must exist at least one critical point $\gamma^* \in (0, 1)$ such that the government is indifferent between the policies.[21] To interpret this condition we define the Pareto frontier when a policy $x = T$ or t is used as $V^x - v^0 = \Omega^x(G^x - g^0)$.[22] So the slope of the frontier in Figure 4 is $1/\Omega'^x$. As we show in the Appendix when we solve and simplify (12) we obtain

$$\lim_{\gamma \to 0} (1/\Omega'^t)/(1/\Omega'^T) > \lim_{\gamma \to 0} \Omega^T/\Omega^t. \tag{13}$$

As we argued before the slope of the Pareto frontier captures the bargaining position. So it is natural to define the ratio of those slopes on the left-hand side of (13) as the *improvement in the government's bargaining position from using the inefficient policy*. The ratio of the lobby's utilities on the right side can then be

[21] Given that g^N is linear in γ, as seen in (9), we could check that when γ^* exists it is unique by confirming whether g^{Nt} is strictly concave for the particular policy t considered. In general if there are multiple γ^* we can simply take the minimum of them when (12) holds to show that when $\gamma \in (0, \gamma^*)$ the government chooses t.

[22] For example, when only lump-sum transfers are used, $\Omega^T(\cdot)$ is $-\frac{1-\beta}{a\beta}(G - g^0) + v^m - v^0$.

interpreted as the *reduction in bargaining surplus from using the inefficient policy*. We are now ready to state the following proposition.

PROPOSITION 3. (Government choice of inefficient policy as the unique form of transfer)

a. *Given a discrete choice a weak government prefers a relatively inefficient transfer policy in bargaining with SIGs if the resulting improvement in the government's bargaining position exceeds the reduction in bargaining surplus.*
b. *Moreover, there are strong enough governments* ($\gamma \in (\gamma^*, 1]$) *that always choose the relatively efficient transfer policy.*

The second part of the proposition is straightforward: The bargaining surplus is higher under the relatively efficient transfer. Thus a strong enough government, i.e., one with a high γ, prefers it since it can appropriate most of that surplus. This is clearly illustrated in Figure 4. In other words, if the government has most of the bargaining power, the reduction in total surplus from using t is the more important effect since the government appropriates a large share of it. Conversely, if the government is weak it is likely to gain from switching to an inefficient policy because it is not obtaining much of the surplus and thus the improvement in bargaining position is the dominant consideration.

To better understand the sufficient condition in part (a) of the proposition, consider Figure 4. A critical value γ^* exists if we can take a line through g^m that is tangent to the Pareto frontier for t. Using a reasoning similar to that in the proof of Proposition 1 the solution under T or t, at $N(\gamma = \gamma^*)$ and $N^t(\gamma = \gamma^*)$, respectively, will then entail the same utility for the government. Keeping all else constant we can see that if the surplus under t, Ω^t, is sufficiently small then the point v^{mt} would be close to v^0 and no such tangent would exist. A similar argument can be made to show the importance of the steepness of the Pareto frontier in ensuring that γ^* exists. Consider now a weak government that obtains $g^N(\gamma < \gamma^*)$ under the efficient transfer. Evaluating the slope of the concave Pareto frontier for the inefficient policy at that point, A, we can see that it is steeper than the slope of the dotted line through g^m and A. So the government payoff is higher under t when $\gamma \in (0, \gamma^*)$.

In general the existence of a γ^* that satisfies (11) must be checked for specific pairs of policies. The simulation in the Appendix shows that the condition is satisfied for the policies we use to illustrate the results of the model—lump-sum transfers versus production subsidies—when the marginal benefit of lobby goods to the politician falls sufficiently fast. This condition requiring Ψ to be sufficiently concave should be key in determining if the condition holds for other pairs of policies as well.

We can use Proposition 3 to determine the government's optimal transfer policy as a function of γ when it has more than two alternatives. For example, we can first compare the production subsidy to the lump-sum transfer; if we find the production subsidy is chosen for $\gamma \in (0, \gamma^*)$, we can subsequently compare the production subsidy with a tariff. For any set of redistributive policies that can be efficiency ranked, we could find the range of γ for which each of them is the government's preferred policy.

Proposition 3 also contains an interesting testable prediction, which we discuss in Section 5.

4. ALTERNATIVE FIRST-STAGE CHOICE MECHANISMS

Up to now, we have assumed that the government unilaterally chooses the type of transfer policy in the first stage. However, in some cases it is more realistic to model such choices as the outcome of a political mechanism that also involves other agents. Therefore in this section we consider two alternative mechanisms. First, we suppose that citizens elect the policymaker who then chooses what type of transfer to use and subsequently bargains with the lobbies. Second, we allow individual SIGs to bargain with the incumbent government in the first stage. Considering alternative choice mechanisms shows that the use of an inefficient policy may arise as an equilibrium outcome even when the politician does not choose them unilaterally.

4.1. *Representative Democracy.* The setup for the election of policymakers is simple. Voting is costless (and sincere in a two-candidate election), with a voter's choices depending only on the characteristics of the candidates. Candidates differ only in their given and known bargaining power γ since this is a key feature for the equilibrium use of inefficient policies. The candidate who is elected chooses the policy restriction that maximizes his objective function—given by equation (5)—and then bargains with lobbies. The bargaining power of a given politician is identical relative to all SIGs and in both stages.[23]

There are three groups of voters with potentially different voting preferences: organized owners of capital, unorganized owners of capital, and workers. Since consumer prices are given the latter two groups are affected by the transfers only through the tax burden imposed to pay for them, which is on a per capita basis. Therefore all voters that are not organized into SIGs have identical preferences over policy outcomes. We assume that these voters form a majority, so that the median voter, who is decisive in determining the electoral outcome, chooses the candidate who delivers the lower tax burden.

In a pure democracy where voters choose policy directly, the median voter would choose to prohibit all transfers to SIGs. In a representative democracy, we assume that voters do not have the power to bind a policymaker to such an action, which would be against his self interest. Nor could any candidate credibly commit to make no transfers in exchange for lobby goods once elected since all candidates

[23] Differences between politicians in their bargaining power with SIGs may reflect their political experience, position within their party, or the strength of the party itself in either a majority or coalition government. Our discussion of possible determinants of γ in Section 5 will clarify why it can differ across politicians and why politicians must take at least part of it as given so that the range of γ in any given country may be limited by its institutions.

value lobby goods and place a finite weight, a, on social welfare.[24] Similarly, we assume that citizens cannot constrain the elected policymaker's choice of transfer policy. If a policymaker prefers to use lump-sum transfers, voters cannot induce him to use production subsidies or vice versa. In sum, candidates cannot commit or be bound to do something other than what is in their self-interest as policymakers.

The fact that unorganized voters and policymakers have opposing preferences on the use of transfers implies that it is crucial to model the first stage carefully. The policy outcomes would be quite different under a pure or direct democracy (where the median voter chooses no transfers) versus the more realistic representative democracy (where the politician implements transfers). Moreover, as we show below, the preferences of unorganized voters and politicians can also differ on the type of transfer.

If both candidates prefer the same redistribution policy, then unorganized voters would prefer the candidate with higher bargaining power because he obtains more of the surplus and so he can implement a lower transfer to the SIGs. We refer to this advantage of stronger candidates as the *pure bargaining power effect*. Therefore there are two necessary conditions if voters are to ever elect the candidate with lower bargaining power. First, his preferred transfer policy must be different from the other candidate, so the interesting elections are the ones contested by a politician with $\gamma^t < \gamma^*$ who prefers t and one with $\gamma^T > \gamma^*$, who prefers T (see Proposition 3). The second necessary condition is that the median voter is better off under the inefficient policy when the politician in power has $\gamma^t < \gamma^*$. The following lemma establishes these preferences.

LEMMA 2 (Unorganized voter preferences over policies). *Voters who are not organized into SIGs prefer the inefficient policy to the efficient one under any politician with bargaining power $\gamma \in [0, \gamma^w]$, where $\gamma^w > \gamma^*$.*

To understand these preferences consider first a politician with bargaining power equal to γ^*. By definition his payoff, $G = aW(\gamma^*) + \Psi(C(\gamma^*))$, is identical under t and T. Moreover, C must be strictly lower under t than T, since t is less efficient and hence elicits fewer lobby goods. Therefore, at γ^*, social welfare under t, W^t, must be strictly higher than under T, W^t. Intuitively, social welfare under t is higher at γ^* because the level of transfers under the inefficient policy is smaller and so is the costly collection of taxes.[25] This is also true for all $\gamma < \gamma^*$ since the government payoff is higher under t than T in those cases. The result also holds

[24] A policymaker has the ability to extract lobby goods from SIGs, which gives him different preferences than workers and unorganized capital owners. Hence, though we could think of a candidate starting out as a citizen with given preferences over transfers, the transformation to policymaker in itself changes those preferences. Drazen and Eslava (2006) make a similar point in considering a policymaker's preferences over goods targeted to some SIGs at the expense of others.

[25] From the voters' point of view, the benefit of the inefficient policy is to reduce the equilibrium level of transfers and so it is indeed like "throwing sand in the wheels." However, they can only get a policymaker to implement this outcome if it is his preferred outcome and a policymaker prefers the inefficient instrument not because it is sand in the wheels and reduces the total surplus, but *in spite* of it.

for some $\gamma^w > \gamma^*$ since W^t is strictly higher than W^T at γ^* and both functions are continuous in γ.

Lemma 2 shows that the preferences of the policymaker and the median voter over the type of transfers do not coincide for some values of γ—for $\gamma \in [\gamma^*, \gamma^w]$ the former prefers the inefficient whereas the policymaker prefers the efficient transfer. Hence, in those cases the unorganized voters would like to constrain him to use the inefficient policy, but in a representative democracy they cannot do so. This generates an incentive for these voters to prefer a candidate with a lower bargaining power, $\gamma^t < \gamma^*$, who will implement the inefficient policy. The question is whether this incentive is ever sufficiently large to offset the pure bargaining power effect described above. The following proposition shows that it is provided that *candidate γ^t is not too weak relative to γ^T* (i.e., $\gamma^T - \gamma^t$ is sufficiently small).

PROPOSITION 4 (Use of inefficient policies in a representative democracy). *Consider a two candidate election for the politician who bargains with SIGs in the second stage and can choose between no transfers, an efficient transfer, or the inefficient one in the first stage. A candidate with $\gamma^t < \gamma^*$ is elected and implements the inefficient policy when he faces a candidate with $\gamma^T > \gamma^*$ if the unorganized voters form a majority and γ^t is not too weak relative to γ^T.*

Hence, in a representative democracy not only will there always be transfers to SIGs in equilibrium (though unorganized voters, who are assumed to form the majority, oppose them), but the policymakers that are elected may precisely be the ones that choose the inefficient transfer policy. This explanation of inefficient transfers in a democracy contrasts with models that fail to provide a motive for a politician to prefer inefficient policies or that do not allow him to participate in the first stage choice mechanism as an independent actor.

Moreover, the conflict of interest between voters and policymakers over the optimality of transfers will imply in some cases a conflict over the preferred instrument when voters cannot directly constrain policymakers. As Proposition 4 shows, this may lead voters to elect a weaker candidate to represent them. Hence, though voters always prefer a stronger bargainer if they can also dictate which policy is used, they may elect a weaker one when they have no control over the choice of transfer policies.

4.2. *Bargaining with Policymakers.* There are numerous ways to model the government's interaction with the lobby in the first stage. Our main objective here is to ask if the inefficient policy is used when we eliminate the asymmetry in Section 3 where the government could make a take-it-or-leave-it offer on the cap or policy choice. We therefore maintain the rest of the structure of the model and simply allow each SIG and the government to bargain in the first stage over the form of transfer. We also explain why inefficient forms of transfer can arise even if the government and lobby interact repeatedly. Throughout we assume that it is too costly for all the SIGs to coordinate in their efforts to bargain with the government in the first stage, so that the government deals with each bilaterally.

This allows us to remain consistent with the original setup and contrast the results with those obtained when the government had all the bargaining power in the first stage.

Consider first the case of a cap on efficient transfers when inefficient policies are also available, as discussed in Section 3.2. As shown in Proposition 2, when the government can choose caps it sets a binding cap on T provided neither party has all the bargaining power in the second stage. If instead we allowed each individual SIG to set the cap, each would choose a nonbinding cap. Each of these outcomes can be seen as the extreme when the government's bargaining power in the first stage, γ_1, is one or zero. This may lead us to think that a cap will be present as long as the government has some bargaining power in the first stage. But, as we show in our working paper, that is not true.

In particular, we show that if the government has more bargaining power during the first, or "constitutional" stage than in the second stage, i.e. if $\gamma_1 > \gamma$, then the outcome is still a cap on T and the use of the inefficient transfer. Briefly, the intuition is as follows. In the special case where $\gamma_1 = \gamma$ allowing for bargaining in the first stage leads to the unconstrained Nash solution. Thus, in this case only the efficient policy is used because the Nash solution is efficient and the Nash product being maximized is the same in the first and second stages. This is also true when we give the lobby more weight in the first stage since its payoff is maximized when T is not capped. However, if we increase the government power in the first stage, so $\gamma_1 > \gamma$, then according to the Nash product in the first stage it is "efficient" to increase the government's payoff (relative to the case when $\gamma_1 = \gamma$) and this can done via the cap.[26]

We think this is an interesting result that is not immediately obvious. It proves that two naive conjectures about introducing bargaining in the first stage are incorrect: that it either always eliminates the cap (because Nash bargaining is efficient) or that it only eliminates it if the lobby has all the bargaining power in that stage. There are several reasons why politicians may have higher bargaining power in the constitutional rather than in the implementation stage. First, what is bargained over is formally under the control of the government—for example, a particular type of legislation or commitment via an international agreement. Second, some SIGs will not be present in the first stage.

Thus far we have considered the choice of first stage restrictions in a static context, which excludes repetition and thus history dependent strategies. One possible objection to the previous result in this section is that in the first stage there are cases with unexplored joint gains from bargaining and repeated interaction implies that the lobby could find a way to "bribe" the government into relaxing

[26] The analysis is more complex with binary choice of policies, since the result of first stage bargaining cannot be a policy somewhere between the policy preferred by the government and that preferred by the lobby. One way of representing the possible outcome of bargaining when choices are discrete in the first stage is to allow the government to choose the policy with probability ρ and the lobby with probability $1 - \rho$. Previously we assumed $\rho = 1$ and showed that, under the conditions in Proposition 3, the equilibrium policy is the inefficient one. More generally, if whenever the government has some bargaining power it has a nonzero probability of being able to choose the policy then we still observe the inefficient policy with probability ρ if the conditions in Proposition 3 hold.

the cap in the first stage. Whether this leads to the fully unconstrained outcome depends on how exactly the repeated game is modelled, which we leave for future research. However, two broad points suggest that the use of inefficient policies would remain in some repeated game setups.

First, if utility is not transferable, as we have assumed so far, then the maximum "bribe" the lobby is willing to pay may be lower than the minimum value the government requires to give up the cap. Second, even if we consider fully transferable utility, the question is whether the unconstrained outcome is self-enforcing. The answer is no, unless the government and lobby place sufficient weight on future payoffs, which is the inducement for cooperating, e.g., for the government not to set its preferred cap after receiving a bribe today. As is common in repeated games the discount factor reflects a pure rate of time preference and the probability that the game continues. Thus the unconstrained outcome is not self-enforcing when governments have a low enough probability of remaining in office.

In sum, inefficient redistribution policies can arise in equilibrium even if their opponents—the SIGs—are allowed to influence the policy choice mechanism in the first stage.

5. FROM THEORY TO EMPIRICS: PREDICTIONS, MEASUREMENT, AND DATA

We now discuss some policy choices consistent with our arguments and with some broad predictions of the model. We then describe a more specific prediction of the model and how it could be econometrically tested in a way that distinguishes it from alternative explanations.

One example of caps on transfers is in agricultural policy. In the 1930s the U.S. federal government initiated an agricultural policy with the objective of providing income support to farmers. Historically the transfers have been based on a variety of price distorting policies such as price supports, production subsidies, and trade policies. In 1996 the Freedom to Farm Act introduced direct payments to farmers subject to annual caps and the 2002 Farm Security and Rural Investment Act tightened some of the payment limits in the 1996 Act and included a cap on individual programs. The OECD (2005, p. 3) also reports that the EU and other member countries are moving towards more efficient decoupled payments to farmers. As we describe more carefully below, our model would broadly predict such a switch if the agricultural sector is losing bargaining power relative to the government. This may be plausible since the share of agriculture in total employment (and GDP) has fallen considerably in developed countries.

A potentially credible way for a government to commit to limits in the use of redistribution policies is to be bound by international agreements that are costly to break. The Stability and Growth Pact that constrains European Union governments' budget deficits and debt levels provides one example. These constraints have been used to increase the government's leverage in negotiations with domestic SIGs as suggested by our model. In Portugal, for example, the government has used the Pact as a key argument to limit wage increases in the public sector when negotiating with unions. Such limits do not necessarily apply to other less efficient transfers to those workers who can lobby for nonwage benefits related to leave time, health care, or retirement regulations.[27]

Trade agreements provide another important example of commitment. The World Trade Organization constrains members production subsidies and allows them to bind their tariffs at a ceiling level, under the threat of tariff retaliation if that commitment is broken. Similarly regional trade agreements allow a country to commit to a limit on its use of trade barriers. Our model provides a rationale for commitment via such international agreements that is distinct from the usual one that appeals to time inconsistency problems.[28] Moreover, currently one of the main concerns in trade agreements is that as the limits on subsidies, tariffs, and other basic measures of protection are set other, *even less efficient* methods of redistribution, such as quantity restrictions, goods' standards, and other nontariff barriers that discriminate against foreign products, are increasingly used. This is consistent with the prediction of our model that once governments commit to a limit on a redistribution policy SIGs find and pursue redistribution via relatively less efficient ones.

5.1. *Inefficient Policies and Bargaining Power: Predictions and Measurement.* In order to econometrically test our model and distinguish it from other explanations for the use of inefficient policies we need to focus on the role of bargaining power of a government relative to SIGs. As shown in Proposition 3 and illustrated in Figure 4, a sufficiently strong government (or politician) prefers the more efficient policy, while other governments prefer the less efficient one. To test if any such relationship is present we must first define and measure the two key variables: the relative use of inefficient policies and bargaining power. Since this relationship is only present in our model we don't provide details on how to test alternative models.[29]

Empirically implementing such a test requires us to first rank alternative policies in terms of their efficiency. One area where this is possible is transfers to farmers. Farm subsidies that are directly linked to current output and input levels—so-called market price supports—are widely seen as more distorting than other direct payments based on farm area or past output. Using these data the OECD calculates the share of transfers to farmers that accounts for market price supports in a variety of countries, years, and products. This issue is central in agricultural policy where 30% of farm receipts in OECD countries are due to some form

[27] "Portugal Chafes Under the Yoke of Austerity" *Financial Times* September 25, 2002. We are not arguing that this was the main motive for countries to sign this agreement but to the extent that governments have used it in this way it suggests it may have been one of the motives.

[28] See, for example, Staiger and Tabellini (1987) and Maggi and Rodriguez-Clare (1998). In our approach the gain to the government from self-restraint is explained by the improvement in its bargaining position relative to the SIGs.

[29] To test the disguised transfer argument in Coate and Morris (1995) one could focus on whether improved information about politicians and/or policies leads to a reduction in inefficient transfers. Their model and ours are clearly not nested and, as discussed in Section 1.1, the Coate and Morris model is best suited to one-off projects, whose efficiency must be uncertain and will therefore be difficult to measure. Our model on the other hand applies to policies whose relative efficiency is much easier to measure, as we describe in this section.

of government transfer and the share of market price supports is still over 70% (OECD, 2005, p. 2).

Trade policy is another area where it is possible to rank alternative transfers according to their efficiency. It is well known that tariffs are generally an inefficient transfer instrument. Even if a production externality is present, a production subsidy is more efficient because it avoids distorting the consumer price. However, there isn't systematic data on production subsidies outside of agriculture (many of them are in fact outlawed by the WTO, in what could be interpreted as a commitment device to limit transfers, as argued by Chandra, 2007). But there is data on quotas and other nontariff trade barriers (NTBs) that are often even less efficient than a tariff. These NTBs can be converted into an advalorem tariff equivalent, which can be used to construct the share of the less efficient trade policy (NTBs) in total protection (tariff plus NTBs). This share is considerable and on average it increases the restrictiveness of trade policy in the world by 70% relative to tariffs alone (Kee et al., 2006). There is substantial variation in this measure both over countries and products that can easily be examined.[30]

Measuring the government's bargaining power relative to SIGs is not simple, but we can provide broad guidance and some specific suggestions for alternative proxies. Binmore et al. (1986) show that the Nash bargaining framework can be interpreted as a bilateral game of alternating offers, where the bargaining power parameter, γ, reflects the relative discount factors of agents or the probability of an exogenous breakdown in bargaining.[31] In our context, γ may thus reflect the probability a government assigns to being forced out of office (or the uncertainty of its tenure in office), so that refusing an offer from the lobby now may lead to no bargain at all before it leaves office. Therefore a government that perceives that it is likely to lose the next election may view itself as having little bargaining power and thus be more likely to choose inefficient means of redistribution. Measures of tenure uncertainty could include constitutional provisions about the timing of elections or the nature of government itself, with, for example, unstable coalitions having less bargaining power than single-party majority governments.

A similar argument can be made for SIGs. If a SIG represents an industry i then the government's bargaining power relative to it, γ_i, is higher if that industry is new, dying, or more generally faces very uncertain times—so that the probability of remaining in business in the absence of government transfers is small. Hence direct measures of expected longevity, or measures of liquidity and volatility of profits across industries, may be correlated with the SIG's (unobserved) bargaining power. The importance of financing for firms (or industries) to remain in operation could confer the government considerable bargaining power in countries where it also controls access to credit through public banks. Any given industry (or other type of SIG) also discounts the future more heavily in countries with poor protection of property rights where they are more likely to accept

[30] Limão and Tovar-Rodriguez (2007) provide a theoretical and empirical analysis of the choice between tariffs and NTBs that builds on our framework.

[31] The wage bargaining literature has used a similar interpretation of γ to justify alternative empirical determinants of the relative bargaining power of unions vs. firms (cf. Dorian, 1992).

the government's offer sooner when there is a higher risk of expropriation. Thus combining industry information with the widely available indices of weak property rights protection and government control of the financial sector can also provide proxies for bargaining power. Since the model's prediction refers to a comparison of governments with high versus intermediate or low bargaining power, we would construct a categorical variable based on percentiles of the data, which would also reduce measurement error in this variable.

In short, we believe that the model generates testable predictions that differentiate it from other models. It applies to important transfer policies and can be tested by exploiting variation over time, countries, and industries using currently available data.

6. CONCLUSIONS

We present a model of policymaking that makes explicit two key elements that are crucial in predicting whether inefficient policies will be used. The first is the choice mechanism over the sets of policies; the second, the policy preferences of all agents who can influence that choice. Policymaking is a two-stage process: In the first stage the set of constraints on policy instruments is chosen, and in the second stage, the government bargains with SIGs over the level of the policy instruments. Our results show the importance of considering the policymaker as an independent agent in both stages.

In such a world, a key consideration is the bargaining position of the government relative to the lobbies, where a crucial feature is that neither side has all the bargaining power and utility is not transferable. The government will benefit if it can commit itself to offer lower benefits to the SIG for any given amount of lobby goods that the SIG provides. As we demonstrated, this commitment increases the government's payoff by improving its bargaining position. However, if the government caps or forgoes the use of one instrument, lobbies will find other, generally less efficient ways to bargain with the government. Hence, equilibrium redistribution is characterized by the use of inefficient instruments. If only one policy can be used then we show that a weak government chooses the inefficient transfer whereas a strong government chooses the efficient one. This is an interesting prediction that is unique to our model and could be empirically tested.

The model yields a number of interesting results not only for the use of inefficient policies when the government can unilaterally choose which to use, but also when these decisions are not made unilaterally. Even when the policy framework is bargained over, inefficient policies may still be used in equilibrium. When elections are used in the first stage of policymaking, direct versus representative democracy can have diametrically opposed implications for the use of inefficient policies by the government. In a representative democracy transfers occur in equilibrium and, more interestingly, voters may prefer the candidate with lower bargaining power (who uses the inefficient transfer) to one with higher bargaining power against SIGs (who would use the efficient transfer). This occurs even though voters are rational, fully informed, and vote solely on the basis of the effect of the redistribution policy.

The model also provides a rationale for commitment via international agreements other than as a solution to time inconsistency problems, as is often suggested. In our approach the gain to the government from self-restraint (which might be achieved via international agreements) is explained by the improvement in its bargaining position relative to the SIGs.

We chose a specific application to demonstrate a general mechanism that appears to be commonly used in practice by governments: restrictions on the amount they can offer in a subsequent bargain. We showed that the basic insight that the government faces a trade-off between the improvement in bargaining position and reduction in bargaining surplus is not specific to lump-sum transfers and production subsidies. It extends to any pair of policies that can be ranked according to their transfer efficiency. As pointed out above, it can also apply in different political economy settings provided that the key bargaining elements are present. Thus it would be interesting to apply this insight to analyze how normative and positive predictions of various policy models would be affected if they allow for the policy set to be endogenously chosen.

Finally, our results highlight some important methodological issues about the interaction of governments and SIGs. First, models that assign all the bargaining power to either party and assume utility is transferable, e.g. through unlimited cash contributions, will fail to explain interesting outcomes, which suggests there is a high value to investigating alternative approaches to the interaction between governments and SIGs. Second, models that leave the government in the background may be inadequate in predicting the type of policies that will be used, and especially why utility maximizing elected politicians may choose inefficient policy instruments even under full information.

APPENDIX

A. *Formal Definition of the Political Equilibrium.* In this section, we provide a more formal definition of the political equilibrium described in Section 3.2. As we point out in Section 2 the structure allows us to consider the government's bilateral interaction with each lobby i separately. So the definition applies for each lobby and we suppress the subscript i. The set $\{\hat{T}^c, \hat{T}, \hat{t}, \hat{C}\}$ forms a subgame perfect Nash equilibrium of this game if and only if caps are chosen to satisfy

$$\hat{T}^c \equiv \arg\max_{T^c} G(\hat{T}(T^c), \hat{t}(T^c), \hat{C}(T^c)) \tag{A.1}$$

and the second stage policies maximize the Nash product s.t. cap and Pareto frontier:

$$\begin{aligned}\{\hat{C}, \hat{T}, \hat{t}\} &\equiv \arg_{\{\hat{C}, \hat{T}, \hat{t}\}} \max(G(T, t, C) - g^0)^\gamma (V(T, t, C) - v^0)^{1-\gamma} \\ &\text{s.t. } \hat{T} \le \hat{T}^c;\ (G(.), V(.)) \in P^e;\ G \ge g^0 \text{ and } V \ge v^0,\end{aligned} \tag{A.2}$$

where $g^0 \equiv \max_{T \ge 0, t \ge 0} G(T, t, C)$ and $v^0 \equiv \max_{C \ge 0} V(T, t, C)$. The utilities (G, V) belong to the set P^e iff they are feasible and efficient, i.e. $\nexists\, (G, V)$ with $T \in [0, \hat{T}^c]$

that yields $G(T, t, C) \geq G(\hat{T}, \hat{t}, \hat{C})$ and $V(T, t, C) \geq V(\hat{T}, \hat{t}, \hat{C})$ with at least one strict inequality.

B. *Efficiency Ranking of Transfer Policies.*

LEMMA 1. *A production subsidy t is an inefficient transfer policy relative to T iff no production externality is present.*

PROOF.

Sufficiency: Consider the case where no externality is present, so that the economically optimal level of t is $t^* = 0$. Deriving a contract curve in $T - t$ space for any given level of C, the definition requires that such a curve contain no points such that $t > 0$. For this to be true, it must be the case that $t > 0$ implies no gains from bargaining. This requires

$$-[G_t / G_T] \mid_{dG=0} < -[V_t / V_T] \mid_{dV=0}$$

$$[\pi'(p + \hat{t})\beta + t\pi''(p + t)]/\beta > \pi'(p + \hat{t}).$$

This is always satisfied given the convexity of the profit function. Note that these equations imply that at $t = 0$ we have $G_t / G_T = V_t / V_T$.

Necessity: Suppose a positive production externality is present. The optimal level of subsidy to address the externality is given by $t^{ext} : G_t^{ext} = 0$. Where G^{ext} is the government objective reflecting the externality. For $t \geq t^{ext}$ to be inefficient, it must be the case that when $t \geq t^{ext}$,we have

$$\text{(B.1)} \qquad \left[- G_t^{ext} / G_T^{ext} \leq -V_t / V_T \right]_{t \geq t^{ext}}$$

$$\left[G_t^{ext} / (a\beta / (1 - \beta)) \leq -\pi_i'(p + \hat{t}) \right]_{t \geq t^{ext}}.$$

But since $G_t^{ext}(t = t^{ext}) = 0$ by the definition of t^{ext} and $\pi'(p + t = t^{ext}) > 0$, (B.1) cannot hold for $t = t^{ext}$. Hence, t is *not* inefficient when an externality is present according to the definition in the text. Note however that the condition in (B.1) will be satisfied for some sufficiently high $t > t^{ext}$. ■

C. *Proofs.*

PROPOSITION 1. (Government cap on efficient transfers)

Sufficiency: Suppose that $\gamma \in (0, 1)$. We need only show the existence of a cap such that $T^c < T^N$ and $G(T^{Nc}, C^{Nc}) > G(T^N, C^N)$. The solution is illustrated in Figure 3. We first show that the constrained Pareto frontier is strictly concave. On the basis of that, we then show that $g^{Nc} > g^N$. The constrained Pareto frontier in Figure 3 coincides with the original one for $T \leq T^c$ and thus its slope is simply G_T / V_T up to point (C^N, T^c). From (6) we have $G_T / G_C = V_T / V_C$ at (C^N, T^c) so that $G_T / V_T = G_C / V_C$. The rest of the constrained frontier is strictly interior to the unconstrained frontier and has a slope of G_C/V_C, reflecting the ratio of changes in welfare as the amount of the lobby good provided changes. Moreover, $G_C(C^N)/V_C = -\Psi'(C^N) > -\Psi'(C < C^N) = G_C(C < C^N)/V_C$, from the definitions of G and V as well as $\Psi'' < 0$, so the constrained frontier is strictly concave. Now define point A in Figure 3 as the intersection of the constrained frontier and $G = g^N$. Since the constrained frontier is strictly concave and $g^{mc} = g^m$ for $T^c \geq T^0$ (see Figure 2), the segment connecting g^m and A is everywhere below the constrained Pareto frontier.

Consider then an auxiliary problem where the Pareto frontier is defined by the straight line through g^m and A, which has some slope m. For *any* linear Pareto frontier the government equilibrium utility is $g^N - g^0 = \gamma\ (g^m - g^0)$ (from (9)). Since the straight line through g^m and A is a rotation of the original Pareto frontier inwards around g^m, and since $g^m - g^0$ and γ are unchanged in the auxiliary problem, the equilibrium government utility is also unchanged. Therefore if we derive the first-order condition for this auxiliary problem as we do for (8) we obtain $-\ U_V/U_G\,|_A = m$. Strict concavity of the constrained frontier implies that at $A, m > G_C/V_C\,|_A$, the slope of the constrained frontier at A. Therefore, the equilibrium point N^C lies to the northwest of A, implying $g^{Nc} > g^N$.

Necessity. If $\gamma = 1$ then the unconstrained solution is $g^m \equiv Max_{C,T}\ G$ s.t. $V = V^0$. The equilibrium transfer is $T^N(\gamma = 1) = T^0$. A strictly binding cap entails that the government's utility is now $g^{mc} \equiv Max_{C,T} G$ s.t. $V = V^0$ and $T^c < T^0$, the extra constraint implies that $g^{mc} < g^m$.

If $\gamma = 0$ then the second stage Nash bargaining solution is $G^{Nc}\ (T^{Nc}, C^{Nc}) = G(0, 0)$. The government is therefore indifferent among all values of T^c, which implies that there exist $T^c \geq T^N$ (that is, caps that are not strictly binding) that are subgame perfect equilibria. ■

PROPOSITION 2. (Government cap on efficient transfers and use of inefficient transfers)

a. T^c binds iff the government does not have all the bargaining power.

In the political equilibrium $\hat{T}^c$ must satisfy the following FOC: $dG/dT^c = 0$, where $dG/dT^c \equiv G_C C_{T^c} + G_T T_{T^c} + G_t t_{T^c}$. Note that $T_{T^c} = 1$ since a marginal increase in the binding cap T^c will induce an equivalent increase in the transfer. Thus, to show the gain from capping T, a proof similar to that in Proposition 1 applies provided that the Pareto frontier is strictly concave for some binding cap, $T^c < T^N$, when t is available.

The slope of the Pareto frontier is G_T/V_T if T^c is not binding. If T^c binds then any further increases in the utility of the lobby must take place via changes in C being exchanged for t, since as we will see $\hat{t} > 0$. Thus, if T^c binds, the slope is $(G_t dt - G_C dC)/(V_t dt - V_C dC) = G_t/V_t$ since the equilibrium definition requires t and C to be set efficiently, i.e., for $G_t/G_C = V_t/V_C$ Therefore we have

$$\lim_{t \to 0} G_t/V_t = G_T/V_T > [G_t/V_t]|_{t>0} \tag{C.1}$$

where the first equality is due to the definition of G and V. We show this in the proof of Lemma 1 and it implies that for some binding $T^c > T^0$ the unconstrained utility frontier for efficient transfer—the dashed line in Figure 3—has the same slope as the constrained one at the point where $t \to 0$ (not depicted). The inequality follows from the definition of t being inefficient relative to T. Thus for some $T^c > T^0$ the constrained Pareto frontier is strictly concave around $t \to 0$ and we can apply the proof of Proposition 1 to show that $\hat{T}^c$ binds.

b. $\hat{t} > 0$ in equilibrium.

Under the unconstrained optimum the MRS of the policies for the government and lobby are equalized to maximize the joint gain from bargaining, which requires $G_T/G_C = V_T/V_C$ from (6). If the optimal constrained solution was $\hat{t} = 0$ then T^c would be identical to the cap in proposition 1 and $C < C^N$, $T^c < T^N$ so $G_T/G_C > V_T/V_C$ (since $G_{CC}, G_T < 0$ and $G_{TT} = V_{TT} = V_{CC} = 0$). So, in the second stage there are strictly positive joint unexplored gains from exchanging efficient transfers for lobby goods. This implies that $\hat{t} > 0$, since when $t = 0$ this policy is just as efficient as T as show in Lemma 1.

c. For governments that are not too weak $\hat{T}^c > 0$.

Consider the case where $G(T^N(\gamma), 0) \geq G(0, t^{Nt}(\gamma))$, which is satisfied if either

(a) there exists a $\gamma^* > 0$ (defined in (11) by the equality of the government payoffs under T or t) and $\gamma \geq \gamma^*$ (see Proposition 3) or
(b) a $\gamma^* > 0$ does not exist, in which case $G(T^N(\gamma), 0) > G(0, t^{Nt}(\gamma))$ is true for all $\gamma > 0$ since it holds at $\gamma = 1$ and, by the definition of γ^*, there are no cases for which $G(T^N(\gamma), 0) = G(0, t^{Nt}(\gamma))$.

In part (a) of this proposition we show $G(\hat{T}^c(\gamma), \hat{t}(\gamma)) > G(T^N(\gamma), 0)$ for all $\gamma \in (0, 1)$. These two inequalities imply

$$G(\hat{T}^c(\gamma), \hat{t}(\gamma)) > G(0, t^{Nt}(\gamma)) \tag{C.2}$$

if γ^* either does not exist or it exists and $\gamma \geq \gamma^*$. Now suppose that the optimal cap for the government in this case is $\hat{T}^c = 0$. Then in the second stage there would be gains from bargaining and $\hat{t} > 0$ (part b of this proposition). Moreover, since $T = 0$ and t is not constrained we would have $\hat{t} = t^{Nt}$ and so $G(\hat{T}^c(\gamma), \hat{t}(\gamma)) = G(0, t^{Nt}(\gamma))$. But this contradicts (C.2) when γ^* does not exist or when it exists and $\gamma \geq \gamma^*$. When γ^* exists, we also obtain a contradiction for some governments with $\gamma = \gamma^l < \gamma^* < 1$. To see this note that the benefit from constraining T is strictly positive (i.e., $G(\hat{T}^c(\gamma), \hat{t}(\gamma)) > G(T^N(\gamma), 0)$ for all $\gamma \in (0, 1)$) whereas $G(T^N(\gamma), 0)$ and $G(0, t^{Nt}(\gamma))$ are respectively continuous in γ. ■

PROPOSITION 3. (Government choice of inefficient policy as unique form of transfer)

a. When $\gamma = 0$ we have $G(0, t^{Nt}(\gamma), C^{Nt}(\gamma)) = G(T^N(\gamma), 0, C^N) = g^0$. Equation (12) is thus sufficient to show (10) is satisfied for $\gamma \in (0, \gamma^*)$.

To evaluate (12), we first use the implicit function theorem to obtain $\lim_{\gamma\to 0} dg/d\gamma = \lim_{\gamma\to 0} -\hat{L}_{G\gamma}/\hat{L}_{GG}$ where $\hat{L}$ is the Nash product evaluated at the solution of the following program

$$\text{Max}_{G\geq g^0} L \equiv (G-g^0)^{\gamma}(\Omega(G-g^0))^{1-\gamma}$$

The FOC $L_G = 0$ is

$$\gamma\left(\frac{\Omega}{G-g^0}\right)^{1-\gamma} + (1-\gamma)\left(\frac{G-g^0}{\Omega}\right)^{\gamma}\Omega' = 0$$

$$G-g^0 = -\frac{\Omega}{\Omega'}\frac{\gamma}{1-\gamma}$$

Using this we have $\hat{L}_{G\gamma} = \hat{L}/(1-\gamma)(\hat{G}-g^0)$ and $\hat{L}_{GG} = [-\gamma/(1-\gamma) + (1-\gamma)\hat{\Omega}''(\hat{G}-g^0)^2/\hat{\Omega}]\hat{L}/(\hat{G}-g^0)^2$, which we use to obtain after some simplification

$$\lim_{\gamma\to 0} d\hat{g}/d\gamma = \lim_{\gamma\to 0} -\hat{L}_{G\gamma}/\hat{L}_{GG} = \lim_{\gamma\to 0} -\hat{\Omega}/\hat{\Omega}'$$

Therefore (12) reduces to (13) in the text.

b. At $\gamma = 1$ we have $g^m > g^{mt}$ thus the government chooses T. Since the inequality is strict and G is continuous in γ (G is continuous in the policies and $(t^{Nt}(\gamma), C^{Nt}(\gamma))$ and $T^N(\gamma)$ are continuous in γ) we can find a $\overline{\gamma} < 1$ s.t. $g^N(\overline{\gamma}) = g^{Nt}(\overline{\gamma})$. If (11) has a unique solution, then $\overline{\gamma} = \gamma^*$. Otherwise $\overline{\gamma}$ is the maximum γ that satisfies (11). ■

LEMMA 2. (Unorganized voters' preferences over policies)

We show this in two steps. First, the difference in welfare for unorganized voters across policies depends only on the amount of tax they pay to cover transfers. Second, that tax is higher under T if $\gamma \leq \gamma^w$.

Step 1: For the unorganized voters, the income gross of taxes depends only on their labor share and, if they have fixed factors, the world price, neither of which is affected by T or t. So both income and consumer surplus of nonnumeraire goods (which depends only on each good's world price) are independent of the redistribution policy. This implies that the difference in welfare for unorganized voters between t and T is the taxes they pay. Since taxes are lump-sum this group must pay the fraction of taxes not paid by the voters organized into SIGs, i.e., they pay $1-\alpha = 1-\sum_{i\in L}\alpha_i$ of the taxes. Therefore, the difference in welfare across policies for workers, denoted by ℓ, and unorganized factor owners, j, is

$$\sum_{j\notin L}(W_j^t(\gamma) - W_j^T(\gamma)) + W_\ell^t(\gamma) - W_\ell^T(\gamma) = \frac{1-\alpha}{1-\beta}(\tau^T(\gamma) - \tau^t(\gamma))$$

where the equilibrium welfare for j is defined as $W_j^t(\gamma) \equiv W_j(0, t^{Nt}(\gamma))$ and $W_j^T(\gamma) \equiv W_j(T^N(\gamma), 0)$, similarly for workers. This difference is nonnegative iff $\tau^T(\gamma) \geq \tau^t(\gamma)$ or, using the definitions in Section 2, iff

$$\sum_{i\in L} T_i^N(\gamma) \geq \sum_{i\in L} t_i^{Nt}(\gamma)\pi_i'(p_i + t_i^{Nt}(\gamma)) \tag{C.3}$$

so γ^w is implicitly defined as the lowest $\gamma > \gamma^*$ where this expression holds with equality. We now show that if γ^* exists (i.e., under the conditions in Proposition 3) then a $\gamma^w > \gamma^*$ also exists.

Step 2: To show when (C.3) holds we first show that on aggregate, $W^t > W^T$. To do so, we first show that $C_i^{Nt} < C_i^N$ for all $i \in L$. Since the logic is the same for all i we omit the subscript. From (7) we have $\Psi'(C^N) = \frac{a\beta}{1-\beta}$ when only T is used. The contract curve when only t is used is defined by $\frac{G_t}{G_C} = \frac{V_t}{V_C}$, implying that $\Psi'(C^{Nt}) = \frac{a\beta}{1-\beta} + \frac{at\pi''(p+t)}{(1-\beta)\pi'(p+t)}$. Therefore $\Psi'(C^{Nt}) - \Psi'(C^N) = \frac{at\pi''(p+t)}{(1-\beta)\pi'(p+t)} > 0$ at any given γ, where the inequality follows from π' and $\pi'' > 0$. So $C^{Nt} < C^N$ because $\Psi'' < 0$.

To show that $W^t(\gamma) \geq W^T(\gamma)$ for all $\gamma \leq \gamma^*$ and some $\gamma > \gamma^*$ we first consider $\gamma \leq \gamma^*$. From the definition of γ^* in (11) we have $G(0, t^{Nt}(\gamma), C^{Nt}(\gamma)) \geq G(T^N(\gamma), 0, C^N)$ for $\gamma \leq \gamma^*$ so, from the definition of G in (5) we then have

$$W^t(\gamma) - W^T(\gamma) \geq \frac{\Psi(C^N) - \Psi(C^{Nt}(\gamma))}{a} > 0$$

where the first inequality is true for $\gamma \leq \gamma^*$ and the second follows from $C_i^{Nt} < C_i^N$ for all i and γ. Since the last inequality is strict and W is continuous in γ there also exist some $\gamma > \gamma^*$ s.t. $W^t > W^T$.

To verify (C.3), we use $W^t(\gamma) \geq W^T(\gamma)$, and the definition of W to obtain the following expression for all $\gamma \leq \gamma^*$ and some $\gamma > \gamma^*$ (after cancelling out common terms)

$$\sum_{i\in L} \pi_i(p_i + t_i^{Nt}(\gamma)) - \frac{\tau^t(\gamma)}{1-\beta} \geq \sum_{i\in L} \pi_i(p_i) + \sum_{i\in L} T_i^N(\gamma) - \frac{\tau^t(\gamma)}{1-\beta}$$

Simplifying and rearranging we obtain

$$\begin{aligned}\frac{\beta}{1-\beta}\sum_{i\in L} T_i^N(\gamma) &\geq \sum_{i\in L}\left[\pi_i(p_i) - \pi_i(p_i + t_i^{Nt}(\gamma))\right] + \frac{\sum_{i\in L} t_i^{Nt}(\gamma)\pi_i'(p_i + t_i^{Nt}(\gamma))}{1-\beta} \\ &> \sum_{i\in L} -t_i^{Nt}(\gamma)\pi_i'(p_i + t_i^{Nt}(\gamma)) + \frac{\sum_{i\in L} t_i^{Nt}(\gamma)\pi_i'(p_i + t_i^{Nt}(\gamma))}{1-\beta} \\ &= \frac{\beta}{1-\beta}\sum_{i\in L} t_i^{Nt}(\gamma)\pi_i'(p_i + t_i^{Nt}(\gamma))\end{aligned}$$

where the inequality in the second line is due to $\pi'' > 0$. To see this we use a first order approximation and note that since $\pi'' > 0$ we have $\pi_i(p_i) > \pi_i(p_i + t_i^{Nt}(\gamma)) - t_i^{Nt}(\gamma)\pi_i'(p_i + t_i^{Nt}(\gamma))$. Replacing this expression for $\pi_i(p_i)$ and simplifying we obtain the second line. Therefore $\sum_{i\in L} T_i^N(\gamma) > \sum_{i\in L} t_i^{Nt}(\gamma)\pi_i'(p_i + t_i^{Nt}(\gamma))$ for all $\gamma \leq \gamma^*$ and some $\gamma > \gamma^*$, which according to (C.3) implies that unorganized voters prefer t.

PROPOSITION 4. (Use of inefficient policies in a representative democracy)

Both candidates have preferences given by G in (5) so they value lobby goods. The value of these goods is initially higher than the cost of transfers (that is, $\lim_{C\to 0} \Psi'(C) > a\beta/(1-\beta)$), so there is a surplus to bargain over with *each* individual SIG in the second stage, as is clear from Figure 1.

Therefore for any $\gamma > 0$ the politicians are better off with some transfers since $g^N(\gamma > 0) > g^0$. As we have shown in Proposition 3 when γ^* exists then a politician with $\gamma^t \leq \gamma^*$ prefers t (weakly if $\gamma^t = \{0, \gamma^*\}$) and T if $\gamma^T > \gamma^*$.

Consider two candidates $\gamma^t = \gamma^* - \delta < \gamma^* + \delta = \gamma^T$. We now show that the unorganized voters prefer the inefficient policy if γ^t is not too weak relative to γ^T, i.e., if $\gamma^T - \gamma^t = 2\delta$ is sufficiently small. In Lemma 2 we showed that the difference in welfare for unorganized voters across policies depends only on the tax revenue they must pay. This now depends both on the policy and the bargaining power of the politician

$$
\begin{aligned}
&\sum_{j\notin L}\left(W_j^t(\gamma^t) - W_j^T(\gamma^T)\right) + W_\ell^t(\gamma^t) - W_\ell^T(\gamma^T) \\
&\quad = \frac{1-\alpha}{1-\beta}\left(\tau^T(\gamma^T = \gamma^* + \delta) - \tau^t(\gamma^t = \gamma^* - \delta)\right) \\
&\quad = \frac{1-\alpha}{1-\beta}\left[\tau^T(\gamma^*) - \tau^t(\gamma^*) + \left[\frac{\partial \tau^T(\gamma^*)}{\partial \gamma} + \frac{\partial \tau^t(\gamma^*)}{\partial \gamma}\right]\delta + \xi(\delta)\right] \\
&\quad > 0 \text{ for all } \delta \in (0, \bar{\delta}),
\end{aligned}
$$

where the second line is the Taylor expansion of τ^T and τ^t around γ^* (so ξ is the difference between any higher order terms, i.e., $\Sigma_{n=2,3,\ldots} \frac{\partial^n \tau^T(\gamma^*)}{\partial \gamma^n}\delta^n - \frac{\partial^n \tau^t(\gamma^*)}{\partial \gamma^n}\delta^n$). The last inequality follows from the fact that $\tau^T(\gamma^*) > \tau^t(\gamma^*)$ (proved in Lemma 2) and, because $\tau^T(\gamma)$ and $\tau^t(\gamma)$ are continuous functions at γ^*, this difference offsets the higher order terms for a sufficiently small $\delta \in (0, \bar{\delta})$. To see that $\tau^T(\gamma)$ and $\tau^t(\gamma)$ are continuous recall that $\tau^T(\gamma^*) = \sum_{i\in L} T_i^N(\gamma^*)$ and each T_i^N is a continuous function of γ. Similarly, $\tau^t(\gamma) = \sum_{i\in L} t_i^{Nt}(\gamma)\pi_i'(p_i + t_i^{Nt}(\gamma))$ is continuous in γ since t_i^{Nt} is continuous in γ at γ^* and π_i' is continuous in prices. ■

D. *Simulation.*

The following simulation shows that the condition in Proposition 3 can be satisfied so the government prefers production subsidies over lump-sum transfers when Ψ is sufficiently concave.

ASSUMPTIONS: $\Psi \equiv C^{\psi}$, $\psi \in (0,1)$; $q \equiv k^{1-\alpha} l^{\alpha} \Longrightarrow \pi(p+t) = (1-\alpha)(p+t)k((p+t)\alpha)^{\frac{\alpha}{1-\alpha}}$, $\alpha = 0.5$.

Slope condition for efficient transfer

$$\text{(D.1)} \qquad \lim_{\gamma \to 0} -\Omega^T/\Omega'^T = \lim_{\gamma \to 0} (V - v^0)\Psi'(C^N) = (T^m - C^N)a\beta/(1-\beta).$$

The first equality is due to the definition of Ω, the second is due to the first-order condition in (6). The last equality follows from the definition of V^{mT}, where T^m represents the maximum transfer the lobby can extract and is defined by

$$G(T=0, t=0, C=0) = G(T^m, t=0, C^N)$$
$$T^m = \Psi(C^N)/[a\beta/(1-\beta)].$$

Using (D.1), Ψ and the solution to C^N in (6) we obtain the general condition to be evaluated:

$$\text{(D.2)} \qquad \lim_{\gamma \to 0} -\Omega^T/\Omega'^T = \Psi(C^N) - C^N a\beta/(1-\beta)$$
$$= \left(\frac{1-\psi}{\psi}\right) \frac{a\beta}{1-\beta} \exp\left[(\psi - 1)^{-1} \ln \frac{a\beta/(1-\beta)}{\psi}\right].$$

Slope condition for the inefficient transfer

$$\text{(D.3)} \qquad \lim_{\gamma \to 0} -\Omega^t/\Omega''^t = \lim_{\gamma \to 0} (V - v^0)\Psi'(C^{Nt})$$
$$= \lim_{\gamma \to 0} (V^{mT} - v^0) \frac{a(\beta\pi'(p+t) + t\pi''(p+t))}{(1-\beta)\pi'(p+t)}.$$

The first equality is due to the definition of Ω; the expression for $\Psi'(C^{Nt})$ in the second equality is derived from the efficiency condition: $G_t/G_C = V_t/V_C$. Using the definition of V we obtain $V^{mt} - v^0 = \pi(p + t^N(\gamma = 0)) - C^{mt} - \pi(p)$ where C^{mt} is the minimum level of the good provided by the lobby required to maintain the government at the reservation utility. Using the definition of G and the condition $G(T=0, t=0, C=0) = G(T=0, t=t^N(\gamma=0), C^{mt})$ we can write C^{mt} as

$$\text{(D.4)} \qquad C^{mt} = \Psi^{-1}(-a(\pi(p + t^N(\gamma = 0)) - \pi(p)$$
$$- t\pi'(p + t^N(\gamma = 0))/(1-\beta))).$$

TABLE A.1
SIMULATION RESULT FOR THE CHOICE OF LUMP-SUM VERSUS PRODUCTION SUBSIDIES

	$\lim_{\gamma\to 0} -\frac{\Omega^x}{\Omega^{x\prime}}$		
ψ	$x = t$		$x = T$
1/2	0.46	$<$	0.75
1/5	0.72	$>$	0.70

Parameters: $a = p = k = 1$, $\beta = 0.25$, $\alpha = 0.5$, $\gamma = 0$.

Using (D.3), $\Psi, \pi(p+t)$, and (D.4) we obtain:

(D.5)

$$\lim_{\gamma\to 0} -\frac{\Omega^t}{\Omega'^t} = \left[\frac{a(\beta\pi'(p+t^N) + t^N\pi''(p+t^N))}{(1-\beta)\pi'(p+t^N)}(\pi(p+t^N) - \pi(p) - C^{mt})\right]_{\gamma=0}$$

$$\lim_{\gamma\to 0} -\frac{\Omega^t}{\Omega'^t} = \left[\frac{a(\beta k((p+t^N)) + t^N k))}{(1-\beta)k(p+t^N)} \times \{0.25(p+t^N)^2 k - 0.25p^2 k - (-a(0.25(p+t^N)^2 k - 0.25p^2 k - 0.5t^N k/(1-\beta)))^{1/\psi}\}\right]_{\gamma=0.}$$

To calculate this we require the equilibrium t, which is obtained using the efficiency condition $G_t/G_C = V_t/V_C$ and (D.4):

$$t^N : \Psi^{-1}(-a(\pi(p+t) - \pi(p) - t\pi'(p+t)/(1-\beta))) = \Psi'^{-1}\left(\frac{a(\beta\pi'(p+t) + t\pi''(p+t))}{(1-\beta)\pi'(p+t)}\right)$$

$$t^N : (-a(0.25(p+t)^2 k - 0.25p^2 k - 0.5tk(p+t)/(1-\beta)))^{1/\psi} = \left(\frac{1}{\psi}\left(\frac{a(\beta k(p+t)\alpha + tk)}{(1-\beta)k(p+t)}\right)\right)^{-1/(1-\psi)}.$$

Evaluating (D.2) and (D.5) at the parameter values shown in Table A.1, we obtain the results listed therein.

REFERENCES

BARON, D., "Majoritarian Incentives, Pork Barrel Programs, and Procedural Control," *American Journal of Political Science* 35 (1991), 57–90.

BEARD, C. A., *An Economic Interpretation of the Constitution of the United States* (New York: The Free Press, 1913).

BECKER, G., AND C. MULLIGAN, "Deadweight Costs and the Size of Government," *Journal of Law and Economics* 56 (2003), 293–340.

Binmore, K., A. Rubinstein, and A. Wolinsky, "The Nash Bargaining Solution in Economic Modelling," *Rand Journal of Economics* 17 (1986), 176–88.

Buchanan, J. M., and G. Tullock, *The Calculus of Consent* (Ann Arbor: University of Michigan Press, 1962).

Chandra, P. "WTO Accession as Commitment: Theory and Evidence from the Choice of Redistribution Policies," University of Maryland Dissertation, 2007.

Coate, S., and S. Morris, "On the Form of Transfers to Special Interests," *Journal of Political Economy* 103 (1995), 1210–35.

Dixit, A., and J. Londregan, "Redistributional Politics and Economic Efficiency," *American Political Science Review* 89 (1995), 856–66.

——, and ——, "The Determinants of Success of Special Interests in Redistributive Politics," *Journal of Politics* 58 (1996), 1132–55.

——, G. M. Grossman, and E. Helpman, "Common Agency and Coordination: General Theory and Application to Government Policy Making," *Journal of Political Economy* 105(4) (1997), 752–69.

Dorian, D., "Bargaining Power and Wage-Employment Contracts in a Unionized Industry," *International Economic Review* 33(3) (1992), 583–606.

Drazen, A., and M. Eslava, "Pork Barrel Cycles," NBER Working Paper 12190, 2006.

Fiorina, M., "Universalism, Reciprocity, and Distributive Policymaking in Majority Rule Institutions," in J. Crecine, ed., *Research in Public Policy Analysis and Management*, Volume 1 (Greenwich, CT: JAI Press, 1981).

Grossman, G. M., and E. Helpman, "Protection for Sale," *American Economic Review* 84 (1994), 833–50.

Kee, H., A. Nicita, and M. Olarreaga, "Estimating Trade Restrictiveness," World Bank Policy Research WP 3840, 2006.

Limão, N., and P. Tovar-Rodriguez, "Policy Choice: Theory and Evidence from Commitment via International Trade Agreements," Mimeo, University of Maryland, 2007.

Maggi, G., and A. Rodriguez-Clare, "The Value of Trade Agreements in the Presence of Political Pressures," *Journal of Political Economy* 106(3) (1998), 574–601.

Mitra, D., "Endogenous Lobby Formation and Endogenous Protection: A Long-run Model of Trade Policy Determination," *American Economic Review* 89(5) (1999), 1116–34.

North, D., "Economic Performance through Time," *American Economic Review* 84 (1994), 359–68.

OECD, "Agricultural Policies in OECD Countries," (Paris: OECD, 2005).

Rodrik, D., "Taxes, Subsidies, and Welfare with Endogenous Policy," *Journal of International Economics* 21 (1986), 285–99.

——, "Political Economy of Trade Policy," in G. M. Grossman and K. Rogoff, eds., *Handbook of International Economics*, Volume 3 (Amsterdam: North-Holland, 1995), 1457–94.

Shepsle, K., and B. Weingast, "Political Preferences for the Pork Barrel: A Generalization," *American Journal of Political Science* 25 (1981), 96–112.

Staiger, R. W., and G. Tabellini, "Discretionary Trade Policy and Excessive Protection," *American Economic Review* 77 (1987), 823–37.

Tsebelis, G., *Veto Players: How Political Institutions Work* (Princeton: Princeton University Press, 2002).

Tullock, G., *Economics of Income Redistribution* (Boston MA: Kluwer-Nijhoff, 1983).

Weingast, B., K. Shepsle, and C. Johnsen, "The Political Economy of Benefits and Costs: A Neoclassical Approach to Distributive Politics," *Journal of Political Economy* 89 (1981), 642–64.

Wilson, J., "Are Efficiency Improvements in Government Transfer Policies Self-Defeating in Political Equilibrium," *Economics and Politics* 2 (1990), 241–58.

Chapter 8

Inequality and endogenous trade policy outcomes ☆

Nuno Limão [a,*], Arvind Panagariya [b,1]

[a] *Economics Department, University of Maryland and CEPR, College Park 20742, USA*
[b] *School of International and Public Affairs, Columbia University, 420 West 118th Street, New York NY 10027, USA*

Received 8 March 2004; received in revised form 23 April 2006; accepted 11 July 2006

Abstract

An enduring puzzle in international economics is why trade interventions are biased in favor of import-competing rather than export sectors and therefore restrict trade. In this paper, we show that if the government's objective reflects a concern for inequality then trade policy generally exhibits an anti-trade bias. Importantly, under neutral assumptions, the mechanism that we analyze generates the anti-trade bias independently of whether factors are specific or mobile across sectors. The mechanism also generates an anti-trade bias between large countries even after they sign reciprocal trade agreements that eliminate any terms-of-trade motivation for the use of trade protection.

Keywords: Anti-trade bias; Inequality; Protectionism; Trade policy

JEL classification: F1; H2

☆ We thank Stephanie Aaronson, Pravin Krishna, Devashish Mitra, Thierry Verdier, two anonymous referees and participants at the Econometric Society Summer meetings in Evanston for their useful comments and suggestions. We are particularly grateful to the editor, Jonathan Eaton, for the extreme help and extensive comments on an earlier version of the paper.
* Corresponding author. Tel.: +1 301 405 7842.
E-mail addresses: Limao@econ.umd.edu (N. Limão), ap2231@columbia.edu (A. Panagariya).
[1] Tel.: +1 212 854 5354; fax: +1 212 854 5765.

0022-1996/$ - see front matter © 2006 Elsevier B.V. All rights reserved.
doi:10.1016/j.jinteco.2006.07.004

Originally Published in *Journal of International Economics* 72, pp. 292–309.

1. Introduction

An enduring puzzle in international trade is why trade policy has an anti-trade bias (Rodrik, 1995).[2] The conventional explanations focus on some motive to redistribute income but fail to address why the policy makers would prefer to redistribute in favor of the import rather than the export sector. Ironically, the current leading political economy model–Grossman and Helpman (1994) (GH)–actually predicts a pro-trade bias (Levy, 1999).

In this paper, we demonstrate that if the government objective reflects a preference for equity then its trade policy will exhibit an anti-trade bias (ATB) on average. Although trade policy is not the first-best instrument to reduce inequality it is one with a relatively low political cost. In the opinion polls, it continues to receive substantial public approval. This is true not only in the US (Freeman, 2002) but in other countries as well. In fact, the perception that trade causes inequality is often used as one of the central arguments of the "anti-globalization" movement (Sen, 2002; Ravallion, 2003). Moreover, the fact that import protection is often higher in sectors with a large share of low-skill, low-wage workers, strongly suggests that many governments take inequality into account when setting trade policy.[3]

As a prelude to our basic argument, consider the thought experiment that Levy (1999) uses to establish a pro-trade bias in the GH model. Assume two non-numeraire goods, 1 and 2, completely symmetric in consumption and production. Let their initial prices in terms of the numeraire good equal unity. When the world prices are also unity, there is no trade. If we now decrease the specific factor endowment of good 1 and increase that of good 2 by the same proportion the economy will import 1 and export 2. As GH show, if capital owners in sectors 1 and 2 are organized, they lobby and obtain a tariff and an export subsidy respectively. However, given the larger output in the export sector, the subsidy is larger than the import tariff and thus exports expand by more than imports contract implying a pro-trade bias.[4]

Our analysis differs from GH in two key respects. First, we employ the standard two-sector general-equilibrium model that admits the usual substitution possibilities between the import and

[2] The anti-trade bias in developing countries is apparent from the observation that trade reform by them has been followed by an expansion of their trade and more generally for other countries by the focus of the GATT/WTO negotiations on the removal of trade *barriers* rather than trade stimuli. Rough estimates of tariffs versus subsidies in industrial goods for the United States do point to an anti-trade bias: the estimated ad valorem equivalent of the main tax incentives for US exporters, such as the Foreign Sales Corporation Tax, was 1% in 1996 (Desai and Hines, 2000, p.34) whereas the ad valorem equivalent tariff was 2.2% <www.usitc.gov>. As Panagariya (2005) has pointed out recently, contrary to popular perceptions, even agriculture turns out to be subject to much higher levels of tariffs than export subsidies worldwide.

[3] See for example Baldwin (1985) for evidence on the US and Ray (1981) for the US, Canada, UK, Germany, Belgium, Italy, France and Japan. Goldberg and Pavcnik (2004) report a similar finding for many developing countries. Baldwin (1985) concludes that "models [of trade policy] that include behavior based either on long-run self-interest or concern for the welfare of other groups and the state are also necessary to account for the actions of voters and public officials." (p.174) Dutt and Mitra (2002) find that lagged inequality has a positive and significant effect on the tariff level for capital-abundant countries in a cross-section. They find the opposite for labor-abundant ones. More broadly, in a review of the literature on fairness Fehr and Schmidt (2001, p.1) conclude that there is now "overwhelming [experimental] evidence that systematically refutes the self-interest hypothesis [that all people are exclusively motivated by their material self-interest]. The evidence suggests that (...) concerns for fairness and reciprocity cannot be ignored in social interactions."

[4] The GH model does not rule out the *possibility* of ATB. For instance, if there is only one non-numeraire good, the only factor that lobbies is the one specific to this sector. If this good is imported then there is an ATB. But this is generated by denying the export sector the right to lobby since it uses only labor, which is assumed not to lobby.

export sectors. This is important because the ATB puzzle is inherently a general equilibrium issue about redistribution across these sectors.[5] Second, we model a concern for inequality in the government's objective. As we show in Limão and Panagariya (2004), the first modification by itself introduces the possibility of ATB when, as in GH, the government assigns a larger weight to the specific factors in its objective function. If the government weighs all factors equally, however, the general-equilibrium model generally leads to neither anti- nor pro-trade bias. In the present paper, we show that incorporating the concern for inequality introduces ATB even when the government does not favor one or more factors over others.

Thus, begin with a standard two-sector specific-factors economy that is a replica of the world. To neutralize any other motives for ATB assume that the economy is small and the two sectors are initially symmetric. This implies that the relative price of good 1 under autarky is unity at home and abroad and there is no incentive for trade. If the autarky distribution of income among the three production factors is equal, there is initially no incentive to set a tariff or import subsidy even if the government has an inequality concern.[6]

Next, allow an exogenous reduction in the relative price of good 1 in the rest of the world so that the small country now imports good 1 and exports good 2. In the absence of any intervention, the price change causes a decline in the share of K_1 (the factor specific to the import sector 1) in GDP and a rise in the share of K_2. The share of labor in GDP may rise or fall but its change is bounded by the changes of the specific factors. As a result, in the free trade equilibrium, K_2 has the highest share, followed by labor and then K_1. The introduction of a tariff increases the domestic price of the import and this reverses some of the inequality. Thus trade policy exhibits ATB if the government has some concern for inequality.

Perhaps less obviously, a tariff will be the outcome even if the trade shock is not a price change. We demonstrate that other common trade shocks (e.g. shocks to endowments or Hicks-neutral technical change) also lead a government with a concern for inequality to adopt a protectionist policy. The intuition is simple. All these shocks reduce the income of the factor used specifically in the import sector and increase it for the one used in the export sector. The change for the mobile factor share is generally bounded by these two changes. The tariff has the exact opposite effect so it can undo the inequality generated by a variety of shocks. We develop our results in parallel for the specific-factors and the Heckscher–Ohlin (HO) model. This is important because the HO model may be more relevant in determining trade policy preferences in some countries and certainly in longer time horizons, as recent evidence shows (Scheve and Slaughter, 2001; O'Rourke, 2003).

The role of inequality in generating an ATB is best shown in a small symmetric economy where all other motives are neutralized. However, these exact size and symmetry conditions are unlikely to be met in practice. Therefore, to determine whether inequality can explain the ATB observed in a majority of countries, we analyze the case of countries that are large or have any arbitrary initial income distribution. The results extend to a two-country context after we neutralize the terms-of-trade motive for protection. In the general case where preferences, technologies and endowments are unrestricted and therefore permit any initial distribution of income, we may obtain either a pro- or an anti-trade bias. However, we can still establish a

[5] In the GH quasi-linear setup all substitution occurs between the numeraire and non-numeraire goods. According to Dixit et al. (1997, p.754) "the assumption of quasi-linearity makes the model unsuitable for analyzing distribution and transfer policies that are of the essence in public finance and political economy."

[6] Unless otherwise stated, we assume throughout that the ownership of each factor is equally divided among equal number of individuals so that the equality of factor shares leads to an entirely equal income distribution.

likelihood result. We show that if all autarkic income distributions are equally likely, the probability of ATB exceeds 0.5.

One interesting point about the ATB result in the asymmetric case is that it does not require that opening to trade will increase inequality. This is important because in theory moving from autarky to free trade can increase or decrease inequality. Moreover, the recent evidence of increases in trade volumes on inequality is ambiguous.[7] Our results also highlight the potentially important endogeneity problem with some recent studies that try to estimate the effect of trade policy reforms on inequality.[8]

The existing literature on ATB in trade policy is sparse. Eaton and Grossman (1985) show that ATB can result when a government uses trade policy as insurance to maximize expected welfare across different realizations of the terms-of-trade (TOT). The role for trade policy arises due to the absence of perfect insurance markets and ex-post differences in individual welfare resulting from the irreversible allocation of capital between the sectors based on ex-ante TOT. The insurance motive and hence ATB in their model disappears if capital is mobile across sectors, i.e. in the long run.[9] We view the insurance motive for protection as more appropriate for explaining short-term contingent protection, e.g. safeguards, rather than the long-term bias of trade policy towards import protection. As such our model is motivated by a concern for inequality. To sharpen this distinction, our model has no uncertainty and the factor owners have constant marginal utility of income. Moreover, we show that ATB is present even in the long run when capital is freely mobile across sectors.

Mayer (2002) relies on a revenue motive to generate ATB. Although the high administrative cost of raising revenue from domestic taxes is an important reason for the use of tariffs in the early stages of development its importance is negligible for developed countries. Moreover, the revenue motive cannot explain the frequent use of quantity constraints, which generally do not generate revenue. Tovar-Rodriguez (2005) shows that the pro-trade bias prediction in the GH model is reversed if individuals are sufficiently loss averse.[10]

[7] Barro (2000) finds a positive correlation between openness and inequality in a panel of countries. Dollar and Kraay (2004) find small or no effects. For a survey of the effect of trade on wage inequality see Feenstra and Hanson (2003).

[8] Goldberg and Pavcnik (2004) report that most recent work on developing countries finds that trade reforms coincide with increases in relative inequality. Milanovic and Squire (2005) find some evidence that tariff reductions increase inequality in poor countries and the reverse in rich ones.

[9] Eaton and Grossman (1985) appeal to moral hazard and adverse selection to justify the absence of insurance markets. However, as Dixit (1989) shows, when the underlying failure that leads to the missing markets is explicitly modeled the welfare effects of trade policy as insurance can be ambiguous. The social welfare maximization in Eaton and Grossman can be given further micro-foundations in a political economy framework. For example, Rotemberg (2003) assumes that individuals are altruistic and so vote on a trade policy as if maximizing a social welfare function. He then shows that a tariff emerges if the mobile factor is unaffected by a tariff and is the median voter. The result relies on capital immobility and decreasing marginal utility, as in Eaton and Grossman.

[10] Building on the informal argument in Olson (1983), a recent body of literature (e.g. Grossman and Helpman, 1996) formally analyzes the incentives to lobby for protection in sunset versus sunrise industries. In the sunrise industries, the incentive to lobby declines since new entrants would share in the rents so created without having to pay the costs of lobbying. In sunset industries, the only way to maintain normal profits even in the absence of entry may be protection so that free riding on the cost of lobbying may be overcome. This literature does not directly address the issue of ATB, however, unless we equate the sunset industries with import-competing industries and sunrise industries as export industries. But at least within a model that assumes perfect competition, this equation is uncomfortable since in equilibrium, both types of industries make normal profits. Other models, notably Mayer (1984) and Ethier (2004), predict ATB under certain conditions. But these are possibility results since in neither case is there a *presumption* that those conditions are more likely to be satisfied.

Conceptually, it is also important to distinguish between a government objective that exhibits concern for inequality and one that exhibits a status quo bias, such as Corden's (1974, pp 107–9) "conservative social welfare function". As Corden puts it, the latter requires that "any significant absolute reductions in real incomes of any significant section of the community should be avoided." He attributes the *maintenance*, rather than the *introduction*, of many tariffs to such an objective function. The government objective we model differs from a conservative objective function along at least two important dimensions. First, it exhibits symmetry across different individuals with identical incomes. Second, it places a positive value on the decrease in incomes of some groups if this helps to redistribute income towards lower-income groups. Therefore, the two objective functions generate quite different implications for ATB, as we show in the Appendix.[11]

The paper is organized as follows. In Section 2, we outline the model and provide general conditions for ATB. In Section 3 we prove the basic result that the same shock that leads a country to trade also causes ATB if the government has a concern for inequality. In Section 4 we extend the result to the large and asymmetric economy. In Section 5, we conclude.

2. The model

2.1. Economic structure

Consider an economy with two goods, $i=1, 2$, produced according to a constant returns technology. We label the import good (determined endogenously) as 1 and let t denote the import tariff ($t>0$) or subsidy ($t<0$). By choice of units, we set the world price of each good equal to unity so the domestic price of the import is $1+t$. The supply-side is summarized by the standard revenue function $R(1+t, 1;\bar{\mathbf{J}})$, where throughout, the first two arguments refer to the prices of goods 1 and 2 respectively. The factor endowment vector–denoted by $\bar{\mathbf{J}}$–is equal to $(\bar{K}_1, \bar{K}_2, \bar{L})$ for the specific factors model and $(\bar{K}, \bar{L})$for the HO model.

There is specialization in the ownership of each factor and we represent the utility of individuals that own factor j by $U^j=U(\mathbf{C}^j)$ where $\mathbf{C}^j$ denotes the consumption vector of group j. Preferences are identical for all groups and $U(.)$ is linear homogeneous. The consumption decision of group j is summarized via a standard expenditure function, $e(1+t, 1)U^j$. Finally, we assume that tariff revenue is redistributed in exact proportion to each group's earned factor incomes in order to neutralize its use for redistribution purposes.[12] The expenditure–revenue equality for each group j is then given by

$$e(.)U^j = \theta^j\Big[R(.) + t\Big(e_1(.)\sum\nolimits_j U^j - R_1(.)\Big)\Big]\ \forall_j \tag{1}$$

where e_1 (.) and R_1 (.) are the partial derivatives with respect to the domestic price of good 1. The term in square brackets represents total income, which is equal to the sum of revenue from production, $R(.)$, and trade taxes. We denote the share of factor j in earned income by θ^j. It is defined as

$$\theta^j \equiv R_j(.)\bar{J}/R(.)\ \forall_j \tag{2}$$

[11] The importance of the conservative social welfare function in perpetuating tariffs once granted for revenue reasons can be easily overstated. Changes in technology, domestic policies, endowments, etc., constantly shift the fortunes of individuals. It is difficult to argue under such shocks that tariffs are held in place for decades to maintain the status quo.

[12] Symmetrically, if the outcome is a subsidy, each factor owner bears a burden in proportion to its earned income.

where $\bar{J}$ is an element of the endowment vector $\bar{\mathbf{J}}$ defined above and R_j (.) is the partial derivative of R(.) with respect to factor j and therefore the return received by its owner.

For any given tariff, we can solve Eq. (1) for each group's utility level to obtain

$$U^j = \theta^j[R(.)-tR_1(.)]/[e(.)-te_1(.)] \; \forall_j \tag{3}$$

The key question we address next, therefore, is how t is determined.

2.2. Equilibrium trade policy

We describe the political economy side of the model via a political support function (Hillman, 1982; Long and Vousden, 1991), which, as GH and others have shown, can be obtained by modeling the interaction of lobbies and the government from first principles. This representation allows us to focus directly on the conditions for ATB and has the advantage of accommodating alternative theories of demand for trade policy.[13]

Thus, taking $\mathbf{U}$ as the vector of utilities implied by Eq. (3), we denote the government's objective by

$$G = G(\mathbf{U}(t)) \tag{4}$$

The equilibrium tariff maximizes Eq. (4). To determine if there is ATB we examine the first order condition at $t=0$

$$[\mathrm{d}G/\mathrm{d}t]_{t=0} = [R(.)/e(.)]_{t=0}\left[\sum_j G_j(.)\theta_t^j\right]_{t=0} \tag{5}$$

where θ_t^j is the partial derivative of the share in Eq. (2) with respect to t. The marginal contribution of each factor owner's utility to the government's objective is denoted by the partials G_j. The latter play a key role in determining the ATB and henceforth we refer to G_j (t=0,.) as the *political weight* of factor j. So, a tariff is preferred to an import subsidy if the political weighted sum of the changes in factor shares due to the tariff is positive. In the next section we show that a concern for inequality generates endogenous political weights that satisfy this condition and thus such a concern yields a trade policy with ATB. To do so it is useful to re-write Eq. (5) in a form that highlights the redistribution effects of a tariff by noting that the factor shares sum to unity, and so the sum of their partials with respect to t is zero.

$$[\mathrm{d}G/\mathrm{d}t]_{t=0} = [R(.)/e(.)]_{t=0}\left[\sum_j (G_j - G_L)\theta_t^j\right]_{t=0} \tag{6}$$

Combining Eq. (6) with the standard result that a tariff increases the income share of the factor used intensively in the import sector and lowers it for the factor used intensively in the export sector, we obtain sufficient conditions for ATB. We summarize these in Lemma 1, on which we rely to analyze the effect of inequality on ATB. This lemma could similarly be used to investigate if an ATB arises under alternative government objectives.

Lemma 1. *(General conditions for anti-trade bias) In a two-sector economy where the government maximizes a political support function G(**U**(t)) the trade policy has an anti-trade bias*

[13] Most models do not explain why trade policy is chosen for redistribution (Rodrik, 1995). The same is true of this model. However, trade policy may be the optimal redistribution instrument. Feenstra and Lewis (1991) show this when the government is uncertain about individual endowments.

if either (a) the factor that is used intensively in the import sector has a larger political weight than the factor used intensively in the export sector and the two factors are fully mobile across sectors or (b) the specific factor used in the import sector has a larger political weight than the specific factor used in the export sector and the political weight of the mobile factor is bounded by the two.

Proof. Labeling the import as $i=1$, $t>0$ represents an import tariff and it increases the domestic price of 1. When capital is sector-specific the tariff simultaneously increases the return to K_1 and decreases the return to K_2 and thus $\theta_t^{K1}>0>\theta_t^{K2}$, a standard result of the specific factors model. When both factors are mobile then the tariff increases the return to the factor used intensively by the import good and reduces it for the other factor-the standard Stolper–Samuelson effect-thus $\theta_t^K>0>\theta_t^L$ if the import good is K-intensive and $\theta_t^K<0<\theta_t^L$ otherwise. From Eq. (6) it is then obvious that the sufficient conditions for the government to choose $t>0$ are the following

(a) When factors are mobile and the import good is capital-intensive the political weights must satisfy

$$[G_K>G_L]_{t=0} \tag{7}$$

or $G_K<G_L$ if the import is labor-intensive. With two mobile factors this condition is also necessary for $t>0$.

(b) When capital is sector-specific, L is mobile and good 1 is the import the political weights must satisfy

$$[G_{K1}\geq G_L\geq G_{K2}]_{t=0} \tag{8}$$

with at least one strict inequality. □

3. Inequality and anti-trade bias

We now show that if the government's objective reflects a concern for inequality then the resulting endogenous political weights satisfy the conditions in Lemma 1 and the trade policy exhibits an ATB.

3.1. Inequality and the government's objective

We model the government's political support function as follows.

$$G(\mathbf{U})\equiv\alpha(-I(\mathbf{U}))+(1-\alpha)W(\mathbf{U}) \tag{9}$$

where $I(\mathbf{U})$ measures inequality and we define its properties below. The level of overall utility is measured by $W(\mathbf{U})$. To focus on the role of inequality in generating ATB we assume throughout that $W(\mathbf{U})$ is free of any distributional considerations and takes a simple form: the sum of individual utilities.[14] We next introduce

[14] In the longer version of the paper we allow W(.) to take a more general form, which explicitly incorporates other political-economy considerations and give rise to different political weights across factors even if the government has no concern for inequality. For expositional simplicity and clarity, we exclude these considerations here and focus on the simpler case. The longer version is available upon request.

Definition 1. A government has a concern for inequality if $G(\mathbf{U})$ and $I(\mathbf{U})$ in Eq. (9) satisfy the following properties:

- **(a)** Relevance: The government places a strictly positive weight on reducing inequality. Formally, $\alpha \in (0,1]$.
- **(b)** Anonymity: The inequality measure is independent of the identity of individuals and thus symmetric in its arguments. Formally, $I(U^j=a,\ U^{j'}=b,.)=I(U^j=b,\ U^{j'}=a,.)$ for all $j \neq j'$.
- **(c)** Dalton principle: Any regressive transfer increases inequality. Formally, $I(U^j-\delta,\ U^{j'}+\delta,.)>I(U^j,\ U^{j'},.)$ whenever $U^j \leq U^{j'}$ for all $\delta>0$ and $j \neq j'$.
- **(d)** Relative income principle: Equal proportionate changes in the utilities of all individuals leave the inequality measure unchanged. Formally, $I(\beta\mathbf{U})=I(\mathbf{U})$ for $\beta>0$.

In sum, a government has a concern for inequality if it values reductions in a "good" measure of inequality, i.e. one that satisfies the textbook requirements given by the anonymity, Dalton and relative-income principles. Throughout we assume that an identical and constant number of individuals own each factor.[15]

The political weights now reflect the impact of a change in the utility of factor owners on the inequality and aggregate welfare measures. However, since $W(.)$ is the sum of utilities the marginal effect, W_j, is identical for all factors j. So when the government has a concern for inequality the condition for ATB in Eq. (6) is:

$$[\mathrm{d}G/\mathrm{d}t]_{t=0} = [R(.)/e(.)]_{t=0}\left[\sum_j \alpha(I_L - I_j)\theta^j_t\right]_{t=0} \tag{10}$$

Clearly a deviation from free trade occurs only when the government has a concern for inequality. But to show that this implies a tariff rather than an export subsidy we must prove that the endogenous political weights satisfy the conditions in Lemma 1. We first focus on the case of a small symmetric economy in order to neutralize any other possible motives for ATB and then generalize to the large and the asymmetric economy cases.

3.2. Inequality and anti-trade bias in a small, symmetric economy

We model the initial equilibrium such that the country has no incentive either to trade or to use trade policy. We then introduce shocks either to prices, endowments or technologies that generate an incentive to trade and ask whether they also cause the government to adopt a trade policy that exhibits ATB.

The decision to use a tariff depends on its effect on inequality. More precisely, it depends on the effect on inequality of a small redistribution from factor j to L—the term $I_L - I_j$ in Eq. (10). Inequality increases if labor has a higher utility than j and decreases otherwise, as we show in the following lemma.

Lemma 2. *If $I(U)$ is differentiable and satisfies the anonymity and Dalton principles then $\partial I/\partial U^{j'} - \partial I/\partial U^j > 0$ if $\theta^{j'} \geq \theta^j$ for all $j \neq j'$.*

[15] We can normalize this number to unity without loss of generality provided we invoke the population principle, which is also a common requirement for a good inequality measure. This principle requires the inequality measure to remain unchanged when we multiply the number of individuals in each income group by the same number.

Proof. See the Appendix.

This lemma shows how the Dalton principle, that a regressive transfer increases inequality, can be used to derive the marginal effect of trade policy on inequality. One point to note is that the utility of j is a multiple of his factor share and that multiple is common to all factors (see Eq. (3)). This and the assumption of a constant number of individuals implies that throughout we need only compare the factor shares in income to determine if a transfer between two types of factor owner increases inequality.[16] With this we can demonstrate

Proposition 1. *(Inequality and anti-trade bias): Consider a small economy that initially has identical factor income shares and is identical to the rest of the world. If the government has a concern for inequality then shocks to the following variables generate trade and a trade policy that exhibits anti-trade bias: (a) world price (SF and HO), (b) Hicks neutral technology (SF and HO); (c) endowments in the HO model, and (d) specific factor endowments provided the elasticity of substitution between factors in each sector is at least unity.*

Proof. Complete symmetry with the rest of the world in the initial equilibrium ensures that, at $t=0$, there is no trade. Moreover, equal income shares imply that initially $t=0$ is optimal. The shocks in (a)–(d) cause the country to trade if $t=0$. Thus we need only show that those shocks also cause the endogenous political weights to satisfy the conditions for ATB in Lemma 1. For the HO model we require Eq. (7) to hold if the import is capital-intensive, which is equivalent to $\alpha(I_L - I_K) > 0$ when the government maximizes Eq. (9) since $W_L = W_K$. If the government has a concern for inequality then $\alpha > 0$ (relevance) and $I(.)$ satisfies the Dalton principle. Therefore if $\theta^K < \theta^L$ after the shock we can apply Lemma 2 and obtain $I_L - I_K > 0$. As we describe below the shocks (a)–(d) lead to a reduction in θ^K relative to θ^L if the import is K-intensive, so when the initial factor shares are identical, these shocks imply that $\theta^K < \theta^L$. An analogous argument applies if the import is labor intensive (due to the anonymity principle).

Similarly, in the case of the SF model we require the weights to satisfy Eq. (8), which simplifies to $\alpha(I_L - I_{K1}) \geq 0 \geq \alpha(I_L - I_{K2})$ (with at least one strict inequality). These conditions are satisfied since, when good 1 denotes the import, the shocks in (a)–(d) lead to $\theta^{K1} < \theta^L < \theta^{K2}$, as we show below. □

Starting from a no-trade equilibrium characterized by equal factor shares, a shock to prices, technology or endowments will generate trade and also generate inequality. The question is whether that inequality is reduced through the use of a tariff or import subsidy. To see the result within the HO model, consider first the effect of shocks to the relative world price of good 1 or endowments. If the world price of good 1 falls then it is imported and, if it is K-intensive, then $\theta^K < \theta^L$ in the new equilibrium because of the Stolper–Samuelson effect. A similar pattern of inequality results if there is an increase in the labor endowment such that the K-intensive good is imported.[17] Therefore, after either of these trade shocks the government will set a tariff to reduce inequality. An analogous argument applies if the import is L-intensive.

In the case of a Hicks-neutral technology shock the change in the factor shares depends only on the change in the relative factor price at given world prices. An improvement in the production technology

[16] The common multiple in Eq. (3) linking factor shares to utilities and the relative income principle ensure that $I(\mathbf{U})$ is equal to $I(\boldsymbol{\theta})$ and therefore we can focus on the factor shares.

[17] The increase in endowments in the small country does not affect world prices and therefore the domestic prices also remain unchanged. This implies that the wage to rental ratio remains constant (provided the country does not specialize) and thus the share of labor to capital income rises if the labor endowment increases. Recall that we maintain the number of individuals constant throughout so an increase in labor endowment refers to effective units of labor.

of good 2 increases the supply of 2 and decreases that of 1 at constant prices (Johnson, 1955) so 2 becomes the export and 1 the import. The relative demand for the factor used intensively in the import decreases and so does its relative price. So the income share of the factor used intensively in good 1 falls due to the improvement in technology in 2. The resulting increase in inequality is reduced by a tariff.

Consider next the specific-factors model. Because there are three groups and the effect of the tariff on the mobile factor is generally ambiguous it is no longer obvious that the government can use it to offset inequality due to the trade shocks. However, we now show that it will generally be able to do so because these trade shocks affect the specific factors' income by more than labor's and the same is true of the tariff. In the case of a reduction in the world price of good 1 it is evident that a tariff can reverse the resulting inequality because it works as the price change itself. We now turn to the less obvious case of technology and endowment shocks.

A positive Hicks-neutral shock to good 2 leads to its export and increases the share of labor. It also induces some workers to move out of sector 1 thus reducing θ^{K1}. The labor movement partially offsets the initial increase in wages due to the technical change, which implies that θ^L does not rise by as much as θ^{K2}. The latter increases both because of the technical change and the increased labor supply to sector 2. Thus after this shock we have $\theta^{K1} < \theta^L < \theta^{K2}$. This pattern of inequality generates endogenous political weights that satisfy condition (8) in Lemma 1. So the government imposes a tariff on good 1 to reverse some of this inequality. Finally, we also obtain this ordering of income shares and ATB if there is a shock to the specific factors. In this case we require an additional restriction on the elasticity of substitution between factors to ensure that the change in the labor share does not exceed the change in the share of the specific factor whose endowment changes.[18]

The basic insight from Proposition 1 is that all the standard shocks that generate trade in the SF and HO models tend to reduce the income of the factor used intensively (or specifically) in the import sector and do the opposite for the export sector. An import tariff has the reverse effects. Therefore a concern for inequality provides an explanation for the ATB of trade policy. The result is clear and unambiguous for a small economy when we rule out initial asymmetries across factors but it extends to more general cases.

4. Extensions

The key reason to focus on a small economy with income shares that are initially symmetric was to neutralize any other motives for ATB and highlight the role of inequality. However, the exact size and symmetry conditions in Proposition 1 are unlikely to be met in practice. Therefore, to determine whether inequality can explain the ATB actually observed in a majority of countries we extend Proposition 1 to cases when countries are not small and can have any initial income distribution.

4.1. Anti-trade bias in large countries with reciprocal trade liberalization

There is increasing evidence that even small countries have some effect on the prices at which they trade.[19] Therefore we now relax the assumption that world prices are exogenous. For

[18] For example if K_2 increases then θ^{K2} increases at given prices and so does θ^L. As labor moves to sector 2, θ^{K1} falls. The proportionate change in the share of K_2 is greater than that of labor's after an increase in the endowment of K_2 if and only if $\sigma_2 \geq 1 - \sigma_1 L_1 / L_2 - \theta^{L2}(p_2 Q_2 / R)/\theta^L$ where σ_i is the elasticity of substitution in production, L_i is the labor in sector i, θ^{Li} is labor's share in producing i and $p_2 Q_2$ is the value of good 2. Therefore, $\sigma_i \geq 1$ is sufficient to ensure that $\theta^{K1} < \theta^L < \theta^{K2}$ after the endowment shock. The condition follows from algebraic manipulation of these expressions, which can be found, for example, in Bhagwati et al. (1998).

[19] For example, Broda et al. (2006) estimate that both large *and* small countries face finite foreign export supply elasticities for many of their imports.

simplicity we consider a world with two identical countries, home and foreign, that are initially completely symmetric and have identical income shares of all factors. The equilibrium relative price of good 1 is then unity. Because of the initial symmetry there is no motive for trade and the identical income shares of all factors imply that there is initially no motive for a tariff or subsidy.

Endowment and technology changes are now the relevant trade shocks since world prices are endogenous. Since analogous arguments apply to the HO and SF models here we describe only one, an endowment shock in the SF model. Suppose we transfer a fraction of K_2 from foreign to home and a similar fraction of K_1 from home to foreign. Given the symmetry in technology between the sectors, the integrated world equilibrium is unchanged and the free trade price is again unity with home exporting 2 and importing 1. Because the increase of K_2 is exactly offset by the reduction in K_1 and the free trade price remains unity, the real wage and thus the total labor income is unchanged. With the price and wage unchanged, the real return to capital in each sector is also unchanged. So, we have $\theta^{K1} < \theta^{L} < \theta^{K2}$ at home and $\theta^{K1*} > \theta^{L*} > \theta^{K2*}$ in foreign at $t = t^* = 0$. It is simple to establish that symmetric Hicks-neutral technology shocks lead to a similar ranking of shares. For the small economy case this ranking of factor shares was sufficient to establish the conditions for political weights required for ATB in Lemma 1. But we must show whether those are also the relevant conditions for ATB in a large economy.

Given that the countries can now affect world prices their governments have a unilateral incentive to set a tariff. To suppress this motive for an ATB we assume that the tariffs are chosen cooperatively, i.e. to maximize the sum of the objective function in Eq. (9) for the two countries. This assumption implies that the governments internalize the costs imposed on each other from using a tariff to try to improve their terms-of-trade. Moreover, symmetry ensures that the equilibrium tariffs the countries choose are identical and thus leave the world price unchanged at unity. It is then clear that the tariffs are determined by purely internal considerations and precisely as though each country were small. Therefore the conditions for ATB in Lemma 1 and the basic analysis in Subsection 3.2 apply here as well. Since the result is quite similar to Proposition 1 we omit it.[20]

4.2. Anti-trade bias in a small economy: the asymmetric case

We now demonstrate how inequality generates ATB in a more general setting. We show that if initially any factor owner in a small country is as likely to be better or worse off than any other then the probability of using a tariff when trade starts exceeds 0.5. The large country extension can be done along the lines of the last section.

As before, we choose an initial equilibrium with no trade by letting the economy be a replica of the rest of the world. We denote the probability density function (p.d.f.) of the possible initial distribution of factor shares by $f(\boldsymbol{\theta})$.[21] Assuming the p.d.f. is continuous, the probability of an economy starting with perfect equality is exactly zero and we must focus precisely on the cases characterized by initial inequality. To ensure that there is an identical probability that any factor is better or worse off than any other we assume that $f(\boldsymbol{\theta})$ is symmetric. We also assume that the p.d.f. has positive mass on any interval over its support so that its associated cumulative density function $F(\boldsymbol{\theta})$ is strictly increasing. We can now state

[20] We state and prove the result for the large countries more formally in our working paper, Limão and Panagariya (2002).

[21] Since we are not restricting the initial distribution it is possible that the government of this economy would try to induce trade through the use of subsidies. We rule this out by assuming that trading costs are initially prohibitive. In our working paper we examine the case where it is precisely the reduction in such costs that causes trade.

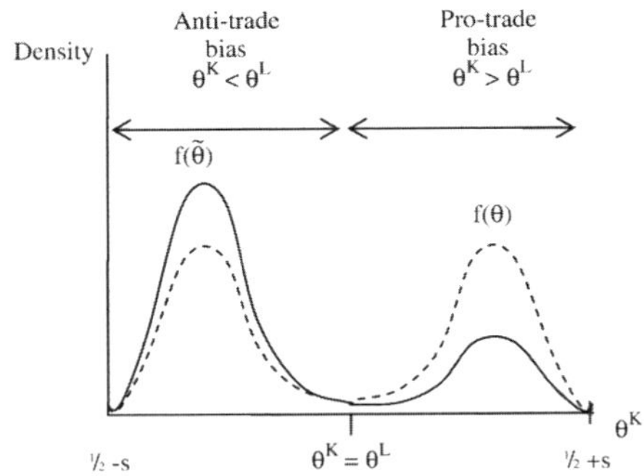

Fig. 1. Initial and post-trade shock share distributions (K-intensive import).

Proposition 2. *(Anti-trade bias with initial inequality): Consider a small economy that is initially identical to the rest of the world and has initial factor income shares that are characterized by a continuous and symmetric p.d.f., $f(\boldsymbol{\theta})$, and a strictly increasing c.d.f., $F(\boldsymbol{\theta})$. If the government has a concern for inequality and neutral expectations about the effect of trade policy on the mobile factor's share in the SF model then shocks to the following variables generate trade and a trade policy that exhibits an anti-trade bias with probability higher than 0.5: (a) world price (SF and HO), (b) Hicks neutral technology (SF and HO); (c) endowments (HO) and (d) specific factor endowments.*

Proof. See the Appendix.

The intuition for the result is simple to illustrate graphically. Consider the initial p.d.f. ($\boldsymbol{\theta}$) represented by the dashed line in Fig. 1. For the HO model this represents the full distribution. It is continuous, initially symmetric and its density is strictly increasing, but otherwise arbitrary. As we have noted previously a shock that leads good 1 to be imported decreases the share of the factor that it uses intensively, say capital. If initially the share of capital was lower than labor's then that will also be the case after the shock. Moreover, even if the capital share was initially slightly higher than labor's, its share after the shock will be lower. Therefore the post-shock density, labelled $f(\tilde{\theta})$, reflects the increased probability that $\theta^K < \theta^L$. This probability now exceeds one half. As we show in Section 3 this relationship between the shares is the necessary and sufficient condition for the government to set $t > 0$ in the HO model. Therefore the probability that the trade policy exhibits ATB also exceeds one half-so an ATB is more likely than a pro-trade bias.[22]

Two comments are in order to explain the result in the context of the SF model. First, recall from Lemma 1 that one of the conditions for ATB is for the political weight to be higher for the factor in the import relative to the export sector. According to Lemma 2 this occurs when the factor share in the import sector is lower. To see that the probability of this event is greater than one half we can use the simplex in Fig. 2 that represents the domain for all possible distributions. After any shock (a)–(d) that leads to trade we have seen that the change in the share for the specific factor in the export sector increases the most followed by labor's and finally by θ^{K1}, which always declines. So for an arbitrary economy with initial distribution at point S^0 the distribution moves in the direction of the arrow. If we were to represent the joint density on the

[22] The proof does not require the support to be fixed nor the mass change to be "smooth" as illustrated in Fig. 1.

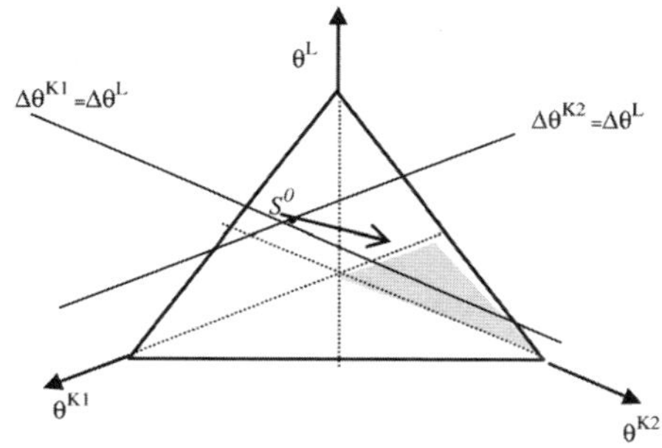

Fig. 2. Income distribution and anti-trade bias in the SF model.

simplex the symmetry requirement would imply that the probability would initially be identical for economies left and right of the θ^L axis. Therefore *all* economies that are initially characterized by $\theta^{K1} < \theta^{K2}$ will remain so, and their density increases after the shock because of economies such as the one represented by S^0.

The second point to note is that knowing the relative shares of the specific factors is sufficient (and necessary) to determine the ATB in the SF model if the government has neutral expectations about the effect of the tariff on the return to the mobile factor. This neutrality condition implies that the government assumes the effect of the tariff on the labor share, θ_t^L, is zero in deciding on the trade policy stance and therefore uses the tariff only if it reduces inequality between the specific capital owners, as is clear from Eq. (10). Thus, since the probability that $\theta^{K1} < \theta^{K2}$ after the shock is greater than one half so is the probability of an ATB in the SF model.[23]

There are two reasons for focusing on the neutral expectations case. First, it is a natural baseline given that it is the most neutral assumption. Second, it may be the relevant case in the setting of policy. Unlike the effect of the tariff on the share of capital income the effect of the tariff on the labor share for a given economy may change over time and the government may not know it at any particular point. It may therefore make its decision based on its expected value of θ_t^L. If it assigns identical probabilities to an increase or decrease and identical absolute values once they are realized then the expected value is zero.[24]

We conclude this subsection by noting the important point that ATB does not depend on the initial trade shock increasing inequality. To see this start again at point S^0 in Fig. 2 and consider a

[23] Note that, unlike Proposition 1, the endowment shock in Proposition 2 does not require a constraint on the elasticity of substitution. This is due to the government's neutral expectations about the effect of the tariff on the mobile factor share.

[24] If the realized value of $\theta_t{}^L$ in the economies discussed above were not always zero there would be cases in which the trade policy would reduce the government's objective ex-post. If governments were extremely averse to this outcome they may choose only to use trade policy if the sufficient conditions in Lemma 1, which are independent of $\theta_t{}^L$, are satisfied. In this case the probability of ATB is still higher than a pro-trade bias. To see this note that the sufficient conditions for ATB correspond to the shaded triangle in Fig. 2 and those for a pro-trade bias correspond to the mirror image left of the θ^L axis. The shocks (a)–(d) in Proposition 2 imply a movement in the direction described for an economy such as S^0. Therefore if an economy is not initially in the region where a pro-trade bias necessarily exists, it cannot be there after the shock. Moreover, some economies in that region are displaced from it by the shock (assuming a continuous and strictly increasing distribution). Conversely, the economies initially in the shaded area where there is necessarily ATB must remain there and its density will in fact increase as the shock pushes others in that direction.

shock that inverts the capital shares but maintains labor's unchanged. Inequality has remained unchanged but the government now sets $t>0$. Similarly we can find cases when inequality falls or increases due to the trade shock and the government still sets a tariff. The intuition is simple. Under autarky there is a latent demand for redistribution but, since only trade policy is available and the economy does not trade, no redistribution occurs. Once the economy starts to trade the government can deploy trade policy. It is important that our results do not hinge on a particular direction of the effect of trade on inequality because the empirical evidence on that issue is mixed, particularly when we look across different countries.

5. Conclusion

In this paper, we show that if the government has an inequality concern then trade policy will generally exhibit an ATB. Despite the existence of more efficient policies to redistribute income, there is considerable empirical evidence that trade policy, which often favors low-skill, low-wage workers, continues to be used for this purpose. Therefore the motive we focus on appears to be an important determinant of trade policy.

A concern with inequality is obviously not the only reason behind the ATB and if we want to address other questions, such as the variation in protection *within* industries in the import sector, we must model the demand side of protection explicitly. Given that ATB is one of the most prominent and nearly universal features of trade policy its motive is likely to interact with other determinants and have important implications in explaining other empirical regularities in the structure of protection. Therefore it is important to ensure that the models that guide such estimation can also predict ATB.

Our analysis is based on inequality across the income shares of various factors of production, which translates into inequality across individuals only if they own equal amounts of a single factor. However, it is possible to extend this framework to analyze the effects of concentrated ownership of factors, as we show in Limão and Panagariya (2002). We believe that our analysis may have interesting implications for the current debate on the effect of trade liberalization on inequality. This literature has generated a considerable amount of conflicting evidence. Our focus on the effect of inequality as a cause for an important feature of trade policy suggests that more attention needs to be given to reverse causality.

Appendix A. Proofs

Lemma 2. If $I(.)$ is differentiable then the second order expansion around the equilibrium prior to a transfer from j to j' is

$$I(U^j-\delta, U^{j'}+\delta) = I(U^j, U^{j'})-[I_j(U^j, U^{j'})-I_{j'}(U^j, U^{j'})]\delta+\varphi \qquad \text{all } j\neq j' \tag{A1}$$

Where $I_j = \partial I/\partial U^j$ and φ represents the second order terms.

If $U^j \leq U^{j'}$ then, according to the Dalton principle in part (c) of Definition 1, we have

$$I(U^j-\delta, U^{j'}+\delta)-I(U^j, U^{j'})>0 \tag{A2}$$

Combining Eq. (A2) with Eq. (A1) and rearranging we obtain

$$I_j(U^j, U^{j'})-I_{j'}(U^j, U^{j'})<\varphi/\delta = (I_{jj}+I_{j'j'})\delta/2-I_jI_{j'}\delta \tag{A3}$$

Where the last equality uses the definition of the second order terms in φ.

Because the Dalton principle applies for all δ it must also apply as $\delta \to 0^+$. The RHS of the last expression in Eq. (A3) approaches 0 as $\delta \to 0^+$ whereas the LHS is unchanged (recall that the derivatives of $I(.)$ are taken around U^j and $U^{j'}$, which are independent of δ). Thus $I_j - I_{j'} < 0$ if $U^j \le U^{j'}$, which is equivalent to requiring that $\theta^j \le \theta^{j'}$ (see Eq. (3)). This applies to all $j \neq j'$ due to the anonymity principle in Definition 1. □

Proposition 2. *Anti-trade bias with initial inequality*

When $t=0$, there is no trade in the initial equilibrium. Ruling out the initial use of trade policy to induce trade, the shocks in (a)–(d) cause the country to trade. To show that $Pr(t>0)>1/2>Pr(t<0)$ we must first calculate the probability for any given trade shock, which we denote by Δx, and sum it over all the possible economies.

$$\Pr(t>0|\Delta x) = \int_{\theta\in\Theta} \Pr(t>0|\Delta x, \boldsymbol{\theta}) f(\boldsymbol{\theta}) \mathrm{d}\boldsymbol{\theta} \tag{A4}$$

We then subtract the value for $\Pr(t<0|\Delta x)$ and show that the difference is positive for any given shock so that if we integrated over all types of shock (i.e. $\Delta x>0$ or $\Delta x<0$ for the different possible shock variables x indicated in (a)–(d)) we would obtain $\Pr(t>0)>1/2>\Pr(t<0)$. With more than two factors the term $\mathrm{d}\boldsymbol{\theta}$ indicates integration over the shares over which the initial distribution is defined and Θ represents its support. Thus we define $\Delta\Pr$ as $\Pr(t>0|\Delta x)-\Pr(t<0|\Delta x)$. It is equal to

$$\Delta\Pr = \int_{\theta\in\Theta} [\Pr(t>0|\Delta x, \boldsymbol{\theta}) - \Pr(t<0|\Delta x, \boldsymbol{\theta})] f(\boldsymbol{\theta}) \mathrm{d}\boldsymbol{\theta} \tag{A5}$$

Using Eq. (10) we can relate the probability of ATB to factor shares. In the HO model we require

$$\mathrm{sign}[\mathrm{d}G/\mathrm{d}t]_{t=0} = \mathrm{sign}[\alpha(I_L - I_K)\theta_t^K]_{t=0} > 0 \tag{A6}$$

From Lemma 1 we know that $t>0$ if sign $(I_L - I_K)_{t=0} > 0$ when the import is K-intensive. This condition is not only sufficient but also necessary for $t>0$ since when the import is K-intensive we have $\theta_t^K > 0$. Both signs are reversed if the import is L-intensive. For the SF model the government's decision depends on its expectation of $\theta_t^{\ L}$. Since the true value may be positive or negative if the government does not know it and places identical weight on both alternatives then on average it expects $\theta_t^L = 0$.[25] This implies that $\theta_t^{K1} = -\theta_t^{K2}$ because $\theta_t^{K1} + \theta_t^{K2} = -\theta_t^L$. Using this we can simplify Eq. (10) to obtain

$$\mathrm{sign}[\mathrm{d}G/\mathrm{d}t]_{t=0} = \mathrm{sign}\left[\alpha(I_{K2} - I_{K1})\theta_t^{K1}\right]_{t=0} > 0 \tag{A7}$$

According to Lemma 2 $I_{K2} > I_{K1}$ iff after the shock we have $\tilde{\theta}_{K1} < \tilde{\theta}_{K2}$ Therefore, we can write $\Delta\Pr$ as

$$\Delta\Pr = \int_{\theta\in\Theta} [\Pr(\tilde{\theta}^{K1} < \tilde{\theta}^{K2}|\Delta x, \boldsymbol{\theta}) - \Pr(\tilde{\theta}^{K1} > \tilde{\theta}^{K2}|\Delta x, \boldsymbol{\theta})] f(\boldsymbol{\theta}) \mathrm{d}\boldsymbol{\theta} \tag{A8}$$

[25] Limão and Panagariya (2004) show that $\theta_t^{\ L} < 0$ if $\theta^{L1}\sigma_1 / \theta^{11} < \theta^{L2}\sigma_2 / \theta^{22}$ and non-negative otherwise, where θ^{ji} represents factor j's share in the production of good i and σ_i represents the factor elasticity of substitution in the production of i.

A similar expression applies for the HO model if we relabeled K_1 and K_2 to represent the factors used intensively in the import and export sectors respectively. A shock that causes good 1 to become the import ensures that all economies with $\theta^{K1} < \theta^{K2}$ in the initial equilibrium have $\tilde{\theta}^{K1} < \tilde{\theta}^{K2}$ in the post-shock equilibrium but the shock causes some economies with $\theta^{K1} = \theta^{K2}$+c initially to have $\tilde{\theta}^{K1} < \tilde{\theta}^{K2}$. This is clear if we take $c \to 0^+$. The existence of such economies is assured by the assumption that $f(\boldsymbol{\theta})$ is continuous and $F(\boldsymbol{\theta})$ is strictly increasing. The symmetric initial distribution of economies then implies that, once we integrate over the full support, the mass of economies with $\tilde{\theta}^{K1} < \tilde{\theta}^{K2}$ after any shock (a)–(d) is higher than the one with $\tilde{\theta}^{K1} > \tilde{\theta}^{K2}$. □

Appendix B. Status quo bias vs. inequality concern

In Proposition 1 we start from a symmetric situation and the tariff partially moves the income distribution back to it. Therefore, we may question whether the same result can be obtained by a government's desire to maintain the status quo, i.e. the utilities prior to the trade shock. We now show that a status quo bias (SQB) is not sufficient to generate ATB in the same situations where ATB is generated by an inequality concern. To do so assume that now $-I(.)$ in Eq. (9) reflects the governments concern for the status quo. More specifically,

Definition 2. A government has a status quo bias if (a) $\alpha \in (0,1]$ and (b) $-I(U^j = U^{j\text{sq}},.) > -I(U^j = U^{j\text{sq}} - \delta,.)$ for each j and $\delta \in (-\infty, \infty)$.

There are three key differences relative to the government with a concern for inequality. First, a government with a SQB does not necessarily weight utilities across different groups symmetrically even when they have identical incomes. Second, the government now favors transfers even if they are regressive provided that they move each group involved towards its respective status quo utility. Third, the government's objective is lowered if all utilities change relative to the status quo even if they do so in the same proportion. Thus, the three key properties of the inequality function are not satisfied by a government with a status quo bias—it does not imply symmetry and it violates the Dalton and relative income principles.

To compare the outcome under a SQB with the inequality result in Proposition 1 consider first a shock to world prices. Since the tariff can exactly offset the change in the world price it can move each factor towards the initial status quo utility. So taking the pre-trade utilities as the status quo a shock to world prices that leads the country to trade also causes ATB if the government has a SQB. This holds whether factors are mobile or not and therefore the outcome when the trading shock is external is similar to the one under an inequality concern.

An important aspect of Proposition 1 was that the inequality concern led to ATB for various shocks that lead to trade and not simply a shock to world prices that can be undone by a tariff. A SQB is not sufficient for ATB precisely because these other shocks that cause ATB under an inequality concern do not necessarily cause it under a SQB. There are two fundamental reasons for this. First, a government with a SQB would like to move individuals back towards their original utility levels and a tariff (or subsidy) will change the utilities of at least a pair of factor owners in different directions. So if the initial trading shock does not change the utilities of that pair of factor owners in opposite directions the tariff or subsidy cannot bring both towards the status quo. To illustrate this consider the case of an increase in an endowment, e.g. labor, in the HO model as analyzed in Proposition 1. At constant world prices factor prices are constant and so is income for capital owners. Therefore the utility for capital owners is unchanged at the status quo after the trade shock and that of workers increases. A tariff will increase U^K and lower U^L given that the country now imports the capital intensive good. But it is possible that for a government with a SQB a small increase in utility towards the status quo is much more valuable if close to it then a similarly small increase when already far removed. This is possible because a SQB places no restriction on symmetry and it allows for the marginal cost from moving away from the status quo to be diminishing.[26] Given this we cannot determine if the same endowment shock that lead to ATB under the inequality concern causes an anti or pro-trade bias under a SQB.

The second, and somewhat related, reason is that in the SF model the tariff has an ambiguous effect on the utility of the mobile factor. So, if a particular shock, e.g. an increase in a specific factor, leads to an increase in labor's utility, and the conditions were such that a tariff decreased it, then the tariff would move labor towards the status quo but a subsidy would be required if the shock were a decrease in the specific factor. So, again the SQB is not sufficient to determine the bias of trade policy.

References

Baldwin, R., 1985. The Political Economy of U.S. Import Policy. MIT Press, Cambridge, MA.

Barro, R., 2000. Inequality and growth in a panel of countries. Journal of Economic Growth 5, 5–32.

Bhagwati, J., Panagariya, A., Srinivasan, T.N., 1998. Lectures on International Trade, 2nd ed. MIT Press, Cambridge, MA.

Broda, C., Limão, N., Weinstein, D., 2006. Optimal Tariffs: The Evidence. NBER WP 12033.

Corden, W.M. 1974. Trade Policy and Economic Welfare. Oxford University Press, Oxford: Clarendon Press.

Desai, A., Hines Jr., J.R., 2000. The Uneasy Marriage of Export Incentives and the Income Tax. NBER WP 8009.

Dixit, A., 1989. Trade and insurance with imperfectly observed outcomes. Quarterly Journal of Economics 104 (1), 195–203.

Dixit, A., Grossman, G., Helpman, E., 1997. Common agency and coordination: general theory and application to government policy making. The Journal of Political Economy 105 (4), 727–769.

Dollar, D., Kraay, A., 2004. Trade, growth and poverty. Economic Journal 114 (493), 22–49.

Dutt, P., Mitra, D., 2002. Endogenous trade policy through majority voting: an empirical investigation. Journal of International Economics 58, 107–133.

Eaton, J., Grossman, G., 1985. Tariffs as insurance: optimal commercial policy when domestic markets are incomplete. Canadian Journal of Economics 18 (2), 258–272.

Ethier, W., 2004. Trade policies based on political externalities: an exploration. PIER Working Paper 04-006.

Feenstra, R., Hanson, G., 2003. Global Production Sharing and Rising Inequality: A Survey of Trade and Wages. In: Choi, E.K., Harrigan, J. (Eds.), Handbook of International Trade. Blackwell, Malden, MA, pp. 146–185.

Feenstra, R.C., Lewis, T.R., 1991. Distributing the gains from trade with incomplete information. Economics and Politics 3, 21–40.

Fehr, E., Schmidt, K., 2001. Theories of fairness and reciprocity: evidence and economic applications. CEPR discussion paper 2703.

Freeman, R., 2002. The Battle over Labor Standards: a Report from the Front. Presented at the First Roundtable: Labor Standard and Trade, IDB and Latin American Trade Network, Buenos Aires, September 20, 2002.

Goldberg, P., Pavcnik, N., 2004. Trade, inequality, and poverty: what do we know? In: Collins, Susan M., Graham, Carol (Eds.), Globalization, Poverty, and Inequality. Brookings Institution Press.

Grossman, G., Helpman, E., 1994. Protection for sale. American Economic Review 84 (4), 833–850.

Grossman, G., Helpman, E., 1996. Rent dissipation, free riding, and trade policy. European Economic Review 40, 795–803.

Hillman, A., 1982. Declining industries and political-support protectionist motives. American Economic Review 72 (5), 1180–1187.

Johnson, H.G., 1955. Economic expansion and international trade. Manchester School 23, 95–112.

Levy, P., 1999. Lobbying and international cooperation in tariff setting. Journal of International Economics 47, 345–370.

Limão, N., Panagariya, A., 2002. Why is there an anti-trade bias in trade policy? WP 02-03. UMD Center for International Economics.

Limão, N., Panagariya, A., 2004. Anti-trade bias in trade policy and general equilibrium. Contributions to Economic Analysis and Policy 3 (1) Article 14.

[26] Research on reference dependent utilities finds experimental evidence of diminishing sensitivity for individuals.

Long, N., Vousden, N., 1991. Protectionist responses and declining industries. Journal of International Economics 30 (1–2), 87–103.
Mayer, W., 2002. Systematic political grass-root support for tariffs. Review of International Economics 10 (4), 657–670.
Mayer, Wolfgang, 1984. Endogenous Tariff Formation. American Economic Review 74 (5), 970–985.
Milanovic, B., Squire, L., 2005. Does tariff liberalization increase wage inequality? Some empirical evidence. NBER Working Paper 11046.
Olson, M., 1983. The political economy of comparative growth rates. In: Mueller, D.C. (Ed.), The Political Economy of Growth. Yale University Press, New Haven.
O'Rourke, K., 2003. Heckscher–Ohlin Theory and Individual Attitudes Towards Globalization. NBER WP 9872.
Panagariya, Arvind, 2005. Liberalizing Agriculture, Foreign Affairs, Special Edition, pp. 56–66.
Ravallion, M., 2003. The debate on globalization, poverty, and inequality: why measurement matters. World Bank Policy Research Working Paper 3038. World Bank, Washington, DC.
Ray, E.J., 1981. Tariff and non-tariff barriers to trade in the United States and abroad. The Review of Economics and Statistics 63 (2), 161–168.
Rodrik, D., 1995. Political economy of trade policy. In: Grossman, Gene M., Rogoff, Kenneth (Eds.), Handbook of International Economics, vol. 3. North-Holland, Amsterdam, pp. 1457–1494.
Rotemberg, J., 2003. Commercial policy with altruistic voters. Journal of Political Economy 111 (1), 174–201.
Scheve, K., Slaughter, M., 2001. What determines individual trade-policy preferences? Journal of International Economics 54, 267–292.
Sen, A., 2002. Globalization, inequality and global protest. Development 45 (2), 11–16.
Tovar-Rodriguez, 2005. The Effects of Loss Aversion on Trade Policy: Theory and Evidence. University of Maryland, Dissertation.

Part III
Externalities and Linkage of Cooperation Across Policies

Chapter 9

Trade policy, cross-border externalities and lobbies: do linked agreements enforce more cooperative outcomes?

Nuno Limão*

Economics Department, University of Maryland, College Park MD 20742, U.S.A.

Received 16 January 2003; received in revised form 17 April 2004; accepted 30 August 2004

Abstract

We analyze whether linking international cooperation in trade policy to environmental policy (or other issues with nonpecuniary externalities) promotes more cooperation in both policies, or whether cooperation in one is strengthened at the expense of the other. In the context of self-enforcing agreements, we show that if the policies are independent in the government's objective function, then linkage promotes cooperation in one policy at the expense of the policy that is easier to enforce under no-linkage. However, if the linked policies are not independent and if these policies are strategic complements, then linkage can sustain more cooperation in both issues than no-linkage. The policies are strategic complements only if (i) the production externality has cross-border effects; (ii) the weight on the externality cost is high; (iii) import competing lobbies are not "powerful".

Keywords: Trade; Linkage; Environment; Labor; Cross-border externality, repeated games

JEL classification: F13; F18; F42; H23; H77

1. Introduction

In trade policy agreements, trade concessions are increasingly made conditional on cooperation in nontrade issues, what is known as "linkage". This trend is clear in

* Tel.: +1 301 405 7842; fax: +1 301 405 3542.
E-mail address: limao@econ.umd.edu.

0022-1996/$ - see front matter
doi:10.1016/j.jinteco.2004.08.009

Originally Published in *Journal of International Economics* 67, pp. 175–199.

multilateral, bilateral, and regional trade agreements. Multilaterally, compliance with intellectual property rights is now enforced through the threat of import barriers, sanctioned by the World Trade Organization (WTO).[1] Moreover, the trend to link will surely intensify. At the end of the last multilateral trade liberalization round, a long list of issues was proposed for similar treatment by the WTO including investment and competition policy, as well as labor and environmental standards. Therefore, linkage has become one of the most important and contentious issues in trade policy.[2]

Perhaps the most obvious role of linkage in agreements is not as an enforcement tool but rather as a side payment. If cooperation on an individual issue benefits country A but hurts B, then the agreement requires either a transfer to B or cooperation in a different issue that benefits B. The use of linkage as a side payment when there are asymmetric benefits across countries is important in the case of regional trade agreements between large and small countries (Abrego et al., 2001 and Limão, 2002b), and it has also been analyzed in the context of environmental agreements (Cesar and de Zewe, 1996).[3]

Despite the prominence of linkage in policy debates, there is little theoretical support for it in terms of its impact on enforcement. The majority of work in the trade literature focuses on static standard trade models to examine what is the impact of harmonizing labor or environmental standards on factor and goods prices or welfare for different countries and economic agents.[4] In this context, one of the most frequent objections to linkage, arising from the optimal policy targeting literature, is that "trade policy measures are usually not the best instruments for achieving social objectives" (Anderson, 1998, p. 244). However, we argue that the important policy question behind linkage is whether the threat of tariffs is effective in *enforcing* more cooperation in another agreement and vice versa. This question cannot be addressed by the targeting literature, which has no basic predictions regarding enforcement.

To explain the motivation and consequences of linkage from an enforcement perspective, we must first understand two key features of international cooperative agreements. First, one of their main objectives is to internalize the costs of countries' actions. When countries impose tariffs, they do not internalize any costs this may have

[1] Bilaterally, the United States and the EU attach investment, environmental and labor clauses to trade preferences given to developing countries via the Generalized System of Preferences. Regionally, NAFTA includes an environmental and a labor agreement.

[2] Including nontrade clauses in trade agreements is not an entirely new phenomenon (Charnovitz, 1998). The main difference is the willingness to enforce those clauses and the availability of effective mechanisms to do so such as the dispute settlement system of the WTO. Certain multilateral environmental agreements such as the Montreal Protocol on CFCs include the threat of trade restrictions in response to noncompliance. However, some of these measures are inconsistent with GATT rules and therefore according to the European Commission "...problems could arise if a country imposed a trade measure for environmental purposes on another WTO member which had not signed the multilateral environmental agreement. The EU wants WTO members to agree that this should not be allowed to happen"<http://trade.info.cec.int/europa/2001newround>.

[3] See also Horstmann et al. (2001) for the effects of linkage in the context of Nash bargaining. Conconi and Perroni (2000) use a cooperative approach to study the effect of linkage on blocking coalitions in a three-country model. For an early analysis of linkage in the political science literature, see Sebenius (1983).

[4] See, for example, Esty (1994) and the volumes edited by Bhagwati and Hudec (1996) and Anderson and Blackhurst (1992).

on foreigners, such as lower export prices. Reciprocal trade liberalization agreements allow countries to internalize these terms-of-trade effects (TOT; Bagwell and Staiger 1999). Similarly, cooperative agreements on issues with nonpecuniary negative externalities are required if that externality has a cross-border effect. Second, international cooperative agreements must be self-enforcing given the absence of a supranational authority to punish violators. That is, these agreements are subject to incentive constraints (IC) which balance the gains of deviating from the agreement against the ensuing losses from retaliation. If countries are not sufficiently patient, then the cooperative first-best is not feasible since the IC bind. Now, since the relevant set of IC for an agreement depends on which policies are available for retaliation, then so must the degree of cooperation.

Given the nature of the agreements considered for linkage, it is clear that understanding its impact on enforcement is crucial. In this regard, one of the central objections put forward by opponents of linkage in trade agreements—that it will lower cooperation in trade policy—is very relevant.[5] Therefore, the central question we ask is the following. Must linkage of trade and nontrade policies cause a reallocation of enforcement or can it actually create enforcement? That is, if in an international agreement we allow for retaliation across two policies, must cooperation in one always be strengthened at the expense of less cooperation in the other, or can linkage sustain more cooperation in both?

To answer this, we focus on a two-country model where the traded goods generate a negative production externality which can have a cross-border effect. The noncooperative equilibrium features inefficiently high tariffs and low externality taxes (e-taxes henceforth) from a global perspective; governments overcome this through cooperative agreements. We assume a status quo of no-linkage, that is retaliation occurs policy-by-policy; hence, for example, noncooperation in e-taxes leads to a punishment in e-taxes but not in tariffs. We then contrast the set of subgame perfect equilibrium policies under no-linkage with those achieved under a linkage regime where noncooperation in *either* policy can trigger punishment in *either* or *both* policies.[6]

Under linkage, the only relevant IC is the one requiring that the gains from deviating in both policies are no higher than the gain from cooperating in both, since if a country decides to deviate in any, it is punished in both, hence it would not be optimal to deviate in only one. Under no-linkage, there are additional IC because of the possibility of deviation in each individual policy. Thus, at a no-linkage solution, the sum of the gains from deviating in each policy cannot exceed the sum of the gains from cooperating in them. Therefore, the joint IC does not bind and linkage creates enforcement if, at the no-linkage solution, the following holds. First, the joint gain from deviation is lower than the sum of

[5] In summarizing the objections to linkage Anderson (1998, p. 244) states that "this activity can lead to an escalation in trade disputes...undermining the global trading system.".

[6] The TRIPs agreement in the WTO allows for the removal of trade concessions if there is an infringement of intellectual property. But the reverse is also explicitly allowed as shown by the WTO's authorization for Ecuador to ignore its TRIPs obligations towards the EU as a retaliation against the EU's trade policy on bananas (WTO Doc. WT/DS27/ARB/ECU on <http://www.wto.org>).

gains from individual deviations, and second, the joint gain from cooperation is higher than the sum of the individual gains from cooperation.

To determine when linkage creates enforcement, we show that if the linked tariffs and e-taxes are strategic complements, so that an increase in tariffs raises the marginal benefit of e-taxes, then the gain from a simultaneous deviation to higher tariffs and lower e-taxes, which occurs under linkage, is lower than the sum of the gains from deviations in each individual policy. Moreover, we also show that for a number of objective functions, including the one in our trade model, strategic complementarity is also sufficient to ensure that the gains from cooperating in both policies exceed the sum of the gains of cooperating in either.

Our main result is not specific to this trade model. It can be applied to other economic problems with a similar structure where agents must enter self-enforcing contracts to repeatedly deal with a cooperation problem over multiple issues that are related even before linkage. The focus on issues that are related, in the sense that we cannot write payoffs for each issue as a function of a single policy, distinguishes our linkage result from previous work. Our approach is motivated by the work on multimarket collusion by Bernheim and Whinston (1990; BW), who show that by aggregating incentive constraints from unrelated markets (so that profits in market A depend only on prices in that market), oligopolists can always achieve at least as much collusion in each market but never more in both.[7] Spagnolo (1999a) extends BW by allowing oligopolists to value the profits from the unrelated markets using a concave function and shows linkage will then enforce more collusion in both markets. Spagnolo (1999b) maps this last result into an international context by interpreting profits as payoffs to unrelated issues that are valued nonlinearly by governments entering into self-enforcing international agreements. However, the payoffs for governments of various policies considered for linkage in international agreements are actually related. Since such cases are particularly important in the trade setting—for example, tariffs on autos and environmental standards in the auto industry—we had to extend and modify previous results in a nontrivial way.

Thus, in our model, where issues are related, linkage can create enforcement and if the new feasible set includes the global optimum, then the equilibrium features more cooperation in both policies. However, if the global optimum is not self-enforcing under linkage, then, even if more cooperation in both policies is *feasible*, the equilibrium may still entail a reallocation of enforcement. To clearly characterize when reallocation occurs and which policy it benefits, we analyze a limit case of our model where, although the e-issue is still trade-related, the policies are independent because the different components of their cross-effect on the government's objective function offset each other. We show that in this case, no creation is possible and linkage always leads to reallocation when there is sufficient asymmetry in the enforceability of each issue under no-linkage. Moreover, if under no-linkage tariffs are easier to enforce than e-taxes, i.e., relatively closer to their cooperative optimum, then linkage leads to more cooperation in e-taxes at the expense of higher tariffs. Although a reallocation of enforcement can occur even if the linked issues are related, this does not imply linkage will have a negative

[7] Phillips and Mason (1992) provide experimental evidence in support of BW.

welfare effect since that reallocation will further cooperate on the issue that is more difficult to enforce.[8]

In the trade literature our result on the creation of enforcement stands in contrast to Ederington (2002), who analyzes a model where social welfare-maximizing governments have access to a tariff and a production tax that addresses an externality with no cross-border effect. He shows that linkage does not enforce more cooperation, because the tariff is the most effective instrument to address the TOT effect. Bagwell and Staiger (2001) also conclude that when the only cross-border externality is due to the TOT, governments simply need to negotiate a market access commitment and should then be free to independently set any policy addressing domestic externalities provided this does not erode the market access negotiated in the WTO, which they argue is ensured by current rules.[9] Independently from our work, Ederington (2001) incorporates a cross-border externality into a parametrized version of his earlier model. He shows that linkage sustains the first best solution at the same discount factor as no-linkage when only import sector policies are available. In contrast, our result implies that linkage can sustain more cooperation. In addition to differences in the setup, e.g., our government is not necessarily a welfare maximizer, one important assumption generating the difference in results is that we allow governments to reoptimize after a deviation under no-linkage—a natural assumption since when policies are interdependent, their cooperative levels depend on the actual value of the other policy. Moreover, our analysis applies even if countries can never sustain the first-best. This is crucial because if no-linkage already sustains the first-best, then countries have no incentive to switch to linkage and because it allows us to address the concerns of policymakers as to whether linkage necessarily causes a reallocation of enforcement.

In addition to deriving the general conditions for creation and reallocation of enforcement, our other main goal is to show when they are satisfied by this trade model. We find that for the foreign policies to be strategic complements in the home government's objective, the nontrade issue must have cross-border spillovers and be sufficiently valued. This implies that for a pair of poor countries, which may place a low weight on the production externality, linkage is unlikely to create enforcement. We also find that import-competing lobbies cannot be too "powerful"; that is, they cannot have too much weight in the objective function, otherwise the domestic tariffs and e-taxes become strategic substitutes. This last result occurs because when a sector's supply increases due to tariff protection, the marginal benefit of lowering the production tax is higher because it affects a higher volume of production. When import lobbies are given sufficient weight in the objective function, this cross-effect is the dominant one.

The structure of the paper is as follows. In Section 2, we introduce the model and derive the noncooperative and cooperative equilibria; in Section 3, we derive the conditions under which linkage reallocates and creates enforcement; in Section 4, we

[8] A similar result applies to cases where the issues are both unrelated and valued additively, as shown by BW for the case of oligopolies, since such cases imply that the policies are independent. However, independence of policies does not imply the issues are unrelated as is clear from the limit case of our model.

[9] Bagwell and Staiger (2001) abstract from enforcement issues.

analyze when these conditions hold in the trade model; and in Section 5, we summarize and discuss the results. All proofs are in the Appendix.

2. Model

2.1. Setup

Each of the two countries produces two homogeneous goods, i=x,y, where x denotes home's import. When countries trade, the consumer and producer prices at home are, respectively, $q_i = p_i^{\mathrm{W}} + \tau_i$ and $p_i = p_i^{\mathrm{W}} + \tau_i - e_i$, where p_i^{W} is the "world" price, τ is a specific import tariff, and e_i a unit production tax. Home's excess demand is then $M_i \equiv D_i(q_i) - S_i(p_i)$.[10] Denoting the foreign variables with "*", p_i^{W} is determined by the usual market clearing condition and is therefore a function of the policy variables:

$$M_i\left(p_i^{\mathrm{W}}, \tau_i, e_i\right) + M_i^*\left(p_i^{\mathrm{W}}, \tau_i^*, e_i^*\right) = 0 \tag{1}$$

We assume that countries have market power, and export taxes are unavailable.[11] The world price is decreasing in tariffs and increasing in production taxes since tariffs depress imports and e lowers world supply. Tariffs raise domestic prices for consumers and producers. Production taxes raise domestic consumer prices but lower producer prices since the direct producer tax effect dominates the rise in p_i^{W}.

$$\partial p_i^{\mathrm{W}}/\partial\tau_i<0;\ \partial q_i/\partial\tau_i = \partial p_i/\partial\tau_i>0;\ \partial p_i^{\mathrm{W}}/\partial e_i>0;\ \partial q_i/\partial e_i>0;\ \partial p_i/\partial e_i<0 \tag{2}$$

One important aspect of import lobbies not yet fully examined in the literature is their impact on the enforcement of trade agreements when nontrade policies are under negotiation. Thus, the first step is to ask if lobbies are relevant at all in the choice of enforcement regime, and to address it, we leave the lobbying mechanism implicit and focus directly on a reduced form objective function for the government, W=W_x+W_y, that allows an extra weight to be placed on producer surplus in the import sector relative to consumer surplus and tax revenue. In the expression below, we have $\lambda_i \geq 1$ in the import sector and λ_i=1 in the export sector.[12] The government's objective also accounts for the nontrade issue, which we model as a negative production externality. Throughout, we also refer to the government's objective function as aggregate welfare, although we must bear in mind that the government does not necessarily weight all agents' welfare equally.

$$W_i \equiv \int_{q_i}^{\infty} D_i(q_i)\mathrm{d}q_i + \lambda_i \int_0^{p_i} S_i(p_i)\mathrm{d}p_i + \tau_i M_i + e_i S_i - \psi_i \Psi_i(S_i + \alpha_i S_i^*) \tag{3}$$

In the absence of production externalities, ψ_i=0, this objective function represents the reduced form of a political contributions model, such as Grossman and Helpman

[10] We assume these functions are linear in own prices.

[11] For evidence of market power in trade, see Knetter (1993) and Chang and Winters (2002).

[12] It is straightforward to extend the model to include export lobbies.

(1994).[13] We assume that Ψ is twice differentiable and convex and $\Psi_i(0)=0$. The nonnegative weights, ψ_i, may differ across countries or sectors thus reflecting different strengths of environmental lobbies or the different valuation by each country of the externality. The geographical scope of the externality is captured by α-positive if the externality has a cross-border effect, zero otherwise. This parameter may be interpreted more broadly as the relative weight placed on the foreign source of the externality.[14]

To focus on one important motivation for linkage, the asymmetry in enforceability between trade and nontrade policies, we rule out other potential motivations for linking agreements. More specifically, we assume symmetry across countries, such that home and foreign import (and export) sectors are mirror images of each other, that is, $W_i=W_j^*$ for $i\neq j$.[15] Moreover, for ease of exposition, we initially assume that domestic production in the export sector produces no externality, but foreign production does, hence $\Psi_y=\Psi_y(\alpha S_y^*)$ and, by symmetry, $\Psi_x=\Psi_x(S_x)$. This allows us to initially abstract from e-taxes in the export sectors. In the Appendix, we show that this assumption is not essential for the main results.

One crucial point to note is that it is impossible to write any subcomponents of the governments' objective, e.g., producer surplus or the production externality cost, in terms of only the tariff or the e-tax. The nontrade issue is inherently trade-related, because changes in the tariffs change prices and therefore equilibrium supply levels.

2.2. Noncooperative vs. fully cooperative equilibrium

In our model, in addition to the cooperation problem in trade generated by the TOT externality, governments also face a cooperation problem due to the presence of the negative production externality. Governments overcome these cooperation problems through repeated interaction, and we now characterize the Nash equilibrium of the stage game that is repeated.

Home chooses taxes in the import sector to maximize Eq. (3), taking foreign policies as given.[16] We drop the subscript, x, and unless otherwise stated, the policies refer to home's

[13] Staiger (1995). In Grossman and Helpman (1994), the government's objective is $W^{\mathrm{GH}}=a\bar{W}+c$, where $\bar{W}$ is social welfare, c is political contributions and a is the marginal rate of substitution between the two. In W_x the term $\lambda-1$ can be directly interpreted as the inverse of a when factor ownership is extremely concentrated. Thus, underlying our model is the basic general equilibrium structure used in Grossman and Helpman (1994). We augment this by modelling a production externality that enters additively in utility and assuming that the revenues from the e-tax are distributed lump-sum to obtain Eq. (3).

[14] For instance, the existence of slave or child labor anywhere in the world may generate per se a "psychological cost"; α can then represent the weight placed on the such conditions abroad relative to home. The weight and scope of the production externality are likely to change over time as scientific knowledge about the externality evolves or as we become aware of foreign practices that induce "psychological costs".

[15] Limão (2002b) analyzes the gains from linkage in an enforcement context when countries forming regional integration agreements are asymmetric and have different bargaining powers.

[16] The necessary first-order conditions are given in Appendix A.2.

import sector. Given the symmetry, the following noncooperative equilibrium also applies to the foreign import sector policies.[17]

$$\tau^N = p^w/\varepsilon \quad ; \quad e^N = \psi\Psi' - (\lambda - 1)S/S' \tag{4}$$

In the absence of import lobbies, the optimal e-tax is equal to the marginal cost of the externality, otherwise the e-tax is lower than $\psi\Psi'$. The Nash tariff is inversely related to the elasticity of the foreign excess demand, $\varepsilon \equiv p^w M^{*\prime}/M^*$; it does not reflect the extra weight placed on producers directly since the producer tax is the most efficient instrument to transfer surplus to those producers.[18] Neither policy reflects the cross-border scope of the externality, because home ignores this effect on foreign, and foreign does not create an externality in home's import sector. Finally, note that because the nontrade issue is trade-related, the policies are generally jointly determined even before any strategic relation through linkage is present.

The fully cooperative policies for these governments are found by choosing the cooperative tariffs and e-taxes, τ^c and e^c that maximize their joint objective. This is equivalent to maximizing Eq. (3) after imposing symmetry, $W^c = W_x(\tau^c, e^c) + W_y(\tau_y^* = \tau^c, e_y^* = e^c)$. The first-order conditions (in Appendix A.2) yield:

$$\tau^g = 0 \quad ; \quad e^g = \psi\Psi' + \alpha\psi^*\Psi^{*\prime} - (\lambda - 1)S/S' \tag{5}$$

The difference between the Nash and global cooperative policies confirms that the externalities which countries must resolve arise due to market power in trade and the cross-border effect of the production externality. Therefore, the underlying motivation for cooperative agreements is independent of the existence of import lobbies. However, we will show that lobbies can alter the benefits of cooperation in an agreement and will therefore be important in the comparison of the linkage and no-linkage enforcement regimes.[19]

3. Effects of linking trade to nontrade agreements

3.1. Two enforcement regimes: linkage and no-linkage

The absence of a supranational authority to punish violators implies that international agreements must be self-enforcing. Therefore, the outcome of such agreements depends on the enforcement regime, i.e., on which policies are available to enforce cooperation. We now analyze the effects of two important enforcement regimes: linkage and no-linkage. Our central question is whether a switch to linkage must result in a reallocation of enforcement across issues or if this trade-off can ever be avoided through the creation of enforcement. As we note in the Introduction, a reallocation of enforcement occurs if greater cooperation on

[17] In the general equilibrium model implicit in the analysis there is a numeraire good, which maintains the balance of payments equilibrium. This allows us to focus on individual sectors in isolation.

[18] The equilibrium value of τ^N is indirectly affected by λ through the impact of e on the world price.

[19] A cooperative agreement on e-taxes may be necessary even if the production externality is purely domestic because the production tax affects world prices. The WTO's agreement on subsidies deals precisely with domestic policies and tries to prevent market access concessions from being eroded through the use of secondary trade barriers. See Copeland (1990) and Bagwell and Staiger (2001) on this issue.

nontrade issues occurs at the expense of higher tariffs or vice versa. A creation of enforcement occurs if under linkage more cooperation in both policies becomes feasible.

Cooperative self-enforcing agreements are well characterized by certain repeated games.[20] The indefinitely repeated stage game is the Nash game described, and we assume that each government observes the other governments actions at the end of each period. We focus on symmetric, subgame perfect, stationary Nash equilibria and adopt the simplest trigger strategies that maintain such equilibria-infinite Nash reversion—the exact trigger depends on whether the policies are linked or not. The payoffs are given by W discounted at the rate $\delta=\bar{\delta}\rho<1$, where $\bar{\delta}$ reflects a proper discount factor, and ρ the probability that the game continues for one more period.

Under a linkage regime, noncooperation in *either* issue can be met with punishment in *either* or *both* issues.[21] That is, a government implements the cooperative level of a particular policy in period t as long as, in all previous periods, the history of play for all players in that policy was one of cooperation. Otherwise, the government reverts to the Nash levels in *either* or *both* linked policies. In the most cooperative linkage agreement, if a government decides to deviate in any policy, it finds it optimal to deviate in all linked policies (Abreu, 1988). The reason for this is that the most cooperative policies will be sustained by the most painful punishment which entails punishment in both policies.[22] In sum, although under linkage, governments can deviate and punish using any combination of tariffs and e-taxes, it is not optimal for them to pursue deviations in individual policies. Thus, we need only consider cooperation, deviation, or Nash in all policies. Since symmetry allows us to express everything in terms of the home country variables, the period payoffs are:

$$W^{C\tau e}\left(\tau_x^c, e_x^c\right) \equiv W_x\left(\tau_x^c, e_x^c\right) + W_y\left(\tau_y^{*c} = \tau_x^c, e_y^{*c} = e_x^c\right)$$

$$W^{D\tau e}\left(\tau_x^c, e_x^c\right) \equiv W_x\left(\tau_x^N, e_x^N\right) + W_y\left(\tau_y^{*c} = \tau_x^c, e_y^{*c} = e_x^c\right)$$

$$W^{N\tau e} \equiv W_x\left(\tau_x^N, e_x^N\right) + W_y\left(\tau_y^{*N} = \tau_x^N, e_y^{*N} = e_x^N\right) \tag{6}$$

In these expressions, (τ_x^c, e_x^c) denotes the policy values during a period of cooperation in both policies and (τ_x^N, e_x^N) the Nash values. The period gain from cooperation, $\omega^{\tau e}(\tau_x^c, e_x^c) \equiv W^{C\tau e} - W^{N\tau e}$, represents the difference between the cooperative and the Nash payoffs. The period gain from deviation, $\Omega^{\tau e}(\tau_x^c, e_x^c) \equiv W^{D\tau e} - W^{C\tau e}$, is given by the

[20] See Dixit (1987) and Bagwell and Staiger (1990) for trade applications and Barret (1994) for environmental ones.

[21] As the GATT's former director of legal affairs makes clear in Roessler (1998, p. 226).

[22] The one period gain from deviating in either policy cannot exceed the gain to deviating in both by the definition of a Nash best response. Stating that a government knows it will be punished in both policies implicitly assumes that the threat of punishment in both policies is a credible one. This threat achieves the most cooperative policies. However, ex post the threat may not be realized. To deal with this issue we could model renegotiation-proof strategies (Farrell and Maskin, 1989) and verify whether they affect our results by checking if it reduces the feasible degree of cooperation under linkage differently from no-linkage.

difference between the deviation and cooperation payoffs. In choosing the cooperative policies, the following incentive constraint must be satisfied each period:

$$\Omega^{\tau e}(\tau_x^c, e_x^c) \leq \frac{\delta}{1-\delta}\omega^{\tau e}(\tau_x^c, e_x^c) \tag{7}$$

This condition, henceforth $\mathrm{IC}^{\tau e}$, states that for each country, the net gain from deviating in any one period must not exceed the discounted value of the net benefit from future cooperation. If governments are sufficiently patient, $\mathrm{IC}^{\tau e}$ does not bind at the global maximum. We assume that the discount factor is small enough that this constraint binds at the global optimal policies in Eq. (5), but large enough that cooperation improves on the Nash values. This is the empirically relevant case, since we do not observe full cooperation in either trade or e-issues.[23]

In a no-linkage regime, governments retaliate policy-by-policy; hence, for instance, their response to a deviation in e-taxes is to revert to Nash in e-taxes but not in tariffs. If a deviation occurs in several policies, then the response is to revert to Nash in each of the policies deviated in. This corresponds to the current regime for environmental and labor standards in relation to the trade agreements in the WTO. The payoffs under cooperation, deviation, and punishment in all policies are defined by Eq. (6), as before. When the deviation and punishment occur only in the trade policy, we have the following payoffs:

$$W^{D\tau}(\tau_x^c, e_x^c) \equiv W_x(\tau_x^r, e_x^c) + W_y(\tau_x^c, e_x^c)$$

$$W^{N\tau} \equiv W_x(\tau_x^r(e_x^{n\tau}), e_x^{n\tau}) + W_y(\tau_x^r(e_x^{n\tau}), e_x^{n\tau})$$

We can define analogous payoffs for a deviation and punishment in the e-tax by interchanging the variables. Fig. 1 clarifies at which points the payoffs are being evaluated. Start at a cooperative point, such as NL. From NL, a deviation in tariffs places home at D_x^τ with domestic tariffs given by the Nash reaction, τ^r, evaluated at the original cooperative e-tax and foreign policies at (τ_x^c, e_x^c).[24] Partial cooperation follows a deviation in tariffs. That is, countries stop cooperating in tariffs but continue to cooperate in e-taxes so that in the period following a deviation in tariffs, the new equilibrium value for the e-taxes is found at N^τ, where countries choose e^c to maximize cooperative welfare given tariffs are set at τ^r.

[23] The severity of this constraint depends importantly on how long it takes to start a punishment after a deviation occurs, which in turn depends on two factors. First, the speed of detection of the deviation, which is not long for transparent trade policies, e.g., tariffs, but may be long when it applies to the enforcement of certain domestic policies such as environmental standards. Second, the initiation of punishment can be delayed by bureaucratic delays in implementing new legislation or by consultations between the countries to ascertain if a deviation did occur. For example, while the WTO was ruling on the legality of the U.S. steel tariffs of 2002 other countries were unable to retaliate. Thus, the United States enjoyed the "benefits" of that deviation for several months.

[24] Since the equilibrium values of the tariffs and e-policies are not independent a deviation in one policy must eventually lead to a change in the equilibrium value of the other. We assume that if this adjustment were to happen simultaneously with the deviation then foreign would consider that home deviated in the two policies. Therefore, in the period that home deviates in tariffs (e-taxes) it does not simultaneously adjust the level of its e-tax (tariff), unless it wishes to deviate in all policies.

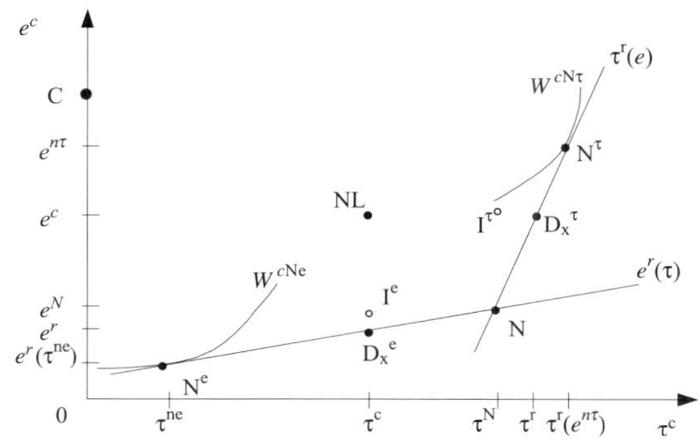

Fig. 1. Cooperation and deviation strategies under no-linkage.

Graphically this corresponds to the tangency point of W^c and the Nash FOC, $\tau^r(e)$, if the IC for the e-tax does not bind.[25]

The period gains from joint cooperation and deviation are unchanged, hence the relevant incentive constraint is the one in Eq. (7). The gains from cooperation and deviation in tariffs, assuming cooperation in e-taxes, are, respectively, $\omega^\tau \equiv W^{C\tau e} - W^{N\tau}$ and $\Omega^\tau \equiv W^{D\tau} - W^{C\tau e}$. The gains from cooperation and deviation in e-taxes are defined analogously. Under no-linkage governments are subject to three incentive constraints, which now reflect the possibility of deviation in the tariff or e-tax individually, or in both simultaneously.

In both enforcement regimes, the governments' problem is to choose the cooperative levels of tariffs and e-taxes that maximize their joint objective function subject to the relevant set of incentive constraints. Given the symmetry of the model, it is sufficient to focus on one country, and, since the problem is stationary, it is equal each period. Thus, the solution set under linkage and no-linkage is, respectively:

$$\Phi^l \equiv \arg\max_{\tau_x^c, e_x^c} \left\{ \omega^{\tau e}\left(\tau_x^c, e_x^c\right) : \mathrm{IC}^{\tau e} \right\} \tag{8}$$

$$\Phi^{nl} \equiv \arg\max_{\tau_x^c, e_x^c} \left\{ \omega^{\tau e}\left(\tau_x^c, e_x^c\right) : \mathrm{IC}^{\tau e}, \mathrm{IC}^{\tau}, \mathrm{IC}^{e} \right\} \tag{9}$$

Since the objective function is the same and under no-linkage an extra two incentive constraints must be met, we can see immediately that all cooperative tariff and e-tax vectors feasible under no-linkage are also feasible under linkage. Thus, in a symmetric equilibrium, aggregate welfare under linkage is never lower than under no-linkage for either country. The key to this result is that in a no-linkage regime, a government can deviate in either or all policies, hence there are unconstrained deviation possibilities but constrained punishment possibilities since only the policies deviated in are subject to punishment. By contrast, under linkage, there are unconstrained deviation possibilities and unconstrained punishment

[25] If it does bind, then N^τ is given by the intersection of the e-tax iso-incentive constraint and τ^r. Assuming that, when there is only partial cooperation in policy k, countries first choose k cooperatively and then set the other policy is reasonable here because countries can always change the policy that is being set noncooperatively. See Copeland (1990) on a similar point.

possibilities. Therefore, under linkage, we can always find punishments at least as painful as under no-linkage. This was the basic intuition underlying the results in BW in the context of multimarket collusion when markets are unrelated.

The previous result does not tell us if a regime switch to linkage can create enforcement or if it must lead to a reallocation of enforcement, and consequently whether linkage will lead to lower cooperation in tariffs or e-taxes. Moreover, it does not ensure that aggregate welfare under linkage is strictly higher than under no-linkage. We now turn to these questions.

3.2. Reallocation of enforcement

To isolate the reallocation effect of linkage, we consider a benchmark case where tariffs and e-taxes are independent, i.e., $\partial^2 W/\partial \tau_x \partial e_x = \partial^2 W/\partial \tau_y^* \partial e_y^* = 0$. As we show in Section 4, this is a special case of our model where the pecuniary and nonpecuniary effects are exactly offsetting. Therefore, although the e-tax can be independent of the tariff, according to the definition above, the e-issue can still be trade-related, since changes in tariffs continue to affect supply and thus the level of the externality directly.

The following definitions are useful in establishing the first proposition. The slope of the linkage incentive frontier in $\tau^c - e^c$ space represents the marginal change in tariffs required to maintain incentive compatibility given a marginal change in e-taxes, hence we refer to it as the marginal rate of substitution in enforcement. We say that tariffs are easier to enforce than e-taxes if, under no-linkage, the discount factor required to sustain the global optimum in tariffs, δ_τ, is lower than δ_e. Thus, δ_τ is defined by the tariff IC evaluated at the global optimum for tariffs, $\Omega^\tau(\tau^g, .) = \frac{\delta_\tau}{1-\delta_\tau}\omega^\tau(\tau^g, .)$; δ_e is similarly defined.

Propositon 1. (*Reallocation of enforcement*).

(a) *If tariffs and e-taxes are independent and their MRS in cooperative welfare and enforcement are not equalized under no-linkage, then a switch to linkage leads to a reallocation of enforcement.*

(b) *If tariffs are easier to enforce than e-taxes under no-linkage, then linkage lowers cooperation in tariffs and raises cooperation in e-taxes for all $\delta \in (\delta_\tau, \delta_e)$ and some $\delta < \delta_\tau$. The opposite is true if e-taxes are easier to enforce.*

The intuition for part (a) is that if the discount factor is low enough, i.e., if $\delta \le \min(\delta_\tau, \delta_e)$, then both of the individual IC bind at the no-linkage solution, NL. The FOCs for the linkage problem defined in Eq. (8) require that the MRS of the policies in welfare and enforcement be equalized. Thus, if at NL the cooperative isowelfare curve is not tangent to the incentive frontier, then linkage leads to an aggregate welfare improvement by eliminating the individual IC. The switch to linkage entails a reallocation of enforcement, because at NL, the linkage IC must also bind when the policies are independent. Therefore, starting at NL, an increase in e^c, for example, implies that the gain to deviating in the e-tax now exceeds the gain to cooperating, violating the linkage IC. But if at the higher e-tax both countries increase τ^c towards its Nash level, the incentive to deviate in the e-tax remains unchanged, due to independence, but the incentive to deviate in tariffs and therefore the overall incentive to deviate is lowered.

To understand part (b), suppose that tariffs are easier to enforce and that free trade is just feasible under no-linkage. At NL, a small increase in cooperative tariffs has no first-order effect (from the FOC for τ^g) and creates slack in the overall IC, which can be reallocated towards increasing e-taxes under linkage. Since the increase in e-taxes creates a first-order gain, this reallocation leaves governments strictly better off. By continuity of the functions, there also exists some δ lower than δ_τ for which this is true.

If tariffs are easier to enforce than e-taxes, then the analysis above provides a formal justification in terms of enforcement for the reallocation concerns put forth by opponents of linkage within the WTO.[26] However, this analysis applies to the linkage of independent policies, which is a limit case when the e-issue is trade-related, as in our model. Thus, we now analyze the case when the linked policies are not independent.

3.3. Creation of enforcement

If the policies are not independent, can the linkage IC hold with slack at the no-linkage solution, that is can linkage create enforcement? We now derive the conditions to answer this question in the affirmative so that linkage can always yield a strictly higher aggregate welfare than no-linkage. Moreover, we show this can occur without any trade-off in cooperation across the issues.

Suppose we find the optimal (and feasible) cooperative tariffs and e-taxes under no-linkage, Φ^{nl}. Then, linkage can sustain more cooperation in both policies if the linkage IC does not bind at Φ^{nl}. A *sufficient* condition for this is that the following holds at Φ^{nl}:[27]

$$\Omega^{\tau e} \leq \Omega^{\tau} + \Omega^{e} \tag{10}$$

$$\omega^{\tau e} \geq \omega^{\tau} + \omega^{e} \tag{11}$$

with at least one inequality being strict. These are sufficient since they imply that:

$$\Omega^{\tau e} \leq \Omega^{\tau} + \Omega^{e} \leq \frac{\delta}{1-\delta}(\omega^{\tau} + \omega^{e}) \leq \frac{\delta}{1-\delta}\omega^{\tau e} \tag{12}$$

with the middle inequality resulting from the fact that Φ^{nl} is implemented and therefore self-enforcing. The proposition stating the conditions for the creation of enforcement relies

[26] Since we model the nontrade issue as inherently trade related there is no simple condition characterizing which policy is easier to enforce. In a simpler model where the issue is not trade-related, so the payoffs for cooperation in each policy can be written independently, there is a simple argument why tariffs are easier to enforce: the effective discount factor for trade agreements may be higher, $\bar{\delta}\rho_\tau > \bar{\delta}\rho_e$. The probability of continuing a trade agreement may be higher than for certain environmental problems because technological progress can eliminate the environmental problem, e.g., moving from coal to solar powered plants eliminates emissions. Alternatively, a more realistic model with several countries may generate differential motives for free-riding in the different individual agreements and generate predictions about which policy is easier to enforce. On this issue, see Barret (1994) and the WTO report on the environment (1999, p.7).

[27] This condition follows the approach in Spagnolo (1999a) who focuses on the case of independent stage game payoffs.

on two lemmas establishing the conditions for Eqs. (10) and (11) to hold. To do so, we recall the definition of supermodularity.

Definition 1. (*Supermodularity*). A function $W(s)\ R^n \rightarrow R$ is (strictly) supermodular in $s \in S$ if:

$$W(s) + W(\tilde{s})(<) = W(\max(s, \tilde{s})) + W(\min(s, \tilde{s}))\forall(s, \tilde{s}) \in S$$

Intuitively supermodularity states that pairing the lowest strategies (e.g., low tariffs with low e-taxes) and the highest ones yields a higher payoff than when other combinations of those strategies is played. Therefore, it captures the idea of complementarity between the policies.

Lemma 1. (*Relative gains from deviation*). *If the objective function, W, is (strictly) supermodular in the linked domestic policies, then* $\Omega^{\tau e}(<)=\Omega^{\tau}+\Omega^{e}$.

To understand the intuition behind Lemma 1, first note that a continuously differentiable function is strictly supermodular in (τ_x, e_x) if and only if $\partial^2 W/\partial\tau_x\partial e_x > 0$ (Topkis, 1979). Thus, strict supermodularity in the domestic-linked policies reduces to a requirement that those policies are strategic complements. Assume this is the case, then a country incurs an extra cost when it deviates jointly, that is, when it increases tariffs and reduces e-taxes, that is not present if it deviates only in one individual policy. When tariffs are increased, the marginal benefit of deviating in e-taxes, i.e., decreasing them, falls. Thus, linking, by "forcing" deviation in both policies, lowers the temptation to deviate in any given policy.[28,29]

To establish the conditions for Eq. (11), note that we can use the definitions of the gains from cooperation to rewrite it as $W^{C\tau e}+W^{N\tau e} \leq W^{N\tau}+W^{Ne}$. That is the sum of home's objective (jointly in the import and export sectors) under cooperation (NL in Fig. 1) and no-cooperation (N) must not exceed the sum of the objective evaluated when there is partial cooperation (N^{τ} and N^{e}). If W is supermodular in the linked domestic and foreign policies, then we can see from the definition of supermodularity and Fig. 1 that we can establish $W^{C\tau e}+W^{N\tau e} \leq W^{I\tau}+W^{Ie}$. Thus, we must also verify whether supermodularity ensures the following partial cooperation condition: $W^{I\tau}+W^{Ie} \leq W^{N\tau}+W^{Ne}$. The issue that arises when the linked issues are intrinsically related is that the Nash phase in tariffs occurs

[28] The gain from deviating under linkage is always at least as large as *either* of the gains from deviating in tariffs or e-taxes individually. This occurs because deviation under linkage requires countries to play their best response in both policies.

[29] Lemma 1 builds upon a result in Spagnolo (1999a) but differs in two respects. He considers two issues each with an independent prisoner's dilemma structure and material payoffs Π_1 and Π_2 which take different values depending on whether agents cooperate or not. These payoffs are evaluated according to $U(\Pi_1,\Pi_2)$ and it is shown that the gains from deviation under linkage are lower than the sum of the gains from deviation if U is submodular in (Π_1,Π_2). The first, trivial, difference occurs because, in our model, the deviations in the linked policies occur in opposite directions (higher tariffs, lower e-taxes); therefore, we require supermodularity as opposed to submodularity. The second, and more substantive, difference occurs because an important set of issues linked are intrinsically related and therefore we cannot write Π_1 and Π_2 separately. Because in our model the linked issues are intrinsically related, lemma 1 also shows that the "movement" from $I^{\tau}(I^{e})$ to $D^{\tau}(D^{e})$, in Fig. 1, improves aggregate welfare. Such a movement would not take place if the issues were unrelated and the policies set independently during the stage game.

at N^{τ} not at I^{τ}, and for e-taxes, it occurs at N^{e} not at I^{e}.[30] This raises the question of whether supermodularity is sufficient to establish the relative gains from cooperation. We now show that supermodularity is in fact sufficient for establishing the relative gains from cooperation for a nontrivial set of objective functions.

Lemma 2. (*Relative gains from cooperation*). *If the objective function, W, is supermodular in the linked domestic policies and strictly supermodular in the linked foreign policies, then* $\omega^{\tau e}>\omega^{\tau}+\omega^{e}$. *Moreover, there exist objective functions, W, strictly supermodular in both the linked domestic and foreign policies such that* $\omega^{\tau e}>\omega^{\tau}+\omega^{e}$.

The intuition is the following. When W is supermodular in domestic policies and strictly supermodular in the linked foreign policies, the simultaneous increase in foreign tariffs and decrease in e-taxes that occurs during a punishment under linkage carries an extra cost which is not present if each of the punishments was carried out individually at points I^{τ} and I^{e}. This complementarity increases the severity of the Nash punishment under linkage and explains why $W^{C\tau e}+W^{N\tau e}<W^{I\tau}+W^{Ie}$. Let's now turn to the partial cooperation condition. When W is supermodular in domestic policies, then the deviation and Nash levels of a given policy coincide. Hence, for example, in Fig. 1 the individual best-response functions would be perpendicular and intersect at N. However, if W is also strictly supermodular in the linked foreign policies then, when foreign increases its tariff, home would like foreign to increase its e-tax as well. This implies that in Fig. 1 the tariff under partial cooperation would be τ^{N}, but the optimal level of the cooperative e-tax for that tariff differs from e^{c} (the level at which I^{τ} is evaluated) and therefore $W^{I\tau}<W^{N\tau}$. Similarly, $W^{Ie}<W^{Ne}$ so that the partial cooperation condition is satisfied. Given that the condition for the gains from cooperation holds strictly when W is strictly supermodular in foreign policies and supermodular in domestic policies, it also holds for some positive levels of complementarity between the domestic policies, as we state in the second part of the lemma and prove in the Appendix.

With Lemmas 1 and 2 and the following definition, we state the main proposition of this section.

Definition 2. (*Creation of enforcement*). Linkage creates enforcement if $\Omega^{\tau e}<\frac{\delta}{1-\delta}\omega^{\tau e}$ *at* Φ^{nl}, that is, if it can enforce both lower tariffs and higher e-taxes than no-linkage.

Proposition 2. (*Creation of enforcement*). *If the objective function, W, is supermodular in the domestic policies and strictly supermodular in the foreign policies, then linkage creates enforcement. Moreover, there exist objective functions, W, strictly supermodular in both domestic and foreign policies such that linkage creates enforcement.*

Proof. Follows directly from Eq. (12) and Lemmas 1 and 2.

The conditions above are sufficient for linkage to yield a strictly higher aggregate welfare than no-linkage, such that no trade-off in cooperation across the issues is

[30] We also discuss this issue in page 13. This constitutes another important difference relative to earlier work. In the case of independent payoffs, studied by Spagnolo (1999a), the readjustment of policies after a deviation does not arise because the policies on different issues are not related during the stage game. In that case I^{τ} and I^{e} exactly coincide with N^{τ} and N^{e} in Fig. 1 and the partial cooperation condition is trivially satisfied with equality.

necessary. This proposition does not rule out the possibility that the optimal linkage solution entails a reallocation of enforcement, which may happen if there is a strong asymmetry in the enforceability of the policies. However, the key point is that the creation of enforcement allows for a strictly higher aggregate welfare level without a need for the reallocation of enforcement, since the direction of change for the cooperative policies is (locally) unrestricted.

4. Structural conditions for the creation of enforcement

We now show when the supermodularity conditions that are sufficient for the creation of enforcement hold in our trade model. The objective is to give guidelines as to what "types" of e-issues (i.e., with a national or a cross-border scope; highly valued or not) and countries (developed or developing; with powerful import lobbies or not) satisfy the complementarity conditions. We analyze these dimensions because of their importance in policy debates of linkage in the context of the WTO.[31]

4.1. Strategic complementarity of domestic tariffs and e-taxes

To determine whether own tariffs and e-taxes are strategic complements in the import sector (x), we first differentiate W, which yields: $W_\tau=(1+p_\tau^{\mathrm{w}})(\tau M'+(e-\psi\Psi')S')-p_\tau^{\mathrm{w}}M+(\lambda-1)(1+p_\tau^{\mathrm{w}})S$. The subscripts now denote partial derivatives unless the function has only one argument in which case a prime is used. The first term, $(1+p_\tau^{\mathrm{w}})$, represents the positive effect of the tariff on domestic prices; $\tau M'$ represents the fall in tariff revenue due to lower imports; eS' represents the increase in e-tax revenue due to higher production; $\psi\Psi' S'$ the increase in externality cost and $-p_\tau^{\mathrm{w}}M$ refers to the positive change in the TOT. The final term reflects the presence of import lobbies. If governments place additional weight on producer surplus in the import sector, then an increase in tariffs has an added benefit in the form of increased producer surplus. The cross-derivative is then:[32]

$$W_{\tau e}=\Big(1+\underset{+}{p_\tau^{\mathrm{w}}}\Big)S'+\Big(-\underset{+}{p_\tau^{\mathrm{w}}}M_e\Big)+\Big(-\underset{+}{\psi\Psi_{\tau e}}\Big)+(\lambda-1)\Big(p_e^{\mathrm{w}}-\underset{-}{1}\Big)(1+P_\tau^{\mathrm{w}})S' \tag{13}$$

The first term represents a strategic revenue effect; when domestic supply expands due to higher tariffs, the marginal benefit of increasing e-taxes increases, so this effect is positive. The second one represents a strategic TOT effect, and it is positive; higher e-taxes expand home imports, which is more valuable at the lower world prices delivered by the increased domestic tariff. The strategic externality effect, $-\psi\Psi_{\tau e}$, can be decomposed into two factors, the change in the marginal cost of the externality due to higher e-taxes, $-(p_e^{\mathrm{w}}-1)S'\psi\Psi''$, and the domestic tariff effect on the externality, $(1+p_\tau^{\mathrm{w}})S'$. The latter

[31] Limão (2002a) analyzes the actual adoption of linkage by different governments in more detail.

[32] Recall that we assume linear demand and supply functions, which is standard in similar analysis of strategic effects of trade policies and implies that the cross derivative of world prices with respect to tariffs and e-taxes is zero.

factor is positive since higher tariffs increase the domestic supply and thus the level of the externality. The domestic e-tax effect on the externality $(p_e^w-1)S'$ is negative. Thus, the strategic externality effect is positive since the loss function is convex. The last term in Eq. (13) is the strategic lobby effect, which is negative. It captures a basic intuition, likely to be present in other models with import-competing lobbies, that when production expands due to tariff protection, the marginal benefit of increasing direct taxes on the producers is lower because it affects a higher volume of production.

With the following definition, we can summarize the conditions for complementarity between domestic tariffs and e-taxes. We say that a country has powerful import lobbies if $\lambda \geq \bar{\lambda}$, where $\bar{\lambda}$ is defined by $W_{\tau e}(\bar{\lambda},.)=0$. That is a country has powerful import lobbies if the weight placed on producer surplus is at least as high as the critical value at which domestic tariffs and e-taxes are independent. We show that such a weight exists and is nontrivial, in the sense that it requires governments to actually give extra weight to import producers.

Proposition 3. *Domestic tariffs and e-taxes are strategic complements in the domestic objective function, W, if and only if a country does not have powerful import lobbies.*

The existence of a threshold point, $\bar{\lambda}$, is simple to show, since the extra weight on import producers affects only the strategic lobby effect and all of the other strategic terms depend only on exogenous parameters.[33] Thus, if the weight equals one, the lobby effect disappears, but, if it is sufficiently large, this effect dominates all others and domestic tariffs and e-taxes become strategic substitutes.

As we show in Lemma 1 the condition in Proposition 3 is sufficient to compare the incentives to deviate under linkage and no-linkage. Therefore, by determining when the domestic policies are complementary, import lobbies affect whether linkage creates enforcement. To compare the cooperation gains, we must also analyze the interaction of the foreign policies in W.

4.2. Strategic complementarity of foreign tariffs and e-taxes

Once again we drop the subscripts, all conditions and variables now refer to home's export sector, y. Differentiating W, we find two negative effects of a foreign tariff increase on domestic welfare: $W_{\tau^*}=-p_{\tau^*}^w M+(-\psi\Psi'(1+p_{\tau^*}^w)\alpha S^{*\prime})$. The first term is the cost due to a reduction in home's export prices, i.e., the usual TOT effect. The second term is the extra externality cost when there is a cross-border effect, since higher foreign tariffs lead to an expansion in foreign production. The cross-derivative is given by:

$$W_{\tau^* e^*} = \Big(\underset{-}{-p_{\tau^*}^w M_{e^*}}\Big) + \Big(\underset{+}{-\psi\Psi_{\tau^* e^*}}\Big) \tag{14}$$

The strategic TOT effect, $-p_{\tau^*}^w M_{e^*}$, is negative. An increase in foreign tariff reduces world prices for domestic's exports, thus an increase in foreign e-taxes becomes less valuable since it expands domestic exports at a reduced world price. The strategic externality effect

[33] Assuming that $\Psi'''=0$, which is the case if Ψ is quadratic for example.

is now $-\psi\Psi_{\tau^*e^*}=-(p^{\mathrm{w}}_{e^*}-1)\alpha S^{*\prime}\psi\Psi''(1+p^{\mathrm{w}}_{\tau^*})\alpha S^{*\prime}$. It consists of the change in marginal cost of the externality due to changes in the e-tax, $-(p^{\mathrm{w}}_{e^*}-1)\alpha S^{*\prime}\psi\Psi''$, weighted by the positive foreign tariff effect on the externality level, $(1+p^{\mathrm{w}}_{\tau^*})\alpha S^{*\prime}$.[34] Consider the critical value $\bar{\psi}$ such that the policies are independent, i.e., $W_{\tau^*e^*}(\bar{\psi},.)=0$. We say that the externality is sufficiently valued if $\psi>\bar{\psi}$.

Proposition 4. *Foreign tariffs and e-taxes are strategic complements in the domestic objective function, W, if and only if the production externality is sufficiently valued and is not purely domestic.*

The key to this result is that when we focus on the pecuniary effects alone, the foreign policies are strategic substitutes, which require the externality effect in the export sector to be positive. This is the case because when the loss function is convex the marginal benefit from reducing the externality level is greater at higher levels of the externality. Since an increase in foreign tariffs increases the level of the externality, it also increases home's marginal benefit from a foreign increase in e^*, because the latter reduces S^*. When the externality is sufficiently valued, this effect dominates the pecuniary one. More importantly, the proposition rules out purely domestic production externalities, since in that case no externality effect exists and therefore foreign policies are strategic substitutes.

The conditions for supermodularity in the last two propositions can be exactly satisfied by a range of parameter combinations in our trade model. Since we can also find combinations such that the policies are independent these propositions also confirm that the analysis in Section 3.1 does apply to a special case of our trade model, although the production externality is trade-related.

5. Conclusions

We started by asking if linking trade policy to other cooperative agreements can ever result in the creation of enforcement rather than always leading to the reallocation of enforcement. We show that the fear of reallocation of enforcement pervasive in the trade literature on linkage is justified if the linked policies are independent because it is quite likely that the trade and nontrade policies are asymmetric in their enforceability. Moreover, if under no-linkage it is relatively easier to cooperate on tariffs than on e-taxes, the reallocation entails more cooperation on nontrade issues at the expense of higher tariffs. Thus, the model helps explain both the recent demands for linkages with trade policy by lobbies for different e-issues and the respective opposition. If the main goal of the WTO remains multilateral trade liberalization, then our result also lends support to this institution's current practice which, except in the area of intellectual property, avoids retaliation across unrelated issues that are typically characterized by independent policies.

However, in switching to a linkage regime, reallocation is not inevitable if policies are not independent to begin with. We show that linkage creates enforcement if the objective function is supermodular in linked policies. This result can be applied to a number of

[34] If we had also allowed for export lobbies then Eq. (14) would include an additional negative term: $(\lambda-1)p^{\mathrm{w}}_{\tau^*}p^{\mathrm{w}}_{e^*}S'$.

economic problems where agents must enter self-enforcing contracts to repeatedly deal with a cooperation problem over multiple issues that are related even before linkage. Obvious candidates are other international cooperative agreements, e.g., on health issues, transport infrastructure. Other applications include firm collusive behavior across interdependent markets (e.g., due to economies of scope or vertical integration) or when there is more than one instrument of collusion in the same market (e.g., price and advertising). Self-enforcing contracts are also pervasive in developing countries where the lack of rule of law often renders binding legal contracts too costly.

We show that the issues for which linkage creates enforcement must have cross-border effects and be sufficiently valued to offset strategic pecuniary effects. These conditions are sufficient when import lobbies are not "powerful". We believe that both the increase in the weight placed on environmental (and other nontrade issues) and the broader interpretation of the scope of their externalities are changing the strategic relation between policies. This can partially explain the increasing demand for linkage, as well as its origin in developed countries. If the externality weight rises with income, that is, if clean air is a normal good, our result suggests that this phenomenon will intensify.

Our analysis is also quite relevant for regional integration agreements. First, one of our basic assumptions—a country's market power in trade—is most plausible at the regional level since transport costs segment markets. Second, more issues have regional rather than global cross-border effects. Thus, there is more scope for the creation of enforcement through linkage regionally. This may explain why linkage in regional integration agreements has been more frequent and less contentious than in the WTO.

Enforcement is not the only factor in the decision to link agreements, but it is certainly an important one. By analyzing linkage from an enforcement perspective, we show that it need not necessarily reduce cooperation in trade policy. One practical concern in implementing linkages is that institutions, such as the WTO, are not equipped to decide on certain nontrade issues. However, in our model, linkage would require only that WTO rules allow the threat to use trade sanctions to enforce certain specific agreements and vice versa. This is compatible with a world order where there exist functional clubs to deal with each specific issue, e.g., the environment, with one or more global coordinating clubs to deal with linkages among issues.[35] Potential drawbacks from linkage may arise from redistribution problems due to within and across country asymmetries and from different degrees of imperfect monitoring of compliance that can potentially cause an escalation in trade disputes.[36] Both of these issues should be fully addressed in the enforcement context used in this paper. It is clear that demands for linkage will not soon fade. Thus, rather than allow the unilateral abuse of trade sanctions, we must understand how to use multilateral threats of noncooperation, in both trade and other issues, to promote more cooperative outcomes.[37]

[35] As suggested, for example, by Lawrence et al. (1996, p. 107).

[36] According to our calculations based on data from Reinhardt (2000).the number of WTO disputes involving nontrade issues tripled from 1994–1999 relative to the previous four years largely due to the inclusion of intellectual property issues in the WTO. However, it is too early to determine if the disputes will reduce cooperation in trade policy or if their number will fall once countries adapt their levels of cooperation in intellectual property.

[37] See Hufbauer et al. (1990) for a thorough review of the U.S.'s use of trade sanctions.

Acknowledgement

I thank two anonymous referees, Stephanie Aaronson, Jagdish Bhagwati, Alessandra Casella, Gernot Doppelhoffer, Josh Ederington, Helen Milner, Rohini Pande, Eric Reinhardt, Mike Riordan, Xavier Sala-I-Martin, Giancarlo Spagnolo, Robert Staiger, David Weinstein, and Gerald Willmann. I am also grateful for comments and suggestions from participants in seminars at the Econometric Society meeting (Atlanta), Georgetown, NYU (Inter-university Conference), Penn State, Stanford University, University of British Columbia, University of Maryland, World Bank, and Yale University. I am particularly indebted to Kyle Bagwell and Don Davis for their support. The usual disclaimer applies.

Appendix A

A.1. Proofs

Proof of Proposition 1.

(a) If $\delta \leq \min(\delta_\tau, \delta_e)$, then the necessary FOC for the interior linkage solution, Φ^1, are $\frac{W_\tau + W_{\tau*}}{W_e + W_{e*}} = \frac{W_\tau + \delta W_{\tau*}}{W_e + \delta W_{e*}}$ and $\Omega^{\tau e}(\tau^c, e^c) = \frac{\delta}{1-\delta}\omega^{\tau e}(\tau^c, e^c)$. Thus, if the MRS are not equalized at the no-linkage point, it is not a linkage solution. Reallocation must then occur because at the no-linkage solution (NL), we have $\Omega^{\tau e} = \frac{\delta}{1-\delta}\omega^{\tau e}$ and $\frac{\partial e^c}{\partial \tau^c}|\Omega^{\tau e} = \frac{\delta}{1-\delta}\omega^{\tau e} > 0$. To show $\Omega^{\tau e} = \frac{\delta}{1-\delta}\omega^{\tau e}$ at NL note that when policies are independent we have $\Omega^{\tau e}(\tau^c, e^c) = \Omega^\tau(\tau^c, e^c) + \Omega^e(\tau^c, e^c)$ and $\omega^{\tau e}(\tau^c, e^c) = \omega^\tau(\tau^c, e^c) + \omega^e(\tau^c, e^c)$ (independence corresponds to the case when W is not strictly supermodular, and so these equalities are proved precisely in Lemmas 1 and 2 below). Thus, $\Omega^{\tau e} = \frac{\delta}{1-\delta}\omega^{\tau e}$, because the individual incentive constraints bind at NL. To show $\frac{\partial e^c}{\partial \tau^c}|\Omega^{\tau e} = \frac{\delta}{1-\delta}\omega^{\tau e} > 0$ note that $\frac{\partial e_c}{\partial \tau_c}|\Omega^{\tau e} = \frac{\delta}{1-\delta}\omega^{\tau e} = -\frac{W_\tau + \delta W_{\tau*}}{W_e + \delta W_{e*}} = -\frac{\partial(\Omega^\tau - \frac{\delta}{1-\delta}\omega^\tau)/\partial \tau^c}{\partial(\Omega^e - \frac{\delta}{1-\delta}\omega^e)/\partial e^c}$, where the first equality employs the definitions of $\Omega^{\tau e}$ and $\omega^{\tau e}$, and the second the definitions of Ω^τ, ω^τ, Ω^e, and ω^e. At NL the individual incentive constraints bind therefore $\partial(\Omega^\tau - \frac{\delta}{1-\delta}\omega^\tau)/\partial \tau^c < 0$ and $\partial(\Omega^e - \frac{\delta}{1-\delta}\omega^e)/\partial e^c > 0$, hence $\frac{\partial e^c}{\partial \tau^c}|\Omega^{\tau e} = \frac{\delta}{1-\delta}\omega^{\tau e} > 0$.

(b) If $\delta = \delta_\tau$ then $\tau^c = 0$ and $W_\tau + W_{\tau*} = 0$ whereas $-\frac{W_\tau + \delta W_{\tau*}}{W_e + \delta W_{e*}} > 0$ and an increase in τ and e until $\frac{W_\tau + W_{\tau*}}{W_e + W_{e*}} = \frac{W_\tau + \delta W_{\tau*}}{W_e + \delta W_{e*}}$ is optimal. By continuity of W and of the incentive frontier $\exists$ $\delta < \delta_\tau$, such that the reallocation still occurs from tariffs to e-taxes. The same argument holds if at NL there is slack in IC^τ, i.e., $\delta_\tau < \delta < \delta_e$. □

Proof of Lemma 1. $\Omega^{\tau e} \leq \Omega^\tau + \Omega^e \Leftrightarrow W_x^{C\tau e} + W_x^{D\tau e} \leq W_x^{D\tau} + W_x^{De}$ where $C\tau e$, $D\tau e$, $D\tau$, De are defined at points NL, N, D^τ, and D^e in Fig. 1. Adding and subtracting both $W_x(\tau^N, e^c)$ and $W_x(\tau^c, e^N)$ to the RHS of the equivalence relation above, we have $s_x + a_x \leq 0$, where:

$$s_x \equiv W_x(\tau^c, e^c) + W_x(\tau^N, e^N) - \{W_x(\tau^N, e^c) + W_x(\tau^c, e^N)\} \tag{A1.1}$$

$$a_x \equiv W_x(\tau^N, e^c) - W_x(\tau^r, e^c) + \{W_x(\tau^c, e^N) - W_x(\tau^c, e^r)\} \tag{A1.2}$$

As we show in Section 2.2, $\tau^c<\tau^N$ and $e^c>e^N$. Thus, max $[(\tau^c,e^c),(\tau^N,e^N)]=(\tau^N,e^c)$ and min $[(\tau^c,e^c),(\tau^N,e^N)]=(\tau^c,e^N)$. Therefore, if W is (strictly) supermodular in τ,e (or, what is equivalent, $W_{x\tau e}(>)=0$), then $s_x(<)=0$. Moreover, $a_x\leq 0$, since τ^r is the best response to e^c and similarly for e^r relative to τ^c. □

Proof of Lemma 2.

Claim 1. *If W is supermodular in (τ_x,e_x) and (τ_y^*,e_y^*) and the partial cooperation condition, $W^{I\tau}+W^{Ie}\leq W^{N\tau}+W^{Ne}$, holds then $\omega^{\tau e}\geq\omega^\tau+\omega^e$.*

Proof of Claim 1. $\omega^{\tau e}\geq\omega^\tau+\omega^e \Leftrightarrow W^{C\tau e}+W^{N\tau e}\leq W^{N\tau}+W^{Ne}$. Rewriting this expression as $s+a\leq 0$ where:

$$s\equiv W(\tau^c,e^c)+W(\tau^N,e^N)-\{W(\tau^N,e^c)+W(\tau^c,e^N)\} \tag{A1.3}$$

$$\begin{aligned} a&\equiv W(\tau^c,e^N)+W(\tau^N,e^c)-\{W(\tau^{ne},e^r(\tau^{ne}))+W(\tau^r(e^{n\tau}),e^{n\tau})\}\\ &=W^{Ie}+W^{I\tau}-(W^{Ne}+W^{N\tau}) \end{aligned} \tag{A1.4}$$

(Strict) supermodularity ensures $s(<)=0$, and the partial cooperation condition states that $a\leq 0$ so $s+a\leq 0$. □

Claim 2. *If the objective function, W, is supermodular in the linked domestic policies and strictly supermodular in the linked foreign policies then $\omega^{\tau e}>\omega^\tau+\omega^e$. Moreover, there exist objective functions, W, strictly supermodular in both the linked domestic and foreign policies such that $\omega^{\tau e}>\omega^\tau+\omega^e$.*

Proof of Claim 2. W is supermodular in (τ_x,e_x) iff $W_{x\tau e}=0$ (given that W is continuous and twice differentiable). If $W_{x\tau e}=0$ then, in Fig. 1, τ^r and e^r are, respectively, vertical and horizontal and therefore $\tau^r(e^{n\tau})=\tau^N$ and $e^r(\tau^{ne})=e^N$. This implies that I^τ and N^τ (I^e and N^e) share the same tariff, τ^N, (e-tax, e^N). Now, if the individual IC for the e-tax (tariff) holds at I^τ (I^e), which we show below is true, then I^τ (I^e) is feasible when countries choose N^τ (N^e). Therefore, $W^{I\tau}+W^{Ie}\leq W^{N\tau}+W^{Ne}$, moreover this inequality is strict if W is strictly supermodular in (τ_y^*,e_y^*), since then the optimal cooperative e-tax (tariff) at I^τ (I^e) differs from that at NL. Therefore, $\omega^{\tau e}>\omega^\tau+\omega^e$ since, from Claim 1, $s<0$ if W is supermodular in (τ_x,e_x) and strictly supermodular in (τ_y^*,e_y^*).

To show the existence of W with $W_{x\tau^*e^*}>0$ and $W_{x\tau e}\in(0,\varepsilon]$, i.e., strictly supermodular in (τ_y^*,e_y^*) and (τ_x,e_x), such that $\omega^{\tau e}>\omega^\tau+\omega^e$ note that $\lim_{\varepsilon\to 0+}e^r(\tau^{ne})=e^N$ and $\lim_{\varepsilon\to 0+}\tau^r(e^{n\tau})=\tau^N$. Given that W is continuous, a $\varepsilon>0$ exists such that $W^{I\tau}+W^{Ie}\leq W^{N\tau}+W^{Ne}$ and therefore, from Claim 1, $\omega^{\tau e}>\omega^\tau+\omega^e$ follows.

To conclude, we show that IC^τ and IC^e are satisfied at I^e and I^τ, respectively. First, note that when there is partial cooperation in one policy, the other policy's IC becomes irrelevant. Intuitively, IC^τ holds at I^e because it held at NL and, since $e^N<e^c$, we have that at NL the gains from deviation are at least as high and the gains from cooperation lower than at I^e. We show this for the two cases in the lemma.

Case 1. W is supermodular in domestic policies and strictly supermodular in foreign policies.

$\Omega^\tau(\tau^c,e^c)=\Omega^\tau(\tau^c,e^N)$. By expanding and rearranging, we have $\Omega^\tau(\tau^c,e^c)-\Omega^\tau(\tau^c,e^N)=-s_x=0$ where s_x is defined in (A1.1), and the last equality is proved in Lemma 1.

$\omega^{\tau}(\tau^{c},e^{c})<\omega^{\tau}(\tau^{c},e^{N})$. By expanding and rearranging, we have $\omega^{\tau}(\tau^{c},e^{c})-\omega^{\tau}(\tau^{c},e^{N})=s<0$, where the inequality is proved in Claim 1.

Thus, under Case 1, IC^{τ} does not bind at I^{e} and therefore $W^{Ie}<W^{Ne}$, since at N^{e} the countries have chosen the optimal cooperative tariff given $e=e^{N}$. A similar proof applies to show that IC^{e} does not bind at I^{τ} and therefore $W^{I\tau}<W^{N\tau}$.

Case 2. W is strictly supermodular in both domestic and foreign policies.

$\Omega^{\tau}(\tau^{c},e^{c})>\Omega^{\tau}(\tau^{c},e^{N})$. By expanding and rearranging, we have $\Omega^{\tau}(\tau^{c},e^{c})-\Omega^{\tau}(\tau^{c},e^{N})=-\{s_{x}+W_{x}(\tau^{N},e^{c})-W_{x}(\tau^{r},e^{c})\}>0$. As we show in Lemma 1, strict supermodularity in domestic policies ensures that $s_{x}<0$, moreover $W_{x}(\tau^{N},e^{c})-W_{x}(\tau^{r},e^{c})<0$ since τ^{r} is the best-response to e^{c}.

$\omega^{\tau}(\tau^{c},e^{c})<\omega^{\tau}(\tau^{c},e^{N})$ also holds for some W strictly supermodular in both domestic and foreign policies. By expanding and rearranging, we have $\omega^{\tau}(\tau^{c},e^{c})-\omega^{\tau}(\tau^{c},e^{N})=s+W^{I\tau}-W^{N\tau}<0$, where $s<0$, from Claim 1. Moreover, as we show for Case 1, if $W_{y\tau^{*}e^{*}}>0$ and $W_{x\tau e}=0$ then $W^{I\tau}<W^{N\tau}$, therefore we must have that $\lim W_{x\tau e\rightarrow 0^{+}}(W^{I\tau}-W^{N\tau})\leq 0$.

Thus, under Case 2, IC^{τ} does not bind at I^{e} for $W_{y\tau^{*}e^{*}}>0$ and $W_{x\tau e}\in(0,\bar{\varepsilon}]$. Therefore, $W^{Ie}<W^{Ne}$, since at N^{e} the countries have chosen the optimal cooperative tariff given $e=e^{N}$. A similar proof applies to show that IC^{e} does not bind at I^{τ} and therefore $W^{I\tau}<W^{N\tau}$. □

Proof of Proposition 3. $\partial W_{\tau e}/\partial\lambda=(p_{e}^{w}-1)(1+p_{\tau}^{w})S'$ as long as $\Psi'''=0$, thus, using the results in Eq. (2), $\partial W_{\tau e}/\partial\lambda<0$ for all λ. From the definition of powerful import lobbies if $\lambda=\bar{\lambda}$, then $W_{\tau e}=0$ thus if such a $\lambda>1$ exists then we have $W_{\tau e}>0$ for $\bar{\lambda}>\lambda\geq 1$. As we describe above, $W_{\tau e}(\lambda=1)>0$ which implies that a $\lambda>1$ exists and is unique, for given values of the other exogenous parameters, because $\partial W_{\tau e}/\partial\lambda$ is linear in λ. □

Proof of Proposition 4. $\partial W_{\tau^{*}e^{*}}/\partial\psi=-(p_{e^{*}}^{w}-1)(\alpha S^{*\prime})^{2}(1+p_{\tau^{*}}^{w})\Psi''$ as long as $\Psi'''=0$. Thus, since we assume $\Psi''>0$, if $\alpha>0$ then $\partial W_{\tau^{*}e^{*}}/\partial\psi>0$ for all ψ, by using the results in Eq. (2). By definition $W_{\tau^{*}e^{*}}(\bar{\psi})=0$, thus if such a ψ exists then we have $W_{\tau^{*}e^{*}}(\psi>\bar{\psi})>0$. As we describe above, $W_{\tau^{*}e^{*}}(\psi=0)<0$ which implies that a $\psi>0$ exists and is unique, for given values of the other exogenous parameters, since $\partial W_{\tau^{*}e^{*}}/\partial\psi$ is linear in ψ. □

A.2. Analytical details

A.2.1. Necessary conditions for Nash and global optimal policies.

The expressions below represent the FOC for the Nash policies.

$$W_{\tau}=0:\left(1+P_{\tau}^{w}\right)[\tau M'+(e-\psi\Psi'+(\lambda-1)S/S')S']-p_{\tau}^{w}M=0 \qquad (A2.1)$$

$$W_{e}=0:\left(p_{e}^{w}-1\right)[e-\psi\Psi'+(\lambda-1)S/S']S'+\tau S'+p_{e}^{w}(\tau M'-M)=0 \qquad (A2.2)$$

The expressions below represent the FOC for the global optimal policies.

$$W_{\tau}^{c}=0:\left(1+p_{\tau}^{w}\right)[\tau M'+(e-(\psi\Psi'+\alpha^{*}\psi^{*}\Psi^{*\prime})+(\lambda-1)S/S')S']=0 \qquad (A2.3)$$

$$W_{e}^{c}=0:\left(p_{e}^{w}-1\right)[(e-(\psi\Psi'+\alpha^{*}\psi^{*}\Psi^{*\prime})+(\lambda-1)S/S')S']+\tau S'+p_{e}^{w}\tau M'=0 \qquad (A2.4)$$

A.2.2. Supermodularity conditions

Impact of domestic e-taxes on domestic imports (sector x):

$$M_e = (D' - S')p_e^{\mathrm{w}} + S' = M'p_e^{\mathrm{w}} + S' = \frac{S'M^{*\prime}}{(M' + M^{*\prime})} > 0 \tag{A2.5}$$

where $p_e^{\mathrm{w}} = -S'/(M' + M^{*\prime})$ by applying the implicit function theorem to (1).

Impact of foreign e-taxes on domestic exports (sector y):

$$M_{e^*} = p_{e^*}^{\mathrm{w}} M' \tag{A2.6}$$

A.3. General model

A common concern surrounding import lobbies in debates over linkage is that "traditional protectionist groups will manipulate environmental concerns in order to reduce competition from imports" (Anderson and Blackhurst, 1992, p.20). This issue does not arise in the simpler version of our model because the foreign country's production externality occurs only in home's export sector. Therefore, a producer in the import competing sector does not benefit from a higher foreign e-tax, e_y^*, since it does not affect the price of home's imported good. We briefly discuss the extension of our model that covers such cases by allowing the externality and spillovers to occur in all sectors. For details and proofs of the main results, see Limão (2002a). The basic change is to allow for production externalities in both sectors in each country. Given the existence of externalities in the export sectors e_y and e_x^* become relevant instruments. The government's objective function, $\tilde{W}$, is obtained by not restricting the use of e-taxes in the export sector in the original expression in Eq. (3).

Lemma 1 extends with no changes to the general model because the objective function is additive in the different production sectors. The main change in Lemma 2 is to augment the strategy space in the supermodularity definition to include e_y and e_x^*. Once we do this, it is possible to show that if the objective function, $\tilde{W}$, is supermodular in $(\tau_x,e_x),(\tau_x,e_x^*),(\tau_y^*,e_y)$ and strictly supermodular in (τ_y^*,e_y^*) then linkage creates enforcement. Moreover, there exist objective functions, $\tilde{W}$, strictly supermodular in $(\tau_x,e_x),(\tau_x,e_x^*),(\tau_y^*,e_y)$, and (τ_y^*,e_y^*) such that linkage creates enforcement. Thus, the basic result on the creation of enforcement holds in this more realistic setting.

In addition to the two complementarity conditions examined in the simpler model, we must also ensure that both (τ_x,e_x^*) and (τ_y^*,e_y) are strategic complements with respect to $\tilde{W}$. Moreover, the strategic externality terms in the original conditions in (13–14) now account for the effect of the policy changes on the total supply of that externality, e.g., $S_x+\alpha_x S_x^*$ in home's import sector. The key point is that there still exist parameters such that the objective function is strictly supermodular in the linked policies. Thus, the sufficient conditions for linkage to create enforcement hold even if we allow for externalities and production taxes in both the import and export sectors provided that the government does not place too much weight on import producers.

References

Abrego, L.E., Perroni, C., Whalley, J., Wigle, R.M., 2001. Trade and environment: bargaining outcomes from linked negotiations. Review of International Economics 9 (3), 414–428.

Abreu, D., 1988. On the theory of infinitely repeated games with discounting. Econometrica 56, 383–396.

Anderson, K., 1998. Environmental and labor standards: what role for the WTO? In: Krueger, Anne (Ed.), The WTO as an International Organization. University of Chicago Press, Chicago.

Anderson, K., Blackhurst, R. (Eds.), The Greening of World Trade Issues, vol. xvii. University of Michigan Press, Ann Arbor, p. 276.

Bagwell, K., Staiger, R., 1990. A theory of managed trade. American Economic Review 80, 779–795.

Bagwell, K., Staiger, R., 1999. An economic theory of GATT. American Economic Review 89 (1), 215–248.

Bagwell, K., Staiger, R., 2001. Domestic policies, national sovereignty and international economic institutions. Quarterly Journal of Economics 116 (2), 519–562.

Barret, S., 1994. Strategic environmental policy and international trade. Journal of Public Economics 54 (3), 325–338.

Bernheim, B.D., Whinston, M.D., 1990. Multimarket contact and collusive behavior. The Rand Journal of Economics, 1–26.

Bhagwati, J., Hudec, Robert., (Eds.), 1996. Fair Trade and Harmonization: Pre-requisites for Free Trade? Vol.I. MIT Press, Cambridge, xi, p. 598.

Cesar, H., de Zewe, A., 1996. Issue linkage in global environmental problems. Economic Policy for the Environment and Natural Resources: Techniques for the Management and Control of Pollution. Elgar, Cheltenham, UK, pp. 158–173.

Chang, W., Winters, Alan, 2002. How regional blocs affect excluded countries: the price effects of Mercosur. American Economic Review 92 (4), 889–904.

Charnovitz, S., 1998. Linking topics in treaties. Journal of International Economic Law 329, 329–343.

Conconi, P., Perroni, C., 2000. Issue linkage and issue tie-in in multilateral negotiations. Journal of International Economics 57 (2), 423–447.

Copeland, B.R., 1990. Strategic interaction among nations: negotiable and non-negotiable trade barriers. Canadian Journal of Economics 23 (1), 84–108.

Dixit, A., 1987. Strategic aspects of trade policy. In: Bewley, T. (Ed.), Advances in Economic Theory. Cambridge University Press, pp. 329–362.

Ederington, J., 2001. Global Environmental Agreements and Trade Sanctions. Manuscript. University of Miami.

Ederington, J., 2002. Trade and domestic policy linkage in international agreements. International Economic Review 43 (4), 1347–1367.

Esty, D., 1994. Greening the GATT: Trade, Environment, and the Future. Institute for International Economics, Washington, DC.

Farrell, J., Maskin, E., 1989. Renegotiation in repeated games. Games and Economic Behavior 1 (4), 327–360.

Grossman, G., Helpman, E., 1994. Protection for sale. American Economic Review 84 (4), 833–850.

Horstmann, I., Markusen, J.R., Robles, J., 2001. Multi-Issue Bargaining and Linked Games: Ricardo Revisited or No Pain No Gain. NBER WP, vol. 8347.

Hufbauer, G., Clyde, S., Jeffrey, J., Elliott, K. Ann, 1990. (second ed.). Economic Sanctions Reconsidered: History and Current Policy, vol. xxiii. Institute for International Economics, Washington, DC, pp. 298.

Knetter, M., 1993. International comparisons of price-to-market behavior. American Economic Review 83 (3), 473–486.

Lawrence, R., Bressand, A., Ito, T., 1996. A Vision for the World Economy. Brookings Institution.

Limão, N., 2002a. Trade Policy, Cross-border Externalities and Lobbies: Do Linked Agreements Enforce More Cooperative Outcomes? University of Maryland, Center for International Economics. WP 02-01.

Limão, N., 2002b. Are Preferential Trade Agreements with Non-trade Objectives a Stumbling Bloc for Multilateral Liberalization? University of Maryland, Center for International Economics. WP 02-02.

Phillips, O.R., Mason, C.F., 1992. Mutual forbearance in experimental conglomerate markets. The Rand Journal of Economics, 395–414.

Reinhardt, E., 2000. The Determinants of GATT/WTO Dispute Initiation, 1948–1998. Mimeo, Emory University.

Roessler, F., 1998. Domestic policy objectives and the multilateral trade order: lessons from the past. In: Krueger, A. (Ed.), The WTO as an International Organization. University of Chicago Press, Chicago.

Sebenius, J.K., 1983. Negotiation arithmetic: adding and subtracting issues and parties. International Organization 37 (2), 281–316.

Spagnolo, G., 1999a. On interdependent supergames: multimarket contact, concavity, and collusion. Journal of Economic Theory 89 (1), 127–139.

Spagnolo, G., 1999b. Issue Linkage, Delegation and International Policy Cooperation. University of Cambridge. DAE WP 9913.

Staiger, R., 1995. In: Grossman, Gene, Rogoff, Kenneth (eds.), International Rules and Institutions for Trade Policy in Handbook of International Economics, vol. III. Elsevier, North-Holland, pp. 1451–1495.

Topkis, D., 1979. Equilibrium points in nonzero-sum n-person submodular games. Siam Journal on Control and Optimization 17, 773–787.

World Trade Organization 1999. Trade and Environment. http://www.wto.org.

Chapter 10

Are Preferential Trade Agreements with Non-trade Objectives a Stumbling Block for Multilateral Liberalization?

NUNO LIMÃO
University of Maryland and Centre for Economic Policy Research

First version received October 2003; *final version accepted November* 2006 (*Eds.*)

In many preferential trade agreements (PTAs), countries exchange not only reductions in trade barriers but also cooperation in non-trade issues such as labour and environmental standards, intellectual property, etc. We provide a model of PTAs motivated by cooperation in non-trade issues and analyse its implications for global free trade and welfare. We find that such PTAs increase the cost of multilateral tariff reductions and thus cause a stumbling block to global free trade. This occurs because multilateral tariff reductions decrease the threat that can be used in PTAs and thus the surplus that can be extracted from them. By explicitly modelling the interaction between preferential and multilateral negotiations, we derive a testable prediction and provide novel econometric evidence that supports the model's key prediction. The welfare analysis shows that the current World Trade Organization rules allowing this type of PTAs may be optimal for economically large countries, thus the model can predict the rules we observe. We also analyse alternative rules that constitute a Pareto improvement.

1. INTRODUCTION

Preferential trade agreements (PTAs) are currently among the most important instruments of international economic policy. Since 1995 at least 130 new PTAs were created worldwide, more than doubling the number created in the previous 50 years. More than a third of world trade is estimated to be carried out under them. Traditionally, PTAs are studied simply as a reciprocal reduction of trade barriers, such as tariffs, among a set of countries. However, such reductions are often not the only or even the main motivation for PTAs. Many PTAs require cooperation on issues that are not related to trade policy. The most obvious such agreement is the European Union (E.U.) and its predecessors, which requires countries that want to accede to change their behaviour on a broad set of issues such as environmental and labour standards, intellectual property, human rights, etc. As we describe below, this is far from an isolated case.

Economists generally support free trade, that is, non-preferential trade liberalization, but there is no such consensus about the preferential liberalization that characterizes PTAs. The key concern is that PTAs may be "stumbling blocks" to multilateral liberalization (Bhagwati, 1991); that is, PTAs may halt or reverse the process that has allowed members of the General Agreement on Tariffs and Trade (GATT)/World Trade Organization (WTO) to reduce their multilateral tariffs by over 90% in the last 60 years (Staiger, 1995). One important channel through which this can occur is when PTA partners try to prevent reductions in their preference margins. This leads them to oppose multilateral liberalization because it entails a reduction of tariffs that apply to all partners and thus it erodes preference margins. This problem was foreseen by Johnson (1967) and nearly caused the collapse of multilateral negotiations in 2004, prompting the International

821

Originally Published in *Review of Economic Studies* 74, pp. 821–855.

Monetary Fund to create a special lending programme aimed at developing countries "to mitigate concerns (...) that broad-based tariff liberalization might erode the value of their preferential access to important export markets".[1]

Given the prevalence and importance of non-trade issues in PTAs, it is important to have a model that allows us to analyse their effects on trade and non-trade issues, welfare, and the international rules that govern globalization. Among other things, the model we develop generates interesting insights about the number and membership of PTAs and their effect on cooperation on non-trade issues. To demonstrate the importance of PTAs with non-trade objectives, we examine the central concern with PTAs: how they change the incentives of countries to pursue global free trade. We find robust empirical evidence for the model's prediction that these PTAs cause a stumbling block to multilateral trade liberalization (MTL).[2]

Before presenting our specific results, we show the importance of non-trade issues by describing how prevalent and important they are in the preference programmes of the U.S. and E.U. The reason to focus on them is simple: since they are the two largest traders, any effects of their PTAs on their MTL will have worldwide effects. The scope of the non-trade issues and their importance in motivating individual PTAs vary. For example, the U.S. PTA with Canada and Mexico contained clauses on the enforcement of intellectual property rights as well as labour and environment provisions. The latter two, despite being added as side agreements, were important in their approval by the U.S. congress. All seven PTAs the U.S. has negotiated since then have included chapters on enforcement of intellectual property, labour, and environmental standards. Compliance with these and other criteria is required in order for Caribbean, African, and dozens of other developing countries to be eligible for U.S. trade preferences. Failure to comply has led some of them to lose preferential access to the U.S.[3] Although it is difficult to precisely quantify and assess the relative importance of these non-trade issues in motivating PTAs, some cases are unambiguous. For example, the recent wave of U.S. "... free trade agreements in the Middle East carry out the recommendation in the 9/11 Commission Report..." that "... a comprehensive US strategy to counter terrorism should include economic policies that encourage development, more open societies, and opportunities for people to improve the(ir) lives".[4] The U.S. trade preferences to Andean countries—currently named the "Andean Trade Promotion and Drug Eradication Act"—were enacted specifically to ensure their cooperation in combating drug production and trafficking. The examples above focus on the U.S. because it is the subject of our empirical analysis, but many exist for the E.U. as well.[5]

1. IMF Press Release No. 04/73, 13/04/04.

2. The possibility that linkage of preferences to cooperation on non-trade issues could slow down multilateral liberalization has also been conjectured by international trade lawyers. Trebilcock and Howse assert that: "By failing to respond to the demand for a social clause within the WTO [enforcing labor rights through the threat of trade sanctions], the Organization has simply created an incentive for developed countries to make fewer offers for tariff cuts on an MFN basis in future rounds of negotiations (especially on products of interest to developing countries), so as to preserve the impact that comes from being able to grant–and withdraw–[preferential] GSP treatment" (1999, pp. 462–463).

3. For example, according to the U.S. Generalized System of Preferences (GSP) handbook some countries have lost eligibility for trade preferences under that programme "because of worker rights or intellectual property concerns", p. 6. Accessed at www.ustr.gov/assets/Trade_Development/Preference_Programs/GSP/asset_upload_file267_8359.pdf. In 2005, the U.S. revoked Cote d'Ivoire's eligibility for trade preferences under the AGOA programme because of its failure to comply with the U.N.'s cease-fire resolution. Morocco enacted a comprehensive new labour law recently, and according to U.S. trade negotiators, it was "the prospect of a free trade agreement with the United States [that] helped to forge a domestic consensus for labour law reform in Morocco, spurring reform efforts that had been stymied for more than 20 years." Accessed at www.ustr.gov/Document_Library/Fact_Sheets/2004/Morocco_FTA_Leads_to_Progress_on_Labor_Reform.html.

4. The U.S. has negotiated PTAs with Jordan, Morocco, and Bahrain. It is negotiating with Oman and United Arab Emirates. Its objective is to establish a Middle East Free Trade Area by 2013. Accessed at www.ustr.gov/Document_Library/Press_Releases/2005/October/United_States_Oman_Conclude_Free_Trade_Agreement.html.

5. The E.U. seeks cooperation in non-trade issues via its preferential agreements, even when they do not entail full membership. See Winters (1993) and Grilli (1997) for details on such conditions in the E.U.'s Eastern European,

Quantifying the exact economic importance of cooperation on non-trade issues in trade agreements is very difficult given that many are public goods. In fact, an important objective of this paper is to provide evidence that they are sufficiently important to change the multilateral tariffs the U.S. sets on the rest of the world. The official U.S. agency in charge of the economic analysis of its PTAs admits that the effect of most of those issues is not quantifiable.[6] However, there is indirect evidence from multilateral negotiations in the WTO that suggests they are quite important. For instance, the attempt by developed countries to link cooperation in labour standards to MTL in the WTO was met by the opposition of developing countries and was one of the main causes for the failure to start a new trade round in 1999 in Seattle. Thus, the issue is important enough to forego the gains from MTL. McCalman (2001) provides more specific evidence on the importance of non-trade issues. He estimates the net present value of the transfers that would occur across countries from stronger enforcement of patents, which is now required by the WTO. The net transfer to the U.S. is \$4·5 billion (1988 dollars). For developing countries, the transfers are negative and large: about \$1 billion for Brazil and half a billion dollars each for India and Mexico. According to McCalman, these transfers are of the same order of magnitude as the estimated net welfare gains from reciprocal trade liberalization in the last trade round.

We model non-trade issues as the key motive for PTAs between a country with a large import market, *Large*, that offers tariff reductions to a "regional" partner in exchange for the latter's cooperation in non-trade issues, which we model as regional public goods. We show that these PTAs have an important effect on multilateral tariffs and welfare. Most importantly, these PTAs create an incentive for *Large* to maintain higher multilateral tariffs. Intuitively, the PTA is valuable to *Large* because it allows it to extract cooperation in the non-trade issue. To do this it must offer a preference to the regional partner, that is, a tariff below the multilateral tariff that it applies to all WTO members. This implies that reductions in this multilateral tariff lower the preference margin that *Large* can offer in the PTA and consequently the level of cooperation it can extract. Therefore, these PTAs—currently allowed by WTO rules—are a stumbling block to multilateral liberalization, that is, they generate an incentive to maintain higher multilateral tariffs.

There is a theoretical literature that analyses if PTAs are stumbling blocks to MTL.[7] It focuses on traditional trade models where countries exchange reductions in trade barriers, ignoring PTAs driven by cooperation in non-trade issues, which are the focus of our analysis.[8] This difference has two important implications. First, the existing literature cannot explain the formation of many PTAs. Second, in those traditional models the only direct effect of a PTA is to change quantities and prices of the traded goods, and it is only when such changes occur that the PTA changes the incentives for multilateral tariff setting. But many trade preferences are extended by economically large countries to small ones, and these are unlikely to affect quantities and prices in the large country. So, according to the traditional models these agreements should have no effect on the multilateral tariffs of large countries. In contrast, the stumbling block effect predicted by our model is present for the large and increasing number of agreements, where the partner is relatively small in economic terms, for example, Colombia

Mediterranean, and GSP programmes. More recently, the E.U. has actually implemented what it calls "special incentive arrangements" whereby developing countries can apply for additional preferential tariff reduction if they satisfy certain labour, environmental, or drug combat criteria. On the importance of the exchange of trade preferences for cooperation in non-trade issues, see also Jackson (1997, p. 160), Perroni and Whalley (2000), and World Bank (2000).

6. As is clear from its evaluation of the agreement with the central American countries for example, see p. 117 at http://hotdocs.usitc.gov/docs/pubs/2104f/pub3717.pdf.

7. Interesting contributions include Levy (1997), Bagwell and Staiger (1998), and Krishna (1998).

8. Schiff and Winters (1998) and Bond and Park (2002) study PTAs that stress non-trade issues, typically modelled as a side payment. However, they do not analyse their interaction with multilateral trade agreements.

relative to U.S., provided that it is important in terms of the non-trade issue, for example, the war on drugs.

We also derive precise comparative statics and testable predictions from the model. This is an important and unique feature of our paper since the traditional models of the effect of PTAs on multilateral tariffs have generated few testable predictions and almost no empirical evidence. Our model's key prediction is that, once the PTA is signed, *Large*'s multilateral tariffs increase in the goods exported both by its PTA partner and by the rest of the world relative to those products in the same industry not exported under the PTA. This allows us to construct a good counterfactual for what *Large*'s multilateral tariffs in those PTA products would have been in the absence of those PTAs.

Some of the U.S. PTAs fit the assumptions of the model particularly well, and thus we use them to test the key prediction. Specifically, we analyse the effect of those PTAs on U.S. specific tariff changes negotiated during the last multilateral trade round. We use a difference-in-differences approach over time and across PTA- vs. non-PTA-type goods. The econometric estimates support the key prediction. For the PTAs with non-trade objectives, the U.S. maintained higher multilateral tariffs in PTA-imported goods relative to similar goods imported from the rest of the world. The estimation and robustness tests control for various determinants of multilateral liberalization and address various econometric issues such as the potential for endogeneity arising from possible reverse causation and omitted variable bias. The economic significance is also noteworthy: in the goods exported under the relevant PTAs, these agreements caused an average increase of 33% in the specific tariffs that the U.S. applies multilaterally.[9]

Given the evidence we find for PTAs with non-trade objectives as a stumbling block to MTL, it is important to analyse their welfare predictions and derive implications for WTO rules. We do so from both a positive and a normative perspective. From a positive perspective, the model can explain some features of the current multilateral system. Most significantly, the current WTO rules that permit these PTAs arise endogenously from our model. Large countries, which in practice have chosen such rules in the WTO, prefer them to an alternative regime that forbids these PTAs. In our model, the motive why large states, such as the U.S. and E.U., benefit and thus choose such rules is that they can cooperate with each other in setting multilateral tariffs and thus internalize any effect their PTAs have on those tariffs. However, we also show that when the PTAs cause higher multilateral tariffs they may hurt both the regional PTA partner that cooperates in the non-trade issue and the non-member countries. Therefore, we propose an alternative rule: allowing preferential import subsidies that can be exchanged for cooperation in non-trade issues. We show that switching to these subsidies eliminates the stumbling block effect and generates a Pareto improvement and, according to recent simulation results, would increase the aggregate welfare gains in the current multilateral trade round by about 10% (Limão and Olarreaga, 2006).

The paper is organized as follows. We first show the regional gains to forming PTAs with non-trade objectives. We then show how these PTAs generate a stumbling block to MTL; first illustrating this result in a static model with full enforcement and then proving it in a more realistic dynamic self-enforcing environment. In Section 3, we derive comparative statics and test one of the predictions: that U.S. PTAs with non-trade objectives caused it to set higher multilateral tariffs. In Section 4, we analyse the positive and normative implications of the model for WTO rules. We discuss our results in the conclusion. All proofs are in the appendix.

9. In a recent empirical paper, Limão (2006) explores our comparative static result but focuses mostly on the aggregate effect of U.S. PTAs on its *ad valorem* tariffs. Karacaovali and Limão (2005) do so for the E.U. Both provide some evidence of a stumbling block effect that is complementary to ours. However, we analyse a different form of multilateral trade protection: specific tariffs, which we will see is still important in the U.S. and covers a largely different set of goods.

2. THEORY

2.1. *Model set-up*

We develop a model of regional agreements between countries of asymmetric size in which lower trade barriers are exchanged for cooperation in a non-trade issue. We first describe individual preferences and derive the indirect utilities. We then explain the government's objective and policy instruments. Finally, we write the governments' objective functions in terms of the relevant policy instruments.

Each of the two symmetric regional blocs is composed of two economies, *Large* and *Small*. *Large*'s bigger endowment of the (non-numeraire) goods is the basis for its regional power relative to *Small*. However, *Small* must be important in the non-trade dimension to justify *Large* seeking its cooperation. Thus, we assume that *Small* can produce a public good with a cross-border externality, which is valued by its regional partner, for example, enforcement of human and labour rights, immigration, and environmental laws, etc.

Given the symmetry across regional blocs, we describe only one of them. For simplicity, we assume that countries have the same population, H. Each individual is endowed with one unit of labour—the only factor. The numeraire good is produced with labour according to a constant returns production with a marginal product normalized to unity. In *Large*, each individual is endowed with one unit of each of the non-numeraire goods $i = l, l^*$. Throughout, we use an "*" to denote variables in the other regional bloc. Thus, good l denotes the import good in *Large* and l^* the import for *Large**. In *Small*, each individual is endowed with a fraction $1/k$ of good l and none of l^*; thus, k represents the relative size of the countries in terms of their endowment of l.

The representative consumer in country $j = L$(arge), S(mall) has preferences defined over consumption of the numeraire, c_n^j, the non-numeraire goods, c_i^j, and a public good, E. We write the individual utility as

$$U^j \equiv c_n^j + \sum_i u_i^j(c_i^j) + \overline{\Psi}^j(E^j, E^{\setminus j}). \tag{1}$$

The subutility function for the public good is

$$\overline{\Psi}^j(E^j, E^{\setminus j}) \equiv \lambda^j \Psi(E^j) + \alpha^j \lambda^j \Psi(E^{\setminus j}), \quad \alpha^j, \lambda^j \geq 0, \;\; \Psi' \geq 0, \;\; \Psi'' \leq 0. \tag{2}$$

The weight placed on E, λ^j, varies across countries, and a regional spillover occurs if α^j is positive.[10] We can interpret E as public expenditures to address issues with regional spillovers. Below, we describe how the governments determine its level.

For given prices, taxes, income (denoted by y), and level of E, the individual chooses the quantities of the private goods it consumes to maximize utility subject to a budget constraint, $c_n^j + \sum_i p_i^j c_i^j \leq y^j$. Given the assumptions on the utility, the budget constraint is satisfied with equality, thus individuals demand $d_i^j(p_i^j) = [u_i^{j\prime}(p_i^j)]^{-1}$ of each of the non-numeraire goods. Thus, we write the individual's indirect utility as follows:

$$W^j/H = y^j + \overline{\Psi}^j(E^j, E^{\setminus j}) + \sum_i v_i^j(p_i^j), \tag{3}$$

10. We also assume that $\Psi(0) = 0$, $\lim_{E\to 0} \Psi'(E) = \infty$, and $\lim_{E\to\infty} \Psi(E) \leq \bar{\psi}$.

where the last term represents consumer surplus.[11] An individual's income sources are the wage, the value of the endowment, and net taxes. Net taxes are equal to the *per capita* tariff revenues minus the tax used to finance the public good, e.[12]

We make the following additional assumptions regarding *Small*'s preferences. First, we are interested in the case where it places a smaller weight on E than *Large*. Therefore, without loss of generality, we focus on the extreme case where *Small* places no weight on the public good. Second, we want to focus on a case where the effect of PTAs on multilateral liberalization is driven by the non-trade issue and not changes in trade flows. As we show below, we can neutralize any trade diversion or creation effects from the PTA under a particular trade pattern. A sufficient condition to obtain such a pattern is to assume that *Small* derives no utility from either good l or l^*, it values only the numeraire. Thus, the indirect utility for individuals in *Small* is simply given by their income.

We now describe the government's objective and role. The government sets trade policy and chooses E in order to maximize domestic aggregate welfare. We can incorporate political economy motives for the use of tariffs, but these do not change the qualitative stumbling block results, as we note in Section 2.5.2.

The public good is produced using h_e^j units of labour according to a linear production function: $E^j = b^j h_e^j$. We assume that the population is sufficiently large so that the numeraire is always produced in equilibrium, which fixes the wage at unity. Therefore, the cost of producing E^j is simply h_e^j, the labour bill. According to the government's balanced budget condition, this cost must equal total revenue of the taxes used to fund it, He^j, and so in equilibrium E^j must equal $b^j He^j$. We impose this condition and focus on the government's choice of e^j, the *per capita* tax required to fund E^j.[13]

The trade policy instruments available to the government are specific tariffs on the imported (non-numeraire) goods. The governments also decide on PTAs and multilateral trade agreements and their associated rules. Before analysing the equilibrium agreements, we must show how each government's objective depends on the policy variables, and for this we must describe the trade pattern.

Figure 1 illustrates the trade pattern. The two large countries have similar endowments, and therefore differences in demand determine their trade pattern. We label the good for which *Large* has a stronger preference as l, so it imports l and exports l^*.[14]

Small values only the numeraire good, and so it exports its full endowment of the non-numeraire good, H/k, to *Large*. We assume that the trading costs between a small and a large country in opposite blocs are prohibitive. This simplifying assumption, along with the endowment and preference structure, allows us to neutralize any potential trade diversion and creation effects and thus isolate a distinct effect of PTAs on multilateral tariffs driven by non-trade objectives. To see this clearly, note that *Small* does not set tariffs since they do not import the non-numeraire goods.[15] Since *Small* has no tariff reductions to offer to *Large*, the PTA consists of a tariff reduction by *Large* on *Small*'s exports in exchange for *Small*'s provision of the regional

11. We focus on quadratic subutilities, u_i, which imply linear demands. This can be relaxed for some but not all results.

12. More specifically, if we let w denote the wage, tr the *per capita* tariff revenue and e the tax charged for the public good, then the individual's income is $y^{\mathrm{L}} = w^{\mathrm{L}} + \sum_i p_i^{\mathrm{L}} + \mathrm{tr}^{\mathrm{L}} - e^{\mathrm{L}}$ in *Large* and $y^{\mathrm{S}} = w^{\mathrm{S}} + p_l^{\mathrm{S}}/k + \mathrm{tr}^{\mathrm{S}} - e^{\mathrm{S}}$ in *Small*.

13. The tariff revenue is distributed lump-sum, and we assume that none is used to finance the public good, which maintains the two policies within each country separable in the model.

14. We could alternatively allow the large countries to have identical preferences but endow each with a larger amount than the other in their respective export product. In either case, the balance of payments condition is satisfied through movements of the numeraire good.

15. We can extend the model to provide a motivation for such tariffs in *Small*. However, since reductions in small countries' tariffs are not a central component of the PTAs with large countries that motivate our analysis, we choose not

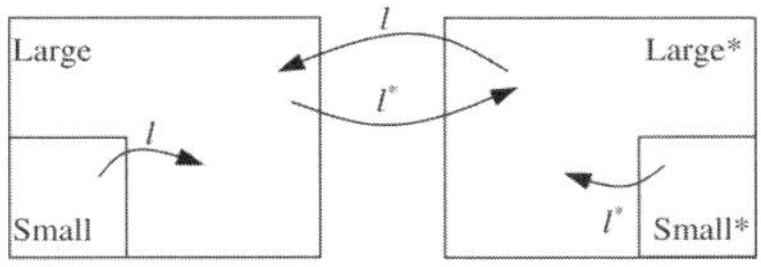

FIGURE 1

The arrows represent the direction of exports of the non-numeraire goods. We assume that trading costs (due to transport or information for example) are prohibitively high between small and large countries in opposite blocks.

public good. Consequently, the only direct effect of the PTA on trade is to increase the price that *Small* receives for the H/k units of good l it exports to *Large*.

To determine the equilibrium prices of goods l and l^*, we first note that *Large* sets a tariff t on imports from *Small* and a tariff τ on imports from *Large**. The price received by *Large** for its export is $p_l^{\mathrm{L}} - \tau$, where p_l^{L} is the domestic price in *Large* and is derived from the market-clearing condition requiring net import demands to sum to zero:

$$M_l^{\mathrm{L}}(p_l^{\mathrm{L}}) + M_l^{\mathrm{L}^*}(p_l^{\mathrm{L}} - \tau) + M_l^{\mathrm{S}} = 0. \tag{4}$$

Net imports are defined by $M_l^j \equiv (d_l^j(p_l^j) - 1)H$ for $j = L, L^*$ and $M_l^{\mathrm{S}} \equiv -H/k$. A condition similar to (4) holds for l^*. These conditions define the domestic prices in *Large* as functions of the tariffs $p_l^{\mathrm{L}}(\tau)$ and $p_{l*}^{\mathrm{L}}(\tau^*)$. These prices are not directly affected by the preferential tariff because the small countries' supplies are perfectly inelastic. It is then simple to show that an increase in τ raises the domestic price in *Large*, p_l^{L}, which includes the tariff. However, it lowers the price net of tariff, $p_l^{\mathrm{L}}(\tau) - \tau$, which is received by exporters in *Large**. For a similar reason, an increase in τ^* lowers the price for *Large*'s exports of l^*. This effect of tariffs is the motive we model for the multilateral trade negotiation in Section 2.5.[16]

We can now write the objective functions for *Small* and *Large* in terms of the policy variables.

$$W^{\mathrm{S}}(t, e^{\mathrm{S}}, \tau) = H\{1 - e^{\mathrm{S}} + (p_l^{\mathrm{L}}(\tau) - t)/k\}, \tag{5}$$

$$\begin{aligned} W^{\mathrm{L}}(t, e^{\mathrm{S}}, \tau, \tau^*, e^{\mathrm{L}}) = {} & H\{1 - e^{\mathrm{L}} + \lambda^{\mathrm{L}}\Psi(b^{\mathrm{L}}He^{\mathrm{L}}) + \alpha^{\mathrm{L}}\lambda^{\mathrm{L}}\Psi(b^{\mathrm{S}}He^{\mathrm{S}})\} - \{M_l^{\mathrm{S}}t + M_l^{\mathrm{L}^*}(\tau)\tau\} \\ & + H\{p_{l*}^{\mathrm{L}}(\tau^*) + v_{l*}^{\mathrm{L}}(p_{l*}^{\mathrm{L}}(\tau^*))\} + H\{p_l^{\mathrm{L}}(\tau) + v_l^{\mathrm{L}}(p_l^{\mathrm{L}}(\tau))\}. \end{aligned} \tag{6}$$

For *Small*, the three terms in (5) represent, respectively, aggregate wages (H), the cost of producing the public good (He^{S}), and export revenue. For *Large*, the terms in (6) represent, respectively, in the first line aggregate wages (H), the cost of producing the public good (He^{L}), utility from the public good, and tariff revenue on imports from *Small* and *Large** ($-\{M_l^{\mathrm{S}}t + M_l^{\mathrm{L}^*}(\tau)\tau\}$). The terms in the second line represent surplus from goods l^* and l.

2.2. *Regional externalities and gains from PTAs*

We begin by examining the incentive to form PTAs with non-trade objectives. The timing of actions is illustrated in Figure 2. First, the rules are chosen; we analyse this in Section 4. Given

to model them. In fact, trade liberalization by the smaller, less developed countries has mostly been a result of a shift in ideology from import substitution towards unilateral liberalization (Ethier, 1998).

16. Implicit differentiation of (4) yields $\partial p_l^{\mathrm{L}}(\tau)/\partial\tau \in (0, 1)$ and $\partial p_{l*}^{\mathrm{L}}(\tau^*)/\partial\tau^* \in (-1, 0)$.

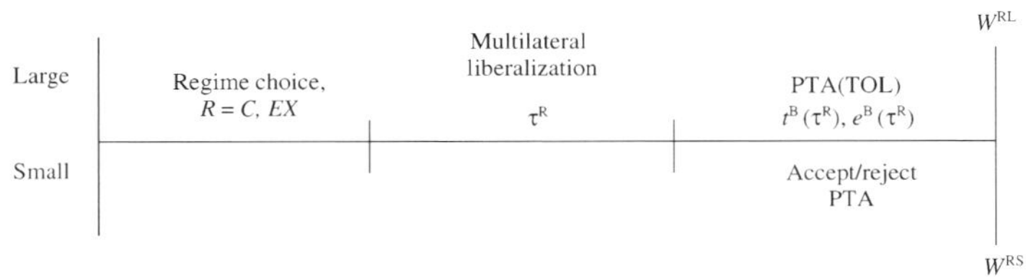

FIGURE 2

Large countries first choose a regime (R), where they either commit to most-favourite-nation rule (MFN) (no PTAs allowed) or not: the preferential trade agreement (PTA) exception. Given the regime, the large countries choose a level for the MFN tariff (τ^R). This is the maximum credible threat that can be subsequently used to make a take-it-or-leave-it offer (TOL) for a PTA, which *Small* can accept or reject. The TOL offer in the final stage is simply the vector (t^B, e^B), the value for *Large*'s preferential tariff on *Small* and a tax level for *Small*'s provision of the public good. The pay-offs are W^{Rj} for regime R and country j.

these rules, the second stage involves the choice of multilateral tariff levels, τ and τ^*, analysed in Section 2.5. In the third stage, a PTA may be formed. This three-stage game takes place each period and is indefinitely repeated.[17]

There exist two externalities in a regional bloc. The first arises through the public good, and the second is the terms-of-trade (TOT) externality: *Large*'s market power in trade implies that by imposing a tariff it can lower the prices received by *Small*'s exporters. These externalities are typically overcome through international self-enforcing agreements. These agreements are sustained by repetition and the threat of non-cooperation. The Nash non-cooperative outcome within a regional bloc in the absence of any constraints is given by a tariff t^N that *Large* sets on *Small* and a level of *Small*'s regional public good, e^{NS}. These are found by maximizing (6) and (5), respectively, taking the other countries policies, including τ, as given

$$t^N = p_l^L(\tau); \quad e^{NS} = 0. \tag{7}$$

The basic intuition is simple. *Small* supplies none of the public good because it does not value it. *Large* increases the tariff until *Small*'s exporters are indifferent between exporting or not. This occurs at the point where the specific tariff equals the price. Since *Small*'s export supply of l is perfectly inelastic, *Large* can use a tariff that just extracts all the surplus and *Small* will still export its full endowment.

In Figure 3, N represents the Nash equilibrium when *Large* can set a discriminatory tariff. As we will show some WTO rules constrain the maximum level of t, so in general we refer to that level as the threat tariff and denote it by t^T. *Small*'s iso-welfare contour at the Nash is labelled $\overline{W}^{NS}$. *Small*'s welfare increases as t or e^S is lowered, reaching the maximum at the origin.[18] *Large*'s welfare is increasing in t and e^S, and its contour at the Nash is $\overline{W}^{NL}$. A PTA with non-trade objectives where *Large* exchanges a reduction in t for an increase in e^S generates a Pareto improvement for the region as a whole, as represented by the shaded area.

17. We implicitly assume that the regional negotiation costs are negligible relative to multilateral ones, which implies that even after multilateral trade negotiations a country can easily sign a PTA. Thus, PTAs are modelled as the last stage of the game. In Section 2.5.2, we show that the key result is independent of the timing of the self-enforcing agreements.

18. The slope is constant because a reduction of t by k increases *Small*'s export price by k and thus its export revenue increases by $kH/k = H$. Since H is the marginal cost for *Small* of increasing e^S, the slope of the iso-welfare is $-k$.

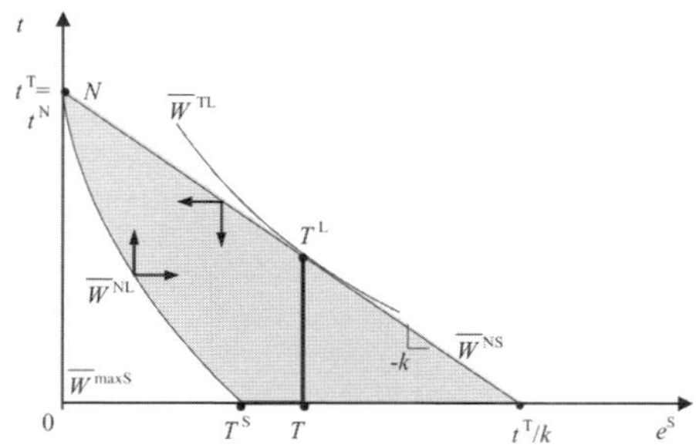

FIGURE 3

Point N denotes the non-cooperative solution to *Large*'s tariff on *Small* and the latter's e-tax. The shaded area represents potential preferential trade agreements (PTAs) which are Pareto improving. The slope of *Small*'s iso-welfare line is $-k < -1$, the ratio of *Large* to *Small*'s endowments. *Large*'s welfare is quasi-linear in t. The segment $T^{S}TT^{L}$ represents PTAs that are both Pareto improving and Pareto efficient. Any efficient bargaining solution must lie on $T^{S}TT^{L}$. If *Large* (*Small*) has all the bargaining power and makes a take-it-or-leave-it offer, then the solution is at T^{L} (T^{S}). The segment TT^{L} is vertical because changes in *Large*'s tariff on *Small* have only tariff revenue effects, which are constant and thus have no impact on the slope of the iso-welfare curves.

2.3. *Interaction of PTAs and multilateral liberalization: the basic mechanism*

We first illustrate one of the key results, the stumbling block effect of PTAs, in a simple setting that ignores enforcement constraints. Once the intuition is clear, we prove it for the more realistic case where enforcement is important and provide a full characterization of the PTA and a welfare analysis of alternative WTO rules.

We start by considering the PTA stage; recall that this is the final stage and thus takes the rules and multilateral tariffs as given. As we noted above, there exist regional gains from trade to be made if *Large* reduces the preferential tariff, t, for an increase in e^{S} by *Small*, as represented by the shaded area in Figure 3. The PTA resulting from an efficient bargaining process must lie on the locus of tangencies represented by $T^{S}TT^{L}$ in that figure. The exact solution depends on the chosen bargaining concept and relative bargaining power. We focus on the case where *Large* has all the bargaining power. This is an important case empirically given the extreme size asymmetries in recent PTAs. If *Large* makes a take-it-or-leave-it (TOL) offer, the solution to the PTA is at T^{L}, which leaves *Small* at its Nash welfare level.[19] More formally, for a given most-favourite-nation rule (MFN) tariff, τ, and threat tariff, t^{T}, the PTA is defined by the following preferential tariff and level of e^{S}:

$$\{t^{B}(t^{T}), e^{B}(t^{T})\} \equiv \underset{t,e^{S}}{\arg\max}\{W^{L}(t, e^{S}, \tau, \tau^{*}, \cdot) : W^{S}(t, e^{S}, \tau) \geq W^{S}(t = t^{T}, e^{S} = 0, \tau)\}. \quad (8)$$

Since *Large* benefits from increases in e^{S} for any given preference, it prefers *Small* to increase e^{S} up to the point where the participation constraint binds, so that *Small* is just indifferent

19. According to the World Bank report on regionalism, the accession policies of North American Free Trade Agreement (NAFTA) and the EU "... can lead to asymmetric agreements in which benefits to developing country candidates are reduced and possibly appropriated by existing members through side conditions on issues such as the environment, labor regulations, and rules of origin" (2000, p. 100). Abrego, Perroni, Whalley and Wigle (2001) estimate the gains relative to non-cooperation of a Nash bargaining outcome in a two-country general computable equilibrium model where a large country trades market access for environmental protection provided by a small country; however, they do not address preferential agreements or the interaction with multilateral liberalization.

between this and a situation where it does not supply the regional good and faces the threat tariff t^{T}. Using the definition of W^{S} in (5), it is simple to confirm that the equilibrium *per capita* cost to *Small* of supplying the regional good, e^{B}, is equal to the *per capita* benefit from the preference margin, $(t^{\mathrm{T}}-t)/k$. Replacing this condition in (8) and taking the first-order condition with respect to t, we can describe the general PTA solution as

$$e^{\mathrm{B}}(t^{\mathrm{T}})=(t^{\mathrm{T}}-t^{\mathrm{B}})/k, \tag{9}$$

$$W_t^{\mathrm{L}}-W_{e^{\mathrm{S}}}^{\mathrm{L}}/k\leq 0, \tag{10}$$

where the subscripts denote partial derivatives. When the PTA is not duty free, (10) holds with equality and has the simple interpretation that the marginal cost for *Large* of decreasing t, $-W_t^{\mathrm{L}}$, equals the marginal benefit from the resulting increase in e^{S}. When the inequality in (10) is strict, the PTA is duty free, which will be significant since it indicates that *Large* would benefit from increasing the preferential margin, $t^{\mathrm{T}}-t^{\mathrm{B}}$, in exchange for additional e^{S}, but it cannot do so by lowering the preferential tariff further when it is already zero and will instead increase the threat tariff, t^{T}. In this section, we focus on the duty-free case, but in Section 2.4 we analyse both and provide sufficient conditions for each to be the equilibrium.

Note that, for a given threat tariff, neither PTA policy in the solution above depends on the MFN tariff directly. But the threat tariff itself is a positive function of the MFN tariff, and this is the source of the interaction between these PTAs and MTL, as we now show.

Thus far, we assumed that *Large* uses the Nash tariff as the threat in the PTA. However, if both countries are members of the WTO, there is an important constraint on the level of this threat. According to the MFN, a country must extend the same tariff on "like-products" to all WTO members. Therefore, the highest credible threat tariff that *Large* can use against *Small* is the multilateral tariff τ. If the MFN rule was strictly enforced, then *Large* would be unable to extend a preferential tariff and have a PTA. However, current WTO rules allow exceptions to MFN, which permit countries to offer preferential tariffs below MFN values. Under such exceptions, the upper bound of the tariff is the "MFN" value. We describe the current rule as a PTA exception to MFN and note that it allows $t\leq\tau$. The value of τ when the PTA is decided is taken as given because it is determined in the previous stage. Therefore, the maximum threat tariff, t^{T}, under the current rules depends on whether *Small* is a WTO member:

$$t^{\mathrm{T}}\begin{cases}\leq\tau, & \text{if } \tau \text{ is set cooperatively and } \textit{Small} \text{ is a WTO member,}\\ =t^{\mathrm{N}}, & \text{otherwise.}\end{cases} \tag{11}$$

Our qualitative analysis still applies if we use τ instead of t^{N} as the threat tariff. The intuition for the stumbling block result should now become clearer. By reducing the multilateral tariff, τ, in the WTO, *Large* reduces the threat tariff it uses in the PTA. When *Small* is a WTO member, that effect on the threat is direct since *Large* uses the maximum threat, $t^{\mathrm{T}}=\tau$, in equilibrium. If the preferential tariff given to *Small* is already at zero, then any reduction in the threat tariff that *Large* can use will cause *Small* to reduce its provision of the public good. It is this extra cost of reducing multilateral tariffs that drives the stumbling block effect. To see this clearly, we must model the MTL process that precedes the PTA stage.[20]

We follow Bagwell and Staiger (1999) who argue that the motive for reciprocal trade liberalization in the WTO is to overcome a TOT externality between large countries. Their view has

20. We focus on the case when *Small* is a WTO member but the effect is also present if it was not and $t^{\mathrm{T}}=t^{\mathrm{N}}$. In this case, the effect of a reduction of τ occurs indirectly by lowering $p_l^{\mathrm{L}}(\tau)$. To see this recall that a reduction in τ causes a fall in $p_l^{\mathrm{L}}(\tau)$ and consequently in the threat tariff.

proved useful in explaining several rules of the world trading system and has therefore gained considerable support among several, although not all, economists.[21] Consistent with this view, much of the MTL occurs between large countries and follows what is known as the principal supplier rule. That is, if *Large* is the largest exporter of a product, say good l^*, to *Large**, then the latter proposes to reduce its tariff on l^*. In exchange, *Large** requests a reduction in the tariff imposed on its export to *Large*, good l. As noted above, the MFN rule requires these reductions to be extended to all other WTO exporters of similar goods. Thus, we model MTL as the reciprocal tariff reduction between the large countries that is extended to the small ones.

Given the symmetry between the two large countries, it is sufficient to focus on one of them and impose the equilibrium condition that their multilateral tariffs are identical, that is, $\tau^* = \tau$. The multilateral tariff set under the PTA exception, τ^{EX}, is then given by

$$\tau^{\mathrm{EX}} \equiv \arg\max_{\tau}\{W^{\mathrm{L}}(t = t^{\mathrm{B}}(t^{\mathrm{T}}), e^{\mathrm{S}} = e^{\mathrm{B}}(t^{\mathrm{T}}), \tau, \tau^* = \tau, \cdot) : t \leq \tau\}. \tag{12}$$

Large always uses the maximum possible threat against *Small* in the PTA. When both are WTO members this is the multilateral tariff, τ^{EX}, so its equilibrium is given by the following first order condition (FOC):

$$\tau^{\mathrm{EX}} : W^{\mathrm{L}}_{\tau} + W^{\mathrm{L}}_{\tau^*} + W^{\mathrm{L}}_{t}\partial t^{\mathrm{B}}/\partial t^{\mathrm{T}} + W^{\mathrm{L}}_{e^{\mathrm{S}}}\partial e^{\mathrm{B}}/\partial t^{\mathrm{T}} = 0. \tag{13}$$

The first two terms represent the effect of increases in the tariffs of *Large* and *Large**. If *Small* did not export this good, these would be the only effects and free trade would be the outcome. The reason is simple, the gain from an increase in own tariffs is achieved by lowering the price paid for imports in the world market. However, this gain occurs at the expense of lower prices received by the exporter. So, when countries are symmetric, any gain for *Large* from a tariff, W^{L}_{τ}, is offset by the cost of facing an identical tariff from *Large** on its exports, $W^{\mathrm{L}}_{\tau^*}$.

When the PTA is duty free, marginal changes in the threat tariff do not affect the preferential tariff, since $t^{\mathrm{B}} = 0$, but they do affect e^{B}. Therefore, in this case the interaction between PTAs and MTL is fully captured by the last term, $W^{\mathrm{L}}_{e^{\mathrm{S}}}\partial e^{\mathrm{B}}/\partial t^{\mathrm{T}}$. This term is positive because increases in t^{T} increase the supply of the public good, e^{B}, which *Large* values. Therefore, the multilateral tariff under the duty-free PTA is higher than in its absence. The magnitude of this stumbling block effect of PTAs depends on the weight that *Large* places on the public good and can therefore be quite high even if *Small*'s exports are negligible.[22]

In Section 3, we derive comparative statics of the multilateral tariff under PTAs relative to the one when they are prohibited and test the resulting prediction. But first we prove the result formally and show how robust it is to alternative enforcement and timing considerations that characterize observed agreements.

21. Although the view in Bagwell and Staiger (1999) has become increasingly accepted, it has faced two criticisms. The first is due to Ethier (2004) who has argued that if the objective of the GATT/WTO was to internalize TOT effects, it should restrict not only import tariffs but also export taxes and yet it does not. This is an interesting point but there may exist a plausible explanation for it. There are at least two potentially important incentives for trade protection: redistributing income to producers, that is, a political economy motive, and a TOT motive (cf. Grossman and Helpman, 1995). In the case of imports, both motives imply a positive tax on imports but in the case of exports they go in opposite directions: the TOT motive implies export taxes but the political economy motive entails export subsidies. This suggests that the GATT/WTO has less of a need to restrict export rather than import taxes explicitly because in equilibrium countries have less of an incentive to pursue TOT gains through exports. The second criticism is that most countries do not have market power in trade and even if they did they would not exert it by raising tariffs. However, there is recent evidence to the contrary on both accounts. Chang and Winters (2002) find that Brazil's increase in tariffs *vis-a-vis* the world relative to Argentina, as they formed Mercosur, caused a decrease in the prices the exporters from the rest of the world received from Brazil. Broda, Limão and Weinstein (2006) estimate that both small and large countries have a reasonable amount of market power across a variety of their imports and find that non-WTO members do set higher tariffs on products where their market power is largest.

22. We can verify that the strategic effect is strictly positive as follows. When the PTA is duty free, we know that (i) $W^{\mathrm{L}}_{e^{\mathrm{S}}}/k > W^{\mathrm{L}}_{t}$ (from (10)) and (ii) $W^{\mathrm{L}}_{e^{\mathrm{S}}}\partial e^{\mathrm{B}}/\partial t^{\mathrm{T}} = W^{\mathrm{L}}_{e^{\mathrm{S}}}/k$ (from (9)) and therefore $W^{\mathrm{L}}_{e^{\mathrm{S}}}\partial e^{\mathrm{B}}/\partial t^{\mathrm{T}} > W^{\mathrm{L}}_{t} = H/k > 0$.

2.4. *Endogenous formation of self-enforcing PTAs*

The solution above ignored enforcement. However, international agreements must be self-enforcing given the absence of an authority to punish a country if it does not comply. If the asymmetry in bargaining power allows *Large* to make a TOL offer, then enforcement becomes a key issue. Intuitively, if the TOL described above can not be directly enforced, then *Small* would accept it, get the higher export price, and not provide the public good. Thus, this PTA solution is not self-enforcing even if *Small* is extremely patient.

Cooperative self-enforcing agreements are well characterized by certain repeated games (cf. Bagwell and Staiger, 1990). We derive the self-enforcing bargaining solution to the PTA when *Large* makes a TOL offer to *Small* for given multilateral tariffs. We assume that governments observe each other's actions at the end of each period and focus on stationary subgame perfect equilibria. We adopt the simplest trigger strategies that maintain such equilibria—infinite Nash reversion. That is, if a deviation occurred then afterwards *Small* sets e^{S} equal to zero and *Large* sets t at the threat tariff defined in (11). The pay-offs for each government are given by their respective welfare functions discounted at a rate δ^j.[23]

More formally, *Large* makes a TOL offer to *Small* specifying t and e^{S} for a given level of the threat tariff, t^{T}, and the multilateral tariff, τ. This offer maximizes the present discounted value of *Large*'s welfare subject to one incentive constraint for each country, IC^j. Since we focus on stationary strategies, we need only maximize welfare each period. We continue to denote the equilibrium values by a superscript B, noting that henceforth it refers to the self-enforcing bargaining solution given by

$$\{t^{\mathrm{B}}(t^{\mathrm{T}}), e^{\mathrm{B}}(t^{\mathrm{T}})\} \equiv \operatorname*{argmax}_{t, e^{\mathrm{S}}}\{W^{\mathrm{L}}(t, e^{\mathrm{S}}, \tau, \tau^*, \cdot) : \mathrm{IC}^{\mathrm{S}}; \mathrm{IC}^{\mathrm{L}}\}. \tag{14}$$

The key difference relative to the solution in (8) is the incentive constraints. The one for *Small*, IC^{S}, requires that its gain from deviating today by not supplying the public good, given by the left side of (15) below, does not exceed the net benefit from future cooperation that arises from facing a lower tariff on its exports. The constraint for *Large* is given by (16), where the left side represents the gain from deviation that would arise from the extra tariff revenue it would collect if it were to increase the tariff on *Small*. In equilibrium, this deviation gain must not exceed the discounted net gain from cooperation that arises from *Small*'s supply of the regional public good—the R.H.S. of (16):

$$W^{\mathrm{S}}(t, e^{\mathrm{NS}}, \tau) - W^{\mathrm{S}}(t, e^{\mathrm{S}}, \tau) \leq \frac{\delta^{\mathrm{S}}}{1-\delta^{\mathrm{S}}}(W^{\mathrm{S}}(t, e^{\mathrm{S}}, \tau) - W^{\mathrm{S}}(t^{\mathrm{T}}, e^{\mathrm{NS}}, \tau)), \tag{15}$$

$$W^{\mathrm{L}}(t^{\mathrm{T}}, e^{\mathrm{S}}, \tau, \cdot) - W^{\mathrm{L}}(t, e^{\mathrm{S}}, \tau, \cdot) \leq \frac{\delta^{\mathrm{L}}}{1-\delta^{\mathrm{L}}}(W^{\mathrm{L}}(t, e^{\mathrm{S}}, \tau, \cdot) - W^{\mathrm{L}}(t^{\mathrm{T}}, e^{\mathrm{NS}}, \tau, \cdot)). \tag{16}$$

In Figure 4, $\overline{\mathrm{IC}}^j$ represents the incentive frontier for country j, that is, the combinations of t and e^{S} that leave j indifferent between cooperating and deviating. In a self-enforcing PTA, *Small* must be left above the Nash welfare level, otherwise the only self-enforcing level for e^{S} is zero. This implies that $\overline{\mathrm{IC}}^{\mathrm{S}}$ is interior relative to $\overline{W}^{\mathrm{NS}}$, that is, relative to *Small*'s iso-welfare contour under no cooperation. The motive is simple: *Small* is now willing to provide less of the

23. It may be possible to design more efficient agreements with non-stationary strategies because when $\delta^{\mathrm{L}} \neq \delta^{\mathrm{S}}$, there is a motive for inter-temporal trading of pay-offs. Moreover, in a paper analysing gradualism in PTAs, Bond and Park (2002) show that under certain cases agreements between asymmetric countries that use non-stationary strategies are more efficient. Our focus on stationary strategies makes the model tractable when we consider the interaction with multilateral liberalization. More efficient agreements should not change the stumbling block result because the PTA would still be valuable to *Large* and thus create an extra cost to lowering the multilateral tariff.

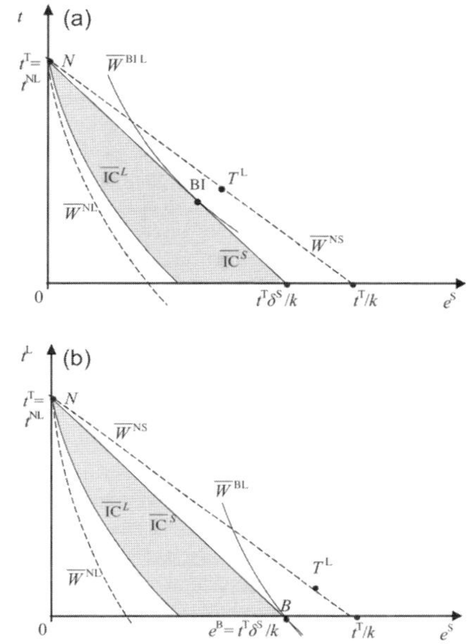

FIGURE 4

The shaded areas represent the set of self-enforcing preferential trade agreements (PTAs) that improve on the Nash (N); it is delimited by each country's incentive frontiers. Point *BI* in 4a represents the self-enforcing take-it-or-leave-it (TOL) PTA solution proposed by *Large* when it is not sufficiently endowed relative to *Small*, that is, when k is not sufficiently high. Under this condition, an alternative solution occurs if *Large*'s IC binds and would lie at the intersection of the incentive frontiers of *Large* and *Small* (*BII* not depicted). In 4b, point B represents the self-enforcing TOL PTA solution proposed by *Large* when it is sufficiently endowed relative to *Small*, that is, when k is sufficiently high.

public good for any given reduction in the preferential tariff because the gains from deviating are enjoyed today whereas future cooperation gains are discounted. Therefore, the bargaining outcomes considered in Section 2.3, those along $\overline{W}^{NS}$, are not self-enforcing for any $\delta^S \in (0, 1)$. The incentive frontier for *Large* holds with equality at $t = t^T$ and it is flatter than $\overline{W}^{NL}$, the reason is also the discounting. Thus, the shaded area between the incentive frontiers of *Large* and *Small* represents the set of self-enforcing PTAs that improve on the Nash. Moreover, since *Large* makes a TOL offer, *Small*'s incentive constraint binds and so the solution is on $\overline{\mathrm{IC}}^S$, otherwise *Large* would increase the preferential tariff or demand a higher e^S. Therefore, $\overline{\mathrm{IC}}^S$ is used to determine e^S as a positive function of the difference between the threat and preferential tariffs.

The shaded areas in Figure 4(a) and (b) show the existence of self-enforcing PTAs that are strictly welfare improving for both countries. The last question we address here is whether the PTA is duty free. This will be an important determinant of whether these agreements are a stumbling block for MTL. As we show in Proposition 1, the PTA is duty free if *Large* is sufficiently endowed relative to *Small*. Before formally stating the proposition, we provide the basic intuition. Recall that we assume that *Small*'s endowment of good l is H/k and *Large*'s is H, which is k times larger. So, the more endowed *Large* is relative to *Small*, that is, the larger k is, the fewer units of *Small*'s exports the preference margin applies to. Therefore, as k increases

Large must lower the preferential tariff in order to be able to extract a given level of e^{S}. For a sufficiently large k, we have a duty-free PTA.[24]

We say that ***Large* is sufficiently endowed relative to *Small* if $k \geq \max(k_1, k_2)$**, where the exact mathematical definitions for the thresholds k_1 and k_2 are provided in the appendix. Here we describe them, starting with the cases where $t^{\mathrm{B}}(t^{\mathrm{T}}) > 0$ and then arguing that as k increases above k_1 or k_2 we obtain $t^{\mathrm{B}}(t^{\mathrm{T}}) = 0$. We need to consider the situation when *Large*'s IC binds and when it does not. First, if *Large*'s IC does not bind, then the solution is at point *BI* in Figure 4(a). This point is defined by the equality of the marginal rate of substitution of the policies in *Large*'s welfare and the substitution of the policies in enforcement for *Small*. In this case, as we increase k, *Small*'s exports, H/k, fall and therefore, for a given level of the tariff and of e^{S}, *Small*'s gain from cooperation falls because the preference margin is applied to fewer exports. Thus, the increase in k implies that a reduction in the preferential tariff is required to maintain a given supply of the public good by *Small*. The increase in k also implies that *Large*'s marginal cost of reducing the preferential tariff falls—it foregoes less tariff revenue—whereas its marginal benefit from the regional public good is unchanged. Thus, the equilibrium preferential tariff falls as k increases. If k reaches a critical value k_1—the level at which the MRS of the policies in welfare in *Large* and enforcement in *Small* are identical and the equilibrium preferential tariff is zero—then the PTA is duty free. This is illustrated by point B in Figure 4(b). When *Large*'s IC does bind, the solution is at the intersection of $\overline{\mathrm{IC}}^{\mathrm{L}}$ and $\overline{\mathrm{IC}}^{\mathrm{S}}$ (not depicted in the figure). Using a reasoning similar to the first case, we can establish a critical value k_2 above which the PTA is duty free. That is, as we raise k it eventually reaches a level k_2 defined by the intersection of $\overline{\mathrm{IC}}^{\mathrm{L}}$ and $\overline{\mathrm{IC}}^{\mathrm{S}}$ when $t^{\mathrm{B}}(t^{\mathrm{T}}) = 0$.

Using the definition above, we characterize the self-enforcing PTAs in the following proposition.

Proposition 1. *(Self-enforcing PTA bargaining solutions):*
The self-enforcing PTA (TOL) bargaining solution for a threat of t^{T} *is* $\{t = t^{\mathrm{B}}(t^{\mathrm{T}}), e^{\mathrm{S}} = e^{\mathrm{B}}(t^{\mathrm{T}})\}$, *where* $e^{\mathrm{B}}(t^{\mathrm{T}}) = \frac{\delta^{\mathrm{S}}}{k}(t^{\mathrm{T}} - t^{\mathrm{B}}(t^{\mathrm{T}}))$ *and*

(i) $t^{\mathrm{B}}(t^{\mathrm{T}}) = 0$ *if and only if Large is sufficiently endowed relative to Small or*
(ii) $t^{\mathrm{B}}(t^{\mathrm{T}}) = t^{BI} : W^{\mathrm{L}}_{e^{\mathrm{S}}}(e^{\mathrm{B}})/W^{\mathrm{L}}_{t} = (W^{\mathrm{S}}_{e^{\mathrm{S}}}/W^{\mathrm{S}}_{t})/\delta^{\mathrm{S}}$ *(IC^{L} does not bind) or* $t^{\mathrm{B}}(t^{\mathrm{T}}) = t^{BII} : t^{\mathrm{T}} - t^{\mathrm{B}} = \delta^{\mathrm{L}} k \alpha^{\mathrm{L}} \lambda^{\mathrm{L}} \Psi(b^{\mathrm{S}} H e^{\mathrm{B}})$ *when* $W^{\mathrm{L}}_{e^{\mathrm{S}}}(e^{\mathrm{B}})/W^{\mathrm{L}}_{t} \geq (W^{\mathrm{S}}_{e^{\mathrm{S}}}/W^{\mathrm{S}}_{t})/\delta^{\mathrm{S}}$ *(IC^{L} binds).*

For given multilateral tariffs, the PTA is strictly welfare improving for both countries relative to no PTA. Thus, in this section we explained the endogenous formation of the many PTAs we observe that are motivated by the desire of large countries to obtain cooperation in non-trade issues. To the extent that WTO rules permit these PTAs, they contribute to their proliferation. Models that ignore non-trade issues cannot explain why developed countries lower their tariffs on products from small countries, particularly when the latter do not reciprocate by lowering their own trade barriers. We now show how these PTAs can cause higher multilateral tariffs.

2.5. *Multilateral trade liberalization*

We model MTL as the second stage of the game, after the rules are set and before the PTAs are signed. The basic structure is similar to Section 2.3. The two large countries choose the

24. The PTA is also duty free if *Large* places a high weight on the public good or if the spillover, α, is important since *Large* is then willing to give up all the tariff revenue for even a small increase in e^{S}.

multilateral tariffs to maximize their joint welfare but now they do so subject to incentive constraints that ensure neither prefers to deviate.[25] We focus on subgame perfect equilibria sustained by the threat of infinite Nash reversion. The exact trigger strategy depends on which rules are chosen, that is on whether governments choose to have a PTA exception to the MFN rule or commit to MFN, which we address in Section 4. Here, we derive the tariffs when the large countries are sufficiently patient such that their incentive constraints for the MTL do not bind. In Section 2.5.2, we extend the analysis to the case when they bind.

2.5.1. PTAs as stumbling blocks to MTL. Given the symmetry between the two large countries, it is sufficient to focus on one and, since the problem is stationary, we can maximize welfare each period. Imposing the symmetry condition, $\tau^* = \tau$, the multilateral tariffs set under the PTA exception, τ^{EX}, and under commitment to MFN, τ^{C}, are, respectively,

$$\tau^{\mathrm{EX}} \equiv \arg\max_{\tau}\{W^{\mathrm{L}}(t = t^{\mathrm{B}}(t^{\mathrm{T}}), e^{\mathrm{S}} = e^{\mathrm{B}}(t^{\mathrm{T}}), \tau, \tau^* = \tau, \cdot) : \mathrm{IC}^{\mathrm{EX}}; t \leq \tau\}, \tag{17}$$

$$\tau^{\mathrm{C}} \equiv \arg\max_{\tau}\{W^{\mathrm{L}}(t, e^{\mathrm{S}} = 0, \tau, \tau^* = \tau, \cdot) : \mathrm{IC}^{\mathrm{C}}; t = \tau\}. \tag{18}$$

When the incentive constraints for the MTL (represented by $\mathrm{IC}^{\mathrm{EX}}$ and IC^{C}) do not bind, there are only two differences between these two maximization programs. First, under a commitment to MFN no PTAs are allowed so $t = \tau$, whereas under the PTA exception the preferential tariff may be lower. Second, under a rule of commitment to MFN *Small* sets $e^{\mathrm{S}} = 0$ because it cannot be compensated by a preferential tariff. Under the PTA exception rule, *Small* can be compensated with a preferential tariff and so it will supply the public good up to some level. Using the fact that the maximum threat that *Large* can use against *Small* (if both are WTO members) is the multilateral tariff, τ^{EX}, we obtain the following when large countries are sufficiently patient, that is, when $\mathrm{IC}^{\mathrm{EX}}$ and IC^{C} do not bind:

$$\tau^{\mathrm{EX}} : W^{\mathrm{L}}_{\tau} + W^{\mathrm{L}}_{\tau^*} + W^{\mathrm{L}}_{t}\partial t^{\mathrm{B}}/\partial t^{\mathrm{T}} + W^{\mathrm{L}}_{e^{\mathrm{S}}}\partial e^{\mathrm{B}}/\partial t^{\mathrm{T}} = 0, \tag{19}$$

$$\tau^{\mathrm{C}} : W^{\mathrm{L}}_{\tau} + W^{\mathrm{L}}_{\tau^*} + W^{\mathrm{L}}_{t} = 0. \tag{20}$$

Note that the condition for τ^{EX} is similar to the one derived in Section 2.3. So the first two terms continue to represent the effect of increases in the tariffs of *Large* and *Large**. Recall that if these were the only effects, then free trade would be the outcome. These two terms are similar for the commitment tariff in (20), but τ^{C} also includes a third term, W^{L}_{t}, which represents an MFN externality effect. This effect arises when *Large* imports the same good from *Large** and *Small* since an increase in τ also increases the tariff on *Small*'s exports thus allowing *Large* to capture extra tariff revenue. Since *Small* is assumed not to offer any reciprocal liberalization in the MTL there is no offsetting effect for this term, which vanishes when *Small*'s exports, H/k, are negligible or equivalently when k is large.

To establish whether τ^{EX} exceeds τ^{C}, we must determine if the last two terms in (19)—which represent the effect of raising the multilateral tariff on the PTA solution—exceed the MFN externality effect, W^{L}_{t}, in (20). The following proposition establishes this and makes use of the following definition. A PTA exception to MFN is a **stumbling block to MTL** if the multilateral tariff under this exception is higher than the tariff under a regime where no such exceptions are allowed, that is, if $\tau^{\mathrm{EX}} > \tau^{\mathrm{C}}$.

25. Because the large countries are symmetric, none "wins" a trade war, that is, none prefers the non-cooperative outcome to free trade. This could happen if the large countries were of asymmetric size, as shown by Johnson (1954). Syropoulos (2002) shows exactly how country size matters for the outcome of tariff wars.

Proposition 2. *(PTAs as stumbling blocks, $\tau^{\mathrm{EX}} > \tau^{\mathrm{C}}$, patient large countries): When large countries are sufficiently patient, a PTA exception to MFN is a stumbling block to MTL if and only if the PTA is duty free.*

The intuition is as follows. Suppose the large countries always set the multilateral tariff at the same level, τ^{C}, independently of whether PTAs are used. This is optimal only if the preference margin that they can offer in the PTA, $\tau^{\mathrm{C}} - t^{\mathrm{B}}(\tau^{\mathrm{C}})$, is sufficiently large to ensure that the small countries provide the amount of the public good that the large countries desire. However, if the PTA is duty free, that is, if the preferential tariff $t^{\mathrm{B}}(\tau^{\mathrm{C}})$ is zero, the large countries would benefit from being able to offer a lower preferential tariff and thus increase the preference margin and extract more cooperation in the non-trade issue. But when $t^{\mathrm{B}}(\tau^{\mathrm{C}}) = 0$, they can only increase the preference margin by increasing the multilateral tariff, so $\tau^{\mathrm{EX}} > \tau^{\mathrm{C}}$.

As pointed out in Proposition 1, the PTA is duty free if *Large* is sufficiently endowed (or values the public good sufficiently). In practice, a number of PTAs are duty free so that condition for the stumbling block effect is likely to be satisfied. In Section 3, we determine when the stumbling block effect is quantitatively significant and its welfare effects on the modelled countries but first we discuss some extensions.

2.5.2. Effect of PTAs on MTL: extensions and qualifications. Proposition 2 can be extended to address various factors. It is also subject to an interesting qualification when countries are impatient so that their incentive constraints in multilateral agreements bind. We provide a brief discussion of these here and provide further details in the appendix available online.

Proposition 2 is robust to including political economy motives for the use of tariffs since the extra terms determining the tariffs would enter similarly in (19) and (20). We can also relax the assumptions of inelastic export supply from small countries and their high trading costs with countries in the opposite regional bloc. These were used to simplify the analysis and highlight the effect that PTAs have on MTL due solely to the non-trade issue. Karacaovali and Limão (2005) extend our model and show that the stumbling block result is robust to these two issues.

Although public goods are more likely to have a regional rather than a global effect, there are some non-trade issues with important global spillovers, for example, global warming, concern with child labour. If countries address these issues "outside" the WTO, as modelled thus far, then we can show that the stumbling block effect of PTAs is still present. In fact, that effect is stronger than in Proposition 2 because large countries have more to gain from the PTA and thus maintain even higher multilateral tariffs (as proved in Limão, 2002). Global spillovers introduce an additional element of cooperation between the large countries and raise the issue of whether countries could use more sophisticated strategies, which we discuss in the appendix.

The stumbling block result is also robust to changes in the timing of the PTA and MTL. To see this, we can collapse the PTA and MTL decisions into a single stage and compare the resulting multilateral tariff with the solution under commitment. The commitment problem is independent of timing because no PTA takes place. But the exception problem changes. The IC for the PTA is still given by (15) and (16) with the threat tariff equal to the multilateral tariff. The solution for all policies is now the following:

$$\{\tau^{\mathrm{EX}}, t^{\mathrm{B}}, e^{\mathrm{B}}\} \equiv \arg\max_{\tau, t, e^{\mathrm{S}}} \{W^{\mathrm{L}}(t, e^{\mathrm{S}}, \tau, \tau^* = \tau, \cdot) : \mathrm{IC}^{\mathrm{EX}}; \mathrm{IC}^{\mathrm{S}}; \mathrm{IC}^{\mathrm{L}}; t \leq \tau\}. \tag{21}$$

We can then show the stumbling block result as in the last section by deriving the FOC and comparing τ^{EX} with the tariff obtained under commitment in (20). We do so in the appendix and show that, when large countries are sufficiently patient, a duty-free PTA is a stumbling block to

MTL even if the preferential and multilateral agreements occur simultaneously. The intuition is identical so we do not repeat it here.

Proposition 2 may be reversed when the large countries are not sufficiently patient. Whether that occurs or not depends on whether large countries can commit to not having PTAs under all circumstances, including during a trade war between these large countries. We discuss the case when problems with enforcement imply that the PTA is a building block to MTL and provide the details in the appendix.

To analyse the enforcement issue, we distinguish between two extreme cases: strong and weak commitment to MFN. Under strong commitment to MFN, countries can costlessly enforce non-discrimination, that is, the same tariff on all partners, so PTAs never take place. Under weak commitment to MFN, there is no instrument to enforce non-discrimination during trade wars between large countries, at which time PTAs can take place. In our set-up, we can interpret weak commitment as the simple elimination of WTO articles that allow exceptions to MFN. Strong commitment would entail a different punishment or an additional rule, such as allowing a third country to punish the warring parties if they also set discriminatory tariffs. The three regimes, PTA exception, weak, and strong commitment to MFN, lead to different incentive constraints and thus different levels of multilateral liberalization.

The multilateral tariff is lower under the PTA exception than under weak commitment to MFN when the IC for the multilateral agreement binds. As we prove in the appendix, the motive for the reversal of the result in Proposition 2 is that under weak commitment the gain from deviating from the multilateral agreement is higher and the gain from cooperating is lower than under the PTA exception. The motive is that under weak commitment, large countries do not sign PTAs while cooperating but do so if they ever engage in a trade war with each other. This possibility provides an extra incentive for them to deviate from the multilateral agreement. Similarly, the gains from cooperation are lower under weak commitment due to the absence of a PTA when the large countries do cooperate. Thus, a multilateral tariff that is just self-enforcing under the PTA exception rule is not self-enforcing under a weak commitment to MFN.

Enforcement considerations reverse the stumbling block result of Proposition 2 in the case of weak commitment. However, we can still obtain the result that the PTA exception is a stumbling block to MTL relative to strong commitment to MFN (Limão, 2002, provides a proof with the exact conditions). The contrasting results under weak and strong commitment to MFN have two related implications. First, they indicate that the stumbling block result does not rest crucially on whether countries are sufficiently patient. Second, they provide the following important warning to governments deciding to commit to MFN. Simply eliminating the current rules that allow exceptions to MFN leads to higher multilateral tariffs if countries are not sufficiently patient. But, with additional rules that credibly sustain a strong commitment to MFN, governments can enforce lower multilateral tariffs.

Modelling the interaction of PTAs and MTL carefully allows us to achieve three objectives. First, to derive the result in Proposition 2 and show how it can be extended and qualified. Second, to determine the welfare ranking of different types of rules for each country, which is not obvious in this environment with externalities, and is done in Section 4. Third, to derive comparative statics and testable predictions that can be used to test the model, which we now do.

3. PREDICTIONS AND EVIDENCE

In this section, we derive comparative statics and show how they can be used to construct a counterfactual, which we employ to provide novel econometric evidence in support of the model. We also discuss additional evidence on the key prediction of the model as well as on auxiliary predictions, which may be useful in validating some of its more specific features.

3.1. *Predictions and construction of a counterfactual*

Since its inception, the GATT has contained exceptions to the MFN rule. So how can we test if a stumbling block effect is present when we have not observed the counterfactual commitment regime? The following proposition allows us to answer this.

Proposition 3. *(Comparative static): Increases in α^{L} or λ^{L} increase the multilateral tariff, τ^{EX}, and the stumbling block effect, $\tau^{\mathrm{EX}} - \tau^{\mathrm{C}}$, if and only if the PTA is duty free.*

Increases in the weight, λ^{L}, or scope of the spillover, α^{L}, imply a higher marginal benefit for *Large* from increases in e^{S}, so *Large* finds it optimal to offer a lower preferential tariff in exchange for the public good from *Small*. However, this is only feasible if the preferential tariff is positive. When the PTA is duty free, *Large* must use a higher threat tariff for *Small* to increase e^{S}. This higher threat is only credible if it does not exceed the multilateral tariff and thus the equilibrium multilateral tariff must increase. The magnitude of the stumbling block effect, $\tau^{\mathrm{EX}} - \tau^{\mathrm{C}}$, increases because the multilateral tariff under commitment, τ^{C} in (20), is independent of α^{L} and λ^{L}.[26]

According to Proposition 3, multilateral tariffs are increasing in the weight that *Large* places on the regional public. Both the weight λ^{L}, a preference parameter, and the degree of the cross-border effect in the issue, α^{L}, generally a fixed characteristic of the issue, are likely to be exogenous relative to the multilateral tariffs. Moreover, it is also unlikely that those parameters affect multilateral tariffs directly through other channels. One potential difficulty is finding good proxies for marginal changes in α^{L} and λ^{L} so we consider a closely related alternative, which is a limit case.[27]

In our model, if α^{L} or λ^{L} is zero we observe no PTA and the equilibrium MFN tariff is equal to the commitment tariff, τ^{C}. When both α^{L} and λ^{L} are positive, a PTA is signed and the MFN tariff is τ^{EX}. Thus, if all else were equal, changes in the MFN tariffs, before and after a PTA, for exports from the small to the large regional partner can provide an estimate of the stumbling block effect. The obvious problem is that all else is not equal. In particular, MFN tariff changes are infrequent and typically take place in negotiation rounds where various other factors affect the multilateral tariff. Thus, we must construct a reasonable counterfactual. To do so we use a control group of products that are similar, for example, in the same industry or sector, to the ones exported by the small partner but are exported only by the rest of the world. We refer to these as non-PTA goods. Adding non-PTA goods is straightforward in our model because of the quasi-linear utility. The resulting objective function, $\widetilde{W}^{\mathrm{L}}$, would reflect these extra goods and the tariffs associated

26. Note that the result also holds if the large countries are not sufficiently patient as we prove in the appendix. Bond, Syropoulos and Winters (2001) show that a deepening of a customs union, that is, an exogenous reduction in its internal tariff, can lead to lower multilateral tariffs. Theirs is a pure trade model, and the results are driven by trade diversion. The fact that the prediction is the opposite of the one in our model clearly shows the importance of modelling PTAs.

27. Throughout, we take α, λ as exogenous. However, it is possible that certain public goods, for example, clean environment, human rights, etc., are normal goods. So we could postulate that λ increases with income and ask whether the source of the increase in income, and thus of λ, affects the result in Proposition 3. If the increase in income was in the form of more numeraire good, the answer is no since none of the tariffs depend on that level. But if it was caused by an increase of *Large*'s endowment of the non-numeraire import relative to *Small*, then the incentives to set tariffs would be affected. In this case, the stumbling block effect would be more likely than if the increase in λ was due to purely exogenous motives (*e.g.* due to a change in preferences). The reason is that if *Large* is initially not sufficiently endowed relative to *Small*, then the PTA that results after an exogenous increase in λ is not duty free and thus there is no stumbling block effect (Propositions 1 and 2). However, if the increase in λ is due to a shock to endowments that is sufficiently strong to ensure that *Large* becomes sufficiently endowed relative to *Small*, then the resulting PTA is duty free and causes a stumbling block effect under the conditions in Proposition 2.

with them. The multilateral tariff for these goods under the exception regime, denoted $\tau^{\mathrm{EX}}_{\mathrm{npta}}$, is defined by the expression below, which is analogous to τ^{C} and captures the reciprocity effect[28]

$$\tau^{\mathrm{EX}}_{\mathrm{npta}} : \widetilde{W}^{\mathrm{L}}_{t_{\mathrm{npta}}} + \widetilde{W}^{\mathrm{L}}_{t^{*}_{\mathrm{npta}}} = 0.$$

Thus, the model strongly suggests a difference-in-differences approach, comparing the changes in MFN tariffs for a given large country of two types of products: the non-PTA goods exported only by the rest of the world (the control group) against those also exported by the PTA partner. This approach is further supported by actual examples that countries respond to concerns of PTA partners by maintaining higher multilateral tariffs on PTA products even though they lower them for similar non-PTA goods.[29]

We now describe the data and econometric approach that we use to test the stumbling block prediction.

3.2. *Data*

Two agreements that fit the assumptions of our model particularly well are the Caribbean Basin Initiative (CBI) and the Andean Trade Preference Act (ATPA). The large partner in both cases is the U.S., and it provides duty-free access to a large set of products exported by the small Caribbean and Andean countries. These countries do not grant preferential treatment to U.S. exports but must comply with various labour standards, respect intellectual property, and, in the case of the Andean countries, assist in the war on drugs. Moreover, the main destination for their exports is the U.S., and these small countries have little direct effect on multilateral trade negotiations.

Both the ATPA (1992) and the CBI (1984) were signed between the last two multilateral trade rounds, the Tokyo Round and Uruguay Round (UR). Moreover, when the Tokyo Round was negotiated, 1973–1979, neither was expected with certainty. However, both were in place in 1994 when the multilateral negotiations for the UR were concluded. Thus, the MFN tariffs the U.S. set in the Tokyo Round should reflect τ^{C} and the ones in the UR should reflect τ^{EX} for the products exported by the CBI and ATPA to the U.S.

We must construct two key variables: a measure of MFN trade protection and the PTA variable. For trade protection, we employ the U.S. specific tariffs collected from the WTO's schedule of tariff concessions during the UR. These data contain the level of the tariff negotiated in the Tokyo Round and UR at the eight-digit harmonized standard, which is the most disaggregate level at which negotiations occur. Since these tariffs are defined as a monetary value per unit, we divide them by the unit value of the product to obtain an *ad valorem* equivalent, which is comparable across products. Table A1 in the appendix provides further details on data sources and variable construction.

28. The MFN externality term present in τ^{C} is now absent since we assume this good is not exported by the small country, and as we noted before that term disappears when its exports are negligible. In a more realistic extension of the model with additional small countries that export this good to *Large* but do not have a PTA with it, such a term is present in determining $\tau^{\mathrm{EX}}_{\mathrm{npta}}$.

29. One of the largest exports from several Caribbean countries to the U.S. is low-valued bottled and bulk rum that enters the U.S. duty free under the CBI. "In WTO tariff negotiations in 1996, U.S. and E.U. negotiators had initially agreed to phase out all tariffs on rum and other 'white spirits' by 2000. Caribbean governments, Administration officials and Members of Congress (...) emphasized to the trade negotiators that such a drastic change in the tariff structure for rum would deal a severe blow to the economies of the USVI, Puerto Rico, and the Caribbean. In response to this outcry (...) the United States agreed to substantially liberalize duties on expensive rum. However, to protect the interests of the USVI and other Caribbean island producers, the United States also agreed to maintain existing MFN duties on low-value bottled and bulk rum." Testimony before the House Committee on Ways and Means. Accessed on June 2003 at http://waysandmeans.house.gov/legacy/trade/107cong/5-8-01/5-8chri.htm.

TABLE 1

Summary statistics

Variables	Mean	S.D.	Min	Max
$\Delta\tau$	−1·46	2·71	−36·3	0
ATPA_CBI	0·361	0·643	0	2
ATPA	0·165	0·371	0	1
CBI	0·196	0·397	0	1
NAFTA	0·704	0·457	0	1
ISRAEL	0·153	0·36	0	1
GSP	0·369	0·483	0	1
RECIPROCITY	−50·3	12·7	−86·6	−2·26
INITIAL τ	3·24	4·64	0·00428	36·3
Excluded instruments				
UNILAT_RED	−28·9	19·3	−79·4	−0·355
EXP GROWTH	130	23·3	10·5	164
TRANSP_COST 94	8·51	6·24	0·318	59
ΔPRICE_90_94	10·9	94·6	−470	736
TC × ΔPRICE	58·4	825	−3644	9385
EX_CBI	0·238	0·426	0	1
EX_ATPA	0·209	0·407	0	1
EX_ISR	0·168	0·374	0	1
EX_GSP	0·733	0·443	0	1

Notes: All variables, except indicators, are in percentages. Number of observations: 929. After excluding the special sections (21 and 22), there exist data for 1331 unique eight-digit tariff lines for which the U.S. sets a positive specific tariff before the Uruguay Round. Lines with missing or zero imports from every U.S. partner must be dropped because they are required to construct the transport cost and price variables ($n = 1011$). The sample is reduced to 1000 due to missing preference data. Missing tariff reduction and GDP growth data for some partners used to construct reciprocity and growth variables reduces the sample to 931. Two industries have a single observation in the sub sample of 931, thus reducing the sample to 929, which is used in the main specifications.

An important motive to focus on specific tariffs is that they are a relatively important component of protection in the U.S. in the set of products exported under the ATPA and CBI. For example, in the set of products with positive specific tariffs (over 1000) their average *ad valorem* equivalent was about 6·9% with a median of about 1·9%, which indicates some highly protected products where preference margins are high. Moreover, in a large majority of such products there was no other type of tariff, for example, in rum, which is one of the CBI's largest exports. The fraction of exports from ATPA or CBI to the U.S. in 1994 in the products in our sample with positive specific tariffs is about 18% relative to their total exports in products with positive specific or *ad valorem* tariffs. For NAFTA (the U.S. PTA with Canada and Mexico), that figure is less than 9%. Therefore, if the ATPA and CBI cause a stumbling effect we should expect to see it in U.S. specific tariffs.

The other key variable is whether an eight-digit good i is a PTA good, that is, whether it was exported to the U.S. by a PTA partner and received a preference in 1994. So in Table 1, which provides summary statistics, ATPA corresponds to the PTA variable for the Andean countries, etc. The reason for choosing 1994 is the following. In 1994, the negotiations for the UR, which defined the current level of MFN tariffs, had just been concluded, and it was implemented in the period 1995–1999. The U.S. did not conclude any new PTAs in the period 1995–2001, so we assume that at the time the UR final negotiations took place, 1992–1993, the only U.S. PTAs that could affect its MFN tariffs were those PTAs in place by 1994. We do not choose a date between 1995 and 1999 because whether a good is exported by a PTA partner and receives a preference in that period may depend on the MFN tariff, which may generate an endogeneity problem as we discuss below.

Using these data, we can calculate some preliminary statistics. The average specific tariff reduction for goods that the U.S. did not import under PTAs was approximately 2·2 percentage points. The reduction for the set of PTA goods exported under the ATPA or CBI to the U.S. was 1·4. The difference of 0·8 is statistically significant according to a t-test (S.E. = 0·35) and provides preliminary evidence of a relative increase of the MFN tariff in PTA goods. The difference does not appear to be driven by any single industry since several industries have both PTA and non-PTA goods. However, to properly address this issue and also to test if this difference reflects a spurious correlation or a causal effect of these PTAs we employ the following econometric approach.

3.3. *Econometric approach*

As noted above, when the Tokyo Round was negotiated neither the ATPA nor the CBI was expected with any certainty. However, both were in place when the UR was concluded. Thus, we take the Tokyo Round tariff to reflect the model's commitment level and the UR tariff as the exception level. We then take the difference for each product i over time and denote it by $\Delta\tau_i$ to write the basic estimating equation as

$$\Delta\tau_i = \pi \,\mathrm{PTA}_i + \Delta\mathbf{x}_i\beta + u_i, \tag{22}$$

where PTA_i is the indicator variable for the PTA goods and therefore the main prediction is that π is positive if the PTA causes a stumbling block. Econometrically, π measures the average difference in the reduction in tariffs of PTA vs. non-PTA goods. To ensure that this measure is not biased, we require that the MFN tariff changes of non-PTA goods provide a reasonable counterfactual for the PTA goods in the absence of PTAs. Therefore, we control for some important variables, in $\Delta\mathbf{x}$, which we describe in detail below. The tariff change measure we use is the log growth of the tariff factor, $\Delta\ln(1+\tau_{it})$, which, given that we use the *ad valorem* equivalent, provides a useful economic interpretation in terms of price changes that we explore in Section 3.5. But the results are identical when we use simple differences.

To establish causality we must address the potential endogeneity arising from reverse causation in (22). The negotiated MFN tariff changes—the dependent variable in (22)—were implemented in 1995–1999 so they should not affect whether the good was exported by a PTA in 1994. However, the tariff changes may have affected whether a good received a preference in 1994 because when some of those preferences were negotiated (*e.g.* ATPA in the early 1990s), they were expected to be in place for some part of the 1995–1999 period, while the MFN tariff changes were due to be implemented. So if those MFN tariff changes were expected, they could have affected which goods received preferences.[30] Therefore, we instrument for the PTA variable using whether the good was exported in 1994 by the PTA partners to the U.S. whether or not it received a preference. The instrument is correlated with the PTA variable but excludes the potentially endogenous component, that is, the preference. We also test the validity of this instrument by employing additional excluded instruments that predict whether a good is likely to be exported by the ATPA and CBI. These instruments are transport cost levels and changes in the U.S. prices at the border (exclusive of tariffs) between 1990 and 1994.[31]

30. For example, suppose that during the ATPA negotiations there is product for which the Andean countries expect the U.S. to reduce its MFN tariff, and thus any preference margin, to zero while in another they expect no change for reasons unrelated to its PTAs. The Andean countries are then more likely to lobby for a preference in the latter, which would generate a positive correlation between the PTA good variable and the MFN tariff change.

31. Goods with higher average transport costs to the U.S. are more likely to be supplied by the relatively closer, lower transport cost, countries, such as the members of the ATPA and CBI. Increases in the U.S. border prices of a good between 1990 and 1994, while U.S. MFN tariffs were constant, will increase the probability that any given country exports the good to the U.S.

Our econometric approach is similar to Limão (2006) in its use of difference-in-differences and choice of instruments. However, there are a number of important differences, two of which we highlight here. First, the objective of that paper is to model multilateral negotiations empirically and estimate the effect of aggregate U.S. PTA variables on its *ad valorem* tariffs; so it contains no theory and it focuses mostly on whether a good is subject to preferences in any or every PTA rather than the specific PTAs that fit our theory.[32] Second, and perhaps more importantly, here we employ different data. More specifically, we analyse a different trade policy—specific rather than *ad valorem* tariffs—and (as a result) a significantly different sample of goods.

The differences in the sample and trade policy measure are important for at least two reasons. First, although average U.S. *ad valorem* tariffs are among the lowest in the world, it has relatively high specific tariff rates, so high they are often criticized in WTO reports, particularly by developing countries whose products are disproportionately hit.[33] Second, because they were not subject to any *ad valorem* tariff, nearly two-thirds of the products in our sample are not included in Limão (2006). As we describe in Section 3.2, these products constitute an important part of the exports of ATPA and CBI. Moreover, the new wave of U.S. PTAs with non-trade objectives is precisely with developing countries that export similar goods so it is essential to include those goods. If our empirical test for them fails, the theory is seriously thrown into doubt.

3.4. *Estimation results*

Table 2 provides the estimates for the stumbling block effect, the coefficient π in (22). To address potential endogeneity problems, we employ the instrumental variables approach just described. We also discuss formal tests of endogeneity and the instruments that further justify this procedure and present alternative specifications to test the robustness of the results.

In addition to employing instrumental variables (IV) there are three other features common to all specifications in Table 2, which we note before discussing the estimates. First, the sample contains all the products that were subject to positive specific tariffs before the UR and therefore could potentially be given a preference.[34] Second, since both the ATPA and the CBI receive preferences in the exact same goods in this sample we restrict their PTA effect to be identical. So ATPA_CBI is constructed as the sum of ATPA and CBI as defined above. We test this restriction for all specifications and the data do not reject it.[35] Third, lobbying for protection typically occurs at the industry level and can affect how large the tariff reductions are. To account for these, as well as other unobservable industry characteristics that could influence the changes in MFN tariffs and bias the PTA coefficient, we include a full set of industry dummies.

Column 1 of Table 2 contains the estimates for the basic specification. The stumbling block effect is positive, as predicted by the model, and significant at the 1% level. There was an average increase of 0·53 in the MFN tariff factor for goods exported under either the ATPA or the CBI relative to the non-PTA goods. The magnitude of the effect is not negligible since the average reduction in the non-PTA goods—the average over the estimated industry effects—was −1·65,

32. It reports a single specification with all the individual PTA variables, which provides some complementary evidence for the theory in this paper.

33. For example, as recently as 2001 the WTO's trade policy review of the U.S. stated that "High specific and compound rates on agri-food and tobacco products, clothing, footwear and headgear and textiles continued to act as barriers to trade, and were of great concern to developing countries" p. 23 of document WT/TPR/M/88 at www.wto.org.

34. There are two reasons to focus on products with positive tariffs before the UR. First, all the tariffs in the sample that were initially zero remained unchanged and are likely to share an unobserved common characteristic. Thus, including those observations could bias the estimates if the proportion of zero tariffs is different for PTA goods relative to the rest of the goods. Second, when the MFN tariff is zero there is often no information about whether a preference exists, since it is in effect irrelevant at that point. We can address this by setting the preference variable to zero and including all observations. We did so and found that the parameter of interest, π, was still positive and statistically significant.

35. We can identify the effects separately because the ATPA and CBI do not export the same goods.

TABLE 2

IV Estimates of stumbling block effect

Dependent variable: $\Delta\tau$		(1)	(2)	(3)	(4)	(5)	(6)
ATPA_CBI (π)†		0·533	0·552	0·511	0·440	0·329	0·522
		(0·152)	(0·148)	(0·152)	(0·142)	(0·136)	(0·167)
RECIPROCITY†			0·017	0·018	0·005	0·021	0·018
			(0·010)	(0·010)	(0·011)	(0·010)	(0·011)
NAFTA				0·263	0·203	0·072	0·298
				(0·237)	(0·197)	(0·242)	(0·270)
ISRAEL†				0·089	0·058	0·152	0·159
				(0·269)	(0·227)	(0·274)	(0·297)
GSP†				−0·171	0·069	−0·843	−0·222
				(0·462)	(0·397)	(0·524)	(0·514)
INITIAL $\tau^\dagger$				−0·192			
				(0·107)			
Mean reduction^a	gross	−1·65	−1·68	−1·80	−1·80	−1·32	−1·89
	net	na	−0·82	−0·89	−1·53	−0·26	−0·98
Mean price effect^b	gross	68%	67%	72%	76%	75%	72%
	net	na	33%	43%	71%	−25%	47%
No. of observations		929	929	929	929	919	929
No. of parameters		17	18	21	22	62	21
Hansen's J $(p)^c$		0·16	0·26	0·22	0·13	0·43	0·24
Exogeneity $(p)^d$		0·00	0·00	0·00	0·00	0·00	0·00
Equality $(p)^e$		0·78	0·91	0·77	0·10	0·46	0·67

Notes: Heteroskedasticity robust standard errors in parentheses. Section/industry dummies included but not reported. (a) Estimated average tariff factor growth for non-PTA products taken as the average of the industry effects weighted by their share of observations in the sample. The estimates in the rows labelled "gross" include the growth due to the average change in the reciprocity variable in the sample, whereas "net" excludes it. (b) Measure of relative growth of world prices due to CBI and ATPA when there is imperfect pass through ($\zeta_{\text{pta}} \approx \zeta_{\text{npta}} < 1$), calculated as $(\pi + c)/c$ where c is the mean tariff reduction for non-PTA goods using the measures gross or net of the reciprocity effect. (c) Test of over-identifying restrictions. Probability at which we reject the null hypothesis that the excluded instruments are uncorrelated with the error term, and correctly excluded from the estimated equation. (d) Durbin–Wu–Hausman specification test for the exogeneity of the variables marked with a "†". Probability value at which we reject the consistency of OLS. (e) Wald test of the null hypothesis of equality between the CBI and ATPA parameters in unrestricted versions of each specification. Specification in column (5) identical to (3) except we use harmonized standard two-digit industry dummies instead of section dummies. These results require us to drop 10 other industries with a single observation. Specification in column (6) uses the difference in the *ad valorem* equivalent of the specific tariff as the dependent variable.

as indicated in the row labelled "mean reduction". Before providing an economic quantification, we provide diagnostic and robustness tests for this result.

The first-stage regression results in column 1 of Table 3 indicate that the instruments explain a considerable amount of the variation in the endogenous PTA variable. The R^2 is 0·84, and we strongly reject the null of insignificance of the excluded instruments. The sign of the significant instruments is as expected: whether a good is exported is positively correlated with whether it is exported and receives a preference; higher average transport costs with all partners predict that the regional partners, with relatively lower costs, are more likely to export the good. Moreover, the over-identifying restriction test supports the orthogonality of the instruments relative to the error and their exclusion. The p-value is 0·16, given in the row labelled "Hansen's J (p)" in Table 2. This strongly suggests that the estimates from the parsimonious specification reflect a causal relationship rather than a spurious correlation due to reverse causation or omitted variable bias. Nonetheless, it is important to test if the result is robust to the inclusion of other variables, particularly if these can help rule out plausible alternative explanations for the finding.

TABLE 3

First-stage regressions for basic and preferred specifications

Specification Table 2	(1)	(3)			
Dependent variable	ATPA_CBI	ATPA_CBI	RECIPROCITY	GSP	ISRAEL
EX_CBI	0·791	0·798	0·370	−0·045	0·040
	(0·026)	(0·026)	(0·513)	(0·034)	(0·010)
EX_ATPA	0·769	0·785	1·081	0·071	−0·002
	(0·027)	(0·027)	(0·528)	(0·035)	(0·011)
TRANSP_COST 94	0·006	0·006	−0·012	0·004	0·000
	(0·002)	(0·002)	(0·033)	(0·002)	(0·001)
ΔPRICE_90_94	−0·000	−0·000	−0·000	−0·000	−0·000
	(0·000)	(0·000)	(0·004)	(0·000)	(0·000)
TC × ΔPRICE	0·000	0·000	0·000	0·000	0·000
	(0·000)	(0·000)	(0·000)	(0·000)	(0·000)
NAFTA		−0·026	1·40	0·038	0·009
		(0·023)	(0·446)	(0·030)	(0·009)
EX_GSP		−0·025	0·181	0·476	−0·009
		(0·024)	(0·464)	(0·031)	(0·009)
EX_ISR		−0·037	−1·05	0·072	0·908
		(0·027)	(0·535)	(0·036)	(0·011)
UNILAT_RED		−0·003	0·688	0·002	−0·001
		(0·001)	(0·014)	(0·001)	(0·000)
EXP GROWTH		0·002	−0·188	−0·002	0·000
		(0·001)	(0·011)	(0·001)	(0·000)
No. of observations	929	929	929	929	929
Adjusted R^2	0·84	0·84	0·99	0·61	0·92
F-test exc. IV (p-value) [a]	0·00	0·00	0·00	0·00	0·00

Notes: Heteroskedasticity robust standard errors in parentheses. Section/industry dummies included but not reported. (a) Probability value for the F-test of the null hypothesis that the excluded instruments are jointly insignificant.

The first important product-level control variable that we must analyse is reciprocity in tariff negotiations, which, as discussed in Section 2, is a central part of the trading system. Omitting reciprocity raises an important concern about our estimate of π. The members of ATPA and CBI are developing countries so at least a subset of the goods they export is common to other developing countries. If that subset is large and those other developing countries have not liberalized much, then the U.S. would have little motive to lower its tariffs in those products even in the absence of a stumbling block effect. That is, we would find a smaller reduction by the U.S. in those products exported by developing countries and attribute it to the PTA when it is really an MFN externality effect, of the type found in our model. We can test if this is the case by controlling for reciprocity.[36]

The reciprocity variable is constructed as a measure of market access "concessions" that is consistent with the practice in multilateral tariff negotiations. It is defined at the product level as a weighted average of the aggregate tariff reductions of U.S. trade partners. The weights vary by product and are given by those partners' export shares on product i into the U.S. Since the negotiation for reducing U.S. tariffs in product i occurs only with its principal suppliers, only the top five exporters are taken for each product.

The theory predicts a positive sign for the reciprocity variable. If a country offers relatively larger concessions, then the U.S. reciprocates through larger MFN tariff reductions in the

36. It is also possible that these U.S. PTAs may affect how much MTL the non-PTA countries are willing to negotiate, which then has an indirect effect on the U.S.'s own liberalization. The reciprocity variable controls for this indirect effect, allowing us to estimate direct effect that the theory highlights.

products it imports from that country. This generates another potential source of endogeneity due to reverse causation since the total tariff reduction by that country will, through reciprocity, partially depend on the U.S.'s reductions. We address this by instrumenting for reciprocity similarly to Limão (2006). The instrument is the unilateral portion of the total tariff reductions of U.S. partners that were eventually offered at the UR. More specifically, several countries undertook unilateral trade liberalizations between 1986 and 1992. They were unilateral because they were undertaken outside of GATT negotiations, without an expectation that they would be reciprocated since the very completion of the UR was in doubt until 1992. However, when the final multilateral cuts were negotiated, between 1992 and 1994, the unilateral reductions undertaken from 1986 to 1992 were retroactively reciprocated because they had taken place after the official start date of the round (Finger *et al.*, 2002, p. 121). Therefore, we employ the unilateral liberalization by GATT/WTO members between 1986 and 1992 as an instrument for what was eventually used as a basis for their reciprocal liberalization—the amount between 1986 and 1995. We also use the exporter countries' gross domestic product (GDP) growth between 1977 and 1990 as an instrument for their liberalization.

Column 2 of Table 2 contains the estimates when controlling for reciprocity. This determinant has the expected positive effect, larger liberalization by exporters of a particular good to the U.S. causes the U.S. to reciprocate by lowering its own MFN tariffs in that good. The effect is quantitatively significant since if there were no liberalization by other countries, that is, if the reciprocity variable was zero, then the estimated mean reduction is only $-0{\cdot}82$ for non-PTA goods, which is about half of the effect we find without reciprocity. Although reciprocity has a significant impact on the average reduction, it does not affect the sign, significance, or magnitude of the stumbling block estimate, which is now 0·55 instead of 0·53.

In addition to the industry effects, which we include throughout, and reciprocity, other U.S. PTAs may be a potential determinant of its MTL. In 1994, the U.S. also provided preferences under the NAFTA (Canada and Mexico), the GSP (various developing countries), and Israel. Since our objective is to stay as close as possible to the assumptions of the model, we chose not to focus on these agreements. Both Canada and Mexico and the group of GSP beneficiary countries have non-negligible market shares in the U.S. and direct impact in multilateral negotiations. This is not true of Israel but it has a special relation with the U.S., and it is one of the largest recipients of U.S. official aid, which implies that in this case preferences are not required to "purchase" Israeli cooperation in non-trade issues. This explains our focus on the ATPA and CBI: their characteristics fit particularly well with the theoretical model. However, we should control for the other agreements to ensure that the effect of the ATPA and CBI is not driven by other agreements with similar PTA goods.

Column 3 of Table 2 controls for the key determinants in $\Delta\mathbf{x}$: industry effects, reciprocity, and other PTAs. The stumbling block effect for the agreements that fit the assumptions of our model remains positive and significant at 1%. The reciprocity effect is also unchanged. The effect of the other agreements is statistically insignificant. Although controlling for the other PTAs in this sample and for this measure of protection does not change the results, we believe that conceptually this is the best specification since it ensures that the control group of non-PTA goods is defined with respect to goods that are not exported under any PTA. Therefore, the additional robustness results discussed below will be based on this specification.[37]

37. Limão (2006) examines *ad valorem* tariffs and finds evidence of a stumbling block effect in the U.S. that is stronger for products in which PTA partners have large export values and that it is present for GSP and NAFTA in addition to the CBI and ATPA. This along with our finding here that for products subject to specific tariffs the effect is only significant for the ATPA and CBI provides additional supporting evidence for the model once we note that NAFTA and GSP have a lower share of their exports in products where the U.S. applies specific tariffs than the ATPA and CBI.

Finally, we note that, for the preferred specification (3), the first-stage results (in the last four columns of Table 3) strongly support the instruments we use both in terms of their explanatory power and expected sign. This is the case for the PTA and reciprocity variables. The over-identifying restrictions test does not reject the hypothesis that the excluded instruments are orthogonal to the error and correctly excluded.[38]

3.5. *Quantification*

To provide some interpretation and economic quantification of the importance of the estimated effect recall the following. First, π measures the average difference in the reduction in tariffs of PTA vs. non-PTA goods. Second, conditional on the determinants in $\Delta\mathbf{x}$, the reduction in tariffs for non-PTA goods captures the reduction that would have occurred in the PTA goods in the absence of a PTA, that is, under commitment to MFN. So we can ask what was the relative magnitude of the reduction in tariffs for PTA goods under the exception vs. what it would have been under commitment. We find that magnitude is large: it ranges from 43% to 72% in our preferred specification (column 3 of Table 2). We obtain this from calculating $(\pi + c)/c$, where c is the estimated mean reduction for non-PTA goods and π is the PTA parameter in (22). With no stumbling block effect, π would be zero and this relative magnitude is 100%. So the larger the stumbling block effect the lower this statistic is. The stronger effect of 43% corresponds to goods exported by countries that did not lower their tariffs, that is, it calculates c net of the reciprocity effect, $-0{\cdot}89$. Since the change for the PTA goods was (0·5–0·89), we have $(\pi + c)/c = 0{\cdot}43$. The estimate of 72% includes the reciprocity effect.[39]

The relative magnitudes above also have an interpretation as "mean price effects" as we label them in Table 2. Since we calculate an *ad valorem* equivalent to the specific tariff, the domestic price of a good in the U.S. can be written as $p = p^*(1+\tau)$, where p^* is the world price. When there is full pass through from tariffs to domestic prices, the world price remains unchanged and so the ratio of the growth in domestic price for a PTA and a similar non-PTA good is simply $\Delta \ln p_{\text{pta}}/\Delta \ln p_{\text{npta}} = \Delta \ln(1+\tau_{\text{pta}})/\Delta \ln(1+\tau_{\text{npta}})$. Using (22), this expression is equal to $(\pi + c)/c$. This expression also provides an approximate measure of the relative world price effects for goods when there is imperfect pass through, that is when some of the tariff reductions are passed to exporters in the form of higher prices, as we assumed in the theoretical model. In this case, we have $\Delta \ln p^*_{\text{pta}}/\Delta \ln p^*_{\text{npta}} \approx (\pi + c)/c$ provided that the pass-through rate across PTA and non-PTA goods is similar.[40] This implies that a country that is not a member of the ATPA or CBI but exports the same goods to the U.S. received only 43%–72% of the price increase relative to a situation where the U.S. did not have those preferential agreements.

Using the theoretical model, we can also calculate the counterfactual average tariff level for PTA goods in the absence of PTAs. To do so we start with the average tariff from the Tokyo Round for ATPA or CBI goods in the sample. This was 3·3% for goods with positive MFN

38. We treat the ISRAEL and GSP variables as endogenous for the same reason presented for the ATPA and CBI: the selection of goods receiving preferences may depend on expected MFN tariff changes. Since for NAFTA all the products in the sample receive preferential treatment, this issue does not arise and we treat it as exogenous. We omit the first-stage results for ATPA_CBI and RECIPROCITY for specification (2) in Table 2 for space considerations and because they are very similar to those for specification (3). They are available upon request.

39. These two estimates provide information about different counterfactuals. Strictly speaking, we do not know what value the reciprocity variable would have taken in the absence of PTAs so we can either ask about this relative effect if the U.S. had unilaterally changed its tariffs without responding to its partners in the UR, the estimates net of reciprocity (43%), or ask what the effect was given the observed level of reciprocity (72%).

40. Define the pass through as $\zeta_i \equiv \Delta \ln p_i/\Delta \ln(1+\tau_i)$, where i = pta or npta. Then, since we can write the domestic price as $\ln p_i = \ln(1+\tau_i) + \ln p^*_i$, we have $\zeta_i = 1 + \Delta \ln p^*_i/\Delta \ln(1+\tau_i)$. We can then write the ratio of world price effects as $\Delta \ln p^*_{\text{pta}}/\Delta \ln p^*_{\text{npta}} = [\Delta \ln(1+\tau_{\text{pta}})/\Delta \ln(1+\tau_{\text{npta}})](\zeta_{\text{pta}} - 1)/(\zeta_{\text{npta}} - 1) \approx (\pi + c)/c$ if $\zeta_{\text{pta}} \approx \zeta_{\text{npta}} < 1$.

tariffs. We then subtract the average change that would have taken place in the absence of PTAs, calculated from our counterfactual as the estimated average reduction in non-PTA goods gross of reciprocity, −1·8%. Thus, the predicted U.S. MFN tariff level for ATPA or CBI goods in the absence of these agreements is 1·5%. The stumbling block effect added 0·5 percentage points, thus causing the average tariff level on those PTA goods to be 33% higher.

3.6. *Robustness tests and additional evidence*

We now test the robustness of the results with respect to additional regressors and alternative definitions of the dependent variable. We also discuss additional evidence for the E.U.

The average initial MFN tariff for the ATPA and CBI PTA goods in the sample is higher than for non-PTA goods. This could bias the stumbling block estimate upwards if products with higher initial tariffs were associated with certain unobservable characteristics, for example, strong lobbies in industries specialized in very specific products, that simultaneously cause higher initial tariffs and smaller reductions. To test if this affects our estimates, we include the initial tariff as an endogenous regressor and re-estimate the preferred specification. The estimates in column 4 of Table 2 indicate that products with higher initial tariffs actually had significantly larger rather than smaller reductions. The stumbling block effect remains positive and significant, and it is statistically indistinguishable from the previous estimate.[41]

It is possible that the industry dummies we included thus far do not fully capture the political economy effects or other industry characteristics that affected the tariff reductions. Therefore, in column 5 we include a finer set of dummies: one for each two-digit industry of the harmonized system in the sample that divide the HS-8 digit products into 96 possible industries. Note that this is a strict test because it eliminates a considerable amount of the variation in the tariff measure and leaves us with an average of 15·5 observations per industry with which to identify differences between PTA and non-PTA goods. Nonetheless, we continue to find that the stumbling block result is positive and significant.

The estimated effect, π, is also unchanged if instead of taking the difference of the log tariff factor we use the difference of the tariffs. This is clear from column 6 where the estimate of 0·52 has the immediate interpretation that the MFN tariff for a PTA good exported by the ATPA or CBI increased by one half a percentage point relative to the non-PTA goods. If exported by both, the increase was 1 percentage point and it fully offset other motives for reduction (−0·98 was the average decrease for non-PTA).

We conclude this section with a brief discussion of additional evidence that supports our theoretical model. Karacaovali and Limão (2005) use data for the E.U. to estimate a structural equation derived by extending our theoretical model. They find that the E.U.'s PTAs caused it to maintain higher multilateral tariffs in PTA goods. Interestingly, they also estimate that the effect is not present in goods that face a positive preferential tariff, that is, PTA goods that do not benefit from duty-free status. Recall that duty-free status is an important condition to obtain the stumbling block effect in Proposition 2, and thus the finding provides strong support for a fairly specific prediction of our model.[42] They also find no stumbling block effect for the goods exported by countries that became E.U. members, which is another prediction of the extended model since there are extensive cash transfer mechanisms among E.U. members and thus trade preferences need not be used as transfers.

41. Since we previously had more excluded instruments than endogenous variables, we do not require any additional instruments to identify the initial tariff in the first stage; its R^2 is 0·43 and we reject the insignificance of the instruments with a p-value of 0·0001.

42. We cannot test that prediction with the U.S. data because none of the PTA goods under ATPA and CBI in our sample face positive preferential tariffs.

4. IMPLICATIONS FOR WTO RULES

The evidence strongly supports the theoretical prediction that U.S. and E.U. PTAs have caused a stumbling block effect. Therefore, it is important to analyse the welfare consequences of such agreements and the implications of our model for WTO rules. We do so from both a positive and a normative perspective. From a positive perspective, we show how the model can explain two features of the current system. First, the current regime of exceptions to MFN. Second, the recent attempt to change this regime and move cooperation in non-trade issues into the WTO, which was generally supported by large developed countries and opposed by small developing ones. From a normative perspective, we analyse the welfare consequences of different rules and propose a new rule, allowing import subsidies, that constitutes a Pareto improvement relative to the current exception to MFN.

4.1. *Positive implications*

We have analysed trade agreements under two alternative rules or regimes: MFN commitment or exception. We now show which emerges in equilibrium. Until recently, developing countries often complained that most GATT/WTO rules were decided by developed countries (Srinivasan, 1999). We capture this by allowing large countries to choose the trading rules in order to maximize their own joint welfare. By ranking the pay-offs for the large countries under the alternative regimes, we show which they chose in the initial stage. We then contrast it to the small countries' preferred regime.

Proposition 4. *(Welfare ranking of regimes):*

(i) When large countries are sufficiently patient

A. the PTA exception regime welfare dominates commitment to MFN for large countries

B. the PTA exception regime welfare dominates commitment to MFN for small countries if the PTA is not duty free or if small countries are not sufficiently patient.

(ii) When large countries are sufficiently patient and the PTA is duty free, then there exist some sufficiently patient small countries for which commitment to MFN welfare dominates the PTA exception regime.

Let us first consider the result for *Large*. As we have shown in Section 2.4, *Large* gains from a PTA for a given multilateral tariff. Since a PTA that is not duty free has no effect on the multilateral tariff (Proposition 2), it is clear that *Large* chooses a rule that allows PTAs in that case. However, when large countries are sufficiently patient they prefer the exception regime even if the PTA affects the multilateral tariff. This occurs because their IC for the MTL does not bind and thus they continue to choose the cooperative tariff that maximizes their joint welfare. This allows them to internalize the effects of each other's PTAs on their MTL. Thus, the model predicts the regime we observe since it was large countries that chose the current GATT/WTO rules regarding MFN commitment.

It is also interesting to ask what the welfare ranking of regimes is for small countries from both a normative and a positive perspective. In the last 10 years, as the WTO replaced the GATT, the power of small developing countries in the world trading system appears to have increased (Mattoo and Subramanian, 2004). So, even if large countries still set the agenda, it is plausible that smaller ones have acquired some veto power. Proposition 4 answers whether small countries support the current set of rules.

Small prefers the exception regime when the PTA is not duty free. In that case, the agreement does not affect multilateral tariffs and, as shown in Section 2.4, for given multilateral tariffs, the

PTA is strictly welfare improving for *Small*. However, when the PTA is duty free there is an offsetting effect for them. The multilateral tariff is higher and thus so is the threat tariff. When *Small* is not sufficiently patient, it can extract enough surplus through the PTA to achieve a higher welfare under the exception regime (since its threat to stop cooperating is more credible). But as part (ii) of the proposition shows, there exist sufficiently patient small countries for which an increase in the threat tariff allows *Large* to demand a significant increase in their supply of the public good. This leaves *Small* worse off than if no PTAs were allowed.

Thus far, the focus has been on whether the model predicts one of two alternative rules. But there are other plausible and empirically important alternatives. Recently, the U.S. and the E.U., for example, supported linking cooperation on non-trade issues to multilateral tariffs in the WTO. This has been vigorously opposed by most small developing countries. Our model provides an explanation for both positions. According to the proposals, linkage in the WTO can be translated into our model as allowing *Large* to threaten *Small* with a tariff above the multilateral tariff. Thus, in our model the threat tariff used if *Small* stops supplying the public good can now be higher than τ. In the absence of a prohibition of preferential treatment, from the perspective of our model, the only difference between the PTA exception rule and linkage in the WTO is that the latter allows large countries to use a higher threat tariff against small ones. Our model then predicts that large countries favour linkage in the WTO and *Small* opposes it because the higher threat, which is not implemented along the equilibrium path, allows *Large* to extract more cooperation from *Small* at any given tariffs that are implemented in equilibrium. Thus, our model predicts the recent attempt to move cooperation in non-trade issues into the WTO—both the support of large developed countries and the opposition of small developing ones.[43]

4.2. *Normative implications*

To analyse the normative implications of the model for WTO rules, it is useful to start with a welfare benchmark for the rules. As we noted before, if the PTA is not duty free then the multilateral tariffs remain unchanged. In this case, the PTA actually delivers the exact same solution as the unconstrained first best, that is, the solution is identical to one where large countries make direct transfers of the numeraire to "purchase" *Small*'s supply of the regional public good. The reason is simple: the quasi-linearity of preferences and the inelastic export supply imply that a preference is simply a transfer of income that causes *Small* to supply the regional good but distorts no other decision. However, when the PTA is not duty free it distorts the MFN tariff, which raises the question of what alternative rules could be used.

One criterion is for the alternative to eliminate the stumbling block effect. If *Large* could use lump-sum transfers to ensure that *Small* provides the public good, there would be no motive for a PTA and consequently no stumbling block. But, to the extent that we do observe PTAs there must exist a constraint that prevents countries from simply using lump-sum transfers.[44]

43. An interesting alternative would be to allow for linkage in the WTO but simultaneously require that no preferences be given to small countries. The choice between this and the PTA exception for large countries is no longer obvious. The threat tariff they can use under linkage is higher but what is important in determining how much they can extract from *Small* is the difference between that threat and the actual tariff charged on *Small*'s exports. That difference is $t^{N}(\tau)-\tau$ under linkage and $\tau^{EX}-t^{B}(\tau^{EX})$ under the exception. When $t^{N}(\tau)-\tau$ is sufficiently large, then large countries prefer to link in the WTO. Otherwise they prefer the PTA exception. Suppose then that cooperation in multilateral tariffs is gradual as we have observed it in the last 60 years. This means that initially the difference between cooperative and non-cooperative tariffs is small and it increases over time. In this case, our model predicts that, all else equal, large countries are increasingly more likely to try to pursue linkage in the WTO.

44. For example, if some individuals in the preference granting country do not value the cooperation then they will oppose a direct transfer to obtain it. This is more difficult with the indirect transfer that arises with the preference because trade policy is not revised every year whereas budgets are. Moreover, the indirect transfer through a preferential tariff may be somewhat more "disguised" than the direct transfer. In the receiving country, cash from a direct transfer may end

Another obvious alternative is eliminating the WTO articles that allow exceptions to MFN, that is, implementing commitment to MFN. However, this would be opposed by the large countries, as we show in Proposition 4.

A more interesting normative criterion is for the alternative rule to generate a Pareto improvement relative to the PTA exception. Allowing import subsidies, that is, negative preferential tariffs, would satisfy this criterion. It is simple to understand why import subsidies improve the welfare of large countries. As we note after Proposition 2 in offering a preferential margin, the large countries always prefer to use lower preferential tariffs than higher multilateral tariffs. A lower preferential tariff works as a cash transfer and does not distort any economic decisions in *Large*, but the higher multilateral tariff distorts the consumption of the non-numeraire goods and moves them away from the optimum. By removing the non-negativity constraint on preferential tariffs, that is, allowing import subsidies, the large countries no longer need to distort the multilateral tariff. When that non-negativity constraint is binding, that is, when the PTAs are duty free, these countries will gain from the switch. *Small* also prefers to be compensated via an import subsidy rather than face a higher threat in the form of higher multilateral tariffs.[45]

Just as the exception rule delivers the unconstrained first best when the PTA is not duty free, the import subsidy delivers the first best even if the PTA was duty free (before a subsidy is implemented). In addition to generating a Pareto improvement for the PTA members, the subsidy would also generate a welfare improvement for non-members that export goods similar to the small countries to *Large* since their exports would now face lower multilateral tariffs. This would be an important advantage since the costs of PTAs for non-members are generally an important criterion in designing WTO rules on PTAs.

The welfare cost from maintaining these preferences instead of an import subsidy scheme is estimated by Limão and Olarreaga (2006). They apply a general computable equilibrium model to disaggregated trade data to estimate the welfare impact of lost multilateral liberalization by the U.S., E.U., and Japan due to their PTAs. They find that the aggregate gains in the trade round currently under negotiation would increase by about 10% even if we consider only the preference schemes those countries use for the least developing countries. Moreover, they find that all groups of countries would gain from the switch.[46]

5. CONCLUSION

Trade is not the only motivation for PTAs, cooperation in issues not directly related to trade is often just as important. Thus far, these other motives and the effects of such agreements have

up in a politician's pocket and thus not provide the incentives for the intended supply of cooperation. For example, one of the stated aims of the U.S. in providing preferences to the Andean countries is to raise the relative price to activities other than drug production.

45. Although the argument for *Small* is less obvious, the basic intuition can be made clear without going into much detail. Recall from Proposition 1 that *Small*'s equilibrium supply of the public good is $e^{\mathrm{B}} = (\delta^s/k)(\tau - t^{\mathrm{B}})$. A given increase in the preferential margin, $\tau - t^{\mathrm{B}}$, has the same cost to *Small* in terms of the extra amount of e it must provide. This aggregate marginal cost is $H\delta^s/k$, which is independent of whether the increase in $\tau - t^{\mathrm{B}}$ is due to an increase in τ or a decrease of similar magnitude in t^{B}. However, the benefit in terms of export value depends on which of these tariffs changes. *Small* obtains $(p^{\mathrm{L}}(\tau) - t^{\mathrm{B}})H/k$ for its exports so a marginal decrease in the preferential tariff increases *Small*'s welfare by H/k. But, for a given t^{B}, the benefit of a marginal increase of similar magnitude in τ is $(\partial p/\partial \tau)H/k$. The higher tariff generates an increase in the domestic price but that pass through is less than one because *Large* has market power and this tariff is imposed on goods from *Large** so $\partial p/\partial \tau < 1$. To close this argument, we need to show that the equilibrium decrease in the preferential tariff under the subsidy is not smaller than the increase in the multilateral tariff. This will indeed be the case because it is relatively more costly for *Large* to use the multilateral tariff. By starting from a situation where the PTA is just duty free and increasing α or λ, we can show that the increase in the multilateral tariff under the exception is smaller in magnitude than the fall in the preferential tariff.

46. More specifically, they combine the stumbling block estimates of Limão (2006) to calculate the effects of the additional MTL that would result if the preferences of these three countries were replaced by import subsidies.

generally been ignored. We cannot continue to ignore these non-trade objectives in PTAs since they are now both pervasive and quite explicit. More importantly, when we account for the non-trade motives behind many PTAs we can better explain which are formed and their consequences on the multilateral system.

We show that PTAs have important effects on the multilateral trading system—and in particular on multilateral tariffs of large countries—even if the agreement is signed with an economically small country. The model allows us to map the outcome from different rules into an empirical test of whether PTAs with non-trade objectives cause a stumbling block to MTL. The novel evidence we present strongly supports the model. In the goods exported under the relevant PTAs, these agreements caused an average increase of 33% in the specific tariffs that the U.S. applies multilaterally. This and other recent evidence indicates that PTAs formed by the U.S. and the E.U. have caused them to maintain higher multilateral tariffs.

The model correctly predicts the current set of rules for PTAs in the WTO. However, the welfare analysis shows that even though the current rules are optimal for large countries they are not necessarily so for small PTA partners and non-members. This provides a strong motivation for the WTO to regulate PTAs more carefully, for small countries to seek a more active rule in determining WTO rules and to explore alternatives such as import subsidies.

APPENDIX. PROOFS OF PROPOSITIONS IN TEXT

Proposition 1. *Self-enforcing PTA bargaining solutions.*

In the text we define that *Large* is sufficiently endowed relative to *Small* if $k \geq \max(k_1, k_2)$, where k_1 is defined by $\left\{\frac{W^{\mathrm{L}}_{e^{\mathrm{S}}}(k_1)}{W^{\mathrm{L}}_t} = \frac{W^{\mathrm{S}}_{e^{\mathrm{S}}}}{W^{\mathrm{S}}_t}\frac{1}{\delta^{\mathrm{S}}}\right\}\Big|_{t=0,e^{\mathrm{S}}=\frac{t^{\mathrm{T}}\delta^{\mathrm{S}}}{k_1}}$. Rewriting the IC in (16) and (15) as $\Omega^j \leq \frac{\delta^j}{1-\delta^j}\omega^j$, then k_2 is defined by $\left\{\Omega^{\mathrm{L}}(t, e^{\mathrm{S}}, k_2) = \frac{\delta^{\mathrm{L}}}{1-\delta^{\mathrm{L}}}\omega^{\mathrm{L}}(t, e^{\mathrm{S}}, k_2)\right\}\Big|_{t=0,e^{\mathrm{S}}=\frac{t^{\mathrm{T}}\delta^{\mathrm{S}}}{k_2}}$. Using (5), (6), and (16), our conditions reduce to $\{\alpha^{\mathrm{L}}\lambda^{\mathrm{L}}\delta^{\mathrm{S}}Hb^{\mathrm{S}}\Psi'(b^{\mathrm{S}}He^{\mathrm{S}})\}|_{e^{\mathrm{S}}=t^{\mathrm{T}}\delta^{\mathrm{S}}/k_1} = 1$ for k_1 and $\{\alpha^{\mathrm{L}}\lambda^{\mathrm{L}}\delta^{\mathrm{L}}\Psi(b^{\mathrm{S}}He^{\mathrm{S}})\}|_{e^{\mathrm{S}}=t^{\mathrm{T}}\delta^{\mathrm{S}}/k_2} = t^{\mathrm{T}}/k_2$ for k_2.

Forming the Lagrangian with μ^j and ϕ^g as the multipliers for the incentive and non-negativity constraints, respectively, we have the following necessary conditions for $j = L, \mathrm{S}$ and $g = t, e^{\mathrm{S}}$:

$$\partial W^{\mathrm{L}}/\partial g - \sum_j \mu^j\left(\partial\Omega^j/\partial g - \frac{\delta^j}{1-\delta^j}\partial\omega^j/\partial g\right) + \phi^g = 0,$$

$$\mu^j\left(\Omega^j - \frac{\delta^j}{1-\delta^j}\omega^j\right) = 0, \quad \phi^g g = 0, \quad \mu^j \geq 0, \;\; \phi^g \geq 0.$$

First, if $\Omega^{\mathrm{S}} < \frac{\delta^{\mathrm{S}}}{1-\delta^{\mathrm{S}}}\omega^{\mathrm{S}}$ at the solution then an increase in e^{S} is feasible and optimal, which implies that $\Omega^{\mathrm{S}} = \frac{\delta^{\mathrm{S}}}{1-\delta^{\mathrm{S}}}\omega^{\mathrm{S}} \Leftrightarrow e^{\mathrm{B}} = \frac{\delta^{\mathrm{S}}}{k}(t^{\mathrm{T}} - t^{\mathrm{B}})$, using the definitions in (5) and (15).

If $k = k_2$, then, by definition, $\Omega^{\mathrm{L}} = \frac{\delta^{\mathrm{L}}}{1-\delta^{\mathrm{L}}}\omega^{\mathrm{L}}$ at $t^{\mathrm{B}} = 0, e^{\mathrm{B}} = \frac{\delta^{\mathrm{S}}t^{\mathrm{T}}}{k}$, thus in Figure 4 $\overline{\mathrm{IC}}^{\mathrm{L}}$ and $\overline{\mathrm{IC}}^{\mathrm{S}}$ would intersect at $t = 0$. An increase in k relaxes IC^{L} at any given t^{T} since it reduces $\Omega^{\mathrm{L}} = \frac{H}{k}(t^{\mathrm{T}} - t)$ and increases $\omega^{\mathrm{L}} = \frac{\delta}{1-\delta}\left(-\frac{H}{k}(t^{\mathrm{T}} - t) + H\alpha^{\mathrm{L}}\lambda^{\mathrm{L}}\Psi(b^{\mathrm{S}}He^{\mathrm{S}})\right)$. Thus, $\Omega^{\mathrm{L}} \leq \frac{\delta^{\mathrm{L}}}{1-\delta^{\mathrm{L}}}\omega^{\mathrm{L}}$ at $t^{\mathrm{B}} = 0, e^{\mathrm{B}} = \frac{\delta^{\mathrm{S}}t^{\mathrm{T}}}{k}$ iff $k \geq k_2$. The FOC then yields $W^{\mathrm{L}}_{e^{\mathrm{S}}}/W^{\mathrm{L}}_t \geq W^{\mathrm{S}}_{e^{\mathrm{S}}}/W^{\mathrm{S}}_t\delta^{\mathrm{S}}$. Now, if $k > k_2$ then IC^{L} does not bind and e^{B} is determined by $W^{\mathrm{L}}_{e^{\mathrm{S}}}/W^{\mathrm{L}}_t = W^{\mathrm{S}}_{e^{\mathrm{S}}}/W^{\mathrm{S}}_t\delta^{\mathrm{S}}$. A further increase in k lowers t^{B} but not e^{B} (because $W^{\mathrm{L}}_{e^{\mathrm{S}}}/W^{\mathrm{L}}_t = W^{\mathrm{S}}_{e^{\mathrm{S}}}/W^{\mathrm{S}}_t\delta^{\mathrm{S}}$ is independent of k). If in addition $k = k_1 \geq k_2$, then $W^{\mathrm{L}}_{e^{\mathrm{S}}}/W^{\mathrm{L}}_t = W^{\mathrm{S}}_{e^{\mathrm{S}}}/W^{\mathrm{S}}_t\delta^{\mathrm{S}}$ at $(t^{\mathrm{B}} = 0, e^{\mathrm{B}} = \delta^{\mathrm{S}}t^{\mathrm{T}}/k)$. Thus, since we rule out $t^{\mathrm{B}} < 0$ it must be that, at the given t^{T}, $e^{\mathrm{B}} = \delta^{\mathrm{S}}t^{\mathrm{T}}/k$ falls and therefore at $k \geq k_1$ we have $W^{\mathrm{L}}_{e^{\mathrm{S}}}/W^{\mathrm{L}}_t > W^{\mathrm{S}}_{e^{\mathrm{S}}}/W^{\mathrm{S}}_t\delta^{\mathrm{S}}$.

If $k < k_2$, then, by definition, $\overline{\mathrm{IC}}^{\mathrm{L}}$ and $\overline{\mathrm{IC}}^{\mathrm{S}}$ intersect at $t > 0$ and two cases arise. First, if $\Omega^{\mathrm{L}} < \frac{\delta^{\mathrm{L}}}{1-\delta^{\mathrm{L}}}\omega^{\mathrm{L}}$ at $(t^{\mathrm{B}}, e^{\mathrm{B}})$, then e^{B} is determined by $W^{\mathrm{L}}_{e^{\mathrm{S}}}/W^{\mathrm{L}}_t = W^{\mathrm{S}}_{e^{\mathrm{S}}}/W^{\mathrm{S}}_t\delta^{\mathrm{S}}$ and t^{B} by $e^{\mathrm{B}} = \frac{\delta^{\mathrm{S}}}{k}(t^{\mathrm{T}} - t^{\mathrm{B}})$. Second, if $\Omega^{\mathrm{L}} = \frac{\delta^{\mathrm{L}}}{1-\delta^{\mathrm{L}}}\omega^{\mathrm{L}}$, then $t^{\mathrm{T}} - t^{\mathrm{B}} = \delta^{\mathrm{L}}k\alpha^{\mathrm{L}}\lambda^{\mathrm{L}}\Psi(b^{\mathrm{S}}He^{\mathrm{B}})$ by using (6) and (16). In the second case, the FOC requires $W^{\mathrm{L}}_{e^{\mathrm{S}}}/W^{\mathrm{L}}_t \geq W^{\mathrm{S}}_{e^{\mathrm{S}}}/W^{\mathrm{S}}_t\delta^{\mathrm{S}}$. ‖

Proposition 2. *PTAs as stumbling blocks, $\tau^{EX} > \tau^{C}$.*

If large countries are sufficiently patient s.t. neither IC^{EX} nor IC^{C} binds, then (19) and (20) are necessary to determine τ^{EX} and τ^{C} (they are also sufficient since the respective second derivatives are negative). Evaluating (20) at τ^{EX}, we obtain $\left\{W_t^{L}\left(1-\frac{\partial t^{B}}{\partial t^{T}}\right)-W_{e^{S}}^{L}\frac{\partial e^{B}}{\partial t^{T}}\right\}|_{\tau^{EX}}$. We must consider two cases:

Case 1. *PTA is not or is "just" duty free at t^{T} if $t^{B}(t^{T}=\tau^{EX})\geq 0 \wedge t^{B}(t^{T}\to\tau^{EX+})>0$*

From implicit differentiation of either (t^{BI}, e^{B}) or (t^{BII}, e^{B}) in Proposition 1, we obtain $\partial t^{B}/\partial t^{T}=1$ and $\partial e^{B}/\partial t^{T}=0$.

$\therefore \left\{W_t^{L}\left(1-\frac{\partial t^{B}}{\partial t^{T}}\right)-W_{e^{S}}^{L}\frac{\partial e^{B}}{\partial t^{T}}\right\}|_{\tau^{EX}}=0 \Rightarrow \tau^{EX}=\tau^{C}$.

Case 2. *PTA is duty free at t^{T} if $t^{B}(t^{T}=\tau^{EX})=0 \wedge t^{B}(t^{T}\to\tau^{EX+})=0$*

From implicit differentiation of either (t^{BI}, e^{B}) or (t^{BII}, e^{B}) in Proposition 1, we obtain $\partial t^{B}/\partial t^{T}=0$ and $\partial e^{B}/\partial t^{T}=\frac{\delta^{S}}{k}$. Thus, $\{W_t^{L}(1-\frac{\partial t^{B}}{\partial t^{T}})-W_{e^{S}}^{L}\frac{\partial e^{B}}{\partial t^{T}}\}|_{\tau^{EX}}<0$ because $\frac{W_{e^{S}}^{L}}{W_t^{L}}>\frac{W_{e^{S}}^{S}}{W_t^{S}}\frac{1}{\delta^{S}}=\frac{k}{\delta^{S}}$ (Proposition 1).

$\therefore \left\{W_t^{L}(1-\frac{\partial t^{B}}{\partial t^{T}})-W_{e^{S}}^{L}\frac{\partial e^{B}}{\partial t^{T}}\right\}|_{\tau^{EX}}<0 \Rightarrow \tau^{EX}>\tau^{C}$. ||

Proposition 3. *Comparative statics.*

We need to consider only the effect of α^{L} since λ^{L} enters W^{L} symmetrically.

A. IC^{EX} and IC^{C} not binding
First, $d\tau^{C}/d\alpha=0$ since under commitment no PTA occurs. Implicit differentiation of (19) yields

$$\frac{d\tau^{EX}}{d\alpha}=\frac{\partial\left(W_t^{L}\frac{\partial t^{B}}{\partial t^{T}}+W_{e^{S}}^{L}\frac{\partial e^{B}}{\partial t^{T}}\right)/\partial\alpha}{-\partial^{2}W^{L}/\partial(\tau)^{2}},$$

$$\operatorname{sign}\left(\frac{d\tau^{EX}}{d\alpha}\right)=\operatorname{sign}\left(\partial\left(W_t^{L}\frac{\partial t^{B}}{\partial t^{T}}+W_{e^{S}}^{L}\frac{\partial e^{B}}{\partial t^{T}}\right)\Big/\partial\alpha\right),$$

where the second line follows from the concavity of $W^{L}(t=t^{B}, e^{S}=e^{B}, \tau, \tau^{*}=\tau, \cdot)$ in τ. Similarly to Proposition 2 we must consider two cases.

Case 1. $t^{B}(t^{T}=\tau^{EX})\geq 0 \wedge t^{B}(t^{T}\to\tau^{EX+})>0$.

From Proposition 1, $\frac{\partial t^{B}}{\partial t^{T}}=1$ and thus $\frac{\partial}{\partial\alpha}\left(\frac{\partial t^{B}}{\partial t^{T}}\right)=0$. Moreover, $\frac{\partial e^{B}}{\partial\tau}=0$ and $\frac{\partial}{\partial\alpha}(W_t^{L})=0$ since $W_t^{L}=H/k$.
$\therefore d\tau^{EX}/d\alpha=d\tau^{C}/d\alpha=0$.

Case 2. $t^{B}(t^{T}=\tau^{EX})=0 \wedge t^{B}(t^{T}\to\tau^{EX+})=0$.

From Proposition 1, $\frac{\partial t^{B}}{\partial t^{T}}=0$ and thus $\frac{\partial}{\partial\alpha}\left(\frac{\partial t^{B}}{\partial t^{T}}\right)=0$. Moreover, $\frac{\partial}{\partial\alpha}\left(\frac{\partial e^{B}}{\partial\tau}\right)=0$ since $\frac{\partial e^{B}}{\partial\tau}=\delta^{S}/k$ and $\frac{\partial}{\partial\alpha}(W_t^{L})=0$ since $W_t^{L}=H/k$.
$\therefore \partial\left(W_t^{L}\frac{\partial t^{B}}{\partial t^{T}}+W_{e^{S}}^{L}\frac{\partial e^{B}}{\partial t^{T}}\right)\Big/\partial\alpha=(\delta^{S}/k)\partial(W_{e^{S}}^{L})/\partial\alpha>0 \Rightarrow d\tau^{EX}/d\alpha>d\tau^{C}/d\alpha=0$. ||

B. IC^{EX} and IC^{C} bind: see Section A.2.4 of online appendix.

Proposition 4. *Welfare ranking of regimes*
(i) A. When large countries are sufficiently patient, the PTA exception regime welfare dominates commitment to MFN for large countries.

To prove this, we show that we can rewrite the commitment problem in a form that is identical to the exception problem except it has an additional constraint. Rewriting the problem in (18) by explicitly allowing large countries to

TABLE A1

Data description and sources

Variable	Definition/description	Source[a]
$\Delta\tau$	$=\ln[(1+\tau_{it}/p_i)/(1+\tau_{it-1}/p_i)]$; $\tau_{it,t-1}$: U.S. specific bound tariff (t: post-UR, $t-1$: pre-UR). p_i: Average price for HS 8-digit product i over all exporters of i to the U.S. between 1989–99.	WTO, Feenstra, Romalis and Schott (2002)
INITIAL τ	$=\tau_{it-1}/p_{it}$	WTO, Feenstra *et al.* (2002)
PTANAME	=1 if HS-8 good i exported to U.S. under the PTA (1994)	Feenstra *et al.* (2002)
ATPA_CBI	= ATPA + CBI	Feenstra *et al.* (2002)
EX_PTA	=1 if HS-8 good i exported to the U.S. by the respective PTA partner whether or not the product received a preference (1994)	Feenstra *et al.* (2002)
s^k_{iT}	Partner k's export share of top five exporters of HS-8 good i to U.S. in 1990	Feenstra *et al.* (2002)
RECIPROCITY	$\sum_k s^k_{iT}\ (\sum_j \Delta\tau^k_{jt} w^k_j)$, where $(\sum_j \Delta\tau^k_{jt} w^k_j)$: Partner k's aggregate multilateral liberalization; $\Delta\tau^k_{jt} \equiv$ % change 1995–1986; $w^k_j \equiv$ Share of good j in k's imports	Finger, Reincke and Castro (2002)
UNILAT_RED	$\sum_k s^k_{iT}\ (\sum_j \Delta\tau^k_{jt} w^k_j - \sum_j \Delta\tau^{rk}_{jt} w^k_j)$, where $\Delta\tau^{rk}_{jt} \equiv$ % change 1995–1992	Finger *et al.* (2002)
ΔPRICE_90_94	Mean price change (1990–1994) for HS-8 good i exported to U.S.	Feenstra *et al.* (2002)
TRANSP_COST 94	Mean transport cost for HS-8 good i exported to U.S. in 1994	U.S.ITC
TRANSP_COST$\times\Delta$PRICE	= TC $\times$ Δ PRICE_90_94	
EXP GROWTH	$=\sum_k s^k_{iT} \ln(\text{GDP}^k_{90}/\ \text{GDP}^k_{77})$. Growth in partner k's GDP.	PWT 6.1

Notes: (a) PWT, Penn World Tables; U.S. ITC, United States International Trade Commission; WTO, World Trade Organization.

propose PTAs under commitment, the equilibrium solution is still $\tau = \tau^{C} = t$ and $e^{S} = 0$. Note that $e^{B}(t^{T}) = \frac{\delta^{S}}{k}(t^{T} - t^{B}(t^{T})) = 0$ because the constraint $t = \tau$ means both that $t^{B}(t^{T}) = \tau$ and t^{T} cannot be higher than τ:

$$\tau^{C} \equiv \arg\max_{\tau}\{W^{L}(t = t^{B}(t^{T}), e^{S} = e^{B}(t^{T}), \tau, \tau^{*} = \tau, \cdot) : \mathrm{IC}^{C}; t = \tau\}. \tag{23}$$

When large countries are sufficiently patient, their IC in the MTL does not bind and the only difference between the program for τ^{EX} in (17) and the one for τ^{C} in (23) is that in the latter the constraint $t = \tau$ binds because the PTA is welfare improving at any given multilateral tariff.

Therefore, since (23) and (18) are equivalent, we have $W^{L}(\tau^{EX}, \cdot) > W^{L}(\tau^{C}, \cdot)$ for $\delta^{S} > 0$. ||

To prove parts (i)B and (ii) of Proposition 4, it is useful to restate the proposition in a form that is exactly equivalent to the text:

When large countries are sufficiently patient and *Small is not sufficiently patient, it prefers the PTA regime.*

When large countries are sufficiently patient and Small is sufficiently patient:

(i) *it prefers the PTA regime if the PTA under $\tau^{EX}(\delta^{S})$ is not duty free* ($W^{EXS} > W^{CS}$).

(ii) *there exists a $\delta^{S} \in (p_{\tau}, 1)$ s.t. Small prefers the commitment regime if the PTA under $\tau^{EX}(\delta^{S})$ is duty free* ($W^{EXS} < W^{CS}$).

We show that a necessary and sufficient condition for $W^{EXS} > W^{CS}$ is

$$\delta^{S} < 1 - \frac{(\tau^{EX} - \tau^{C})(1 - p_{\tau}^{L})}{\tau^{EX} - t^{B}(\tau^{EX})} = \begin{cases} 1, & \text{when the PTA at } \tau^{EX} \text{ is not duty free,} \\ p_{\tau}^{L} + \frac{\tau^{C}}{\tau^{EX}}(1 - p_{\tau}^{L}) < 1, & \text{when the PTA at } \tau^{EX} \text{ is duty free.} \end{cases}$$

Moreover, $\delta^{S} < p_{\tau}^{L}$ is a sufficient condition for $W^{EXS} > W^{CS}$ since $\min\left(1 - \frac{(\tau^{EX} - \tau^{C})(1 - p_{\tau}^{L})}{\tau^{EX} - t^{B}(\tau^{EX})}\right) \geq p_{\tau}^{L}$, where $p_{\tau}^{L} \equiv \partial p_{l}^{L}/\partial\tau$ and all the prices in the expressions immediately above and below correspond to *Large*'s import good, l, so we drop the subscript:

$$\begin{aligned} W^{EXS} - W^{CS} &= \left\{\frac{H}{k}(p^{L}(\tau^{EX}) - t^{B}(\tau^{EX}) - He^{B}(\tau^{EX}))\right\} - \frac{H}{k}(p^{L}(\tau^{C}) - \tau^{C}) \\ &= \frac{H}{k}(p^{L}(\tau^{EX}) - t^{B}(\tau^{EX}) - (p^{L}(\tau^{C}) - \tau^{C}) - \delta^{S}(\tau^{EX} - t^{B}(\tau^{EX}))) \\ &= \frac{H}{k}(p^{L}(\tau^{EX}) - p^{L}(\tau^{C}) - (\tau^{EX} - \tau^{C}) + (\tau^{EX} - t^{B}(\tau^{EX}))(1 - \delta^{S})) \\ &= \frac{H}{k}((\tau^{EX} - t^{B}(\tau^{EX}))(1 - \delta^{S}) - (\tau^{EX} - \tau^{C})(1 - p_{\tau}^{L})). \end{aligned}$$

In the first line, we use (5); in the second, we use IC^{S} from the proof of Proposition 1 to substitute e^{B}; in the third, we add and subtract τ^{EX}. The fourth line follows from the linearity of prices in tariffs that implies $p^{L}(\tau^{EX}) - p^{L}(\tau^{C}) = (\tau^{EX} - \tau^{C})p_{\tau}^{L}$. Solving for δ^{S} we obtain $\delta^{S} < 1 - \frac{(\tau^{EX} - \tau^{C})(1 - p_{\tau}^{L})}{\tau^{EX} - t^{B}(\tau^{EX})}$.

Therefore, when the PTA is not duty free at τ^{EX}, $\tau^{EX} = \tau^{C}$

$\Rightarrow \delta^{S} < 1$ is necessary and sufficient for $W^{EXS} > W^{CS}$.

Therefore, when $t^{B}(\tau^{EX}) = 0$, $\tau^{EX} > \tau^{C}$

$\Rightarrow \delta^{S} < 1 - \frac{(\tau^{EX} - \tau^{C})(1 - p_{\tau}^{L})}{\tau^{EX}} = \{p_{\tau}^{L} + \frac{\tau^{C}}{\tau^{EX}}(1 - p_{\tau}^{L})\} \in (p_{\tau}, 1)$ is necessary and sufficient for $W^{EXS} > W^{CS}$, thus a $\delta^{S} \in (p_{\tau}, 1)$ exists s.t. *Small* prefers the commitment regime. ||

Acknowledgements. I thank Piyush Chandra, Rod Ludema, John Mclaren, Helen Milner, Arvind Panagariya, Michael Riordan, David Weinstein, Eric Van Wicoop, and participants at seminars in UPenn, the USITC, NBER Summer Institute 2003, and the World Bank for comments. I am grateful to Stephanie Aaronson, Kyle Bagwell, and Don Davis for helpful discussions. I especially thank the editor, Maitreesh Ghatak, and two anonymous referees for extremely useful suggestions. The usual disclaimer applies.

REFERENCES

ABREGO, L. E., PERRONI, C., WHALLEY, J. and WIGLE, R. M. (2001), "Trade and Environment: Bargaining Outcomes from Linked Negotiations", *Review of International Economics*, **9** (3), 414–428.

BAGWELL, K. and STAIGER, R. (1990), "A Theory of Managed Trade", *American Economic Review*, **80**, 779–795.

BAGWELL, K. and STAIGER, R. (1998), "Will Preferential Agreements Undermine the Multilateral Trading System?", *Economic Journal*, **108** (449), 1162–1182.

BAGWELL, K. and STAIGER, R. (1999), "An Economic Theory of GATT", *American Economic Review*, **89** (1), 215–248.

BHAGWATI, J. (1991), *The World Trading System at Risk* (Princeton: Princeton University Press).

BOND, E. W. and PARK, J. (2002), "Gradualism in Trade Agreements with Asymmetric Countries", *Review of Economic Studies*, **69** (2), 379–406.

BOND, E., SYROPOULOS, C. and WINTERS, A. (2001), "Deepening of Regional Integration and Multilateral Trade Agreements", *Journal of International Economics*, **53**, 335–361.

BRODA, C., LIMÃO, N. and WEINSTEIN, D. (2006), "Optimal Tariffs: The Evidence" (NBER Working Paper No. 12033, National Bureau of Economic Research).

CHANG, W. and WINTERS, A. (2002), "How Regional Blocs Affect Excluded Countries: The Price Effects of Mercosur", *American Economic Review*, **92** (4), 889–904.

ETHIER, W. (1998), "Regionalism in a Multilateral World", *The Journal of Political Economy*, **106** (6), 1214–1245.

ETHIER, W. (2004), "Political Externalities, Non-Discrimination, and a Multilateral World", *Review of International Economics*, **12** (3), 303–320.

FEENSTRA, R., ROMALIS, J. and SCHOTT, P. (2002), "U.S. Imports, Exports and Tariff Data, 1989–2001" (NBER Working Paper No. W9387, National Bureau of Economic Research).

FINGER, J. M., REINCKE, U. and CASTRO, A. (2002), "Market Access Bargaining in the Uruguay Round: Rigid or Relaxed Reciprocity?", in J. Bhagwati (ed.) *Going Alone: The Case for Relaxed Reciprocity* (Cambridge, MA: MIT Press) 111–135.

GRILLI, E. (1997), "EU Trade and Aid Policies Towards the LDCs and CEECs", in A. M. El-Agra (ed.) *Economic Integration Worldwide* (London: Macmillan Press) 135–174.

GROSSMAN, G. and HELPMAN, E. (1995), "Trade Wars and Trade Talks", *Journal of Political Economy*, **103** (4), 675–708.

JACKSON, J. (1997) *The World Trading System: Law and Policy of International Economic Relations*, 2nd edn (Cambridge, MA: MIT Press).

JOHNSON, H. (1954), "Optimum Tariffs and Retaliation", *Review of Economic Studies*, **21**, 142–153.

JOHNSON, H. G. (1967), *Economic Policies Toward Less Developed Countries* (Washington DC: Brookings Institution).

KARACAOVALI, B. and LIMÃO, N. (2005), "The Clash of Liberalizations: Preferential vs. Multilateral Trade Liberalization in the European Union" (World Bank Research Working Paper No. 3493).

KRISHNA, P. (1998), "Regionalism and Multilateralism: A Political Economy Approach", *Quarterly Journal of Economics*, **113**, 227–251.

LEVY, P. (1997), "A Political-Economic Analysis of Free-Trade Agreements", *American Economic Review*, **87** (4), 506–519.

LIMÃO, N. (2002), "Are Preferential Trade Agreements with Non-Trade Objectives a Stumbling Block for Multilateral Liberalization?" (UMD CIE Working Paper No. 02-02, University of Maryland Center for International Economics).

LIMÃO, N. (2006), "Preferential Trade Agreements as Stumbling Blocks for Multilateral Trade Liberalization: Evidence for the US", *American Economic Review*, **96** (3), 896–914.

LIMÃO, N. and OLARREAGA, M. (2006), "Trade Preferences to Small Developing Countries and the Welfare Costs of Lost Multilateral Liberalization", *World Bank Economic Review*, **20** (2), 217–240.

MATTOO, A. and SUBRAMANIAN, A. (2004), "The WTO and the Poorest Countries: The Stark Reality" (IMF Working Paper No. WP/04/81, International Monetary Fund).

MCCALMAN, P. (2001), "Reaping What you Sow: An Empirical Analysis of International Patent Harmonization", *Journal of International Economics*, **55** (1), 161–186.

PERRONI, C. and WHALLEY, J. (2000), "The New Regionalism: Trade Liberalization or Insurance?", *Canadian Journal of Economics*, **33** (1), 1–24.

SCHIFF, M. and WINTERS, A. (1998), "Regional Integration as Diplomacy", *World Bank Economic Review*, **12** (2), 271–295.

SRINIVASAN, T. N. (1999), "Developing Countries in the World Trading System: From GATT, 1947, to the Third Ministerial Meeting of WTO, 1999", *The World Economy*, **22** (8), 1047–1064.

STAIGER, R. (1995), "International Rules and Institutions for Trade Policy", in G. Grossman and K. Rogoff (eds.) *Handbook of International Economics*, Vol. III (Amsterdam: North-Holland) 1495–1551.

SYROPOULOS, C. (2002), "Optimum Tariffs and Retaliation Revisited: How Country Size Matters", *Review of Economic Studies*, **69** (3), 707–727.

TREBILCOCK, M. J. and HOWSE, R. (1999) *The Regulation of International Trade*, 2nd edn (London: Routledge).

WINTERS, A. (1993), "Expanding EC Membership and Association Accords", in K. Anderson and R. Blackhurst (eds.) *Regional Integration and the World Trading System* (Harvester Wheatsheaf) 104–125.

WORLD BANK (2000) *Regional Integration Agreements* (Washington DC: World Bank).

Chapter 11

Size inequality, coordination externalities and international trade agreements

Nuno Limão [a], Kamal Saggi [b,*]

[a] University of Maryland, NBER and CEPR, United States
[b] Vanderbilt University, United States

ARTICLE INFO

Article history:
Received 24 February 2012
Accepted 24 May 2013
Available online 15 June 2013

JEL classification:
F13
F42
K33
O1
O24

Keywords:
Trade agreements
Tariffs
Bonds
Fines

ABSTRACT

Developing countries now account for a significant fraction of world trade and two-thirds of the membership of the World Trade Organization (WTO). However, many are still individually small and thus have a limited ability to bilaterally extract and enforce trade concessions from larger developed economies even though as a group they would be able to do so. We show that this coordination externality generates asymmetric outcomes under agreements that rely on bilateral threats of trade retaliation – such as the WTO – but not under agreements extended to include certain financial instruments. In particular, we find that an extended agreement generates improvements in global efficiency and equity if it includes the exchange of bonds prior to trading but not if it relies solely on ex post fines. Moreover, a combination of bonds and fines generates similar improvements even if small countries are subject to financial constraints that prevent them from posting bonds.

1. Introduction

International trade relations between developed and developing countries have often been adversarial. As early as 1947, some developing countries were denouncing the United States' proposals for the predecessor of the World Trade Organization (WTO) as "serving the interests of developed countries and undermining the development prospects of poor countries" (Srinivasan, 1999, p. 1050). More recently, the Uruguay Round was seen by most developing countries as having produced a multilateral bargain that is biased heavily in favor of developed countries. Partly to rectify the perceived imbalance of the Uruguay Round outcome, the Doha *Development* Round was launched in 2001 with the idea that it would put the interests of developing countries at the forefront.[1]

Developing countries now account for two-thirds of the 157 WTO members (up from 11 in the GATT) and over a third of world trade and have increasingly begun to demand a more active voice in multilateral negotiations. However, they still face considerable challenges in translating such demands into tangible outcomes: despite having been launched over a decade ago, the Doha Round has yet to be concluded. In this paper we analyze a key problem that developing countries face in

* Corresponding author. Tel.: +615 322 3237.
E-mail addresses: Limao@econ.umd.edu (N. Limão), k.saggi@Vanderbilt.Edu, ksaggi@gmail.com (K. Saggi).

[1] The Doha ministerial declaration of November 2001 states: "We recognize the need for all our peoples to benefit from the increased opportunities and welfare gains that the multilateral trading system generates. The majority of WTO members are developing countries. We seek to place their needs and interests at the heart of the Work Programme adopted in this declaration."

0014-2921/$ - see front matter © 2013 Elsevier B.V. All rights reserved.
http://dx.doi.org/10.1016/j.euroecorev.2013.05.006

Originally Published in *European Economic Review* 63, pp. 10–27.

trying to achieve a more favorable outcome in international trade negotiations—i.e. the presence of a *coordination externality* among themselves. Even though developing countries are now large on aggregate, most are still individually small and thus have a limited ability to bilaterally extract and enforce trade concessions from larger developed economies. We show that under standard agreements that rely on bilateral threats of trade retaliation – such as the WTO – this coordination externality generates asymmetric outcomes that are less favorable to developing countries (as well as globally) than those obtained under an agreement extended to include certain types of financial instruments.

The traditionally dominant role of large countries in the world trading system is partly due to the bilateral and reciprocal nature of negotiations in international trade agreements such as the GATT/WTO. The key idea is the following: if the European Union (EU) wants the United States (US) to lower its tariffs on EU exports then it must reciprocate with lower tariffs on goods it imports from the US. However, this reciprocal exchange relies on the presence of relatively symmetric market power on both sides: while a tariff reduction by a country with a sufficiently high import share and market power increases the price received by foreign exporters, no significant bilateral concessions occur when the reduction is undertaken by a small country.[2] Market power is also essential in enforcing cooperation since the threat to abandon the agreement and increase tariffs on the part of a country that lacks such power is not credible and therefore fails to act as a useful deterrent. Thus, *bilateral asymmetries* in market power undermine international cooperation and may explain why some exports from (smaller) developing countries (e.g. in agriculture, textiles, some manufactures) have historically faced relatively higher tariffs in (larger) developed countries. By undermining cooperation, this asymmetry can also lead to higher tariffs by developing countries but, as long as they remain small as a group, the large countries do not lose much from this, which may explain why the latter have not pushed developing countries to liberalize further until recently.[3]

Most formal analyses of the GATT/WTO focus on two large countries.[4] The focus on this canonical case has yielded important insights and was a reasonable approximation until the Uruguay Round since up to that point GATT/WTO negotiations were led primarily by the US and Europe (cf. Schott, 2009). However, the global economic landscape has changed significantly with the emergence of the BRICs—Brazil, Russia, India and China. From 2000 to 2009 alone the world import share of the largest traders, the US and EU, fell from 43% to 34% (54–42% if we also include Japan and Canada) and their bilateral trade accounts for less than 20% of their total trade.[5] The relative decline of the US and EU in world trade suggests that it is important to analyze international trade agreements between multiple countries of asymmetric size, something that we focus on in this paper.

While some of the recent decline of the US and EU in world trade is mirrored in the rise of the BRICs – particularly China – there is also a longer trend driven by other developing countries' trade liberalization and growth.[6] This is important in motivating the coordination externality underlying our model since this externality is most relevant if several countries jointly account for a non-negligible amount of exports of a larger country. For example, if we exclude Japan, Australia and China, the next top 10 Asian destinations in 2009 accounted for 13% of total US exports but their median share was only 1.3% (the largest is Korea with less than 3%). Another case in point is South and Central America: while the region jointly accounts for 10% of US exports all but one country accounts for less than 1% (the only exception is Brazil, whose share is 2.5%). More broadly, if the US were to negotiate only with the top five destinations for its products it would cover only 64% of its exports, with the analogous figure for the EU being even smaller, 44%.[7]

Our model highlights the role of *bilateral size asymmetry* in international trade agreements by focusing on two "regions" of equal size with one containing a single country (Large) and the other multiple countries, each of whom individually has less market power in trade. Large exports a single good, x, to all small countries and imports a different good in return. The bilateral size asymmetry generates lower tariffs and welfare for the smaller countries in the absence of an agreement because their tariff choices are subject to a coordination externality, i.e. when setting its tariff on good x each small country ignores any positive terms-of-trade effect that its tariff has on all other *importers* of the same good. We then show that this

[2] For evidence of the positive relationship between market power and either import shares or GDP see Broda et al. (2008).

[3] In fact, if the asymmetry is sufficiently large, the large country would be strictly better off by not cooperating (cf. Johnson, 1953–1954). An additional explanation for relatively higher tariffs by the large developed countries on exports of small developing countries is that historically the latter have tended not to take an active role in multilateral trade negotiations. One reason for such non-participation and higher tariffs by large countries arises when, as in our setup, a large country imports the same good from many small countries. Ludema and Mayda (2009) show how the WTO's MFN rule requiring the importer to set the same tariff on all exporters lowers the incentive for the latter to participate in reciprocal negotiations in an attempt to minimize reductions in their own tariffs. Since this incentive is well understood theoretically we abstract from it (by assuming all exporters either participate or not) and focus instead on the coordination externality.

[4] See for example Mayer (1981), Grossman and Helpman (1995) and Bagwell and Staiger (1999). The latter also considers a third large country to study tariff discrimination.

[5] Authors calculations based on data from the WTO's "International trade statistics 2010". We treat the EU as a single country since it has a common tariff and negotiates as a block. Thus, world imports exclude flows within EU-27.

[6] As the Director General of the WTO notes "Between 1973 and 1997 the developing countries' share of manufactured imports in developed markets tripled—from 7.5% to 23%. What these figures reflect is the developing world's truly remarkable integration into the global economy over the past three decades." Source: Ruggiero (1999) accessed at ⟨http://www.wto.org/english/news_e/pres99_e/pr122_e.htm⟩. Besedes and Prusa (2011) examine the sources of export growth for 46 countries between 1975 and 2003.

[7] Moreover, the recent increases in this dispersion measure suggest an increasingly important role for the coordination externality among importers of US goods. For example, the top five US destinations in 2000 accounted for 70% of its exports but those in 2009 only accounted for 64%. At the industry level we see a similar trend with over 2/3 of HS 2 industries showing declines averaging 7 percentage points in the share of top five destinations (the average for those with an increase was about 4 p.p.).

imbalance remains even if countries cooperate through a standard trade agreement that relies on the threat of tariff retaliation because cooperation is ultimately sustained by the threat of non-cooperative tariffs, which are subject to the coordination externality.[8] The small countries would gain from jointly threatening higher tariffs to punish any deviation by Large but this threat is not credible: in the event the agreement breaks down, each small country has an individual incentive to free ride on the others if they were to try punishing the large country via a jointly optimal Nash tariff.

In the model all countries have identical *income per capita* in the absence of trade policies. When trade policy is used it generates an asymmetry in income per capita: increasing it for the larger country and reducing it for the smaller ones when cooperation is based on tariff retaliation alone. The most parsimonious way to show this result involves a "developing" region with K countries and a "developed" one with a single large country, but a similar insight should hold as long as the representative country in the developed region was larger. Given this, and the current distribution of world trade – where about half is accounted for by a large number of developing countries – we think it is reasonable to identify the region with more countries as the developing one.[9] Moreover, as we discuss next, the type of reforms proposed to standard trade agreements to address the size asymmetry issue have mainly originated with developing countries.

Next, we examine how standard agreements – i.e. those based on tariff retaliation alone – can be reformed to counter the coordination externality and generate more efficient and equitable (i.e. symmetric) outcomes. More specifically, we extend the standard trade agreement to include financial instruments such that a country that deviates must incur a monetary cost, such as paying a fine or losing a bond that it previously posted. Some such instruments have been proposed in the WTO, particularly by developing countries arguing that their limited market power prevents them from using tariffs to obtain proper compensation in case of a violation.

Before explaining why and how such extended agreements may generate more efficient and equitable outcomes, we describe some of the ongoing debate surrounding the use of financial instruments in trade agreements. The situation confronting developing countries is well illustrated by the case in which Ecuador challenged the preferential treatment that the EU accorded to banana exporting nations that were its former colonies. The US too had challenged the EU's regime and, like Ecuador, was authorized to impose retaliatory tariffs on the EU. However, while the US was in a good position to make use of this authorization, Ecuador simply did not import enough from the EU to be able to effectively retaliate in tariffs. If it had done so it would have simply imposed a distortion on itself without much harm to the EU. Given this, Ecuador went so far as to seek WTO approval to cross-retaliate in the area of intellectual property by not allowing local producers of red wine to use the 'Bordeaux' label and by allowing local firms to produce unauthorized copies of hit European recordings.[10]

The idea that financial compensation could be used as means for settling international trade disputes has a long history—in fact it was discussed during the original GATT 1947 negotiations. While the GATT did not adopt this idea, calls for its usage have resurfaced periodically. For example, in 1964 Brazil and Uruguay formally suggested its consideration and the idea was floated and discussed also during the Uruguay Round negotiations (Mercurio, 2009). While the dispute settlement system of the WTO has yet to embrace financial compensation as a mandatory trade remedy, it does allow for 'voluntary compensation' as an alternative to trade retaliation. Financial compensation was actually used in the *US-Copyright* dispute between the US and the EU. This case was filed by the EU to challenge US laws that exempted small businesses such as restaurants and bars from paying royalties when playing copyrighted music (Grossman and Mavroidis, 2004). The EU challenged these laws on the grounds that they were inconsistent with Article 9.1 of the Trade Related Intellectual Property Agreement (TRIPS). The WTO panel ruled that at least part of the exemptions granted by the US were indeed in conflict with TRIPS. Instead of amending its laws to make them WTO compliant, the US entered into discussions with the EU in order to find a mutually agreeable level of financial compensation.[11]

In recent years, the use of financial compensation has also become more common in bilateral trade agreements. For example, Mercurio (2009) notes that in several recent free trade agreements involving the United States – and countries such as Australia, Chile, and Singapore – the signatories have agreed to a format under which a non-compliant country can stop the complainant country from instituting retaliatory measures by paying an annual 'monetary assessment', much like in the *US-Copyright* case between the US and the EU.

In case of a trade dispute it is typically more efficient to use financial compensation than a distortionary instrument such as a tariff, provided the compensation can be enforced. What existing proposals and their analyses typically neglect however, and what we focus on, is the more difficult question of how financial compensation can be enforced and whether such instruments can deter deviations and generate more cooperation ex ante.[12] We show that agreements extended to

[8] We should note that tariff retaliation at the WTO is permitted as a last resort after negotiations between the affected parties have failed and any panel ruling calling for compliance has gone unheeded by the defendant.

[9] About 51% of world imports in 2009 were accounted for by the US, EU and eight other high income countries (Japan, Canada, Korea, Australia, Switzerland, Norway, New Zealand and Israel). The remaining half of world imports was accounted for by a very large number of developing countries since the BRICs together accounted for only about 16% of world imports.

[10] For an elaborate discussion of the legal and economic arguments in favor of financial compensation as a means for settling trade disputes see Bronckers and Van Den Broek (2005). A comprehensive overview of the various aspects of the dispute settlement process in the WTO is provided by Lawrence (2003).

[11] Ultimately, the two sides could not come to agreement and had to resort to binding WTO arbitration, which determined the annual level of compensation that the US would have to pay to the EC so long as its laws remained incompatible with TRIPS.

[12] The financial transfers do not have to come directly from the country that violates the agreement. For example, Mexico has proposed that countries should be allowed to sell their right to retaliate to others that possess more market power to retaliate. This proposal has been analyzed by Bagwell et al.

include specific financial instruments can enhance cooperation and generate outcomes that are more symmetric relative to a standard trade agreement. In particular, we show these improvements occur when countries exchange bonds *prior to trading and agree to forfeit them in case of a violation*. The use of bonds in this fashion accomplishes two important tasks. First, by requiring a high enough bond to be posted ex ante, we remove the incentive of the large country to deviate (so as not to forfeit its bond). Second, the use of bonds neutralizes the tariff coordination externality amongst small countries. It does so because if the large country deviates then any one of the small countries can, and will, keep the bond that the large country posted with it and doing so has *no effect on the values of bonds held by any other small countries*.[13]

We also show that the specific choice of the financial instrument is crucial since the obvious alternative, i.e. a monetary fine, does *not* improve on the standard agreement *when used in isolation*. The reason is that for the fine to be paid by the violating country it must still be enforced by small countries through the threat of tariff retaliation, which is subject to the coordination externality. Relative to Limão and Saggi (2008), the crucial novel element in our present paper is the presence of the coordination externality among small countries, each of which is not in a position to credibly threaten tariff retaliation. As noted earlier, this scenario is an apt description of the situation confronting developing countries at the WTO.

There are potentially important obstacles in reforming standard agreements to include financial instruments. The main obstacle that we consider is the limited ability countries might have to post bonds with trading partners. We show that our main results are robust to the presence of some bond constraints even if they are severe for small countries provided the extended agreement includes both bonds (posted by the large country) *and* fines that are paid in the event of a deviation. However, if the bond constraint is also severe for the large country then this extended agreement must rely on fines alone and it yields the same outcome as the standard trade agreement that relies only on tariff retaliation. The intuition for this result is that the payment of fines can ultimately only be enforced by the threat of tariffs (if no bonds were posted).[14]

Our basic approach is common in the literature on trade agreements: we model such agreements as an equilibrium outcome of repeated interaction between governments. However, most of this literature ignores the role of financial instruments. An exception is Bagwell and Staiger (2005) who show that if governments face private anticipated shocks then cash transfers can help enforce more cooperative tariffs. However, Limão and Saggi (2008) show that their result will not hold if we instead consider fines enacted in the case of a deviation. The fact that different types of financial instruments lead to different levels of tariff cooperation highlights the importance of carefully modeling each of their roles in international trade agreements. Unlike these two papers, we examine countries that are asymmetric in their market power and show this generates a role for bonds, that is absent in Limão and Saggi (2008). Park (2000) also examines cooperation between asymmetric countries but focuses on a case where there is a single small country with *no* market power and one large country; he shows that cash transfers from the former to the latter can help enforce lower tariffs. This purchase of market access by a single infinitesimally small country is fundamentally different from the coordination externality among many small countries that we analyze and argue is empirically relevant. Thus the results we find are naturally different, e.g. we find that cooperation in tariffs can be achieved without requiring the small countries to purchase market access from the large country.

The paper is structured as follows. In Section 2 we set up the model and describe the policy externalities. In Section 3 we derive the policy and welfare impacts of standard agreements, contrast them with the extended agreements and analyze the implementation issues that may arise. We conclude in Section 4. All proofs are in the Appendix.

2. Setup and trade policy externalities

2.1. Setup

The economic structure within each country is a standard one in the analysis of trade agreements (cf. Limão and Saggi, 2008). However, instead of focusing on two symmetric countries, we allow for multiple asymmetric countries. To clearly highlight the role of size asymmetries we focus on a single large country trading with a finite number of small countries, $K>1$, where the latter are identical among themselves.

Given that preferences and technologies are identical across countries, we describe the setup in detail for the large country (using variables without asterisks), and then point out any modification for the small ones. Each country can produce two homogeneous goods, $i=x, y$ and a numeraire, n. Individual utility over the consumption levels, c, of these goods is given by $u \equiv c_n + \sum_i u_i(c_i)$. Since utility is quasi-linear and separable, the demand function for good i depends only on its own price and is the same for all individuals so we denote aggregate demand by $D_i(p_i)$.

(*footnote continued*)
(2007) in an auction framework that assumes the violation has already occurred and a country has "earned" the right to retaliate against another (offending) country. They show that in some cases it is the offending country that wins that auction so the transfer is direct but that is not always the case.

[13] We further show that this benefit of bonds relative to the standard agreement is eliminated when there are just two symmetric countries, which is the special case that Limão and Saggi (2008) study. Thus, the underlying asymmetry among trading partners is necessary for bonds to enhance the scope for cooperation.

[14] This extends one of the basic insights in Limão and Saggi (2008) – that allowing for fines does not improve cooperation relative to standard agreements – to a setting with asymmetric countries.

Each unit of the numeraire, c_n, is produced with a constant returns to scale technology using only labor. Each non-numeraire good is also produced with a constant returns technology but it uses both labor and a specific factor. We denote the supply function for non-numeraire goods by $S_i(p_i)$, omitting its dependence on the specific factor endowment since both labor and specific capital endowments are assumed constant and inelastically supplied.

We assume that the large country is a mirror image of the set of small countries so it imports one of the non-numeraire goods, which we label y, and exports the other, x. Under trade, the domestic import price in the large country is then $p_y = p_y^w + \tau$ where p^w is the "world" price and τ is a specific import tariff on y, which satisfies an MFN constraint, i.e. it does not discriminate by country of origin. The large country's imports of y are then $M_y \equiv D_y(p_y) - S_y(p_y)$ and its world price is determined by the market clearing condition

$$M_y(p_y^w + \tau) + \sum_k M_y^{*k}(p_y^w) = 0 \tag{1}$$

where M_y^{*k} denote exports of good y by each of the k small countries. An analogous condition applies to good x.

We assume that no export policies are available so trade policy is described by the level of the import tariff in each country. Reductions in the large country's import demand affect the world price of y and it is simple to verify that in this setup an increase in the large country's tariff lowers the world price, $p_y^w(\tau)$, and raises the domestic one. Similarly, if the K small countries jointly increased their tariffs on x they would reduce its world price; i.e. small countries as a whole also have market power in trade.

The government chooses trade policies that maximize the political objective function below, which reflects social welfare and allows for extra weight ($\lambda_i \geq 1$) on specific factor owners[15]

$$W(\tau, \boldsymbol{\tau}^*) \equiv \sum_i \left[\int_{p_i}^{\infty} D_i(p_i)\, dp_i + \lambda_i \int_0^{p_i} S_i(p_i)\, dp_i + \tau_i M_i(p_i) \right] + L \tag{2}$$

where we recall that the tariff τ affects W both directly through tariff revenue, the term $\tau_y M_y$, and through its effect on home prices; whereas the effect of small countries' import tariffs, $\boldsymbol{\tau}^*$, is indirect and occurs only through the world price, $p_x^w(\boldsymbol{\tau}^*)$. In Eq. (2), the first term in parenthesis is consumer surplus; the second term can be interpreted as producer surplus or the quasi-rents accruing to the fixed factor owners; and the last term, L, is simply the total wage income of the large country when the wage is unity. This objective function is concave in τ and decreasing in each of the elements of $\boldsymbol{\tau}^*$.[16]

Each of the individual small countries has an objective function, which is denoted by W^{*k}. It has the same functional form as (2) so we do not rewrite it but simply note that it is evaluated using the prices and endowments in each k. To simplify the exposition and focus on the size asymmetry we now describe some restrictions. Each of these K small countries owns a constant fraction ($1/K$) of its region's population (L^*) so $L^{*k} = L^*/K$ and of its specific inputs. Moreover, given identical preferences, technologies and political parameters in the region ($\lambda_i^{*k} = \lambda_i^*$), the only potential difference that can arise across W^{*k} is if some k faces different prices because it sets or faces different tariffs than the others. It will often be useful to focus on equilibria where all small countries set the same tariff, $\tau^* = \tau^{*k}$ for all k and face the same tariff exporting to Large, τ, which can be different from τ^*. In this case prices and quantities are identical for all k so, given constant returns, the aggregate variables for the region are $Z_i^* \equiv \sum_k Z_i^{*k}(p_i^{*k}) = KZ_i^{*k}(p_i^*)$ (where $Z^* = D^*, S^*, M^*$). Moreover, the aggregate political welfare in the region when $\tau_i^{*k} = \tau_i^*$ and $\lambda_i^{*k} = \lambda_i^*$ is $W^* \equiv \sum_k W^{*k} = KW^{*k}$.

We also assume that the two regions as a whole have equal populations ($L = L^*$) and equal supplies of fixed factors in their respective import and export sectors. This symmetry assumption implies that the "aggregate" import market power of small countries is no different from that of the large country. This underlying symmetry across regions simplifies our exposition but is not crucial for our results; the same is true of our assumption of equal political weights in each region ($\lambda_y = \lambda_x^* = \lambda$) and their absence in the respective export sectors ($\lambda_x = \lambda_y^* = 1$).[17]

2.2. Trade policy externalities among asymmetric countries

The large country's Nash tariff is obtained by maximizing (2) while taking the small countries' tariffs as given. Since we do not model export policies we drop the good subscript, i, and any subscripts below denote partial derivatives. The large country's Nash tariff on y solves

$$\tau^N \equiv \underset{\tau}{\operatorname{argmax}}\, W(\tau, \boldsymbol{\tau}^*) \tag{3}$$

Recalling that the equilibrium prices are a function of tariffs, the first order condition for τ is

$$-Dp_\tau + \lambda S p_\tau + M + \tau M' p_\tau = 0 \tag{4}$$

[15] This can be obtained as the reduced form of a political economy model such as Grossman and Helpman (1994).

[16] We assume that there is sufficient labor to ensure a positive supply of the numeraire so that the wage rate in the economy is fixed by the marginal productivity of labor in the numeraire, which is normalized to unity.

[17] A more important assumption we make is that the political economy parameter is fixed and public information. For an interesting analysis of the role of the WTO where that is not the case see Beshkar (2010).

Using $M=D-S$, $M'\equiv dM(p)/dp$ and $p_\tau = p_\tau^w + 1$ and the elasticity expressions defined below we obtain a Nash tariff in ad-valorem terms, $\tau^N/p^w(\tau)$, implicitly defined by

$$\frac{\tau^N}{p^w(\tau)} = \frac{1}{\varepsilon(\tau)} + (\lambda-1)\frac{S(\tau)/M(\tau)}{\xi(\tau)} \tag{5}$$

We show the potential dependence of the endogenous variables on the tariff. We do so for clarity in the formula but will omit it below for notational simplicity. The first term, $1/\varepsilon \equiv M^*/(p^w M'^*)$, is the inverse of the elasticity of the aggregate export supply curve of small countries (since τ applies to all small countries) and it reflects the large country's terms-of-trade (TOT) motive for the use of tariffs. The second term reflects a political economy motive that is increasing in the extra weight placed on specific factor owners (λ) and decreasing in the large country's import demand elasticity ξ where $\xi \equiv -(\partial M/\partial p^w)(p^w/M) = -M'p^w/M$.

If the small countries cannot successfully coordinate their tariff choices, then the Nash tariff of an individual small country in its import sector (x) is

$$\frac{\tau^{*Nk}}{p^w} = \frac{1}{\varepsilon^{*k}} + (\lambda-1)\frac{S^{*k}/M^{*k}}{\xi^{*k}} \tag{6}$$

where all the variables are defined similarly to τ^N in (5) but from the perspective of country k, as detailed in the Appendix.

A country's import tariff lowers the price received by exporters of that good, this is the standard negative *terms-of-trade externality*, which we will confirm below is a central reason for a trade agreement. However, the outcome of that agreement will depend on another externality that is present when there are several countries importing the same good, what we will refer to as a *coordination externality*. To understand it suppose that small countries could coordinate their tariffs choices in order to maximize their region's aggregate objective, $\sum_k W^{*k}$, then their *coordinated* Nash tariff, denoted by $\tau^{*Ncoord}$, would be given by (6) evaluated at the *aggregate* regional quantities (S^*/M^*) and elasticities, ε^* and ξ^*. We argue that small countries set a higher tariff when acting jointly than individually because their market power is higher under coordination. We show this by contradiction. Suppose τ^{*Nk} and $\tau^{*Ncoord}$ are identical and then evaluate the TOT and political economy components of welfare. Note that given the symmetry across small countries we have the same τ^{*Nk} across all of them and thus the same price, therefore $(S^{*k}/M^{*k})/\xi^{*k} = (S^*/M^*)/\xi^*$, so with $\tau^{*Nk} = \tau^{*Ncoord}$ and thus equal prices the political economy component is also identical. However, at any given tariff and prices we can show that $1/\varepsilon^{*k} < 1/\varepsilon^*$ if $K > 1$. The intuition for this is simple, when small countries set their tariffs independently, each small country does not take into account the positive TOT benefits that accrue to other small countries. As might be expected, this coordination externality is increasing in the number of countries.

The empirical relevance of the expressions above in tariff policy setting requires at least three pieces of evidence. First, countries should have at least some market power in imports. Second, prior to trade agreements countries should set higher tariffs on products with higher market power. Third, larger countries (in terms of GDP or import quantities) should have more market power than smaller countries. Evidence for each of these is provided by Broda et al. (2008).[18] Evidence for the third point is particularly relevant for this paper since as we divide a region of given size each of the resulting K countries will have lower GDP and imports than the whole region and lower market power, $1/\varepsilon^{*k}$.

As we noted before, to highlight the size differences it is useful to keep other factors constant. If we assume symmetry across regions in their respective import and export sectors then two other implications emerge. First, since $\tau^N = \tau^{*Ncoord}$ the lack of coordination among small countries implies that their respective tariffs are lower than that of the large country. Note that the tariff τ^N applies to good y and is independent of the tariffs that small countries set on x because (i) the utility function is quasi-linear and separable and (ii) the only mobile factor is labor and its factor price is pinned down by its productivity in the numeraire sector. The second implication of symmetric regions is as follows. Under an agreement without enforcement problems countries could choose tariffs to maximize their joint objective $W + KW^{*k}$ and, if regions were symmetric, this would be equivalent to maximizing the objective of either region after imposing $\tau = \tau^*$. Thus we obtain

$$\tau^G \equiv \underset{\tau^C}{\operatorname{argmax}}\, W(\tau^C, \boldsymbol{\tau}^* = \tau^C) \tag{7}$$

so the globally optimal ad-valorem tariff $\tau^G/p^w(\tau^G)$ (derived in the appendix) is

$$\frac{\tau^G}{p^w(\tau)} = (\lambda-1)\frac{S(\tau)/M(\tau)}{\xi(\tau)} \tag{8}$$

It is simple to see that $\tau^G/p^w < \tau^N/p^w$. The difference between the Nash and globally cooperative policies confirms that market power in trade leads to international externalities motivating the need for a trade agreement (Bagwell and Staiger, 1999). Note also that even in the presence of an international agreement, countries may choose to have positive tariffs due to internal political economy distortions (i.e. when $\lambda > 1$).[19]

[18] They also find evidence of a positive impact of the political economy component, captured by $(S/M)/\xi$.

[19] Broda et al. (2008) provide evidence that countries set higher protection in goods where they have higher market power if they are either non-WTO members or the policy is not subject to strong WTO discipline. Bagwell and Staiger (2011) find that WTO accession leads to greater tariff reductions in products with higher initial import volumes and market power.

Since the globally optimal tariff τ^G is below the level that is optimal for each *individual* country, each country has an incentive to deviate from it and would do so if it faced no punishment. Before addressing how the threat of tariff retaliation can be used to sustain international cooperation, we make an important observation. Note from (6) that if the number of small countries is sufficiently high and governments face no political pressures (i.e. $\lambda=1$), the Nash tariff of each small country in the absence of coordination among them, τ^{*Nk}, approaches zero. Under such circumstances, a small country neither can individually offer *any* tariff reduction to the large country nor can it credibly threaten the large country with any tariff retaliation in case the latter reneges on a cooperative trade agreement. Thus, as K increases so does the coordination externality and this lowers the incentive of the large country to enter into any agreement that relies only on uncoordinated tariff retaliation to enforce cooperation. Naturally if K is so high that the value of τ^{*Nk} is close to the global optimum τ^G then the large country would always prefer not to cooperate at all. On the other hand, an individual small country has a much stronger incentive to cooperate since it has limited ability to manipulate its TOT. In what follows, we assume that $K\in(1,\overline{K}]$, i.e. there is more than one "small" country (thus the asymmetry) but not so many of them as to make their cooperation unattractive to the large country.[20]

3. Trade agreements among asymmetric countries

3.1. Standard agreements: asymmetric outcomes under tariff retaliation

We now examine the role of agreements in enforcing tariff cooperation between asymmetric countries. We show that if standard agreements, which rely solely on tariff threats, cannot sustain the globally optimal tariff for all countries then the outcome is an asymmetric one with the large country setting a higher tariff than the small ones (Proposition 1). The asymmetry is driven by the coordination externality previously highlighted. In the next section, we show that if we go beyond the enforcement instruments in standard agreements and include financial ones, namely bonds, then we can both improve cooperation and make the outcome more equitable by sustaining the symmetric global tariff (Propositions 2 and 3).

Consider an infinitely repeated game where the stage game delivers the Nash tariffs previously derived, i.e. τ^N and τ^{*Nk}. Assume that countries observe each other's actions at the end of each period. The strategy for each country is to cooperate until any country deviates by raising its tariff. Any such deviation is followed by a punishment of n periods during which the country that originally deviated faces Nash tariffs on its exports and demonstrates its willingness to restart cooperation by setting a cooperative tariff level. If this occurs then cooperative tariffs are set by all after the n periods, otherwise the agreement breaks down and countries permanently revert to Nash tariffs.

To find the lowest cooperative tariff that is *weakly renegotiation proof* (or simply *WRP*) we first define each country's payoffs under the alternative situations that can arise. We focus on WRP strategies for three reasons. First, taking account of the WRP constraint is intuitively appealing since it ensures that punishing parties actually have an incentive to implement the punishment. Second, temporary punishments are more realistic in the context of disputes in the WTO than infinite Nash reversion after any deviation (the latter is a possibility but we view it as the ultimate punishment corresponding to an unraveling of the GATT/WTO system that results from member countries not following its rules). The third reason is to easily contrast the results with Limão and Saggi (2008) who also employ this approach.[21]

Let $\boldsymbol{\tau}^{*N}$ represent the vector of Nash tariffs composed of each of the (uncoordinated) small countries' equilibrium values, τ^{*Nk}. In the absence of cooperation, the payoff to the large country equals its government's objective evaluated at non-cooperative tariffs

$$W^N \equiv W(\tau^N, \boldsymbol{\tau}^{*N}) \tag{9}$$

The cooperative tariff vector (to be found) for the small countries is represented by $\boldsymbol{\tau}^{*C}$ and its representative element, τ^{*Ck}, will be common to all k during periods of cooperation since these countries are identical. We denote the large country's cooperative tariff by τ^C so the cooperative payoff of the large country is

$$W^C \equiv W(\tau^C, \boldsymbol{\tau}^{*C}) \tag{10}$$

If the large country deviates, it does so by imposing its optimal Nash tariff τ^N, which we recall is non-discriminatory and so applies to all small countries. In that period, the small countries are still setting cooperative tariffs.[22] The deviation payoff to the large country in the period is

$$W^D \equiv W(\tau^N, \boldsymbol{\tau}^{*C}) \tag{11}$$

[20] A sufficient condition for the large country to accept setting a tariff below its Nash and at (or above) its global optimum in exchange for small setting $\boldsymbol{\tau}^{*G}$ is for $W(\tau^G, \boldsymbol{\tau}^{*G}) \geq W(\tau^N, \tau^{*Nk}(K))$, which holds strictly when $K=1$. There are sufficient free parameters in the model to ensure that the condition also holds for some $K>1$. But there is some $\overline{K}$ such that $\tau^{*Nk}(K)$ is so low that the condition above holds with equality and thus we assume that $K\in(1,\overline{K}]$.

[21] A further motive is that Ludema (2001) shows that the reliance on reciprocity during dispute settlement at the WTO implies that only trade agreements that are renegotiation proof can be sustained in equilibrium.

[22] The large country's deviation tariff level is independent of the level for the small ones because of the separability across sectors.

According to the strategy we consider if the large country deviates, then in *each* of the n punishment periods its payoff is $W^P \equiv W(\tau^C, \boldsymbol{\tau}^{*N})$

We can then define the large country's continuation payoff after a deviation as

$$V^\tau \equiv \sum_{t=1}^{n} \delta^t W^P + \sum_{t=n+1}^{\infty} \delta^t W^C \tag{12}$$

i.e. it undergoes punishment for n periods after which cooperation resumes. Given these payoffs, the incentive compatibility (IC) constraint for the large country to cooperate is

$$W^D + V^\tau \le \frac{W^C}{1-\delta} \tag{13}$$

That is, the sum of the payoff from a deviation, W^D, and the continuation payoff, V^τ, should not exceed the present value of the stream of cooperative payoffs.

Since the per period punishment payoff is lower than the Nash payoff, i.e. $W^P < W^N$, the punishment phase is subgame perfect only if it is not profitable for the country that is being punished (in this case the large country) to simply abandon the agreement and revert to Nash tariffs forever. So V^τ must be at least as large as the Nash payoff in order for the cooperative equilibrium to be *WRP*

$$V^\tau \ge \frac{\delta}{1-\delta} W^N \tag{14}$$

Because $W^C > W^P$, the longer the punishment phase n, the lower the continuation payoff V^τ. Therefore, the maximum punishment phase that is *WRP* is found by equating the continuation payoff V^τ to the RHS of (14). We define this maximum punishment period as $n^{\max}$, and it is implicitly given by

$$V^{\tau\ \min} \equiv \delta \frac{1-\delta^{n^{\max}}}{1-\delta} W^P + \frac{\delta^{n^{\max}+1}}{1-\delta} W^C = \frac{\delta}{1-\delta} W^N \tag{15}$$

Therefore, the lowest cooperative *WRP* tariff is obtained at $n^{\max}$ and implicitly defined when (13) holds with equality. Given the maximum *WRP* punishment it is also simple to see that this cooperative tariff level would also be obtained under an alternative strategy where if any country deviates then they all permanently revert to Nash. To see this clearly, we substitute $V^{\tau\ \min}$ in (13) and use the definitions for W^D, W^N and W^C to obtain

$$W(\tau^N, \boldsymbol{\tau}^{*C}) + \frac{\delta}{1-\delta}(\tau^N, \boldsymbol{\tau}^{*N}) \le \frac{W(\tau^C, \boldsymbol{\tau}^{*C})}{1-\delta} \tag{16}$$

which is identical to the large country's incentive constraint under infinite Nash reversion. Thus the lowest self-enforcing tariff under infinite Nash reversion or *WRP* is implicitly defined when (16) holds with equality.

To understand the effect of the coordination externality on cooperation, note that the worst punishment that uncoordinated small countries can inflict on the large one is for each to revert to its individual Nash tariff, τ^{*Nk}, which is lower than their coordinated punishment tariff, $\tau^{*Ncoord}$. Therefore, for any given cooperative tariff, the total payoff of deviating for the large country, as given by the LHS of (16), is greater relative to the case where small countries coordinate their tariff decisions. In other words, the lack of coordination between small countries increases the large country's incentive to deviate, which is one component of the asymmetric outcome. The other component arises because the coordination externality reduces the incentive of each small country to deviate since the short-term gain from such a deviation is smaller relative to coordination.[23] To see this more explicitly we now derive the IC for each small country.

We use $\boldsymbol{\tau}^{*Dk}$ to denote the tariff vector of a small country k when it deviates. To clearly isolate and understand the role of the coordination externality we first describe what are the alternative deviation possibilities one could consider. First, consider a full coordination scenario, that is suppose that we allowed small countries to act as a single country (e.g. if they formed a customs union that maximized their joint welfare under cooperation, deviation and punishment periods). Under this scenario, $\boldsymbol{\tau}^{*Dk}$ is the same for all k and simply reflects their Nash tariff and it would be equal to τ^N, i.e. Large's non-cooperative value (since the regions are symmetric). Therefore, not surprisingly, the IC for each of the k countries and Large would be identical under full coordination and the setting would be the same as in Limão and Saggi (2008), who show there is no role for bonds. Second, consider a scenario where all small countries happen to deviate at the same time but cannot coordinate on the level of the optimal tariff, so they choose the level that maximizes their *individual* government objectives. In this case $\boldsymbol{\tau}^{*Dk} = \boldsymbol{\tau}^{*N}$ so it is the same for all k but evaluated at τ^{*Nk}, the uncoordinated Nash value previously derived. Finally, consider an alternative scenario with individual and uncoordinated deviations where we require all other countries to be cooperating in the period when any small country deviates. In this case $\boldsymbol{\tau}^{*Dk}$ will include the non-cooperative tariff for country k evaluated at the prices that result when the other small countries are still cooperating.

We focus on the second scenario described above for two reasons. First, it allows us to isolate the coordination externality since the only difference relative to the case where the small countries act as a unified decision maker is that

[23] The incentive to deviate by the small countries is also reduced by the fact that reversion to Nash is more costly to them, which implies that if they would deviate the large country would impose a relatively harsher punishment that would still be WRP.

they deviate and punish using $\tau^{*Nk} < \tau^{*Ncoord}$. Second, the results are qualitatively similar if we focus on individual deviations instead.[24]

Following the derivation for the large country, the IC of a small country is given by

$$W^{*k}(\tau^C, \boldsymbol{\tau}^{*Dk}) + \frac{\delta}{1-\delta} W^{*k}(\tau^N, \boldsymbol{\tau}^{*N}) \leq \frac{W^{*k}(\tau^C, \boldsymbol{\tau}^{*C})}{1-\delta} \tag{17}$$

We use these incentive constraints to establish the first result, which is a building block to showing that the coordination externality leads to asymmetric tariffs in standard agreements.

Lemma 1 (*Asymmetric cooperation incentives under standard agreements*). *The large country's payoff is higher than the respective aggregate payoff to K uncoordinated small countries under* (i) *a deviation from a given symmetric cooperative tariff, i.e.* $W(\tau^N, \boldsymbol{\tau}^{*C}) > \sum_k W^{*k}(\tau^C, \boldsymbol{\tau}^{*Dk})$ *at* $\tau^C = \tau^{*Ck}$ *and* (ii) *under non-cooperative tariffs, i.e.* $W(\tau^N, \boldsymbol{\tau}^{*N}) > \sum_k W^{*k}(\tau^N, \boldsymbol{\tau}^{*N})$.

It is worth relating Lemma 1 to the recent literature on tariff *wars*. Zissimos (2009) obtains a similar result in a Heckscher–Ohlin model of North–South trade where each region comprises many (similar) countries. In his model, holding constant the number of countries in the North at one, if the number of countries in the South increases then the tariffs set by individual Southern countries falls below their jointly optimal tariff, so that the South necessarily loses from a tariff war when it is composed of many countries. He notes that the asymmetry between the two regions in terms of number of countries is crucial for this result: indeed, in a two-country set-up Syropoulos (2002) has shown that a sufficient condition for a country to be better off under a non-cooperative tariff war relative to free trade is that its relative size be sufficiently large. These papers focus on the outcome of trade wars whereas we use Lemma 1 as a building block to analyze alternative self-enforcing trade agreements.[25]

Lemma 1 fixes the cooperative tariff at a fixed symmetric level to highlight the fact that the larger country may have a weaker incentive to cooperate than the uncoordinated small countries.[26] We now show that this coordination externality not only generates an imbalance in market power across countries but also generates asymmetric cooperative tariffs (and thus unequal welfare outcomes) in a trade agreement enforced by the threat of tariff retaliation. As will be clear enforcement is only an issue if the large country is not sufficiently patient to sustain the global optimum tariff in a standard agreement, i.e. if $\delta < \delta_G$ where δ_G is implicitly defined to ensure that the incentive constraint in (16) is satisfied at τ^G.

Proposition 1 (*Asymmetric outcomes under standard agreements*). *In a standard trade agreement supported by the threat of tariff retaliation, the most cooperative tariff set by a large country exceeds the tariff set by each of the K uncoordinated small countries: i.e.* $\tau^C > \tau^{*Ck}$ *whenever the large country is not sufficiently patient to sustain the globally optimal tariff* ($\delta < \delta_G$) *and thus this agreement yields higher welfare for the large country than for the set of small ones, i.e.* $W(\tau^C, \boldsymbol{\tau}^{*C}) > KW^{*k}(\tau^C, \boldsymbol{\tau}^{*C})$.

Proposition 1 emphasizes the asymmetry in market power across countries and how this asymmetry leads to an outcome that is skewed in favor of the large country when tariff cooperation is sustained solely on the basis of tariff retaliation. We next consider how the use of financial instruments alters the scope for cooperation as well as the welfare of each country.

3.2. Extended agreements: efficiency and equity with financial instruments

We now show how the coordination externality can be offset when we extend the set of enforcement instruments to allow for certain type of financial instruments. We show that such an extended trade agreement generates (i) an improvement in global welfare relative to the standard agreement and (ii) more symmetric welfare outcomes across countries.

First, we consider the exchange of bonds as a means for sustaining cooperation when countries pursue the following strategy. Countries start cooperating by posting a bond with each of its import sources. At the end of a period, if the countries have cooperated then they "return" their respective bonds. If a country deviates from the cooperative tariff, it loses

[24] More specifically, in a supplementary appendix we show that the IC for small countries under individual deviations does not bind when evaluated at the solution under simultaneous deviations. Moreover, the type of deviations for small countries does not affect whether or not the IC for the large country binds at the global optimum, which is the source of the inefficiency in the standard agreement. We thank an anonymous referee for suggesting that we clarify this point.

[25] In a recent paper, Syropoulos and Dinopoulos (2012) show that when there are three countries and international income transfers are not possible, a relatively small country may prefer an equilibrium with tariffs over free trade provided that the tariffs used are non-discriminatory in nature, as is required by the core WTO rule of MFN. See also Saggi and Yildiz (2010) where a small country is the one that prevents the obtainment of free trade when liberalizing countries cannot tariff discriminate and must extend any tariff concessions to non-participating countries on an MFN basis. In their model, the possibility of forming FTAs induces the smaller country to vote in favor of free trade since such FTAs are worse from its perspective than MFN based liberalization amongst other countries.

[26] The prediction of higher protection for the larger country in our model would seem to contradict the fact that large developed WTO members typically have lower *average* tariffs. We could easily change the model to replicate this fact if we allowed for lower political pressure for protection, (i.e. λ) in these countries relative to the small ones. We could also introduce an additional block of countries (one large and another K small) and allow for additional goods that are mainly traded between the two large countries, such that the prediction would then be that large countries have relatively higher tariffs on goods that they import from small countries than from large ones, a fact that has been documented. Our model abstracts from these considerations to focus directly on the coordination externality.

its bond. For cooperation to resume, the deviating country must return the present discounted value of the bond of the injured country. If it does so in the period after the deviation occurs, then tariffs return to the cooperative level. If it does not, cooperation breaks down and all countries switch to their optimal Nash tariffs.

To understand the basic insight, consider a situation where each country has a similar discount factor, just below the level required for the large country to sustain the global optimum under a standard agreement, (i.e. δ is just below δ_G). Recall that in that case the small countries are still patient enough to sustain the global optimum so their IC holds with slack. If we then allowed the large country to post a bond with a value exceeding what it receives from the collection of small countries then its incentive to deviate declines (it stands to lose more from forfeiting its bond) so it could sustain a lower cooperative tariff. While this bond would also increase each small country's incentive to deviate, they could still sustain the same cooperation as before since the incentive constraint of each small country had slack at the initial symmetric tariffs $\tau^C = \tau^{*Ck} = \tau^G$ for some $\delta < \delta_G$. We demonstrate this intuition formally below.

Suppose the large country posts a bond of value b^k (in units of the numeraire) with each of the small countries it imports from, and receives $\sum_k b^{*k}$ from them. Since all small countries are ex ante identical we assume from the start that when cooperating they each post a bond of equal value, $b^{*k} = b^*$, and receive an equal share of the large country's bond, $b^k = b/K$. The *WRP* incentive constraint for the large country and *each* of the small countries are respectively given by

$$W(\tau^N, \boldsymbol{\tau}^{*C}) - b + Kb^* + V^b \leq \frac{W(\tau^C, \boldsymbol{\tau}^{*C})}{1-\delta} \tag{18}$$

$$W^{*k}(\tau^C, \boldsymbol{\tau}^{*Dk}) - b^* + b/K + V^{*b} \leq \frac{W^{*k}(\tau^C, \boldsymbol{\tau}^{*C})}{1-\delta} \tag{19}$$

where their respective continuation payoffs are defined as

$$V^b \equiv -\frac{\delta K b^*}{\delta} + \frac{\delta W(\tau^C, \boldsymbol{\tau}^{*C})}{1-\delta} \tag{20}$$

$$V^{*b} \equiv -\frac{\delta b}{\delta K} + \frac{\delta W^{*k}(\tau^C, \boldsymbol{\tau}^{*C})}{1-\delta} \tag{21}$$

The first term in the large country's continuation payoff V^b equals the present value of the bonds posted by the small countries that must be returned by the large country for cooperation to resume and the second term is the present discounted value of its payoff under cooperation. A similar interpretation applies to a small country's continuation payoff V^{*b}.

We now derive the minimum bond values required to enforce the global optimum assuming the *WRP* constraint is satisfied (which we will verify below). To do so, we substitute these continuation payoffs into (18) and (19) respectively and solve for b^g and b^{*g}

$$b^g = W(\tau^N, \boldsymbol{\tau}^{*G}) - W(\tau^G, \boldsymbol{\tau}^{*G}) \tag{22}$$

$$b^{*g} = W^{*k}(\tau^G, \boldsymbol{\tau}^{*Dk}) - W^{*k}(\tau^G, \boldsymbol{\tau}^{*G}) \tag{23}$$

These bond values are quite intuitive: the minimum bonds required to achieve globally optimal tariffs are equal to each country's TOT gain of deviating from those tariffs. Further note that the large country requires a larger bond than the set of K small countries. That is, $b^g > Kb^{*g}$ since $W(\tau^N, \boldsymbol{\tau}^{*G}) > KW^{*k}(\tau^G, \boldsymbol{\tau}^{*Dk})$ (as proved in Lemma 1) and $W(\tau^G, \boldsymbol{\tau}^{*G}) = KW^{*k}(\tau^G, \boldsymbol{\tau}^{*G})$ (due to symmetry). In sum, since the large country deviates to an optimal tariff, τ^N, that is larger than the optimal tariff of a typical small country (τ^{*Nk}), its TOT gain from deviating is larger than the corresponding total gain of K uncoordinated small countries. Therefore, the large country must post a larger bond, i.e. $b^g > Kb^{*g}$, which reduces its incentive to deviate relative to that under tariff retaliation thereby opening up the possibility of increased cooperation.

The final step is to show that there is some $\delta < \delta_G$ such that tariff retaliation does *not* enforce globally optimal tariffs whereas the bonds b^g and b^{*g} do while also satisfying the *WRP* constraint. Let $b^{\max}$ be the bond value that equates the continuation payoff of a small country V^{*b} in (21) to its payoff from abandoning the agreement $W^{*k}(\tau^N, \boldsymbol{\tau}^{*N})\delta/(1-\delta)$. We have

$$V^{*b} = -\frac{b^{\max}}{K} + \frac{\delta W^{*k}(\tau^C, \boldsymbol{\tau}^{*C})}{1-\delta} = \frac{\delta W^{*k}(\tau^N, \boldsymbol{\tau}^{*N})}{1-\delta}$$

$$b^{\max} = K\frac{\delta[W^{*k}(\tau^C, \boldsymbol{\tau}^{*C}) - W^{*k}(\tau^N, \boldsymbol{\tau}^{*N})]}{1-\delta} \tag{24}$$

In other words, if the bond posted by the large country exceeds $b^{\max}$, then a typical small country is better off cheating on the agreement and abandoning it altogether since its continuation payoff falls below what it gets outside the agreement.

Similarly, let $b^{*\max}$ be the value of the bond posted by a small country that equates the large country's continuation payoff V^b in (21) to $W(\tau^N, \boldsymbol{\tau}^{*N})\delta/(1-\delta)$, i.e. its payoff from abandoning the agreement. We have

$$V^b = -Kb^{*\max} + \frac{\delta W(\tau^C, \boldsymbol{\tau}^{*C})}{1-\delta} = \frac{\delta W(\tau^N, \boldsymbol{\tau}^{*N})}{1-\delta} \tag{25a}$$

$$Kb^{*\max} = \frac{\delta[W(\tau^C, \boldsymbol{\tau}^{*C}) - W(\tau^N, \boldsymbol{\tau}^{*N})]}{1-\delta} \tag{25b}$$

Note that since $W(\tau^N, \boldsymbol{\tau}^{*N}) > KW^{*k}(\tau^N, \boldsymbol{\tau}^{*N})$, we have that $b^{\max} > Kb^{*\max}$ at any symmetric cooperative tariff. The intuition for this is clear: due to its greater market power, abandoning the agreement is relatively more attractive to the large country and therefore a smaller (aggregate) bond on the part of small countries is necessary to ensure that the large country prefers to resume cooperation by returning bonds of small countries as opposed to abandoning the agreement. In other words, since cooperation is relatively less attractive to the large country, it is willing to suffer a relatively smaller punishment to resume cooperation (as measured by the value of bonds it has to repay to resume cooperation).

As before, if the bonds posted by the small countries exceed $Kb^{*\max}$, the continuation payoff of the large country is too low for it to prefer to resume cooperation as opposed to abandoning the agreement altogether. The two *WRP* constraints together ensure that the bonds required to sustain the global optimum $(\tau^G, \boldsymbol{\tau}^{*G})$ are not so high that countries prefer to abandon the agreement altogether

$$b^g \le b^{\max}(\tau^G, \boldsymbol{\tau}^{*G}) \quad \text{and} \quad b^{*g} \le b^{*\max}(\tau^G, \boldsymbol{\tau}^{*G})$$

First consider $b^g \le b^{\max}(\tau^G, \boldsymbol{\tau}^{*G})$. Since $b^g = W(\tau^N, \boldsymbol{\tau}^{*G}) - W(\tau^G, \boldsymbol{\tau}^{*G})$ we can use the definition of δ_G and re-arrange (16) to obtain

$$b^g = \frac{\delta_G[W(\tau^G, \boldsymbol{\tau}^{*G}) - W(\tau^N, \boldsymbol{\tau}^{*N})]}{1-\delta_G}$$

From the symmetry of W and KW^{*k} at the global optimum we can rewrite b^g as

$$b^g = \frac{\delta_G[KW^{*k}(\tau^G, \boldsymbol{\tau}^{*G}) - W(\tau^N, \boldsymbol{\tau}^{*N})]}{1-\delta_G} < K\frac{\delta_G[W^{*k}(\tau^G, \boldsymbol{\tau}^{*G}) - W^{*k}(\tau^N, \boldsymbol{\tau}^{*N})]}{1-\delta_G} = b^{\max}(\tau^G, \boldsymbol{\tau}^{*G}) \tag{26}$$

The last inequality follows from the coordination externality, which implies that $W(\tau^N, \boldsymbol{\tau}^{*N}) > KW^{*k}(\tau^N, \boldsymbol{\tau}^{*N})$ for $K > 1$, as proved in Lemma 1. Since the RHS in the last line is equal to $b^{\max}$ evaluated at the globally optimal tariffs and it is continuous in δ, we have that when $K > 1$ there exist $\delta < \delta_G$ s.t. $b^g \le b^{\max}(\tau^G, \boldsymbol{\tau}^{*G})$, where we recall that b^g is independent of δ. Intuitively, the inequality above says that at the critical discount factor where the large country's incentive constraint just binds under tariff retaliation, (i.e. at $\delta = \delta_G$), the bond b^g that the large country has to post in order to sustain cooperation over the global optimum is less than the maximum bond $b^{\max}(\tau^G, \boldsymbol{\tau}^{*G})$ that satisfies the *WRP* constraint at globally optimal tariffs (which equals the present discounted value of cooperation to small countries as a whole discounted by one period).

Now consider $b^{*g} \le b^{*\max}$. Using the value for b^{*g} in (23) on the LHS we have

$$\begin{aligned} Kb^{*g} &= K[W^{*k}(\tau^G, \boldsymbol{\tau}^{*Dk}) - W^{*k}(\tau^G, \boldsymbol{\tau}^{*G})] < W(\tau^N, \boldsymbol{\tau}^{*G}) - W(\tau^G, \boldsymbol{\tau}^{*G}) \\ &= \frac{\delta_G[W(\tau^G, \boldsymbol{\tau}^{*G}) - W(\tau^N, \boldsymbol{\tau}^{*N})]}{1-\delta_G} = Kb^{*\max} \end{aligned} \tag{27}$$

where the first inequality follows from $W(\tau^G, \boldsymbol{\tau}^{*G}) = W^*(\tau^G, \boldsymbol{\tau}^{*G})$ (by symmetry) and $W(\tau^N, \boldsymbol{\tau}^{*G}) > W^*(\tau^G, \boldsymbol{\tau}^{*Dk})$ for $K > 1$, as proved in Lemma 1. The equality on the second line follows from the definition of δ_G. Since the RHS in the last line is equal to $Kb^{*\max}(\tau^G, \boldsymbol{\tau}^{*G})$ in (25b), and is continuous in δ_G, we have that when $K > 1$ there exists a $\delta < \delta_G$ s.t. $b^{*g} \le b^{*\max}(\tau^G, \boldsymbol{\tau}^{*G})$. Intuitively, the last inequality says that at the critical discount factor where the large country's incentive constraint just binds under tariff retaliation, (i.e. at $\delta = \delta_G$), the collective value of the bonds posted by small countries required to sustain cooperation over the global optimum is less than the present discounted value of cooperation to the large country (discounted by one period).

The main result can now be stated:

Proposition 2 (*Improved cooperation and symmetric outcomes with bonds*). *In a trade agreement extended to include bond exchange as an enforcement instrument the large country and the K uncoordinated small countries can sustain the globally optimal tariffs* ($\tau^C = \tau^{*Ck} = \tau^G$) *even if they cannot enforce it under a standard agreement. Therefore, for some* $\delta < \delta_G$, *the extended agreement generates* (i) *an increase in welfare for the small countries*; (ii) *a global increase in welfare and* (iii) *a more equitable outcome relative to the standard agreement.*

The first part of the proposition follows directly from what we showed above: that there exist WRP bonds that sustain the global optimum for at least some $\delta < \delta_G$. Since the global optimum tariffs are symmetric it follows that the outcome is more equitable than under the standard agreement where the large country sets higher tariffs than the small ones (part iii). Moreover, the tariffs for the large country are lower under the extended agreement and those for the small countries are no higher (at least for some $\delta < \delta_G$) so welfare is higher for small countries (part i) and globally since $W + KW^{*k}$ is concave and decreasing in tariffs above the global optimum.

To understand the intuition behind Proposition 2 it is useful to consider an extreme case where $K=1$ so the asymmetry disappears. In that case the bonds that can support the global optimum can only be *WRP* if $\delta = \delta_G$, as we can see from (26) and (27) but if the two symmetric countries are that patient then they can sustain τ^G in a standard agreement. More generally, if $\delta < \delta_G$ and two symmetric countries exchange bonds then their incentives to deviate remain unchanged because their bonds are of equal value (as shown in Limão and Saggi, 2008). However, if countries are asymmetric then we can require one to post a bigger bond than its smaller partner to offset its incentive to deviate from cooperative tariffs.

This increases the incentive to deviate by the smaller country (to keep the bigger bond) but the threat of future tariff retaliation prevents it from doing so.

This proposition provides an enforcement rationale for why some small countries have advocated for trade agreements to be extended to include financial instruments. In our model, the reason why bonds can help cooperation is that tariffs and bonds have rather different properties from an enforcement perspective. Namely, only tariffs are subject to a coordination externality: their non-cooperative levels reflect the individual small country's TOT motive and ignore the spillover TOT effects on other small countries. So if Large deviates against all small countries then they set a positive tariff that is above the cooperative level but lower than if they were to coordinate their punishment and internalize all the TOT effects on each other; thus the standard agreement fails to enforce the global optimum. The coordination externality is not present with bonds since, conditional on a sufficiently large bond being posted by Large with each of the small countries, if Large deviates then all that each small country has to do is keep the bond that it already received. The decision to keep the bond by a single small country has *no effect on the values of bonds held by others.*

It is worth discussing more broadly why bonds can assist with cooperation when there are asymmetries across countries. While we focus on size asymmetry due to its empirical relevance and in order to highlight the coordination externality that appears to be an important feature of the current world trading system, it is clear that other types of asymmetries could generate a motive for the use of bonds in improving cooperation. For example, bonds can improve cooperation if there are differences in political economy pressures for protection across countries that lead to different non-cooperative tariffs or if patience levels differ across countries so that incentive constraints of relatively impatient countries are harder to satisfy.[27] The basic intuition for the role for bonds in the presence of such type of asymmetries is that bonds posted by those that are less willing to cooperate can help *transfer enforcement power* to countries that are more willing to do so.

We now discuss possible obstacles to reforming standard agreements to include financial instruments.

3.3. Agreement reform

There are potentially important obstacles in reforming standard agreements to include financial enforcement instruments. One would be the cost of setting up and administering a system with financial instruments. However, the proposals by different WTO members to implement such schemes suggest that this may not be prohibitively costly. Therefore, the main obstacle we focus on is the limited ability and/or willingness to post bonds with trading partners. We show that even severe "bond constraints" for small countries can be overcome to achieve the outcomes in Proposition 2 if we design the extended agreement to also include fines. However, if the bond constraint is also severe for the large country then this extended agreement will result in the same asymmetric outcome as the standard one. These results highlight the importance of formally modeling alternative instruments to successfully reform standard agreements. We also discuss how to overcome another potential obstacle; namely, that the large country may prefer the standard agreement whereas the small countries prefer the extended one.

It is not difficult to motivate or provide a simple formal model of why certain countries may be unable or unwilling to post a large bond at the start of a period in order to induce another country to set a more cooperative tariff. Therefore, instead of committing to a specific motive for this we instead assume that countries face exogenous "bond constraints", i.e. $b<b^g$ and $b^*<b^{*g}$, and in Proposition 3 we show that the outcome in Proposition 2 can be achieved even if the small countries post *no bond at all* and the large one posts a bond that is of a value smaller than b^g but still positive. So bond constraints may not be an important obstacle to reform a standard agreement even if they are very severe for small countries (if $b^*=0$). However, in order for agreements to generate efficient and symmetric outcomes in the presence of bond constraints we need to include another financial instrument in the trade agreement, i.e. a fine. The advantage of fines over bonds is that the latter must be posted every period before trading starts whereas fines need only be paid if a deviation ever occurs and are therefore not subject to the same type of financial constraint that bonds are. This raises the question if we need bonds at all in an extended agreement with fines and in Proposition 4 we also constrain $b=0$ to show that they must be included and posted by the large country.[28]

To understand why fines can overcome bond constraints on small but not large countries we must explain why *WRP* fines face an enforcement issue relative to bonds. Namely, the deviating country has to be induced to pay the fine, whereas the bond is already in the hands of its partner and is thus automatically foregone. Thus fines require some threat of tariff retaliation if they are not paid. We model this tariff threat as a last resort that would only ever materialize if the agreement

[27] As a concrete example, consider cooperation between two countries (Home and Foreign) that are symmetric along all dimensions except their discount factors. Suppose that if both countries had a discount factor of δ_G they could sustain the global optimum in a standard agreement but Home's discount factor is below this critical level while Foreign's is above it, i.e. $\delta<\delta_G<\delta^*$. As a result, Home's IC does not hold at the global optimum but Foreign's IC has some slack in it. This asymmetric situation generates a role for Home to post a bond that would lower its incentive to deviate and thus improve the maximum sustainable cooperation. Suppose Home posts a bond such that its IC just binds at the global optimum. The bond increases Foreign's incentive to deviate, but if Foreign is sufficiently patient, its IC will continue to hold at the global optimum in the presence of the bond.

[28] One simple way to model the "bond constraints" is to assume that production of the numeraire can only take place after policies are set so none of it is available for the initial bonds. If we want the larger country to be able to post some bond we can allow it to have some endowment of the numeraire available at the start of the period. To maintain symmetry we can allow for a similar endowment for the K small countries that is only available after the policies are set so it affects only their ability to post a bond.

breaks down. So, the large country will find it easy to enforce large fines, which prevents small ones from deviating even if they post no bond ($b^*=0$). But small countries will not have the same ability due to the coordination externality.

Proposition 3 summarizes the results when the extended agreement includes fines and countries face some bond constraints.

Proposition 3 (*Improved cooperation and symmetric outcomes with fines and bond constraints*). *In a trade agreement extended to include WRP fines and constrained bond exchange* ($b \in [\tilde{b}^g, b^g)$; $b^* \in [0, b^{*g})$) *the large country and the K uncoordinated small countries can sustain the globally optimal tariffs* ($\tau^C = \tau^{*Ck} = \tau^G$) *even if they cannot enforce it under a standard agreement. Therefore, for some* $\delta < \delta_G$, *there is a* $\tilde{b}^g > 0$ *such that this agreement generates* (i) *an increase in welfare for the small countries;* (ii) *a global increase in welfare and* (iii) *a more equitable outcome relative to the standard agreement. Furthermore these results hold even if the small countries face severe bond constraints, i.e. if* $b^*=0$.

A corollary is that if the bond constraints were also severe for the large country, i.e. $b=0=b^*$, then Proposition 3 would not hold since $\tilde{b}^g > 0$ unless $\delta = \delta_G$. In fact, under such severe bond constraints, the outcome would be the same as that under the standard agreement. The intuition is straightforward: the outcome under the standard agreement is ultimately determined by the threat of the agreement breaking down and thus infinite tariff reversion, which is the same threat that enforces fines so the two yield the same IC. Proposition 4 summarizes this result.

Proposition 4 (*Equivalence of standard and extended agreements with fines under severe bond constraints*). *A trade agreement extended to include WRP fines and subject to severe constraints on bond exchange* ($b=b^*=0$) *yields the same outcomes as those in Proposition 1 for a standard trade agreement supported by tariff retaliation.*

This last result makes it clear that an extended agreement has to be carefully designed to include the relevant instruments. In this case, what is needed is a bond posted by the large country that removes the need for small countries to coordinate on a particular tariff level in case a retaliation is required. This result extends Proposition 2 of Limão and Saggi (2008), which showed that fines do not enhance cooperation relative to tariff retaliation between two *symmetric* countries. Here, we show that in the absence of bonds, fines do not enhance the cooperation even in this setting with asymmetric countries.

We now turn to the choice of agreement. Any of the agreements considered thus far increases the payoffs for *each* of the countries relative to non-cooperation. This should be clear for the small countries. The large country will also be better off relative to non-cooperation if, as we assume throughout, there is a finite number of small countries. However, large and small countries can have different preferred agreements since for some $\delta < \delta_G$ we obtain $\tau^C > \tau^{*Ck} = \tau^G$ under the standard agreement (Proposition 1) and $\tau^C = \tau^{*Ck} = \tau^G$ under the extended agreements with $\tilde{b}^g$ (Propositions 2 and 3). Therefore, the small countries prefer the extended agreement but the large country prefers the standard one since $W(\tau, \boldsymbol{\tau}^{*G})$ is increasing in its own tariff when $\tau < \tau^N$. This raises the question of which agreement would be adopted. If ex ante transfers were available then we would expect the extended agreement to be adopted since it generates the highest global political welfare (Propositions 2 and 3).

One may then ask how to implement this reform in terms of the model and in practice. In this model of agreements with financial instruments, it seems reasonable to allow for transferable utility (via an ex ante transfer of the numeraire good). If we were to then model an initial stage where countries bargain (efficiently) over the type of agreement (standard or extended) and the associated value of the ex ante transfer, then the extended agreement would be adopted. The value of the transfer from each small country would depend on the precise details of the initial bargaining. If the large country had all the bargaining power then it may be able to extract the full additional gain of the extended agreement relative to the standard one. However, there is no reason to believe this is the only distribution of bargaining power. First, small countries are not negligible in size individually and may also be able to exert their collective power at the negotiation stage even if they cannot coordinate their tariffs after a trade war breaks out. Second, in practice negotiation outcomes are affected not only by relative size but also by the fairness of outcomes, which is a goal of the Doha Round. In sum, if ex ante transfers using the numeraire are possible then it is plausible that the extended agreement would be adopted.

The issue is more complicated if, as considered in the last two propositions, small countries are constrained in their transfers of the numeraire. Note that even if these constraints are severe they do not necessarily *eliminate* the possibility that an extended agreement is adopted. As we argued in the last paragraph, the amount of the transfer will reflect not just the benefit of the extended agreement relative to the standard one but also the initial bargaining procedure; so even a small ex ante transfer may be enough to adopt an extended agreement with large benefits.[29] More generally, if transfers are required but the small countries are constrained in terms of the numeraire then a narrow interpretation of our results is that they show the extended agreement provides a potential Pareto improvement. However, we have also clearly identified the potential constraint to implementing this agreement: the ex ante transfer of the numeraire. One way to overcome this constraint is to enrich the model to allow transfers to take the form of an initial concession by small countries in non-trade issues. One example of this was the acceptance by developing countries of the TRIPS agreement in the Uruguay Round, which many viewed as a transfer from developing to developed countries.

[29] In fact, we could consider an alternative initial stage choice mechanisms where the agreements are put to a vote in the WTO such that the larger number of small countries would imply that their preferred outcome is implemented without *any* transfers.

Naturally any transfer that makes the extended agreement more attractive for the large country also reduces some of its attractiveness to the small ones and would not generate symmetric welfare outcomes. But the small countries would still enjoy higher welfare than under non-cooperation or the standard agreement.

4. Conclusion

The multilateral trading system has changed dramatically since 23 founding members signed the GATT in 1947. The WTO now comprises 157 members, many of which are small individually but jointly account for a substantial fraction of trade. The recent emergence of the BRICs and the longer trend of trade liberalization across the developing world has eroded the relative standing of the US and EU in world trade. These salient changes in the global economic landscape have also started to alter the dynamic underlying multilateral trade negotiations. Whereas the first eight rounds of trade negotiations saw limited participation from developing countries and were led primarily by the USA and the EU, the most recent, and currently ongoing, round of negotiations – i.e. the Doha Round – puts (or at least claims to put) the interests of developing countries at center stage.

The increasingly dispersed pattern of world trade along with the increased participation of developing countries at the WTO suggests that the standard two-country paradigm underlying formal models of international trade agreements may no longer adequately capture actual trade negotiations. In this paper we analyze one basic problem that arises under this "new trade order": a *coordination externality* among countries that import a common good. The externality is strongest when each importer is bilaterally small relative to the exporter, but would have a reasonable degree of market power if it were to coordinate its tariff choices with other importers. This coordination externality implies that smaller countries have less of a threat to use tariffs and therefore a limited ability to bilaterally extract and enforce cooperation from larger countries. Thus international cooperation based on the threat of tariff retaliation yields an asymmetric equilibrium outcome that is biased in favor of the large country.

We examine the use of financial instruments as a means for resolving this coordination externality and the asymmetric outcome that results because of it. To this end, we consider an extended trade agreement under which countries post bonds prior to trading, with the understanding that a country violating the agreement would forfeit its bond. We show that the use of bonds in this fashion does not suffer from the coordination externality that characterizes the tariff choices of small countries. Indeed, we find that when the trade agreement is extended to allow for bonds, the resulting outcome is preferable from both an efficiency and equity perspective.[30] Since the implementation of such an extended agreement might be problematic due to the inability to post bonds (especially on the part of small countries) we show that our results hold even if small countries do not post *any* bonds at all provided the extended agreement allows for fines. Furthermore, the use of such fines also allows the large country to post a smaller bond.

The new trade order arising from the decline of the US and EU relative to several smaller developing countries in the world trading system raises a number of interesting questions and challenges. We argue that to adequately address these new issues, one needs to go beyond the canonical economic theories of agreements. In this paper, we construct a model that isolates a specific issue that is arguably central to the new global economic landscape: a coordination externality. Future research should consider the implications of such an externality for WTO rules and for the process via which trade concessions are exchanged, e.g. whether to add other instruments to enforce joint punishments and/or adjust the bilateral reciprocity principle. This externality also highlights the incentive of smaller countries to coordinate on a common external tariff via the formation of a customs unions. Future research could extend our approach by allowing for discriminatory tariffs in order to analyze the interaction between preferential and multilateral liberalization in the presence of bonds.[31] Finally, this new trade order seems to be one where bilateral trade shares and patterns are both dynamic and uncertain, two dimensions that should be better incorporated in future research on trade agreements.

Acknowledgment

We would like to thank Theo Eicher and two anonymous referees for their very useful comments and suggestions.

[30] Although we do not consider this in our model, posting bonds with a third party may also help improve cooperation. For example, if bonds of sufficient value are deposited in an escrow fund, tariff retaliation is no longer necessary for sustaining cooperation since the bond posted by the violating country can be used to compensate the injured country. Such an escrow scheme was in fact proposed by Chile in its bilateral trade agreement with the US. "Chile Looks for Monetary Sanctions as Enforcement Mechanism", INSIDE U.S. TRADE 13, 11/11/2002.

[31] While some countries have tried to do so (e.g. Mercosur) customs unions are difficult to negotiate and are thus unlikely to eliminate the need for alternatives such as financial instruments in the WTO. For an interesting analysis of links between preferential and multilateral liberalization in the absence of other enforcement mechanisms see Ornelas (2005) and Syropoulos and Dinopoulos (2012).

Appendix A

A.1. Nash tariff for smaller countries

The tariff in (6) is obtained by solving the following first-order condition for τ^{*k}, where all variables correspond to their import, x:

$$W^k_{\tau^{*k}} = 0 : (1 + p^w_{\tau^{*k}})[\tau^{*k} M'^{*k} + (\lambda - 1)S^{*k}] - p^w_{\tau^{*k}} M^{*k} = 0$$

$$\tau^{*k} = \frac{p^w_{\tau^{*k}}}{1 + p^w_{\tau^{*k}}} \frac{M^{*k}}{M'^{*k}} - (\lambda - 1)\frac{S^{*k}}{M'^{*k}}$$

where here and below we use $M'^c \equiv dM^c(p^c)/dp^c$ for each country c's import derivative w.r.t. own price and recall that with a specific tariff $\partial M^{*k}(p^w + \tau^{*k})/\partial \tau^{*k} = \partial M^{*k}(p^w + \tau^{*k})/\partial p^w = M'^{*k}$.

To obtain $p^w_{\tau^{*k}}$ we implicitly differentiate the market clearing condition for x holding all other tariffs constant

$$M(p^w) + \sum_{j \neq k} M^{*j}(p^w + \tau^{*j \neq k}) + M^{*k}(p^w + \tau^{*k}) = 0$$

$$p^w_{\tau^{*k}} = -\frac{M'^{*k}}{M' + \sum_{j \neq k} M'^{*j} + M'^{*k}} \Leftrightarrow \frac{p^w_{\tau^{*k}}}{1 + p^w_{\tau^{*k}}} = \frac{-M'^{*k}}{M' + \sum_{j \neq k} M'^{*j}}$$

Replacing in the first order condition and simplifying we obtain

$$\frac{\tau^{*k}}{p^w} = \frac{-M'^{*k}}{M' + \sum_{j \neq k} M'^{*j}} \frac{M^{*k}}{p^w M'^{*k}} - (\lambda - 1)\frac{S^{*k}/M^{*k}}{M'^{*k} p^w / M^{*k}}$$

$$\frac{\tau^{*k}}{p^w} = \frac{1}{\varepsilon^{*k}} + (\lambda - 1)\frac{S^{*k}/M^{*k}}{\xi^{*k}}$$

where the last line uses the following definitions of k's import elasticity, ξ^{*k}, and what we refer to as its residual foreign export supply elasticity, ε^{*k} respectively:

$$-\xi^{*k} \equiv -\frac{\partial M^{*k}}{\partial p^w} \frac{p^w}{M^{*k}} = \frac{-M'^{*k} p^w}{M^{*k}}$$

$$1/\varepsilon^{*k} \equiv \frac{M + \sum_{j \neq k} M^{*j}}{p^w (M' + \sum_{j \neq k} M'^{*j})}$$

A.2. Relationship between elasticities of individual small countries and regional aggregate

Notice that if all k have the same tariffs then the individual country and regional import demand elasticities are identical

$$\xi^{*k} = -M'^{*k} p^w / M^{*k} = -(M'^{*}/K) p^w / (M^{*}/K) = \xi^{*}$$

However, the market power of individual small countries, as measured by the inverse of their residual foreign export supply elasticity, is lower than the region's, i.e. $1/\varepsilon^{*k} < 1/\varepsilon^{*}$ whenever $K > 1$ since

$$\frac{1}{\varepsilon^{*k}} \equiv \frac{M + \sum_{j \neq k} M^{*j}}{p^w (M' + \sum_{j \neq k} M'^{*j})} < \frac{M}{p^w M'} \equiv \frac{1}{\varepsilon^{*}} \tag{28}$$

The inequality follows since at any given tariff and world prices (i) the numerator on the LHS of the inequality is lower in absolute value than the one on the RHS (recall that $M < 0$ and $\sum_{j \neq k} M^{*j} > 0$ for the good exported by Large) and (ii) the denominator on the LHS of the inequality is larger in absolute value (since both M' and $\sum_{j \neq k} M'^{*j}$ are negative).

Global optimum tariffs (Eq. (8)): These are obtained by solving the following first-order condition for τ^C:

$$W_\tau(\tau^C) + W_{\tau^*}(\tau^* = \tau^C) = 0 : (1 + p^w_\tau)[\tau^C M' + (\lambda - 1)S] = 0$$

Proof of Lemma 1. To see (i) recall that if all small countries set equal tariffs then $\sum_k W^{*k} = KW^{*k}$ and this "regional" welfare measure is mirror symmetric to W so if $\tau^C = \tau^{*Ck}$ and $\boldsymbol{\tau}^* = \tau^N$ for all small countries we have the equality below

$$W(\tau = \tau^N, \boldsymbol{\tau}^* = \tau^C) = KW^{*k}(\tau = \tau^C, \boldsymbol{\tau}^* = \tau^N)$$
$$> KW^{*k}(\tau = \tau^C, \boldsymbol{\tau}^{*Dk})$$

where the inequality arises because $\tau^N = \tau^{*Ncoord}$ maximizes KW^{*k} for a given τ^C and the elements of $\boldsymbol{\tau}^{*Dk}$ are τ^{*Nk}, which are smaller than $\tau^{*\,Ncoord}$ (from (6) when $K > 1$).

To see (ii) note that symmetry implies that

$$W(\tau^N, \boldsymbol{\tau}^* = \tau^N) = KW^{*k}(\tau^N, \boldsymbol{\tau}^* = \tau^N)$$

which implies that

$$W(\tau^N, \boldsymbol{\tau}^{*N}) > W(\tau^N, \boldsymbol{\tau}^* = \tau^N) = KW^{*k}(\tau^N, \boldsymbol{\tau}^* = \tau^N)$$

This is because $\boldsymbol{\tau}^{*N} = \tau^{*Nk}$ for all K and it is smaller than τ^N (from (6)) and so the export price obtained by the large country is higher relative to when it faces τ^N in all small countries. Furthermore, we have

$$KW^{*k}(\tau^N, \boldsymbol{\tau}^* = \tau^N) > KW^{*k}(\tau^N, \boldsymbol{\tau}^{*N})$$

This is because $\boldsymbol{\tau}^* = \tau^N$ for all K maximizes the aggregate payoff of small countries for any given tariff of the large country, not $\boldsymbol{\tau}^{*N}$ whose elements compose of K tariffs each of which equals $\tau^{*Nk} < \tau^{*Ncoord}$. Combining the last two inequalities we obtain $W(\tau^N, \boldsymbol{\tau}^{*N}) > \sum_k W^{*k}(\tau^N, \boldsymbol{\tau}^{*N})$. □

Proof of Proposition 1. Suppose that $\delta = \delta_G$ so that by definition the incentive constraint of the large country (16) holds with equality when each country sets its tariff to equal the globally optimal tariff τ^G. The incentive constraint for a typical small country is similar to (16), except that small country exporters face a higher tariff relative to that faced by exporters from the large country, i.e. $\tau^N > \tau^{*Nk}$, and the payoff of each small country is divided by K (but K cancels out because it enters similarly on both sides of the IC). Thus, the cooperative payoff for the small countries as a group is equal to that for the large one (due to symmetry) and the payoffs for small countries from deviating are smaller, as shown in Lemma 1. This means that at δ_G, where (16) holds with equality, *there must be slack in the corresponding IC for each small country*. If we lower δ below δ_G then the large country's incentive constraint (16) no longer holds at τ^G. So under tariff retaliation, the global optimum is not feasible for $\delta < \delta_G$. But the corresponding constraint for each small country continues to hold and has slack, at least for some $\delta < \delta_G$.

Since, by definition, for any $\delta < \delta_G$ tariff retaliation cannot sustain τ^G, to prove Proposition 1 we need only to show that when $\delta < \delta_G$ the lowest self-enforcing cooperative tariffs used are such that $\tau^C > \tau^{*Ck}$. We prove this by contradiction. Assume that the lowest self-enforcing cooperative tariffs for all countries are the same, i.e. $\tau^C = \tau^{*Ck}$ and such that the IC of the large country (16) binds.[32] We then show that if $\tau^C = \tau^{*Ck}$ then the IC of a small country (17) has slack implying that such a tariff is not the most cooperative tariff on the part of small countries. Since the RHS of (16) is equal to K times the RHS of (17) at $\tau^C = \tau^{*Ck}$ (due to symmetry) we need only to show that the LHS of (16) exceeds K times the RHS of (17), which is done in Lemma 1. Given this there must be some $\tau^{*Ck} < \tau^C$ for small countries that is still self-enforcing since the reduction in τ^{*Ck} reduces the slack in (17) without violating the large country's IC in (16).

Given the asymmetry in the cooperative tariffs, the large country will have a higher welfare than the collection of small ones even though they are mirror images and there is constant returns to scale in production.[33] □

Proof of Proposition 2. See the text. □

Proof of Proposition 3. To prove Proposition 3 we need only to show that for some $\delta < \delta_G$ the global optimum can be sustained using bonds $b^* = 0 < b^{*g}$ and $b < b^g$. Once that is done the results in (i)–(iii) follow directly from the same arguments in Proposition 2. Consider the following strategy: similarly to before, each country must first post a bond in order for cooperation to begin. We will focus on the case where the total value of this bond is $\tilde{b} > 0$ for the large country (equally divided among the K small countries) whereas b^* is arbitrarily small, in practice $b^* = 0$. If a country deviates, it loses its bond but keeps any foreign bond(s) it may hold. But now, if a deviation were to occur then cooperation resumes only after a fine is paid by the deviating country. The incentive constraints for the large and each of the small countries are respectively

$$W(\tau^N, \boldsymbol{\tau}^{*G}) - \tilde{b} + V^{\tilde{b}} \le \frac{W(\tau^G, \boldsymbol{\tau}^{*G})}{1-\delta} \tag{29}$$

$$W^{*k}(\tau^G, \boldsymbol{\tau}^{*N}) + \tilde{b}/K + V^{*\tilde{b}} \le \frac{W^{*k}(\tau^G, \boldsymbol{\tau}^{*G})}{1-\delta} \tag{30}$$

and the minimum continuation payoffs for each are

$$V^{\tilde{b}} \equiv -\delta f + \frac{\delta W(\tau^G, \boldsymbol{\tau}^{*G})}{1-\delta} \quad \text{and} \quad V^{*\tilde{b}} \equiv -\delta f^* + \frac{\delta W^{*k}(\tau^G, \boldsymbol{\tau}^{*G})}{1-\delta}$$

[32] It is clear that we need not consider the case where $\tau^C > \tau^{*Ck}$.

[33] This is not to say that the welfare distribution across countries is *more* unequal under the agreement than under non-cooperation since the Nash policies are also asymmetric. In fact, if $\delta = \delta_G$ the agreement sustains the symmetric global optimum and so generates a more equal welfare distribution than non-cooperation. By continuity, this must also be true for at least some $\delta < \delta_G$.

where f and f^* are the fine values paid by the large and small countries respectively. As before, we require the continuation payoff to be *WRP* in that no country prefers to abandon the agreement altogether. This implies that the minimum continuation payoff for each country must be no lower than the payoff obtained under non-cooperation

$$V^{\tilde{b}\ \min} \equiv -\delta f^{\max} + \frac{\delta W(\tau^G, \boldsymbol{\tau}^{*G})}{1-\delta} = \frac{\delta W(\tau^N, \boldsymbol{\tau}^{*N})}{1-\delta} \tag{31}$$

$$V^{*\tilde{b}\ \min} \equiv -\delta f^{*\ \max} + \frac{\delta W^{*k}(\tau^G, \boldsymbol{\tau}^{*G})}{1-\delta} = \frac{\delta W^{*k}(\tau^N, \boldsymbol{\tau}^{*N})}{1-\delta} \tag{32}$$

These constraints pin down the maximum fine that each country is willing to pay and re-arranging them we can interpret that maximum fine to be the net present discounted value of cooperation

$$f^{\max} = \frac{W(\tau^G, \boldsymbol{\tau}^{*G}) - W(\tau^N, \boldsymbol{\tau}^{*N})}{1-\delta}$$

$$f^{*\ \max} = \frac{W^{*k}(\tau^G, \boldsymbol{\tau}^{*G}) - W^{*k}(\tau^N, \boldsymbol{\tau}^{*N})}{1-\delta}$$

Replacing $V^{\tilde{b}\ \min}$ in (29) by $\delta W(\tau^N, \boldsymbol{\tau}^{*N})/(1-\delta)$ allows us to solve for the minimum bond required to sustain globally optimal tariffs

$$\tilde{b}^g = W(\tau^N, \boldsymbol{\tau}^{*G}) + \frac{\delta W(\tau^N, \boldsymbol{\tau}^{*N})}{1-\delta} - \frac{W(\tau^G, \boldsymbol{\tau}^{*G})}{1-\delta}$$

To clearly see the relationship between this and the bond required without fines we rewrite the expression above and use the value of b^g in (22) to obtain

$$\tilde{b}^g = \underbrace{[W(\tau^N, \boldsymbol{\tau}^{*G}) - W(\tau^G, \boldsymbol{\tau}^{*G})]}_{=b^g} - \frac{\delta}{1-\delta}[W(\tau^G, \boldsymbol{\tau}^{*G}) - W(\tau^N, \boldsymbol{\tau}^{*N})[< b^g \tag{33}$$

The inequality $\tilde{b}^g < b^g$ holds because the second term in parenthesis (i.e. $W(\tau^G, \boldsymbol{\tau}^{*G}) - W(\tau^N, \boldsymbol{\tau}^{*N})$) is positive whenever the number of small countries is small enough that the large country prefers a cooperative trade agreement to a trade war, which is our assumption throughout (see footnote 20). Intuitively, when fines can be used in conjunction with bonds, the large country can post a lower bond because the threat of the maximum fine $f^{\max}$ (off the equilibrium path) ensures that its continuation payoff is no higher than when fines are not used (since it equals $\delta W(\tau^N, \boldsymbol{\tau}^{*N})/(1-\delta)$ in either case) while the posting of zero bonds by small countries implies that its short term gain of deviating from cooperation is lower relative to the case without fines. It should also be clear that for $\delta < \delta_G$ we have $\tilde{b}^g > 0$ since if $\delta = \delta_G$ then $\tilde{b}^g = 0$ and reducing δ reduces the gains from cooperation, which is the second term in (33).

To show that $\tilde{b}^g$ does not violate the incentive constraint for small countries in (30) we replace $\tilde{b}^g$ and $V^{*\ b\ \min}$ into (30) and rearrange it to obtain

$$W(\tau^N, \boldsymbol{\tau}^{*G}) + \frac{\delta W(\tau^N, \boldsymbol{\tau}^{*N})}{1-\delta} + K\left[W^{*k}(\tau^G, \boldsymbol{\tau}^{*N}) + \frac{\delta W^{*k}(\tau^N, \boldsymbol{\tau}^{*N})}{1-\delta}\right] \le \frac{W(\tau^G, \boldsymbol{\tau}^{*G})}{1-\delta} + K\frac{W^{*k}(\tau^G, \boldsymbol{\tau}^{*G})}{1-\delta} \tag{34}$$

This is simply the sum of the IC in the standard agreement given by (16) and (17) when evaluated at the global optimum. We know that at δ_G the IC for the large country holds with equality at τ^G (by the definition of δ_G) and the IC for each small country holds with slack (Proposition 1) so (34) holds strictly at δ_G and continuity ensures it must also hold for some $\delta < \delta_G$. □

Proof of proposition 4. Substitute the minimum continuation payoffs for the extended agreement, $V^{\tilde{b}\ \min}$ and $V^{*\tilde{b}\ \min}$, and set $\tilde{b} = 0$ in the IC in (29) and (30). Evaluating these at a general cooperative tariff level (instead of requiring it to be the global optimum) we obtain the IC under the standard agreement, (16) and (17). □

Appendix B. Supplementary data

Supplementary data associated with this article can be found in the online version at http://dx.doi.org/10.1016/j.euroecorev.2013.05.006.

References

Bagwell, K., Staiger, R., 1999. An economic theory of GATT. American Economic Review 89 (1), 215–248.

Bagwell, K., Staiger, R., 2005. Enforcement, private political pressure, and the GATT/WTO escape clause. Journal of Legal Studies 34 (2), 471–513.

Bagwell, K., Staiger, R., 2011. What do trade negotiators negotiate about? Empirical evidence from the world trade organization. American Economic Review 101 (4). 1283–73.

Bagwell, K., Mavroidis, P., Staiger, R., 2007. Auctioning countermeasures in the WTO. Journal of International Economics 73 (2), 309–332.

Besedes, T., Prusa, T., 2011. The role of extensive and intensive margins and export growth. Journal of Development Economics 96 (2), 371–379.
Beshkar, M., 2010. Optimal remedies in international trade agreements. European Economic Review 54 (3), 455–466.
Broda, C., Limão, N., Weinstein, D., 2008. Optimal tariffs and market power: the evidence. American Economic Review 98 (5), 2032–2065.
Bronckers, M., Van Den Broek, N., 2005. Financial compensation in the WTO: improving the remedies of WTO dispute settlement. Journal of International Economic Law 8, 101–126.
Grossman, G., Helpman, E., 1994. Protection for sale. American Economic Review 84 (4), 833–850.
Grossman, G., Helpman, E., 1995. Trade wars and trade talks. Journal of Political Economy 103, 675–708.
Grossman, G., Mavroidis, P.C., 2004. United States—Section 110(5) of the US copyright act, recourse to arbitration under article 25 of the DSU: would've or should've? Impaired benefits due to copyright infringement. World Trade Review 2, 233–249.
Johnson, H.G., 1953–54. Optimum tariffs and retaliation. Review of Economic Studies 21, 142–153.
Lawrence, R., 2003. Crimes and Punishments? Retaliation Under the WTO. Institute of International Economics, Washington, DC.
Limão, N., Saggi, K., 2008. Tariff retaliation versus financial compensation in the enforcement of international trade agreements. Journal of International Economics 76, 48–60.
Ludema, R., 2001. Optimal international trade agreements and dispute settlement procedures. European Journal of Political Economy 17, 355–376.
Ludema, R., Mayda, Anna M., 2009. Do countries free ride on MFN? Journal of International Economics 77 (2), 137–150.
Mayer, W., 1981. Theoretical considerations on negotiated tariff adjustments. Oxford Economic Papers 33, 135–153.
Mercurio, B., 2009. Why compensation cannot replace trade retaliation in the WTO dispute settlement understanding. World Trade Review 8 (2), 315–338.
Ornelas, E., 2005. Trade creating free trade areas and the undermining of multilateralism. European Economic Review 49 (7), 1717–1735.
Park, J.-H., 2000. International trade agreements between countries of asymmetric size. Journal of International Economics 50, 473–495.
Saggi, K., Yildiz, H., 2010. Bilateralism, multilateralism, and the quest for global free trade. Journal of International Economics 81, 26–37.
Schott, J., 2009. America, Europe, and the new trade order. Business and Politics 11 (3), 1–22.
Srinivasan, T.N., 1999. Developing countries in the world trading system: from GATT, 1947, to the third ministerial meeting of WTO, 1999. The World Economy 22 (8), 1047–1064.
Syropoulos, C., 2002. Optimum tariffs and retaliation: how country size matters. Review of Economic Studies 69, 707–727.
Syropoulos, C., Dinopoulos, E., 2012. Multi-country Tariff Wars and Trade Agreements. Mimeo.
Zissimos, B., 2009. Optimum tariffs and retaliation: how country numbers matter. Journal of International Economics 78, 276–286.

Chapter 12

Tariff retaliation versus financial compensation in the enforcement of international trade agreements ☆

Nuno Limão [a,*,1], Kamal Saggi [b,2]

[a] University of Maryland, Department of Economics, CEPR, NBER, United States
[b] Southern Methodist University, United States

ARTICLE INFO

Article history:
Received 22 February 2006
Received in revised form 18 March 2008
Accepted 26 March 2008

Keywords:
Dispute settlement
WTO
Tariffs
Monetary fines
Bonds
Policy coordination

JEL classification:
F13
F42
K33
H77

ABSTRACT

We analyze whether financial compensation is preferable to the WTO's current dispute settlement system that permits injured member countries to impose retaliatory tariffs. We show that, ex-post, monetary fines are more efficient than tariffs in terms of granting compensation to injured parties but fines suffer from an enforcement problem since they must be paid by the violating country. If fines must ultimately be supported by the threat of tariffs, they fail to yield a more cooperative outcome than the use of tariffs alone. Furthermore, the exchange of bonds between symmetric countries also does not improve enforcement relative to retaliatory tariffs.

1. Introduction

One of the major goals of the World Trade Organization (WTO) is to reduce policy barriers to international trade. Yet, its dispute settlement system allows members to raise tariffs in response to trade violations committed by other members. Although retaliation is permitted only as a last resort, the fact that the WTO even permits tariff increases appears to be a direct contradiction of its goal of freer trade. This contradiction as well as the fact that many small countries cannot effectively retaliate via tariffs have lead to calls for alternative trade dispute remedies.[3]

☆ The views expressed are those of the authors. We thank the editor, two anonymous referees, Stephanie Aaronson, Piyush Chandra, Kyle Bagwell, Chad Bown, Bernard Hoekman and Petros Mavroidis for useful discussions and comments. We gratefully acknowledge the financial support of the UK's Department for International Development.

* Corresponding author. Tel.: +301 405 7842.
E-mail addresses: limao@econ.umd.edu (N. Limão), ksaggi@smu.edu (K. Saggi).

[1] I gratefully acknowledge the financial support of the World Bank and IMF Research Groups, which hosted me during part of this research. The views expressed in this paper are those of the authors and not of these institutions.

[2] Tel.: +214 768 3274.

[3] See Hoekman and Kostecki (2001) for a good overview of the WTO's dispute settlement procedures. Lawrence (2003) notes that WTO rules are designed to preserve the existing balance of concessions (i.e. to maintain reciprocity). Ethier (2003) argues that the role of the WTO's dispute settlement procedure is "not to facilitate punishment: It is to constrain it."

0022-1996/$ – see front matter
doi:10.1016/j.jinteco.2008.03.005

Originally Published in *Journal of International Economics* 76, pp. 48–60.

There are at least two possible reasons why the WTO's Dispute Settlement Understanding (DSU) permits tariff retaliation. First, the threat of retaliation might encourage members to comply with WTO rules: in the absence of any fear of foreign retaliation, members would be tempted to raise their trade barriers whenever so urged by their import lobbies. Second, tariff retaliation may allow an injured country to obtain partial compensation by either improving its terms-of-trade and/or by benefiting those import competing sectors that are favored due to political economy considerations. Of course, even if tariff retaliation helps enforce cooperation and/or enable compensation in trade agreements, it may not necessarily be the optimal instrument for achieving these objectives. In principle, monetary fines payable by a country that violates WTO rules could have both a deterrent effect and a compensatory one while simultaneously avoiding the well-known inefficiencies of tariffs. Our goal in this paper is to evaluate whether the use of fines and bonds can improve upon the WTO's current dispute settlement system based on retaliatory tariffs.

The idea that trade disputes be settled via financial compensation has gained substantial attention in recent years with several new proposals to reform the DSU in the Doha Round, which is still under way.[4] Similar proposals were made in the early 1960s by Uruguay and Brazil who wanted less developed countries to be provided with financial compensation for GATT violations committed by developed countries. Moreover, as .Dam (1970) notes, the principle of financial liability to injured parties underlies domestic laws across the world and its use in international law seems natural.

Desirable as it may seem, the implementation of financial compensation faces important hurdles. We address what we think is the major hurdle: *enforcing such a system*. How does one ensure that the required fine, whatever it is ruled to be, is actually paid by a violating country? While an injured country can implement retaliatory tariffs without requiring any cooperation from a violating country, such is not the case for fines. Ultimately, a violating country has to agree to pay the fine and it will only do so when it is in its best interest since there exists no supra-national authority that can enforce the payment of the fine.[5] This enforcement problem with financial compensation is clearly reflected in the current DSU — it allows for compensation but does not specify the form it must take. Article 22.2 of the DSU states that the compensation must be mutually agreed upon and if it is not, an injured country can apply for retaliation. The only case that we know of where a dispute resulted in monetary compensation was when the US was found guilty of non-payment of royalties by US firms to the EU. This shows that while financial compensation is possible under the DSU, it simply has not been agreed to in most trade disputes that have come before the WTO.[6]

An important objective of this paper is to analyze the effectiveness of alternative dispute remedies in maintaining relatively low trade barriers. We also analyze the effectiveness of the different systems from the perspective of compensating injured countries. In so doing, we argue that one needs to account not only for how a remedy is able to enforce cooperation but also *how the remedy itself can be enforced*. For fines to succeed in enforcing low tariffs and providing compensation, it is crucial that they be backed by a supporting instrument that is not controlled by a violating country. Retaliatory tariffs are the obvious choice for such a *supporting* instrument. However, we show that a system where retaliatory tariffs are used to support the payment of fines yields no more cooperation than one that uses tariffs alone to retaliate against violations.

The equivalence of fines and tariff retaliation in terms of enforcement suggests that both mechanisms yield the same payoffs. However, we show that this is only true if there are no deviations from cooperation. When such deviations occur, and they clearly do in practice, we show that fines supported by tariffs have an advantage over tariff retaliation as a primary remedy. Namely, the payoff to an injured country is higher under fines even though the cost of the penalty for a violating country is unchanged. Thus we show that switching to fines generates a Pareto improvement in the presence of shocks that result in disputes. The underlying rationale for this result is that tariffs are an inefficient form of compensation: the welfare gain they generate for an injured country with market power is always less than the welfare cost they impose on the country that commits the original violation.[7]

Given the aforementioned result regarding the equivalence of fines and tariffs from an enforcement perspective, it is important to ask whether alternative financial mechanisms can help sustain greater cooperation. To this end, we ask whether international cooperation can be sustained by a system where countries exchange bonds of a given amount, with the understanding that a country's bond will be forfeited in case it commits a trade violation. We find that the exchange of bonds between symmetric countries does not improve enforcement relative to a system based solely on retaliatory tariffs. This is because a deviating country has no incentive to return the other country's bond and the extra benefit of deviating on bonds is exactly offset by the cost of losing one's own bond.

Our paper is related to the literature on the enforcement of trade agreements, early contributions to which are reviewed in Staiger (1995). Since then there have been several important contributions and here we briefly note some that are particularly relevant for our paper. Park (2000) studies cooperation between a large and a small country (which has no market power) and shows, among other things, that trade agreements where the small country can make direct transfers can enforce lower tariffs. This is because the threat of terminating the transfer payment gives the small country more leverage than a tariff retaliation. The "purchase" of market access to a large country by a small one is an interesting and relevant result when this transfer is understood

[4] For example, Bronckers and Van Den Broek have argued strongly in favor of financial compensation as a means of settling trade disputes (see editorial in the Financial Times, 06/24/04 and Bronckers and Van Den Broek, 2005).

[5] Another hurdle might be an informational one: determining the financial loss incurred by an exporter. However, a similar issue occurs under the current tariff retaliation system. For more recent discussions by legal scholars on improvements of the WTO's DSU and use of monetary compensation see Shaffer (2003) and Hudec (2002).

[6] However, monetary fines have recently been introduced by the US in its preferential trade agreements with Singapore, Chile, the central American countries, and Australia. More specifically, in these agreements, monetary fines are typically a preferred form of compensation when there is a violation related to the trade or intellectual property right provisions.

[7] In a different context, Hoekman and Saggi (2007) argue that since most developing countries lack the institutional capacity for fighting foreign export cartels via antitrust enforcement, developed countries ought to ban such cartels in return for tariff concessions or some monetary compensation. Cartelization creates an inefficiency much like the use of a tariff by a large country in that the loss suffered by the injured party exceeds the gain of the other party.

as a concession in a non-trade issue, as invoked by Park and explicitly analyzed by others (e.g. Limão, 2007). However, in this paper we focus on examining alternative enforcement mechanisms in a setting with large symmetric countries.

In addition to proposals to switch to financial compensation, which we analyze, there have also been others. For example, Mexico has proposed injured countries to be allowed to trade their retaliation rights, i.e. to "sell" them to countries that have sufficient market power to credibly threaten tariff retaliation. Bagwell et al. (2007) analyze this proposal in an auction framework where a country has "earned" the right to retaliate against another (offending) country and wants to sell this right as opposed to retaliating itself (perhaps because it has no market power in trade with the offending country). In one of the auctions they consider, the offending country – the target of retaliation – is permitted to bid to retire the right of retaliation, and in effect is induced to pay the injured country cash compensation in order to keep the right of retaliation out of the hands of other countries who would use it. In this way, Bagwell et al argue that such an auction could harness the retaliatory measures in the WTO to make credible the payment of cash compensation by large industrial countries (who have violated WTO rules) to small least-developed countries (who are injured by these violations). This point is related to our findings here, in that both there and here the threat of tariffs is required to make the payments of financial compensation credible. But our emphasis is very different: Bagwell et al do not model the deviation that creates the right of retaliation that is then auctioned, and their focus is on how auctions might multilateralize this threat to facilitate compensatory payments between countries of asymmetric power and size. In contrast, we focus on the potential role of financial compensation in allowing countries of similar size to implement lower tariffs in a self-enforcing agreement.

Yet an alternative role for financial instruments in trade agreements is considered by Bagwell and Staiger (2005). They show that if governments face anticipated political economy shocks that are private information, then allowing for cash transfers helps to enforce more cooperative tariffs. We also extend our model to include private, anticipated shocks and show that the types of fines we consider do not enforce more cooperation in that setting. The difference in the results occurs because we consider fines that are enacted only in the case of a deviation whereas in Bagwell and Staiger (2005) the financial transfers are used only as long as countries cooperate. The fact that different types of "financial instruments" lead to different tariff cooperation highlights the importance of carefully modelling each of their roles in international trade agreements.

Following most of the literature, we model trade agreements as the sub-game perfect equilibria of repeated games. But rather than focusing on infinite Nash reversion in tariffs as a form to punish violations we focus on renegotiation proof agreements, which better captures the WTO as argued by Ludema (2001). He notes that most trade disputes in the WTO have been settled through negotiations and whenever sanctions have been used, their level has been in accordance with the principle of reciprocity. He then shows that this important feature of disputes in the WTO implies that only those trade agreements that are renegotiation proof are sustained in equilibrium.[8]

The structure of the paper is as follows. In Section 2 we introduce the model and derive the tariff levels in the absence of enforcement problems. In Section 3 we introduce the alternative enforcement mechanisms and contrast the degree of trade liberalization that they can each enforce. We also show the ex-post efficiency of fines relative to tariff retaliation as a form of compensation when trade disputes occur after unanticipated shocks. Furthermore, we discuss how the results extend to the case of anticipated shocks and how different types of financial instruments lead to different outcomes when such shocks are private information. In Section 4 we summarize the results and discuss possible extensions.

2. Model

Given that the issue of alternative enforcement mechanisms is not yet well understood we focus on the simple case of two symmetric countries (home and foreign). Each country produces two homogeneous goods, $i=x, y$ as well as a numeraire good, n. Individual utility over the consumption level, c, of three goods is given by

$$u \equiv c_n + \sum_i u_i(c_i)$$

Since utility is quasi-linear, the demand function for good i depends only on its own price and is similar for all individuals so we denote aggregate demand at home by $D_i(p_i)$, where $D_i'(p_i)<0$. Each unit of the numeraire good c_n is produced with constant returns to scale technology using only labor, which is available in fixed supply, L. Each good i is produced with a constant returns technology using both labor and a specific factor; each specific factor is available in fixed supply. We denote the supply function for good i by $S_i(p_i)$ where $S_i'(p_i)>0$.

Let x denote home's import. Under trade, domestic import prices are given by $p_x = p^w + \tau$ where p^w is the "world" price and τ is a specific import tariff on x. Home's excess demand is then $M_i \equiv D_i(p_i) - S_i(p_i)$. Denoting foreign variables with an asterisk (*) the world price for home's import is determined by the market clearing condition

$$M_x(p_x^w + \tau) + M_x^*(p_x^w) = 0 \tag{1}$$

A similar condition applies to foreign's import good, y. We assume that no export policies are used so that trade policy is simply described by the level of the import tariff in each country, τ and τ^*. Moreover, we assume that countries have market power in trade so

[8] A broader question is why a third party such as the WTO and its dispute system is needed at all if trade agreements are self-enforcing. Maggi (1999) argues that the role of the WTO is to disseminate information about violations. Klimenko, Ramey, and Watson (2008) argue that the WTO can facilitate cooperation by helping countries to condition their negotiations on the history of cooperation. This role is important when there are ongoing negotiations with outcomes that can differ depending on whether the history is one of cooperation or disputes.

that their optimal tariffs are positive. It is then simple to verify that, in this setup, increasing the tariff on good x lowers the world price, $p_x^w(\tau)$, and raises the domestic one. Given the symmetry a similar relationship holds for the effect of τ^* on the prices of good y.[9]

We focus directly on a reduced form objective function for the government that may allow extra weight (measured by $\lambda_i \geq 1$) to be placed on specific factor owners.

$$W\left(\tau,\tau^*\right)=\sum_i\left[\int_{p_i}^{\infty}D_i(p_i)dp_i+\lambda_i\int_0^{p_i}S_i(p_i)dp_i+\tau_iM_i(p_i)\right]+wL \tag{2}$$

where we recall that τ affects W both directly through tariff revenue, the term $\tau_x M_x$, and through its effect on home prices; whereas the effect of τ^* is indirect and occurs only through the world price, $p_y^w(\tau^*)$. The first term in brackets is consumer surplus. The second one captures producer surplus (weighted by λ) or alternatively the quasi-rents accruing to the fixed factor owners. The last term, wL, is the total wage income. We assume that L is large enough to ensure a positive supply of the numeraire and so the wage rate in the economy is fixed by the marginal productivity of labor in the numeraire good, which in the absence of labor taxes we normalize to unity. Therefore, W can be interpreted as a reduced form of a political contributions model such as Grossman-Helpman (1994).[10]

The Nash tariff, denoted by τ^N, is obtained by maximizing (2) while taking the other country's tariff as given. Since we do not model export policies the good subscript, i, can be dropped so any subscripts below denote partial derivatives. Let

$$\tau^N=\arg_\tau \max W\left(\tau,\tau^*\right) \tag{3}$$

Recalling that the equilibrium prices are a function of the tariff, the first order condition is

$$-Dp_\tau+\lambda Sp_\tau+M+\tau M_P p_\tau=0 \tag{4}$$

Using $M=D-S$, $p_\tau=p_\tau^w+1$ and re-arranging the above we obtain

$$(p_\tau^w+1)\left[\tau M_P+(\lambda-1)S\right]-Mp_\tau^w=0, \tag{5}$$

which implies that the Nash tariff in ad-valorem terms, $\tau^N/p^w(\tau)$, is implicitly defined by:

$$\frac{\tau^N}{p^w(\tau)}=\frac{1}{\varepsilon(\tau)}+(\lambda-1)\frac{S(\tau)/M(\tau)}{\xi(\tau)} \tag{6}$$

We explicitly show the potential dependence of the various terms on the tariff. We do so for clarity in the formula but will omit them below for notational simplicity. The first term, $1/\varepsilon$ is defined as $\frac{M^*}{p^w M_p^*}$ and represents the inverse of the foreign export supply elasticity and it reflects the terms-of-trade motive for the use of tariffs. The second term reflects a political economy motive that is increasing in the extra weight placed on specific factor owners (λ) and decreasing in home's import demand elasticity ξ where $\xi\equiv-\frac{\partial M}{\partial p^w}\frac{p^w}{M}=-M_P p^w/M$. Given symmetry, the foreign country's import tariff is the same, i.e. $\tau^N=\tau^{*N}$.

At the other extreme, if cooperation was not subject to any enforcement problems, countries would choose tariffs that maximize their joint objective $W+W^*$. This is equivalent to maximizing the objective of either one once we employ symmetry and note that $\tau=\tau^*$. Thus we obtain

$$\tau^G\equiv\arg_{\tau^c}\max W\left(\tau^c,\tau^*=\tau^c\right) \tag{7}$$

which implies that the globally optimal ad-valorem tariff $\tau^G/p^w(\tau^G)$ is given by

$$\frac{\tau^G}{p^w(\tau)}=(\lambda-1)\frac{S(\tau)/M(\tau)}{\xi(\tau)} \tag{8}$$

It is clear that the optimal cooperative tariff is lower than the non-cooperative tariff (i.e. $\tau^G/p^w<\tau^N/p^w$). The difference between the Nash and globally cooperative policies confirms that market power in trade leads to international externalities that can potentially be resolved by trade agreements.[11] Moreover, it points out that even in the presence of an international agreement, countries may choose to have positive tariffs due to internal political economy distortions. Since the globally optimum tariff is below the level that is optimal for each *individual* country, each country has an incentive to deviate from it and would do so if it faced no punishment. We now address how countries can enforce cooperation.

[9] Broda, Limão and Weinstein (in press) estimate that several countries have considerable market power in trade and use it to set higher tariffs prior to their WTO accession.

[10] In Grossman-Helpman (1994) the government's objective is $W^{GH}=a\bar{W}+c$, where $\bar{W}$ is social welfare, c is political contributions and a is the marginal rate of substitution between the two. In W the term $\lambda-1$ can be directly interpreted as the inverse of a when factor ownership is extremely concentrated.

[11] This role for the WTO is argued in Bagwell and Staiger (1999). Bagwell and Staiger (2006) provide evidence for their theory by showing that WTO accession leads to greater tariff reductions in products with higher initial import volumes.

3. Enforcement of trade agreements

The absence of a supra-national authority to punish violators implies that international agreements must be self-enforcing. Cooperative self-enforcing agreements are well characterized by certain repeated games.[12] We begin with the standard approach in the literature of using the threat of tariff retaliation to enforce cooperation and then contrast its outcome with alternative enforcement mechanisms.

3.1. Supporting cooperation via tariff retaliation

Consider an infinitely repeated game where the stage game delivers the Nash tariff in the previous Section. Assume that governments observe each other's actions at the end of each period. The strategy employed by countries is to start by cooperating until one deviates by raising its tariff. Any deviation is followed by a punishment phase of n periods after which cooperation is resumed. We model punishments as being temporary because this is clearly more realistic than infinite Nash reversion. Although the latter is a possibility, we view it as the ultimate punishment corresponding to an unravelling of the GATT/WTO system that results from member countries not following its rules. The more common occurrences are trade disputes that are met with temporary punishments.

To find the lowest cooperative tariff that is renegotiation proof we must first define the payoffs to each government under the alternative situations that can arise. In the absence of cooperation, the payoff to each country equals the government's objective evaluated at the non-cooperative tariffs:

$$W^N = W\left(\tau^N, \tau^{*N}\right) \tag{9}$$

Similarly, when countries cooperate, i.e. set their tariffs at τ^c and τ^{*c} (determined below), the payoff to each is given by:

$$W^C = W\left(\tau^c, \tau^{*c}\right) \tag{10}$$

If a country deviates, it does so by imposing its optimal Nash tariff τ^N on its trading partner who, in that period, still utilizes the cooperative tariff, τ^{*c}. The payoff to a country in the period it deviates is therefore given by

$$W^D = W\left(\tau^N, \tau^{*c}\right) \tag{11}$$

Given the symmetry, in equilibrium $\tau^c = \tau^{*c}$ and $\tau^N = \tau^{*N}$, where τ^N is defined by Eq. (6).[13] Since we allow for renegotiation after a deviation we must model the punishment phase before cooperation is resumed. We assume that countries agree that a deviation will be followed by n periods of punishment where the country that deviated faces τ^{*N} on its exports and must show its willingness to restart cooperation by setting its own import tariff at the cooperative level $\tau^c < \tau^N$. The per-period payoff for the deviating country during the punishment phase is therefore

$$W^P = W\left(\tau^c, \tau^{*N}\right)$$

Given the above payoffs, it is straightforward to show that the static tariff game has a Prisoner's Dilemma structure since the following two sets of inequalities are satisfied:

$$W^D > W^C > W^N > W^P \tag{12}$$

$$W^C + W^{*C} > W^P + W^{*P}\left(\tau^c, \tau^{*N}\right) \tag{13}$$

where $W^{*P}(\tau^c, \tau^{*N})$ is foreign's payoff when home is being punished. The inequality $W^D > W^C$ reflects the incentive to deviate from the static cooperative outcome. It is guaranteed in our model by the fact that when home cooperates its tariff is below its reaction curve so switching to τ^N generates a welfare gain during the deviation period. The inequality $W^C > W^N$ requires a country to prefer the cooperative to the non-cooperative outcome where both countries set τ^N; and this is ensured by the fact that countries are symmetric so the higher non-cooperative tariffs have no impact on their terms-of-trade but introduce a deadweight loss. The inequality $W^N > W^P$ simply says that during the punishment phase of the repeated game, the punished country's payoff is below the static Nash level W^N, which holds since τ^c is not home's best-response to τ^{*N}. Finally, inequality (13) requires that cooperative tariffs yield a higher *joint* welfare than an outcome where either country is being punished thus precluding countries from

[12] See Dixit (1987) and Bagwell and Staiger (1990) for example.

[13] The deviation value of the tariff is independent of the other country's policy, i.e. the best-response functions are horizontal. This is due to the quasilinear demand structure and the fact that there are no export policies. In a different setup, e.g. one with import and export policies, the deviation value of the tariff would be lower or higher than τN depending on whether it was a strategic complement or substitute of the foreign export tax.

optimally choosing to alternate in punishing each other instead of cooperating. This condition, as we will see, is crucial in showing the compensation role for fines. It is automatically satisfied in our setup because the difference between the cooperative and Nash tariffs simply reflects a terms-of-trade motive that involves a deadweight loss so home's cost from being punished W^C-W^P always exceeds foreign's terms-of-trade gain, $W^{*P}-W^{*C}$.[14]

Define the continuation payoff after a deviation as:

$$V^{\tau} \equiv \sum\nolimits_{t=1}^{n} \delta^t W^P + \sum\nolimits_{t=n+1}^{\infty} \delta^t W^C \tag{14}$$

Given these payoffs, the following incentive compatibility (IC) constraint must be satisfied

$$W^D + V^{\tau} \leq \frac{W^C}{1-\delta} \tag{15}$$

which is identical for the symmetric countries. That is, the sum of the payoff of a deviation, W^D, and the continuation payoff, V^{τ}, should not exceed the payoff of cooperation, which is discounted by $\delta<1$.

Since $W^P<W^N$ the punishment phase is subgame perfect only if it is not profitable for the country that is being punished to simply abandon the agreement and revert to Nash forever. So we require that V^{τ} exceed the discounted Nash payoff in order to be *weakly renegotiation* proof (WRP):[15]

$$V^{\tau} \geq \frac{\delta}{1-\delta} W^N \tag{16}$$

Because $W^C>W^P$, the longer the punishment phase, the lower is V^{τ}. Therefore the maximum punishment that is WRP is found by increasing n to lower the continuation payoff until it is equal to the RHS of Eq. (16). We define this value as $n^{\max}$, which is implicitly given by

$$V^{\tau\min} \equiv \delta \frac{1-\delta^{n^{\max}}}{1-\delta} W^P + \frac{\delta^{n^{\max}+1}}{1-\delta} W^C = \frac{\delta}{1-\delta} W^N \tag{17}$$

To confirm that the lowest cooperative tariff that is WRP is identical to the one under infinite Nash reversion we can replace Eq. (17) in Eq. (15) to obtain

$$W^D + \frac{\delta}{1-\delta} W^N \leq \frac{1}{1-\delta} W^C \tag{18}$$

The lowest self-enforcing tariff under infinite Nash reversion or WRP is implicitly defined when Eq. (18) holds with equality. This serves as a convenient benchmark against which alternative enforcement mechanisms can be compared. Since we are interested in cases where the threat of tariff retaliation is insufficient to enforce the global optimum, we consider discount factors δ low enough that tariff retaliation alone cannot sustain τ^G. In the symmetric case above this requires $\delta<\delta_g$, where δ_g is defined when Eq. (18) holds with equality at $\tau=\tau^*=\tau^G$.

3.2. Fines and tariff retaliation

We now consider the effect of switching from tariff retaliation to a monetary fine to punish deviations from a trade agreement. One key difference between these options is that the fine must be voluntarily paid by the deviating country whereas retaliatory tariffs are imposed by the other country. This means that if the country that deviates decides *not* to pay the fine, the only thing the other country can ultimately do is to revert to non-cooperation in tariffs, which in our model is equivalent to leaving the agreement altogether. Given this, the most cooperative tariff that can be achieved with fines is determined as follows.

After a deviation, a country must pay a fine equal to f units of the numeraire, which the government collects via a lump-sum tax. Cooperation in tariffs resumes the same period the fine is paid. It is reasonable to suppose that if the fine is paid, the transfer occurs in a single period. Thus we set $n=1$ without loss of generality since we can always alter the value of the fine, f, to mimic the effects of changes in n. The incentive constraint is then similar to the one we had previously, with the possible exception of the continuation payoff that is now V^f:

$$W^D + V^f \leq \frac{W^C}{1-\delta} \tag{19}$$

[14] Note that under W^P home sets τ^c and faces τ^{*N}, which is also the outcome that occurs if foreign were to deviate. Thus in our setup W^P corresponds exactly to the "sucker" payoff and W^{*P} to foreign's deviation payoff that are more commonly used in defining these inequalities. We thank an anonymous referee for prompting us to include these inequalities explicitly.

[15] Farrell and Maskin (1989) and Van Damme (1989) show that using the following punishment as part of the strategy is WRP: the party that deviates accepts to be punished and during that period it plays cooperatively. In this case clearly $W^P<W^N$. The WRP concept requires the strategy not to be Pareto dominated (i.e. $W^{*P}>W^{*C}$) so that cooperation does not Pareto dominate the punishment phase for the injured party. When this is the case, the foreign country is better off when home is punished than under cooperation but home is worse off.

The continuation payoff V^f is now the cost of the fine, $-\delta f$, plus the stream of cooperative payoffs

$$V^f \equiv -\delta f + \frac{\delta}{1-\delta} W^C \tag{20}$$

If we ignore the renegotiation constraint, there exists a sufficiently large f that delivers the global optimum, τ^G. However, we must ensure that the punishment payoff is WRP. Also, since in the absence of tariff retaliation a deviating country has no incentive to pay the fine, there must be a punishment for not doing so. In the context of our model, the only punishment that the other country can impose is to increase its tariff. Therefore the WRP constraint is defined with respect to the payoff under infinite Nash reversion and it requires that

$$V^f \geq \frac{\delta}{1-\delta} W^N \tag{21}$$

Thus WRP requires the maximum fine, $f^{\max}$, and the resulting minimum payoff that the deviating country can be held to, $V^{f\min}$, to be

$$V^{f\min} \equiv -\delta f^{\max} + \frac{\delta}{1-\delta} W^C = \frac{\delta}{1-\delta} W^N \tag{22}$$

which implies that the maximum fine that is WRP is the present discounted value of cooperation in the trade agreement, i.e.

$$f^{\max} = (W^C - W^N)/(1-\delta) \tag{23}$$

By substituting $V^f = V^{f\min}$ in Eq. (19) we can obtain the lowest cooperative tariff that is WRP when fines are enforced by the threat of abandoning the agreement altogether. This gives

$$W^D + \frac{\delta}{1-\delta} W^N \leq \frac{W^C}{1-\delta} \tag{24}$$

which is identical to the constraint under tariff retaliation in (18). We summarize this result in the following proposition.

Proposition 1. *(Enforcement equivalence of tariffs and fines): In a trade agreement between two symmetric countries, the most cooperative tariff that can be enforced by tariff retaliation is equal to the tariff that can be enforced with WRP fines.*

The basic intuition behind this result becomes clear after we note two points. First, since the fine must be paid by the violating country it must find it in its best interest to do so. Therefore, the fine itself needs to be enforced. In the absence of additional instruments this enforcement must rely on the threat of infinite tariff retaliation, i.e. the breakdown of the trade agreement. Second, the maximum punishment that is WRP is the payoff that the deviating country would get if it abandoned the agreement. This is true of the value of the fine paid and the cost imposed by temporary tariff retaliation. Thus both alternatives yield the same cooperative tariff.

There is one important corollary of Proposition 1. Since the most cooperative tariff is identical under these two mechanisms, the payoffs are also exactly the same. This is because thus far we have not introduced any deviations in equilibrium and, along the equilibrium path, countries always obtain the cooperative payoff W^C (that depends only on the level of the cooperative tariff). In Section 3.4 we show that if deviations do occur, the payoffs under the two mechanisms are different. Before doing so, we analyze whether an alternative enforcement mechanism can improve cooperation relative to the ones analyzed above.

3.3. Exchanging bonds

Fines are not the only financial enforcement mechanism. An interesting alternative to consider is the use of bonds that countries forfeit if they violate a trade agreement. This type of scheme has actually been proposed in the context of trade agreements so we now consider how effective it would be in improving tariff cooperation.[16]

Suppose that at the beginning of every period each country posts a bond of value b (measured in terms of the numeraire good) that it forfeits in case it commits a violation. Assume also that countries observe this and cooperate only if such a bond is posted by both of them. Naturally, once bonds are posted, countries are free to decide whether to cooperate on tariffs or not. If either country does not post a bond, both play Nash in tariffs forever (we later discuss the case where the punishment phase is finite). We assume there is no third party that can hold the bonds so that governments must post them with each other. If at the end of a period both countries have cooperated then they "return" their bonds to each other, otherwise the country that deviated loses its bond. In the

[16] In its bilateral trade agreement with the US, Chile proposed a scheme where each member would fund an escrow account and forfeit some of it if it violated the agreement ("Chile Looks for Monetary Sanctions as Enforcement Mechanism", INSIDE U.S. TRADE 13, 11/11/2002). This effectively amounts to posting a bond with a third party and we discuss this possibility in our working paper. Here we focus on the exchange of bonds, i.e. the case when no outside enforcement institution is available to hold bonds or is too costly to use.

exposition we abstract from the possibility of countries keeping the foreign bond without ever posting their own, since as we discuss at the end of the section and show in the appendix this does not change the key results.

Under infinite Nash reversion, if a country deviates in tariffs it will be optimal for it not to return the other country's bond. In this case, the equilibrium tariff remains unchanged relative to the case of no bonds. To see this, note that the incentive constraint is given by:

$$\left(W^D + b^* - b\right) + \frac{\delta}{1-\delta}W^N \leq \frac{W^C}{1-\delta} \tag{25}$$

where the payoff under Nash reversion is the same as before since under no cooperation both countries simply set their tariffs at τ^N and bonds are irrelevant. The functional form of the cooperation payoff is also unchanged because we assume that if countries cooperate they receive their bond and consume it at the end of the period (and we assume no discounting within the period). The key difference is the deviation payoff, which is now given by the original value, W^D, net of the value of the bond that is lost, $-b$ and the one not returned, b^*. However, if, as we expect due to symmetry and stationarity, the optimal bond is the same for both countries (i.e. $b^* = b$), the constraint in Eq. (25) is identical to the one in Eq. (18) and thus the resulting cooperative tariff is equal to that under infinite Nash reversion.

Now consider the case where the punishment phase is finite. Countries start cooperating by initially posting a bond b with each other. If a country deviates from the cooperative tariff, it loses its bond. For cooperation to resume, the deviating country must return the present discounted value of the bond of the injured country, b^*/δ. If it does so in the period after the deviation occurs, tariffs return to the cooperative level. The incentive constraint for cooperation can be written as:

$$W^D + b^* - b + V^b \leq \frac{W^C}{1-\delta} \tag{26}$$

We can again write the minimum continuation payoff that is WRP:

$$V^{b\min} \equiv -\frac{\delta b^{*\max}}{\delta} + \frac{\delta W^C}{1-\delta} = \frac{\delta}{1-\delta}W^N$$

which implies a maximum bond of

$$b^{*\max} = b^{\max} = \delta\frac{W^C - W^N}{1-\delta} \tag{27}$$

Replacing this in Eq. (26) we obtain an IC for the lowest cooperative tariff under bonds that is exactly the same as in Eq. (25), which we already noted yields the same tariff as infinite Nash reversion. Therefore we have the following proposition:

Proposition 2. *(Enforcement under tariffs versus exchanged bonds): In a trade agreement between two symmetric countries, the most cooperative tariff that can be enforced by tariff retaliation is equal to the tariff enforced by WRP bonds exchanged between them.*

Our formulation regarding the use of bonds deserves further discussion. We assume that if either country does not post a bond, both play Nash in tariffs. What if one country receives a bond and decides not to post any in return so that the agreement breaks down and both countries revert to their Nash tariffs? This possibility does not change the result in the last proposition. In the appendix we provide the additional incentive constraint arising from deviation in bonds and show that it allows for bonds up to $b^{IC} = (W^C - W^N)/(1-\delta)$ to be sustained. As a result this IC does not bind for bonds of lower value such as $b^{\max}$ in Eq. (27).

Alternatively we could have allowed countries the *option* of exchanging bonds without any penalty if they did not do so. Note, however, that while our formulation may not be necessary to obtain Proposition 2, this result is if anything stronger under our approach — i.e. we have shown that even if we "coerce" countries to use bonds the outcome is no better than if tariffs alone are used. Note that we "coerce" countries to use bonds via the threat of Nash reversion in tariffs so this is achieved as an *equilibrium* outcome and in a way that is consistent with the rest of our model. Absence such a tariff threat there would effectively be no punishment for a country that failed to provide (or return) a bond after receiving one. Thus, the alternative specification where countries are simply given the option of posting bonds could not help enforce more cooperation on tariffs than the one we use.

3.4. Compensation under alternative mechanisms

As we note in the Introduction, WTO dispute settlement remedies have both an enforcement and a compensation role. Thus far we have focused only on the enforcement aspect and shown that enforcement cannot be improved by replacing the current system with fines or bonds alone. When the most cooperative tariff under that alternative mechanism is identical so is the payoff to governments. The reason is that our model thus far assumes perfect foresight and no shocks, so that no violations occur in equilibrium — i.e. no disputes actually arise. One consequence of this is that the potential inefficiency of tariffs relative to financial compensation in the event of a trade dispute cannot be addressed. We now extend our model to address this issue and show that if a dispute is triggered by a violation, fines can generate *higher compensation* for the injured country at the same cost to the violator even if the cooperative tariff enforced is identical. For ease of exposition we illustrate this result for the punishments considered thus far but then prove it also holds for the less severe punishments often contemplated by the DSU.

In what follows, we illustrate our point in the simplest possible way. We assume governments believe the set of parameters are fixed and base their policies on those fixed values, e.g. a certain level of political pressure, λ in Eq. (2). We then consider the impact of a shock that is unanticipated by the government and perfectly observable by all. If this shock implies higher political pressure, i.e. $\lambda^H > \lambda$, then it generates an incentive for a higher tariff than the cooperative level previously set. Moreover, we assume the shock is temporary, so in the following period λ returns to the original level and thus the government continues to believe that will be the relevant value to base future policies on. Such a shock and the resulting tariff increase would likely trigger a dispute and a ruling against the country because tariffs are bound at a maximum numerical value in the WTO and not on a contingent set of parameters.[17]

The question we ask is the following: Given that a country deviates from the agreement due to an unanticipated shock, under which mechanism is the continuation payoff higher? We focus on fines supported by tariffs so as to yield the same enforcement outcome as temporary tariff retaliation. Since we focus on the most cooperative tariff, the minimum payoff that the deviating country can be held to is the discounted Nash payoff, $W^N\delta/(1-\delta)$. The question then is whether this alternative yields a higher compensation for the *injured country*. The continuation payoff for the injured country under temporary tariff retaliation when the most cooperative WRP is implemented is

$$V^{*\tau} \equiv \delta W^{*P}\frac{1-\delta^{n^{\max}}}{1-\delta} + \frac{\delta^{n^{\max}+1}}{1-\delta}W^{*C} \tag{28}$$

where we recall that the payoff for the injured country under the punishment phase $W^{*P}(\tau^c, \tau^{*N})$ exceeds $W^{*C}(\tau^c, \tau^{*c})$ because the punishment involves the injured setting its optimal tariff $\tau^* = \tau^N$ and the other country setting its cooperative tariff, τ^c.

Under a fine supported by infinite Nash tariff reversion the payoff analogous to (28) is

$$V^{*f} \equiv \delta f^{\max} + \frac{\delta}{1-\delta}W^{*C} \tag{29}$$

This payoff reflects the received fine and the immediate resumption of cooperation with a payoff W^{*C} per period, identical to the one in Eq. (28) since we derived that both sustain the same cooperative tariff. Therefore the compensation under fines is higher than under tariff retaliation if and only if the expression in Eq. (29) exceeds Eq. (28). This yields the following condition for the fine:

$$f^{\max} > \frac{1-\delta^{n^{\max}}}{1-\delta}\left(W^{*P} - W^{*C}\right) \tag{30}$$

With this condition we are ready to compare the compensation properties of each mechanism and rank them. Since we consider unanticipated shocks we think that a reasonable ranking of the two can be established by comparing their payoffs under cooperation and their continuation payoffs if a shock does occur. Denoting the equilibrium WRP cooperative levels of tariffs under fines and tariff retaliation by τ^{Cf} and $\tau^{C\tau}$ we use the following definition. *A trade agreement enforced by fines generates a Pareto improvement relative to one using tariffs if the following inequalities hold: (i)* $W^C(\tau^{Cf}) \geq W^C(\tau^{C\tau})$; *(ii)* $W^{*C}(\tau^{Cf}) \geq W^{*C}(\tau^{C\tau})$; *(iii)* $V^f \geq V^\tau$; *and (iv)* $V^{*f} \geq V^{*\tau}$ *with at least one holding strictly.* We can now state the following.

Proposition 3. *(Compensation properties and ranking of tariffs versus fines): (a) In the presence of unanticipated shocks, e.g. to the political economy parameter* λ*, a trade agreement between two symmetric countries that is enforced by WRP fines supported by tariffs yields higher compensation for the injured country* ($V^{*f} > V^{*\tau}$) *and generates a Pareto improvement relative to a similar agreement enforced by tariff retaliation alone. (b) The results in (a) are independent of restrictions on the severity of the punishment (i.e. they hold for* $n < n^{\max}$ *or* $f < f^{\max}$*) whenever the tariff retaliation and fine mechanisms enforce the same cooperative tariff.*

The first part of the proposition says that the continuation payoff for the injured country after a shock is higher under fines, i.e. the inequality in Eq. (30) always holds. We show this in the appendix, below we provide the intuition. The Pareto improvement is then a corollary of the higher continuation payoff and of Proposition 1. In Proposition 1 we show that fines and tariffs enforce the same cooperative tariff so $W^C(\tau^{Cf}) = W^C(\tau^{C\tau})$ for home and similarly for foreign due to symmetry. Moreover, we also showed that the WRP continuation payoff that a country is held to in equilibrium is the same under the two alternatives, $V^f = V^\tau$. So fines generate a Pareto improvement. The last part of the proposition shows the same result holds even if punishments are less severe provided we consider punishments that enforce similar tariffs.

To see why inequality (30) always holds, note that when the WRP constraint under fines binds then $f^{\max}$ is given by Eq. (23), which due to symmetry is also equal $(W^{*C} - W^{*N})/(1-\delta)$. Using this and the definition of the payoffs we can rewrite Eq. (30) as

$$\frac{W^{*C} - W^{*N}}{1-\delta} > \frac{1-\delta^{n^{\max}}}{1-\delta}\left(W^*\left(\tau^c, \tau^{*N}\right) - W^*\left(\tau^c, \tau^{*c}\right)\right) \tag{31}$$

The value of the fine received by the injured country (i.e. the left hand side) is equal to the present discounted value of cooperation in the trade agreement relative to infinite Nash reversion. This value needs to exceed any temporary gains that the injured country

[17] A potential reason for this in the WTO is the difficulty of writing an agreement that is conditional on political economy parameters that are likely to be hard to observe by other countries.

can obtain by raising its tariff during the punishment phase of $n^{\max}$ periods. The latter gain is simply the terms-of-trade benefit that it obtains from using its Nash tariff relative to the cooperative one. By using the definition for $n^{\max}$ in Eq. (17) and simplifying we can show this condition always holds. The underlying reason is that while tariffs can also transfer income by changing the terms-of-trade, they lead to a deadweight loss whereas fines do not.

The objective in this section is to determine if fines have an advantage over tariff retaliation when both enforce the same degree of tariff cooperation. In this context, considering the punishment that leads to the most cooperative tariffs seems a natural benchmark since Proposition 1 shows that under this type of punishment both tariff retaliation and fines deliver identical enforcement. However, since the WTO's DSU can restrict punishment to be less severe, it is worth asking how such a restriction affects our results regarding compensation. The last part of Proposition 3 shows that our results hold for all punishments that yield the same cooperative tariffs under fines and tariff retaliation.

Consider, for example, the case when the tariff punishment period is $n^p \in [1, n^{\max}]$ so that it may be less severe than before and can be chosen to match a range of alternative payoffs for either the violating country or the injured one (e.g. n^p can be chosen to allow the injured country to impose higher tariffs for a sufficient period as to "withdraw substantially equivalent concessions"). To hold constant the degree of enforcement across the two mechanisms and to focus on compensation, consider a fine equal to f^p, which delivers the same cooperative tariff as tariff retaliation when $n = n^p$. This fine is easily found by requiring the continuation payoffs for a country that deviates to be identical under the alternative mechanisms, i.e. $V^{\tau}(n^p) = V^f(f^p)$. It is then simple to show that compensation for the injured country is higher under fines relative to tariff retaliation if and only if a condition exactly analogous to Eq. (30) holds. The only difference being that it is now evaluated at n^p (and f^p), which can be restricted to fall below the maximum value $n^{\max}$ (and $f^{\max}$). Such a condition holds for exactly the same reasons as those described above.

Proposition 3 captures an important insight about the role of fines as a compensation mechanism. We chose the simplest setup to show it, i.e. one where the deviation is caused by a shock to λ that is unanticipated by the government. This means that the government places a zero probability on such a shock and is therefore indifferent between fines and tariffs *ex-ante*. However, this does *not* mean that such a shock has a zero probability of actually occurring, it only means that the government beliefs about λ may be proved wrong at any given point in time and when that occurs fines do generate a Pareto improvement *ex-post*. However, if governments are frequently proved wrong they may learn to anticipate some shocks and we now discuss this possibility.

3.5. *Tariffs versus fines under anticipated shocks*

Thus far we have shown that fines supported by tariff retaliation do not yield more cooperation than tariff retaliation alone, but fines yield a Pareto improvement in the presence of unanticipated shocks since they are more efficient in compensating the injured party. However, some shocks are anticipated and this raises two questions. First, do our results have any implications for the scenario where shocks are anticipated by governments? Second, are our results robust to changes in model structure that allow it to directly tackle anticipated shocks? We now argue that the answer to both of these questions is a qualified yes.

The compensation result in Proposition 3 is also relevant when political economy shocks are anticipated provided there are contracting costs. To see this suppose that the government knows the true distribution of λ. Let that distribution take $N+1$ possible values, one being λ_p, with probability p, and the remaining N alternative values each having identical probability $(1-p)/N$. Then, if contracting costs are high and increasing in the number of states of nature and if p is sufficiently high, then the governments may optimally choose a simple agreement based on the most likely value, λ_p. In sum, although our compensation result was derived under unanticipated shocks, we think that its insight may also operate under more realistic settings where shocks are anticipated and there are contracting costs. Rather than modeling these new features, which deserve a paper of its own, we now discuss an extension of the model that directly tackles anticipated shocks.

To clearly contrast our results with those in the literature we now describe the impact of fines in the context of a closely related model that considers anticipated shocks; we provide the details in an Appendix available on request. Bagwell and Staiger (2005) (henceforth BS) show that certain types of financial transfers can enhance tariff cooperation by allowing a country with high political pressure to raise its tariff while simultaneously compensating its trading partner. In their model, governments experience anticipated political shocks to λ that create incentives for raising tariffs. They show that when countries can set a tariff-transfer combination in each period, they are able to implement fully efficient tariffs. Their formulation of transfers as an integral part of tariff-setting is conceptually quite different from ours in that we model fines as a retaliation or ex-post compensation. Interestingly, these two alternative formulations of financial compensation require different rules and instruments to be available in trade agreements and, more importantly, lead to rather different outcomes. Indeed, when we integrate our type of retaliatory fines into the setup of BS we find that the use of such fines yields *no* more tariff cooperation than the use of tariff retaliation alone.

Following BS, suppose that each government's political economy parameter, λ, is private information and is identically and independently distributed over time. For simplicity, as in Bagwell (2007), assume that λ equals λ_H with probability π_H and λ_L with probability $\pi_L \equiv 1-\pi_H$ where $\lambda_H > \lambda_L$. One can then calculate Nash tariff values that depend on λ, $\tau^N(\lambda)$. One difference is that now strong tariff bindings (i.e. fixed levels of the cooperative tariff) are dominated by weak bindings, i.e. setting a maximum tariff (see BS). Intuitively, a weak binding helps address the terms-of-trade externality while *also* providing governments the flexibility to change tariffs to respond to political pressure (up to some maximum). Thus we follow their paper and focus on a weak tariff binding. This means that if a government's Nash tariff falls below the weak binding, denoted by τ^W, it utilizes the Nash value, $\tau^N(\lambda)$, and otherwise it applies the agreed binding.

Now consider a repeated game setting where countries cooperate on the *optimal* weak binding. To examine the alternative enforcement mechanisms we need to define the payoffs under deviation. Bagwell (2007) shows that countries only have an incentive to deviate when $\lambda=\lambda_H$ since the optimal weak binding level turns out to be higher than a country's Nash tariff when $\lambda=\lambda_L$. That payoff is given by

$$W\left(\tau^N(\lambda_H), \tau^{*c}(\lambda, \tau_o^W), \lambda = \lambda_H\right) \tag{32}$$

In the benchmark case when countries use infinite Nash reversion and no transfers, Bagwell (2007) shows there is a discount factor $\delta \equiv \delta^W < 1$ such that the IC below is satisfied with equality at the global cooperative weak binding, $\tau^c(\lambda, \tau_o^w)$.

$$W\left(\tau^N(\lambda_H), \tau^{*c}(\lambda, \tau_o^W), \lambda = \lambda_H\right) + \frac{\delta E_{\lambda,\lambda^*} W\left(\tau^N(\lambda), \tau^{*N}\left(\lambda^*\right), \lambda\right)}{1-\delta} \leq \frac{E_{\lambda,\lambda^*} W\left(\tau^c(\lambda, \tau_o^W), \tau^{*c}\left(\lambda^*, \tau_o^W\right), \lambda\right)}{1-\delta} \tag{33}$$

The discounted Nash payoff (the second term on the LHS) and the cooperation payoff (the term on the RHS) correctly capture the expectation over the political economy parameters.

Instead of facing infinite Nash reversion, we assume that countries that deviate face n periods of punishment. Similarly to what we have seen in Sections 3.1 and 3.2, this implies that the discounted Nash payoff in Eq. (33) should be replaced by a continuation payoff, denoted by $E_{\lambda\lambda^*}V^\tau$ in the case of tariff retaliation and $E_{\lambda\lambda^*}V^f$ in the case of fines. The main difference relative to our earlier definition of these continuation payoffs is that we must now take expected values over any terms that depend on λ.[18]

In equilibrium it must still be the case that the minimum expected continuation payoff that can be imposed on a country that deviates is the expected discounted Nash payoff (otherwise the country would be better off by simply abandoning the agreement). This ensures that the IC under WRP tariffs or fines would be identical to Eq. (33) and so, when $\delta=\delta^W$, those IC hold with equality at $\tau^c(\lambda, \tau_o^w)$, i.e. either enforcement mechanism leads to the exact same cooperative tariff even with anticipated shocks.

To contrast our result with the one in BS note that at δ^W countries set their optimal cooperative tariffs when $\lambda=\lambda^H$ but still set their Nash tariffs along the equilibrium path when $\lambda=\lambda_L$. The latter are jointly inefficient but, in the absence of other instruments being used along the equilibrium path, this inefficiency is a necessary cost to pay to enforce a weak binding where $\tau_o^w > \tau^N(\lambda_L)$.[19] Since in our setup fines are used only when the weak binding is broken they do not affect the level of the applied tariff when $\lambda=\lambda_L$ (so that inefficiency remains). By contrast, BS allow governments to make transfers to each other at the time that they apply their individual tariffs and show that these transfers can help sustain the efficient tariffs even if $\lambda=\lambda_L$.

Intuitively, the existence of the transfer in BS expands the number of available instruments that can be used to sustain cooperation and thus the set of feasible payoffs (something that does not happen with the retaliatory fines considered by us) and this allows for more tariff cooperation. Furthermore, in BS if a country violates the tariff binding it reverts to its Nash tariff without needing to pay any fine or transfer. By contrast, in our model, a fine is stipulated to be paid *only* when a country breaks the tariff binding, i.e. the fine is used as a punishment for sustaining the cooperative equilibrium. As a result, the enforcement of the fine itself becomes a central issue in our model. The fact that different types of "financial instruments" lead to different levels of tariff cooperation highlights the importance of carefully modelling each of their role in international trade agreements.

4. Conclusion

The opinion that the WTO's dispute settlement system needs improvement is widespread. In particular, there is much concern about the use of tariff retaliation as the sole mechanism for dealing with member countries that fail to comply with a WTO ruling against them. In this paper, we analyze alternative mechanisms based on financial compensation and argue that one of the major problems in their implementation is enforcement.

Ultimately, the enforcement of monetary fines may require some type of retaliatory instrument and in that case, fines fail to yield any more cooperation than tariffs. Thus, despite their problems, a desirable aspect of retaliatory tariffs is that they are controlled by injured parties and can be used in the event a violating country fails to comply with the ruling of a WTO panel. We also analyze whether bonds can improve cooperation relative to tariff retaliation and show they cannot do so when exchanged between symmetric countries. An interesting question to address in future research is how this result changes with asymmetric countries.[20]

We also showed that fines have an advantage over tariff retaliation as a primary remedy: if a violation does occur, the payoff to an injured country is higher under fines even though the cost of the penalty for a violating country is unchanged. The intuition is simple: tariffs are an inefficient form of compensation because the welfare gain they generate for an injured country with market power is always less than the welfare cost for the country facing the tariff punishment. We established this ex-post efficiency of

[18] The other difference is that now they are defined over the weak binding tariffs.

[19] Since $\tau^G(\lambda_H) > \tau^N(\lambda_L)$ and $T^G(\lambda_L)=0$, the low type country has no incentive to cheat – it is free to use its optimal Nash tariff and has to pay no transfer for doing so. Thus cooperation hinges on the high type country.

[20] Posting bonds with a third party may improve cooperation between symmetric countries. As we discuss in our working paper if bonds are deposited in an escrow fund (i.e. with a third party), tariff retaliation is no longer necessary since the bond posted by the violating country can be used to compensate the injured country. As we noted earlier, such an escrow scheme was proposed by Chile in its bilateral trade agreement with the US. Future research should develop a model that fully accounts for the role of a third party in this context.

fines in the case of unanticipated shocks and argued it could be extended to more realistic cases. Moreover, we discussed how different types of financial compensation leads to different outcomes under private information, which illustrates the importance of carefully modelling alternative instruments.

Future research should build on these insights to determine whether the WTO's dispute system should move to financial compensation as the primary remedy. In our view, several aspects related to the ex-ante efficiency of tariffs as an enforcement mechanism deserve to be modelled carefully in the future. First, the level of compensation under fines deserves attention. If fines were required to deliver the exact same level of compensation to the injured country as it would obtain under tariff retaliation, then equilibrium tariffs would actually be higher under fines. The logic is similar to Proposition 3 but now it applies to the violating country: a given amount of compensation received is less costly to the violating country if it can pay it with a fine instead of having to face higher tariffs on its exports during the punishment period. Second, the enforcement advantage of tariff retaliation would be even stronger if injured countries can select the goods on which they retaliate, as observed in recent cases where retaliating parties chose products concentrated in swing states. By targeting states with greater political influence, tariffs may be more effective in generating pressure through exporters for the violating government to comply with the WTO's ruling. As Lawrence (2003) notes, parties often retaliate in a fashion that maximizes incentives for compliance. Third, this advantage of tariffs relative to fines can be further reinforced when fines are raised via general taxation because then the punishment for violating the trade agreement is dispersed and can go unnoticed. Future research on the optimal design of enforcement mechanisms should extend our analysis to incorporate these ex-ante efficiency arguments of tariffs relative to fines.

Appendix A. Proofs

A.1. Proposition 2 (robustness to bond deviation)

The basic proposition is proved in the text but here we prove the claim in the text that its result is robust to deviations in bonds. More specifically, we show that deviations in bonds that lead to a breakdown of the agreement, i.e. infinite reversion to Nash tariffs, do not affect the result in Proposition 2. The additional IC if a country keeps the foreign bond, b^*, and does not post its own, reflects the fact that both immediately go to Nash in tariffs, i.e.

$$\left(W^N + b^*\right) + \frac{\delta}{1-\delta}W^N \leq \frac{W^C}{1-\delta}$$

this implies that the maximum bond that satisfies this IC is equal to

$$b^{*IC} = \frac{W^C - W^N}{1-\delta}$$

It is then immediate to see that the maximum bond that is WRP in Eq. (27) is lower than b^{*IC} and thus it also satisfies the "bond" IC above, that is

$$b^{*\max} = \delta\frac{W^C - W^N}{1-\delta} \leq b^{*IC} = \frac{W^C - W^N}{1-\delta}$$

So the extra IC for deviating in bonds alone does not bind under the WRP case and the proposition in the text remains unchanged. □

We can also add that the result under infinite reversion described earlier in that section holds, with a slight qualification requiring that the maximum bond countries would ever choose would be b^{*IC}. Any higher (symmetric) bonds do not affect the original IC in Eq. (25) but increase the incentive to deviate in bonds and would thus require a higher cooperative tariff in equilibrium for the bond IC to be satisfied, thus bonds above b^{*IC} would actually lead to less cooperation in tariffs.

A.2. Proposition 3: Higher compensation: $V^{*f}(f) > V^{*\tau}(n)$

Proposition 1 shows that we obtain $\tau^{Cf}(f = f^{\max}) = \tau^{C\tau}(n = n^{\max})$. Consider now some arbitrary $n^p \in [1, n^{\max}]$ and a corresponding fine f^p defined by $V^f(f^p) = V^\tau(n^p)$, as given in Eqs. (14) and (20). These punishments also imply the equilibrium cooperative tariff is identical across enforcement mechanisms, i.e. $\tau^{Cf}(f = f^p) = \tau^{C\tau}(n = n^p)$, as is clear from the constraints in Eqs. (15) and (19). When $n^p = n^{\max}$ we have $f = f^{\max}$ since $V^f(f^{\max}) = \frac{\delta}{1-\delta}W^N = V^\tau(n^{\max})$, so $n^p = n^{\max}$ is a special case and we prove the general result for n^p. For a given n^p we obtain the following f^p by employing the definitions in Eqs. (14) and (20) and $\tau^{Cf}(f = f^p) = \tau^{C\tau}(n = n^p)$

$$V^\tau(n^p) = V^f(f^p)$$
$$f^p = \frac{1-\delta^{n^p}}{1-\delta}(W^C - W^P)$$

The payoffs $V^{*\tau}(n)$ and $V^{*f}(f)$ are defined in Eqs. (28) and (29) when $f=f^{\max}$ and $n=n^{\max}$. The definition is the same at $f=f^P$ and $n=n^P$ and so $V^{*f}(f^P)>V^{*\tau}(n^P)$ iff

$$\delta f^P+\frac{\delta}{1-\delta}W^{*C}\left(\tau^{Cf}\right)>\delta W^{*P}\left(\tau^{C\tau},\tau^{*N}\right)\frac{1-\delta^{n^P}}{1-\delta}+\frac{\delta^{n^P+1}}{1-\delta}W^{*C}\left(\tau^{C\tau}\right)$$

Since $\tau^{Cf}(f=f^P)=\tau^{C\tau}(n=n^P)$ we simplify this to obtain the expression in (30) in the text and now show it must hold for the general case.

$$f^P>\frac{1-\delta^{n^P}}{1-\delta}\left(W^{*P}-W^{*C}\right)\Leftrightarrow W^C-W^P>W^{*P}-W^{*C}$$

where the second line uses the value of f^P found above. The last line can be re-arranged to obtain inequality (13). As we describe in the text this holds because the difference between the cooperative and Nash tariffs simply reflects a terms-of-trade motive that involves a deadweight loss so home's cost from being punished, W^C-W^P, always exceeds foreign's terms-of-trade gain, $W^{*P}-W^C$.

Pareto improvement. Our definition of Pareto improvement in the text is satisfied if (*i*) $W^C(\tau^{Cf})=W^C(\tau^{C\tau})$; (*ii*) $W^{*C}(\tau^{Cf})=W^{*C}(\tau^{C\tau})$; (*iii*) $V^f=V^\tau$; and (iv) $V^{*f}>V^{*\tau}$. Since the last inequality was just shown we need only show the first three equalities. From Proposition 1 we know that $\tau^{Cf}=\tau^{C\tau}$ for $n^{\max}$ and $f^{\max}$. Therefore $W^C(\tau^{Cf})=W^C(\tau^{C\tau})$. Given symmetry we also have $W^{*C}(\tau^{Cf})=W^{*C}(\tau^{C\tau})$. As we show in Section 3.1, Eq. (17), $V^\tau=V^{\tau\min}=\frac{\delta}{1-\delta}W^N$. In Section 3.2, Eq. (22) shows that V^f is also equal to that value. Thus, under the most cooperative tariff we have $V^\tau=V^f$. By definition of n^P and f^P we have $V^\tau(n^P)=V^f(f^P)$ and as shown above this implies $\tau^{Cf}(f=f^P)=\tau^{C\tau}(n=n^P)$ so conditions (*i*); (*ii*) and (*iii*) also hold for the general case. □

References

Bagwell, K., 2007. Self-Enforcing Trade Agreements and Private Information. Mimeo.
Bagwell, K., Staiger, R., 1990. A theory of managed trade. American Economic Review 80, 779–795.
Bagwell, K., Staiger, R., 1999. An economic theory of GATT. American Economic Review 89 (1), 215–248.
Bagwell, K., Staiger, R., 2005. Enforcement, private political pressure, and the GATT/WTO Escape Clause. Journal of Legal Studies 34 (2), 471–513.
Bagwell, K., Staiger, R., 2006. What do trade negotiators negotiate about? Empirical Evidence From the World Trade Organization, NBER Working Paper Series No. 12727. National Bureau of Economic Research, Cambridge, MA.
Bagwell, K., Mavroidis, P., Staiger, R., 2007. Auctioning countermeasures in the WTO. Journal of International Economics 73 (2), 309–332.
Broda, C., N. Limão, Weinstein, D., in press. Optimal tariffs and market power: the evidence. American Economic Review.
Bronckers, M., Van Den Broek, N., 2005. Financial compensation in the WTO: improving the remedies of WTO dispute settlement. Journal of International Economic Law 8, 101–126.
Dam, K.W., 1970. The GATT Law and International Economic Organization. The University of Chicago Press, Chicago.
Dixit, A., 1987. Strategic aspects of trade policy. In: Bewley, T. (Ed.), Advances in Economic Theory. Cambridge University Press, pp. 329–362.
Ethier, W.J., 2003. Intellectual Property Rights and Dispute Settlement in the World Trade Organization. Mimeo.
Farrell, J., Maskin, E., 1989. Renegotiation in repeated games. Games and Economic Behavior 1 (4), 327–360.
Grossman, G., Helpman, E., 1994. Protection for sale. American Economic Review 84 (4), 833–850.
Hoekman, B.M., Kostecki, M., 2001. The Political Economy of the World Trading System. Oxford University Press, New York, NY.
Hoekman, B., Saggi, K., 2007. Tariff bindings and bilateral cooperation on export cartels. Journal of Development Economics 83, 141–156.
Hudec, R., 2002. The adequacy of WTO dispute settlement remedies: a developing country perspective. In: Mattoo, Aaditya, Hoekman, Bernard, English, Philip (Eds.), Development, Trade, and the WTO: A Handbook. The World Bank, Washington, D.C.
Klimenko, M., Ramey, G., Watson, J., 2008. Recurrent trade agreements and the value of external enforcement. Journal of International Economics 74 (2), 475–499.
Lawrence, R., 2003. Crimes and punishments? Retaliation under the WTO. Institute of International Economics, Washington, D.C.
Limão, N., 2007. Are preferential trade agreements with non-trade objectives a stumblingblock for multilateral liberalization? Review of Economic Studies 74 (3), 821–855.
Ludema, R., 2001. Optimal international trade agreements and dispute settlement procedures. European Journal of Political Economy 17, 355–376.
Maggi, G., 1999. The role of multilateral institutions in international trade cooperation. American Economic Review 89 (1), 190–214.
Park, J.-H., 2000. International trade agreements between countries of asymmetric size. Journal of International Economics 50, 473–495.
Shaffer, G., 2003. How to make the WTO dispute settlement system work for developing countries: some proactive developing country strategies. International Centre for Trade and Sustainable Development, Working Paper No. 5.
Staiger, R., 1995. In: Grossman, Gene, Rogoff, Kenneth (Eds.), International rules and institutions for trade policy. . Handbook of international economics, vol. 3. Elsevier, North-Holland, pp. 1495–1551.
Van Damme, E., 1989. Renegotiation-proof equilibria in repeated prisoners' dilemma. Journal of Economic Theory 47, 206–217.

Part IV
Policy Externalities Across Agreements: Multilateral vs. Preferential Liberalization

Chapter 13

Preferential Trade Agreements as Stumbling Blocks for Multilateral Trade Liberalization: Evidence for the United States

By NUNO LIMÃO*

Nearly all countries are currently part of preferential trade agreements (PTAs).[1] The importance of PTAs is difficult to overstate, and thus understanding their effects has become a central concern. During the late 1980s and early 1990s multilateral trade negotiations were stalled while the United States and the European Union successfully pursued PTAs. This triggered the question of whether PTAs promote or slow multilateral trade liberalization (MTL) or, as Jagdish Bhagwati (1991) puts it, whether PTAs are a "building block" or a "stumbling block" to MTL. After a decade of theoretical work on that question, no consensus has been reached and there is a surprising absence of empirical evidence on it. We use detailed data on U.S. tariffs to provide the first systematic evidence that the direct effect of U.S. PTAs was to generate a stumbling block to its own MTL.

PTAs can affect MTL through various channels. They can divert scarce negotiation resources, alter the number of negotiating parties and their bargaining power, and affect a country's optimal multilateral tariffs in all or a subset of goods. In Section I we discuss the theoretical literature. We argue that it has generated interesting insights but almost no econometrically testable predictions because of its focus on comparing aggregate MTL with and without PTAs. Since, at one point, we observe a country's MTL only when it either has PTAs or does not, it is difficult to construct a convincing counterfactual for estimation. To address this, we argue that if PTAs affect MTL, that effect is strongest on PTA goods, i.e., the subset of goods that a country *imports* under its PTAs, and thus we propose estimating the direct effect of the PTAs on a country's MTL by using non-PTA goods as the counterfactual for the outcome in the absence of PTAs. Briefly, in our model a country has an incentive to maintain higher *multilateral* tariffs on PTA products relative to *similar* products that it imports only from non-PTA partners. Moreover, the multilateral tariff on non-PTA goods post PTAs is equal to what it would have been in similar PTA goods prior to PTAs, which provides theoretical support for our counterfactual interpretation.

The prediction could be tested using a cross-section of tariffs at the product level. But, to ensure that we construct a good counterfactual, we must control for unobserved product characteristics. Thus, we use the time dimension as well and compare the changes in U.S. multilateral tariffs in PTA versus non-PTA goods between the Tokyo and Uruguay Rounds, with most of the U.S. PTAs having been implemented in between them.[2] By using tariff changes at the

* Department of Economics, University of Maryland, 4118 F Tydings Hall, 20742 MD, and Center for Economic Policy Research (e-mail: limao@wam.umd.edu). I thank the anonymous referees, Stephanie Aaronson, Kyle Bagwell, Richard Baldwin, Andrew Bernard, Piyush Chandra, Caroline Freund, Gordon Hanson, Bernard Hoekman, Jon Haveman, Pravin Krishna, Arvind Panagariya, Robert Staiger, Alan Winters, and seminar participants at Columbia University, the Empirical Investigations in International Trade Conference, the NBER Summer Institute 2003, Princeton University, the University of Pennsylvania, USITC, and the World Bank for comments and/or discussions. The usual disclaimer applies. I gratefully acknowledge Baybars Karacaovali for research assistance and the support of the University of Maryland General Research Board through the Summer Research Award. Part of this research was conducted while visiting the World Bank's Trade Research Group. I am grateful for their hospitality and financial support.

[1] From 1948 to 1994 there were 124 notifications to the WTO of distinct PTAs by its members. Since 1995 there have been at least an additional 130. The WTO estimates that 300 PTAs will be in force by 2005 (www.wto.org).

[2] The U.S. multilateral tariffs were largely constant between these rounds because they were bound by agreement. Changing them between rounds would have implied an additional cost to the United States: higher tariffs on its exports as other countries could retaliate since, according to Article XXIV, countries can't raise multilateral tariffs after

Originally Published in *The American Economic Review* 96(3), pp. 896–914.

product level, we can also control for *all* determinants of tariff changes that occur at the industry level. These industry characteristics—emphasized in various theoretical models—explain a good part of the cross-sectional industry variation of trade protection.[3] Thus, our ability to control for them is important in ensuring that the PTA and non-PTA goods that we compare are similar.

We find that a stumbling block effect is present. We estimate that the U.S. cuts in *multilateral* tariffs were smaller for products that it imported under its PTAs relative to similar products that it imported only from nonmembers. That is, the direct effect of the U.S. PTAs was to cause the most-favored-nation (MFN) tariffs for its PTA goods, which are nearly 90 percent of all goods in the sample, to remain higher than they would have been in the absence of those PTAs. The effect is stronger for goods that the United States imports from all its PTAs or goods that constitute relatively larger shares of a given PTA partner's exports to the United States. Moreover, the effect is robust to reverse causation, which can arise if the choice of goods that receive preferences depends on MFN tariff changes. We address the endogeneity by using several instruments—which we justify and test—such as transport costs and world price variables, as well as whether the product was exported by a PTA partner before the multilateral tariff changes.

By pursuing PTAs, the United States may have also changed the level of MTL of the countries it negotiated with in the last round, which in turn has an indirect additional effect on U.S. tariffs if there is reciprocity in multilateral trade negotiations. To control for this indirect effect, we must model tariff reciprocity empirically. This allows us to isolate the direct effect of the U.S. PTAs on its own MTL, i.e., the effect that is independent of other countries' MTL.[4] Reciprocity is a key concept in the GATT and forms the cornerstone of the main economic models of MTL (Kyle Bagwell and Robert W. Staiger, 1999a). Thus far, however, there is no systematic evidence that countries respond with larger tariff cuts when offered larger tariff reductions by their partners; so testing this is interesting in its own right. We test and find that partner countries' reciprocal tariff reductions are endogenous, and argue that the timing and mode of the last multilateral negotiations provide a good instrument. After instrumenting, we find reciprocity for U.S. products not subject to nontariff barriers (NTBs). We also argue that reciprocity may amplify the direct stumbling block effect of U.S. PTAs.[5]

Using the estimated effect of PTAs on tariff reductions, we quantify the impact on domestic U.S. prices and world prices. In the absence of PTAs, the changes in prices for PTA goods due to U.S. tariff changes would, by definition, be

PTAs. Moreover, given the timing of some of its PTAs in the early 1990s, the United States could simply wait and not reduce the multilateral tariffs on PTA goods by as much in the Uruguay Round (ongoing from 1986–1994) thus avoiding a penalty from retaliation.

[3] Daniel Trefler (1993); Pinelopi K. Goldberg and Giovanni Maggi (1999). Most studies are cross sectional; John H. Cheh (1974), Howard P. Marvel and Edward J. Ray (1983), and Robert E. Baldwin (1985) are exceptions, examining the determinants of U.S. tariff cuts at the industry level in previous trade rounds.

[4] There are opposing arguments for whether the U.S. PTAs made other countries more or less likely to liberalize in the Uruguay Round (UR). The objective of some proponents of PTAs in the United States was to use them to bring other trading partners to the table in the UR. However, others, such as the U.S. trade representative under Reagan (William E. Brock), viewed PTAs as a distinct alternative path to MTL and not necessarily as a tactic to force others to negotiate in the GATT. Whether the outcome corresponded to either of these objectives is unknowable because we did not observe the outcome in the absence of U.S. PTAs. We do know that previous rounds were completed in the absence of significant U.S. involvement in PTAs, so the probability of such an event was not zero. Given this, and the fact that nearly all theoretical work focuses on the effect of a country's PTAs on its own MTL, the best we can do is to control for the observed level of aggregate MTL of other countries and estimate the direct effect of U.S. PTAs on its own MTL net of that. We also provide bounds for the total stumbling block effect that incorporate the indirect effect and suggest that the direct effect we focus on is the dominant one.

[5] The only attempt we know of to measure reciprocity at all is that of J. Michael Finger et al. (2002). They calculate that in the UR the weighted tariff reductions concessions of several countries were not balanced by concessions they received. Since other trade instruments and nontrade issues were also negotiated, this finding is not surprising. Moreover, their finding does not preclude the product reciprocity that we estimate, which requires a positive correlation between tariff concessions exchanged by pairs of countries, but not necessarily a balance.

the same as for similar non-PTA goods. With PTAs, we estimate that the price effects for goods the United States imports under any of its PTAs were, on average, only 52 percent of those in similar non-PTA goods. Using our counterfactual interpretation, this implies that the price change for PTA goods could have been twice as high in the absence of the direct effect of these PTAs. If the good was imported from every PTA, the effect was even smaller—23 percent. Furthermore, we find a similar quantitative effect when we separate the PTA with Mexico and Canada (NAFTA) from all other PTAs; we also find that even individual agreements with small countries had a significant effect.

In the next section, we discuss the theoretical literature and the testable prediction. In Section II we present the empirical model. In Section III we estimate and quantify the importance of the direct stumbling block effect. We summarize the results and discuss some implications in the last section.

I. Theory and a Testable Prediction

One strand of the literature models the decision of a country signing a PTA as endogenous and studies how this affects the country's *own* binary decision to pursue free trade multilaterally. Philip I. Levy (1997) shows that the median voter may reject multilateral free trade after voting for a PTA, even though he would have accepted it if no PTA had been available. Gene M. Grossman and Elhanan Helpman (1995) show that when producers form lobbies, the PTAs most likely to arise are those with partners that have relatively higher costs of production, thus causing trade diversion. Pravin Krishna (1998) arrives at a similar conclusion in a different setup and argues that these PTAs can reduce the incentive for multilateral free trade. This occurs because the export rents they generate disappear when countries liberalize multilaterally, and so the producers that benefit from those rents oppose MTL. Other authors derive the equilibrium level of multilateral tariffs showing that they may be higher or lower in the presence of PTAs. For example, Bagwell and Staiger (1999b) show how, in a repeated game, PTAs are a stumbling block if countries are very patient, and are a building block otherwise. Given the inherent complexity in modeling PTAs, it is unsurprising that both outcomes are possible.[6]

The theoretical work has produced interesting insights but no consensus, thus increasing the need for empirical evidence. The problem is that the predictions of most of these theories are extremely difficult to test econometrically. The initial research that identifies MTL with free trade effectively focuses on whether a PTA changes the probability of a country participating in a multilateral round. This is a fine theoretical approach, but by itself it cannot answer if we expect that PTAs promote or slow down MTL because, given a round, the degree of liberalization may vary because of PTAs. Perhaps recognizing this last point, several authors focus instead on deriving directly the level of the multilateral tariff with and without PTAs. The difficulty with testing the latter (and the former) is that we never observe the counterfactual, e.g., if a country has PTAs during a particular round, it is impossible to observe how much liberalization it would have undertaken in the absence of those PTAs.

The ideal testable prediction would focus on a counterfactual that is observed and still allow us to infer the level of multilateral tariffs in a given product or set of products with and without PTAs. Our proposal to get as close as possible to this is to explore the cross-sectional variation of tariffs in a country. More specifically, we propose to use a theory that predicts that, after controlling for product characteristics, two products have the same multilateral tariff unless either is imported under a PTA. The tariff for the non-PTA good can then be used as the counterfactual for what the tariff would have been for a PTA good in the absence of PTAs. The estimated difference in tariffs between the two goods measures the impact of PTAs on the MTL of PTA goods.[7]

[6] There are other important contributions; for a survey, see L. Alan Winters (1999). A different strand started by Paul Krugman (1991) analyzes the welfare path for exogenously expanding trading blocs; Jeffrey Frankel et al. (1996) develop extensions of it.

[7] One could compare the aggregate MTL of a country in different multilateral rounds—one round where it had PTAs and the other without. But with so many other possible determinants of aggregate MTL, it would be hard to con-

Limão (2002) provides a fully specified model of the interaction of PTAs and MTL that is useful from an empirical perspective for two reasons. First, it delivers the type of testable prediction just described. Second, it provides a motive as to why even the PTAs with small countries (from a trade perspective) may cause a large country to change its multilateral tariffs. The latter feature is important because many of the U.S. PTA partners are small and other models would predict they have no effect on the U.S. MTL because such models are driven by the effects of the PTAs on trade volumes and prices, which are absent if the PTA partner is small.[8] The U.S. benefit from PTAs with small countries is derived from the cooperation it extracts in nontrade issues, which it "pays for" with trade preferences.[9] Below we argue that the basic mechanism generating a stumbling block in this model extends to models where nontrade issues are not necessarily important.

In Limão (2002) there are two symmetric regional blocs, each containing two countries, *Large* and (PTA) *Partner*. There exist two externalities within each bloc. First, both governments can provide a public good with regional spillovers. *Partner* places a negligible weight on the public good, which results in an underprovision from *Large*'s perspective. Second, *Large* can use a tariff to depress the price of *Partner*'s exports. They can internalize these effects via a PTA where *Large* lowers its tariffs on *Partner*'s exports in exchange for an increase in the latter's provision of the public good, i.e., cooperation in nontrade issues.[10]

The large countries in the two blocs also face a terms-of-trade externality between them and internalize it via multilateral trade negotiations. These negotiations occur prior to the PTAs and maximize the two large countries' joint objective.[11] According to the MFN in the WTO, a multilateral tariff reduction between two members must be extended to all members. WTO rules allow for exceptions, however, where *Large* can offer a preferential tariff to *Partner* lower than MFN.

The stumbling-block effect should now be clear. If *Large* negotiates a multilateral tariff of zero in the goods it imports from *Partner*, it cannot offer a preferential tariff reduction. By raising the multilateral tariff on PTA goods slightly, *Large* incurs no first-order cost and it gains, since it can offer a preference to *Partner* and induce it to supply some of the regional public good.[12] This extra benefit from higher multilateral tariffs is not present in similar goods that are not imported from *Partner*. Moreover, the model assumes that the non-PTA good enters utility in a quasi-additive way, so it is neutral about whether it is a complement or a substitute for the PTA good, which implies that

vincingly attribute any differences in MTL solely to PTAs. A similar concern applies if we try to compare the aggregate liberalization of countries with and without PTAs, as illustrated by Faezeh Foroutan (1998). She finds lower average MFN tariffs for Latin American countries with PTAs after the Uruguay Round but says that no causality can be drawn from such a correlation because those countries were moving away from import substitution during the 1990s, which implied considerable unilateral liberalization independent of any effects from PTAs. Our identification strategy is to assume that, conditional on other countries' MTL, the set of non-PTA goods has a similar multilateral tariff with or without PTAs. We believe that, on average, this condition is more plausible than either of the ones required to use aggregate data, e.g., than assuming that in the absence of PTAs the United States would have had the same aggregate MTL as Japan in the UR or that it would have had the same aggregate MTL as itself in the previous round when it had fewer PTAs.

[8] The share of total U.S. imports in 1994 for products that were given preferential treatment was 12 percent for NAFTA, but only 3 percent for GSP and less than 0.4 percent for Israel, as well as for ATPA and CBI (www.usitc.gov/ave.pdf, accessed 06/03).

[9] Current examples include U.S. agreements with Jordan, the Andean countries, and other Latin American and Caribbean countries, and the preferential treatment to developing countries through the GSP.

[10] The PTA is modeled such that it does not directly affect prices or trade volumes of any good subject to tariffs in *Large;* its only direct trade effect is to increase the price that *Partner* receives for the fixed amount of its exports. Thus, the impact of this PTA on multilateral tariffs is present even for small partners. Baybars Karacaovali and Limão (2005) extend the model to show that the stumbling block effect is also present if the PTA directly causes changes in the trade volumes.

[11] *Large*'s tariff may also be partially due to internal political economy motives. This does not affect the results qualitatively, as shown in Karacaovali and Limão (2005).

[12] We assume that *Large* cannot simply make a transfer payment to obtain the regional public good from *Small.* If *Large* faced no such constraint then we should not observe several current PTAs where trade preferences are exchanged for cooperation in nontrade issues.

the optimal multilateral tariff for non-PTA goods is unaffected by the PTA. The empirical work requires a weaker assumption for the use of non-PTA goods as the counterfactual (see footnote 17).

Governments recognize the strategic effect described above and take it into account during negotiations. Both the United Nations Conference on Trade and Development (UNCTAD) and beneficiary countries of the U.S. Generalized System of Preferences (GSP) program regularly express the concern that MTL in certain products causes an "erosion of preferences" in the goods they export to the United States.[13] Moreover, there is anecdotal evidence that the United States responds to these concerns by maintaining higher multilateral tariffs on PTA products, even though it lowers the tariffs for similar products not exported by PTA partners. A perfect example of this occurred with low-valued rum the United States imports duty-free from the Caribbean. When the United States and the European Union started to negotiate the elimination of their multilateral tariffs on spirits, the Caribbean governments lobbied the United States and eventually ensured that the multilateral tariff was maintained on one of their main exports: low-valued rum. The U.S. tariff on other types of rum and spirits was lowered as originally planned, which indicates that non-PTA goods may be a good counterfactual for the outcome in the absence of a PTA.[14]

Some PTAs fit the specific assumptions of this model closely, and thus the prediction we test applies directly to them.[15] But, the basic insight may also apply to PTAs where the gains for *both* partners are more directly related to trade, e.g., NAFTA. Lowering multilateral tariffs reduces the preferential margins that can be offered. If these preferences have value for the PTA members, then there is an extra cost to reducing multilateral tariffs in those products. The conjecture that this strategic incentive is also present in models addressing only trade issues is supported by the results in Bagwell and Staiger (2004).[16]

II. Empirical Model

Our empirical model of the U.S. MFN tariff is given by the following linear approximation:

$$(1)\quad \tau_{it} = \phi G_i z_T + \phi_2 z_T + \phi_3 G_i + \alpha_t + \alpha_i + \alpha_{It} + \beta(b_t - b_t^k)1_i^k + (-\rho * ma_t^k)1_i^k + \varepsilon_{it}$$

$$i = 1, \ldots, N;\ t = 1, 2,$$

where τ_{it} is a measure of the U.S. MFN-bound ad valorem tariff rate negotiated in period t on product i. The indicator G_i denotes whether i is exported to the United States under a PTA and the indicator z_T is equal to one after the PTA and zero before it. Thus ϕ is the coefficient of interest—positive if the PTA causes an increase in the U.S. MFN tariff on PTA goods relative to non-PTA goods. To ensure that the MFN tariffs of non-PTA goods provide a reasonable counterfactual for the PTA goods in the absence of PTAs, we must control for several factors. First, we control for all unobserved product characteristics through a full set of product dummies,

[13] According to the international trade director of the General Accounting Office, policymakers in the United States are clearly aware of the impact of an "erosion of preferences" on the willingness of PTA partners to cooperate on nontrade issues (GAO/T-GGD-94-174, June 20, 1994).

[14] Testimony before the House Committee on Ways and Means, May 8, 2001. Accessed June 2003 on http://waysandmeans.house.gov/legacy/trade/107cong/5-8-01/5-8chri.htm.

[15] The PTAs with the Caribbean (CBI) and Andean (ATPA) countries, for example, fit the key assumptions: (a) the largest trade partner for both is the United States, which provides duty-free access to their exports; (b) ATPA and CBI do not provide preferential trade access to U.S. goods but must cooperate on labor standards, intellectual property enforcement, and the war on drugs; (c) those PTAs are small in terms of both the U.S. import share and their small direct effect on multilateral trade negotiations; (d) the nontrade issues that ATPA and CBI cooperate in are important to the United States. Israel and the GSP also fit some of the assumptions.

[16] They analyze accession to the WTO in the context of a pure trade model that uses a sequential bargaining mechanism similar to Limão (2002) and show that it can cause WTO members to hold back tariff reductions on goods exported by countries expected to accede to the WTO.

α_i. Second, we control for all time-varying unobserved characteristics of the group of goods i in each industry I during period t—captured by α_{It}. This set of time-varying industry dummies captures tariff determinants that are emphasized by various theories (e.g., import penetration, labor intensity, and lobbying strength of domestic industries versus their foreign counterparts). The last two variables in (1) control for bargaining and reciprocity effects related to multilateral trade negotiations, which vary over time and products as we now describe.[17]

To estimate the direct effect of PTAs on the U.S. MTL, we relax the symmetry assumption of the theoretical model and also allow for multiple non-PTA countries to negotiate multilaterally with the United States. Thus we control for any indirect effects on the U.S. MTL that arise from other countries changing their MTL in response to the U.S. PTAs. In (1), 1_i^k is an indicator for whether country k exports good i to the United States and therefore the last two variables exhibit product variation since each country k exports different sets of goods. These variables measure two important determinants of tariff changes during multilateral negotiations: the U.S. bargaining power relative to country k and product reciprocity. We initially assume the United States is negotiating with a single country, k, and generalize this to multiple countries below. To describe and model bargaining and reciprocity it is useful to difference (1) across the last two multilateral rounds[18]:

$$(2) \qquad \Delta\tau_{it} = \phi G_i + \phi_2 + \Delta\alpha_t + \Delta\alpha_{It} + \beta\Delta(b_t - b_t^k)1_i^k + (-\rho * \Delta ma_t^k)1_i^k + \Delta\varepsilon_{it} \quad i = 1, \ldots, N.$$

Some theories of GATT recognize the potential importance of bargaining power but do not model its determinants.[19] Thus, we will take a broad and simple view of bargaining power and argue that, conditional on the other variables, country k exporting good i is expected to obtain a relatively larger cut in the U.S. tariff if, when comparing across the two trade rounds, either of the following holds: (a) country k is relatively better prepared for the negotiation, perhaps because it has more resources to dedicate to it; (b) k imports more of the U.S. goods such that it has relatively high market power. Relative economic size is crucial in both of these, and so we use relative GDP changes as a broad proxy for these and possibly other changes in bargaining power across rounds.[20] Thus, the prediction is that

[17] According to the model in (1), if we could identify ϕ_2 econometrically we could actually test the maintained hypothesis that the tariff for the non-PTA products is a good counterfactual, since $\phi_2 = 0$ implies that the PTA had no effect on the tariff of non-PTA goods. However, the United States changed its MFN tariffs only after negotiating the multilateral rounds, so we can't identify ϕ_2 separately from the aggregate tariff change in each round, which is captured by α_t. According to the model in Section II, ϕ_2 is zero if the non-PTA goods are additively separable from PTA goods in the utility. Although in practice this may not be a valid assumption for each and every non-PTA good, it is also not necessary to ensure that on average the MFN tariff of non-PTA goods is unaffected by PTAs (once we condition for the U.S. response to other countries' MTL). For example, if a non-PTA good is a substitute for a PTA good, then a richer model is likely to predict a higher multilateral tariff for it as well, but it would predict a lower tariff if they are complements. Any given non-PTA good will have both substitute and complements in the sample and econometrically the requirement is simply that those second-order effects average to zero, not for each good but for all.

[18] To interpret the estimate of ϕ as the effect of PTAs on tariffs and be clear about the identification strategy, it is useful to start with the equation in levels and understand the timing of events. In (1), $t = 1$ corresponds to the final negotiation of the Tokyo Round (1977–1978) and $t = 2$ to the final stage of the negotiation of the UR (1993–1994). For ATPA $T = 1991$–1992. Similarly NAFTA, Israel, and CBI were initiated after the Tokyo Round, so differencing equation (1) between $t = 1, 2$ leads exactly to (2) for those four agreements. Some GSP preferences were in place by the Tokyo Round and thus possibly reflected in the MFN tariff at $t = 1$. The United States tightened the eligibility criteria for GSP between the two rounds, however, which requires a higher MFN tariff on GSP products to offset the extra cost on GSP countries imposed by the tighter criteria. Therefore, we may interpret ϕ in (2) for GSP as an increase in the stumbling-block effect.

[19] Bagwell and Staiger (1999a), for example, model reciprocal trade negotiations and argue that the initial stage is precisely the determination of a specific world price vector, which is the outcome of bargaining.

[20] This proxy should be reasonably positively correlated with the effects it tries to capture. First, the gain from negotiating a given reduction in another country's tariffs is increasing in the total amount of exports, so an increase in size increases the incentives for a better negotiation team

an increase in k's bargaining power relative to the United States, as proxied by a fall in the log difference of GDP in the United States and country k, $(b_t - b_t^k)$, causes the United States to lower its tariff in the goods exported by k, i.e., $\beta > 0$.

A potentially important determinant of differential liberalization across products is reciprocity—the extent to which the United States reduces its tariffs by more when its partners offer larger tariff reductions. Reciprocity in multilateral negotiations is typically sought in first-differences (Bhagwati, 1991), i.e., negotiators focus on *changes* in protection as opposed to their level; these are often called market access concessions. If product reciprocity is followed, then the larger the *aggregate* market access concession k offers to the United States, i.e., the larger Δma_t^k in (2) is, the larger the U.S. tariff reduction, $-\Delta\tau_{it}$, is on the products exported by k. So if reciprocity occurred, then $\rho > 0$.[21]

To aggregate a country's proposed change in market access over all goods, negotiators in GATT commonly use two methods, which differ in how the tariff changes are weighted.[22] Using either of them, we can express the *aggregate* change in k's market access as $\Delta ma_t^k = \Sigma_j(-\Delta\tau_{jt}^k)w_{jT}^k$, where $-\Delta\tau_{jt}^k$ is the percentage tariff *reduction* by k in each imported good j. For a given weight, larger reductions by k increase market access for the United States and so, if negotiators reciprocate, lead to a lower U.S. tariff in each good i that k exports to the United States.

The last issue to address in the estimation is that of multiple exporters for any good i to the United States. According to the principal supplier rule in the GATT, countries negotiate only with the top exporters; so we aggregate the observations for each good i in (2) over its principal suppliers to the United States using their individual export value as a share of their total value exported to the United States, s_{iT}^k. Using this and the derived market access expression above, we write (2) in terms of estimable coefficients as

$$(3) \qquad \Delta\tau_{it} = \phi G_i + a + a_I + \beta\Sigma_k s_{iT}^k \Delta(b_t - b_t^k) + \rho\Sigma_k s_{iT}^k(\Sigma_j \Delta\tau_{jt}^k w_{jT}^k) + u_i$$

$$i = 1, \ldots, N,$$

where a denotes an intercept that estimates the average MFN tariff change for the excluded industry (miscellaneous manufacturing); and a_I represents the set of included industry dummies. We estimate (3) and test if ϕ is positive. Moreover, if bargaining power and reciprocity are important determinants of multilateral tariff settings, then we expect β and ρ to be positive.

A. *Endogeneity*

To obtain consistent estimates for the parameters in (3), we must address the following potential endogeneity problems associated with the reciprocity and PTA variables.

The reciprocity variable may be subject to reverse causation because, if reciprocity did occur, a fraction of k's tariff reductions would be due to reductions in U.S. tariffs on k's products. We use two related facts about the timing and mode of negotiations in the Uruguay Round to construct an instrument for reciprocity. The market access negotiations started in 1986 but were stalled until 1992, during which period various countries liberalized unilaterally.[23] This decision to liberalize was primarily domestic, e.g., moving away from import substitution strategies, and not conditional on other countries lowering their tariffs,

and also the resources available to it. Moreover, numerous empirical gravity estimates show that GDP is one of the strongest determinants of bilateral imports and exports (more so than GDP per capita, for example). Both of these suggest that a measure of size, rather than income per capita, for example, is more appropriate to capture broad changes in bargaining power.

[21] We may expect to find product reciprocity because, in the UR, negotiators used a product-by-product approach rather than agreeing to reduce tariffs across the board according to a formula (Bernard M. Hoekman and Michel M. Kostecki, 2001, p. 133).

[22] One measure uses k's import share of good j in all of k's imports as the weight. The other is the "trade coverage" measure, which uses the value of k's imports in j as the weight (Hoekman and Kostecki, 2001, p. 124). In the data section, we discuss which we use. See our working paper for more discussion on these.

[23] In the data, all countries show some unilateral liberalization with the least occurring among E.U. members.

i.e., it was not reciprocal. Nonetheless, based on interviews with the negotiating delegations, Finger et al. (2002) report that "according to delegations the informal practice was [... that] countries that had, after 1986, unilaterally reduced their tariffs would be given 'credit' at the round to the extent that they bound these cuts at the round" (p. 121). Therefore, the unilateral liberalization by U.S. partners between 1986 and 1992 was "predetermined" relative to U.S. tariff reductions negotiated between 1992 and 1994 but relevant in affecting the extent of those U.S. cuts, because the United States responded to that unilateral liberalization ex post in the same way it responded to tariff reductions, negotiated in 1992 to 1994, that were explicitly reciprocal. Thus, we use a country's unilateral liberalization (1986–1992) as the instrument for its total liberalization (1986–1995). The negotiated tariffs were implemented between 1995 and 2000.

The preferences captured in the PTA variable may also be endogenous to tariff changes. For NAFTA, all the products in our sample receive preferences, whether or not they are exported by Canada and Mexico; therefore, the identification relies on whether a product is exported by them to the United States. But for the other PTAs, not all goods receive preferences, raising the question of whether the decision to grant a preference in a given good was determined by *changes* in the U.S. MFN tariffs. The first step we take in addressing this issue is to use preferences that were determined before the changes in the U.S. MFN tariff were implemented. Using the "predetermined" preferences may, however, be insufficient if some of those MFN tariff changes were expected. The industry dummies in (3) address this if the main expected differences are across industries. But there may also exist product characteristics that indicate if the tariff *change* will be high or low. For example, a product protected by an NTB on any country can indicate how a tariff will subsequently change. Therefore, we control for the existence of NTBs in estimating (3).

We test and find that using predetermined preferences and industry and product controls does not fully solve this endogeneity problem, so we instrument for G_i. The instruments we use include whether the PTA partners exported the good to the United States before the Uruguay Round *independently* of whether a preference was received. This is a reasonable instrument because it is correlated with the set of goods that are exported *and* receive preferences. Moreover, the decision to export a good prior to that round may be independent of the subsequent MFN tariff *changes* so that the instrument is uncorrelated with the error term in (3).[24] To test the exogeneity of this instrument, we include other instruments that capture whether a particular good is likely to be exported—transport costs and world price changes prior to that round—which are a priori more likely to be exogenous relative to tariff changes implemented after the round is finished. We use the extra orthogonality conditions implied by the last set of instruments to verify the exogeneity of exports as an instrument.

III. Estimation

A. *Data*

Table 1 provides summary statistics for the main variables (we provide detailed definitions for each variable in Appendix Table 1A). By 1994 the United States provided preferences to Canada and Mexico under NAFTA (effective in 1994), Israel (1985), several developing countries under the GSP (1976), Caribbean countries (CBI, 1984) and Andean countries (ATPA, 1992). To test if small PTAs have an individual impact, we construct separate variables corresponding to G_i in (3), e.g., $\text{ISRAEL}_i = 1$ if product i is exported by Israel with a preference in 1994. The fraction of such goods ranges from 0.83 for NAFTA to 0.15 for ATPA. We also construct the union of the individual PTA variables, ANYPTA, to estimate the average stumbling block effect, and their intersection, EVRPTA. These account for 0.89 and 0.049 of the goods.

For the dependent variable, we use the growth of the MFN ad valorem tariff factor, $\Delta \ln(1 + \tau_{it})$, which we can translate into price effects and is therefore more informative about the economic impact of the stumbling block effect than changes in the tariff level. The av-

[24] This is possible because the decision to export may depend mainly on a country's relative resource and factor abundance, and the world price and trading costs associated with that good.

TABLE 1—SUMMARY STATISTICS

Variable	Mean	St. dev.	Min	Max
USLIB	−2.89	3.21	−32.2	3.17
ANYPTA	0.891	0.312	0	1
EVRPTA	0.049	0.216	0	1
ANYPTAxHI_EX	0.197	0.398	0	1
NONAFTA	0.605	0.489	0	1
NAFTA	0.826	0.379	0	1
ATPA	0.145	0.352	0	1
CBI[a]	0.186	0.389	0	1
GSP[a]	0.467	0.499	0	1
ISR	0.279	0.449	0	1
BARPOW	−30.9	21.5	−70.5	93.0
TOTLIB	−51.3	11.3	−89.5	−0.593
TOTxNTB	−16.2	24.4	−81.9	0
NTB	0.324	0.468	0	1
DS	0.047	0.213	0	1

Notes: Number of observations: 5,079. There were 7,853 unique eight-digit tariff lines for which the WTO tariff data were available before and after the Uruguay Round once the special sections (21 and 22) are excluded. The sample is reduced once we exclude the lines for which the MFN tariff was zero before the round ($n = 6800$). Lines with missing or zero imports are dropped because the imports are required to construct TOT and BARPOW ($n = 5227$). Missing data on transport costs and preferences further reduce the sample to 5,079. Please see the working paper for summary statistics of excluded instruments used in first stage regressions.

[a] The members of the ATPA are also beneficiaries under the CBI and GSP. However, we do not include them in the construction of the CBI and GSP variables, both because the benefits under the ATPA are more generous and to minimize multicollinearity problems.

erage negotiated reduction of the U.S. tariff factor was 2.9 percent.

We construct the bargaining power variable as described in the previous section. To construct the reciprocity variable for each country k, $\Sigma_j \Delta\tau_{jt}^k w_{jT}^k$, we use the import weighted average tariff reduction calculated by Finger et al. (2002). It consists of the tariff reductions for each WTO member, k, in the Uruguay Round for each product, j, weighted by that product's import share for each k. They calculate two variants: all tariff reductions from 1986 to 1995 and reductions from 1992 to 1995. From these we construct our measure of unilateral liberalization from 1986 to 1992, which we use as an instrument. We weight both unilateral and total liberalization by the principal exporter share, s_{iT}^k, as described above. On average, the U.S. partners committed to reducing their tariffs by 51 percent in the period 1986–1995 (TOTLIB in Table 1).

B. *Estimates*

Before presenting the regression results, we briefly describe how the dependent variable varies according to its PTA status without any controls. First, consider the basic difference-in-difference estimate. The mean reduction in the MFN tariff *factor* for PTA goods is 2.75 percent. For the non-PTA goods the reduction is 4.03 percent, which is significantly larger.[25] Consider now the entire distribution of the changes. Figure 1 presents kernel density estimates for the two samples, i.e., the "smoothed" histograms. The density for the PTA goods is the dashed line—clearly shifted toward zero. Few PTA goods had reductions of more than 6 percent. That is not the case for non-PTA goods, as is clear from the "fatter" solid left tail. Moreover, the difference in tariff reductions is present within several industries and 69 out of the 93 two-digit harmonized standard industries contain products in both the control and treatment group, which we use to identify ϕ. Thus the result is not driven by any single industry.[26]

Table 2 contains the results from estimating (3). The first two columns provide OLS estimates for comparison purposes. The remaining ones contain different specifications in which we apply a GMM estimator and instrument for the endogenous variables, denoted by the symbol "†." All the specifications include two-digit harmonized standard industry dummies, which we do not report here.[27]

[25] Significant at the 1-percent level according to a simple t-test of difference in means.

[26] These 69 industries span a varied set of products, including agriculture, prepared foods, chemicals, metals, plastics, leather, textiles and apparel, footwear and machinery, and vehicles. In the two-digit industries with non-PTA products, the proportion can be as high as 60 percent and on average it is 12 percent. In our working paper, we provide evidence of the difference in PTA and non-PTA good tariff reductions for each PTA within several separate groups of industries.

[27] We include only products with positive tariffs before the UR for two reasons. First, when the MFN tariff is zero, there is often no information about whether a preference exists, since it is in effect irrelevant. Second, all the tariffs in the sample that were initially zero remained unchanged

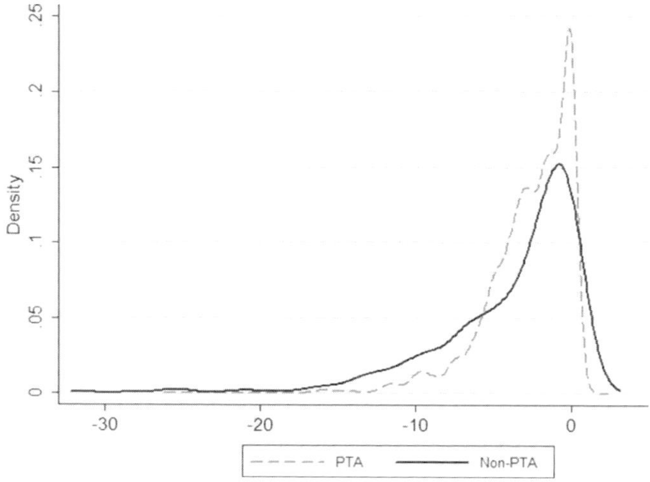

FIGURE 1. DISTRIBUTION OF U.S. MFN TARIFF CHANGES FOR PTA AND NON-PTA GOODS

The first point to note is that the estimate for the coefficient on ANYPTA, ϕ in (3), is positive and significant over the different specifications, which is consistent with a direct stumbling block effect. The OLS estimate for ϕ in column 1 is 0.98; therefore, it is biased downward relative to the IV estimate of 1.28 (column 3). As we discuss below, we cannot reject endogeneity and thus we should focus on the IV estimates.[28]

We may expect the magnitudes of the stumbling block effect to vary over different goods depending on their importance to the United States or its PTA partners. In column 4 we include EVRPTA, which is equal to one for the subset of goods that are exported under every PTA, and find that the effect is 60 percent larger for those products. The rum anecdote for CBI in Section I suggests that the stumbling-block effect should be stronger in products that are important exports for a PTA partner. We test this in column 5 by interacting ANYPTA with an indicator equal to one if the export value of the product exported by a given PTA is above the mean of its total exports to the United States; the effect is 48 percent higher for important exports. The fact that the effect we estimate varies in a sensible and predictable way over different goods provides further support that it is being driven by the PTAs.

If the estimates just described are capturing the effect of only NAFTA, then PTAs with small countries should not affect U.S. multilateral tariffs, as predicted by most standard models. To test this, in column 6 we separate NAFTA from the remaining agreements and find that jointly the agreements with smaller countries also have a significant effect and its magnitude is statistically identical to NAFTA's.[29]

and are likely to share an unobserved common characteristic. Thus, including those observations would bias the estimates if the proportion of zero tariffs is different for PTA goods relative to the rest of the goods. In addition, we include a dummy variable, DS, which accounts for eight-digit tariff lines which were subdivided in the WTO data and which we averaged over; eliminating this dummy does not affect the results.

[28] The estimate for ϕ is also positive and significant if we use the percentage change in tariffs as the dependent variable.

[29] Moreover, the number of goods affected is approximately the same as under NAFTA.

TABLE 2—ESTIMATES OF STUMBLING BLOCK AND MULTILATERAL NEGOTIATION EFFECTS

Dependent variable	OLS		IV-GMM				
USLIB ($\Delta\tau$)	(1)	(2)	(3)	(4)	(5)	(6)	(7)
ANYPTA† (ϕ)	0.982***	0.982***	1.28***	1.33***	1.21***		
	(0.204)	(0.204)	(0.328)	(0.321)	(0.331)		
EVRPTA†		0.004		0.778***			
		(0.139)		(0.219)			
ANYPTA * HI_EX†					0.584***		
					(0.110)		
NONAFTA†						0.710***	
						(0.209)	
NAFTA‡						0.799***	0.815***
						(0.149)	(0.149)
ATPA†							0.398***
							(0.151)
CBI†							0.381***
							(0.141)
GSP†							0.658***
							(0.220)
ISR†							0.010
							(0.097)
BARPOW (β)	0.009***	0.009***	0.009***	0.009***	0.008***	0.009***	0.009***
	(0.002)	(0.002)	(0.002)	(0.002)	(0.002)	(0.002)	(0.002)
TOTLIB† (ρ)	−0.004	−0.004	0.014**	0.015**	0.017***	0.017***	0.018***
	(0.005)	(0.005)	(0.006)	(0.006)	(0.006)	(0.006)	(0.006)
TOT * NTB†	−0.012	−0.012	−0.071***	−0.070***	−0.072***	−0.071***	−0.072***
	(0.008)	(0.008)	(0.011)	(0.011)	(0.011)	(0.011)	(0.011)
NTB	−0.914*	−0.914*	−4.02***	−3.98***	−4.11***	−3.96***	−3.88***
	(0.480)	(0.480)	(0.676)	(0.668)	(0.676)	(0.673)	(0.670)
DS	−0.635***	−0.635***	−0.676***	−0.708***	−0.748***	−0.704***	−0.753***
	(0.168)	(0.168)	(0.170)	(0.170)	(0.170)	(0.166)	(0.169)
Constant (a)	−2.94***	−2.94***	−2.26***	−2.41***	−2.24***	−2.28***	−2.42***
	(0.401)	(0.401)	(0.478)	(0.474)	(0.479)	(0.431)	(0.429)
Observations	5079	5079	5079	5079	5079	5079	5079
Adj. R-sq.	0.18	0.18	—	—	—	—	—
Hansen's Jp[a]	—	—	0.64	0.85	0.73	0.54	0.56
C-stat p[b]	—	—	0.39	0.71	0.66	0.49	0.60
Exogeneity test p[c]	—	—	0.00	0.00	0.00	0.00	0.00
Homosk. p[d]	—	—	0.00	0.00	0.00	0.00	0.00
No. of parameters	98	99	98	99	99	99	102

Notes: Standard errors in parentheses. Harmonized standard two-digit dummies included but not reported.

* Significant at 10 percent.

** Significant at 5 percent.

*** Significant at 1 percent.

[a] Test of overidentifying restrictions. Probability at which we reject the null hypothesis that the excluded instruments are uncorrelated with the error term, and correctly excluded from the estimated equation.

[b] Probability for rejection of the null hypothesis of exogeneity of a subset of f instruments marked with "‡." C-stat = $J^r - J^u$ with a chi-square distribution with f degrees of freedom, where J^r represents the minimized value of the GMM objective function for the restricted and efficient regression (with all overidentifying restrictions) and J^u the value for the unrestricted, inefficient, but consistent regression without the questionable instruments.

[c] Regression-based Hausman specification test for the endogeneity of the variables marked with a "†." Probability value at which we reject the consistency and efficiency of OLS.

[d] Identical result for three versions of the Pagan-Hall homoskedasticity test using the levels of the instruments, the "fitted value" of the dependent variable, and its square.

In column 7 we identify the direct stumbling block effect for each of the individual PTAs, with the exception of Israel, so even PTAs with small countries can individually affect a large country's MFN tariffs. These average effects for each PTA apply to a large number of goods. Even at this disaggregated level, the smaller PTAs export in over 15 percent of the product lines in our sample. Moreover, the United States continues to import from non-PTA partners in nearly all those lines, which indicates that the PTA partner is not the lowest-cost producer.[30] Therefore, the small PTAs have the potential to affect a large number of non-PTA countries and a nonnegligible amount of U.S. trade.

To identify the reciprocity effect, we must address its endogeneity and control for the existence of NTBs. The measure constructed by Finger et al. (2002) does not reflect tariff equivalent changes due to NTB changes, so our tariff reciprocity variable should work as expected for the products with no NTBs. We test and confirm this by interacting the NTB indicator with the reciprocity variable.[31] The IV estimates of reciprocity are positive and significant, ranging from 0.014 to 0.018. So a decrease in the tariff of a U.S. partner that exports good i leads to a decrease in the U.S. tariff of that product. Comparing the insignificant OLS estimates with the IV ones, we see the importance of instrumenting.

Reciprocity, when also followed by other WTO members, may amplify the importance of PTAs as stumbling blocks. Suppose k does not have a PTA with the United States but exports only PTA goods to that country. Reciprocity implies that, to the extent that the direct stumbling block effect lowers the U.S. aggregate MTL, as we argue below, then k offers fewer reductions on the goods it imports from the United States. The United States internalizes this effect on itself when choosing its MTL. But countries that export the same goods will also face k's higher MFN tariff and potentially lower export prices.

The bargaining power elasticity, β in (3), is positive, as predicted, and significant.

C. *Specification Tests and Instrument Choice*

The bottom rows of Table 2 present test statistics for the IV estimation. The Hausman endogeneity tests of the PTA and reciprocity variables, denoted with the symbol "†," reject the consistency of OLS. We reject the null of homoskedasticity for all specifications, which suggests that GMM is more efficient than standard IV. We also cannot reject the validity of the overidentifying restrictions. Finally, because tests of multiple overidentifying restrictions may have low power, we also test a subset of the instruments used and cannot reject their exogeneity.

The instruments in the first-stage regressions explain a significant part of the variation of each of the endogenous variables, and we can reject the null that the instruments are jointly zero. The first-stage regressions for the PTA variables can be interpreted as linear probability models of whether a good is exported to the United States *under* a (or any) preferential program—so some of the results may be interesting in their own right. We omit these tables here due to space constraints, but they are available in the working paper where we discuss them (Limão, 2002).

Whether a PTA partner exported a particular good to the United States before the Uruguay Round may depend on the U.S. MFN tariff *level,* but is unlikely to depend on the subsequent *change* in the tariff. Nonetheless, we test the export variables and their interactions with other instruments and fail to reject the null hypothesis that they are exogenous. We report the p-value for this test in the row in Table 2 labeled "c-stat p."[32] The main instrument for

[30] This could also be due to product differentiation within hs-8 categories.

[31] In products with NTBs, an exporter is less likely to try to get the United States to reduce its tariffs because it will still face the protection from the NTB.

[32] See Fumio Hayashi (2000) for an explanation of this statistic. Testing for the exogeneity of a subset of instruments requires an alternative set, which is considered exogenous a priori. This explains why we also use the average U.S. international transport cost for each good as an excluded instrument. This is a potential predictor for whether a good is exported under the PTA because, conditional on a PTA partner exporting a good to the United States, it will gain more from a preference in that good if there are high average transport costs, since this implies that it will face less competition from the rest of the world in the U.S.

reciprocity is unilateral reduction, as explained previously, and it has a positive and significant effect on total reduction.[33]

D. *Interpretation of Estimates as Price Effects and Quantification*

We first interpret our estimates in terms of price effects and then quantify the direct stumbling block effect and provide bounds on the total effect that incorporates the potential indirect effect through reciprocity.

The domestic price for a traded product subject to an ad valorem tariff τ can be written as $\ln p_t^d = \ln(1 + \tau_t) + \ln p_t^w$. We can then define the pass-through rate from tariffs to domestic prices as

$$(4) \qquad \pi \equiv \Delta \ln p_t^d / \Delta \ln(1 + \tau_t) = 1 + \Delta \ln p_t^w / \Delta \ln(1 + \tau_t).$$

If there is full pass-through, i.e., if $\pi = 1$, then it is simple to show that the stumbling block parameter, ϕ, represents the growth in the U.S. price for a PTA good relative to a similar non-PTA good.[34] Alternatively, the ratio of the domestic price growth of a PTA to a similar non-PTA good is:

$$(5) \qquad \Delta \ln p_{\text{PTA},t}^d / \Delta \ln p_t^d = \Delta \ln(1 + \tau_{\text{PTA},t}) / \Delta \ln(1 + \tau_t) = 1 + \phi/\tilde{a},$$

where $\tilde{a}$ is the estimated average tariff growth for non-PTA products, so the last equality applies to a "benchmark" good with no NTBs and no changes in bargaining power or market access.

We can also provide an interpretation of the results if there is incomplete pass-through, i.e., if $\pi < 1$. This is important since the motivation for countries to seek reciprocal trade liberalization in a number of models is precisely that a reduction in the tariffs of the importing country increases the price received by the exporter (or maintains the terms of trade unchanged, as the importer is also reducing its own tariffs). Mordechai E. Kreinin (1961) estimates that more than two-thirds of U.S. tariff reductions in the Geneva Round were passed on as higher prices to countries exporting to the United States, i.e., a pass-through less than one-third.[35] We do not know of comparable estimates during the last round, but we can provide an estimate of the effect on the relative export prices of PTA versus non-PTA goods exported by non-PTA countries. Rearranging (4), we have $\Delta \ln p_t^w = (\pi - 1)\Delta \ln(1 + \tau_t)$, which we use to derive the ratio of the growth of world prices for a "benchmark" PTA versus a non-PTA good:

$$(6) \qquad \Delta \ln p_{\text{PTA},t}^w / \Delta \ln p_t^w = [\Delta \ln(1 + \tau_{\text{PTA},t}) / \Delta \ln(1 + \tau_t)] * [(\pi_{\text{PTA}} - 1)/(\pi - 1)] \approx 1 + \phi/\tilde{a} \quad \text{if } \pi_{\text{PTA}} \approx \pi < 1.$$

Thus, we obtain an expression similar to (5). However, (6) applies not when $\pi = 1$ but when both π_{PTA} and π are lower than unity, and we are agnostic about their relative size for two goods that differ only in their PTA status.

In Table 3 we apply the interpretations above to quantify the importance of our estimates. Each

market because PTA partners tend to be regional and have transport costs lower than the average. In the first stage, the polynomial of the transport cost variable is jointly significant in explaining the PTA variables across different specifications. For the specification with individual PTAs, we use changes in the world price between 1990 and 1992 as an instrument, as well as its interaction with transport costs.

[33] All the tests of the reciprocity variable are done jointly with its interaction with the NTB variable.

[34] Using the definition of $\ln p_t^d$, equation (4), and recalling that $\Delta \ln(1 + \tau_t)$ is the dependent variable in (3), we obtain $\Delta \ln(p_{\text{PTA},t}^d) - \Delta \ln(p_t^d) = \Delta \ln(1 + \tau_{\text{PTA},t}) - \Delta \ln(1 + \tau_t) = \phi$, where $x_{\text{PTA},t}$ denotes the value of x when the PTA variable, G, is one.

[35] Further evidence of market power is provided by Won Chang and Winters (2002), who investigate the elimination of internal tariffs between Argentina and Brazil. There is also ample evidence of imperfect pass-through from exchange rates and that the effect is symmetric to that of tariff changes (Robert C. Feenstra, 1989).

TABLE 3—QUANTIFICATION OF THE DIRECT STUMBLING BLOCK EFFECT

Percent	Any PTA[a]	Any & every PTA[b]	Any PTA w/ HI_EX[c]	Individual PTAs[d] NAFTA	ATPA	CBI	GSP
Growth of relative US price of PTA goods if $\pi = 1$, ϕ	1.28	2.11	1.79	0.82	0.40	0.38	0.66
	(0.33)	(0.36)	(0.32)	(0.15)	(0.15)	(0.14)	(0.22)
Relative price growth,[e] $1 + \phi/\bar{a}$	52	23	31	68	84	84	74
	(10)	(13)	(11)	(6.6)	(6.3)	(6.1)	(8.7)
Foreign tariff reduction equivalent,[f] ϕ/ρ	89	145	104	45	22	21	37
	(39)	(59)	(38)	(16)	(11)	(9.9)	(16)
Foreign bargaining power equivalent,[g] ϕ/β	137	223	233	94	46	44	76
	(46)	(60)	(76)	(27)	(20)	(19)	(30)

Notes: Standard errors in parenthesis obtained using the delta method for the nonlinear parameter combinations in the last three rows. Point estimates for ϕ/ρ and ϕ/β vary slightly from Table 2 due to rounding.

[a] Table 2, column 3.

[b] Table 2, column 4, joint effect of ANYPTA and EVRPTA.

[c] Table 2, column 5, joint effect of ANYPTA and ANYPTA * HI_EX.

[d] Table 2, column 7.

[e] Represents relative U.S. domestic price effect of preferential versus nonpreferential good if $\pi = 1$ and world price effect if $\pi_{PTA} \approx \pi < 1$. $\bar{a} \equiv a + (\Sigma_{I \in \iota} a_I)/69$: the estimated average tariff factor growth for non-PTA products over the set ι of 69 industries that contained at least one of them.

[f] Average tariff reduction required by an exporter of a PTA-type good with share of one in order to overcome the preferential effect. If the exporter has a share s, then the effect is $\phi/s\rho$.

[g] GDP growth required by an exporter of a PTA-type good with share of one in order to overcome the preferential effect. If the exporter has a share s, then the effect is $\phi/s\beta$.

row provides an alternative measure, and the columns correspond to the IV specifications in Table 2. The first column uses the estimates in column 3 of Table 2. If we assume $\pi = 1$, then the U.S. domestic price of PTA goods increased by 1.28 percent relative to similar non-PTA goods. The average U.S. domestic price growth for a "benchmark" non-PTA good was approximately −2.67 percent, and therefore the reduction of the domestic price for the PTA good in the United States was only 52 percent of that experienced by the average non-PTA good. Assuming imperfect and similar pass-through, we can use (6) to interpret the relative price growth measures in row 2 as follows. The increase in the export price for a country without a PTA with the United States that exports any of the PTA-type goods is only 52 percent of the price increase for a similar non-PTA good. Using the non-PTA goods as the counterfactual for the absence of PTAs, the results above can be interpreted as the effects of the U.S. PTAs on the prices of the PTA goods.

In the second column we consider the effect for the goods exported by every PTA. The relative price growth is only 23 percent and we can't reject the hypothesis that the average relative price growth for the goods exported by every PTA was as low as zero. For important exports for any PTA, the relative price growth is a mere 31 percent, as shown in the third column. The last set of columns in Table 3 uses the significant estimates for individual PTAs in column 7 of Table 2. The strongest effect is for NAFTA, 68 percent, followed by GSP, 74 percent. The estimates for ATPA and CBI are identical, 84 percent. The upper bound of the 95-percent confidence interval for these PTAs is below 100 percent. So, the price effects for PTA and non-PTA goods are not similar even for ATPA and CBI.[36]

The signing of some U.S. PTAs may have changed the equilibrium level of aggregate MTL of other countries, which, because of reciprocity, provides an indirect channel by which U.S. tariffs are affected. There is considerable disagreement about whether the U.S. PTAs had a positive or negative effect on other countries' willingness to liberalize.

[36] The reason that the individual PTA estimates of ϕ are lower than the estimate for any PTA is that several of the goods exported by the smaller PTAs are also exported under NAFTA.

To compare the relative importance of the direct effect of the PTAs and the indirect effect through reciprocity, we consider a country that does not have a PTA with the United States but exports the same good as a PTA partner. We then ask how much *more* this country must lower its average tariff in order to obtain the same average tariff reduction by the United States in that good as the one received by a country that exports a similar non-PTA good. If that country has an export share to the United States close to one in that good, then the answer is 89 percent for the specification with ANYPTA (Table 3, first column). That number is larger for lower export shares. So, in order to overturn the direct effect we estimate, the extra MTL that PTAs needed to have created in other countries had to be very large, particularly if we note that the median value for the exporters in the sample is only 44 percent.[37, 38]

We can also compare the relative importance of the direct and indirect effects of PTAs in *aggregate* U.S. MTL, i.e., over PTA and non-PTA goods. Although we did not observe the values of aggregate MTL in the absence of the U.S. PTAs, we can consider some bounds on them and then calculate the total effect of the U.S. PTAs on its *aggregate* MTL. We take the difference of the expected values over all goods in (3) between the case when PTAs exist, $z_T = 1$ (see equation (1)), and $z_T = 0$. Denoting all remaining variables by a vector $\boldsymbol{x}_i$ we obtain

(7)

$$E(\Delta\tau_{it}|z_T = 1, \boldsymbol{x}_i) - E(\Delta\tau_{it}|z_T = 0, \boldsymbol{x}_i) = \phi E(G_i) + \rho[E(\Sigma_k s^k_{iT}(\Sigma_j \Delta\tau^k_{jt} w^k_{jT}))](1 - \chi) + \beta[E(\Sigma_k s^k_{iT}\Delta(b_t - b^k_t))](1 - \delta).$$

The expression in (7) captures the total stumbling block effect of PTAs as it applies to aggregate U.S. MTL. It reflects the average direct stumbling block effect, $\phi E(G_i)$, and the difference in the multilateral negotiation variables. Since the values of the reciprocity and bargaining variables are unobserved when $z_T = 0$, we write them as some proportion of the observed variables, e.g., χ is $E(\Sigma_k s^k_{iT}(\Sigma_j \Delta\tau^k_{jt} w^k_{jT})|z_T = 0, \boldsymbol{x}_i)/E(\Sigma_k s^k_{iT}(\Sigma_j \Delta\tau^k_{jt} w^k_{jT}))$ and δ is defined similarly for bargaining. The most neutral *initial* assumption is that foreign MTL and bargaining are unaffected by the U.S. PTAs, i.e., $\chi = \delta = 1$, in which case the total effect of the PTAs is simply the average direct effect $\phi E(G_i) = 1.14$ $(=1.28 * 0.89)$.[39] If other countries had liberalized twice as much in the absence of PTAs, $\chi = 2$, then the total effect would be 1.86 $(=1.28 * 0.89 - 0.014 * (-51.3))$ when $\delta = 1$. Even if they had liberalized half as much, $\chi = ½$, the total effect would be 0.78 when $\delta = 1$, so the indirect effect would not offset the direct one. Moreover, these bounds for the total effect are statistically close to the direct effect.[40]

E. *Robustness*

We have already discussed a number of specification and robustness tests. Here, we report two more: robustness to finer industry controls, and an alternative test of our hypothesis that attempts to capture whether there is an important missing variable bias in the estimation.

We reestimate the main specifications in Table 2 using a richer set of industry effects (over 800 four-digit harmonized standard industries). The estimates, presented in our working paper, confirm the main results in Table 2 in terms of the sign and significance of the PTA, bargaining, and reciprocity variables. This provides further evidence that the coefficients in Table 2 are not

[37] The foreign tariff changes are defined as percentage changes of the tariff, not the tariff factor; thus the magnitudes are larger than those for the dependent variable.

[38] A similar statistic for bargaining power shows that a large increase in a country's GDP would have been necessary between the Tokyo and Uruguay Rounds to overcome the stumbling block effect: 94 percent to overcome NAFTA, and over 40 percent for ATPA or CBI. The highest increases in bargaining power in our sample were Singapore (51 percent) and the European Union (43 percent).

[39] This total effect and the estimate of reciprocity suggest that the initial neutral assumption should be revised to say that other countries in fact had less MTL because of these PTAs. Note also that, by considering the expected value of the multilateral variables, we take into account both how the PTAs may affect the probability of the round and the value of reciprocity and bargaining variables if the round is concluded.

[40] The standard error of the estimates is 0.33 for ϕ and 0.31 for $E(G_i)$.

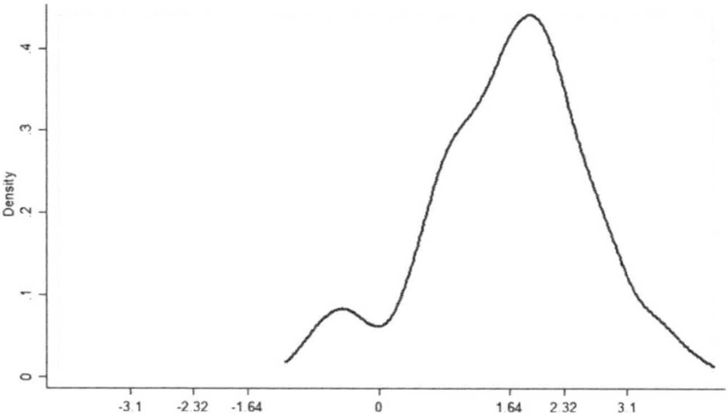

FIGURE 2. EFFECT ON U.S. MFN TARIFFS OF NAFTA GOODS RELATIVE TO RANDOM NON-PTA COUNTRIES

biased by omitted political economy or other industry time-varying effects.

Let us consider an alternative robustness test. If there were no stumbling block effect, then there should be no *systematic* difference in the change in MFN tariffs for products exported by a PTA and any *given* combination of non-PTA countries. To test this, we include an additional control group, a country or combination of countries c that do not have a PTA with the United States, and estimate the following for each:

$$(8) \qquad \Delta\tau_{it} = \delta_c G_i + \eta_c G_{ic} + a_c + a_{ct} + \beta_c \Sigma_k s^k_{iT} \Delta(b_t - b^k_t) + \rho_c \Sigma_k s^k_{iT} \Sigma_j \Delta\tau^k_{jt} w^k_{jT} + u_{ic}$$

$$i = 1, \ldots, N,$$

where G_i is the PTA variable and G_{ic} is one if any of the countries in the group export to the United States, and zero otherwise. The null hypothesis is that $\delta_c = \eta_c$ in each regression. Since we do not know which preferences would be offered if the countries in c had a PTA with the United States, we assume preferences in all goods. Thus the only PTA that we can test against is NAFTA, since it is the only one in which all products in our sample receive preferential treatment. But we can, and do, control for the other PTAs.[41]

We estimate (8) for each combination c using IV-GMM, as in column 6 of Table 2, and find that the coefficient for NAFTA *exceeds* that for the non-PTA partners in 92 percent of the cases. When the point estimate of the difference is negative, it is not statistically significant. To describe the difference and respective signifi-

[41] Although we could use any combination of countries that are not PTA partners, we think this test is more powerful if the control countries are not completely different from the PTA partners we test against (Canada and Mexico). For example, we would not want to generate multiple estimates reflecting combinations of microstates that export a handful of products to claim that in a majority of cases we confirm or reject that $\delta_c = \eta_c$. Thus, we restrict the countries to satisfy at least one of two criteria: either export at least one product in each of the 20 sectors considered, as Canada and Mexico do, or export at least 266 products, which corresponds to approximately 10 percent of the 2,658 lines that Mexico exported to the United States. The criteria are sensible, since the identification depends on differences in the products exported within a given industry. The results are not very sensitive to changes in the criteria, as we describe in the working paper (where we also list the 23 included countries). Many of the countries do not qualify because they benefit from preferences under the GSP. To compare with NAFTA, we construct all possible combinations of one and two countries, a total of 276 combinations.

cance, we plot the z-statistic for $\delta_c - \eta_c$.[42] Figure 2 plots the "smoothed" distribution of all the estimates. If there were no systematic differences, this distribution would be centered around zero. Clearly, the majority of the estimates is positive and significant. Therefore, this test provides further support that the United States did not reduce its MFN tariffs on products imported under NAFTA by as much as on other products not imported from its PTA partners.[43]

IV. Conclusion

Are preferential agreements a stumbling block for a country's multilateral liberalization? This question has been of central concern to economists and politicians in the last 15 years. We provide the first estimates to show that this concern is well founded for the United States. Its PTAs caused smaller reductions in multilateral tariffs of the goods it imported from its PTAs relative to similar non-PTA goods. Taking non-PTA goods as a reasonable counterfactual, this finding implies that the direct effect of the U.S. PTAs was to cause the MFN tariff for its PTA goods to remain higher than they would have been in the absence of PTAs. On average, an exporter to the United States that did not belong to one of its PTAs received only 52 percent as large a benefit (in terms of price increases) if it exported a PTA good instead of a similar non-PTA good. This effect is even stronger if the good was exported by all PTAs or was an important export for a PTA partner.

The direct stumbling block effect is present even for agreements with small countries. This is important because there are many more PTAs that the United States can still sign with small countries, and because such PTAs affect products exported by other small developing countries to the United States. These are countries relative to which the United States is likely to have market power, and thus smaller reductions in U.S. tariffs affect their export price adversely.

We also provide new estimates of tariff reciprocity in multilateral negotiations and solve the potential endogeneity problem associated with it. We confirm that reciprocity is indeed present for products that were not subject to NTBs. If other countries followed reciprocity, then the PTAs signed by the United States may have caused other countries to reciprocate with smaller reductions on U.S. products. It is also possible that the U.S. decision to sign PTAs had an indirect bargaining effect that made other countries more (or less) willing to liberalize. The bounds for the total effect that incorporates this potential indirect effect suggest that the direct one we focus on is a large component. So applying our approach to other countries should be useful in providing incremental evidence. Karacaovali and Limão (2005) do so for the European Union and find similar effects. In sum, although we can't yet definitively answer if PTAs lower worldwide aggregate MTL, we believe that our estimates provide an important starting point and suggest that outcome is likely.

Finally, our approach has the following application. With a new trade round under way, it is important to test if the proposals reflect the same pattern of the Uruguay Round. It may also be desirable to avoid it, both because the stumbling effect is potentially harmful to a number of countries and because it directly violates a 1999 WTO decision that "any preferential tariff treatment implemented pursuant to this Waiver [of the MFN rule for the purpose of preferential tariff treatment for LDCs ...] shall not constitute an impediment to the reduction or elimination of tariffs on a most-favored-nation basis."[44] This was precisely the waiver that the United States obtained to implement ATPA, for example. One simple way to ensure that this would not occur is to use the empirical model in this paper to evaluate tariff concession proposals.

[42] We estimate (8) in a modified form, $\delta_c G_i + \eta_c G_{ic} = (\delta_c - \eta_c)G_i + \eta_c(G_{ic} + G_i)$, so we test $\delta_c = \eta_c$ directly using a z-statistic.

[43] The level of the NAFTA coefficient, δ_c, is also informative. It is always positive and significant, and its median value is 0.74—within less than a standard error of the value estimated in Table 1. We also include the variable for PTAs other than NAFTA. That coefficient is also always positive and significant, and its median value is also within less than a standard error of the 0.71 estimate in Table 1.

[44] In WT/L/304, p. 2, accessed April 2003 on www.wto.org/english/docs_e/legal_e/waiver1999_e.pdf.

TABLE 1A—DATA DESCRIPTION

Name	Variable in model (3)	Data/description	Source[a]
USLIB	$\Delta\tau_{it}$	$\ln(1+\tau_{it}) - \ln(1+\tau_{it-1})$; τ_{it}: US ad valorem bound rate (post-UR). τ_{it-1} US ad valorem base rate (pre-UR)	WTO
ANYPTA	G_i	=1 if exported to the US under any preferential trade agreement before UR implemented (1994)	NBER/Feenstra et al. (2002)
EVRPTA		=1 if exported to the US under all its preferential trade agreements (1994)	" "
ANYPTAxHI_EX		=1 if exported to the US under any preferential trade agreement before UR implemented (1994) and export value of good *i* from each given PTA exceeds the mean export value of that PTA to the US in all goods	" "
NONAFTA		=1 if exported to the US under any preferential trade agreement except NAFTA (1994)	" "
PTA (NAFTA, etc.)		=1 if exported to the US under each of the respective PTAs (1994)	" "
s_{iT}^k		Partner *k*'s export share of top 5 exporters of *i* to US	" "
BARPOW	$\Sigma_k s_{iT}^k \Delta(b_t - b_t^k)$	$\Sigma_k s_{iT}^k \Delta(\ln \text{GDP}_t^{\text{US}} - \ln \text{GDP}_t^k)$	PWT 6.1
$\Sigma_j \Delta\tau_{jt}^k w_{jT}^k$		where $\Delta\tau_{jt}^k \equiv$ percent change 95 − 86 $\approx \ln(\tau_{j95}^k/\tau_{j86}^k)$; $w_{jT}^k \equiv$ share of good *j* in *k*'s imports	Finger et al. (2002)
$\Sigma_j \Delta\tau_{jt}^{\prime k} w_{jT}^k$		where $\Delta\tau_{jt}^{\prime k} \equiv$ percent change 95 − 92 $\approx \ln(\tau_{j95}^k/\tau_{j92}^k)$	Finger et al. (2002)
TOTLIB	$\Sigma_k s_{iT}^k \Sigma_j \Delta\tau_{jt}^k w_{jT}^k$	$\Sigma_k s_{iT}^k(\Sigma_j \Delta\tau_{jt}^k w_{jT}^k)$	
UNILIB		$\Sigma_k s_{iT}^k(\Sigma_j \Delta\tau_{jt}^k - \Sigma_j \Delta\tau_{jt}^{\prime k}) w_{jT}^k$	
NTB		=1 for HS 8-digit product *i* if the US had any NTB on it applied to *any* country in 1993	UNCTAD TRAINS
DS		=1 if 8-digit line is subdivided	WTO

Note: Please see the working paper for summary statistics of excluded instruments used in first-stage regressions.

[a] Abbreviations: PWT, Penn World Tables; USITC, United States International Trade Commission; WTO, World Trade Organization; UNCTAD, United Nations Conference on Trade and Development; UR, Uruguay Round.

REFERENCES

Bagwell, Kyle and Staiger, Robert W. "An Economic Theory of GATT." *American Economic Review*, 1999a, *89*(1), pp. 215–48.

Bagwell, Kyle and Staiger, Robert W. "Regionalism and Multilateral Tariff Co-Operation," in John Piggott and Allan D. Woodland, eds., *International trade policy and the Pacific Rim: Proceedings of the IEA conference held in Sydney, Australia*. London: Macmillan Press, 1999b, pp. 157–85.

Bagwell, Kyle and Staiger, Robert W. "Backward Stealing and Forward Manipulation in the WTO." *National Bureau of Economic Research, Inc., NBER Working Papers: No. 10420, 2004.*

Baldwin, Robert E. *The political economy of the US import policy*. Cambridge, MA: MIT Press, 1985.

Bhagwati, Jagdish. *The world trading system at risk*. Princeton: Princeton University Press, 1991.

Chang, Won and Winters, L. Alan. "How Regional Blocs Affect Excluded Countries: The Price Effects of Mercosur." *American Economic Review*, 2002, *92*(4), pp. 889–904.

Cheh, John H. "United States Concessions in the Kennedy Round and Short-Run Labor Adjustment Costs." *Journal of International Economics*, 1974, *4*(4), pp. 323–40.

Feenstra, Robert C. "Symmetric Pass-through of Tariffs and Exchange Rates under Imperfect Competition: An Empirical Test." *Journal of International Economics*, 1989, *27*(1–2), pp. 25–45.

Feenstra, Robert C.; Romalis, John and Schott, Peter K. "U.S. Imports, Exports, and Tariff Data, 1989–2001." National Bureau of Economic Research, Inc., NBER Working Papers: No. 9387, 2002.

Finger, J. Michael; Ingco, Merlinda D. and Reincke, Ulrich. *The Uruguay Round: Statistics on tariff concessions given and received.* Washington, D.C.: World Bank, 1996.

Finger, J. Michael; Reincke, Ulrich and Castro, Adriana. "Market Access Bargaining in the Uruguay Round: How Tightly Does Reciprocity Constrain?" in Jagidish Bhagwati, ed., *Going alone: The case for relaxed reciprocity in freeing trade.* Cambridge and London: MIT Press, 2002, pp. 111–35.

Foroutan, Faezeh. "Does Membership in a Regional Preferential Trade Arrangement Make a Country More or Less Protectionist?" *World Economy*, 1998, *21*(3), pp. 305–35.

Frankel, Jeffrey A.; Stein, Ernesto and Wei, Shang-Jin. "Regional Trading Arrangements: Natural or Supernatural." *American Economic Review*, 1996, *86*(2), pp. 52–56.

Goldberg, Pinelopi K. and Maggi, Giovanni. "Protection for Sale: An Empirical Investigation." *American Economic Review*, 1999, *89*(5), pp. 1135–55.

Grossman, Gene M. and Helpman, Elhanan. "The Politics of Free-Trade Agreements." *American Economic Review*, 1995, *85*(4), pp. 667–90.

Hayashi, Fumio. *Econometrics.* Princeton: Princeton University Press, 2000.

Hoekman, Bernard M. and Kostecki, Michel M. *The political economy of the world trading system: The WTO and beyond.* 2nd ed. Oxford: Oxford University Press, 1995.

Karacaovali, Baybars and Limão, Nuno. "The Clash of Liberalizations: Preferential versus Multilateral Trade Liberalization in the European Union." The World Bank, Policy Research Working Paper Series: No. 3493, 2005.

Kreinin, Mordechai E. "Effect of Tariff Changes on the Prices and Volume of Imports." *American Economic Review*, 1961, *51*(3), pp. 310–24.

Krishna, Pravin. "Regionalism and Multilateralism: A Political Economy Approach." *Quarterly Journal of Economics*, 1998, *113*(1), pp. 227–51.

Krugman, Paul R. "Is Bilateralism Bad?" in Elhanan Helpman and Assaf Razin, eds., *International trade and trade policy.* Cambridge, MA: MIT Press, 1991, pp. 9–23.

Levy, Philip I. "A Political-Economic Analysis of Free-Trade Agreements." *American Economic Review*, 1997, *87*(4), pp. 506–19.

Limão, Nuno. "Are Preferential Trade Agreements with Non-trade Objectives a Stumbling Block for Multilateral Liberalization?" University of Maryland, Center for International Economics Working Paper No. 02-02, 2002, www.wam.umd.edu/~limao/lspta_ciewp0202.pdf.

Limão, Nuno. "Preferential Trade Agreements as Stumbling Blocks for Multilateral Trade Liberalization: Evidence for the US." Center for Economic Policy Research, CEPR Discussion Papers: No. 4884, 2005.

Marvel, Howard P. and Ray, Edward J. "The Kennedy Round: Evidence on the Regulation of International Trade in the United States." *American Economic Review*, 1983, *73*(1), pp. 190–97.

Trefler, Daniel. "Trade Liberalization and the Theory of Endogenous Protection: An Econometric Study of U.S. Import Policy." *Journal of Political Economy*, 1993, *101*(1), pp. 138–60.

Winters, L. Alan. "Regionalism vs. Multilateralism," in Richard Baldwin, Daniel Cohen, André Sapir, and Anthony J. Venables, eds., *Market integration, regionalism and the global economy.* Cambridge: Cambridge University Press, 1999, chap. 2.

Chapter 14

The clash of liberalizations: Preferential vs. multilateral trade liberalization in the European Union☆

Baybars Karacaovali [a], Nuno Limão [b,c,d,*]

[a] *Department of Economics, Fordham University, Bronx, NY 10458, United States*
[b] *Department of Economics, University of Maryland, College Park, MD 20742, United States*
[c] *NBER, United States*
[d] *CEPR, United Kingdom*

Received 5 December 2006; received in revised form 26 February 2007; accepted 26 July 2007

Abstract

Preferential trade agreements (PTAs) are characterized by liberalization with respect to only a few partners and thus they can potentially clash with, and retard multilateral trade liberalization (MTL). Yet there is almost no systematic evidence on whether the numerous existing PTAs actually affect MTL. We provide a model showing that PTAs hinder MTL unless they entail accession to a customs union with internal transfers. Using product-level tariffs negotiated by the European Union (EU) in the last two multilateral trade rounds we find that several of its PTAs have clashed with its MTL. However, this effect is absent for EU accessions. Moreover, we provide new evidence on the political economy determinants of trade policy in the EU.

Keywords: Preferential trade agreements; Customs unions; Multilateral trade negotiations; MFN tariff concessions; Reciprocity

JEL classification: D78; F13; F14; F15

1. Introduction

Over 130 preferential trade agreements (PTAs) were formed between 1995 and 2005—more than in the previous 50 years combined. Nearly all countries are currently members of at least one PTA and at least a third of world trade is

☆ We thank, without implicating, two anonymous referees, Stephanie Aaronson, Piyush Chandra, Alan Deardorff, Kishore Gawande, Juan Carlos Hallak, Bernard Hoekman, Marcelo Olarreaga, Robert Staiger, Patricia Tovar-Rodriguez and Alan Winters for helpful discussions and comments. We also thank the participants at the seminars in Michigan State University and University of Michigan as well as at the Midwest International Economic Group Conference (St. Louis, November 2004), the ASSA meetings (Philadelphia, January 2005), and the International Trade and Finance Association 15th International Conference (Istanbul, Turkey, May 2005). Marcelo Olarreaga and John Romalis generously shared some of the data. Nuno Limão gratefully acknowledges the financial support of the World Bank and IMF Research Groups, which hosted him during part of this research. The views expressed in this paper are those of the authors and not of those institutions.
* Corresponding author. Department of Economics, University of Maryland, College Park, MD 20742, United States. Tel.: +1 301 405 7842; fax: +1 301 405 3542.
E-mail addresses: karacaovali@fordham.edu (B. Karacaovali), limao@econ.umd.edu (N. Limão).

0022-1996/$ - see front matter
doi:10.1016/j.jinteco.2007.07.003

Originally Published in *Journal of International Economics* 74, pp. 299–327.

carried out under such agreements. Although most economists favor multilateral trade liberalization (MTL), there is no such consensus on the desirability of preferential liberalization. The original concern with PTAs was their ambiguous effect on welfare: positive if the preferential partner is more efficient than the rest of the world but negative otherwise (Viner, 1950). During the late 1980s and early 1990s, MTL was stalled while the United States and the European Union pursued PTAs, generating much debate on whether PTAs are a "building block" or a "stumbling block" towards MTL (Bhagwati, 1991). This issue was also prominent in the latest multilateral round since several developing countries fear that MTL will erode the preferences provided to them.[1]

An important source of concern with PTAs is that they can hurt non-members. One direct channel by which this occurs is if the PTA members divert their import demand away from the non-members and this effect is large enough to reduce non-members' export prices. There is evidence of trade diversion (Romalis, 2007) and also some direct evidence that PTAs do lower export prices for non-members (Chang and Winters, 2002). This and other costs to non-members due to discrimination disappear if the preference is fully eroded by MTL. Thus, it is crucial to determine if PTAs hold back MTL and entrench these costs, particularly given that a large share of world trade is not yet covered by any preferences. After much debate there is still no theoretical consensus about and scant empirical evidence of a "clash of liberalizations". We use product-level protection data to estimate the impact of European Union PTAs on its multilateral liberalization in the last multilateral trade round and find evidence of such a clash. The effect is present for all European Union (EU) preferential agreements except those involving full accession where the partner becomes a EU member. Both findings are predictions of our model as we explain below.

There are several compelling reasons for focusing on the EU. First, given that the EU is the world's largest trader, its trade policy surely affects non-members. Second, as we discuss below, the EU has different types of preferential agreements, which allows us to theoretically derive and test a rich set of predictions. Finally, although the EU accounts for at least a fifth of world trade, there is hardly any empirical evidence on the formation of the EU's trade policy in general and none that analyzes how its PTAs affect its MTL.[2]

Most of the early theory focuses on PTAs that are purely motivated by trade related issues and then analyzes their effect on MTL assuming that MTL implies free trade. Therefore, that research centers on how PTAs affect the binary choice between free trade and no MTL, and it effectively asks whether PTAs make a multilateral trade round more or less likely (cf. Krishna, 1998; Levy, 1997). Assuming that a round leads to free trade and focusing on the probability of a round simplifies the analysis but generates predictions that are very difficult to test because these rounds are so infrequent. Moreover, countries can choose to conclude a multilateral round with considerable liberalization or one with almost none. Thus, the focus should be on whether PTAs affect the change in multilateral tariffs and not simply the probability of a round.[3]

The model we develop, which builds on Limão (2007), captures key features of the multilateral system and of recent PTAs, and generates several specific predictions that we test. The main one is that multilateral tariffs are higher on goods that a country imports duty-free from preferential partners (PTA goods, henceforth) than on otherwise similar goods (non-PTA goods). The basic intuition for this result is the following. Suppose the EU offers preferential duty-free access in a set of goods to a certain country. The latter benefits from facing lower tariffs than its competitors; the fact that the EU signs the PTA indicates that its member governments value it at given multilateral tariffs. If the EU eliminated its multilateral tariff on that same set of goods, it would effectively eliminate the PTA that it valued. We show that this additional cost of MTL is only present for the subset of PTA goods and affects multilateral tariff levels only when the preferential tariff is already zero since otherwise, the preferential tariff can be reduced to maintain the preferential margin. The model also predicts that there is no stumbling block effect if the PTA involves full accession

[1] The latest round was launched in 2001 and according to an article in the leaders section of the *Economist* magazine, a factor that may lead to its collapse is that "Poor countries with preferential access to rich world markets want to make sure that freer trade will not reduce these preferences" ("Talking the Talk", July 17th 2004, p. 14). However, the *possibility* that these preferences would reduce MTL is not new: it was a concern raised when the generalized system of preferences to developing countries was originally proposed (Johnson, 1967, p. 166).

[2] Constantopoulos (1974) and Riedel (1977) examine some determinants of protection of individual members before accession to the EU and Tavares (2001) analyzes the determinants of the EU's common external tariff. Those authors use industry data and we are not aware of any paper that has thus far analyzed product level protection in the EU.

[3] Bagwell and Staiger (1999a) analyze two opposing effects of PTAs on the equilibrium multilateral tariff *level* in a self-enforcing model. They show that PTAs are a stumbling block if countries are very patient and a building block otherwise. Another approach is due to Krugman (1991) who analyzes the welfare path for exogenously expanding trading blocs, which Bond and Syropoulos (1996) also analyze. Winters (1999) surveys this literature.

because the EU can now easily offset any reduction in preferential margins due to MTL through a direct cash transfer to the preferential partner.

The central motive for the EU to offer trade preferences in this theoretical model is to extract concessions from its PTA partners on areas not directly related to trade. This is a key feature of many of the PTAs the EU had in place in 1994, as we describe in Section 2, and so we employ this model's structural equation for the equilibrium trade policy as the basis for our estimation. However, the empirical analysis will include all of the EU's PTAs and we will explain how our instrumental variables approach can address omitted variable issues that could arise when other motives for PTAs are important.

Using detailed tariff data we find that the EU's PTAs generated a stumbling block for its MTL in the last trade round. More specifically, the EU reduced its multilateral tariffs on goods not imported under PTAs by almost twice as much as on its PTA goods, as predicted by the model. We ensure that the results are robust to reverse causation and other possible sources of endogeneity by employing an IV-GMM estimator and testing for the exogeneity of different variables and the validity of our instruments. The stumbling block effect we estimate is stronger for goods that were exported by all of the EU's PTA partners. Various robustness tests provide further support for the baseline estimates. The effect is not present for goods with a positive preferential tariff or in EU accessions, which are two important auxiliary predictions of our model. In sum, EU accessions in the 1980s and 1995 did not significantly hinder (or promote) its MTL but all of the other PTAs in place in 1994 hindered its MTL. Both types of agreements are important for the EU so it is useful to recall that the latter are the source of the stumbling block effect.[4]

The results are also economically significant. The estimates imply that the average increase on prices received by exporters to the EU due to its multilateral tariff changes was only about half for PTA goods relative to other goods. Moreover, according to the theoretical model, our estimate represents not only the current wedge in the tariffs between PTA and non-PTA goods but also what the actual tariff wedge for the set of PTA goods would be relative to the counterfactual where the EU has no preferences for that *same* set of goods. That wedge is about 1.4 percentage points whereas the current average tariff for PTA goods in our sample is 4.7%.

There is a small but growing literature on this important question. Limão (2006) provides detailed evidence of a "clash of liberalizations" for the US in the Uruguay Round. His approach is similar to ours but we test a number of additional predictions that are relevant for the EU and we follow the structural equations more closely. However, it is possible that in other countries PTAs lead to lower protection against non-members. Foroutan (1998) finds lower average non-preferential tariffs for Latin American countries with PTAs after the Uruguay Round. She notes that no causality can be drawn from such a correlation because those countries were moving away from import substitution during the 1990s, which implied considerable unilateral liberalization independently of any effects from PTAs. Two other interesting papers on Latin America go much farther than establishing univariate correlations. Bohara et al. (2004) estimate that the Argentine unilateral tariffs were lower in industries where the value of imports from MERCOSUR to value added in Argentina was highest. Estevadeordal et al. (2006) provide a systematic study for ten Latin American countries and find that preferences were associated with lower non-preferential tariffs in the period of 1990 to 2001. None of these three papers model multilateral negotiations so there is no systematic evidence that PTAs lead to more multilateral liberalization. Even if such evidence is found for Latin American and some other countries, it will be difficult to overturn the concern that PTAs slow down MTL because the current evidence supports this conclusion for two of the largest traders, the EU and the US, which are central to this controversy.

Reciprocity in tariff changes is a key feature of our model and also of the leading economic theory of the GATT (Bagwell and Staiger, 1999b). However, some economists question whether it is followed in practice (Finger et al., 2002). We empirically model the multilateral negotiation process and find that reciprocity was followed in the last trade round: the EU's tariff reductions were largest for products exported by countries that provided greater increases in market access. Finally, we model and provide novel evidence of the EU's internal political economy determinants of trade policy. The EU places some, but not much, additional weight on producer than consumer welfare. In this respect our findings are similar to structural estimates of the Grossman and Helpman (1994) model that also find small values for the US.

The paper is organized as follows. We start with a brief description of the EU's trade policy formation that guides the theoretical and empirical modelling. In Section 3, we model the interaction between PTAs and MTL and derive the

[4] A narrow measure of their relative importance is total exports to the EU in 1994, which were about twice as high for the non-acceding PTA partners relative to the ones that acceded in the 1980s and 1995. Since 1995 the EU has pursued both types of PTAs.

main theoretical predictions. In Section 4, we first discuss our strategy for empirical identification and then analyze and quantify the estimation results. In the final section we summarize the main results and discuss their implications. All the proofs and details regarding the data are in the Appendix.

2. The European Union's trade policy

Before its expansion in 2004, the EU's membership was composed of 15 countries that accounted for one third of the world output and more than 20% of world trade. The EU succeeded the European Communities that started in the 1950s as a customs union. Currently, its members form a single market with free movement of goods, services, capital, and labor. There is also a very strong element of cooperation between members in non-trade policies, particularly in issues with regional spillovers such as immigration, environment, development of poorer regions, foreign policy, and judicial matters.

The key actors in the formation of the EU trade policy are the European Commission and the Council. The Commission proposes, negotiates and enforces trade policy on behalf of the members. The Council, where each member's government is represented, is the decision maker with the power to approve or reject the Commission's proposals for trade policy negotiations and their eventual outcome. That is, the Council is decisive in approving the common external tariff that the Commission negotiates in multilateral trade rounds as well as any preferential treatment it negotiates with non-EU members.

The EU's expansion of preferential trade treatment has occurred both through increased membership—initially 6 countries and 15 by the time of our analysis (now 27)—and through numerous PTAs with non-members. Table A1 in the appendix provides some details about all of the latter that were in place by 1994 including their abbreviations—here we note only a few key points. First, several of the EU's PTAs do not require the partner to lower their tariffs. Second, many of these PTAs, e.g. preferences to developing countries through GSP and ACP, seek, and at times explicitly require, cooperation in non-trade issues such as labor standards, human rights, migration control, and combat against drugs. The PTAs with the Mediterranean countries are also similar in nature and are aimed at addressing issues with regional externalities, such as immigration.[5] These features are explicitly captured by our model. Several of the countries that benefit from this preferential treatment fear that MTL on the part of the EU will erode these preferences. Thus, they have at times opposed MTL but the EU itself has used the same argument to avoid liberalizing, which is central to our model.[6]

In the estimation we also consider the remaining preferences the EU had in place before the Uruguay Round: to EFTA members that did not eventually join the EU and to some Central and East European economies. These did involve reciprocal trade preferences. However, the East European countries had to comply with several side conditions such as environmental and intellectual property regulations. For the EU, the benefits of these side conditions along with the political integration in Western Europe likely outweighed the preferential treatment provided to the EU exports. A similar argument applies to the accession of Greece, Spain and Portugal to the EU. So our model will focus on this exchange of preferences on the part of the EU for cooperation in non-trade issues, appropriately modified in the cases of accessions where a common external tariff is applied.

3. Theory

In this section, we show how PTAs can induce higher non-preferential (i.e. MFN) tariffs. The model captures key features of the EU's PTAs, as previously described, by extending Limão (2007) along several important dimensions. First, we model a political economy motive for the use of tariffs, which is an important determinant of the cross-sectional tariff structure. Second, we allow for different types of PTAs, both without a common external tariff and with it as well as direct cash transfers across members. In Karacaovali and Limão (2005) we provide additional microfoundations for various parts of the model and show how the results extend in different directions. Here we focus

[5] According to Jackson (1997, p. 160) "during the last twenty-five years or so the experience of the GSP in the GATT system has been that the industrialized countries often succumb to the temptation to use the preference systems as part of 'bargaining chips' of *diplomacy*." The conditionality of EU's concessions in exchange for cooperation has further been documented for instance in Grilli (1997).

[6] A stark example was the European Commission's argument that a cut in the price support of about 25% in EU sugar was not tenable because it would cause an income loss of 250 million euros to ACP countries, some of whom export sugar to the EU under preferential treatment. European Commission (2000), "Commission Proposes Overhaul of Sugar Market," Brussels, October 4th 2000, IP/00/1109.

on the simplest model that can provide a number of new predictions about PTAs that are relevant for the EU and derive the structural equations that guide the estimation.

3.1. Setup

We first describe the basic economic structure and trade pattern. We then model the government's objective and show how it depends on multilateral and preferential tariffs as well as the supply of regional public goods, which motivate the cooperation in non-trade issues behind many of the EU's PTAs.

Each of the two symmetric regional blocs is composed of two economies, which we denote by $j=L, S$. All variables in the "foreign" bloc are denoted with an "*". Each country produces a numeraire using labor—the only factor—in a constant returns process with productivity normalized to unity. The numeraire is freely traded so the wage is equal to unity in all countries. The supply of non-numeraire goods is fixed and equal to $X_i^j \geq 0$ units of good i in country j.

For expositional purposes we maintain the trade pattern as simple as possible and illustrate the basic results using only two goods (in addition to the numeraire). Country L imports good 1 from both L^* and the regional partner, S. Symmetrically, L^* imports good 2 from L and S^*. The small countries, S and S^*, only export to their respective regional bloc partners and we assume that the prices they receive by exporting are above the maximum threshold price that consumers in S and S^* are willing to pay. Thus, effectively the equilibrium demand for non-numeraire goods in S and S^* is zero, which, along with the fixed supply, implies that their net exports are price inelastic. This allows us to show that a PTA can lead to a stumbling block effect even if it takes place with small countries and leads to no changes in their export volume. This assumption is analytically convenient and also plausible for some but not all EU agreements, as we can see in Table A1. However, the qualitative results are similar if we relax this elasticity assumption, as we show in Karacaovali and Limão (2005).

Country L sets a specific tariff τ_1 on the imports from L^* and a preferential tariff $\pi_1 \leq \tau_1$ on S. The equilibrium domestic price in L for its import, p_1, is then derived from the market clearing condition:

$$M_1(p_1) + M_1^*(p_1 - \tau_1) + M_1^s = 0 \tag{1}$$

where $M_1(\cdot) \equiv D_1(p_1) - X_1$ and $M_1^*(\cdot) \equiv D_1^*(p_1 - \tau_1) - X_1^*$ are the net import demand functions for L and L^*; M_1^s is the respective function for S, which in equilibrium is $-X_1^s$ given that $D_1^s = 0$ as described above. We assume that S^* has no endowment of good 1. The domestic price in L^* for its export is simply the price in L net of the tariff, $p_1 - \tau_1$. A similar market clearing condition holds for good 2, which is imported by L^*. Thus the domestic prices in L and L^* for their respective imports can be written as functions of their own tariffs, i.e. $p_1(\tau_1)$ and $p_2^*(\tau_2^*)$. Implicitly differentiating Eq. (1) we can show that an increase in τ_1 lowers the exporter price, $p_1 - \tau_1$, and increases p_1. Note that because the net exports of S and S^* are price inelastic, the equilibrium prices are not directly affected by the preferential tariffs.

We now model the government objective and then derive the multilateral tariff in the absence of PTAs. In this part of the exercise we can abstract from the objective of small countries and so defer its presentation until Section 3.2.2, where we analyze the case with PTAs. Thus we also simplify the notation by dropping the country superscript for L's variables. The government in L sets trade policy and chooses the tax rate, e, to finance expenditures on a public good in order to maximize the following political support function

$$\begin{aligned} G(\tau, \pi, \tau^*, e^s, e) \equiv 1 &- \left[\tau_1 M_1^*(p_1(\tau_1) - \tau_1) + \pi_1 M_1^s\right] + \left[\upsilon_1(p_1(\tau_1)) + \upsilon_2(p_2(\tau_2^*))\right] \\ &+ \left[\omega_1 p_1(\tau_1) X_1 + \omega_2 p_2(\tau_2^*) X_2\right] + \left[\Psi(e, e^s) - e\right] \end{aligned} \tag{2}$$

We have normalized the size of the population to one so the first term represents aggregate labor income. The second set of terms in brackets represents tariff revenue. The $\upsilon_i(\cdot)$ terms represent consumer surplus, which depend only on the good's own domestic price.[7] The first set of terms in brackets on the second line represents a weighted value of endowments, where $\omega_i \geq 1$. Note that if $\omega_i = 1$ for all i, the objective reduces to a standard social welfare function.

[7] We assume that the underlying consumer utility is additively separable and throughout we focus on a quadratic form of each good's subutility for L and L^* that gives rise to linear demand curves.

Therefore $\omega_i - 1$ can be interpreted as a political economy weight the government places on suppliers.[8] Since we do not have data on export subsidies, and they are generally not permitted by the WTO, we focus on the case where the large countries do not have a motive to use them in the first place, i.e. $\omega_2 = 1$. This does not affect the stumbling block effect we derive. Note also that we can easily extend the objective in Eq. (2) to incorporate multiple import and export goods by simply adding their contributions to consumer surplus, endowment value and tariff revenue analogously to goods 1 and 2. Subsequently, when we extend the model in this way, the tariff vectors, τ, π and τ^* will contain multiple elements.

The key difference between this government objective and the ones commonly found in other trade policy applications is the last set of terms in brackets on the second line. The first term, $\Psi(e, e^s)$, represents the benefit from expenditures on issues with a regional spillover such as the environment, human and labor rights, immigration, etc. We assume that this function is concave and separable in the provision of the local and regional public goods. The direct cost is captured by $-e$, the value of the lump-sum tax (measured in terms of the numeraire) that is used to finance the public good in L.

3.2. Preferential vs. multilateral trade liberalization

3.2.1. MFN tariffs without preferences

We first derive the MFN tariffs when PTAs are not allowed, which provides the natural benchmark to determine if PTAs hinder multilateral liberalization. Following Bagwell and Staiger (1999b), we model reciprocal trade liberalization in the WTO as a cooperative outcome between countries that generates a gain from overcoming a terms-of-trade externality.[9] Accordingly, most of the negotiations occur between large countries and follow what is known as the principal supplier rule: if, for a given product, country L is the largest exporter to L^*, then L^* proposes a tariff reduction to L in that product in exchange for L's tariff reduction on L^*'s exports to L. The MFN rule then requires this reduction to be extended to all other WTO exporters of similar goods. Given that both the EU and the rest of the world are several times larger than most of the EU's individual PTA partners we take L and L^* as the principal suppliers. In the estimation section we relax this assumption.

The large countries choose multilateral tariffs to maximize their joint objective. Given the symmetry we can concentrate on maximizing L's objective after imposing the condition that tariffs in their respective import sectors are equal, $\tau^* = \tau$. We abstract from enforcement considerations such as the ones addressed in Limão (2007). The equilibrium multilateral tariffs in the absence of a PTA are given by

$$\tau^m \equiv \arg\max_{\tau} \{G(\tau = \tau^*, \pi, \tau^*, e^s, .) : \pi = \tau\} \tag{3}$$

where the constraint $\pi = \tau$ precludes PTAs and, when L imports only good 1 we have $\tau^m = \tau_1^m$. In the appendix we use the first-order condition (FOC) to derive the advalorem equivalent tariff, $t^m = \tau^m/p$, since it is the focus of our empirical work. For good $i = 1$ this tariff is implicitly given by

$$t_i^m = (\omega_i - 1)\frac{X_i/M_i}{\varepsilon_i} + \frac{M_i^s}{M_i^* + M_i^s}\frac{1}{\varepsilon_i^*} \tag{4}$$

where ε_i denotes L's import demand elasticity and ε_i^* is the foreign export supply elasticity it faces.[10] If good i is not exported by the regional partner, i.e. if $M_i^s = 0$, this expression is similar to several political economy models (Helpman, 1999). The tariff is increasing in the political economy weight, ω_i, and the inverse of the import penetration ratio, X_i/M_i. This term is weighted by the import elasticity for standard Ramsey taxation reasons. The last term

[8] This is a reduced form that can be obtained as a special case from a model where lobbying is given micro-foundations, such as in Grossman and Helpman (1994), provided that in that model the ownership of the specific factors is concentrated. In Karacaovali and Limão (2005) we show that Eq. (2) can be obtained as the objective for the EU that arises from bargaining between independent EU-member governments—a fair representation of the EU's trade policy formation, as we describe in Section 2.

[9] Bagwell and Staiger (2006) provide evidence for their theory by showing that WTO accession leads to greater tariff reductions in products with higher initial import volumes. Broda, Limão and Weinstein (2006) estimate that several countries have considerable market power in trade in certain goods and use it to set higher tariffs prior to their WTO accession.

[10] Both of these are evaluated at the equilibrium tariff. Their definitions are $\varepsilon_i \equiv -M_i'p_i^*/M_i$ and $\varepsilon_i^* \equiv [\partial(M_i^* + M_i^s)/\partial p_i^*] \times [p_i^*/(M_i^* + M_i^s)]$. Note that import demand elasticities are typically estimated with respect to the domestic price but we define it slightly differently for the purpose of the model discussion and derivations. However, our empirical implementation will take this into account explicitly. See Table A3 for details.

represents an MFN externality effect and leads to higher tariffs. It arises if S does not participate in MTL directly because the MFN clause requires L and L^* to lower their tariffs on imports from all partners even if some did not reciprocally lower their own tariffs.

In the empirical work we must address the fact that the EU sets tariffs on multiple goods. The expression in Eq. (4) applies in such a setting to any good i that is not subject to a preference, i.e. whenever $\tau_i = \pi_i$, and whether PTAs are allowed or not. The reason for this is the additive separability of goods in the government's objective and the symmetry across regional blocs. These two assumptions imply that L can reciprocate any tariff reduction by L^* on the symmetric import sector independently of what occurs in the remaining goods. That is if L also imported an additional good, $i=3$, symmetric to L^*'s import of $i=4$, there would be an additional FOC for τ_3 independent of the one for the original import, τ_1. We relax this symmetry assumption in the empirical section. But it is useful to keep in mind that Eq. (4) captures the benchmark equilibrium rate for the subset of products in which S either does not export or does not receive any preferences even when PTAs are already pursued. Thus, we use these "non-PTA" goods as a control group in the estimation.

3.2.2. MFN tariffs with preferences

We first model preferential tariffs and then determine their effect on multilateral tariffs. The PTA between L and S is characterized by a bargaining solution where L grants preferential tariffs, $\pi \leq \tau$, in exchange for an increase in S's provision of the regional public good. To capture the asymmetry in size and bargaining power between the EU and its PTA partners we allow L to make a take-it-or-leave-it offer to S.

Country S also maximizes a political support function, G^s, given by a weighted sum of income net of the cost of providing the public good, $1-e^s$, and the value of the endowment, which is exported to L.

$$G^s(\pi, \tau, e^s) \equiv 1 - e^s + (p_1(\tau_1) - \pi_1)\omega_1^s X_1^s \tag{5}$$

In the absence of a PTA we have $e^s=0$ since we simplify by assuming that S places no weight on the regional activity valued by L. When S is a WTO member, the highest credible threat tariff that L can use is to revert to the MFN tariffs, i.e. set $\pi=\tau$, as required by the WTO rules. So, for a given MFN tariff, S will accept to participate in the PTA if

$$G^s(\pi = \pi^p, \tau, e^s = e^p) \geq G^s(\pi = \tau, \tau, e^s = 0) \tag{6}$$

Since L extracts all the bargaining surplus from the PTA, the bargaining equilibrium level of e^s, denoted by e^p, is increased until this participation constraint holds with equality. This yields the following equilibrium level of e^s for a given preferential tariff margin of $(\tau_1 - \pi_1)$:

$$e^p = (\tau_1 - \pi_1)\omega_1^s X_1^s \tag{7}$$

Intuitively, L can require S to collect an amount of the lump-sum tax e^p (used to supply the regional public good) that is as high as the value that S places on the revenue transfer from L due to the preference. Higher weight is given to products with larger political influence in S. If S exports multiple goods then the expression on the right-hand side of Eq. (7) would be a sum over the goods it exports to L.[11]

The governments in L and L^* choose multilateral tariffs as before with a key difference. Now they take into account the effect that these tariffs have on the PTA by changing the preferential margin and consequently the provision of the regional public good in Eq. (7). Hence, the equilibrium MFN and preferential tariffs are given by

$$\{\tau^{mp}, \pi^p\} \equiv \arg\max_{\tau,\pi} \{G(\tau = \tau^*, \pi, \tau^*, e^s, .) : \pi \leq \tau; e^s = e^p\} \tag{8}$$

[11] When L sets the MFN tariffs it assumes that S accepts the PTA and that if S were to renege on it, then L would remove the preference and set its tariff on S equal to the MFN tariff originally agreed upon with L^*. This is perhaps easier to understand in a setup where cooperation is maintained due to repeated interaction, as in our working paper. In the repeated setup case we simply require that if at a future date S stops supplying the regional good, then the large countries do not renegotiate their MFN tariffs. We think this is a plausible assumption in practice given the costs of renegotiating MFN tariffs between rounds. Nonetheless, we can also consider the alternative when the threat point in Eq. (6) uses the equilibrium MFN tariff without a PTA. This alternative introduces some changes but we obtain similar qualitative results and in particular the condition that we will show is key for obtaining a stumbling block effect–a duty-free preferential tariff–is still necessary in this case (proof available on request).

As we show in the appendix (Section A.1) this yields the following equilibrium advalorem MFN tariff for a good exported by S to its PTA partner, $t_i^{mp} = \tau_i^{mp}/p_i^*$.

$$t_i^{mp} = \left(G_{e^s}\partial e^p/\partial\tau_i - X_i^s\right)\frac{1}{M_i p_i'}\frac{1}{\varepsilon_i} + (\omega_i - 1)\frac{X_i/M_i}{\varepsilon_i} + \frac{M_i^s}{M_i^* + M_i^s}\frac{1}{\varepsilon_i^*} \tag{9}$$

The key difference relative to the tariff if PTAs were forbidden, t_i^m, is the first term, which captures the potential for a stumbling block effect due to the PTA, i.e. the potential for $t_i^{mp} > t_i^m$. To interpret and sign this effect, note that $1/M_i p_i' \varepsilon_i$ is positive, so the sign depends only on whether $G_{e^s}\partial e^p/\partial\tau_i > X_i^s$. That is on whether the marginal benefit for L of increasing the preferential margin and obtaining additional e^s, exceeds the marginal cost from lost tariff revenue, X_i^s. This depends on whether the preferential tariff is positive or not. To see this we can use the FOC for the preferential tariff, π_i, that requires

$$-(G_{e^s}\partial e^p/\partial\pi_i + G_{\pi_i}) \geq 0 \tag{10}$$

When the equilibrium preferential tariff is zero, we are at a corner solution and so this condition holds with strict inequality. In this case the marginal benefit to L of *increasing* the preferential margin exceeds the marginal cost but it cannot increase the margin by lowering the preferential tariff when it is already at zero, therefore it increases the MFN tariff. So the PTA has a stumbling block effect when the preferential tariff is already zero. If the PTA good is imported under a positive preferential tariff then Eq. (10) holds with equality and so the MFN tariff is unchanged, i.e. $t_i^{mp} = t_i^m$. To see this formally we note that $\partial e^p/\partial\tau_i = -\partial e^p/\partial\pi_i$ (Eq. (7)) and $G_{\pi_i} = X_i^s$ (Eq. (2)) such that $G_{e^s}\partial e^p/\partial\tau_i - X_i^s = -(G_{e^s}\partial e^p/\partial\pi_i + G_{\pi_i})$. A sufficient condition for a corner solution in the PTA is for L to place enough weight on S's provision of the regional good.

In sum, the intuition for the stumbling block effect is as follows. When the marginal benefit for L of increasing e^s is higher than the cost in terms of the foregone tariff revenue, L prefers to increase the preferential margin given to S and it initially does this by reducing the preferential tariff. However, once the preferential tariff is at zero, the preferential margin can only be increased by raising the MFN tariff and that is the optimal action for L.

A natural definition of the stumbling block effect is the difference of the MFN tariffs with and without PTAs.

$$t_i^{mp} - t_i^m = \left(G_{e^s}\omega_i^s - 1\right)\frac{X_i^s}{M_i p_i'}\frac{1}{\varepsilon_i} \geq 0 \tag{11}$$

The focus of the estimation is to identify this term and test if it is positive. Before we describe exactly how we test this and other predictions we briefly note how this effect is also present in more realistic setups.

If the large countries also placed a political economy weight on their exporters then, in the absence of export subsidies, the equilibrium MFN tariff would be lower. This occurs because each country now places a higher weight on price increases for its exporters. It is simple to show that the export "lobby term" that arises in this case is identical with or without PTAs so it does not affect the stumbling block effect.

When we relax the inelastic export supply assumption for S, the difference between the MFN tariffs with and without PTAs includes an additional term due to the trade volume effect. More specifically, the PTA causes an increase in S's exports to L and a decrease of L^*'s exports to L, which causes a decline in the MFN tariff. This channel is similar to the tariff complementarity in Bagwell and Staiger (1999a). The extra trade term attenuates but does not fully offset the stumbling block effect, as we show in our working paper.

We also test two other interesting predictions that follow from the model. First, if the effect is present, then it should be stronger for the PTA goods that are more important exports of S to L since a given margin applies to a higher export volume. Second, when S exports multiple goods, the effect is still present in the set of goods where the preferential tariff is zero but not where it is positive. In the latter case the preferential tariff can be lowered, which is less costly to L than increasing the MFN tariff in *that* good but leads to the same benefit for S.

The last result with multiple goods may not be immediately obvious but we prove it in the appendix (Section A.2); here we provide the intuition. The EU can and often chooses to provide preferences for only a subset of products and for some of them it sets positive preferential tariffs, e.g. in agreements that do not fall under GATT article XXIV. Why would the EU ever increase the margin in good 1 by distorting its MFN tariff if it could increase its overall transfer to S by lowering the preferential tariff in some other good it imports, say good 3? According to this model the EU would do so when an increase in the preferential margin to good 1 is more valuable to S because its suppliers have more political influence, i.e. $\omega_1^s > \omega_3^s$. So, even though the cost to L of increasing the margin for good 1 by distorting the MFN may be slightly higher, so is the benefit in terms of the amount of regional public good it obtains, as we can see in Eq. (7). In sum, with multiple goods we must consider the EU's optimal allocation of preferences across goods, which depends on the political weights in S. The model predicts that the stumbling effect is present in the set of goods where the preferential tariff is zero but not in those where it is positive. Thus the model not only provides us with a structural equation to guide the estimation but also a set of predictions that are not obvious from the outset.

3.2.3. Common external tariff and direct transfers

Most results on PTAs depend on whether they have a common external tariff (c.f. Cadot et al., 1999; Bagwell and Staiger, 1999a). Given that between the Tokyo and Uruguay Rounds—the period we analyze in the empirical work—the EU accepted new members that share its common external tariff (CET), we extend the model to analyze the effect of such accessions on MTL.

The use of a CET raises several interesting questions; e.g. which is the optimal country in the union to decide on the CET (Syropoulos, 2002) and, more importantly for our purposes, how the tariff revenue is to be distributed over the different countries, e.g. if all goods enter the EU via one port, does that country receive all the revenue? Clearly not; so PTAs with a CET must agree on revenue transfer mechanisms. Therefore, one key difference relative to other PTAs is the existence of a mechanism for transfers, which L can also use to "purchase" the supply of the regional good. We note that the willingness to implement such transfer schemes is often limited, which along with the need to agree on a CET explains why customs unions are rare relative to other PTAs. The implicit costs in the use of direct transfers explain why we ruled them out in deriving the stumbling block effect in the absence of a CET.[12] However, those countries that can agree on a CET clearly do not face prohibitive costs of direct transfers since they use them to redistribute revenue. So the PTA solution must now explicitly allow transfers.[13]

As we prove in the appendix (Section A.1.2), the stumbling block effect disappears under this case. However, despite the ability to use transfers, a preferential rate may still be used because, for given multilateral tariffs, L is indifferent between a transfer *and* preferential tariff reductions. At a given MFN tariff, the cost for L of a reduction in a preferential tariff π is simply the lost tariff revenue, which is no more costly than transferring an equivalent amount in the numeraire good. The difference relative to the PTA without a CET is that now if, at $\pi=0$, S is still not providing "enough" e^s, the optimal solution is for L to increase the transfer rather than the MFN tariff, since the latter distorts the prices. Thus, in equilibrium the MFN tariff is not affected by this type of a PTA.

When S exports multiple goods there is another feature of a PTA with a CET that makes a stumbling block effect less likely even in the absence of transfers. Customs unions are usually formed between partners in the same region, so their trade values are often large across many goods. Often in these agreements, and certainly for the EU accessions that we consider, the preferential tariffs cover all goods and are set to zero. This feature may be due to different constraints, e.g. compliance with GATT article XXIV (under which EU accessions fall), some cost of maintaining border controls to levy positive preferential tariffs on a subset of goods when all other goods and factors are freely mobile, etc. The constraints that lead L to set duty-free preferences on most of S's exports make it less likely that L would also need to set a higher MFN tariff (or make transfers) to obtain the regional public good relative to a situation where L is unconstrained in the choice of preferential rates for individual goods. In sum, the broad application of duty-free rates in EU accessions lowers the need to distort the MFN tariff to increase the preference margin in specific goods.

[12] Using direct transfers may also not be the most efficient way to transfer resources to other countries, as the aid vs. trade literature highlights, or to reward cooperation since the direct transfer may end up in the pockets of a politician without providing the best incentives for cooperation. For example, one of the stated aims of the US in providing preferences to the Andean countries is to raise the relative price of activities other than drug production. Alternatively, the partner country government may place a positive political economy weight on its exporters, $\omega_i^s > 1$, such that it benefits more from a preference that increases the income in good i than a lump-sum transfer of identical value to the government's coffers. Political economy constraints that reduce the effectiveness of direct transfers relative to preferences are present in practice, otherwise we would not observe several of the current preference schemes.

[13] In fact, the transfer is the only difference relative to the PTA without a CET since, in the simple case we consider here, S does not consume any non-numeraire goods so the CET is not binding for S. In the working paper we show that the result is identical if S consumes some of its export and the CET binds for it.

4. Estimation

4.1. Predictions and identification

We now derive the model's estimating equation, point out its main predictions and analyze how it is identified.

The general expression for the MFN tariff on a product i at time t nests the case where the good receives a preference (Eq. (9)) or not (Eq. (4)). Simplifying the notation by using x_i for $\frac{X_i/M_i}{\varepsilon_i}$, m_i for $\frac{M_i^s}{M_i^*+M_i^s}\frac{1}{\varepsilon_i^*}$ and ϕ_i for the stumbling block term, $\left(G_{e^s}\omega_i^s - 1\right)\frac{X_i^s}{M_i p_i'}\frac{1}{\varepsilon_i}$ in Eq. (11), we have :

$$t_{it} = \phi_{it} I_{it} + (\omega_{it} - 1)x_{it} + m_{it} \tag{12}$$

where, according to the model, I_{it} is an indicator for whether good i is imported from a preferential partner and receives a zero preferential rate at time t. The econometric model in error form is then

$$t_{it} = \phi_t I_{it} + \beta_t x_{it} + m_{it} + u_{it} \tag{13}$$

where $E(u_{it}|x_{it}, m_{it}, I_{it})=0$ and β_t measures the average extra weight the government places on importers. The key parameter is ϕ_t, which measures the *average* stumbling block, i.e. the average difference of MFN tariff levels with and without PTAs as defined in Eq. (11); the central question is whether it is positive. We also augment the econometric model to test three other predictions. Namely that this effect is: (i) stronger for goods with higher PTA exports; (ii) not present for goods with a positive preferential tariff and (iii) not present for goods exported by countries that recently joined the EU and have access to transfers.

The theoretical model captures key features of trade policy determination. However, it is parsimonious and possibly not fully specified, e.g. tariffs may be affected by foreign lobbies and tend to be highly persistent, which may be due to various unobserved product effects. Such effects may also influence whether a good receives a preference and thus generate an omitted variable bias. We address this by estimating the model in differences and employing instrumental variables. Since the model focuses on MFN tariffs, which the EU changes very infrequently, we take the difference between the MFN tariffs negotiated in the Uruguay Round (UR) and those in place before it. The latter were largely set during the Tokyo Round since the WTO shows no record of renegotiation for the EU between these rounds.

Estimation in differences can still provide an estimate of the *level* of the stumbling block effect given the timing and properties of certain EU PTAs. Some PTAs were not in place during the Tokyo Round, so $I_{it-1}=0$ for certain goods, and so the EU's multilateral tariff in the goods exported by those countries should not have been affected. This is also true for several products of PTAs that were in place at $t-1$ because the EU did not offer duty-free access to several goods. As we describe in Table A1 there have been important extensions in the coverage of preferences between rounds.[14] Moreover, the range of products that each PTA can expect to export has increased substantially as trade costs fell. In sum, a large range of products changed status from $I_{it-1}=0$ to $I_{it}=1$ and when we difference Eq. (12) for those products and write it in error form we obtain

$$\Delta t_i = \phi_t I_{it} + \beta \Delta x_i + \Delta m_i + \Delta u_i \tag{14}$$

where we assume the weights, ω_i, are time-invariant—an assumption that we test and find to be reasonable in our working paper. Therefore, in this case β and ϕ_t have the same interpretation as in the level equation (Eq. (13)). Fig. 1 illustrates why this is the case. We plot the tariffs for two goods that are similar except that one becomes a PTA good between the Tokyo and Uruguay rounds. The tariff increase up to the dashed line, i.e. $t^{mp} - t^m$, indicates the stumbling block effect predicted by the model if the preference is duty-free. The EU may choose not to change the bound multilateral tariff immediately because this would impose a renegotiation cost (as well as the costs from higher tariffs on EU products that other countries would be allowed to set) but, when the new round occurs, the difference in the reduction in the two products reflects the stumbling block effect. That is $(t^m - t^{m\prime}) - (t^m - t^{mp\prime}) = t^{mp\prime} - t^{m\prime} = \phi_t$. The same prediction applies to goods that, at the time the UR was negotiated, were expected to have a duty-free preference.

[14] For instance, the preferences have been expanded through a number of revisions for MED, ACP, GSP, EFTX, which are the agreements that initially took effect before the Tokyo Round. These revisions also included new requirements on cooperation relating to human rights and democracy from all recipients (Brown, 2002; Raya, 1999). In addition to that, the European Economic Area with EFTA in 1992 provided a much deeper economic integration between partners.

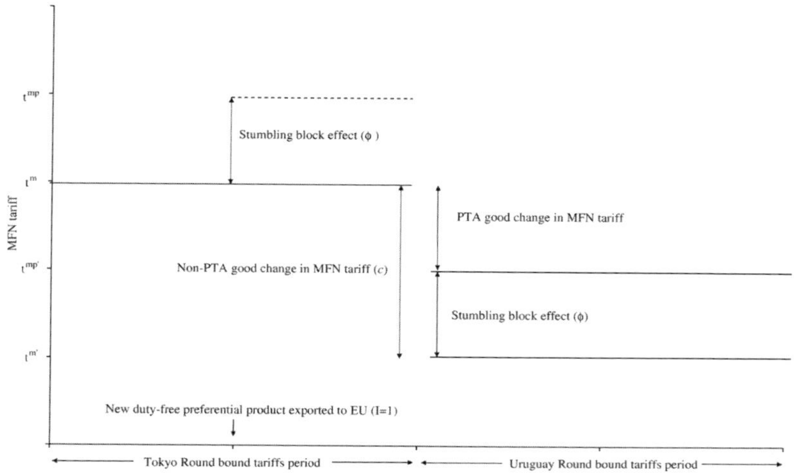

Fig. 1. Identification of the stumbling block effect through MFN tariff changes.

Some products were already PTA goods during the Tokyo Round and therefore did not change status. In this case an OLS estimate of the parameter on I_{it} in Eq. (14), call it $\tilde{\phi}$, reflects a weighted average of the level effect for new PTA goods and the change in the stumbling effect for the existing PTA goods. We show this in Section A.3 of the appendix where we also argue that $\tilde{\phi}$ represents a downward biased estimate of the level effect, ϕ_t. The basic reason is the attenuation bias due to measurement error. For continuing PTAs we do not have information on which subset of products were already PTA goods at $t-1$. Thus an instrument that is correlated with the new PTA goods in I_{it} but not the existing ones reduces or eliminates this bias. A comparison of OLS and alternative IV estimates supports this view, as we will show.

One potentially important determinant that is not explicitly reflected in Eq. (14) is reciprocity—the extent to which the EU lowered its tariffs in response to other countries' reductions in the UR. Reciprocity is an important principle in WTO negotiations and a basic feature of our theoretical model; it is not reflected in Eq. (14) because we assumed symmetry across the regional blocs and then solved for the equilibrium tariff. By relaxing this assumption and controlling explicitly for reciprocity we minimize the possibility for omitted variable bias.

We follow Limão (2006) who constructs a measure of market access concessions that is consistent with the practice in multilateral tariff negotiations. The variable is defined at the product level as $R_i=\sum_k s^k_{it}[\sum_j w^k_j \Delta t^k_j/t^k_{jt}]$ where $\Delta t^k_j/t^k_{jt}$ is the percentage tariff reduction by a non-EU country k in good j and w^k_{jt} is the import share of good j in total imports of k. Therefore the term in brackets captures country k's average concession, which is multiplied by the export share of a principal supplier k in good i to the EU, s^k_{it}. An exporter is a principal supplier of good i if it is one of the top 5 exporters of good i to the EU. The prediction is that if k offers relatively larger concessions, then the EU reciprocates through larger MFN tariff reductions in the products it imports from k. We also test and find that the results are similar if we follow the structural model more literally and do not include this variable.

The final issue in deriving the estimating equation is data availability for the MFN externality variable, m. We do not have a bilateral record of which countries negotiated with the EU on each 8-digit product during the trade rounds and therefore we cannot construct the exact variable, Δm. But we proxy for it by using information on the share of small exporters by product, i.e. the share of those countries that are not one of the top-5 exporters in product i to the EU. Increases in this share between the rounds imply that the probability of an MFN externality increases, since the EU would have to negotiate with more exporters each of whom now has a higher incentive to free-ride. We consider the change in this share between 1994 and 1989, the earliest year when this 8-digit data is reported. If the change in this period is sufficiently large, then it will be positively correlated with the change over the full period between rounds. We capture this by constructing an indicator variable, P, for whether the change in this share for good i is above the median change.[15] The model then predicts a positive coefficient on this variable.

Introducing the proxy for Δm and augmenting Eq. (14) to explicitly account for reciprocity yields our basic estimating equation:

$$\Delta t_i = c + \phi_t I_{it} + \beta \Delta x_i + \rho R_i + \mu P_i + \upsilon_i \tag{15}$$

where we include a constant term, c, and modify the error term to explicitly allow for the measurement error in classifying new PTA goods (and possibly in the proxy and reciprocity variables). Since we are interested in establishing causality, we now discuss how we address the potential endogeneity issues in estimating Eq. (15).

The most important endogeneity concern is reverse causation since the preference may depend on MFN tariff changes, e.g. if a PTA partner expects a small MFN reduction in a product, it is more likely to request a preference in it than in a product where it expects a large MFN reduction. To tackle this we employ instrumental variables. The central variable is the PTA good indicator, $I_i^{\text{pta}} = PR_i^{\text{pta}} D_i^{\text{pta}}$, which is equal to one if good i faces a zero preferential tariff, i.e. $PR_i^{\text{pta}} = 1$, and that PTA partner exports it to the EU, $D_i^{\text{pta}} = 1$. Since the main reverse causation concern arises due to the preference component, the main instrument we employ for I_i^{pta} is D_i^{pta} for the year 1994 regardless of whether it receives a preference or not. This instrument is clearly correlated with I_i^{pta} but we expect it to be uncorrelated with the error term in Eq. (15) since the changes in the MFN tariff we use as a dependent variable are implemented starting only in 1995. When we consider goods exported duty-free under any or every PTA we adjust the instrument accordingly so it reflects whether good i was exported by any or every PTA.

To predict whether a good was likely to receive a preference around the time of the UR, we also include as an instrument whether the EU set non-tariff barriers on the good in 1993. A country is more likely to request a preference in a good if it expects that otherwise it would be subject to an NTB. This effect would be magnified if the country already exported this product and the NTB applied to all countries (the variable D^{ntball}), hence we interact these two variables as well. These instruments are motivated by two related effects. First, an NTB can reduce the price received by exporters to the EU and a good that receives a preference is less likely to face an NTB. Second, NTBs tend to raise domestic prices in the EU, which is the price that the preferential exporter receives if it faces a zero preferential tariff and no NTBs. Since setting an NTB on all partners can also indicate some other good characteristic that may affect MFN tariff changes, we also show that the results are robust to dropping the instruments that include D^{ntball} and its interactions.

The IV-GMM approach we employ allows us to carefully test the exogeneity of these instruments via alternative over-identifying restriction tests. The set of over-identifying restrictions that permits us to perform these tests arise from including other instruments, such as "world" price changes between 1992 and 1994, which are unlikely to depend on the changes in MFN tariffs that only take place in the subsequent years. There are two related channels by which price changes help to predict the identity of a PTA good, I_i^{pta}. First, a PTA partner is more likely to export a good in 1994 if between 1992 and 1994 there were large price increases that now allow the exporter to overcome any fixed trading costs in i. Second, the benefit of receiving a preference on some fixed level of exports X_i^s rather than facing an advalorem MFN tariff t_i is equal to $p_i^w t_i X_i^s$, so it is increasing in the world price. Thus increases in p_i^w raise the incentive for the PTA partner to negotiate a preference in this good. Since these effects are likely to vary with the price changes, we allow for non-linearities by also including higher order terms.

Another benefit of the IV-GMM approach is that it allows us to address potential omitted variables bias. This could arise for a number of reasons including the possibility that some of the EU's PTAs reflect additional motives not modeled in the theory. So, the IV approach allows us to include all of the EU's preferential programs in 1994 in our empirical analysis and obtain estimates for the stumbling block effect, ϕ, even when other motives for PTAs are present. We cannot rule out the theoretical possibility that under alternative motives for PTAs, our exclusion restrictions for the instruments are invalid. But ultimately this is an empirical question, which we address with the over-identification restriction tests just described and by testing the robustness of the results to excluding different sets of instruments.

The variable that captures the political economy effect, Δx, is likely to depend on the MFN tariffs since it involves the production/import ratio weighted by the import demand elasticity, all of which are functions of the EU's domestic prices and hence its MFN tariffs. Therefore, we employ the levels of these variables before the MFN tariff is implemented, e.g. 1978 for

[15] The estimation results do not change when we employ 75th or 90th percentiles instead.

x_{t-1} and 1992 for x_t. If these variables exhibit persistence over time, using the lag values will not address the endogeneity so we also instrument Δx. We employ the change in a measure of scale economies (value added/number of firms) and its interaction with the average world price change in the *industry* between 1992 and 1994. All else equal, industries with large fixed costs of entry and thus high economies of scale are likely to have higher X/M.[16] World price changes in 1992–94, on the other hand, directly affect domestic prices, which are important determinants of all the components of x, i.e. X, M, and ε but do not depend on the tariff changes on the left hand side, which are implemented only after 1994.

Finally, the reciprocity variable is another potential source of endogeneity due to reverse causation since the total tariff reduction by other WTO members in the UR partially depends on EU reductions. Our instrument is the unilateral portion of the total tariff reductions that were eventually offered at the UR. More specifically, several countries undertook unilateral trade liberalization between 1986 and 1992. Their liberalization was unilateral because it was undertaken outside of GATT negotiations without an expectation that it would be reciprocated since, the very completion of the round was in doubt until 1992. However, when the final multilateral cuts were negotiated, between 1992 and 1994, the unilateral reductions undertaken from 1986 to 1992 were explicitly reciprocated because they had taken place after the official start date of the round (Finger et al., 2002). Therefore, we employ the unilateral liberalization by WTO members between 1986 and 1992 as an instrument for what was eventually used as a basis for their reciprocal liberalization—the total liberalization between 1986 and 1995.

4.2. Data

In Table A3 we provide detailed definitions of the variables, their construction, and sources; Table A2 contains summary statistics. Here we note some of its salient characteristics. We employ the advalorem MFN tariffs from the WTO schedules of concessions, and the preferential tariffs from UNCTAD, both at the 8-digit Harmonized Standard (HS) level.[17] To construct the reciprocity variable, we employ the data in Finger et al. (2002). They use the available tariff reductions for each WTO member during the UR, and aggregate it from the product level into country-averages. We take these average country concessions and construct a product specific measure of reciprocity by using those countries' export shares to the EU by 8-digit product (from EUROSTAT).

We use data on production and other industry-level variables for constructing x and its instruments. This data is available for individual EU members and we aggregate it as suggested by the theoretical model.[18] UNIDO's industrial database provides the most comprehensive source covering all EU members and dating back to 1978. It is collected at the industry level and hence more aggregated than the trade and tariff data. We use clustering at the industry level to correct the standard errors for this fact.[19] Since UNIDO does not provide production data for agriculture, we exclude those products, but processed agricultural products are included. Given the prevalence of non-tariff barriers and EU subsidies in agriculture we don't believe this is a drawback since an analysis that focuses on tariffs without taking these other forms of protection into account could be inappropriate for agriculture.

[16] According to the model, and similar to Grossman and Helpman (1994), once we have accounted for the size effect, x, in the protection equation, other variables, such as scale, should have no direct effect and can thus be excluded. This is the rationale in Goldberg and Maggi (1999) to exclude a similar scale variable from the main trade protection equation and use it as an instrument for X/M and political organization.

[17] The model prediction applies to goods that have or are expected to have a duty-free preference when the UR was negotiated. Hence we employ the preferential rates reported for 1996 for all PTAs except where unavailable (EFTA, for which we use 1993). Moreover, we exclude products with a zero MFN tariff before the UR for two reasons. First, when the MFN tariff is zero there is often more noise in the data about whether a preference exists or not, since it is in effect irrelevant. Second, all the tariffs in the sample that were initially zero remained unchanged and are likely to share an unobserved common characteristic. Thus, including those observations would bias the estimates if the proportion of zero tariffs is different for PTA goods relative to the rest of the goods.

[18] In Karacaovali and Limão (2005) we show that Eq. (2) can be obtained as the objective for the EU that arises from bargaining between independent EU-member governments, which suggests that we should simply add production for each industry over the EU members to obtain X_i and divide it by aggregate imports in i. The weight, ω_i, can then be interpreted as an average of the individual member weights, $(\omega_i - 1) = \sum_c (\omega_i^c - 1)\xi_i^c$ where ω_i^c is individual member c's weight for a given producer and ξ_i^c is the production share in the EU.

[19] In calculating the variable $(X_i/M_i)/\varepsilon_i$ the remaining variables that we employ are at the same level of aggregation as the production data. The fact that this data is more aggregated could potentially introduce some measurement error. Although we cannot rule out this possibility, we note that it may not be such an important concern for the following reason. If the EU negotiators use the production data at the most disaggregated level available for most of its members, as we do, then our measure is actually the relevant one. The interpretation of β is now as the average EU-wide extra weight taken over the different industries rather than products. We are comfortable with this interpretation, since producers tend to organize at the industry level to lobby for protection. This is particularly true in the EU, where there is more variation in protection across industries than within them. Therefore, to the extent that the extra weight reflects a political economy motive, the best way to identify it is at the industry level.

Table 1
EU tariff levels and changes in the Uruguay round: distribution by industry

ISIC code	Sector name	Before UR		After UR		Change		
		Mean	Std. Dev.	Mean	Std. Dev.	Mean	Std. Dev.	Coef. variation
311	Food products	0.16	0.09	0.11	0.07	0.05	0.03	0.55
313	Beverages	0.11	0.04	0.07	0.02	0.04	0.02	0.51
314	Tobacco	0.42	0.20	0.25	0.12	0.17	0.09	0.52
321	Textiles	0.10	0.03	0.07	0.02	0.03	0.02	0.77
322	Wearing apparel except footwear	0.13	0.03	0.11	0.03	0.02	0.01	0.47
323	Leather products	0.05	0.02	0.03	0.02	0.02	0.01	0.56
324	Footwear except rubber or plastic	0.10	0.05	0.09	0.04	0.01	0.01	1.50
331	Wood products except furniture	0.06	0.02	0.02	0.03	0.04	0.01	0.31
332	Furniture except metal	0.06	0.01	0.01	0.02	0.05	0.01	0.28
341	Paper and products	0.09	0.02	0.04	0.02	0.04	0.02	0.39
342	Printing and publishing	0.09	0.03	0.05	0.02	0.05	0.02	0.36
351	Industrial chemicals	0.08	0.03	0.06	0.02	0.03	0.03	1.08
352	Other chemicals	0.07	0.02	0.03	0.03	0.04	0.03	0.81
353	Petroleum refineries	0.05	0.02	0.03	0.02	0.02	0.01	0.53
354	Miscellaneous petroleum and coal products	0.04	0.02	0.03	0.03	0.01	0.01	0.85
355	Rubber products	0.05	0.02	0.03	0.02	0.02	0.01	0.53
356	Plastic products	0.11	0.05	0.08	0.05	0.03	0.02	0.63
361	Pottery china earthenware	0.08	0.03	0.06	0.03	0.02	0.01	0.58
362	Glass and products	0.07	0.03	0.05	0.03	0.03	0.01	0.46
369	Other non-metallic mineral products	0.05	0.02	0.02	0.02	0.02	0.01	0.38
371	Iron and steel	0.06	0.02	0.00	0.01	0.05	0.02	0.39
372	Non-ferrous metals	0.06	0.02	0.04	0.03	0.02	0.01	0.67
381	Fabricated metal products	0.06	0.02	0.03	0.02	0.03	0.01	0.50
382	Machinery except electrical	0.05	0.01	0.02	0.01	0.03	0.01	0.48
383	Machinery electric	0.06	0.03	0.03	0.02	0.03	0.02	0.55
384	Transport equipment	0.08	0.05	0.05	0.05	0.02	0.02	0.75
385	Professional and scientific equipment	0.06	0.01	0.03	0.02	0.03	0.01	0.41
390	Other manufactured products	0.06	0.02	0.03	0.02	0.03	0.02	0.50
	Total	0.08	0.05	0.05	0.04	0.03	0.02	0.73

Advalorem tariff rates are reported. The total number of observations in our sample is equal to 6294. Products with zero initial tariff rates are excluded from the sample as explained in the text.

In Table 1, we present the tariff levels and their changes for our sample. Although our analysis is conducted at the product level, we provide some statistics aggregated by industry. The highest tariff rates before and after the UR appear in the tobacco sector: an average of 42 and 25% respectively. The lowest pre-UR tariffs are in the miscellaneous petroleum and coal products sector with 3.9%, whereas the iron and steel industry became the least protected in terms of tariffs after the UR, 0.4%. The footwear sector experienced the least liberalization, 0.8 percentage points, and tobacco the highest, 17. Note also that there is a considerable amount of variation in tariff changes both within industries, with coefficients of variation between 0.28 and 1.5, and across industries, with a coefficient of variation of 0.44.

4.3. Estimation results

The unconditional mean reduction in MFN tariffs by the EU during the UR was 4.4 percentage points for non-PTA goods but only 2.9 for goods exported duty-free by any PTA partner. A simple *t*-test confirms that the difference of 1.5 percentage points, with a standard error of 0.1, is statistically significant. This difference may be due to other factors that are correlated with the PTA variable. Therefore, in Table 2 we present the estimates of the parameters in Eq. (15). In order to address the endogeneity issues discussed above, we use the two-step efficient generalized method of moments estimator (IV-GMM), which is robust to heteroskedasticity with an undetermined form and we cluster at the industry level.

4.3.1. Stumbling block estimates

The indicator variable $I^{\text{any}0}$ in Table 2 takes the value one if the EU imports the good from *any* partner at a duty-free preferential rate. It excludes countries that acceded as full EU members after the Tokyo Round, which we estimate

Table 2
Impact of EU preferences on MFN tariffs: main predictions

	IV-GMM			OLS
	(1)	(2)	(3)	(4)
$I^{\text{any0}\dagger}$	0.015***	0.015***	0.011***	0.013***
$(\phi^{\text{any0}}>0)$	(0.003)	(0.003)	(0.002)	(0.001)
$I^{\text{evy0}\dagger}$		0.007***		
$(\phi^{\text{evy0}}>0)$		(0.002)		
$I^{\text{hiexp}\dagger}$			0.005***	
$(\phi^{\text{hiexp}}>0)$			(0.002)	
$R^{\dagger}$	0.006*	0.005*	0.006**	0.010***
$(\rho>0)$	(0.003)	(0.003)	(0.003)	(0.002)
$\Delta x^{\dagger}$	0.004*	0.003**	0.003**	0.000
$(\beta>0)$	(0.002)	(0.001)	(0.001)	(0.000)
P	0.001	0.000	0.001	0.001*
$(\mu>0)$	(0.001)	(0.000)	(0.001)	(0.000)
Constant	−0.034***	−0.034***	−0.036***	−0.038***
(c)	(0.005)	(0.004)	(0.003)	(0.002)
Observations	6294	6294	6294	6294
Hansen's J p-val[a]	0.506	0.567	0.569	n/a
C-stat p-val[b]	0.729	0.562	0.553[e]	n/a
Endogeneity p-val[c]	0.517	0.248	0.270	n/a
Heterosked. p-val[d]	0.000	0.000	0.000	0.000
$1+\phi/c$[e]	0.55(0.41, 0.68)	0.58 (0.47, 0.69)	0.69 (0.56, 0.81)	0.66 (0.60, 0.71)
$1+(\phi+\phi^{\text{evy, hi}})/c$[e]	n/a	0.39 (0.21, 0.56)	0.56[f] (0.44, 0.68)	n/a
Schwarz info.	−7.58	−7.60	−7.61	−7.68

Robust standard errors clustered at the 3-digit ISIC level in parentheses. * significant at 10%; ** significant at 5%; *** significant at 1%. The model's parameter and sign predictions are indicated in parentheses below each variable. IV-GMM obtained from an instrumental variable efficient generalized method of moments estimator. OLS obtained from Cragg's heteroskedastic ordinary least squares estimator. See Table 4 with the first stage regressions for the list of instruments.

[a] Hansen–Sargan test of over-identifying restrictions. Probability value for the null hypothesis that the excluded instruments are uncorrelated with the second stage error term, and correctly excluded from the estimated equation.

[b] Difference in Sargan (C) statistic. Probability value for the rejection of the null hypothesis of exogeneity of a subset of f instruments marked with "‡" in Table 4. The first stage regression results for specification (3) are similar to those of (2) in Table 4 but employ the export indicator for high exports, D^{hiexp}, instead of D^{evy}. The statistic used is $C=J^{\text{r}}-J^{\text{u}}$ with a chi-square distribution of f degrees of freedom where J^{r} represents the minimized value of the GMM objective function for the restricted and efficient regression (with all over-identifying restrictions) and J^{u} the value for the unrestricted, inefficient but consistent regression without the questionable instruments.

[c] Endogeneity test of the variables marked with a "†" based on the C statistic. Probability value at which we reject the consistency and efficiency of OLS.

[d] Pagan–Hall heteroskedasticity test. Probability value for the null hypothesis that the disturbance is homoskedastic.

[e] Confidence intervals calculated using the delta method.

[f] The value for the combined effect of I^{any0} and I^{hiexp}.

separately as suggested by the theory. The coefficient for I^{any0} provides an estimate of ϕ and we find that it is positive and significant at the 1% level under all specifications. This provides evidence of a smaller reduction in the EU's MFN tariffs for its PTA goods (with a zero preferential tariff) relative to its non-PTA goods as predicted by the model. The effect is similar if we use I^{any}, which is equal to one if the good has any preference. But we will focus on a baseline that uses I^{any0} as the model requires and test if the effect is different for goods with positive preferences. Before quantifying the importance of this stumbling block effect, we test other predictions.[20]

The model also predicts a stronger stumbling block effect for important exports of a PTA partner. We test this by introducing an additional variable, I^{hiexp}—I^{any0} interacted with D^{hiexp}, where D^{hiexp} is one if the share of a PTA partner's exports in good i relative to its total exports to the EU is above a certain threshold. In column 3 of Table 2 we

[20] A potential cost of using data that is finely disaggregated is that it is more likely to suffer from product misclassification when a shipment is recorded. We try to minimize this problem by classifying a good as being exported by a PTA to the EU only if the value registered in that year is above a certain low threshold. In our estimations, we employ the 5th percentile of the value of a given PTAs' exports in that year as the threshold. The baseline results using a different threshold, the 10th percentile, are similar. The results without imposing any threshold are identical and reported in our working paper.

Table 3
Impact of EU preferences on MFN tariffs: auxiliary predictions

	IV-GMM		
	(1)	(2)	(3)
$I^{\text{any0}\dagger}$	0.015***		
$(\phi^{\text{any0}}>0)$	(0.003)		
I^{afs}	0.002		
$(\phi^{\text{afs}}=0)$	(0.002)		
I^{spg}	−0.001		
$(\phi^{\text{spg}}=0)$	(0.001)		
$I^{\text{any}\dagger}$		0.013***	
$(\phi^{\text{any}}>0)$		(0.003)	
$I^{\text{pos}\dagger}$		−0.026	
$(\phi^{\text{pos}}+\phi^{\text{any}}=0)$		(0.032)	
$I^{\text{gsp}\dagger\text{f}}$			0.003***
$(\phi^{\text{gsp}}>0)$			(0.001)
$I^{\text{gspl}\dagger\text{f}}$			0.003***
$(\phi^{\text{gspl}}>0)$			(0.001)
$I^{\text{acp}\dagger\text{f}}$			0.000
$(\phi^{\text{acp}}>0)$			(0.001)
$I^{\text{eftx}\dagger\text{f}}$			0.002***
$(\phi^{\text{eftx}}>0)$			(0.001)
$I^{\text{med}\dagger\text{f}}$			0.002***
$(\phi^{\text{med}}>0)$			(0.001)
$I^{\text{cec}\dagger\text{f}}$			0.002***
$(\phi^{\text{cec}}>0)$			(0.001)
$\Delta x^{\dagger}$	0.003**	0.004*	0.003**
$(\beta>0)$	(0.002)	(0.002)	(0.001)
$R^{\dagger}$	0.006*	0.008*	0.008***
$(\rho>0)$	(0.004)	(0.004)	(0.003)
P	0.001	0.001	−0.000
$(\mu>0)$	(0.001)	(0.001)	(0.000)
Constant	−0.035***	−0.030***	−0.028***
(c)	(0.004)	(0.005)	(0.003)
Observations	6294	6294	6294
Hansen's J p-val[a]	0.495	0.559	0.159
C-stat p-val[b]	0.722	0.446	0.114
Endogeneity p-val[c]	0.525	0.399	0.210
Heterosked. p-val[d]	0.000	0.000	0.000
$1+\phi/c^{\text{e}}$	0.57 (0.47, 0.66)	0.57 (0.42, 0.72)	n/a
$1+\sum\phi^{\text{pta}}/c^{\text{e}}$	n/a	n/a	0.53[f] (0.37, 0.69)
$\phi^{\text{pos}}+\phi^{\text{any}}=0$ p-val	n/a	0.68 (accept)	n/a
Schwarz info.	−7.60	−7.56	−7.64

All the notes to Table 2 apply. For the specification in the last column, we employ export indicators for each PTA, D^{pta}, instead of D^{any}. The following coefficient restrictions are employed in the last column, $\phi^{\text{gsp}}=\phi^{\text{gspl}}$, $\phi^{\text{eftx}}=\phi^{\text{cec}}$, based on a test failing to reject their equality. (a)–(e): See notes to Table 2. (f) Calculated for a product exported under every program. The other values, with confidence intervals in parentheses, are GSP and GSPL: 0.88 (0.82, 0.94), ACP: 0.99 (0.93, 1.06), MED: 0.92 (0.87, 0.97), EFTX and CEC: 0.93 (0.88, 0.97).

estimate that such an *extra* effect is present and significant. The results are qualitatively similar if we use different thresholds such as the median or 75th percentile instead of the 25th.

Although we did not explicitly model simultaneous PTAs we expect that in such an extension, if a product is exported by several preferential partners, then an increase in the margin of preference that benefits every partner generates a stronger stumbling block effect. In effect, it is equivalent to an increase in preferential exports from a given partner. We test this in column 2 of Table 2 by including an additional variable, I^{evy0}, which is an indicator for whether the EU imports the product at a tariff of zero from *every* preferential partner. We estimate a significant *additional* effect of 0.7 percentage points for this subset of goods.

Standard Hausman tests reject the null of consistency of the OLS estimates for some but not all specifications (the p-value ranges from 0.04 to 0.52 across different specifications). Moreover, there are good reasons to expect the OLS estimates to be biased, both because of reverse causality and measurement error, as we noted in Section 4.1. Therefore we focus on the IV estimates, which may be inefficient but consistent over all the regressions. We also calculated the OLS counterpart for each specification and found that the stumbling block results are qualitatively similar to the IV estimates. In column 4 of Table 2 we confirm this for the baseline specification; the coefficient on I^{any0} is 0.013 and it is significant at 1%. It is smaller than the IV estimate indicating some attenuation bias, which we will further address in the robustness section.

According to the model, MFN tariff changes for products imported from countries that joined the EU between the last two trade rounds should be identical to those of other products. We find this to be true in the data. In column 1 of Table 3 the variables I^{afs} and I^{spg} are indicators for products exported by Austria, Finland, and Sweden and Portugal, Spain, and Greece respectively, which are statistically insignificant. The stumbling block effect generated by the PTAs that do not share a common external tariff with the EU remains unchanged both in magnitude and significance.

According to the model the stumbling block effect is only present for products with a zero preferential tariff. We test this in column 2 of Table 3 where the variable I^{any} takes the value one for the goods imported by the EU at a preferential tariff rate—either zero or positive—whereas I^{pos} is one for the subset of goods with a positive preferential tariff. The sum of these coefficients measures the total effect of a good with a positive preferential tariff and a formal test shows that we cannot reject the hypothesis that the tariff reduction for such goods is identical to the non-PTA goods. This prediction is fairly specific to the model and thus its confirmation provides it strong support.

The estimates presented so far refer to an average effect of all of the EU's PTAs. It is also interesting to test whether the effect is driven by any given PTA in particular. Although there is a positive correlation among the variables for different programs, we do identify a stumbling block effect originating from each in column 3 of Table 3. All individual effects are significant with the exception of the one for ACP, which is nonetheless significant when tested jointly with GSP, a program with preferences highly correlated with those in ACP. It is also worth noting that the effect for PTAs signed after the Tokyo Round, such as CEC where we know for sure that the classification as a new PTA good is not subject to measurement error, is positive and significant.

In Table 4, we present the first stage regressions for some of the main specifications, which indicate that the instruments are jointly significant in all of our specifications with F-statistics higher than 10. Moreover, the rows at the bottom of Tables 2 and 3 labeled "Hansen's J" show that we cannot reject the null hypothesis that the excluded instruments are uncorrelated with the second stage error term, and correctly excluded from the estimated equation at any conventional level of significance. When the set of instruments is large, this test may have low power. Therefore, we also test the subset of instruments that are a priori more likely to be endogenous, such as the export dummy and NTB variables. The results are found in the row "C-Stat" and indicate that we cannot reject the orthogonality of the smaller subsets either.[21]

In sum, the evidence supports not only the model's main predictions but also its auxiliary ones, which rely on variation between PTA and non-PTA goods as well as variation within PTA goods (e.g. every PTA, high exports and positive preferential tariffs). This considerably increases our confidence that the results are not spurious. We will consider a number of additional robustness tests including alternative instruments, sample, and regressors. Since the main message will remain unchanged, we defer this to Section 4.5 and first quantify the effects and discuss the remaining determinants of EU multilateral tariffs.

4.3.2. *Reciprocity and political economy determinants of EU tariffs*

Tariff changes are notoriously hard to predict and in fact most empirical studies that employ a structural approach focus on explaining the cross-section. Nonetheless, given how sparse the evidence is for the EU's trade policy determination, we think that it is interesting to ask whether the remaining variables of our parsimonious model have any explanatory power.

The coefficient on Δx provides an estimate of $\omega - 1$, which can be interpreted as the production weighted average of the extra importance attached to producer surplus relative to social welfare in the EU. We find it to be positive with the IV estimates ranging from 0.003 to 0.004. To our knowledge these are the first such estimates for the EU. Goldberg and Maggi (1999) estimate this extra weight to be approximately 0.014 for the US, whereas Gawande and Bandyopadhyay (2000) estimate a much lower value of 0.0003. Thus, our estimate for the EU lies in between these for the US.[22]

[21] An additional robustness test is to exclude the export dummy and its interactions from the instrument list altogether. Naturally the first stage R-square for the PTA variable falls but the F-statistic of the excluded instruments is still significant at the 1% level since the price variables help to predict PTA goods. The second stage estimate for ϕ^{any0} in this case is also positive and significant at the 1% level and slightly higher than the baseline in column 2 of Table 2.

[22] Goldberg and Maggi (1999) report $1/\omega = 0.986$ (p. 1145) whereas Gawande and Bandyopadhyay (2000) report $1/(\omega - 1)$ (p. 147). In Karacaovali and Limão (2005), we relax the constraint of constant weights across sectors and show that those with higher share of employment and regional concentration receive higher tariff protection, but we also find that the restriction of constant weights (over industries and time) is reasonable for the EU.

Table 4
First stage regressions for main predictions

	Table 2 — Column 1			Table 2 — Column 2			
	I^{any0}	Δx	R	I^{any0}	I^{evy0}	Δx	R
D^{anyexp}‡	0.936***	−0.866***	0.021***	0.933***	−0.003	−0.774***	0.020***
	(0.023)	(0.217)	(0.007)	(0.023)	(0.020)	(0.215)	(0.007)
D^{evyexp}‡				0.035***	0.801***	−0.755***	0.013***
				(0.007)	(0.006)	(0.063)	(0.002)
D^{ntball}‡	0.008	−0.888**	−0.010	0.013	−0.014	−0.974**	−0.009
	(0.041)	(0.388)	(0.012)	(0.041)	(0.036)	(0.383)	(0.012)
$D^{ntball} \times D^{anyexp}$‡	−0.229***	0.506	0.010	−0.251***	0.000	0.319	0.009
	(0.042)	(0.392)	(0.012)	(0.041)	(0.036)	(0.389)	(0.012)
$D^{ntball} \times D^{evyexp}$‡				0.190***	−0.109***	1.497***	0.012*
				(0.026)	(0.022)	(0.240)	(0.007)
Δp_{9294}	−0.003	0.051	−0.004**	−0.002	−0.001	0.035	−0.004**
	(0.006)	(0.059)	(0.002)	(0.006)	(0.005)	(0.059)	(0.002)
$(\Delta p_{9294})^2$	−0.009***	−0.005	0.000	−0.007***	0.000	−0.024	0.001
	(0.003)	(0.028)	(0.001)	(0.003)	(0.003)	(0.027)	(0.001)
$(\Delta p_{9294})^3$	0.002*	−0.007	0.000	0.002*	0.000	−0.004	0.000
	(0.001)	(0.009)	(0.000)	(0.001)	(0.001)	(0.009)	(0.000)
D^{ntb}‡	0.051***	1.014***	0.025***	0.049***	0.020***	1.072***	0.024***
	(0.006)	(0.060)	(0.002)	(0.006)	(0.006)	(0.059)	(0.002)
Δscale	0.189***	−0.497***	−0.032***	0.190***	0.003	−0.550***	−0.031***
	(0.009)	(0.082)	(0.002)	(0.009)	(0.008)	(0.081)	(0.002)
$(\Delta p_{9294})^{avg} \times \Delta$scale‡	−0.362***	−0.917	0.102***	−0.285***	−0.017	−1.465*	0.119***
	(0.085)	(0.803)	(0.024)	(0.085)	(0.074)	(0.797)	(0.024)
R^{uni}	0.041**	−0.075	0.754***	0.042**	0.024	−0.058	0.754***
	(0.017)	(0.163)	(0.005)	(0.017)	(0.015)	(0.161)	(0.005)
P	0.039***	−0.274***	−0.004***	0.036***	0.003	−0.252***	−0.005***
	(0.005)	(0.046)	(0.001)	(0.005)	(0.004)	(0.045)	(0.001)
Constant	−0.039*	−1.129***	−0.275***	−0.042*	0.003	−1.084***	−0.275***
	(0.024)	(0.222)	(0.007)	(0.023)	(0.020)	(0.219)	(0.007)
Observations	6294	6294	6294	6294	6294	6294	6294
Adj. R^2	0.378	0.078	0.792	0.389	0.767	0.100	0.794
Shea's partial R^2	0.323	0.066	0.780	0.342	0.670	0.082	0.783
F-test excl. p-val[a]	0.000	0.000	0.000	0.000	0.000	0.000	0.000

Robust standard errors clustered at the 3-digit ISIC level in parentheses. * significant at 10%; ** significant at 5%; *** significant at 1%. The first stage regression results for specification (3) in Table 2 are similar to those of (2) shown above but employ the export indicator for high exports, D^{hiexp}, instead of D^{evy}.

‡: the subset of instruments further tested for exogeneity. The probability value for the difference in Sargan (C) statistics for these instruments are reported on the row labeled C-stat p-val. in Table 2.

[a] Probability value for the F-test of H_0: The excluded instruments are jointly insignificant. All F-statistics exceed 10.

As we point out in the Introduction, reciprocity is a key variable in the theory behind MTL but there is disagreement about its use in practice. We find that the EU had larger reduction in tariffs on goods exported by trading partners that reduced their own tariffs by a greater amount. Reciprocity may magnify the stumbling block effect, because smaller reductions in the EU will be reciprocated by smaller reductions in the trading partners. Since Limão (2006) also finds reciprocity to be a significant factor in the US multilateral tariff reductions during the UR, we expect that the stumbling block effect of the EU and the US had an indirect effect at least in the reciprocal tariff reductions between the two.

Our proxy for the change in MFN externality term, Δm, is generally positive as predicted but always insignificant. One explanation for this is that the reciprocity variable already accounts for this effect. Since those countries that free-ride will have small average tariff reductions, the EU will "reciprocate" with smaller tariff reductions of its own as well.

4.4. Quantification and interpretation

The simplest interpretation of the coefficient on the PTA variable is that it represents how much the MFN tariff for PTA goods increased relative to the non-PTA goods. Its value is 1.5 percentage points for goods exported under any

PTA and about 2.2 for every PTA. Since the reduction for non-PTA goods was 3.4 percentage points, the magnitude of the stumbling block effect is not trivial.

We can quantify the tariff effect in terms of price changes to assess its economic importance. This type of quantification is important because one key concern with PTAs is that they have an impact on other countries by affecting the prices received by excluded countries, for example by causing higher MFN tariffs, as our model shows. Moreover, there is considerable evidence of imperfect pass-through both from exchange rate changes (c.f. Goldberg and Knetter, 1997) and from tariff changes (c.f. Finger, 1976; Feenstra, 1989).

In the context of the average price effects generated by tariff changes during the UR, the stumbling block effect is not negligible. This is clearest from employing the ratio of the relative (domestic) price growth effects

$$\Delta \ln p^d_{\text{pta}} / \Delta \ln p^d_{\text{mfn}} = \Delta \ln(1 + t^{mp}) / \Delta \ln(1 + t^m) \approx \Delta t^{mp} / \Delta t^m = 1 + \phi / c$$

where c is the estimated average tariff change for non-PTA goods. This equality applies to a "benchmark" good with no changes in either the market access or the elasticity adjusted production/import ratio. If the stumbling block effect completely offsets the average price effect, then $1+\phi/c=0$ and if the price effect for the PTA goods were identical to the non-PTA goods, the statistic would be equal to 1. As we show in the working paper this statistic also measures the relative world price effects for goods where there is imperfect pass-through, that is $\Delta \ln p^w_{\text{pta}} / \Delta \ln p^w_{\text{mfn}} \approx 1+\phi/c$, provided that the pass-through rate for PTA goods is similar to other goods.

The closer $1+\phi/c$ is to zero the stronger the stumbling block effect. For example, a value of 0.5 indicates that a non-PTA country received only half of the export price increase from EU's MFN tariff changes in the UR by exporting a PTA good relative to a similar non-PTA good. An alternative interpretation in light of the theoretical model is that the export price for the PTA goods was half of what it would have been in the absence of EU's PTAs. At the bottom of Tables 2 and 3, the row labeled $1+\phi/c$ provides the estimates of the price effects as well as their confidence intervals. The effect of any PTA is about 0.55 (column 1, Table 2) and it is not very sensitive to controlling for the exports of AFS or SGP (column 1, Table 3) or a positive preferential tariff (column 2, Table 3). The effect for goods exported by every PTA is stronger: 0.39 (column 2, Table 2).

An interesting question is whether our estimates carry any information about the unobserved counterfactual of what the average EU tariff would have been in the absence of any PTAs. A strict interpretation of our estimates according to the theoretical model is that MFN tariffs are 1.5 percentage points higher for PTA goods relative to a counterfactual without PTAs and, since PTA goods represent a large share of our sample, the average over *all goods* is 1.4 percentage points. However, there has also been debate on whether the PTAs pursued by the US and the EU increased or decreased the completion probability of the Uruguay Round (UR). Since multilateral trade rounds are too infrequent, whether PTAs increase or decrease the probability of a round cannot be answered econometrically but we can provide some bounds for our results. For instance, suppose that in the absence of PTAs the UR would not have been completed, and the mere existence of PTAs assured its completion. In this case the *total* stumbling block effect, which incorporates possible changes in the probability of a round, can be shown to be equal to 1.2 percentage points (Karacaovali and Limão, 2005). Thus, even under this extreme assumption, these EU PTAs are a stumbling block and would have been so unless the average reduction in tariffs by other countries had been almost six times larger than what we actually observed. If, on the other hand, the probability of completing the round without PTAs were nearly one and with PTAs it became nearly zero, then the total stumbling block effect would be at least 1.4 percentage points.

Finally, examining the importance of the PTA variable differently, the explained amount of variation in the tariffs across goods which can be attributed to it is significantly higher than the rest of the variables.

4.5. Robustness analysis

We now test whether the stumbling block results given in Table 2 are robust along various dimensions such as the choice of controls, instruments, measurement error in the PTA variable, and the sample. We summarize the results in Table 5, where the first column repeats the basic information from Table 2 for comparison. The first two rows correspond to robustness tests of specification 1 in Table 2, that is ϕ^{any0} and $1+\phi^{\text{any0}}/c$—the quantification discussed in the previous section—respectively. The third and fourth rows present similar statistics when we account for the effect of every PTA, analogously to column 2 of Table 2.

Table 5
Robustness and specification analysis

Robustness procedure:		IV-GMM	IV-GMM (excl. reciproc.)	IV-GMM (sure switch)	IV-GMM (initial tariff)	IV-GMM (excl. 311)	IV-GMM (sure switch & excl. 311)	IV-GMM ("industry" effects)	IV-GMM (sure switch & "industry" effects)	IV-GMM (exclude ntb_all iv)
Specification	Test	(1)	(2)	(3)	(4)	(5)	(6)	(7)	(8)	(9)
Table 2 (1)	ϕ^{any0} (s.e.)	0.015	0.016 (0.003)	0.036	0.018	0.005	0.028 (0.008)	0.007 (0.003)	0.038 (0.007)	0.014
		(0.003)		(0.006)[b]	(0.004)[c]	(0.002)				(0.006)
Table 2 (1)	$1+\phi/c$[a]	0.55	0.56	0.35	0.36	0.79	0.39 (0.25, 0.53)	0.77	0.36	0.48
	(95% CI)	(0.41, 0.68)	(0.41, 0.71)	(0.23, 0.48)	(−0.03, 0.70)[d]	(0.66, 0.92)		(0.61, 0.93)	(0.24, 0.49)	(0.13, 0.83)
Table 2 (2)	ϕ^{evy0} (s.e.)	0.007	0.007 (0.002)	0.006	0.009	0.007	0.006 (0.002)	0.004 (0.001)	0.002 (0.001)	0.009
		(0.002)		(0.002)	(0.002)	(0.002)				(0.003)
Table 2 (2)	$1+(\phi^{evy0}+\phi^{any0})/c$	0.39	0.41	0.28	−0.11	0.52	0.35 (0.16, 0.54)	0.58	0.35	0.24
	(95% CI)	(0.21, 0.56)	(0.22, 0.59)	(0.15, 0.41)	(−0.85, 0.63)	(0.28, 0.78)		(0.45, 0.72)	(0.25, 0.45)	(−0.26, 0.73)
Table 2 (1)	Schwarz info.	−7.58	−7.57	−7.59	−7.45	−7.68	−7.65	−7.72	−7.64	−7.49
	Observations	6294	6294	6294	6294	5875	5875	6294	6294	6294

IV-GMM obtained from an instrumental variable efficient generalized method of moments estimator.

The Hansen–Sargan test of over-identifying restrictions cannot reject the null hypothesis that the excluded instruments are uncorrelated with the second stage error term, and correctly excluded from the estimated equation in any of the specifications, with a p-value of 0.5 or higher in columns 1 through 6 and a p-value of 0.22 or higher in columns 7 through 9. The same is true for the difference in Sargan test for subsets of instruments.

Column (1) replicates the results from columns 1 and 2 of Table 2.

Column (2) drops the reciprocity variable and its instrument from the specifications in columns 1 and 2 of Table 2.

Column (3) employs instruments for the subset of products that are known to have switched status, i.e. uses D^{cec} instead of D^{anyexp} for I^{any0}.

Column (4) includes the initial tariff as an additional endogenous regressor.

Column (5) excludes all products in ISIC 311.

Column (6) excludes all products in ISIC 311 and employs instruments for subset of products that are known to have switched status, as in column 3.

Column (7) includes fixed effects for each of the Harmonized Standard 1-digit classifications.

Column (8) includes fixed effects for each of the Harmonized Standard 1-digit classifications and employs instruments for the subset of products that are known to have switched status, as in column 3.

Column (9) excludes all instruments that are constructed using the D^{ntball} variable.

[a] Measures the relative growth of world prices due to PTAs when the pass-through of tariffs to domestic prices is imperfect and similar for PTA and non-PTA goods, i.e. $\zeta^{PTA} \approx \zeta < 1$. Confidence intervals calculated using the delta method.

[b] We can reject the null that the coefficient is equal to 0.013, the OLS value in Table 2, with a p-value of =0.00.

[c] The coefficient on the initial tariff variable (t_{t-1}) and the associated standard errors for specifications 1 and 2 are respectively: −0.195 (0.111) and −0.143 (0.068).

[d] Refers to the relative growth at the mean initial tariff i.e. $1+\phi/(c+0.0789 * \phi^{ini})$. When we account for the different average initial tariffs which are 0.0757 at $I^{any0}=1$ and 0.128 otherwise, and then calculate $(c+0.0757 * \phi^{ini}+\phi)/(c+0.128 * \phi^{ini})$, we obtain 0.26 (−0.09, 0.61).

We did not derive the reciprocity variable directly from our theoretical model. Thus, we ask whether the main results are affected if we drop it and follow the structural equation more closely. The second column of Table 5 shows that the results are unchanged.

As we describe in Section 4.1 and show in the appendix (Section A.3), there is a potential for misclassification of new PTA goods that may generate attenuation bias. An instrument that is correlated with the new PTA goods in I_{it} but not the existing ones reduces or eliminates this bias and in fact we showed that the OLS estimates were slightly lower than the IV. However, the IV specifications we analyzed thus far are unlikely to fully solve this problem. A better alternative may be to use as instruments those goods that we know are "sure switches" to PTA goods. This is the case for the goods exported by the former communist countries in the CEC group, because this PTA was completely unexpected at the time of the Tokyo Round and in place by the UR. When we use the CEC exports as an instrument for I^{any0}, the stumbling block estimate is 0.036, as shown in column 3 of Table 5. This value is significantly higher than the OLS estimate of 0.013 and also the baseline IV estimate of 0.015, which supports our earlier argument that the misclassification of new PTA goods will if anything lead to an underestimate of the true stumbling block effect. The price effect estimate is now 0.36, which is about 30 percentage points stronger than the OLS estimate.

We do not expect our estimates to be biased due to omitted variables because, even if they are correlated with the included regressors, we instrument, test, and confirm the orthogonality of the excluded instruments relative to the error term. Nevertheless, we want to explicitly address the effect of including the initial tariff rate in the estimation. The average initial MFN tariff for PTA goods in our sample is 7.6%, whereas it is 12.8% for the non-PTA goods. Although in the UR no explicit formula was followed such that higher tariffs would be cut by more than the lower ones, it is certainly a possible outcome and may lead us to find bigger cuts in the non-PTA goods. When we add the initial tariff level as an endogenous regressor, we find that its coefficient is typically negative, so products with higher initial tariffs had slightly bigger cuts, but it is not always statistically significant. Moreover, the initial tariff does not affect the sign, magnitude or significance of the basic stumbling block effect. As shown in column 4 of Table 5, the relative growth effect evaluated at the average initial tariff is at least as large as the ones found in Table 2. Since the main results are not sensitive to the inclusion of the initial tariff and, according to the Schwarz criterion, the specification without it is preferred, we choose to focus on the latter, which also follows our theoretical model more closely.

There is considerable variation across PTAs in the set of goods each exports duty-free to the EU. This fraction in our sample ranges from 0.2 for GSPL to 0.9 for countries that acceded the EU and the median for the PTAs with non-acceding countries, which are our main focus, is 0.58. The fraction of PTA goods exported by *any* PTA is 0.94 and two-thirds of the ISIC three-digit industries contain both PTA and non-PTA goods. The fraction of such goods exported by every PTA is 0.13 spread over three quarters of the industries.

Despite the variation just described, the food products industry, ISIC 311, contains approximately half of all the products in our sample that do not enter the EU duty-free through *any* preferential agreements. Although this category does not include primary agricultural products (it includes processing of food related products), it does share one important characteristic with agriculture: high protection. To the extent that this feature is time-invariant, then it is immediately addressed by the fact that we estimate the equations in differences. Moreover, the initial tariff, which is on average higher for ISIC 311 than for other industries, does not seem to be biasing the results, because, as we have just shown, its inclusion does not affect the results significantly. To investigate whether the stumbling block effect is merely driven by a cross-industry difference in the average tariff cut between ISIC 311 and other industries, we re-estimate the model by dropping the observations in 311. The estimates in column 5 of Table 5 are qualitatively similar to those in Table 2 in terms of the signs and significance of the coefficients.

When we exclude products in ISIC 311 the point estimate for ϕ^{any0} is smaller than the baseline. One reason for the lower estimate for ϕ^{any0} when ISIC 311 is excluded is that the attenuation bias from the measurement error is severely aggravated. The reason is simple, goods that were not PTA goods in the latter period, were also not PTA goods earlier (since preferences and the range of goods exported have increased) so they were correctly classified as no switches. By dropping a large number of these non-PTA goods we increase the fraction of PTA goods and therefore the proportion of potentially misclassified goods. We confirm this in column 6 where we apply the alternative instruments of sure switches described above to the subsample without ISIC 311. The point estimate for ϕ^{any0} is now 0.028, which is statistically indistinguishable from the earlier one in column 3 of 0.036, as is the price effect, 0.39.

For the products in the industries mentioned above, we were able to identify potential problems and test the robustness of the results to excluding them. However, there may exist other unobserved industry characteristics driving tariff changes and they may occur in industries that are defined differently, e.g. by the Harmonized Standard (HS) tariff code. Controlling for unobserved industry characteristics is particularly important when one employs a different empirical approach, which does not follow a structural equation as closely as we do. This is the case in Limão (2006) who controls for "industries" defined by the HS classification when studying the US. Nonetheless, one may ask whether our baseline results are also robust to controlling for such unobserved industry characteristics. Thus, in columns 7 and 8 of Table 5 we include industry effects—broadly defined here by the HS-1 digit classifications. We still obtain a positive and significant stumbling block effect. Since including these HS dummies implies that there is less variation available to identify the effect, it is important to address the measurement error in the PTA variable in order to minimize any attenuation bias. Column 8 does this by employing the sure switch instruments. When we do so, we find that the results are both qualitatively and quantitatively close to the analogous ones in column 3.[23]

It is possible that goods in which the EU has an NTB on all partners share other properties that affect its MFN tariff change. As we previously reported, alternative over-identifying restrictions tests reject this hypothesis. But we can go further and test if this affects our results by dropping all instruments that include the NTB variable, D^{ntball}. The results, shown in the last column, are the same as in the baseline: ϕ^{any0} is 0.014 instead of 0.015 and ϕ^{evy0} is 0.009 instead of 0.007.

The Hansen–Sargan test of over-identifying restrictions cannot reject the null hypothesis that the excluded instruments are uncorrelated with the second stage error, and correctly excluded in any of the specifications, with a p-value of 0.5 or higher in columns 1 through 6 and a p-value of 0.22 or higher in columns 7 through 9. The same is true for the difference in Sargan test for subsets of instruments.

The identity of a PTA good may be correlated with other characteristics that affect tariff changes and this was a key motive for instrumenting the PTA variable and extensively testing the validity of the instruments. However, we go further and now summarize various tests directly related to the identity of the PTA goods. In addition to the one described for ISIC 311, the baseline result is also robust to excluding the export variable from the instrument list and using price changes to predict which goods are exported (see footnote 21). The large share of goods exported by at least one PTA, I^{any0}, is explained by several factors, including the very large and diverse number of PTA partners (over 150) and for some, the low trade costs due to proximity to the EU (e.g. EFTA, MED, CEC). As we see in Table A1, the fraction of HS-8 lines with a duty-free preference varies across PTAs from 70% (GSP) to 94% (EFTA). EFTA exports in 90% of the HS-8 lines and receives preferences in most, so if we recalculate I^{any0} excluding EFTA, its mean falls to 0.78. Given this, we can ask if the baseline result is driven by EFTA by using the redefined I^{any0} variable and including the EFTA variable separately in that regression (adjusting the instruments accordingly). The results are very similar to the baseline, with $\phi^{\text{any0}}=0.016$ and a coefficient on the EFTA variable positive and significant, similar to the one found for the individual PTA results in column 3 of Table 3. Therefore, the various robustness tests provide additional evidence that the identity of the PTA goods does not significantly bias the IV results.

5. Conclusion

We analyze the effects of PTAs on multilateral trade liberalization—a controversial issue where the evidence has been scarce. The model we develop captures key features of the current trading system and provides a rich set of predictions regarding the impact of PTAs on MTL. We derive structural equations of protection that guide the estimation. Using detailed tariff data for the EU during the last two multilateral rounds, we find evidence that its PTAs slowed down MTL. As the model predicts, this occurred only in products with a zero preferential tariff and was not present in agreements with a common external tariff and transfers, i.e. accessions to the EU in the 1980s and 1995. Our model also incorporates domestic political economy motives for tariffs and we find a negative relation between import penetration and tariff levels working through the extra weight that governments place on producer surplus. We also find evidence of multilateral reciprocity.

In the absence of its PTAs, the EU would have lowered its MFN tariff on PTA products by an additional 1.5 percentage points. Since the average reduction for non-PTA products is almost twice as high, the average price effect due to the EU's multilateral tariff changes is 50–60% for PTA goods relative to other goods. We also discuss how this

[23] Limão (2006) controls for industries defined at the finer HS-2 digit level. The EU tariff changes do not permit us to control for such disaggregate industries because the share of the between variation at the HS-2 level is about two times higher in the EU than in the US tariff changes. This also implies that for the EU, the HS-1 effects account for a reasonable share of the tariff change variation relative to the other variables we include, as evidenced by the statistical significance of these HS-1 effects in the regression and the improvement in the Schwarz criterion.

wedge between PTA and non-PTA products provides an estimate of the effect of PTAs on the expected average reductions in *all* products relative to a situation where the EU has no PTAs and show that the effect is at least 1.2 percentage points.

We find no evidence of a stumbling block effect for countries that acceded the EU in the 1980s and 1995. But we do find evidence for all other preferential agreements of the EU in place at the time of the Uruguay Round. Since the EU continues to expand both types of preferences, we think that both results are important. Moreover, the lack of evidence on preferences promoting multilateral liberalization for the EU (or the US) suggests that we should be concerned about a "clash of liberalizations". Similar work that carefully establishes causation is required for other countries. Even if the EU and the US turn out to be the exceptions, this concern has to be still addressed because their share of world trade implies that their PTAs have a potentially large impact on non-members. These estimates suggest that the stumbling block effect may be even worse for the Doha round, which is currently under negotiation. The motive is simple; after the UR, preferences for existing and new PTAs were greatly expanded, partly as a way to counter the preference erosion generated by the lower MFN tariffs.

The inevitable final question is what, if anything, can be done to minimize this clash. The current enthusiasm for PTAs means that prohibiting them is not feasible and we have not shown that doing so would necessarily be optimal either. However, there may be ways to grant preferential treatment that do not slow down MTL. Recall that, according to the model, the effect of PTAs on MTL only occurs when the preferential tariff is zero and cannot be further lowered. From this perspective, the answer is simple: remove the non-negativity constraint on preferential tariffs and allow import subsidies. Limão and Olarreaga (2006) estimate that the additional MTL thus permitted generates a Pareto improvement for the three groups of countries: non-members, and preference granting and receiving countries. This or other proposals that target the source of the problem and take into account the effects on these three groups of countries are the most likely to be accepted by them and minimize any further clash of liberalizations.

Appendix A

A.1. Tariff expressions

A.1.1. No common external tariff

Eq. (4): Consider good $i=1$, which is imported by L from L^* and S, and its symmetric counterpart $i=2$, exported to L^*. Using Eq. (2) we simplify the first-order-condition (FOC) for an interior solution to Eq. (3) and obtain

$$\begin{aligned} G_{\tau_1}+G_{\tau_2^*}+G_{\pi_1} &= -\left[M_1^s+M_1^*+\tau_1(p_1'-1)M_1^{*\prime}\right]-p_1'M_1-\left(p_2^{*\prime}-1\right)M_2+(\omega_1-1)p_1'X_1 \\ &= -\left[\tau_1(p_1'-1)M_1^{*\prime}\right]-(p_1'-1)M_1-\left(p_2^{*\prime}-1\right)M_2+(\omega_1-1)p_1'X_1 \end{aligned} \tag{16}$$

where $p'\equiv\partial p/\partial\tau$, $M^{*\prime}\equiv\partial M^*/\partial p^*$ and we use the market clearing condition in Eq. (1) for $i=1$. Equating to zero and solving for τ_1, we obtain

$$\tau_1^m=\frac{(\omega_1-1)p_1'X_1-(p_1'-1)M_1-\left(p_2^{*\prime}-1\right)M_2}{(p_1'-1)M_1^{*\prime}} \tag{17}$$

To derive Eq. (4) in the text, we do the following. The symmetry implies that $p_1'=p_2^{*\prime}$, $M_1=M_2^*$, and $M_1^s=M_2^{s*}$. Market clearing implies that $M_2^*+M_2^{s*}=-M_2$, where we replace the symmetry conditions to obtain $M_2=-(M_1+M_1^s)$. Finally, we divide Eq. (17) by p_1^*, use $p'=M^{*\prime}/[M^{*\prime}+M']$ (from implicit differentiation of Eq. (1)) and $M_1^{s\prime}=0$) and employ the following elasticity definitions: $\varepsilon\equiv-M'p^*/M$ and $\varepsilon^*\equiv[\partial(M^*+M^s)/\partial p^*]\times[p^*/(M^*+M^s)]=[\partial M^*/\partial p^*]\times[p^*/(M^*+M^s)]$.

Eq. (9): Using Eqs. (1) and (2) and the fact that net exports of S are $X_1{}^s$ in equilibrium, the FOC for τ^{mp} for an interior solution to Eq. (8) is

$$\begin{aligned} G_{e^s}\frac{\partial e^p}{\partial\tau_1}+G_{\tau_1}+G_{\tau_2^*} &= G_{e^s}\frac{\partial e^p}{\partial\tau_1}-\left[M_1^*+M_1+\tau_1(p_1'-1)M_1^{*\prime}\right]-(p_1'-1)M_1-\left(p_2^{*\prime}-1\right)M_2+(\omega_1-1)p_1'X_1 \\ &= G_{e^s}\frac{\partial e^p}{\partial\tau_1}-X_1^s-\tau_1(p_1'-1)M_1^{*\prime}-(p_1'-1)M_1-\left(p_2^{*\prime}-1\right)M_2+(\omega_1-1)p_1'X_1 \end{aligned} \tag{18}$$

Equating to zero and solving for τ_1 we obtain

$$\tau_1^{mp} = \frac{(\omega_1 - 1)p_1' X_1 - (p_1' - 1)M_1 - (p_2^{*\prime} - 1)M_2 + \left[G_{e^s}\frac{\partial e^p}{\partial \tau_1} - X_1^s\right]}{(p_1' - 1)M_1^{*\prime}} \tag{19}$$

To obtain Eq. (9), we apply the symmetry conditions described in the previous derivation, divide Eq. (19) by p_1^*, and employ the same elasticity definitions.

A.1.2. Common external tariff and direct transfers

We show that a stumbling block effect is absent in the presence of direct transfers by focusing on the simpler case when S exports only good 1 and $\omega_1^s = 1$. Allowing a transfer T from L to S under a PTA implies that the participation constraint for S is now $G^s(\pi^p, \tau, e^p) + T \geq G^s(\pi, \tau, e^s = 0)$. Thus the equilibrium level of e^s for a given preference, $\tau_1 - \pi_1$, and transfer, T is

$$e^{\text{pcu}} = T + (\tau_1 - \pi_1)(-M_1^s) \tag{20}$$

The large countries maximize their joint objective net of transfers made to the regional partner.

$$\{\tau^{\text{mcu}}, \pi^{\text{pcu}}, T^{\text{cu}}\} \equiv \underset{\tau,\pi,T}{\arg\max}\ \{G(\tau = \tau^*, \pi, \tau^*, e^s = 0, .) - T : \pi \leq \tau; e^s = e^{\text{pcu}}\} \tag{21}$$

The FOCs for a good obtaining a preference under this program of CET with transfers are

$$G_\tau + G_{\tau^*} + G_{e^s}\frac{\partial e^{\text{pcu}}}{\partial \tau} \leq 0; \quad G_\pi + G_{e^s}\frac{\partial e^{\text{pcu}}}{\partial \pi} \leq 0; \quad G_T + G_{e^s}\frac{\partial e^{\text{pcu}}}{\partial T} \leq 0 \tag{22}$$

where we recall that $G(\cdot)$ is defined by Eq. (2). Evaluating the FOC of the MFN tariff in the absence of preferences, i.e. Eq. (16), at the level of the MFN tariff under the CU in Eq. (22), we obtain

$$\left[G_{\tau_1} + G_{\tau_2^*} + G_{\pi_1}\right]_{G_\tau + G_{\tau^*} + G_{e^s}\frac{\partial e^{\text{pcu}}}{\partial \tau} = 0} = G_{\pi_1} - G_{e^s}\frac{\partial e^{\text{pcu}}}{\partial \tau_1} = G_{\pi_1} + G_{e^s}\frac{\partial e^{\text{pcu}}}{\partial \pi_1} = 0 \tag{23}$$

where the second equality uses Eq. (20). In order to establish the last equality we must show that the FOC for π in Eq. (22) is zero. Suppose it is not, such that $G_\pi + G_{e^s}\frac{\partial e^{\text{pcu}}}{\partial \pi} = -M^s + M^s G_{e^s} = (-1 + G_{e^s})M^s < 0$ when evaluated at $\tau^{\text{mcu}} = \tau^m$. This implies that L would gain by further lowering π but it can only do so until it is zero. However, $G_T + G_{e^s}\frac{\partial e^{\text{pcu}}}{\partial T} = -1 + G_{e^s}$, which is positive if $G_\pi + G_{e^s}\frac{\partial e^{\text{pcu}}}{\partial \pi} < 0$. Thus $\tau^{\text{mcu}} = \tau^m$, $T = 0$ and $\pi = 0$ is not a solution. T must be increased until $-1 + G_{e^s} = 0$, which implies that $G_\pi + G_{e^s}\frac{\partial e^{\text{pcu}}}{\partial \pi} = 0$. Therefore we obtain $\tau^{\text{mcu}} = \tau^m$, $T^{\text{cu}} > 0$ and $\pi = \pi^{\text{pcu}} < \tau^{\text{mcu}}$.

A.2. Stumbling block effects with multiple PTA goods

In Section 3.2.2 we claim that when S exports multiple goods, the stumbling effect is present in the set of goods where the preferential tariff is zero but not in those where it is positive and that this depends on the existence of different political weights in S. We show this for the case when L imports goods 1 and 3 from L^* and S, and the symmetric imports for L^* are $i = 2, 4$. The equilibrium level of e^p in Eq. (7) is now

$$e^p = \sum_{i=1,3} (\tau_i - \pi_i)\omega_i^s X_i^s \tag{24}$$

The FOC for the two MFN and two preferential tariffs arising from the program in Eq. (8) are

$$\begin{aligned} &G_{e^s}\frac{\partial e^p}{\partial \tau_1} + G_{\tau_1} + G_{\tau_2^*} \leq 0; \quad G_{e^s}\frac{\partial e^p}{\partial \tau_3} + G_{\tau_3} + G_{\tau_4^*} \leq 0 \\ &G_{e^s}\frac{\partial e^p}{\partial \pi_1} + G_{\pi_1} \leq 0; \quad G_{e^s}\frac{\partial e^p}{\partial \pi_3} + G_{\pi_3} \leq 0 \end{aligned}$$

The objective is to show that in an equilibrium where both goods receive a preference but there is room for increasing the preferential margin in good 3, i.e. $\pi_3 \in (0, \tau_3)$, then if $\omega_1^s > \omega_3^s$, we have $\pi_1 = 0$, $\tau_1^{mp} > \tau_1^m$, and $\tau_3^{mp} = \tau_3^m$. By construction, the solution for π_3 is an interior one in this equilibrium and therefore its FOC holds with equality and $G_{e^s}\frac{\partial e^p}{\partial \pi_3} = -G_{\pi_3}$. Substituting this in the FOC for π_1 we obtain

$$\left(\frac{-G_{\pi_3}}{\partial e^p/\partial \pi_3}\right)\frac{\partial e^p}{\partial \pi_1} + G_{\pi_1} = -X_3^s\frac{\omega_1^s X_1^s}{\omega_3^s X_3^s} + X_1^s = \left(1-\frac{\omega_1^s}{\omega_3^s}\right)X_1^s < 0$$

where the first equality uses the definition of G and Eq. (24), and the final inequality is due to $\omega_1^s > \omega_3^s$.

The expression for the MFN tariff in good i is still given by Eq. (9) and, as we show in the text, the stumbling block effect is present in that good iff $-(G_{e^s}\partial e^p/\partial \pi_i + G_{\pi_i})>0$. The LHS terms are simply the FOC for π_i and in this equilibrium we know they are equal to zero for good 3 since $\pi_3>0$ and so $\tau_3^{mp}=\tau_3^m$. But this inequality does hold for good 1 and so $\tau_1^{mp}>\tau_1^m$.

If the optimal preferential tariff implied by the FOC is $\pi_3>\tau_3^m$, then L must follow WTO rules and set $\pi_3=\tau_3^m$. In this case we are effectively back to the situation with one PTA good so it is not sufficient for $\omega_1^s>\omega_3^s$ in order to obtain $\pi_1=0$. But provided that in equilibrium we do have $\pi_1=0$ (e.g. because ω_1^s is sufficiently large relative to ω_3^s) then we continue to have the same prediction as before. That is, in the duty-free PTA goods, there is a stumbling block, $\tau_1^{mp}>\tau_1^m$, and in the goods that do not receive a preference, the tariff expression is the same as in the case with no PTAs, so $\tau_3^{mp}=\tau_3^m$.

A.3. Interpretation of estimates for continuing PTAs

By differencing Eq. (12) and assuming time-invariant political weights, we obtain the general econometric model in error form

$$\Delta t_i = \phi_{it}(I_{it} - I_{it-1}) + I_{it-1}\Delta\phi_{it} + \beta\Delta x_i + \Delta m_i + \Delta u_i \tag{25}$$

where $E(\Delta u_i|I_{it}, I_{it-1},\Delta x_{it},\Delta m_{it})=0$. For observations that are not PTA goods at $t-1$ we obtain Eq. (14). EU preferences in PTAs that existed by the Tokyo Round expanded between the two rounds. Moreover, the sets of products that any given country can export have generally increased and if a product was exported in the recent past, the PTA government is likely to expect to export it in the immediate future. Both facts strongly suggest that $I_{it-1}=1$ implies $I_{it}=1$ and since both are binary variables, we have $I_{it-1}=I_{it-1}I_{it}$. This is obvious from the matrix below that shows all the possible combinations for a given product's status and clarifies its practical implication: ruling out the possibility in the last row where a good's status is initially 1 and then changes to 0.

I_{it}	I_{it-1}	$I_{it}I_{it-1}$	$I_{it}-I_{it-1}$
0	0	0	0
1	0	0	1
1	1	1	0
0	1	0	−1

Replacing $I_{it-1}=I_{it-1}I_{it}$ in Eq. (25) and factoring out I_{it} we obtain

$$\Delta t_i = ((1 - I_{it-1})\phi_{it} + I_{it-1}\Delta\phi_{it})I_{it} + \beta\Delta x_i + \Delta m_i + \Delta u_i \tag{26}$$

So an OLS estimate of the parameter on I_{it} for continuing agreements, call it $\tilde{\phi}$, can be interpreted as the average over all goods of $(1-I_{it-1})\phi_{it}+I_{it-1}\Delta\phi_{it}$. This is a weighted average of the current stumbling block for goods with new preferences and the change in the stumbling block of the goods with continuing preferences, as we note in the text. Thus $\tilde{\phi}$ is the average *change* in the stumbling block between rounds, i.e. how much smaller tariff reductions were.

For PTAs signed between rounds, $\tilde{\phi}$ reflects exactly the stumbling block effect *level* since in that case $I_{it-1}=0$. For those PTAs that previously had some subset of goods exported under preferences, $\tilde{\phi}$ generally provides a downward biased estimate of the level effect, ϕ_t. To see this, we simplify Eq. (26) to obtain

$$\Delta t_i = (\phi_{it} - I_{it-1}\phi_{it-1})I_{it} + \beta\Delta x_i + \Delta m_i + \Delta u_i \tag{27}$$

Recall from the model that $\phi_{it-1}\geq 0$, so generally the OLS coefficient on I_{it} will be a downward biased estimate of ϕ_t. This occurs because we should use only true switches to identify ϕ_{it}. But for some agreements we cannot observe which subset of I_t corresponds to true switches (no product data on I_{it-1} for agreements in place before Tokyo Round) so we misclassify some goods with $I_t=1$ as switches even though they had no change in status.

Eq. (27) also indicates how the bias can be ameliorated with IV. When the instrument is correlated with I_t but not with I_{t-1} the term $I_{it-1}\phi_{it-1}$ can be left in the error term and we obtain a consistent estimate of ϕ_t. The programs with new preferences and/or exports, e.g. CEC, have $I_{t-1}=0$ and so are good candidates for instruments.

A.4. Data

Table A1
Details on EU PTAs

Program	Recipients	Start date	Type of preference	Import share 1994	Share in '94 PTA imports	% of duty-free HS-8 lines	Notes/non-trade issues/extensions	Sources
ACP (African, Caribbean, and Pacific)	Over 70 countries, mostly former colonies of EU members	1976	Unilateral PTA	0.5%	1.9%	84%	Colonial ties major motivation. Financial and political cooperation; human rights play a role. (its earliest predecessor Yaoundé in 1963) In 1990 became the first development agreement to incorporate a human rights clause as a 'fundamental' part of cooperation (article 5).	Brown (2002), EU Commission 2004[4]
CEC[1] (Central and East European)	Slovak Republic, Czech Republic, Poland, and Hungary	1992	Bilateral FTA	1.4%	6%	80%	Serves as a transition to full membership. Recipients committed to pass laws such as in intellectual property rights to conform with EU.	Busse (2000)
EFTX	Switzerland, Norway, Iceland, Liechtenstein	1973–1974	Bilateral FTA	5.2%	22.3%	94%	EFTA members excluding AFS. Mainly industrial goods, excludes most agricultural products. Provides further for common competition rules, rules for state aid and government procurement, as well as harmonization of rules and standards for goods and services	EFTA[5] Secretariat 2004
GSP[2] (generalized system of preferences)	More than 100 developing countries	1971	Unilateral PTA	13%	57%	70%	Widest program; includes non-duty-free rates. Preferential rates vary according to competitiveness of the recipient countries. In 1981 the tariff quotas that were initially (in 1971) applied on 'sensitive products' were largely reduced.	Atkinson (1999), EU Commission 2004[4]
GSPL (GSP for least developed)	About 50 of the poorest nations in the world	1971	Unilateral PTA	0.3%	1.2%	77%	Objective: Improving access to global markets for agricultural and industrial goods and services. It's a special arrangement for LDCs under the GSP program.	European Commission 2004
MED[3] (Mediterranean countries)	Algeria, Israel Morocco, Tunisia, Egypt, Jordan, Syria	1975–1977	Unilateral PTA	2.7%	11.3%	81%	Cooperation in social affairs, migration, human rights, and democracy. Preferences on industrial goods only, with strict rules of origin. A redirected Mediterranean Policy (RMP) was initiated in 1992 and substantially increased the amount of development aid and extended EU trade preferences.	EU Commission 2004[4], Raya (1999)
AFS and SPG	EU members joined between Tokyo and Uruguay rounds	See note	Bilateral CU	n/a	n/a	100%	AFS: Austria (1995), Finland (1995), Sweden (1995). SPG: Spain (1986), Portugal (1986), Greece (1981). Accession years in parentheses.	EU Commission 2004[4]

Notes: (1) Romania and Bulgaria signed FTA agreements with the EU in 1993, hence should be part of the CEC category but they are not included in our analysis due to lack of data. (2) There exist special arrangements supporting measures to combat drugs under the GSP program. The recipients are the Andean group (Colombia, Venezuela, Ecuador, Peru, and Bolivia) and the Central American Common Market group (Costa Rica, El Salvador, Guatemala, Honduras, and Nicaragua). The extra concessions data for these groups is not available and hence they are considered only as part of the general GSP program. (3) Lebanon made a unilateral PTA arrangement with the EU in 1977 but it is not included in our estimations due to again lack of data. (4) http://europa.eu/pol/comm/index_en.htm accessed June 2006. (5) http://secretariat.efta.int/ accessed June 2006.

Table A2
Summary statistics

Variable	Mean	Std. Dev.	Min	Max
Δt	−0.030	0.022	−0.268	0.000
I^{any0}	0.939	0.239	0	1
I^{evy0}	0.133	0.339	0	1
I^{any}	0.954	0.210	0	1
I^{pos}	0.015	0.121	0	1
I^{afs}	0.902	0.297	0	1
I^{spg}	0.875	0.330	0	1
I^{hiexp}	0.891	0.311	0	1
I^{gsp}	0.646	0.478	0	1
I^{gspl}	0.190	0.392	0	1
I^{acp}	0.291	0.454	0	1
I^{eftx}	0.870	0.337	0	1
I^{med}	0.508	0.500	0	1
I^{cec}	0.671	0.470	0	1
Δx	−2.004	1.853	−13.884	5.466
R	−0.460	0.118	−0.960	0.000
D^{anyexp}	0.984	0.126	0	1
D^{evyexp}	0.167	0.373	0	1
D^{gsp}	0.899	0.302	0	1
D^{gspl}	0.224	0.417	0	1
D^{acp}	0.333	0.471	0	1
D^{eftx}	0.904	0.294	0	1
D^{med}	0.594	0.491	0	1
D^{cec}	0.810	0.355	0	1
D^{hiexp}	0.948	0.221	0	1
R^{uni}	−0.267	0.139	−0.922	0
D^{ntb}	0.288	0.453	0	1
D^{ntball}	0.096	0.295	0	1
$D^{ntball} \times D^{anyexp}$	0.091	0.288	0	1
$D^{ntball} \times D^{evyexp}$	0.010	0.101	0	1
$D^{ntball} \times D^{gsp}$	0.069	0.253	0	1
Δp_{9294}	0.001	0.461	−3.912	4.874
Δscale	0.307	0.322	−0.351	1.047
$(\Delta p_{9294})^{avg} \times \Delta$scale	0.005	0.032	−0.053	0.126
P	0.502	0.500	0	1
t_{t-1}	0.079	0.046	0.005	0.65

The number of observations in our sample (n) is 6294. There were 8688 non-missing values for Δt (the dependent variable), which reduce to 7784 when we omit the lines with zero initial tariffs. Missing import and market access variables to construct the reciprocity variable reduce the sample to 6837, and missing price data to 6721. Production related data accounts for the remaining missing values and leaves us with $n=6294$.

Table A3
Data sources and definitions

Variable	Definition	Sources
Δt_i	The change in the bound advalorem MFN tariffs between the pre-Uruguay Round (UR) and post-UR periods for the HS 8-digit product i.	WTO
I_i^{any0} $[I_i^{evy0}]$	Equals 1 if HS 8 product i is imported in 1994 and receives a zero preferential rate by EU under any [all for I_i^{evy0}] of its PTAs. Excludes PTAs with CET.	Comext-Trains
I_i^{any} $[I_i^{pos}]$	Equals 1, if HS 8 product i is imported in 1994 and receives either a duty-free or positive preferential tariff rate [a positive preferential rate only for I_i^{pos}].	Comext-Trains
I_i^{afs} $[I_i^{spg}]$	Equals 1 if HS 8 product i is imported by the EU in 1994 from the "recent" members Austria, Finland, or Sweden [Spain, Portugal, or Greece for I_i^{spg}].	Comext
I_i^{hiexp}	An indicator equal to 1 if the exports of any of the PTA partners (excluding the ones with CET) to the EU in HS 8 product i are greater than the 25th percentile of its exports to the EU and are exported under the respective preferential program, i.e. $I_i^{any0} \times D_i^{hiexp}$ (see below)	Comext-Trains

(continued on next page)

Table A3 (*continued*)

Variable	Definition	Sources
R_i	$\equiv \sum_k s_i^k (\sum_j w_j^k \Delta t_j^k / t_{jt}^k)$ change in market access provided by the major exporters of HS 8 product i to EU during UR; where $\Delta t_j^k / t_{jt}^k$ is the percentage tariff reduction by country k in good j between 1986 and 1995, w_j^k is the 1992 import share of good j in total imports of k, and s_i^k is the exports of a principal supplier (a top 5 exporter) k to EU in HS 8 product i as a share of total exports of i from EU's all principal suppliers.	Finger et al. (2002) and authors' calculations from Comext
R_i^{uni}	Reciprocity variable computed only for the unilateral liberalization (between 1986 and 1992) by the major exporters to the EU. The computation is otherwise similar to that of R.	Same as R_i
Δx_I	The EU-wide change in the elasticity adjusted inverse import penetration ratio between 1978 (pre-Tokyo Round) and 1992 (pre-UR), for each 3-digit ISIC industry I. Computed using the 1978 members of the EU. Production values measured in domestic prices, $p_{IT}X_{IT}$, whereas import values measured in world prices, $p_{IT}^{*}M_{IT}$. Our elasticity measure is also evaluated at the domestic prices (and is for the EU as a whole), hence we calculate the measure required by the model as. $x_{It}=X_{It}/M_{It}(M_{It}'/M_{It})p_{It}^{*}=p_{It}X_{It}/p_{It}^{*}M_{It}$ $(M_{It}'p_{It}/M_{It})$.	Kee et al. (2004) Unido, Comtrade and Penn World Tables
P_i	Proxy for the change in the MFN externality effect, Δm. Computed as a dummy equal to one if the change in the share of the non-top 5 exporters in total exports to the EU between 1989 and 1994 is above the median for an HS 8 digit product i.	Comext
$I_i^{\text{pta-name}}$	Equals 1 if EU imports HS 8 product i at a zero preferential rate under the "pta_name" program, which includes GSP, GSPL, ACP, MED, CEC, EFTX.	Comext-Trains
$D_i^{\text{any exp[evy exp]}}$	Equals 1 if HS 8 product i is imported by EU from any [all for $D_i^{\text{evy exp}}$] of its PTA partners in 1994 (regardless of a preference or not).	Comext
D_i^{hiexp}	Equals 1, if HS 8 product i is an important export for a PTA partner (greater than the 25th percentile of its exports to the EU).	Comext
$D_i^{\text{ntball[ntb]}}$	Equals 1 if HS 8 product i is subject to a non-tariff barrier that applies to all exporters [at least one exporter for D_i^{ntb}] of i to the EU.	Trains
Δp_{i9294}	Change in world price of HS 8 product i between 1992 and 94. Computed using unit values for the EU and averaged over all of its exporters.	Comext
Δscale_I	The change in the EU-wide value added/number of firms by ISIC 3 sector I between 1978 and 1992.	Unido
$(\Delta p_{i9294})^{\text{avg}} \times \Delta \text{scale}_I$	Interaction of Δp_{i9294} averaged over industry I and Δscale_I.	Unido-Comtrade

References

Atkinson, B., 1999. Trade policy and preferences. In: Cosgrove-Sacks, C., Scappucci, G. (Eds.), The European Union and Developing Countries. MacMillan Press, London, pp. 305–321.

Bagwell, K., Staiger, R., 1999a. Regionalism and multilateral tariff cooperation. In: Piggott, J., Woodland, A. (Eds.), International Trade Policy and the Pacific Rim. MacMillan Press, London, pp. 157–185.

Bagwell, K., Staiger, R., 1999b. An economic theory of GATT. American Economic Review 89 (1), 215–248.

Bagwell, K., Staiger, R., 2006. What do trade negotiators negotiate about? Empirical Evidence from the World Trade Organization. NBER Working Paper, vol. 12727.

Bhagwati, J., 1991. The World Trading System at Risk. Princeton University Press, Princeton NJ.

Bohara, A.K., Gawande, K., Sanguinetti, P., 2004. Trade diversion and declining tariffs: evidence from Mercosur. Journal of International Economics 64 (1), 65–88.

Bond, E.W., Syropoulos, C., 1996. The size of trading blocs: market power and world welfare effects. Journal of International Economics 40 (3-4), 411–437.

Broda, C., Limão, N., Weinstein, D., 2006. Optimal Tariffs: The Evidence. NBER Working Paper, vol. 12033.

Brown, W., 2002. The European Union and Africa. I.B. Tauris Publishers, London.

Busse, M., 2000. The hub and spoke approach of EU trade policy. Mimeo, Hamburg Institute of International Economics.

Cadot, O., De Melo, J., Olarreaga, M., 1999. Regional integration and lobbying for tariffs against nonmembers. International Economic Review 40 (3), 635–657.

Chang, W., Winters, A., 2002. How regional blocs affect excluded countries: the price effects of Mercosur. American Economic Review 92 (4), 889–904.

Constantopoulos, M., 1974. Labour protection in Western Europe. European Economic Review 5 (4), 313–328.

Estevadeordal, A., Freund, C., Ornelas, E., 2006. Do regional trade agreements promote external trade liberalization? Evidence from Latin America. Mimeo.

Feenstra, R.C., 1989. Symmetric pass-through of tariffs and exchange rates under imperfect competition: an empirical test. Journal of International Economics 27 (1-2), 25–45.

Finger, M., 1976. Effects of the Kennedy Round tariff concessions on the exports of developing countries. Economic Journal 86, 87–95.

Finger, J.M., Reincke, U., Castro, A., 2002. Market access bargaining in the Uruguay Round: rigid or relaxed reciprocity? In: Bhagwati, J. (Ed.), Going Alone: the Case for Relaxed Reciprocity in Freeing Trade. MIT Press, Cambridge MA, pp. 111–135.
Foroutan, F., 1998. Does membership in a regional preferential trade arrangement make a country more or less protectionist? The World Economy 21 (3), 305–336.
Gawande, K., Bandyopadhyay, U., 2000. Is protection for sale? Evidence on the Grossman–Helpman theory of endogenous protection. Review of Economics and Statistics 82 (1), 139–152.
Goldberg, P.K., Knetter, M.M., 1997. Goods prices and exchange rates: what have we learned? Journal of Economic Literature 35 (3), 1243–1272.
Goldberg, P.K., Maggi, G., 1999. Protection for sale: an empirical investigation. American Economic Review 89 (5), 1135–1155.
Grilli, E., 1997. EU trade and aid policies towards the LDCs and the CEECs. In: El-Agra, A.M. (Ed.), Economic Integration Worldwide. MacMillan Press, London, pp. 135–174.
Grossman, G., Helpman, E., 1994. Protection for sale. American Economic Review 84 (4), 833–850.
Helpman, E., 1999. Politics and trade policy. In: Baldwin, R., Cohen, D., Sapir, A., Venables, T. (Eds.), Market Integration, Regionalism and the Global Economy. Cambridge University Press, Cambridge, pp. 86–112.
Jackson, J., 1997. The World Trading System: Law and Policy of International Economic Relations. 2nd edition. MIT Press, Cambridge MA.
Johnson, H.G., 1967. Economic Policies Toward Less Developed Countries. Brookings Institution, Washington DC.
Karacaovali, B., Limão, N., 2005. The clash of liberalizations: preferential vs. multilateral trade liberalization in the European Union. World Bank Policy Research Working Paper, vol. 3493.
Kee, H.L., Nicita, A., Olarreaga, M., 2004. Import demand elasticities and trade distortions. World Bank Policy Research Working Paper, vol. 3452.
Krishna, P., 1998. Regionalism and multilateralism: a political economy approach. Quarterly Journal of Economics 113 (1), 227–251.
Krugman, P., 1991. Is bilateralism bad? In: Helpman, E., Razin, A. (Eds.), International Trade and Trade Policy. MIT Press, Cambridge MA, pp. 9–23.
Levy, P., 1997. A political-economic analysis of free-trade agreements. American Economic Review 87 (4), 506–519.
Limão, N., 2006. Preferential trade agreements as stumbling blocks for multilateral trade liberalization: evidence for the U.S. American Economic Review 96 (3), 896–914.
Limão, N., 2007. Are preferential trade agreements with non-trade objectives a stumbling block for multilateral liberalization? Review of Economic Studies 74 (3), 821–855.
Limão, N., Olarreaga, M., 2006. Trade preferences to small developing countries and the welfare costs of lost multilateral liberalization. World Bank Economic Review 20 (2), 217–240.
Raya, F.J., 1999. A review of the Barcelona Conference and a summary of EU policy objectives. In: Cosgrove-Sacks, C., Scappucci, G. (Eds.), The European Union and Developing Countries. MacMillan Press, London, pp. 193–205.
Riedel, J., 1977. Tariff concessions in the Kennedy Round and the structure of protection in West Germany: an econometric assessment. Journal of International Economics 7, 133–143.
Romalis, J., 2007. NAFTA's and CUSFTA's impact on international trade. Review of Economics and Statistics 89 (3), 416–435.
Syropoulos, C., 2002. On tariff preferences and delegation decisions in customs unions: a Heckscher–Ohlin approach. Economic Journal 112, 625–648.
Tavares, S.C., 2001. The political economy of tariff determination in the European Union. Mimeo, University of Florida.
Viner, J., 1950. The Customs Union Issue. Carnegie Endowment for International Peace, New York.
Winters, A., 1999. Regionalism vs. multilateralism. In: Baldwin, R., Cohen, D., Sapir, A., Venables, T. (Eds.), Market Integration, Regionalism and the Global Economy. Cambridge University Press, Cambridge, pp. 7–49.

Chapter 15

Trade Preferences to Small Developing Countries and the Welfare Costs of Lost Multilateral Liberalization

Nuno Limão and Marcelo Olarreaga

The proliferation of preferential trade liberalization over the last 20 years has raised the question of whether it slows multilateral trade liberalization. Recent theoretical and empirical evidence indicates that this is the case even for unilateral preferences that developed countries provide to small and poor countries, but there is no estimate of the resulting welfare costs. This stumbling block effect can be avoided by replacing the unilateral preferences with a fixed import subsidy, which generates a Pareto improvement. More importantly, this paper presents the first estimates of the welfare cost of preferential liberalization as a stumbling block to multilateral liberalization. Recent estimates of the stumbling block effect of preferences with data for 170 countries and more than 5,000 products are used to calculate the welfare effects of the European Union, Japan, and the United States switching from unilateral preferences for least developed countries to an import subsidy scheme. In a model with no dynamic gains to trade, the switch produces an annual net welfare gain for the 170 countries that adds about 10 percent to the estimated trade liberalization gains in the Doha Round. It also generates gains for each group: the European Union, Japan, and the United States ($2,934 million), least developed countries ($520 million), and the rest of the world ($900 million).

One pillar of the multilateral trading system is nondiscrimination across trading partners: the most favored nation (MFN) principle in the first article of the General Agreement on Tariffs and Trade. But nearly all World Trade Organization (WTO) members also participate in preferential trade agreements. The

Nuno Limão is an assistant professor of economics at the University of Maryland; his email address is limao@econ.umd.edu. Marcelo Olarreaga is a senior economist at the World Bank; his email address is molarreaga@worldbank.org. Both authors are affiliated with the Centre for Economic Policy Research. They thank Stephanie Aaronson, Piyush Chandra, Bernard Hoekman, Kyle Bagwell, George Bermann, Bill Davy, Aaditya Mattoo, Petros Mavroidis, Stefano Inama, Chris Stevens, Alan Winters, three anonymous referees, and participants of the seminar on the World Trade Organization and developing countries at Columbia Law School for helpful comments and discussions. They also thank the U.K. Department for International Development for financial support. A supplemental appendix to this article is available at http://wber.oxfordjournals.org/.

THE WORLD BANK ECONOMIC REVIEW, VOL. 20, NO. 2, pp. 217–240 doi:10.1093/wber/lhj013

Advance Access publication May 17, 2006

Originally Published in *The World Bank Economic Review* 20(2), pp. 217–240.

potential for preferential trade agreements to be a stumbling block to multilateral trade liberalization (MTL) was an important concern during the Uruguay Round (Bhagwati 1991). This article quantifies the welfare effects of the more recent concern during the Doha Round that even unilateral trade preferences provided to small and poor developing countries can slow multilateral liberalization by the large developed countries that provide them. This problem prompted the International Monetary Fund (IMF) to create a special lending program aimed at developing countries "to mitigate concerns... that their balance of payments positions could suffer, albeit temporarily, as multilateral liberalization changes their competitive position in world markets. Chief among these concerns is that broad-based tariff liberalization might erode the value of their preferential access to important export markets" (IMF 2004b).[1]

The concern with preference erosion could affect the level of liberalization, particularly in the Doha Round, for two reasons. First, preference beneficiaries oppose MFN liberalization by countries that grant preferences. Even though erosion is critical only for a specific set of goods and countries, many other countries perceive such losses to be important. These countries can influence the current round because it was designated a "development round," creating the expectation that it would benefit developing countries.[2] Second, developed countries providing preferences may want to maintain them because they can be used as a side payment for cooperation on nontrade issues. Here are two examples. First, in 2000 the European Commission argued that a cut in its price support for sugar was untenable because it would reduce income for developing countries that export sugar to the EU under preferences (European Commission 2000). Second, the United States recognizes that its MFN tariff reductions hinder its ability to extract concessions in terms of enforcing labor, environmental standards, and the like from countries that export under a preference to the United States (Mendelowitz 1994).

1. See also IMF (2004a). According to the WTO's director-general, the IMF's program is "a welcome contribution to the Doha Round, in particular to attaining ambitious market access results" (Panitchpakdi 2004). For an interesting discussion, see Winters (2004). The possibility that preference erosion would reduce MFN liberalization was actually noted long ago; it was a concern voiced by opponents of the Generalized System of Preferences when it was originally proposed (Johnson 1967).

2. This points to the importance of further research and dissemination of basic facts about gains from preferences. There is some debate regarding the effectiveness of preferences in generating additional exports. Haveman and Shatz (2004) provide evidence that the unilateral preferences of the triad economies (the European Union (EU), Japan, and the United States) considerably increased their imports from least developed countries in 2000. Earlier estimates of the Generalized System of Preferences scheme are provided by Sapir (1981) for the EU and by Sapir and Ludenberg (1984) for the United States. UNCTAD (2003), Hoekman, Michalopoulos, and Winters (2004), and Stevens and Kennan (2004) propose several recommendations to fully realize the net benefits of preferences for least developed countries, including ways to improve utilization rates, to relax and harmonize rules of origin, to increase the predictability of preferences by binding them in the WTO, and so on. Many of these recommendations also apply to the alternative of import subsidies proposed here.

Limão (2002) provides a model in which preferences that are extended to small countries can cause large countries to maintain higher MFN tariffs. This stumbling block effect arises because of an important feature of EU and U.S. preference schemes: they require cooperation in nontrade issues such as labor and environmental standards, intellectual property protection, drug enforcement, immigration, and human rights. The appendix contains references to these and other side conditions in various preferential trade agreements. The preferential margins extended to small countries are often a payment for cooperation, which implies that a reduction in MFN tariffs that lowers the preferential margin will be resisted by both the country that receives preferences and the country that grants them.[3]

The following example illustrates the intuition behind the problem and the solution explored here. The U.S. MFN tariff on flowers is 10 percent, but Colombia can export them to the United States at a preferential tariff equal to zero—that is, it has a 10 percent preference margin in the United States. If the United States set its MFN tariff on flowers equal to zero in the Doha Round, it would be unable to provide a preference margin to Colombia to extract cooperation on nontrade issues. Thus, the model predicts that the United States will not reduce this MFN tariff to zero. There is a simple solution to this problem: allow a preferential import subsidy set at a fixed rate, for example, at the level of the current preference margin, 10 percent. If the U.S. charges the MFN tariff on Colombian flowers but pays a fixed subsidy rate of 10 percent to the Colombian producers, all participants are initially indifferent. But the United States could then maintain the fixed subsidy rate and reduce its MFN tariff without the opposition that results from preference erosion and the U.S. desire to extract cooperation through preferences.

In this article the welfare costs of preferences in terms of lost MTL are calculated using the recent estimates of the stumbling block effect generated by U.S. preferences from Limão (2006). Similar estimates are obtained for the EU by Karacaovali and Limão (2005). These estimates are combined with data for 170 countries and approximately 5,000 goods to provide the first welfare estimates of preferential trade agreements as a stumbling block. The welfare effects are calculated from a baseline MFN tariff reduction of 33 percent expected in the Doha Round relative to the subsidy counterfactual, which entails additional reductions by the triad economies (the EU, Japan, and the United States). Given the results in Limão (2006), this additional liberalization is estimated to be about 8 percentage points for goods in which the triad economies offer preferences.

The focus here is on the preferences that the triad economies extend to least developed countries: a subset of preferential trade agreements that fit the assumptions of the theory well. Total annual welfare gains for the 48 least developed countries are estimated at $520 million, with all countries but one

3. The fear that preferential trade agreements could be a stumbling block to MTL has generated a considerable theoretical literature but no consensus. See Bagwell and Staiger (1998), Krishna (1998), and Levy (1997). Winters (1999) provides an excellent review.

gaining. The maximum gain is 6.7 percent of GDP, and the average is 0.38 percent. More important, the countries that most oppose MTL because of its preference erosion effect are estimated to gain the most from the switch. Welfare for the triad economies would increase by nearly $3 billion a year, mainly because of the additional MFN tariff reductions allowed by the subsidy. For the same reason, the rest of the world experiences an annual welfare gain of $900 million, which is important since one concern with preferential trade agreements is their costs on outsiders (Chang and Winters 2002). In relative terms, least developed countries as a group gain the most—over 0.5 percent of GDP a year. Similar gains arise for the least developed countries even if the subsidy causes only 2.8 percentage points of extra liberalization. Both the triad economies and the rest of the world continue to gain under this last scenario.

The aggregate annual welfare gain of $4,354 million adds almost 10 percent to the gains that the model predicts from goods liberalization in the Doha Round without switching to subsidies—that is, relative to the baseline reduction of 33 percent. Moreover, this estimate is likely to be a lower bound of the stumbling block effect of preferential trade agreements. At one extreme, the concern with preference erosion could prevent the completion of the round, costing an additional $47 billion.

Section I discusses recent theoretical and empirical evidence on how preferential treatment to small countries can generate a stumbling block and how it can be addressed by an import subsidy. In Section II the welfare effects are calculated. Section III addresses issues related to the implementation of the import subsidy. Section IV discusses the results. The appendix provides details on the theoretical model and discusses side conditions in preferential trade agreements. The supplemental appendix (available at http://wber.oxfordjournals.org/) provides details regarding the trade model used to simulate the effects, discusses data sources, and provides some descriptive statistics.

I. Preferences as a Stumbling Block to MTL

Preferential trade agreements can affect MFN tariffs through several channels. They can divert scarce negotiation resources and alter the number of negotiating parties and their bargaining power. In the context of unilateral preferences analyzed here, these effects are not as relevant as the concern with preference erosion. That concern has created an important stumbling block to MTL, as can be shown in a model where unilateral preferences are exchanged for cooperation in nontrade issues. The appendix provides such a model, based on Limão (2002), that shows two things. First, the unilateral preferences that large countries use can cause them to maintain higher multilateral tariffs even if those preferences are extended to countries that are small from a trade perspective. Second, an import subsidy resolves this problem.

Three main criteria were used in choosing the counterfactual to analyze the cost of preferences as a stumbling block. It should remove the stumbling block, generate a Pareto improvement in the context of a well-defined model (so that it can be expected to gain the support of WTO members) and be simple enough to permit estimation and implementation.

When the import subsidy is designed to mimic trade preferences, it fulfills these criteria. Eliminating unilateral preferences or replacing them with direct transfers to reward cooperation would remove the stumbling block. However, eliminating preferences altogether is opposed by several countries so it is not as interesting a counterfactual. Cash transfers may not be the most efficient way to transfer resources to other countries, as the aid versus trade literature highlights, or to reward their cooperation.[4] Political economy constraints that reduce the effectiveness of cash transfers relative to preferences are present in practice; otherwise it would be difficult to explain the existence of many preference schemes. For example, preferences may trigger investment in a particular sector and create a longer-lasting constituency when that country lobbies its government to do whatever is necessary to maintain the preferences. Lump-sum transfers could end up in anonymous bank accounts in Switzerland. So, as an alternative to preferences, the subsidy scheme may also dominate direct transfers.

Before the welfare costs of preferences are estimated, some direct evidence for preferential trade agreements as a stumbling block to MTL is provided that is subsequently used in the quantification. The model generates specific testable predictions. At an extreme, if the MFN tariff is zero, no tariff preference can be offered and so no preferential agreement is possible without subsidies. Therefore, to the extent that the EU and the United States value the cooperation in the side conditions of those agreements, reductions in MFN tariffs on products imported from the preferential partner are more costly than reductions in tariffs on other products.

Limão (2006) estimates the effect of U.S. preferential trade agreements on its MFN tariffs by exploring whether the effect occurs only with goods that the United States imports from its preferential trade agreement partners and not with goods that it imports only from the rest of the world. Using tariff data for more than 5,000 products, he finds that U.S. preferential trade agreements generated a stumbling block in the Uruguay Round. He estimates that the U.S. average reduction in MFN tariff for goods exported by any of its preferential trade agreement partners was about half that for other goods. The effect is stronger for products that are exported under all preferential trade agreements or that constitute larger shares of a given preferential trade agreement partner's exports to the United States. These estimates control for several determinants of U.S. tariff changes and carefully establish the direction of causality from the

4. Thus, the proposal here differs from the others that suggest temporary development assistance to the governments of developing countries that are hurt by preference erosion—for example, Hoekman (2004). See McCulloch and Pinera (1977) on the issue of trade and aid issue and Adam and O'Connell (2004) for a more recent analysis.

preferential trade agreements to the MFN tariff changes using instrumental variables.

A switch by the triad economies to a subsidy after the Doha Round would cause them to reduce their tariffs by an additional 8.3 percentage points on the goods for which they provide preferences to least developed countries. This result is obtained by assuming a 33 percent MFN tariff liberalization in Doha on all goods—the average for developed countries in the Uruguay Round—and dividing it by a stumbling block factor of 80 percent calculated from Limão (2006). According to his estimates, the reduction in MFN tariffs for goods that the United States imports from its Generalized System of Preferences beneficiaries was only about 80 percent of what it would have been without such preferences. Thus under the subsidy scheme, triad economies' liberalization in goods where they provide a preference to least developed countries is estimated to be 41.3 percent, an additional 8.3 percentage points relative to the 33 percent baseline liberalization. The sensitivity of the welfare results is analyzed with respect to this estimate.[5]

Karacaovali and Limão (2005) provide similar estimates for the stumbling block effect that apply to the EU's preferential trade agreements. The EU average MFN tariff cut for goods exported by any of its preferential trade agreements was about half that for other goods. They also provide evidence that directly supports the use of an import subsidy as a solution when preferential tariffs are close to zero. Their model predicts that if the preferential tariff is positive, the MFN tariff can still be reduced without affecting the preference margin simply by lowering the preferential tariff by the same amount. This prediction is tested and confirmed for the EU, strongly supporting the argument that by removing the non-negativity constraint for preferential tariffs an import subsidy would indeed eliminate the stumbling block effect.

II. Welfare Estimates of Preferences as a Stumbling Block to MTL

This section first describes the methodology used to quantify the welfare costs of preferences as measured by the gains from switching to an import subsidy. Once

5. More specifically, the stumbling block factor is defined as $f = (\Delta t_p/t_0)/(\Delta t_s/t_0)$, where $\Delta t_p/t_0$ is the growth in the MFN tariffs of a triad economy when preferences are in place and $\Delta t_s/t_0$ is the growth when they are absent. Limão (2006) takes the changes in tariffs on the nonpreferential trade agreement good as the counterfactual for the outcome in preferential trade agreement goods if preferential trade agreements were absent and calculates $\Delta \ln(1+t_p)/\Delta \ln(1+t_s) \approx \Delta t_p/\Delta t_s = f$. Using his estimates leads to $\Delta \ln(1+t_p)/\Delta \ln(1+t_s) = (\tilde{a} + \rho * TOTLIB + \phi)/(\tilde{a} + \rho * TOTLIB) = 0.8$. The variable $TOTLIB$ represents the liberalization by U.S. partners, so ρ captures the reciprocity effect; $TOTLIB$ was 51.3 on average in his sample, so $\rho * TOTLIB = 0.018 * (-51.3)$. The estimates for $\rho = 0.018$ and $\phi = 0.658$ are from the last column of table 1 in Limão (2006), where he controls for the existence of other preferential trade agreements. Using his estimate for the Generalized System of Preferences in table 2, 0.74, yields $\tilde{a} = -2.53 = 0.658/(0.74 - 1)$. The 95 percent confidence interval for the stumbling block factor described above is (0.697, 0.923), which is then used to calculate the high and low scenarios of additional liberalization of 14.3 percentage points and 2.8 percentage points in table 2.

the computed measures are conceptually clear, the estimation is standard. (The formal details of the estimation can be found in the supplemental appendix.) The empirical results are then discussed.

Methodology

First, the budgetary cost for each subsidy-granting country (SGC) is calculated. This is the amount paid to each subsidy-receiving country (SRC), which is an input into the welfare calculation and a measure that may preempt concerns with the budgetary costs of implementation. An import subsidy rate for each good and each SGC must be chosen. Here, this rate is the current preference margin, which provides a convenient benchmark to calculate welfare changes because the initial switch leaves all prices and quantities unchanged. Naturally, alternative subsidy rates are possible and would deliver different results. The first two columns of table 1 list the cost of this subsidy for all goods under current levels of tariffs and trade and under those predicted after the Doha Round, with MFN tariffs assumed to be 33 percent lower. The key budgetary measure is the cost of switching to the subsidy, which is obtained by subtracting the forgone tariff revenue under the current preferences (see column 3 of table 1).

TABLE 1. Budgetary Impact on Triad Economies of Switching to a Subsidy Scheme ($ Millions)

	Cost of Subsidy			
Economy	Current Most Favored Nation Tariff[a]	Post-Doha Most Favored Nation Tariff[b]	Cost of Switch Post-Doha Most Favored Nation Tariff[c]	Preference Erosion Post-Doha Most Favored Nation Tariff[d]
European Union	669	674	208	441
Japan	31	32	6	17
United States	63	64	21	166
Total	763	768	235	624

Note: A decomposition of subsidies and preference erosion by subsidy-receiving countries is provided in appendix table A.1.

[a]Calculated using a subsidy rate for each good equal to the current preference margins in each subsidy-granting country using current prices, quantities, and most favored nation tariffs; see equation (S.1) in the supplemental appendix.

[b]Assumes a 33 percent reduction in most favored nation tariffs by all World Trade Organization members; see equation (S.2) in the supplemental appendix.

[c]Assumes a 33 percent reduction in most favored nation tariffs by all World Trade Organization members; see equation (S.3) in the supplemental appendix.

[d]Uses current preferences and assumes a 33 percent reduction in most favored nation tariffs by all World Trade Organization members; see equation (S.12) in the supplemental appendix.

Source: Authors' analysis based on data discussed in the supplemental appendix.

Second, the preference erosion measure is calculated for each preference-receiving country in each preference-granting country market. If current preferences are maintained, this measure is simply the difference between the extra export revenue due to preferences before and after a 33 percent reduction in MFN tariffs without a subsidy. These values are listed in column 4 of table 1 and by country in appendix table A.1.[6]

Third, and most important, the welfare cost of preferences is calculated by country (table 2 and appendix table A.2). This is the additional welfare gain that would be obtained in the Doha Round if the triad economies switched to an import subsidy.

To calculate all three measures, we need an estimate of the changes in world prices and quantities imported and exported associated with the tariff reductions in the 170 countries in the sample. This is calculated by combining estimates of import demand and export supply elasticities with a simple trade model, which is described in detail in the supplemental appendix. A simple partial equilibrium model is employed for each six-digit tariff line in the Harmonized System. It assumes that each tariff line includes a homogeneous good and that the world market for each is in equilibrium. Neither substitution effects across goods nor income effects are modeled on the demand or the supply side. Although such effects could be incorporated here, recent work suggests that they have little impact on aggregate welfare gains.[7] The aggregate welfare estimate here is similar to those generated using more complex computable general equilibrium models.[8]

Empirical Results

The focus here is on the preferences granted by the triad economies to 48 of the 49 least developed countries under the Generalized System of Preferences (data are not available to compute welfare gains for Kiribati). While these are not the only small countries that the triad economies offer preferences to, they form an interesting subgroup. Data on products at the six-digit harmonized standard level that receive preferences from triad economies

6. These preferences are not fully utilized (Inama 2003), so it is likely to also be the case under the subsidy. Therefore, the estimates of the cost of the subsidy and preference erosion are likely to be an upper bound for the true effects. However, this should not have a large effect on the net welfare calculations since the qualitative effect of imperfect utilization is similar under the subsidy and preference scenarios, and the net welfare effects are the difference between the two.

7. Hoekman, Nicita, and Olarreaga (2006) find that the world welfare gain from a 40 percent cut in MFN tariffs among WTO members is $51 billion without cross-price effects and $59 billion with them. This difference is statistically insignificant when they account for the standard errors associated with the measurement of the elasticities of import demand and export supply. Thus, the exposition of the model in the supplemental appendix is kept simple and clear by abstracting from cross-price effects.

8. For example, assuming a 33 percent liberalization for all WTO members leads to a yearly gain of about $47 billion in our estimation. Francois, van Mejil, and van Tongeren (2005) estimate it to be $45 billion when they apply a 50 percent cut in bound tariffs using a static computable general equilibrium model with constant returns to scale and with an Armington setup.

TABLE 2. Annual Welfare Cost of Least Developed Country Preferences as a Stumbling Block

Economy	Share of GDP[a] (%)	$ Millions[b]		
		Intermediate	Low	High
Triad economies	0.013	2,934	1,048	5,045
European Union	0.027	2,336	849	4,023
Japan	0.006	237	79	415
United States	0.004	361	120	607
Least developed countries[c]	0.518	520	513	526
Bangladesh	0.36	176	173	179
Cambodia	0.60	24	22	25
Lesotho	2.09	18	18	18
Madagascar	1.16	53	53	53
Malawi	6.66	117	117	117
Maldives	0.47	3	3	3
Mauritania	0.61	6	6	6
Mozambique	0.25	9	9	10
Myanmar	1.23	20	19	21
São Tomé and Principe	1.32	1	1	1
Senegal	0.33	17	17	17
Sierra Leone	0.65	5	5	5
Solomon Islands	0.67	2	2	2
Tanzania	0.32	30	30	30
Uganda	0.11	7	7	7
Others		33	31	32
Rest of the world	0.010	900	315	1,721
Total	0.010	4,354	1,888	7,270

Note: See appendix table A.2 for welfare estimates for other least developed countries. Estimates are based on equations (S.6) and (S.11) in the supplemental appendix.

[a]Intermediate welfare gains/GDP, where GDP is for 2002 and in current U.S. dollars.

[b]Assumes a baseline reduction in most favored nation tariffs of 33 percent by all World Trade Organization members plus an additional amount by the triad economies in the products in which they provide preferences to least developed countries. The additional amount is 8.3 percentage points for intermediate, 2.8 percentage points for low, and 14.3 percentage points for high. These three figures are calculated using the estimates in Limão (forthcoming); 8.3 percentage points is calculated from a point estimate, and the extremes represent the 95 percent confidence interval. See the text for details.

[c]The estimates for least developed countries are insensitive to different scenarios because most of their welfare gain is due to the avoided preference erosion under the 33 percent baseline common to all three scenarios.

Source: Authors' analysis based on data discussed in the supplemental appendix.

and on bilateral trade flows and MFN tariffs for all countries are used to calculate changes in prices and quantities due to liberalization. The import and export elasticities at the tariff line for every country are from the article by

Kee, Nicita, and Olarreaga (2004). The exact data sources and years are in the supplemental appendix.

To provide an idea of trade coverage, we should note that in 2001–03 imports from least developed countries totaled on average $8 billion for the EU, $1 billion for Japan, and $7 billion for the United States. According to UNCTAD (2003), 99.8 percent of dutiable EU imports from least developed countries are covered by preferences, as are 53 percent of Japanese imports and 44 percent of U.S. imports. Among least developed countries, Bangladesh and Cambodia are the top beneficiaries of EU and Japanese tariff preferences, and Madagascar and Malawi are the top beneficiaries of U.S. preferences.

The first column of table 1 lists that the cost of the subsidy for the triad economies is $763 million without tariff reductions. This is equal to the tariff revenue currently forgone due to preferences, and it is borne mostly by the EU for three reasons. First, the EU imports larger quantities from least developed countries. Second, EU preferences to least developed countries tend to be more generous, as seen in the supplemental appendix table S.1. Third, the EU MFN tariffs on the type of goods exported by least developed countries tend to be higher.

The second column of table 1 lists the amount of the subsidy after a 33 percent reduction in bound tariffs by all WTO members, $768 million. It is higher than the currently forgone tariff revenue because exports from SRCs increase with the rise in world prices caused by the multilateral tariff reductions.

The third column of table 1 lists the estimates of the budgetary cost to triad economies implied by switching to the subsidy scheme. This cost arises because the tariff charged on imports from SRCs falls but the subsidy rate does not. Moreover, this shortfall applies to a larger value of imports because the MFN tariff reductions increase world prices. The total budgetary cost for the triad economies is only $235 million, and the share borne by Japan and the United States is minimal. This value excludes the impact of any additional MFN tariff reduction that may be possible under the subsidy.

The fourth column of table 1 lists the preference erosion costs that preference-receiving countries suffer in each triad economy market under a 33 percent reduction in MFN tariffs without a subsidy. These erosion costs would be much larger than the budgetary costs for the triad economies to move toward a subsidy. The least developed countries' loss is $624 million, mostly in the EU market. Previous estimates were around $530 million (for example, Subramanian 2004). There are two main reasons for the larger results here. First, the average estimated elasticity of export supply in least developed countries is 5, which is larger than the value assumed by Subramanian for all goods, 1. Second, the MFN tariffs here include *ad valorem* equivalents of specific tariffs, which leads to larger preference erosion.

Estimates by country are summarized in appendix table A.1. They are calculated to help identify the countries that are, or should be, most opposed to MTL based on its impact on preference erosion. If these countries gain considerably by a switch to a subsidy, a large obstacle to liberalization may be removed. The three countries that would face the largest losses in absolute terms due to erosion are Bangladesh ($202 million), Malawi ($151 million), and Madagascar ($63 million). The countries that face the largest losses in share of GDP are Malawi (8.6 percent), Lesotho (2.7 percent), and São Tomé and Principe (1.6 percent). The results also show that losses from preference erosion are concentrated, with 26 of 48 countries losing less than 0.1 percent of GDP.

The triad economies should not be opposed to switching to a subsidy simply because of the budgetary cost; switching would also allow further liberalization. table 2 summarizes estimates of the net welfare impact, including this extra liberalization by the triad economies on products subject to least developed country preferences. The focus here is on the intermediate estimates in the first two columns, which are based on an estimated additional 8.3 percentage points of liberalization; the sensitivity of the results to alternative estimates is discussed below. The annual gain for the triad economies is $2,934 million, meaning that their governments should be in favor of switching. The largest gain, $2,336 million, is for the EU; Japan would gain $237 million and the United States $361 million.[9]

The least developed countries also benefit from switching to the subsidy, with a total gain of $520 million a year. The change in welfare is much larger for least developed countries when measured relative to GDP—about 50 times larger than that for the triad economies. There are 27 least developed countries that will see net welfare changes of less than 0.1 percent of GDP. And Djibouti experiences a marginal loss of $0.07 million due to deteriorating terms of trade associated with liberalization.

Table 2 also lists the least developed countries that are among the top 10 countries that gain the most either in absolute value or as a share of GDP. These countries are also among those that gain the most per capita. The other 33 countries together gain only $33 million. The largest absolute gains for individual least developed countries are for Bangladesh ($176 million), Malawi ($117 million), and Madagascar ($53 million). The largest gains in share of GDP are for Malawi (6.7 percent), Lesotho (2.1 percent), and São Tomé and Principe (1.3 percent). Recall that these were the same countries that stood to lose the most from preference erosion. So if faced with a choice between the preference and the subsidy scheme, least developed countries should support the subsidy scheme and the additional MTL that it entails.

9. The results do not appear to be driven by specific products such as sugar, which, as discussed in the introduction, provides an important example of the effects discussed here. Excluding sugar, the welfare gain for the European is only $72 million less.

The aggregate welfare gain for least developed countries is lower than the preference erosion value in table 1 because preference erosion measures the change in export revenues and ignores any extra costs of production. For individual countries, the gains in table 2 may also be lower than the preference erosion effect in appendix table A.2 because additional MTL by the triad economies occurs in many goods, some of which the SRC may import, implying that it will face a deterioration in its terms of trade, for example, Djibouti and Rwanda.

The rest of the world gains $900 million: 108 countries experience a gain and 11 a loss. But the largest loss, which is for Nigeria, is only $0.6 million. By contrast, gains are as high as $167 million for China. The gains for the rest of the world occur as a result of the additional liberalization from switching to the subsidy.[10]

The aggregate welfare gain of $4,354 million adds nearly 10 percent to the gains that the model predicts from goods liberalization in the Doha Round without switching to a subsidy. Nonetheless, this is likely to be a low estimate of the cost of preferential trade agreements as a stumbling block for MTL because the focus here is on the preferences to least developed countries. The estimates in Limão (2006) suggest that the stumbling block effect is greater when it applies to several preferential trade agreements; if the additional liberalization was about 14 percentage points, the aggregate gains increase to more than $7 billion, as shown in the last column of table 2. Even under the 8.3 percentage points scenario, the welfare estimates are likely to be a lower bound, for several reasons. First, they refer to an annual effect. With the static model used here, if there were no further shocks after the implementation of the subsidy scheme, the discounted welfare effect would be several times higher. Second, to calculate the welfare effects, we employed a static perfect competition model with no externalities, which is well known to provide relatively small gains from trade liberalization. Third, when the effect of the additional liberalization by the triad economies is computed, reciprocity effects are not added. In practice, the triad economies would be expected to attempt to negotiate further reductions from other countries.[11]

Since the additional liberalization of 8.3 percentage points is an estimate, the sensitivity of the results was tested by considering two extreme alternatives that represent its confidence interval: 2.8 percentage points and 14.3 percentage points. Two points stand out. First, most of the change in the aggregate gains, which now range from $2 billion to $7 billion, is due to the

10. For non–least developed countries, the estimates do not include the preference erosion effect caused by the extra 8.3 percent liberalization in the triad economy markets.

11. Under the preference scheme the MFN tariff reductions would result in a lower level of cooperation in nontrade issues by the small countries, which would entail an additional cost to the triad economies that is not computed here.

triad economies—which is not surprising since they are the countries liberalizing.[12] Second, the estimates for the least developed countries remain nearly unchanged because most of their gains arise from the avoided preference erosion under the 33 percent baseline reduction common to all three scenarios. Therefore, from the perspective of least developed countries, the proposal here should be attractive even if the amount of additional liberalization by the triad economies is very small.[13]

III. Implementation, Scope, and Refinement of the Subsidy Scheme

We analyzed the small budgetary cost of switching to the subsidy. The logistical costs of running it are similar to those for preferences because many of the procedures are already in place. However, we now discuss some potential differences in running each scheme and possible refinements to the subsidy proposal.

When the value of the subsidy and that of tariff rate are identical, they have equivalent effects on prices, quantities, and implementation. When the preferential tariff is zero, the exporter receives the domestic price in the preference-granting country, $p^w + t$, where p^w is the world price and t is the MFN tariff, and $p^w + t$ is also the price that the importer pays. Under the subsidy, the preferential exporter receives $p^w + s$, the same as before when $t = s$. The importer pays $p^w + t + s$ before receiving a rebate equivalent to the amount of the subsidy per unit, s. If this occurs at customs, the buyer's price is simply $p^w + t$. Here, the subsidy is implemented as an immediate drawback scheme, which already exists in the triad economies to rebate import duties when the

12. The triad economies' total welfare change can be decomposed into an efficiency and a budgetary effect. The budgetary effect has two components: the first captures the cost of the subsidy relative to the preference under a 33 percent MFN tariff reduction (equation S.5 in the supplemental appendix), and the second captures the extra cost of the subsidy due to the additional liberalization (the term in the last parenthesis of equation S.8 in the supplemental appendix). The efficiency component is given by the remaining terms on the right side of equation (S.8). Under the intermediate scenario of an additional 8.3 percentage points, the first component of the budgetary cost accounts for 8 percent of the $2,934 million welfare change of the triad economies. This increases to 14 percent for the total budgetary cost (14 percent for the EU, 5 percent for Japan, and 24 percent for the United States). Thus, most of the change in their welfare is driven by the efficiency effect.

13. To understand the insensitivity in the welfare effect for the least developed countries, note that it can be decomposed in two terms. As seen from equation (S.11) in the supplemental appendix, the first effect arises from the additional liberalization that occurs only under the subsidy, given by equation (S.10). The second effect is given by the second term in equation (S.11), which captures the difference in welfare changes under the subsidy versus the preference when tariffs fall by 33 percent. Under the preferences, a reduction in MFN tariffs causes a reduction in the welfare for the least developed countries because of erosion, as summarized in table 1. Thus, the second effect captures the role of the subsidy in avoiding preference erosion. In the estimates here this last effect dominates the effect from additional MTL by the triad economies, which accounts on average for only about 2 percent of the total welfare change for individual least developed countries. But there is some heterogeneity across countries in this, and for a few least developed countries, the effect from additional liberalization by the triad economies is actually negative because the additional MTL occurs in many goods, some of which the SRC may import.

imported good is re-exported or used as an input in the production of an exported good.

The discussion above should also make clear that the subsidy is as transparent as the current preferences. Therefore, political economy arguments that the subsidy is more transparent, and thus less likely to be adopted, are not convincing.[14]

But the subsidy may become an issue after an MFN tariff reduction, that is, when $t' < s$. Two differences arise when the MFN tariff rate falls. The first is the direct budgetary cost: customs collects t' per unit and must rebate s. Estimates show this cost is small. However, when the subsidies involve expenditure above the tariff collected on the product from that country, they may need to be in the budget. This could be financed directly from tariff revenue collected on imports from other countries. Moreover, from the domestic legal perspective of the SGC, the budget implications of subsidies are no different from those of the preferences.[15]

The second issue that may arise when $t' < s$ is re-exports. The buyer in the SGC can ship the good back to an agent in the SRC that will re-export it to collect the subsidy again. This is profitable if the excess subsidy, $s - t'$, is high enough to offset the transaction cost, which includes the cost of forging the certificate of origin of the good and the two-way transport cost. For most goods, though, transport costs make re-exporting unprofitable, particularly when the origin country is a least developed country, where transport costs tend to be higher (Limão and Venables 2001). If interest forgone on the sale of the good because of the time in shipment is added, re-exports are very unlikely to be profitable. If re-exports became a problem, one solution would be to implement the subsidy rebate only when the good is sold to the final consumer in the SGC. Since internal sales often incur a sales tax, this would serve as an additional hurdle that would have to be overcome for re-exports to be profitable. In fact, exempting imports from least developed countries from

14. One political problem that governments in SGCs may face is justifying to the import competing producers why they are subsidizing a foreign producer. This is not an issue before the MFN tariff reduction since $t = s$ and so the subsidy is offset by the tariff. But it may be an issue after an MFN reduction, that is, when $t' < s$. This should not be an issue if the MFN reduction was given since the SRCs we consider are small and so the domestic price in the SGC would remain almost unchanged for a given reduction in the MFN tariff under the preference or subsidy. So import competing producers would only oppose the subsidy if indeed the subsidy led to additional MFN liberalization. But this opposition is exactly identical to the import competing sector's opposition to MFN liberalization that arises because of other motives. The countervailing force here is therefore the same: exporters in each of the triad countries would support the subsidy precisely because it allows additional MTL in the remaining triad markets to which they export.

15. In the United States, for example, any foregone tariff revenue from a new preference must be estimated and a replacement in the budget suggested. There are also precedents for the use of import subsidies in the EU—for example, when supplies of sugar available within the Community or a major consuming region are no longer sufficient (Council Regulation 1260/2001, June 19, 2001).

paying such a tax could, under certain conditions, mimic the subsidy and thus be an alternative.[16]

This proposal may apply better to certain countries that are "strategically large," that is, whose cooperation in certain nontrade issues is important. Proposals for a "buy-out" of preferences, either through a lump-sum payment or temporary adjustment assistance through grants (Hoekman 2004) or loans (IMF 2004a and 2004b), are unlikely to work for those countries.[17] For example, the United States had the opportunity to offer only cash for Colombia's cooperation on the war on drugs, and it chose not to. However, the skeptics of the subsidy scheme may want to first experiment by switching only in one sector or a subset of one sector. For example, there may be a stronger case for U.S. preferences to Colombia in the agricultural sector as a way to provide alternatives to growing coca. Moreover, sector-specific experimentation can show whether unexpected implementation problems may arise.

Choosing a fixed subsidy rate equal to the current preference margin yields a convenient benchmark to evaluate the welfare effects of a switch. But alternative subsidy rates can help address other problems with preferences. Preferences may have led to investment in sectors where countries do not have a comparative advantage (Tangermann 2002). A modified subsidy scheme would address this. A fixed subsidy rate that is equal for all products exported to all SGCs could be used to align the pattern of export specialization with relative world prices. This would keep relative prices in the SRC equal to world relative prices.

IV. Conclusion

The recent wave of preferential trade agreements suggests that policymakers find them desirable. But their effect on multilateral liberalization must be estimated and taken seriously. This article describes recent theoretical and empirical evidence that shows how preferential trade agreements can slow multilateral liberalization even when the countries receiving the preference are small. It argues that import subsidies can be used to decouple preferences from MFN tariff liberalization and that subsidies would be supported by the countries receiving and granting preferences.

16. A sufficient condition for this exemption to work exactly in the same way as a subsidy rate of value s is for the existing sales tax rate to be at least as high as the subsidy rate. This condition is not satisfied for some goods with high preference margins (which were chosen as the initial subsidy rate).

17. The IMF's proposed program is in the form of loans to finance temporary adjustment costs if the MFN tariff reductions have a significant effect on the balance of payments in the beneficiary countries. Even if this program compensated for the full amount of preference erosion, it would not be able to deliver the same MFN tariff reduction as the subsidy proposed because after the MFN tariff reduction the granting countries can only threaten to remove a smaller amount of preferences. Thus, they will be able to extract less in the form of side conditions than before the MFN reduction (or subsidy scheme). This implies that the granting countries themselves will offer fewer MFN reductions under the IMF program than under the subsidy scheme.

We provide the first estimates of the welfare costs of preferential trade agreements as a stumbling block to multilateral liberalization. It is $2,934 million per year for the TRIAD if they switched their preferences to least developed countries into fixed import subsidies in the context of the liberalization anticipated in the Doha Round. This occurs because under the subsidy plan triad economies can further reduce their MFN tariffs. The switch would also increase annual welfare in the rest of the world by $900 million. For least developed countries receiving preferences from the triad economies, the gain is $520 million—due mostly to the preference erosion avoided under the subsidy.

The aggregate annual welfare estimate of more than $4 billion adds about 10 percent to the gains that the model predicts from goods liberalization in the Doha Round. This is likely to be a lower bound of the stumbling block effect of preferential trade agreements. At one extreme, the concern with preference erosion could prevent the completion of the round, costing an additional $47 billion a year.

In terms of implementation, the budgetary costs of the subsidy are small, and the logistical costs are in principle not significantly higher than those associated with the current preferences. However, two issues must be addressed: legality in the WTO and the scope of the subsidies. From a legal perspective the subsidies conflict with the MFN principle; but this could be addressed in the same way as preferences: through waivers, the enabling clause, or article XXIV, for example.

In terms of the scope of the subsidy, the question is whether the proposal should extend to all countries that receive unilateral preferences. The basic argument should apply to them as well. Naturally, the budgetary cost for the triad economies would be higher, but the additional MFN tariff liberalization that would result may be enough to offset it. Even more broadly, extending the scheme to members of all preferential trade agreements could be considered. The concern with preference erosion also applies to them, and there is evidence that they have slowed U.S. and EU MFN tariff liberalization. Future research should address this broader question and calculate the welfare costs of other preferential trade agreements.

Appendix

First a simplified version of the model in Limão (2002) is presented to show how unilateral preferences to small countries can cause economies such as the EU and the United States to maintain higher multilateral tariffs and how this incentive disappears when an import subsidy is allowed. The role of side conditions in preferential trade agreements is then discussed.

Preferences to Small Countries as a Stumbling Block to MTL

Assume each regional bloc contains a large and a small country, denoted by L and S. Two externalities exist within each bloc. First, L is affected by the level of an action e that S can undertake at a cost. This is a general way to capture the demand that L has for cooperation in labor, environmental, immigration issues, improvements in governance, and so on. Second, there is a terms of trade externality, that is, L can use a tariff to depress the price of S's exports. Countries in a bloc can internalize these effects through a preferential trade agreement where L lowers its tariffs on S's exports in exchange for an increase in S's provision of e. The preferential trade agreement is modeled so that its only direct trade effect is to increase the price that S receives for its exports.

There are two import tariffs that L chooses: t, the multilateral tariff that it applies to the rest of the world, and $t^{\mathrm{p}} \leq t$, the preferential tariff on that good applied to imports from S. The good that L exports to the rest of the world faces a tariff t^{r}. So the objective function that L maximizes is

$$W^{\mathrm{L}} = W^{\mathrm{L}}(e, t^{\mathrm{p}}, t, t^{\mathrm{r}}) \tag{A.1}$$

where the partial effects are $W_e^{\mathrm{L}} > 0$ and, due to the terms of trade effects, $W_x^{\mathrm{L}} > 0$ for $x = t^{\mathrm{p}}, t$ when evaluated at $x = 0$ and $W_{t^{\mathrm{r}}}^{\mathrm{L}} < 0$.

The objective maximized by S depends on e and the tariffs set by L, which affect the price that S receives for its exports.

$$W^{\mathrm{S}} = W^{\mathrm{S}}(e, t^{\mathrm{p}}, t). \tag{A.2}$$

Under a preferential trade agreement S receives an export price of $p^{\mathrm{w}}(t) + t - t^{\mathrm{p}}$, where $p^{\mathrm{w}}(t)$ is the equilibrium world price, so $p^{\mathrm{w}}(t) + t$ is the price in L. Therefore, $W_{t^{\mathrm{p}}}^{\mathrm{S}} < 0$ and $W_t^{\mathrm{S}} > 0$. But in the absence of a preferential trade agreement, S faces the multilateral tariff and receives only $p^{\mathrm{w}}(t)$, which falls when t is raised and so $W_t^{\mathrm{S}} < 0$. For simplicity, it is assumed that S has no trade in the good exported by L to the rest of the world and thus is indifferent to the level of t^{r}. The balance of payments condition is satisfied through a numeraire good that enters utilities in a quasi-linear way and that L uses to pay for its imports from S.

The crucial assumption that generates a motive for L's preferential treatment for S is that it values e. Take the neutral case where S places neither a positive nor a negative weight on the direct effect of e on itself and assume that this action requires some expenditure by S, which implies a negative marginal benefit in terms of the numeraire. So, if S and L do not cooperate, S does not supply e and L does not provide a preference. They can improve on this outcome through a bargain where L sets $t^{\mathrm{p}} < t$ and S supplies e.[18]

18. Note that for a given t, this bargain may be just as efficient as a lump-sum transfer from L assuming that preferences are quasi-linear so that the tariff revenue that L gives up through the preference has the same effect as an equivalent lump-sum transfer. This would not be the case if S had an upward sloping export supply as assumed in the simulation. However, there can be realistic political economy constraints that would deliver the preference instead of the lump-sum transfer as the constrained first-best policy to be used in exchange for e; here, it is simply assumed that the preference is the only available instrument, and the implications for the multilateral tariff are then analyzed.

In most of the agreements analyzed here L has nearly all the bargaining power relative to S. Therefore, it is sensible to focus on the outcome of a take-it-or-leave-it offer that leaves S at the status quo welfare level. If S is a WTO member, the maximum tariff that L can set is $t^{\mathrm{p}} = t$, due to the MFN rule. Therefore, the status quo welfare will be determined by evaluating t^{p} at t and e at the level that is optimal for S. More specifically, the bargain that L offers must at least satisfy $W^{\mathrm{S}}(e = e^{\mathrm{b}}, t^{\mathrm{p}} = t^{\mathrm{b}} < t, t) \geq W^{\mathrm{S}}(e = 0, t^{\mathrm{p}} = t, t)$. So for a given level of t and t^{p}, the equilibrium level of e^{b} can be written as a function $e^{\mathrm{b}}(t^{\mathrm{p}}, t)$ that is decreasing in the preferential tariff and increasing in the MFN tariff because either movement raises W^{S} and thus allows L to extract a higher level of e. In the simple case the focus is on the fact that net exports of S are constant, implying that, in the function $e^{\mathrm{b}}(t^{\mathrm{p}}, t)$, S cares only about the preferential margin $t - t^{\mathrm{p}}$, so $e^{\mathrm{b}}_t = -e^{\mathrm{b}}_{t^{\mathrm{p}}} > 0$.

WTO countries negotiate reciprocal tariff reductions with their principal suppliers. So if the rest of the world (ROW) is the main supplier of the good that L also imports from S, L negotiates with ROW. To capture this, the equilibrium multilateral tariffs are modeled as the solution that maximizes the joint objective of L and ROW. Moreover, it is assumed that L chooses the preferential tariff simultaneously and that ROW is a mirror image of L, although neither of these assumptions is essential for the result. This implies that the focus can be on solving for t, since it will be equal to t^{r}, and that the effect of t on W^{r} is identical to that of t^{r} on W^{L}. Imposing the equilibrium conditions of symmetry, $t = t^{\mathrm{r}}$, and $e = e^{\mathrm{b}}(t^{\mathrm{p}}, t)$ the joint optimum for L and ROW under a preferential trade agreement is given by the following program and necessary first-order conditions

$$\{\tilde{t}, \tilde{t}^{\mathrm{p}}\} \equiv \arg_{t,t^{\mathrm{p}}} \max W^{\mathrm{L}}(e = e^{\mathrm{b}}(t^{\mathrm{p}}, t), t^{\mathrm{p}}, t, t^{\mathrm{r}} = t) \tag{A.3}$$

$$W^{\mathrm{L}}_{t^{\mathrm{p}}} + W^{\mathrm{L}}_{e} e^{\mathrm{b}}_{t^{\mathrm{p}}} \leq 0 \tag{A.4}$$

$$W^{\mathrm{L}}_{t} + W^{\mathrm{L}}_{t^{\mathrm{r}}} + W^{\mathrm{L}}_{e} e^{\mathrm{b}}_{t} \leq 0. \tag{A.5}$$

To see how a stumbling block can arise when import subsidies are not allowed, let us constrast this with the condition for the tariff in the absence of a preferential trade agreement. Now L has no incentive to provide a preference to S, so $t = t^{\mathrm{p}}$ and $e = 0$, which yields the following solution:

$$t' \equiv \arg_t \max W^{\mathrm{L}}(e = 0, t^{\mathrm{p}} = t, t, t^{\mathrm{r}} = t). \tag{A.6}$$

Using the first-order condition derived for this last problem, $W^{\mathrm{L}}_{t} + W^{\mathrm{L}}_{t^{\mathrm{r}}} + W^{\mathrm{L}}_{t^{\mathrm{p}}} = 0$, to evaluate the first-order condition for t when a preferential trade agreement is present (equation A.5), it can be determined whether $\tilde{t} > t'$. That will be so if the following expression is positive:

$$
\text{(A.7)}\quad \begin{aligned}\left(W_t^{\mathrm{L}} + W_{t^{\mathrm{r}}}^{\mathrm{L}} + W_e^{\mathrm{L}} e_t^{\mathrm{b}}\right)_{t',t^{\mathrm{P}}=0} &\geq \left[W_t^{\mathrm{L}} + W_{t^{\mathrm{r}}}^{\mathrm{L}} + W_{t^{\mathrm{P}}}^{\mathrm{L}}\left(-\frac{e_t^{\mathrm{b}}}{e_{t^{\mathrm{P}}}^{\mathrm{b}}}\right)\right]_{t',t^{\mathrm{P}}=0}\\ &= \left\{(W_t^{\mathrm{L}} + W_{t^{\mathrm{r}}}^{\mathrm{L}})\left[1 - \left(-\frac{e_t^{\mathrm{b}}}{e_{t^{\mathrm{P}}}^{\mathrm{b}}}\right)\right]\right\}_{t',t^{\mathrm{P}}=0} = 0\end{aligned}
$$

where the inequality in the first line reflects the use of equation (A.4). If import subsidies were allowed, t^{P} could continue to be lowered below zero and the inequality above would disappear since an interior solution could be found. But otherwise it is possible to obtain a corner solution in the preferential trade agreement, that is a situation where, at $t^{\mathrm{P}} = 0$, L would like S to increase e. In this case, equation (A.4) holds with a strict inequality. The second line of equation (A.7) is zero in the case considered here, where $-e_{t^{\mathrm{P}}}^{\mathrm{b}} = e_t^{\mathrm{b}}$—that is, when an increase in the MFN tariff has the same effect as a decrease in the preferential tariff, both simply increase the preferential margin. This implies that $\tilde{t} > t'$ if $[W_{t^{\mathrm{P}}}^{\mathrm{L}} + W_e^{\mathrm{L}} e_{t^{\mathrm{P}}}^{\mathrm{b}}]_{t^{\mathrm{P}}=0} < 0$. So import subsidies completely eliminate the need to distort the MFN tariff to maintain a preference margin.

Side Conditions in Preferential Agreements

The Generalized System of Preferences and other unilateral preferences provided by the EU and United States often have side conditions attached that are valued by the preference-granting country and potentially costly to the recipient. That is, these unilateral preferences are not free to developing countries. The Generalized System of Preferences, for example, was designed to promote the development of poorer countries based on an infant industry argument (UNCTAD 1964), but "during the last twenty-five years or so the experience of the GSP in the GATT system has been that for a number of reasons the preference-granting national entities (that is, the industrialized countries) often succumb to the temptation to use the preference systems as part of 'bargaining chips' of diplomacy" (Jackson 1997, p. 160). International trade lawyers have also warned of the possibility that the Generalized System of Preferences will retard the MTL of the developed countries that grant such preferences because of a similar mechanism (Trebilcock and Howse 1999). Failure of Generalized System of Preferences beneficiaries to comply with some of the nontrade issues has cost them their preferential access to the United States.[19]

19. For example, according to USTR (2005), some countries have lost eligibility for trade preferences under Generalized System of Preferences because of worker rights or intellectual property concerns. In 2005 the United States revoked Côte d'Ivoire's eligibility for trade preferences under the African Growth and Opportunity Act because it failed to comply with the U.N. cease fire resolution. Morocco enacted a comprehensive new labor law recently, and according to U.S. trade negotiators, it was "the prospect of a free trade agreement with the United States [that] helped to forge a domestic consensus for labor law reform in Morocco, spurring reform efforts that had been stymied for more than 20 years" (USTR 2004).

Both the EU and the United States explicitly offer reductions in trade barriers in exchange for cooperation on various nontrade issues such as labor, environment, drug trafficking, and intellectual property protection. Examples of these have included the Eastern European and Mediterranean agreements signed by the EU; the U.S. agreements with Jordan, Mexico, and other Latin American and Caribbean countries; and the preferential treatment that the EU and the United States extend to most developing countries through Generalized System of Preferences. This type of agreement is increasingly prevalent, as the new U.S. preferences to Middle Eastern countries make clear.[20]

TABLE A.1. Preference Erosion and Subsidy by Beneficiary Country ($ Millions)

	European Union		Japan		United States	
Subsidy-Receiving Country	Preference Erosion	Subsidy	Preference Erosion	Subsidy	Preference Erosion	Subsidy
Afghanistan	0.28	0.64	0.00	0.00	0.00	0.00
Angola	3.08	4.10	0.07	0.20	0.00	0.00
Bangladesh	193.61	346.86	6.55	11.17	1.90	2.48
Benin	0.61	1.19	0.00	0.00	0.00	0.00
Bhutan	0.04	0.11	0.00	0.00	0.01	0.01
Burkina Faso	0.55	1.19	0.00	0.00	0.00	0.01
Burundi	0.03	0.05	0.00	0.00	0.00	0.00
Cambodia	20.80	41.74	5.40	10.76	0.17	0.33
Cape Verde	0.37	0.75	0.00	0.00	0.07	0.15
Central African Republic	0.56	0.79	0.00	0.00	1.55	0.85
Chad	0.02	0.07	0.00	0.00	0.00	0.00
Comoros	0.04	0.10	0.00	0.00	0.00	0.00
Congo	0.27	0.47	0.00	0.01	0.01	0.02
Djibouti	0.05	0.11	0.00	0.00	0.00	0.00
Equatorial Guinea	0.02	0.04	0.00	0.00	0.00	0.00
Eritrea	0.29	0.45	0.00	0.00	0.00	0.00
Ethiopia	0.87	2.04	0.03	0.06	0.06	0.18
Gambia, The	0.58	0.87	0.05	0.08	0.00	0.01
Guinea	2.59	3.27	0.00	0.00	0.03	0.04
Guinea-Bissau	0.22	0.25	0.00	0.00	0.00	0.00

(*Continued*)

20. See USITC (1994, 1996) for conditions applying to the Andean Trade Preference Act. See Bayard and Elliot (1994) and UNCTAD (2000) for details on conditionality in the Generalized System of Preferences program. See Perroni and Whalley (2000) for details on conditionality in the North American Free Trade Agreement. See Winters (1993) for details on the EU's Eastern European, Mediterranean, and Generalized System of Preferences programs; the Generalized System of Preference programs are also described in UNCTAD (2002).

TABLE A.1. Continued

Subsidy-Receiving Country	European Union		Japan		United States	
	Preference Erosion	Subsidy	Preference Erosion	Subsidy	Preference Erosion	Subsidy
Haiti	0.23	0.37	0.01	0.01	1.08	2.61
Kiribati	n.a.	n.a.	n.a.	n.a.	n.a.	n.a.
Lao PDR	6.77	13.02	0.12	0.30	0.00	0.00
Lesotho	0.25	0.29	0.00	0.00	22.90	18.78
Liberia	0.79	2.27	0.00	0.00	0.01	0.02
Madagascar	45.42	63.52	0.08	0.15	18.14	15.18
Malawi	40.77	39.64	0.01	0.01	110.28	25.42
Maldives	3.84	4.31	0.03	0.04	0.00	0.00
Mali	1.22	1.58	0.00	0.01	0.03	0.05
Mauritania	5.91	8.75	1.28	2.60	0.00	0.00
Mozambique	11.17	14.21	0.00	0.00	0.02	0.04
Myanmar	20.55	37.85	1.79	3.59	0.12	0.33
Nepal	4.78	11.55	0.72	1.88	0.37	0.62
Niger	0.48	0.90	0.00	0.01	0.02	0.04
Rwanda	0.03	0.09	0.00	0.00	0.00	0.01
Samoa	0.03	0.04	0.02	0.02	0.00	0.01
São Tomé and Principe	0.77	0.93	0.00	0.00	0.00	0.01
Senegal	19.68	28.41	0.06	0.13	0.02	0.05
Sierra Leone	5.33	11.27	0.00	0.00	0.02	0.04
Solomon Islands	2.01	2.14	0.20	0.34	0.00	0.00
Somalia	0.04	0.06	0.00	0.00	0.01	0.02
Sudan	0.84	1.41	0.00	0.01	0.00	0.00
Tanzania	28.22	30.98	0.04	0.09	8.29	3.15
Togo	0.55	0.96	0.00	0.00	0.01	0.04
Tuvalu	0.02	0.04	0.00	0.00	0.00	0.00
Uganda	8.12	7.82	0.00	0.00	0.01	0.03
Vanuatu	0.03	0.08	0.08	0.17	0.01	0.02
Yemen	1.12	1.42	0.02	0.04	0.00	0.00
Zambia	6.38	9.72	0.00	0.00	0.40	0.63

n.a., not available.

Source: Authors' calculations based on data discussed in the supplemental appendix.

Table A.2. Changes in Net Welfare by Least Developed Countries

Subsidy-Receiving Country	Total($ Millions)	Per Capita($)	Share of GDP[a](%)
Afghanistan	0.26	0.01	0.01
Angola	2.59	0.2	0.02
Bangladesh	175.72	1.31	0.36
Benin	0.53	0.08	0.02
Bhutan	0.05	0.06	0.01
Burkina Faso	0.48	0.04	0.02

(*Continued*)

TABLE A.2. Continued

Subsidy-Receiving Country	Total($ Millions)	Per Capita($)	Share of GDP[a](%)
Burundi	0.01	0	0
Cambodia	23.55	1.8	0.6
Cape Verde[b]	0.4	0.88	0.06
Central African Republic	1.67	0.44	0.16
Chad	0.01	0	0
Comoros[b]	0.04	0.07	0.02
Congo, Rep.	0.19	0.05	0.01
Djibouti	−0.07	−0.1	−0.01
Equatorial Guinea	0.01	0.02	0
Eritrea	0.25	0.06	0.04
Ethiopia	0.87	0.01	0.01
Gambia, The[b]	0.55	0.4	0.14
Guinea	2.21	0.29	0.07
Guinea-Bissau	0.17	0.12	0.08
Haiti[b]	0.78	0.1	0.02
Kiribati	n.a.	n.a.	n.a.
Lao PDR	6.16	1.13	0.34
Lesotho[b]	18.14	10.26	2.09
Liberia	0.78	0.24	0.15
Madagascar	53.06	3.27	1.16
Malawi	116.94	11	6.66
Maldives	3.05	10.76	0.47
Mali	1.01	0.09	0.03
Mauritania	6.13	2.36	0.61
Mozambique	9.47	0.52	0.25
Myanmar	19.96	2.6	1.23
Nepal	5.43	0.23	0.1
Niger	0.45	0.04	0.02
Rwanda	0.01	0	0
Samoa[b]	0.05	0.29	0.02
São Tomé and Principe	0.65	4.26	1.32
Senegal	17.06	1.73	0.33
Sierra Leone	4.83	0.93	0.65
Solomon Islands	1.84	4.21	0.67
Somalia	0.04	0	0
Sudan	0.53	0.02	0
Tanzania	29.82	0.86	0.32
Togo	0.53	0.11	0.04
Tuvalu	0.01	0	0
Uganda	6.65	0.27	0.11
Vanuatu	0.08	0.39	0.03
Yemen, Rep.	0.84	0.05	0.01
Zambia	5.95	0.59	0.16

n.a., not available.

[a]GDP is for 2002 and in current U.S. dollars.

[b]Excludes changes in tariff revenue due to the lack of tariff data. The direction of the bias is unclear, but it is probably small since changes in tariff revenue represent on average less than 1 percent of the total welfare change.

REFERENCES

Adam, C., and S. O'Connell. 2004. "Aid versus Trade Revisited." *The Economic Journal* 114:150–73.

Bagwell, K., and R. Staiger. 1998. "Regionalism and Multilateral Tariff Cooperation." In J. Piggott and A. Woodland, eds., *International Trade Policy and the Pacific Rim*. London: MacMillan.

Bayard, T., and K. Ann Elliott. 1994. *Reciprocity and Retaliation in US Trade Policy*. Washington, D.C.: Institute for International Economics.

Bhagwati, J. 1991. *The World Trading System at Risk*. Princeton, N.J.: Princeton University Press.

Chang, W., and A. Winters. 2002. "How Regional Blocs Affect Excluded Countries: The Price Effects of Mercosur." *American Economic Review* 92(4):889–904.

European Commission. 2000. "Commission Proposes Overhaul of Sugar Market." IP/00/1109, April 10. Brussels.

Francois, J. H. van Mejil, and F. van Tongeren. 2005. "Trade Liberalization in the Doha Development Round." *Economic Policy* 20(42):349–39.

Haveman, J., and H. Shatz. 2004. "Developed Country Trade Barriers and the Least Developed Countries: The Economic Results of Freeing Trade." In B. Guha-Khasnobis, ed., *The* WTO*, Developing Countries and the Doha Development Agenda*. New York: Palgrave-MacMillan.

Hoekman, B. 2004. "Overcoming Discrimination against Developing Countries: Access, Rules and Differential Treatment." Paper presented at the Cornell Law School and Cordell Hull Institute conference "The Role of the WTO System in the World Economy," July 9–10, Paris.

Hoekman, B., C. Michalopoulos, and A. Winters. 2004. "Special and Differential Treatment of Developing Countries in the WTO: Moving Forward after Cancun." *The World Economy* 27(4):481–506.

Hoekman, B., A. Nicita, and M. Olarreaga. 2006. "Estimating the Effects of Global Trade Reform." In B. Hoekman and M. Olarreaga, eds., *Global Trade Liberalization and Poor Countries: Poverty Impacts and Policy Implications*. Washington D.C.: Brookings Institution Press, and Paris: Institut de Sciences Politiques.

IMF (International Monetary Fund). 2004a. "Fund Support for Trade-Related Balance of Payments Adjustments." Policy Development and Review Department, Washington, D.C. [http://www.imf.org/external/np/pdr/tim/2004/eng/022704.pdf].

———. 2004b. "IMF Executive Board Approves Trade Integration Mechanism." Press Release 04/73, April 13. Washington, D.C.

Inama, S. 2003. "Trade Preferences and the World Trade Organization Negotiations on Market Access." *Journal of World Trade* 37(5):959–76.

Jackson, J. 1997. *The World Trading System: Law and Policy of International Economic Relations*. Second edition. Cambridge, Mass.: MIT Press.

Johnson, Harry G. 1967. *Economic Policies toward Less Developed Countries*. Washington, D.C.: Brookings Institution.

Karacaovali, B., and N. Limão. 2005. "The Clash of Liberalizations: Preferential vs. Multilateral Trade Liberalization in the European Union." Policy Research Working Paper 3493. World Bank, Washington,D.C.

Kee, H. L., A. Nicita, and M. Olarreaga. 2004. "Import Demand Elasticities and Trade Distortions." Policy Research Working Paper 3452. World Bank, Washington, D.C.

Krishna, P. 1998. "Regionalism and Multilateralism: A Political Economy Approach." *Quarterly Journal of Economics* 113(1):227–51.

Levy, P. 1997. "A Political-Economic Analysis of Free-Trade Agreements." *American Economic Review* 87(4):506–19.

Limão, N. 2002. "Are Preferential Trade Agreements with Non-trade Objectives a Stumbling Block for Multilateral Liberalization?" Working Paper 02-02. University of Maryland, Department of Economics, Center for International Economics, College Park.

———. 2006. "Preferential Trade Agreements as Stumbling Blocks for Multilateral Trade Liberalization: Evidence for the US." *American Economic Review*.

Limão, N., and A. Venables. 2001. "Infrastructure, Geographical Disadvantage, Transport Costs and Trade." *World Bank Economic Review* 15(2):451–79.

McCulloch, R., and J. Pinera. 1977. "Trade as Aid: The Political Economy of Tariff Preferences for Developing Countries." *American Economic Review* 67(5):959–67.

Mendelowitz, Allan. 1994. "International Trade: Issues Concerning the Generalized System of Preferences." GAO/T-GGD-94-174, June 20. U.S. General Accounting Office, Washington, D.C.

OECD (Organisation for Economic Co-operation and Development). 2003. *Tariffs and Trade: OECD Query and Simulation Package*. Paris.

Panitchpakdi, Supachai. 2004. "Dr. Supachai Lauds IMF's New Policy." Statement before International Monetary and Financial Committee, April 24, Washington, D.C.

Perroni, C., and J. Whalley. 2000. "The New Regionalism: Trade Liberalization or Insurance?" *Canadian Journal of Economics* 33(1):1–24.

Sapir, A. 1981. "Trade Benefits under the EEC Generalized System of Preferences." *European Economic Review* 15(3):339–55.

Sapir, A., and L. Lundberg. 1984. "The US Generalized System of Preferences and Its Impacts." In A.O. Krueger and R.E. Baldwin, eds., *The Structure and Evolution of US Trade Policy*. National Bureau of Economic Research Conference Report. Chicago, Ill.: University of Chicago Press.

Stevens, C., and J. Kennan. 2004. "Making Preferences More Effective." Briefing Paper. Institute of Development Studies, Brighton, U.K.

Subramanian, A. 2004. "Financing of Losses From Preference Erosion." WT/TF/COH/14. Communication from the International Monetary Fund. World Trade Organization, Geneva.

Tangermann, S. 2002. "The Future of Preferential Trade Arrangements for Developing Countries and the Current Round of WTO Negotiations on Agriculture." Rome: Food and Agriculture Organization.

Trebilcock, M. J., and R. Howse. 1999. *The Regulation of International Trade*. Second edition. New York: Routledge.

UNCTAD (United Nations Conference on Trade and Development). 1964. "Towards a New Trade Policy for Development." Report by the Secretary-General of UNCTAD. New York.

———. 2000. "Generalized System of Preferences: Handbook on the Scheme of the USA." UNCTAD/ITCD/TSB/Misc.58. Geneva.

———. 2002. "Handbook on the Scheme of the European Community." UNCTAD/ITCD/TSB/Misc.25/Rev.2. Geneva.

———. 2003. "Trade Preferences for LDCs: An Early Assessment of Benefits and Possible Improvements." UNCTAD/ITCD/TSB/2003/8. Geneva.

USITC (United States International Trade Commission). 1994. "Andean Trade Preference Act: Effect on the U.S. Economy and on Andean Drug Crop Eradication and Crop Substitution." Washington D.C.

———. 1996. "Andean Trade Preference Act: Effect on the U.S. Economy and on Andean Drug Crop Eradication and Crop Substitution." Washington, D.C.

USTR (Office of the United States Trade Representative). 2004. "Morocco FTA Leads to Progress on Labor Reform." Fact sheet. Washington, D.C. [http://www.ustr.gov/Document_Library/Fact_Sheets/2004/Morocco_FTA_Leads_to_ Progress_on_Labor_Reform.html].

———. 2005. "U.S. Generalized System of Preferences Guidebook." Washington, D.C. [http://www.ustr.gov/assets/Trade_Development/Preference_Programs/GSP/asset_upload_file267_8359.pdf].

Winters, A. 1993. "Expanding EC Membership and Association Accords: Recent Experience and Future Prospects." In K. Anderson and R. Blackhurst, eds., *Regional Integration and the Global Trading System*. New York: St. Martin's Press.

———. 1999. "Regionalism vs. Multilateralism." In R. Baldwin, D. Cohen, A. Sapir, and T. Venables, eds., *Market Integration, Regionalism and the Global Economy*. Cambridge, U.K.: Centre for Economic Policy Research.

———. 2004. "Adjustment Assistance for Trade Liberalization." World Bank, Washington, D.C.